THE CENTURY HISTORICAL SERIES
WILLIAM E. LINGELBACH, *Editor*

A SHORT HISTORY OF AMERICAN DEMOCRACY

THOMAS JEFFERSON

(Courtesy of the American Philosophical Association.)

A SHORT HISTORY OF American Democracy

BY

ROY F. NICHOLS
Professor of History
University of Pennsylvania

AND

JEANNETTE P. NICHOLS
Sometime Professor of History
Wesleyan College

D. APPLETON-CENTURY COMPANY
INCORPORATED
NEW YORK LONDON

476

PRINTED IN THE UNITED STATES OF AMERICA

PREFACE

Teaching needs occasionally call for somewhat shorter textbooks, in which the history of American democracy is closely integrated with the place of the Republic in world affairs. To achieve this purpose this book has been prepared by abridging and combining three earlier books, *The Growth of American Democracy, The Republic of the United States,* and *Twentieth Century United States,* and adding new material. The chapters are made short, so that they may be readily adjusted to varying assignment programs.

Herein is shown the evolution of democratic institutions, as affected by both internal and external forces, including the influence of seventeenth and eighteenth century ideas, the rise of our constitutional procedures and the history of our concepts of liberty. Social movements, such as European immigration, internal migration and the conquest of the land by the people are cultivated, to unearth the roots of our nationality. The impact of the industrial, agricultural and transportation revolutions is discussed. The resulting society is described, with its intimate interactions between agricultural, industrial, sectional and political groups. The story of the testing of national unity in the fire of civil war is related. Military, naval and diplomatic developments are fully treated. In each period the interaction between the United States and other powers in both hemispheres is described, leading up to the emergence of the United States as a world power and her participation in World War I. Thereafter certain aspects of European, Asiatic and Latin American history are included to explain how Communism, Fascism, Nazism and Japanese militarism arose to challenge the republican system of the United States. Throughout attention has been focused on the growth, the needs, and the responsibilities of American Democracy in a world of clashing ideologies.

R. F. N.
J. P. N.

CONTENTS

COLONIES

1492–1763

INDEPENDENCE

1763–1823

RECONSTRUCTION AND LARGE-SCALE ORGANIZATION

1865–1900

LIST OF ILLUSTRATIONS

LIST OF MAPS

COLONIES
1492-1763

CHAPTER I

EUROPE DISCOVERS AMERICA

As millions of American youth set forth in 1943 for the battlefronts of Europe, they are reversing a process which began four hundred and fifty years ago. They are returning to the homes of their ancestors. During the four intervening centuries, across the waters of the Atlantic, have constantly passed people, goods, institutions and ideas. The broad ocean expanse, in many senses a barrier, has proved no less a highway —for the transit of western civilization in both directions. The constant movement has made America in fact a laboratory, for the testing of some ideas conceived in Europe and many more born of the new environment.

A New Age in Europe

Beginning in the twelfth century renaissance, the centers of civilization in Europe began to feel very strongly the urge to experiment. Western civilization had been slowly emerging from the chaos which marked the "dark ages," for institutions like the Christian Church and feudalism had kept a flicker of flame in the lamp of civilization during the barbarian invasions and had brought some order out of disorder. As the growing orderliness made mere existence a less precarious proposition, the fertile-minded could turn their thoughts and plans to other matters than survival. The Renaissance and later the Protestant Revolt are examples of the great forces stirring which led some of the very enterprising to discover America and to make experiment there, also. Taken together, these forces and the conditions they created fostered so many new ideas and desires that they finally rose in a veritable flood, to create and dominate the Modern Age.

Europe's shift from medieval to modern ways of thought and action came through momentous changes. Foremost were six: contacts with strange peoples, intellectual activity, maritime inventions, growth of capitalism, emergence of the middle class, and the rise of national languages and states. Europeans thereby learned more of the world in which they lived, gained greater insight into its possibilities for adventure, profit, power and perfection. To realize these new opportunities, they wandered far beyond their time-honored horizons.

They were in fact forced into new activities, by the constant pressure of outside peoples upon their territory. Saracens, Turks and Mongols at various times had invaded Europe, surging in wherever they could force an entrance. As Europeans sought to defend themselves from the invaders, they could not but grow more conscious of the outer regions of the then known world. Of necessity they laid aside preoccupation with the petty concerns of feudal domains and planned larger undertakings of wide significance.

The sharpest pressure came from the East, whence welled a flood of consequences which at length brought forth America. As far back as the eleventh century the Byzantine Empire, with its capital at Constantinople, was hard pressed by the Turks, who had captured the Holy Land and seemed on the march against Christendom. The Emperor turned to his western Christian brethren for aid and appealed to the Pope. Urban II responded with zeal. He and his predecessors had been in frequent conflict with the secular rulers of Europe, and Urban probably welcomed an opportunity to demonstrate the influence of the papacy. In 1095 he preached a crusade to save the Holy Land and his appeal and those of his successors were heeded. During the next two centuries, no less than seven crusades were undertaken, drawing fighting men to the East from most quarters of Europe.

These soldiers of the Cross through several generations became acquainted with new lands, new people, new customs and new commodities. They saw strange sights, finer things and more comfortable ways of living, which made them realize something of the crudity of their own surroundings. The needs of these expeditions likewise stimulated trade and communication. The great armies had to be fed, equipped and transported on a large scale; those who were responsible had to learn to manage big enterprise. People had to think in terms of greater distances, larger quantities and more dangerous risks. Talk of far places became current as the various contingents of crusaders and traders returned and related their adventures.

In the thirteenth century a second pressure was felt. The Mongols under Jenghis Khan invaded Europe in 1225 and overran Russia. Under the great Khan's successor they crossed Poland and Hungary, penetrating as far west as Silesia. The advance of these formidable tribesmen from the steppes was a greater menace to Christendom than the invasion of the Turks. It was a direct challenge to the Church, and Pope Innocent IV was not slow to grasp it. He acted in the hope that he might stop the Mongolian invaders, enlist them as allies against the Moslems who dominated the Near East and convert them and their Khan to Christianity. He therefore sent an emissary, the Franciscan monk, John of Plano Carpini, who traveled in 1245 into the interior of Asia to the Khan's headquarters at Karakorum. He was the first of a series of envoys and missionaries who went back and forth through Central Asia, penetrating to China. They made converts, established churches and even bishoprics and archbishoprics; furthermore, they wrote of what they saw and what they learned. Their manuscripts were copied and had some small circulation. Europe was beginning to hear current stories about regions farther away than the Near East, tales of lands of fabulous wealth and happiness.

These journeys stimulated trade as adventurous business men followed the monks. Two Venetian merchants, Maffeo and Nicolo Polo, set out in 1260 in search of new markets. They visited Asia and later returned thither with Nicolo's son, Marco. He had manifold experiences in the Far East, notably in China, and did not finally return to Europe until 1295. Fortunes of war made him a prisoner of the rival city of Genoa, and while in durance vile he dictated his memoirs, giving in very racy style a great mass of description of the fabulous East, of Cathay and Cipango (China and Japan), stressing particularly the wealth of gold and jewels which the natives (he said) hardly valued. His manuscript was much copied and his stories passed around from mouth to mouth.

While these contacts with the East were bringing to European minds glowing pictures of those distant lands, the intellectual world was reaching out for the implications of certain geographical concepts of the ancients. The Moslem invasion of Spain and the long occupation of that peninsula by the Moors had brought Arabic culture into Europe. Unlike the ecclesiastical savants of the Latin world of learning, the Arabian scholars were well versed in Greek. They knew the theories of the Hellenistic and Alexandrian scientists regarding the sphericity of the earth. During the twelfth and thirteenth centuries there poured forth from the University of Toledo a series of manuscripts which had currency in France and Italy and attracted Latin scholars. These Arabic works, translated into Latin, contained the Greek scientific ideas, particularly those of Aristotle and Eratosthenes. These concepts were received by the scholars awakening in the glow of the Renaissance, and to the learned world the earth was no longer flat. Scholars calculated the circumference of their newly recovered globe and concluded that perhaps Europe was really not so far from Cathay and Cipango. The adventurous might reach the East by sailing west across the Atlantic.

The new knowledge of the fourteenth and fifteenth centuries also had its practical side. It stimulated inventions which were to promote new ideas and strange discoveries. In the first rank was printing, which became practical by 1462, thus providing the means for disseminating old and new knowledge. The work of the ancient Alexandrian geographer, Claudius Ptolemy, and the treatises of Cardinal d'Ailly contained in his *Imago Mundi*, as well as the adventures of Marco Polo, could be distributed more widely in the latter half of the fifteenth century. Maps likewise were now drawn more accurately, giving many a mariner the benefit of *portolani* or charts which were better, at least, than blind guesses.

Other practical instruments made navigation safer and thus more tempting to those venturing forth on unknown seas. Most seafarers heretofore had clung pretty closely to the shore, and when sailors ventured into the Mediterranean out of sight of land, they depended on the stars for reckoning; woe betide them when clouds hid the sky. The Arabs had devised the compass and the Crusaders had brought it for Christian mariners to test against the usual superstitious opposition to things new. New devices were perfected to calculate latitude and longitude. The astrolabe and the cross-staff were instruments whereby the heights of stars above the horizon might be measured. Clocks had come into use, so that the mariner knowing the height of certain stars and the time could then refer to prepared tables or ephemerides and from them tell where he was. Finally, there were improvements in ship construction. The old many-oared galleys were replaced by vessels with strong masts and high prows and sterns. Though by present-day standards these caravels were of perilously light draft, they carried the discoverers to their destination across the stormy Atlantic and they later bore the first generations of the colonists.

Commerce, like knowledge, profited by contacts with strange peoples of eastern lands. The efforts necessary to supply and transport the crusading armies had increased the wealth and experience of such Italian cities as Venice and Genoa. In fact, their merchants had been largely responsible for some of the later crusades. They had practical control of the growing trade with the Levant. The demand for eastern luxuries and commodities increased as the wealthy learned of them. More Europeans craved spices to improve the taste of their indifferent food, often partly spoiled through lack of preservatives and refrigeration. They wanted perfumes to make less unpleasant their uncleanly homes and persons. They wanted soft silks, gems and drugs. The Venetian and Genoese merchants labored to supply these wants—at a price.

Well-defined trade routes were marked out by the middlemen. Far-eastern goods were brought overland to the Caspian, thence to the Black Sea and finally to Constantinople, or they might be collected at Malacca on the Malay Peninsula and transported on the Indian Ocean to Calcutta and thence through the Red Sea and overland to Alexandria, or into the Persian Gulf and overland via Bagdad to Antioch or Jaffa. At the Mediterranean ports Italian merchants bargained for these wares to carry them to their cities. There, arrangements were made for distributing them through Europe, either by great flotillas

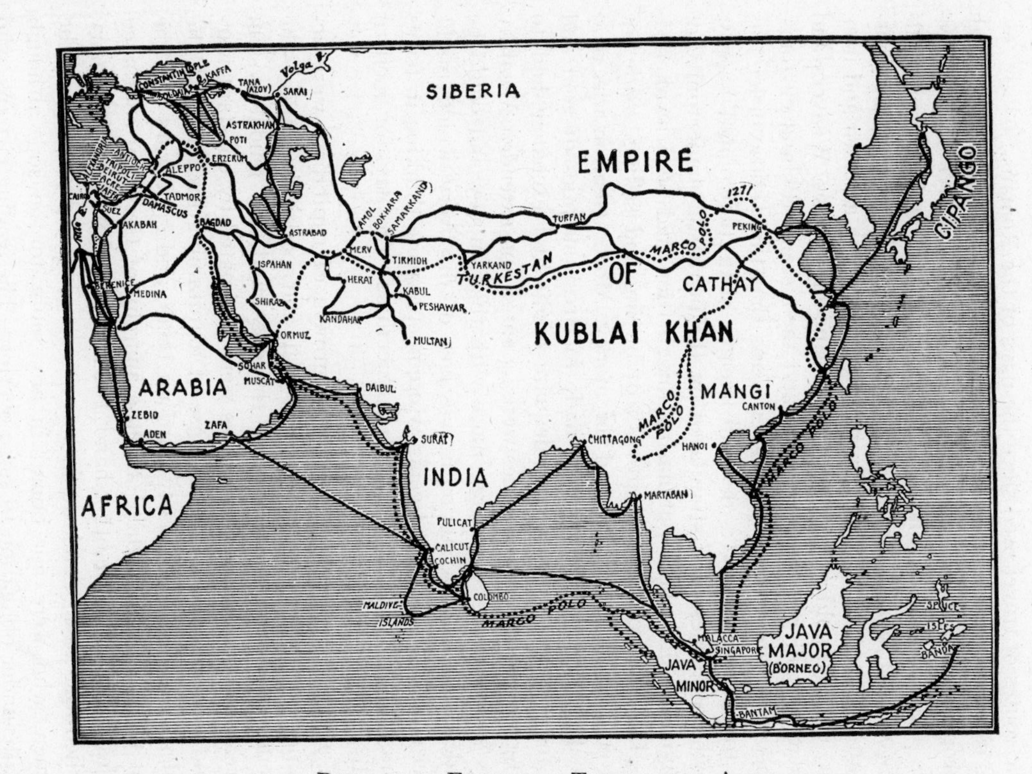

Routes of European Trade with Asia

(From Bolton's *History of the Americas,* by permission of the author and Ginn and Company.)

which sailed boldly out through the Straits of Gibraltar and northward to France, England and the Low Countries, or overland following historic routes of travel used since the days of the Romans.

This expanding trade was met by corresponding activity in the north of Europe. There the Hansa towns developed commerce in the Germanies and Scandinavia and likewise brought fuel and raw materials to the south. In England and the Low Countries the wool trade flourished and there were advances in manufactures, such as cloth and iron, leather, cutlery, gold and silver utensils and ornaments. Weavers and smiths with their guild organization and their standards and customs, had they been alert, might have seen signs that their static order was about to be pressed by a demand greater than they could supply. Everywhere business was stimulated by the increasing importunity of the buying public whose purchasing imagination had been awakened.

This business activity, the growth of buying and selling, made for a greater interest in and demand for money. More attention was paid to coinage and eager search was made for fresh supplies of gold and silver for minting. Also, more adequate credit and exchange had to be perfected and banking services were invented and extended. Wealthy traders were willing to venture more with their money and could be persuaded to risk sums to outfit voyages of discovery which might uncover supplies of gold and gems. More people were thinking in terms of money and profits, shares and partnerships; the days of modern capitalism had begun.

The advance of knowledge and the growth of capitalism were accompanied by a highly significant social and political change—the emergence of the middle class. On the one hand, the feudal system was breaking up; the fighting nobles were decimated by constant warfare and impoverished by the expense of maintaining their forces. The Crusades had been particularly hard on them, and civil wars like the War of the Roses in England and the anarchy of Germany continued their destruction. On the other hand, the increase of trade and industry multiplied the towns and made more numerous and important the townsmen, who were not bound in any sense to the soil, although nominally under obligation to some overlord. The leading citizens, who were wealthy merchants and craftsmen, sought to increase their social and political prestige by the power of their money. Their feudal masters needed cash for their expensive living. Retainers, castles, luxuries were costly and mortgages were heavy burdens. So the nobles sold privileges to the towns. Otherwise the prosperous burghers might maintain soldiers of their own and compel the neighboring barons to respect their pretensions. In this fashion towns and cities gained charters of liberties guaranteeing their independence of feudal exactions.

The new middle class gained more prestige because of a significant political change. As the feudal power waned, kings were emerging who were more than nominal feudal overlords. They were statesmen and military leaders with power. They, too, needed money and sought the financial support of the middle class. In order to ensure a fairly reasonable acquiescence in tax levies, the kings recognized the demands of the middle class for important places in the ancient parliaments in England, France and Spain, and for participation in the tax-levying power. They found the bourgeoisie willing to support monarchs who created policies in aid of trade, who protected merchants by maintaining peace and order, and who sought new raw materials and markets. The king's peace was better than feudal anarchy. The king and his enterprising bourgeoisie had much in common. In fact, this new spirit of enterprise and new vision, the appearance of powerful directing agencies in the new monarchies and the growth of a middle class capable of broad views and vigorous leadership, were the most significant of all the developments leading to the building of a new world.

These new monarchs organized national states; new concentrations of patriotism and power were replacing the loose associations and petty rivalries of the multitude of feudal baronies. These states were situated in western Europe, where people dwelt farthest from the centers of older civilization, where conditions of life were hardest, where supplies were most expensive and most difficult to get. The new nations were marked by speech differences, for there was increasing use of local vernaculars in literature and by government. The distinctive language of each people emphasized their common interest within their realm and the differences between them and their neighbors outside. On the Iberian peninsula were the Hispanic kingdoms, about to consolidate into Spain and Portugal. North of the Pyrenees lay France, in the Low Countries dwelt the Dutch, and across the Channel the English were preparing to create an empire. There was almost constant fighting in this region; the Spanish and Portuguese were bent on driving out the Moors. The French and English were bitterly hostile and for nearly a hundred years, from mid-fourteenth to mid-fifteenth century, were at war. These constant conflicts and rivalries emphasized patriotism and loyalty to one's own king and country and hatred of others. They bred a venturesome group who in intervals of peace yearned for new and daring exploits and were ready servants of ambitious sovereigns. Such were the people who lived on the shores of the great "Ocean Sea," the Atlantic, beyond which scholars held there were strange lands yet undiscovered.

Thus, conditions in the Europe of the thirteenth, fourteenth and fifteenth centuries were changing the outlook of that continent. No longer were old ways satisfying; eyes were turning in new directions. New purposes, new ambitions, new ideas, new hopes were moving

Europe to launch a great migration. Liberated minds were motivated by a new purpose to a burst of creative resourcefulness and enterprise which was to be the great achievement of the Modern Age.

The Discovery of America

The actual discovery of America was directed from a logical base of operations, where there was a most favorable combination of circumstances. In many respects, the Iberian peninsula was the natural point for such activity, for it was nearest the New World and its needs were compelling. The peninsula had been racked by a continuous crusade which, by the fifteenth century, had been going on for 700 years. Ever since the Moslem invasion in 711, the Hispanic Christians had been fighting to drive them back. Their long-drawn-out struggle drained their resources. As they were at the extreme southwestern point of Europe, they were away from the sources of supply fed out by the Mediterranean traders and their import costs were made excessive by high freight rates and middlemen's charges. They themselves had relatively little to export and only a meagre supply of gold with which to meet the adverse balances. If they could find new routes to the East they could free themselves from the Mediterranean yoke. Furthermore, if they could find new supplies of gold for their own exclusive use, they would, so they thought, enjoy prosperity and ease. The warlike and adventurous life of constant crusading, and a lack of good agricultural land and natural resources, made for a way of life that emphasized adventure and deprecated work. Therefore, African slaves were desired to carry on the necessary toil. With the Mediterranean shores controlled by French, Italians or Moslems, it was but natural that the needs and ambitions of these Iberians drove them to dare the little-known waters of the Atlantic.

Their courage in venturing upon this ocean was buoyed up by religious faith. The missionary enterprise of the Church had been kept at high pitch in the Iberian peninsula by constant warfare with the infidel. Legend had it that in the heart of Africa was a great Christian power, the fabulous Prester John. If this potentate could be visited, it might be possible to arrange a union of Christian forces which would drive the Moslems from the north of Africa as well as from the peninsula. Economic need, desire for power, love of adventure and zeal for the faith all united to urge these people so strategically located to make the efforts which were to lead to America.

The Portuguese, situated on the Atlantic coast of the peninsula, led the way. One of their royal family, Prince Henry the Navigator, showed a true scientist's zeal in advancing maritime enterprise. Although he himself never sailed, he built an observatory, called together distant scholars, established a school of navigation and equipped and directed expeditions. The Portuguese efforts culminated in the feat of Bartholomew Diaz; in 1486 he braved the mysteries of the Cape of Good Hope and opened the way to India which his countryman, Vasco da Gama, finally reached in 1497-1498. Soon the Portuguese would be in the isles of the East Indies.

Meanwhile, the success of the Portuguese had inspired an Italian sailor who had come to live among them. Christopher Columbus was a Genoese born about 1451, son of a weaver of wool. Somehow, he found an education as he followed the sea. By the time he was 25 he had come to Portugal and in the years following he sailed to the Canaries, the Azores, the island of Madeira, where he lived briefly, and the Guinea coast. He was tremendously interested in the travel legends and literature, particularly Marco Polo's travels recently available in print. He talked with sailors, learned as he traveled, and the more he learned became the more convinced that the Portuguese idea of seeking Asia by sailing around Africa could be improved upon. Calculating the circumference of the earth, he made an error and figured the distance much less than it really was. Why not sail due west? Having convinced himself, he spent two years trying to persuade the King of Portugal to finance a voyage.

Failing, Columbus, now about 33, set out to try his luck elsewhere on the Iberian peninsula; it then held, besides Portugal, Castile, Aragon and the Moorish kingdom with its stronghold of Granada. The rulers of Castile and Aragon, Isabella and Ferdinand, had united their hands in marriage and their kingdoms in a supreme effort to oust the Moors Their Moorish war had been going on five years when Columbus arrived, and it kept him waiting eight years more. In despair, he despatched his brother to sound out Henry VII of England and in 1492 prepared himself to approach the court of France. That year Granada fell; and the victorious Isabella was ready to listen to intercessors for Columbus. Shrewd, ambitious, commanding and calculating, she agreed to help finance Columbus; her "jewels" were long since gone, and she contributed less than one-fourth of the sum (equivalent to $100,000 in modern money) needed for the venture. But she marked her patronage by making him a grandee and pledging him and his heirs one-tenth of the gold and silver in the new lands. Under such auspices Columbus made his historic voyage of 1492 and became the discoverer of America. Upon this foundation Spain built a huge colonial empire. It once embraced the better part of both American continents: Central America; all of South America except Brazil, which Portugal preëmpted; Florida; Mexico, including Texas; and the wilderness north and west of Texas, including California and reaching approximately to Oregon.

Beginning of French and Dutch Enterprise

The Spanish achievement had many repercussions in Europe and caused other nations to look to America. Spain's power was mightily increased by her new supply of treasure, and she undertook to gain advantage at the expense of her neighbors—France, the Netherlands and England. They had to defend themselves and to seek like sources of power with which to accomplish it. Also, the great gold supply coming into Europe by way of Spain cheapened money and made prices high. The other nations sought to find new gold supplies to keep from economic ruin.

Spain first turned upon France, which was attempting to expand into Italy at her expense. France, beaten and frustrated in Italy, turned to experiment in the possibilities of America. French fishermen and traders from Dieppe, Rouen, Honfleur and St. Malo had visited America as early as 1504, touching at places on the coast from Canada to Brazil. Twenty years later a Florentine, Verrazano, who was something of a pirate preying upon Spanish shipping to and from Mexico, went on an exploring voyage for Francis I of France and for a promoter from Dieppe. He followed the American coast from the 30th to 50th parallel and took possession of it in the name of his patron. Ten years passed, however, before Francis I followed up this exploit by sending Jacques Cartier of St. Malo to explore his new possessions. His explorations of the St. Lawrence valley, 1534-1544, however, resulted in no permanent settlements. The winters were too severe, the climate seemed impossible.

Meanwhile, the religious motive supplanted the dynastic motive in French colonization, for the country was torn by forty years of religious strife and civil war. Many Protestants, called Huguenots, drawn in part from the prosperous middle class, had become wealthy and sought privileges of freedom of worship and political rights. Opposition of the ruling Catholic group to this new class produced political struggles that broke out into massacre and war. The Protestant leaders thought of the possibilities in the New World much as did the English Puritans later, and tried first South and then North America. French merchants had organized a trade to South America and in 1556 the leading Huguenot, Admiral Coligny, patronized a venture in Brazil which lasted a dozen years before the Portuguese ended it. In North America Coligny backed Jean Ribaut in an attempt of 1562 to establish a colony at Port Royal Sound, in what is now South Carolina, and two years later another on the St. John's River in Florida. At this juncture Spain, which had been jealously watching the rise of French Protestant influence, struck at their colonies. They were destroyed with barbarous cruelty and Florida was made a Spanish province with control exercised from St. Augustine, which still stands today, the oldest city in the mainland area of the United States.

The first successful French colony was commercial, rather than imperial or religious, in origin. Two merchants of St. Malo in 1600 won a monopoly from Henry IV and planned a trading-post on the St. Lawrence. They built a fort at the mouth of the Saguenay at Tadoussac and a company followed them there. Fortunately Samuel de Champlain, a pilot, entered their service and quickly emerged as a capable leader. Settlements were made on an island in Passamaquoddy Bay between Maine and New Brunswick and in Acadia (present day Nova Scotia). Champlain crowned his efforts in 1608 by the permanent founding of Quebec. He remained long in Canada, persistently exploring. He discovered the Great Lakes and established the fact that the St. Lawrence was a river, not a strait. Just before his death in 1634 one of his voyageurs, Jean Nicolet, penetrated into Wisconsin. Compared with the Spanish exploits, the French ventures were limited and unsuccessful. Only a few Frenchmen were in the New World in the early years of the seventeenth century, and most of them were scattered along the St. Lawrence.

Spain's advance likewise stimulated the Dutch to colonial effort. They had progressed under the vitalizing forces which were producing the Modern Age. The middle class and townsmen had grown prosperous; their trade and industry had grown proverbial. These citizens used their wealth to great advantage in bargaining with feudal overlords, and a number of thriving cities such as Rotterdam, Utrecht and Delft had gained charters and were practically free city-states. However, when their ruler married the daughter of Ferdinand and Isabella the burghers of the Protestant Netherlands became Spanish subjects. Catholic Spain looked upon the prosperous Protestants with extreme ill favor.

When Philip II became King of Spain in 1556, trouble brewed fast. The Spanish sought to oppress the Dutch by heavy taxes, by demanding that they give up Protestantism and by curtailing their liberties and privileges. In 1566 began a rebellion which resulted in the creation of a Dutch Republic under the leadership of William the Silent. This new union of city-states was officially announced in 1581 but was not recognized by Philip II, who continued efforts to regain them. One of his weapons was commercial. The Dutch had been trading with the East through Portugal, but as Portugal had become a part of Spain, Philip closed this trade to the rebelling Hollanders. Such a policy only stimulated the Dutch traders and sea-rovers to widen their interests. They began in 1595 an attack on the Portuguese East Indies that was entirely successful, resulting in the establishment of the Dutch East Indies seized by the Japanese in the present war. They also turned their attention to Portuguese possessions in America. They had gone to Guiana, just north of Brazil, as early as 1580, and they continued that interest and used it for a base of invasion into Brazil itself.

An East India Company was organized by the Dutch in 1602, and one of its captains, an Englishman, Henry Hudson, explored the North American coast, discovering in 1609 the great river that bears his name. Hudson was soon followed by fur-traders who occasionally camped on Manhattan and sailed up the Hudson to trade with the Indians. The explorations of one of these traders, Adriaen Block, who visited the areas which were to be Connecticut, Rhode Island and Massachusetts, led the Dutch government to give him and his backers a temporary trade monopoly over the Hudson River region. Here a trading-post was established on the future Jersey shore of the river, at Bergen. Henry Hudson had also discovered the Delaware River, later visited by Cornelius May, for whom Cape May was named, and occasional traders sought profit in this valley. Far to the south, Dutch interest expanded in Guiana, where a colony was established, and, as the rivalry with Spanish and Portuguese increased in that region, a new plan to strengthen Dutch interests was formulated. Inspired by the success of the Dutch East India Company and the Hudson River traders, a Dutch West India Company was incorporated (1621) to promote the interests of Holland in the Western Hemisphere by establishing New Netherland, later to be New York. The Dutch were thus in a position to set in motion projects which would rival those of France, Portugal and the slowly awakening English.

In the century and more that had elapsed since Columbus led the first settlers to America, an almost bewildering variety of Spanish, French and Dutch had followed them; and the English were belatedly undertaking to join in the contest for New World benefits. The influences at work in the modern world were responding to and exploiting the potentialities of America. In the changing order of western Europe was spreading the idea that America was a place of opportunity where there was assurance of great wealth, high adventure, a missionary field ripe for the harvest, and a freedom for the individual such as the Old World could never know.

CHAPTER II

THE ENGLISH MIGRATION

The adventurous exploits of Spaniards, French and Dutch but paved the way for the real colonization of the future United States. Their share of influence proved small, compared to that of the sturdy English empire-builders. The latter were slow in turning to America, but their interest once aroused proved extraordinarily fruitful.

English Reluctance to Venture Westward

Full three-quarters of a century England had known of America, for as long ago as 1497 John Cabot, in the pay of Bristol merchants, had sailed west for Asia and had happened upon Newfoundland. Yet none had followed him thither save the fishermen who annually made their catch off the bleak shores of the strange new coast. Scarce a soul dreamed of any other form of venture in America.

There were weighty reasons for English reluctance to turn westward. The British Isles were off in a corner of Europe, and English interests were confined primarily to the islands and to the neighboring shores of the Continent. Such narrow horizons limited the vision of Englishmen, and they did not readily conceive of distant projects. Even had there been the imagination, there was not the means. Expeditions across the Atlantic were likely to be extremely expensive and hazardous and England had little surplus capital; none could be spared for so uncertain a venture. The economy of the nation was still largely feudal. Land was the principal form of wealth and it could not be used for mercantile pursuits. There were one or two ancient companies of merchants, such as the Merchant Adventurers and the Staplers, but their dealings were almost entirely confined to trade in cloth and wool with the nearby Low Countries. Few people made much money, and the English had relatively little to spend and less to invest.

Other circumstances were even more discouraging to far-flung enterprise. The English merchant marine was handicapped. It was poor in ships. Westward sailing was made difficult and tedious by the ill favor of the winds which generally blew toward the east. Also England had powerful enemies, particularly the Spanish, who controlled much of the New World. The Spanish navy dominated the sea-lanes leading to the attractive regions of America and their sea strength was such that if English mariners did set out for the shadowy lands, they must sail far to the north in dangerous waters to avoid their foes. Thus only the forbidding northern shores of America were conveniently accessible, and they offered slight inducement for the risk.

Despite these difficulties, English enterprise at length turned to the western continents. The new spirit of the Modern Age was awakening the English people, who were about to reach great heights in many forms of endeavor. The epoch of Elizabeth was moving towards its zenith; it was an age in which an unsuspected creative talent was to make England a leader in shaping modern civilization.

The mightiest force in the creation of this new spirit was a social change of great significance. The new middle class was taking a prominent place in English life. The old feudal order of privileged and unprivileged was giving way before the enterprise of a number of intelligent and obscure people who were industriously laboring to increase England's wealth and prosperity. Many of the feudal domains were turned into sheep pastures. Quantities of fine woolen cloth were manufactured and carried far abroad by English traders who sold it for gold and silver. A number of Englishmen were growing rich; though they had little fame, their strong boxes were filling with gold coin. They found that money gave them power and influence, which they sought to use to their own advantage as the variety of their investments and interests increased. Also there had been a redistribution of property which freed more wealth for active enterprise. When the Church had been separated from Rome in the reign of Henry VIII, the Crown confiscated much of the large property of the monasteries and a great deal of this wealth passed into the hands of those more adroit in its use; a new fund of capital was at the disposal of business. England was leaving her feudal economy and preparing to take the lead in the rise of modern capitalism which was to dominate the western world.

The influential middle class was courted by those "progressive" monarchs, the Tudors. They encouraged the business men who valued peace and needed prosperity, and who were willing to back with their money a monarch who could keep order and promote their interests outside of England. The Tudors and their advisers saw the need of an adequate merchant marine and lent their help to the new merchant interest in building up a shipping worthy of the new age. Henry VIII had given much attention to the navy and nautical science and patronized experts in maritime affairs. One of his protegés, Fletcher of Rye, in 1539 developed the art of tacking, whereby ships were rigged and maneuvered to sail against the wind. Thereafter, the voyage to the westward was much less difficult a venture. New and larger ships, too, began to fly the English flag, carrying more Englishmen of adventurous tastes across the seas.

Finally England emerged as a European power. The Tudors saw the value to the kingdom and to themselves of foreign influence and sought to promote it by shrewd participation in the crafty intrigues which marked the diplomacy of the day. English diplomats, true servants of their Tudor masters, thrust themselves into the affairs of continental Europe, and Henry VIII crossed swords with Frances I of France, Charles V of Spain and Germany and, in a certain sense, with the Pope himself. For family and religious reasons, the rivalry was keenest with Catholic Spain, the power with the huge empire in America. These new forces were combining to produce an expansive England, setting the stage for the new enterprise of the Elizabethan era.

The organization of large-scale business ventures at the mid-point of the sixteenth century paved the way for a lively interest in America. England was heavily in debt and had to gather large sums to pay foreign creditors. The government just then under the regents of Edward VI was unable to act efficiently. Agriculture was disorganized due to the shift from tilling the soil to raising sheep. Unemployment was widespread, for thousands of tenants had been cast adrift when their fields were turned into sheep pastures. Foreign trade and buyers of British cloth were falling off. In fact, the things England needed cost too much. New export markets and cheaper ways of obtaining imports must be found. Such conditions caused the more progressive London merchants much anxious thought as they discussed the matter among themselves in the year 1552. It became apparent to them that new methods were necessary.

Spain and Portugal were increasing their wealth by ventures in unknown fields; by sailing to the west and southeast they had found riches. Might not England gain what was needed by similar voyages? Capitalists, including members of the Merchant Adventurers, began to plan a new organization for larger operations. Clearly there were but two possible roads to the riches of the east, to the northwest or to the northeast; along other routes the Spanish or the Portuguese blocked the way. So the enterprising London merchants sent out explorers to the northeast (1553-1555), established relations with Russia and formed a new company, the Muscovy or Russian Adventurers; yet Cathay was not discovered.

Meanwhile the public began to think of India and the New World. Englishmen made translations of books about the shadowy continents. Difficulties with France and Spain, especially the latter, were multiplying and jealous England noted the steady supply of wealth which came to Spain from America, to England's disadvantage. In the meantime, Elizabeth had ascended the throne and signs of vigorous policies were not slow in appearing.

As the Muscovy proprietors had not reached Cathay by the northeastern route, they determined to try the northwest; something must be done to cut down the charges of the too numerous foreign middlemen who taxed English trade. So they licensed an experienced explorer, Martin Frobisher, in 1575; but his three voyages failed to find the passage to Cathay, or to discover gold, in the vicinity of Greenland. Sir Humphrey Gilbert tried to plant a colony in Newfoundland and Sir Walter Raleigh one in North Carolina, the Roanoke Island home of Virginia Dare, but all to no avail. In colonization ventures there seemed naught but toil and trouble, while in privateering and pillaging Spanish merchant and treasure ships there was easy wealth. Sir Francis Drake, Cavendish, and other glorious freebooters plundered far and wide, with profit.

Commercial Enterprise Leads the Way

In spite of the disasters attending the ventures of Frobisher, Gilbert and Raleigh the idea of American settlement could not die. Their exploits and those of Drake and the freebooters served as advertising while the stronger forces of economic, social and religious change constantly pressed toward colonization.

The last years of Elizabeth's reign, after the failure of Raleigh's enterprise, were years of commercial stagnation deepened by the long-drawn-out war with Spain. The depression revealed very clearly the existing economic weaknesses, as is the way with depressions. In the first place, England's lack of self-sufficiency was proven once again, for the war kept the kingdom in constant danger of being cut off from some vital source of supply. In the second place, the cost of living had increased so that fixed incomes of the gentry in many cases had become inadequate. Finally, the close of the Spanish war caused demobilization of much of the armed force; many an adventurous soldier found himself footloose and fancy free in the midst of a depression. More than ever did England seem overpopulated. All these conditions pointed toward adventure in fabulous and baffling America.

The revival of interest in the New World was at first largely advanced by the merchants. England found herself in a new position commercially; no longer was she off in a corner. The development of trans-Atlantic navigation by the Spanish had widened and readjusted trading routes and had brought the British Isles much nearer the center of commercial activity. Also, British merchants had learned that individuals were not best fitted to exploit America; corporations must be formed. The East India Company had been organized recently for the exploitation of the far east and capitalists began to plan for like organizations to operate in what might have been termed at that time, the far west. A proposal was made by a powerful group of merchants, soldiers and government officials who contended that, as private colonies had ever been a failure, an undertaking should now be tried by a syndicate under governmental patronage. King James I approved the project and two groups of soldiers and merchants were organized under royal patents issued 10 April 1606, in the business centers of London and Plymouth. Important in these groups were Sir Thomas Smythe, one of the most adventurous business men of the day, Richard Hakluyt, a publicity expert, and military men like Sir Thomas Gates.

The London Company acted most effectively and got together 105 men who in three small ships set sail 20 December 1606 to establish what proved to be the first permanent English settlement in America. Jamestown was the result, and commercial enterprise had started what it was hoped would be a profitable venture.

If it were to succeed, the proposed trading-post must attract settlers, and the London Company sought to advertise the new location. Their efforts were successful in attracting the interest of people from various classes. In the first three years there migrated some 400, mostly of humble origin; only 30 per cent could be classed as gentlemen. Their hardships were intense and once the colony was almost abandoned. The company, however, was several times reorganized, liberal offers of land and self-government were made and the venture persisted.

By the end of the first twenty years some 5,649 persons had at various times come to the colony; and though scarce 2,000 of these were still in Virginia, the colony was on a permanent foundation and an outpost of empire had been established. More important, the idea of America was becoming more attractive in England. The survival of the colony and the advertising of the London and Plymouth Companies were doing their work. America might prove more than a field for trade; it might also be a place for happier and freer living.

The Quest for Liberty

Had English interest been confined to the adventurous and speculative, England's American empire might never have been more than a series of trading-posts and company projects for producing raw materials. But the character of the American nation was to be formed by forces much stronger than love of adventure or desire for wealth. The rise of the middle class and the development of the religious reformation were to be particularly potent in turning English attention to America, not as a source of possible gain, but as an experiment station in the creation of a reformed social order.

Emergence of the middle class was accompanied by many social readjustments, and as society resists change, there were many conflicts and much unhappiness. One of the most fertile fields for struggle was religious. As the middle class sought liberty to live their own lives, they were desirous particularly of religious freedom because the old religion was dominated by the hierarchy and priesthood. During the reign of Elizabeth this conflict was accentuated by the appearance of a strong reform group known as Puritans. They wished to change the manner of worship in the Church of England, to make it more matter of fact and less symbolic, to develop discipline and moral standards of personal conduct, and to lay more emphasis upon the chief reformation tenet that man's relations with God were direct and personal and not conducted through the ministrations of a priesthood.

Most of the Puritans were willing to remain within the established church and work for its reform, in the meantime minimizing the use of the prayer book, simplifying the service and church decoration and placing the emphasis upon preaching. In the matter of church government there were those who sought to reintroduce the practice of appointing elders or chief laymen; their ideal was a presbyterian form in which presbyteries or synods, meetings of the preachers and elders, instead of bishops, would determine matters of church policy. The main body of the Puritans as much as possible put their ideas into practice without actually leaving the Church of England. Naturally, their policies produced a lack of uniformity; in some parishes the conduct of religion varied little from that utilized when the church was loyal to the Pope, while in others, especially in the southeast of England, the pastor and people worshiped in a fashion hardly recognizable to those faithful to the church as established by law.

The conflict of opinion and practice had a wider significance than its effect upon religious observance. The government controlled the church; Elizabeth appointed the bishops and was herself the "supreme governor." The sixteenth century was not a period in which governments willingly tolerated views opposing those officially held; and when Elizabeth displayed impatience with people who sought to modify ritual and government the matter took on a political aspect. Various statutes were passed and orders issued which showed clearly that Elizabeth discountenanced this lack of uniformity; but her displeasure was exhibited only sporadically and the magnitude of her other problems prevented a consistent policy. Nevertheless the Queen's attitude was perfectly apparent and her opponents were often recruited among those whose religious ideas she attempted to modify. Liberty of conscience and freedom of religious observance began to be issues which many who disliked the Queen's policies, her arbitrary rule, her "pomp and vain glory," or her governmental program could use in formulating protest among a large group of sober and industrious people.

As a result, the conflict took on a social as well as a political aspect. The nobles and the tenantry, the country squires and the yeomen, the visible remnants of the old feudal order, were generally content with little religious change, now that the monasteries had been broken up and their lands re-distributed. But the new ideas were very attractive to the townsmen and to the rising merchant class who felt the need of honesty and sobriety in business dealings and knew the wealth-producing possibilities of hard work and who also took a more decided interest in management. To a director in a corporation the idea of a "session" or committee of elders to manage a church was a logical thing. Besides, the small townsmen were no longer feudal in their outlook. As their mercantile horizon widened, and their profits grew, their feeling of importance strengthened; but they were in a society that was still organized along feudal lines and in a church dominated by a hierarchy. They were independent in spirit and fond of their own opinions and did not relish the insignificant place allotted them in the episcopal church organization.

In spite of these general conditions the line must not be too clearly drawn according to region or class. People from all walks of life, even from the nobility and country gentry, became Puritan and many a *nouveau riche* middle-class citizen revered the Church of England as a mark of his own social rise. But neighbor did contend with neighbor, families divided and high churchman and Puritan often refused to remain on speaking terms one with another.

The religious, political and social cleavages became most apparent in the case of a small group who began to appear more prominently in the latter years of Elizabeth's reign. The members of this group were convinced that there must be a return to the early Christian custom of independent, self-governing congregations. For them, they felt, there was no virtue in the Church of England, and conscience demanded that they come out and be separate, worshiping in independent congregations according to their own interpretation of the Scriptures. Though these "Separatists," as they were called, were neither many nor important in wealth or social standing, still they were intense and persistent and were bound to spread. Worse still, from the point of view of the government, they were a bad example. The Church of England was the state church, and the medieval idea of uniformity was still too strong to brook the notion of more than one organization. Separatists were not only schismatic but unpatriotic, and as the Queen sought to subdue those who opposed her rule, she was also determined to destroy those who opposed her church.

The result was an act passed in 1593 designed to curb Puritans as well as Separatists by inflicting punishments of death or banishment upon those who persisted in their faith. Two of their leaders, Barrowe and Greenwood, were hanged at Tyburn. Others were arrested and some few abjured the realm that same year, fleeing to Holland where they established a church in Amsterdam. From these years onward under Elizabeth and James, the lot of Puritan, and more especially Separatist, was less and less pleasant and many thought of emigrating. Some time in these years the idea dawned upon these serious-minded folk that in America where a number of them had made investments, all too profitless as yet, there ought to be a haven of refuge where they with God's help might establish His Holy Commonwealth. Theirs too was a vision, not of empire, but of liberty.

About the time the London and Plymouth companies were formed, a small group of these serious-minded people in the Nottinghamshire village of Scrooby had banded together in a Separatist congregation which, contrary to law, met each Sabbath for independent worship. Many of their neighbors ridiculed them and scoffed at their peculiar ideas; some even went so far as to lodge a complaint. Though local authorities were not disposed to deal severely with them, it became apparent that King James was going to make war upon non-conformity in general. The possibility of serious persecution began to prey upon their minds, already harassed by the torture of the gossip and ridicule of neighbors. Since they were liable to imprisonment, loss of property and banishment, the Scrooby congregation began to talk of a migration to Holland such as had been undertaken a decade previous by the church now at Amsterdam. To leave in a body with their possessions would be no easy matter, for it would call attention to their non-conformity and invite the confiscation of their small property under the law of 1593. They must go secretly; and only after great difficulty and much frustration did they in any measure succeed. Less than a hundred finally congregated in Amsterdam in 1607 and 1608 and moved thence to Leyden.

In the decade following, their number increased to some two hundred, but the peace and prosperity they had anticipated did not come in generous measure. To be sure they were free to worship as they chose, but they were aliens in a strange land, and not very prosperous aliens at that. They began to long for an English community where their children might grow up as Englishmen, for more profitable ways of earning a living, and for that comfort and independence which might come to them in an American community of their own founding.

After much discussion they decided to move to America. In 1619 they obtained permission from the London Company to make a settlement, and received assurance that the King would not interfere with their religious customs. The great problem remaining was funds. They were thrifty and reliable and both Dutch and English promoters were anxious to have them undertake colonization in their territories. Thomas Weston, a London merchant, came to Holland to talk over possibilities and John Carver and Robert Cushman went back to confer in London. Finally an agreement was reached, although its actual details satisfied no one. Weston and some London associates agreed to supply money for the journey and the emigrants were to repay their backers from the fruit of their labors in America.

With these difficult negotiations at length concluded, obstacles were by no means overcome. When the final test came only thirty-five of the Leyden congregation were able and willing to go. Recruits were necessary and sixty-seven were found with difficulty in London who were willing to join the company, for motives which were scarcely religious. With these "Pilgrims" the *Mayflower* at length set sail from Plymouth 6 September 1620. The voyage was long and dangerous, and the ship was driven out of its course so that when the emigrants finally arrived in America they found themselves in the territory of the Plymouth, not the London, Company. There was nothing to do, however, but to make the best of it, and 21 December 1620, they landed at Plymouth and under the leadership of John Carver and William Brewster, ably assisted by one of the recruits, Miles Standish, they began settlement.

For ten years there was not much activity in colonization, but in 1630 a new impetus was given. Charles I was proceeding to rule without Parliament by resorting to arbitrary taxation and ignoring the personal rights of his subjects hallowed by custom. His chief ecclesiastic, Archbishop Laud, attempted to enforce religious uniformity by similar high-handed methods. Economic conditions, too, were bad in southeastern England, the stronghold of the Puritans. Their industries were in a decline and in the towns wages were low and food prices high. "Hard times" throughout England, 1620-1635, discouraged many. The staid and sober Puritan country gentlemen were also disturbed by new social conditions. Their quiet precincts were being invaded by newly enriched traders from London who wished to become landed gentry. These parvenus bought landed estates and introduced extravagant expenditures and "ungodly" ways of life. Puritan squires were not rich enough to compete with this style, had they thought it desirable, and their moral sense was horrified by the new laxity in society. The lot of the Puritan, set about by these attacks upon his standards, was not happy.

A group of such men in 1629 organized as the "Governor and Company of Massachusetts Bay in New England," a stock company similar in many respects to the London Company. The stockholders decided to take their charter and migrate in a body. In the spring of 1630, therefore, sixteen vessels and 1,000 colonists were assembled and sailed to America, where in the vicinity of Boston harbor the colony of Massachusetts Bay was planted.

The migration of the Massachusetts Bay Company was soon imitated by another group, moved by somewhat similar motives. Following the death of Queen Mary in 1558, English Catholics had suffered sporadic persecution. Legally they could not be said to exist, as they had no recognized rights; politically and socially, they were without the pale. At all stages in American enterprise, some of their faith had been interested in establishing a refuge there. Their hope was cherished by Sir George Calvert, a politician of influence under the Stuarts, who had been converted to Catholicism. He had been considering a plan for a colony, wishing both to promote his fortunes and to establish a place where Catholics might have freedom.

He died before he could carry out his plan, but in 1634 his son, the second Lord Baltimore, succeeded. Under a charter procured two years previously, whereby Charles I granted the Baltimores the proprietorship of certain land north of Virginia, to be known as Maryland, a little group of twenty gentlemen, four priests and two hundred laborers founded St. Mary's. However, Calvert's hope was realized only in small part, as Catholics migrated less freely than he desired. To make the colony more prosperous he invited Protestant immigrants, who soon outnumbered their Catholic associates. Religious toleration was maintained, sometimes with difficulty, and the Baltimore family continued their ownership of this slow-growing community.

Shortly after the Maryland settlers began their work, New England itself threw off colonies and began in 1636 to get rid of certain radicals who did not agree with the Puritan order of government. Roger Williams was banished first. He gathered to himself others, who built Providence; and shortly thereafter various free spirits organized Portsmouth, Newport and Warwick. These four towns Roger Williams succeeded in uniting as the colony of Providence Plantations—Rhode Island—and obtained a patent of self-government from commissioners of the Long Parliament in 1643. Here any "otherwise minded" people were welcome.

Less radical but no less independent were the Puritans led by Rev. Thomas Hooker, pastor of the church at Newtown in Massachusetts, who peaceably led his people into the Connecticut Valley to establish Hartford. The fertile valley also attracted Puritans direct from England, who during the 'thirties established several settlements.

By 1640 more than 65,000 Englishmen were in America scattered somewhat as follows:

Massachusetts	14,000
Connecticut	2,000
Rhode Island	300
New Hampshire and Maine	1,500
Maryland	1,500
Virginia	8,000
West Indies	40,000

Figures are faulty and inadequate, and our knowledge of human motives is always incomplete; nevertheless, it can be said that the dominating force in colonization in the twenty years, 1620-1640, had been exerted by those who thought more of religious freedom and liberty of action than they did of dividends or the accumulation of wealth. The Puritans might not numerically be able to account a great or overwhelming majority; but in New England, where at that time had settled most of the English who came to the continental area, their ideas of social ordering dominated.

The score of years marked by the Puritan revolution and Commonwealth, 1640-1660, did not check the tide of migration from England but somewhat changed its character. Civil war and governmental change encouraged three groups in particular to migrate. The Puritans as a group were no longer so much interested in America; their energies were required at home to carry through their political experiment. Some royalist sympathizers now sought refuge, especially after the King was beheaded, in Virginia, where loyalty to the Crown was still popular; their number probably has been overrated. Also a number of peace-loving people, especially of the mercantile class, sought a less troubled field of operations in America, where there was none of this civil war, so hard upon business.

A third group directly stimulated by the war was one of the most important in the colonial migration: indentured servants. Wages were low in England during the first half of the seventeenth century and the labor market was glutted. Many wished to get to the New World, but the fare was high; few laborers, saving their wages for a lifetime, could have accumulated the six to ten pounds necessary to procure passage. In the New World, especially in Virginia and Maryland, labor was scarce and the profits from tobacco tempting. As a result hundreds began to take advantage of a form of migration which met both needs. Numerous men and some women began to make agreements whereby in return for transportation to the colonies they would work for a term of years, usually five, as indentured servants to some colonist willing to pay their passage. At the conclusion of this term of service, freedom and some land or money came to the erstwhile servant and he thereby became a property holder. Such an arrangement was bound to be attractive.

When the civil war broke out many prisoners were sent over as indentured servants by whichever side was in control, and during the period of the Commonwealth many who were captured in the Irish and Scotch wars were likewise despatched. Paupers were gathered from the poorhouses and streets of London. Condemned felons also were occasionally sent over under indenture, to relieve the crowded jails and to experiment in criminal reformation. So well did this idea work that a great number of these settled down to a respectable and industrious life. The wilderness, where there were plenty of land, little to steal and few of the temptations of more advanced civilization, proved an excellent destroyer of criminal proclivities. Under such conditions, either by force or their own free will, some 2,000 indentured servants arrived annually in Virginia alone. Migration, therefore, in the years 1640-1660 was steady but uneventful; no new projects were undertaken, but the shiploads of emigrants continued to distribute themselves among the colonies scattered along the Atlantic shore.

The Projects of the Restoration

A new phase of English migration in the seventeenth century began in 1660 with the restoration of the Stuarts. Some friends of Charles II became interested in planting a colony south of Virginia, so he granted them in 1663 an indefinite tract of land known as Carolina. Thus easily then could monarchs make gifts munificent! Carolina, especially the Albemarle Sound region, had attracted earlier settlers; and Virginia farmers found there were not disturbed by the new proprietors. They were given a government and land privileges similar to those in Virginia. The real interest of the promoters, however, was in a colony which they intended to plant themselves. After much hardship, then almost inevitable, a company of one hundred, augmented by threescore others taken on at Barbados, landed at Charleston harbor in 1670. The settlement here suffered and struggled under indifferent leadership. Emigrants came to both North and South Carolina in the years following, and as the location of Charleston proved highly suitable, that portion of the Carolinas prospered.

While their Carolina project was taking shape, the governing group in England undertook a second and more predatory venture. The Dutch and Swedes were located between the New England and the southern colonies, the first along the Hudson, the second along the Delaware in what now are New Jersey, Pennsylvania and Delaware. By 1660 the Dutch and Swedes numbered some 10,000 souls, none too happy under arbitrary Dutch rule.

Dutch and English rivalry had led during the Commonwealth to hostility which the Restoration government was nothing loath to encourage. All told, the Dutch were a nuisance and a menace to English profits—besides, they were reported as almost defenseless. Charles II therefore in 1664 granted to his brother James, Duke of York, the land between the Connecticut and the Delaware as well as Long Island. The Duke of York immediately sent an expedition under Col. Richard Nicolls to seize the new domain. It was no difficult task, and thus English dominion was consolidated from the St. Lawrence to the undetermined southern boundary of the Carolinas. That portion of the newly acquired territory along the Hudson was renamed New York and the Dutch settlers were permitted to retain their property. Meanwhile, even before Nicolls surprised the Dutch, the Duke of York had been asked by two of his close friends, Lord Berkeley and Sir George Carteret, for some of his new estate. They got the lower portion, between the Delaware and the Hudson, which they named New Jersey.

The last phase of the English migration in the seventeenth century found its motive power in another struggle for freedom of conscience. Religious and social difficulties had by no means been abolished by the Restoration. Dissenters were as numerous as ever and again burdened by oppressive laws. The Catholics, too, were becoming more prominent and no less a man than the Duke of York, the heir apparent, was of their faith. Attempts were made to prevent his accession to the throne and the last years of Charles' reign were disturbed by the Popish plot and like intrigues. But the new migration was not to be particularly Catholic; rather it was an ambitious social experiment which proved the climax of seventeenth-century American enterprise.

England had scarcely been conscious of the emergence of a new Christian sect. Under the leadership of George Fox a small group of vigorous individualists, who to that day seemed strangely radical, was beginning to attract attention. These men and women, known to themselves as the Society of Friends and to others as Quakers, sought extreme simplicity in their relations with God and man. They believed in direct communion with God, by means of the illumination of the "inner light," and in the equality of all. Thus they saw no need of priests and paid scant respect to privilege of any sort. They strove for a democratic, individualistic order of society and worship where all were alike followers of the dictates of conscience. Furthermore, they practiced non-resistance; they refused to fight against their enemies, to enter the army or to pay for military support, and declined to take oaths. These two latter practices naturally brought them into conflict with the civil power, and as they were very free in speech and in proclaiming their views, they were considered dangerous to the peace and safety of the realm. Even during the Commonwealth some of them had been imprisoned and after the Restoration more were persecuted.

Like others before them, they thought of the New World as a refuge. Several of their number, including William Penn, had been interested in New Jersey, but because of the many other groups in that colony they had been unable to organize the type of community they wished. Penn had a larger view. He wished to try the "Holy Experiment" of a Quaker colony under their own ideas of government and social order. As the King owed him a large sum, he petitioned Charles to pay this debt by granting him land on the west shore of the Delaware. Charles agreed readily enough and 4 March 1681 signed a charter for the colony of Pennsylvania. The Duke of York contributed his rights to the land around Delaware Bay. By these acts, in spite of the protests and long-drawn-out opposition of the proprietors of Maryland, Penn and his heirs maintained possession of the territory on the western shore of the Delaware which became the colonies of Pennsylvania and Delaware. Philadelphia was laid out in 1682 and the Holy Experiment was en route to becoming a reality. More tolerant than any other foundation except Rhode Island, it invited all who would come. People from many countries arrived and its growth marked a new and more cosmopolitan phase in the development of the British empire in America.

In such fashion between 1607 and 1682 a series of settlements was planted from Carolina to Maine. In them, by 1690, dwelt some 200,000 people, still predominantly English, all owing allegiance to the British Crown. These seventy-five years of migration had called forth much of endurance and ingenuity. The manner in which the settlers overcame the wilderness and builded communities was to be the first demonstration of a way of life and order of society to be known as American.

CHAPTER III

THE ORGANIZATION OF AMERICAN SOCIAL INSTITUTIONS

The colonies thus established by English enterprise were laboratories where many people worked on the problem of institutions for the new society. Most of those who labored thereon were anxious to create better ways of living than they had known hitherto. They set to work with a zest which was to become a well-known characteristic of their descendants.

European Equipment

These pioneers were equipped for their task with something besides a zeal for new and better ways; they had also the habits and customs of middle or lower-class Englishmen, habits sometimes a hindrance rather than a help. The new-comers were descendants of settled people who had been living in the same towns or farming districts for centuries, in environments which had not encouraged change. The initial shock to all their staid habits had been the determination to come to America; this dislocation made succeeding adjustments easier, but nevertheless the demand of the new environment for change proved ruthless and extremely painful.

Those who undertook the new adventure had a wide variety of notions as to what equipment was necessary. All brought supplies of food and weapons; most possessed tools, quite often for mining, though the wiser transported agricultural implements and seed. A little furniture, a few clothes and a book or two, especially the Bible, could sometimes be stowed into the small ships, and occasionally live stock was forced to share with the emigrants the terrors of the long passage.

Colonists thus equipped were thrust into the task of adjusting themselves to wilderness conditions or perishing. The climate was varied and uncertain, and generally different from the English weather to which they were accustomed. Dangers from exposure and starvation cost the lives of many. Even more difficult was the problem of relations with the aborigines. Scattered over the scene of English settlements in small clearings where they carried on primitive agriculture, roaming through the forest, or fishing by stream and seashore, a sparse semi-nomadic "Indian" population lived in a Stone Age culture. They were loosely organized in tribes and those whom the English colonists first met were generally either the Algonquian or Iroquoian stock. At first the Indians considered the white men as gods but soon were taught a different story, and though they seemed inclined in some localities to be friendly, they soon learned by experience that many of the newcomers were grasping and ruthless. War and massacre resulted.

The two civilizations proved incompatible because of the inability of the Indians to grasp the idea of private property in land. They lived a wandering life; even those who engaged in agriculture stayed in a clearing only a short while. When it became overgrown with weeds, it seemed easier to move to a new clearing than root out the new growth. Also they hunted over wide ranges and the white man's proclivity for cutting down forests and building walls and fences cut off their food supply. The whites often went through the form of land purchase with the Indians, but the latter never understood the principle of perpetual alienation of land, especially when the rum which they received in return was so soon consumed, the cloth worn out, or the trinkets lost. Enraged by the loss of hunting grounds, fired by the white man's alcohol, and stimulated in later days by England's enemies, the Indians reacted with a treacherous and barbarous warfare that became intermittent. The conflict brought out the worst in both races and cost many lives. The colonists gained from the Indians useful agricultural knowledge and skill in woodcraft, but beyond that the natives contributed little to mark the new civilization then in the process of creation.

More important than the material equipment of the colonists were their ideas, habits of thought and purposes. Some few came by force; a great many came to find comfortable means and more satisfactory social position. A notable number came to form new communities based upon their interpretations of Biblical command. Most of the emigrants were convinced that their American experiment meant more freedom and happiness. The importance of this psychological equipment cannot be overestimated. The series of commonwealths which were to become the United States were founded on hope and were the manifestation of a great optimism.

Supplied with such material and psychological equipment, the colonists had to adjust themselves to their new circumstances under a variety of conditions, with the later comers the more fortunate. In the first place, relatively few, when all who came are counted, arrived in regions where no white men had settled. Those who founded Jamestown, landed on Plymouth Rock or disembarked on the shores of Maryland were not numerous, though their lot was most difficult and has been most often described. A second group arrived in the various settlements in the days when they were struggling and discouraged. They found that disease and hardship, disillusionment and hopelessness had joined forces with the wilderness to deplete the morale of those who mournfully greeted them. So the new-comers' task was made doubly hard by the necessity of reviving the drooping spirits of the disheartened. The third class, which arrived after the original settlements in the various colonies had become well established, were by far the most numerous and for them the situation was less difficult. To be sure, many of them went out beyond the settled regions and broke ground for new communities, but their base of operations and supplies was but a relatively few miles away and no Atlantic Ocean separated them from their fellows.

During the first century of colonial experiment, settlements were scattered; communities were isolated and poor. The colonist had to live with a minimum of social organization and without the services of protection, distribution, coöperation and culture which have become so common today as to be taken for granted. The help which one could get from his neighbors or from the shadowy colonial backers in England was relatively small. Therefore the colonist had to become self-reliant and versatile or perish. To make survival possible, he had to organize his environment in such a way as to provide himself with many goods and services today offered by the community. He must protect, feed, clothe and entertain himself, keep himself healthy and ensure a shelter for himself when old. Unless he were to maintain himself as a woodsman and trapper there was but one really effective way to meet all these needs, and that was to establish a home and family. A sturdily built house could also serve as a fortification; a wife and children would provide the comfort, care and labor necessary to make the home a self-sustaining and measurably happy unit. All life centered about the home, and the family became the institution of greatest importance to the colonists.

Home and Family

The first homes, those hastily built on arrival for immediate shelter, were rude enough. In the southern colonies, the relative mildness of the climate made housing a matter of less moment; the first Virginians contented themselves with tents, bough shelters or rude board houses of no permanent character. Brick construction was introduced, though, as early as 1611. In New England, on the other hand, the winters were hard and long, and substantial shelter had to be provided immediately. English habits proved tenacious, and thatch for roofs, which had been used in England where wood was scarce, continued to be used in America despite the fact that wood was plentiful. So the arriving Pilgrims built cottages of rough-hewn boards roofed with thatch, a type of house which persisted for many years, and around Massachusetts Bay conical huts of tree limbs and sod, or thatched cottages were the first dwellings.

Throughout the seventeenth century, in fact, most homes remained very simple, plain, rectangular wooden houses with a large chimney or two. In the North there were steep roofs to shed the snow and cellars for storage, while in the southern planting areas the houses were less strongly constructed and built without cellars. At first, the windows were without glass and were closed by wooden shutters; but as the communities prospered glass was imported or made, and hinged windows with diamond or oblong panes became more common. English ideas of thatched roofs and half-timbered houses filled in with brick or clay gave way to shingles and clapboards; brick construction became less rare. As the colonists prospered they added rooms to their houses or built new ones, and the old one- or two-room cabins were either enlarged by ells and wings or relegated to more humble uses as barns or slave quarters.

In furnishings, too, the homes were "dated"; they revealed how much or little time had elapsed since the occupants arrived on these shores. Their first furnishings were meagre indeed, for only the more fortunate could bring from England a few cherished possessions. The great mass had to get along as best they could with such rude chairs, tables and beds as they could contrive. However crude and comfortless these primitive homes may seem today, it must be remembered that the average Englishman at that time was not much better off. In England glass, chimneys, pewter and silverware and even beds and pillows instead of straw pallets had but recently come into use. In America fuel and building material were plentiful and had there been food in equal plenty the early days of the settlements would not have been so disastrous.

Furnishings improved quite slowly in the seventeenth century. A traveler but rarely saw one of the heavy, ornate pieces then popular in England, a carved cupboard or a huge, four-posted bedstead. Space remained scarce on the crowded immigrant ships and a large chest often was the only piece of furniture brought from "home." That of colonial manufacture was plain and solid, made in the household or by the local carpenter. There was little time for ornamentation or fine work, and less money with which to support skilled cabinet-makers.

Tableware, too, was of the simplest, china was almost unknown and there was little glassware. Wooden trenchers and bowls, pewter plates and mugs or perhaps only gourds, knives, crude spoons and forks in a few instances; such was the "dinner service" of the frontier. The more fortunate treasured some silverware and Boston was able to support several goldsmiths, notably John Hull, who made silver cups, bowls, tankards and other utensils in a manner which gave him the distinction of being the first craftsman of taste. Clothing was plain; rough homespun and linen cloth and often leather or deer skin were the materials. Such apparel was made at home in a very literal sense, for the thread was spun, the cloth woven and dyed, and the garments cut out and sewed by the housewife and her daughters. It was durable rather than decorative. There were, however, a few cherished possessions of finer stuff, colored and embroidered, which had been brought over or imported. On high days and holidays, even among the Puritans, colors were not frowned on, and their assemblies were less somber than tradition might lead us to believe.

Life in the homes thus equipped was simple and monotonous. Frontier existence meant hard work and anxiety, little luxury and much weariness. In the southern colonies were a milder climate and more rude ease, but the Indian menace had to be guarded against and disease took an enormous toll in the first years. Loneliness was perhaps as much a trial in the southern area because the general preoccupation with tobacco planting made isolated plantation existence the way of life for most. In the North, life was less lonely because of the neighborly town organization, but in many parts of this region, especially among the influential ruling class of New England, there was a very serious cast to existence. The life devoted to long days of hard work with no loss of "God's precious time" was an ideal which matched the rigors of the New England climate, the stony nature of the soil and the hardships common to all frontiers. Existence had a monotony which even extended to diet, for the frontier provided little beyond a very plain vegetable fare with some game, wild fowl, fish and wild fruit. Milk, beer and ale of their own brewing, cider, and some imported wine and brandy supplied the colonists with their drink at first; rum and corn whisky were more popular later.

With the scarcity of money and labor and the importance of the self-sustaining family in the colonies, a premium was placed upon large families. Early marriage and many children were the rule, and small boys and girls were trained to help in the manifold tasks which crude agricultural methods and the lack of labor-saving devices made necessary. The high birth-rate, however, was somewhat offset by the heavy toll of disase and infant mortality. Epidemics, such as yellow fever and bubonic plague, climatic diseases such as malaria, and the results of hardship and exposure found the colonists with little resource to resist them.

Doctors were few and such as were in the colonies were often nothing more than quacks. Medical knowledge, even the best in Europe, seems today to have been grossly inadequate and ridden with superstitions and horrid dosings. The colonial doctor used vile concoctions which often made the patient much sicker than had he been left alone, or else resorted to bloodletting and thus weakened him at a time when he needed his strength most. Worst of all was the prevalent belief in witchcraft, which convinced many a sick person that he was bewitched and made him resort to charms and hocus-pocus, even to Indian witch doctors or their practices. The best treatments devised were probably the simple rules and herb remedies which one householder handed on to another and which, while they may not have helped much, still did not have the decidedly harmful effects which the crude medical practice of the day produced. In spite of the toll of disease and the high infant and maternal mortality, due to continual child-bearing, ignorance of child hygiene and superstitious midwifery, longevity records were made. For in the colonial life there were the advantages of plain living, hard work in the open air and simple diet which made the chances of those who survived their twenties favorable to a hearty old age, especially among the men.

Social Structure

Socially, life in small and isolated communities or on scattered farms was the chief characteristic of seventeenth-century existence. Individuals lived in practically self-sustaining social units, three thousand miles across the ocean from England. The small settlements themselves had little to do with one another; roads were few and poor, bridges generally non-existent. Distances were great, and there could be little journeying or communication except by slow horseback and boat travel. The whole persuasion of seventeenth-century life was to urge the settlers to stay within a very circumscribed circle. It was still the day of small things, of local interests, of preoccupation with the all-absorbing problems of simple existence.

In organization, as in environment, the new Anglo-American society became fundamentally different from anything European. The colonies evolved without the prevailing class system of ranks and orders. To be sure, some efforts were made to establish social distinctions; in Maryland and the Carolinas they attempted to create a colonial nobility, and the Spanish and French likewise sought to establish an aristocracy; but in general there were few, particularly in the English colonies, who had titles or social privileges. Some Englishmen who were gentlemen bore the title "master." Skilled workmen and freeholders were known as "goodmen." Such ranking persisted for a while, especially in New England, and certain regulations were instituted to make these distinctions more apparent, by limiting the finery of those of the lesser ranks and permitting the gentlemen and their families more privileges of adornment. Penalties were sometimes exacted for transgressions by reducing men from one estate to another. Such a system could not long survive, however, in a country where land was so easily obtainable and people so scarce; the democracy of widely and generally distributed property ownership gradually replaced the old European scheme. In fact, this is but one example of the many habits and customs, age-old and respected in England, which when transplanted to the New World were modified or obliterated by the new conditions.

The community atmosphere in colonial days varied in the different regions. In the South it was less drab, livelier than in others. Here there were few towns; people lived widely scattered on farms, but they satisfied their delight in meeting by entertaining guests for days at a time. Together they enjoyed visiting, dancing, cardplaying and such cheering liquors as might be available. Thus "southern hospitality" became famous. Court days, when planter families gathered at county-seats, and race meets and hunts, all saw much hilarity.

In the middle colonies the Dutch established a manner of living which was different. They brought with them a lasting sense of good living and recreation. They loved their holidays and ingeniously celebrated them. They brought Santa Claus for Christmas; they provided gaily colored eggs for Easter. They were hilarious at Shrovetide; they made calls on New Year's. On all high days and holidays, as well as in ordinary seasons, there was a great love of food and drink. Fat poultry, delectable cakes, a variety of liquors, all made the stout Dutch tables groan with heaviness and richness. They liked games. Golf was a Dutch importation; bowling and the forerunner of croquet likewise came to America from the Low Countries. Skating and sleighing, so dear to those living along the Dutch canals, naturally found a place in the New Amsterdam.

After the English had conquered the Dutch provinces, and the regions of New Jersey and Pennsylvania were opened, the middle colonies became notably cosmopolitan. Thither migrated many settlers from New England, and large groups of Quakers brought their distinct religious and social interests. Later contingents of Welsh, Irish and Germans added a further variety of customs. These admixtures produced an atmosphere of cosmopolitan tolerance which was to be the distinguishing characteristic of the middle colonies.

In New England the atmosphere was even more distinct—decidedly that which the Puritan founders had created. The center of community life outside the home was the church. Each town was not so much a "body politic" as it was a congregation. The founders had come to their new and difficult environment to carry out a serious purpose—to perform the will of God as revealed to them through the Bible and by the manifestation of God's Holy Spirit to them personally. Life, to many of these sober-minded people, was a continual searching for a knowledge of the will of God. Their belief that each was foredestined either for salvation or damnation gave much cause for introspection; only by searchings of the heart and the detection of signs of grace could one be sure of salvation. Consequently, many sought continually for sure signs of their regeneration. The little time they could spend away from work they wished to use in study of the Scriptures, inward searching and meeting together to hear from their minister his words of admonition, advice and revelation. It was not so much that they disliked pleasure, harmless and otherwise, but they felt it to be a waste of time and a distraction from this all-absorbing quest for the knowledge of their souls' salvation. This vital interest in religion combined with their belief that the province should be God's holy commonwealth, made pleasure of a frivolous and carefree sort suspect in the early days of most New England communities. The church was the place where people met one another frequently and in a very sober and decorous sense it was the social as well as the religious center.

Culturally, the seventeenth century meant the abandonment of many European habits, customs and skills, of which succeeding generations knew less and less, as they adopted new ways better fitted to their strange environment. Most important was the destruction of folk art, the arts and crafts of the home such as embroidering, designing, carving and the like. Those craftsmen who brought with them European skill in these matters found little opportunity to use it and still less stimulus to teach it to a new generation. In this respect, the colonists were much worse off at the end of the first century than at its beginning. The frontier was a destroying agent and fostered a materialistic and practical viewpoint which was to become a predominant characteristic of the American people.

The greatest cultural achievement of the seventeenth century was the establishment of a lasting interest in public education. In the South, settlements were too scattered for much community education. The children were generally taught at home or in small private schoolhouses, maintained very informally by the families in the vicinity, and conducted sometimes by a tutor, sometimes by the parish clergyman or lay reader, sometimes by one of the mothers. In the North, town conditions and Puritan ideals made a more elaborate system possible and desirable.

The Puritans were very much interested in an intelligent and literate community. Their religious authority was based upon Biblical precepts and their community ideal was a group of people able to read, write and debate. Children, therefore, must be taught to read and write, and for good business, ciphering also was necessary. Some of the Puritans were English university men, clergy and laity, and in the early years they provided the schools. By 1647 the Massachusetts Bay colony was ready to make common schools mandatory and passed a law requiring each town to maintain one. The law was not always obeyed, and within twenty years after its passage enthusiasm for education at public expense had somewhat waned; but the ideal had been expressed and was later to flourish mightily.

Even more ambitious were some in the Bay Colony who saw the need for higher education. So in 1636 at Cambridge a college was established, soon called Harvard after its first benefactor, which after some initial hardships and under the enlightened leadership of Henry Dunster, graduated its first class in 1642. The New England university men, mostly from Cambridge, England, cherished this new Cambridge experiment and watched its growth, little dreaming of the elaborate structure of university education which was to develop from it.

By the beginning of the eighteenth century it was apparent that the English colonial experiment was unique, presenting a marked contrast to those of the Spanish and French. While the colonies of these latter powers were prone to depend upon Europe, the English were becoming in large measure independent. There were numerous reasons for this. Not only was there an initial racial and cultural difference between the settlers, but the English had not intermarried with the Indians as had the Spanish and French. More important was the fact that the English mother country neglected the American settlements and forced them to shift for themselves. Under these conditions the pioneers of the first century had laid the foundation for an independent society. Their work, however, was but the beginning.

Mobility of Population

In the years from 1690 to 1763 many changes were wrought. Now that the colonies were stronger and less preoccupied with the first hard problems of wilderness life, the American imagination was less confined. By the end of the first century, many of the colonists were of the second or third generation of those born in the New World and were possessed of native familiarity with American conditions. They were not so cumbered with European training and habits as their elders had been. They were ready to assume social characteristics which marked them as American rather than British. This tendency was accelerated by the fact that the coming of many more non-English was creating a decidedly cosmopolitan atmosphere.

Conditions in Europe were encouraging a new series of migrations to America. Louis XIV of France had inaugurated policies which were to increase the population of the English colonies decidedly. First he determined to drive Protestantism out of his realm in 1685 and shortly thereafter he invaded Germany and ravished the Rhine Valley. Stung by his lash, French and Germans in large numbers fled to America. French Huguenots sought to preserve their religion in the New World and became useful citizens in several of the colonies. The Germans fleeing from their ruined homes came first to New York but as they were badly treated there they soon heeded the persuasion of William Penn's agent. Extensive settlements of Pennsylvania Germans were made near Philadelphia. Others went into the Shenandoah Valley and other regions of the southern back country.

About 1700 another group appeared. The Scotch colonists, settled in the north of Ireland at the beginning of the sixteen hundreds, had prospered economically to such an extent that their industries, especially textiles, had become a menace to English manufactures. Parliament listened to the complaints of home capitalists and placed numerous restrictions upon the Scotch-Irish trade. The loss of livelihood there persuaded many to look to America as a solution of their difficulties. Other strains, Welsh, Irish, Scotch, Hebrew and Swiss came in lesser numbers and mingled their enterprise and varied experiences with those of earlier groups.

These new-comers found the land near the coast occupied, so they went westward beyond the early settlements to new frontiers. There they established new communities and began the continuous process of penetrating ever further into the interior. Constant moving westward to make new homes in the wilderness was to be a dominant American trait. Population increased rapidly. In 1690 there were 200,000, by 1710, 350,000 and in 1760 it is estimated that there were 1,500,000 in the thirteen colonies. The size of the influx of non-English meant that the new American society was not to be formed entirely according to an English pattern but was to be a cosmopolitan fusion, a product of the melting pot.

Rising Standard of Living

This new American society early displayed a characteristic which was to be continuous; its standard of living was to rise constantly. In the eighteenth century there was time to think of standards which had been sadly neglected in the press of wilderness conquest. The various colonies were more experienced in the settled ways of established society and there was a more apparent difference than formerly between rich and poor. Not that this difference was hard and fast, for there was ample opportunity for many a poor man to become rich, but at least in the older regions the rigorous leveling of frontier poverty had passed away. The great mass of the people lived lives which were simple and lacking in unusual features. A larger proportion than in the first century were artisans, small tradesmen and laborers in the towns, who dwelt in plain houses, simply furnished, with church or tavern as social centers. Humble as was their lot most of them lived as independent householders and heads of families. They suffered from no "inferiority complexes."

In the more populous centers there had emerged a substantial class of wealthy and educated people who took the lead in their communities and formed a provincial "society." Their wealth and position led them to seek greater display and comfort and in seeking them they established standards of taste which were to be the first cultural achievements of the American colonists. They demanded better quality and were able to pay for it. Their desire for elegant homes and fine furniture brought about the return of the skill in architecture, cabinet work and decoration which the frontier had for a time almost obliterated.

Pride in building vigorously asserted itself. In the towns fine square houses of wood, brick and stone in the Georgian style pleased the eye; and on the great estates North and South manor and plantation houses became show places. No pains were spared in their decoration; all sorts of fine woodwork and plaster ornamentation were created by workmen who had their own sense of beauty and plenty of time in which to utilize it. The decorated mantels of wood or marble, the carved wainscoting, the graceful stairways which these architects and artisans created have stood the test of time and are widely copied in modern construction. Public edifices too, were created with the same taste and skill. Churches were rebuilt in the new style of Christopher Wren and their picturesque spires and beautiful porches decorated many a village green. Each colony must have its government buildings and the capitols frequently were evidence of the talents of budding architects who understood the "colonial" style. The interiors of fine buildings, public as well as private, were equipped with furniture made according to the graceful designs of the English cabinet-makers of the day, copied and often improved by American artisans. It was an age of simple beauty and dignity.

Not only the home, but the person, demonstrated the quality of American taste. The dress of the wealthy elaborately copied the fashions of Georgian England. Silk, lace, fine linen and embroidery were the style for both men and women; and the ornate fashion of men's attire, in those days of knee-breeches and silk stockings, embroidered waistcoats and silver shoe buckles, is quite beyond the imagination of our modern day. Hair dressing too was an art and the expensive powdered coiffures of the women and the curled wigs of the men made an imposing showing. Much penetrating perfume was an evident substitute for bathing, and in diet the wealthy were as elaborate as in their fashions.

Changing population and standards could not fail to have their effect upon such an important colonial interest as religion. While Anglican and Congregational churches still were legally the state churches in several colonies, there were tendencies toward diversity and toleration. America was more than ever the home of religious liberty. Heretical sects persecuted in early New England were now firmly organized in the middle region; Quakers and Baptists flourished. The Huguenots with their French Protestant congregations, the Jews with their synagogues, the German Protestants with their Moravian, Lutheran, Dunkard and Mennonite sects, all imported godliness in their own versions. Ungodliness, as they understood it, reared its ugly head in the rise of scepticism among followers of the "Age of Reason" which was flourishing in Europe. Among the latter "Natural Law" displaced Calvinism, sometimes through the apparent clarity of its thought and again because people were tired of the older, sterner discipline. Devout clergy and laymen searched for means to regenerate the people and found the country in the frame of mind for a stirring revival. When in 1734 Jonathan Edwards began preaching a return to personal faith and sinless life, his pleas fell on willing ears. Clergy of many sects spent themselves in fervent evangelical sermons. This "Great Awakening" as it was called, was a sort of mental purgative, preparing the colonists for the strange, unexpected happenings and the dangerous experiments of the years encircling 1776. It has been called the "wayshower" of the Revolution.

Education was still closely allied with religion and reflected its condition. The diversity of sects was especially influential in directing the progress of higher education, because as the sects prospered they became more interested in proper instruction. The more orthodox Congregationalists feared that Harvard was becoming too liberal; so in 1701 Yale was founded. Anglicans established William and Mary in Virginia in 1693, and Kings (later Columbia) in New York in 1754. Presbyterians founded Princeton in 1746; the Baptists, Rhode Island College (later Brown) in 1764; the Dutch Reformed, Queens (later Rutgers) in 1766. Interest in Indian education accounts for the establishment of Wheelock's Indian School (1754) at Hanover, New Hampshire, which became Dartmouth in 1769. Indirectly, religion also was responsible for the only non-sectarian establishment of the period. George Whitefield, forerunner of the Methodists, preached through the colonies and aroused an enthusiasm which in 1740 led to establishment of a charity school in Philadelphia; it developed into an academy which in turn became the College of Philadelphia and finally the University of Pennsylvania.

In most of the colleges, instruction was formalized with lessons assigned for memorizing verbatim. The classics, Latin, Greek and now and then Hebrew were emphasized. There was some drill in grammar, rhetoric and declamation, with instruction in logic to aid the formation of rational thought processes, so dear to the learned of that day. Most college boys were taught divinity and ethics. For mathematics there was some arithmetic and geometry, and science was touched lightly in a little astronomy and physics; but these subjects might easily be omitted. When Franklin came to plan for his academy he was enthusiastic over a more realistic curriculum and had more emphasis placed on science. He pushed modern languages in beside the ancient tongues, and courses in history, government and international law gave students there some slight sense of social science. Instruction in agriculture and trade was urged by Franklin in a spirit of modern vocational guidance.

Unfortunately, expanding interest in higher education did not mean corresponding improvement in elementary training. The plans of William Penn, who thought education was a responsibility of the state, and the laws in Massachusetts, Maryland and South Carolina designed to establish school systems, all failed to produce desired results. The decline in the old religious interest and the multiplication of new sects with their own private schools further reduced the urge for a tax-supported system. Besides, the growing wealthy classes north and south preferred to educate their children at their own expense by employing private tutors or by sending them to private academies. They felt that the increase of population made public schools too expensive to the taxpayers. Illiteracy was common; even successful men of affairs and most women had to use their "marks" when executing documents. Nevertheless, the ideal of free schools, though somewhat eclipsed, was not dead and was destined for revival at a later time.

All signs pointed to a broader colonial mental horizon and a less complete preoccupation with problems of mere existence. As more people read, more books were imported, respectable private libraries grew and a few lending libraries appeared in northern and southern colonies. Most important was the veritable revolution in light and heat which had an incalculable effect upon reading habits. Stoves and lamps came in the homes of the more well-to-do to replace fireplaces and candles. Now when the day's work was done, and quite frequently it was no longer such a hard day's work as in the early years, one could sit down comfortably and without eyestrain enjoy the pleasures of reading.

Under such auspices, some literary experiments were initiated; most significant was the beginning of American newspaper history. In 1704 the *Boston News-Letter* made its bow, and Benjamin Franklin issued the first number of the *Pennsylvania Gazette* in 1729; this venture and the pungent aphorisms of his *Poor Richard's Almanac* made him the foremost writer of his day. Other editors arose and by 1756 had established newspapers in all the colonies except New Jersey, Delaware and Georgia. Their papers were generally not very revealing; the four pages had numerous advertisements, much belated European news and a few literary gems of uncertain water. Local items were not numerous because all in the locality knew what was going on. Journalists, however, were beginning to figure in public affairs and to influence public opinion. So much so that the authorities in 1735 sought to muzzle John Peter Zenger, a New York editor. He was arrested and tried for libel because of certain articles appearing in his paper attacking the governor. Andrew Hamilton, a prominent Philadelphia lawyer, was called to his defense, and despite contrary instructions by the judge, the jury refused to convict him. A great victory for the freedom of the press had been won which was to figure significantly as one of the precedents for freedom of expression, so vital to any true democracy.

Clearly, American society was to be one in which home and the family, church and school were to be the principal institutions. The spirit which pervaded it was to be cosmopolitan and free. People from various European nations were contributing abundantly to the original English effort and modifying it. New communities on the frontier were continually created. No ranks or privileges were to be found, and a higher standard of living was constantly achieved. Freedom and democratic equality were the characteristics which the desire of those who crossed the sea and the conditions of the wilderness united to create.

CHAPTER IV

BEGINNINGS OF AMERICAN ECONOMIC LIFE

The economic institutions of the colonies grew out of the primary need for food. In the days of founding each colony planned to bring sufficient supply to feed the settlers until a planting and harvest could be completed. The trading-post colonies even expected to continue dependence upon Europe for most of their food, while they bent their energies to mining, lumbering and even manufacturing. However, their ships were too small and the voyages longer than expected. Also, English merchants were not used to gathering large quantities of suitable food supplies convenient for purchase for such expeditions and frequently adequate provisions were just not available. Consequently the first boatloads of colonists generally arrived with rations running short. Furthermore, many of the first-comers sought too energetically for gold which they never found, as in Virginia, or came too late in the season to plant crops, as in Plymouth. Starvation was too frequent a reality. Had not some of the Indians come to their aid, there would have been few if any survivors in some of the early ventures. These initial hardships and the great distance from Europe taught a much needed lesson. Provision must be made for cultivating the soil and for raising food.

Agricultural Economy

Agriculture became the almost universal occupation of seventeenth-century colonists. European habits of cultivation had to be modified by a wilderness technique. Here the Indian, though despised and feared, was of great help. He raised two plants which should be represented on the American coat-of-arms, so important were they in the founding of the nation. Maize, or Indian corn, could be grown in almost any portion of the thirteen colonies, it could be eaten in a pleasing variety of ways and it became the great food staple of the Atlantic Coast settlements. Tobacco, on the other hand, though it could be widely cultivated only in the southern colonies, was a great money maker. When in 1612 John Rolfe, British husband of the Indian princess Pocahontas, raised the first crop in Virginia, it began its career as the dominant agricultural concern there. Under Indian tutelage the colonists learned to cultivate these two crops.

The first task was to cope with the great forests. Following Indian custom the colonists girdled the trees, planted seed corn in the spaces between and left the trunks to be removed later. The stumps could and did frequently remain indefinitely while crop after crop was sown and gathered in these uneven fields. The colonists following Indian directions planted the corn in hills with fish for fertilizer. Lessons in woodcraft from their strange and treacherous neighbors proved invaluable in hunting and trapping. Turkey and deer meat became staples of diet, and furs provided clothing and income.

European ways of farming were by no means altogether abandoned. English food crops were attempted immediately. The first settlers in both Virginia and New England sought to raise grains of European origin. With oats, rye, barley and hay, they were successful, especially in New England, but with the great staple, wheat, there was trouble. The soil of Virginia proved too rich, and it grew rank, producing little grain. In New England, a successful crop proved very uncertain, the summers were too short and the soil thin and rocky. In fact, after the blight of 1644 and successive years wheat production declined. Corn was too easy and too useful a rival to invite further expensive experiment. The colonists made use of the peas, beans, pumpkins, squash, sweet potatoes and melons which the Indians cultivated, but also introduced good English vegetables such as turnips, onions, carrots and cucumbers. The Pilgrims ordered seed for white potatoes from England as early as 1629, but this staple does not seem to have been common until after the Scotch-Irish immigration about 1700. Wild cherries, plums, grapes and various berries were brought under cultivation. Apple trees were imported from Europe and bore fruit at Boston as early as 1639. The apple became the most popular colonial fruit, for hard cider proved a cheap and easy means of pleasant tippling.

Live stock was brought from Europe immediately. Cows, horses, sheep and hogs were sent to Virginia in 1609 and the New England settlers were not long in bringing over farm animals and poultry. In New England the long winters and lack of fodder made their care difficult, and little attention was paid to maintaining good breeds. The condition of the cattle was generally miserable and the disease and mortality among them became dangerous to the profits and health of the colonists. Under such conditions, the dairying of this early period could not be very important, but hogs flourished on acorns, making salt pork an easy trading staple.

The seizure of New York and the development of the middle colonies brought a more prosperous agricultural area under English control. This region had a soil much better adapted to diversified farming than New England and the farmers in it never became wedded to one crop as did the Virginians and Marylanders to tobacco. The fertile limestone soil of the river valleys and hospitable climatic conditions favored the cultivation of wheat, which soon became the most important crop, averaging more bushels per acre than in England. Other grains, vegetables and fruits also flourished extensively and good pasture land improved live stock raising. Such fertility was a constant invitation to agriculture and many left their rocky New England farmsteads to profit in the midlands.

Intimately connected with the spread of agriculture was the distribution of land. Here the conflict between the feudal and individualistic principles immediately reflected the great social change of the times and the place. Virginia and Plymouth both tried out the feudal concept at first, treating the land as the property of the company or association and the settlers as employees. Plots were assigned to each, and the crop was supposed to be turned over to the authorities and in turn distributed to each according to his needs. Production under such a principle could not flourish in America. Plymouth in 1623 abandoned it. Individuals were granted lands for their unrestricted use, at first as tenants, but before long as owners. When the Massachusetts Bay Company established itself at Boston and vicinity, land was apportioned to each settler, and when new towns or villages were established the colony granted land in fee simple to the new community. The townsmen apportioned some of their acres among themselves, in the meantime holding a reserve as common pasturage or as provision for future comers. In these towns the inhabitants generally owned a small plot about their houses and a larger one away from the center where they cultivated their major crops. Under such a system each man's holdings were relatively small, rarely exceeding one hundred acres, and therefore agricultural labor was less of a problem. A man and his family could generally work a farm.

In the South likewise various methods of land distribution were tried. Virginia, after a seven-year experiment with feudal control, granted land generously, offering it as an inducement to settlers. Those who came themselves received land and those who brought others with them obtained in addition for each man a so-called "head right" of fifty or one hundred acres, paying a small annual rent to the King generally in tobacco. In this way, large estates were made possible at least to a small number. In Maryland, the proprietor made grants in similar manner to stimulate migration; in so doing he maintained nominal ownership of the land, requiring a very small rental to be paid to him. As agricultural labor was a problem in Virginia and Maryland, these colonies were anxious to induce as many as would to come over as indentured servants. So it was provided that at the conclusion of his term, the servant became a landholder, receiving in Maryland a land grant automatically. In such manner in the seventeenth century, Virginia and Maryland became provinces where moderate-sized farms were the order of the day; five hundred acres was an average holding in Virginia. Some large plantations there were and a few Negro slaves, but the day of that economy was not yet.

The middle colonies had a different system. When the English government captured the Dutch settlements they found the ownership of land vested in patroons, or proprietors of great estates, with many of the inhabitants in the Hudson Valley held as tenants. Such a manorial system was continued by the English in New York, and the proprietors in New Jersey and later in Pennsylvania adopted the practice of seeking revenues from quit-rents, though there was little uniformity. Farms under this system were larger than in New England, and tenants more frequent. Tenantry, however, did not suit Americans, and landlords were not happy. In practice much of the so-called rented land was freehold and the quit-rent was placed so low as to be a negligible charge. Nevertheless, even that was begrudged and oftentimes could not be collected. More than 90 per cent of the colonials were farmers and their mode of life bred in them an intense individualism. Landlords were European institutions not relished in free America, and individual ownership became ever more common. Feudal customs could not long survive in the New World.

Thus thousands of farms large and small were scattered over the colonial country-side, but indifferently cultivated. These farmers of the seventeenth century, meanly equipped with spades, hoes, scythes, sickles, flails and only occasionally a plough, carried on their work in wasteful fashion. In the southern and middle colonies land was plentiful and there was no incentive to spare the soil. There was little or no fertilization or rotation of crops; tobacco was raised until the soil became exhausted, then a new field was started. New England agriculture was less haphazard. The rocky hillsides needed more care and the common ownership of reserve lands by the towns made farmers more economical. Some attempt was ventured at conservation by allowing the fields occasionally to lie fallow and to serve as pasture. All told it was a frontier agriculture, crude and wasteful, largely managed by struggling small farmers. The day of scientific agriculture or large-scale management was still afar off.

Industry and Commerce

Industrial life likewise had simple beginnings. Most home furnishings were in fact homemade; each household tried to be self-sustaining. But certain essentials which could not be made in the home had to be procured. Implements, weapons, better utensils and furniture, as well as many luxuries, must be provided either by local ingenuity or by trade. Industry in the colonies had another stimulus—the hope of profit entertained by English backers. The idea that the colonies should prove a source of revenue to English stockholders died hard, and before it perished it fathered a number of experiments in industry. England was getting short of wood and there was hope of transferring the smelting and glass-making works to the New World where fuel was plentiful. Ships' stores and potash for the woolen industry were also sought from the forest.

These hopes served to transport artisans to Virginia as early as 1608, to establish rude factories, and that same year the colony sent back a cargo of iron ore, soap, ashes, lumber, pitch and tar. By 1620 three ironworks had been established and ships' stores, wainscoting, clapboards and potash had been sent back to England at intervals. The profits from tobacco were too tempting, however, and Virginia became a planting rather than an industrial colony. Manufacturing did not cease altogether but it was confined to a few artisans in the infrequent towns or to the plantations. Planters necessarily maintained a number of workers who spun thread and wove cloth, tanned leather and made shoes, brewed and distilled. A well-equipped plantation might also have a carpenter, a glazier, a weaver, a blacksmith, a brickmaker and a cooper. In general it may be said that each farmer knew something of many trades and depended upon Europe when he wanted what he could not make or repair himself. If he could not develop this talent, he went without what he needed.

In New England and later in the middle colonies the same handicraft system prevailed, with the colonial farmer a jack of all trades. But in this northern region towns were more frequent and artisans could made a living plying their trades. Many of the towns held out special inducements to shoemakers, carpenters, blacksmiths and the like to settle among them and Boston soon supported even a goldsmith, in fact, several of them. Besides agriculture was so difficult that New England was forced to manufacture in order to have something to trade for European goods they needed. Lumbering and ship-building started almost immediately, a sawmill was built in what became New Hampshire perhaps as early as 1623 and shipyards were established in the best seaports. Mills for grinding corn being indispensable, windmills succeeded the crude mortar and pestle and by 1633 a water-power mill was built at Dorchester. Salt was manufactured by various processes. A tannery was built in Lynn and John Winthrop of that place worked out an ambitious scheme for an iron furnace, which by 1648 was producing eight tons a week.

Cloth making was also started immediately. Flax was introduced in Massachusetts and linen was manufactured therefrom. However, it was a difficult process and woolen cloth was found easier to make. Farmers began to keep sheep and make homespun. In 1643 some fullers came over from Yorkshire and established a fulling mill at Rowley; by 1675 New England was exporting woolen cloth. There were few things which the New Englanders did not try, and Yankee ingenuity became a byword.

Trade developed hand in hand with industry, to supply implements, arms and ammunition, clothes, leather, glass and in the early years even food. Regular importations from the mother country commenced at once. As the colonies became better equipped, trade in food, clothes and leather was less necessary but imports of luxuries and foreign wares became more important. The southern colonies depended on tobacco to pay their European balances after the first few years. The elaborate machinery whereby the planters exported their crop to London agents, who credited them with the proceeds and then filled their orders for European goods, necessarily left them in debt to their agents and much dissatisfied with British merchants. These debts were a continual source of grievance.

In New England trading was bound to supersede all other economic activity in profit-making possibilities. There was so little which Europe wanted, that concentration on fish, fur and lumber was essential to obtain sufficient purchasing power in England. Plymouth started it by exporting a cargo of beaver skins and clapboards, and exports steadily grew. The waters off the New England coast abounded in fish and a race of fishermen soon came into being to fill cargoes for the Azores and the Catholic countries of southern Europe. Fish and lumber, in the form of barrel or pipe staves, freighted many a trading vessel to those ports and returned laden with wine. Furs were also profitable; New England trappers sought the beaver and other fur-bearing animals so that the merchants might send their pelts to Europe. Colonial skippers became acquainted with European ports.

Intercolonial trade, in course of time, became a source of profit. At first the New England people had disposed of their small surplus at home to the constant stream of new-comers who needed to purchase supplies and labor upon arrival. But by 1640 that stream had diminished in size, prices fell and there was an economic crisis, perhaps the first in British America, during 1641-1642. The enterprising now sought to restore their prosperity by turning to intercolonial trade. New England had more to offer her neighbors, especially in the West Indies, than she had to sell to England. Corn, salt pork, pickled beef, flour, butter, lumber and horses were sent down in exchange for sugar, indigo, cotton, dyewood, hides, cocoa and Spanish iron. The southern colonies, too, could join in the traffic offering tobacco and provisions. Merchants prospered in this trade and moderate wealth became a dream possible of fulfilment. The lure of profit which had been destroyed by early hardship was revived.

Economic Expansion

The colonists trod new paths to wealth in the eighteenth century, as their industry accumulated sufficient capital for more ambitious projects. Commerce became more elaborate and profitable, requiring new facilities. When cargoes had been small, boats of light draft could ply from inlet to inlet and up and down the rivers and creeks; but trade could no longer be carried on so simply. Larger population, greater crops and more extensive needs called for bigger ships, capital, wharves, warehouses, insurance, and more reliable news; such facilities could be supplied only in well-equipped seaports. Also new regulations of the home government, requiring goods to be taxed at regular ports of entry, emphasized the importance of commercial centers. Boston, Philadelphia, New York, Charleston and later Baltimore and Savannah became bustling shipping depots.

Great Britain tried to keep the colonial trade strictly within the empire, but British markets were too limited and the large profits of trade with other countries were too attractive. Colonial ships sailed into many rich waters. One of the most lucrative of these far-flung enterprises took colonial sea-captains up the gold coast of Africa, on a triple exchange of molasses, rum and slaves. Yankee skippers purchased molasses in the West Indies and carried it to New England distilleries to be made into rum. They carried the casks of this stimulant to Africa to trade for Negro slaves, whom in turn they carried back to the West Indies to exchange for molasses. Their profits from this triple traffic were large and it expanded as bigger funds were needed to meet the bills for colonial imports from Europe. Also frequent wars of the period increased the demand for food and raw materials and made privateering against England's enemies a profitable profession. The strong-boxes of the merchants grew heavier and their risks more daring with each new success.

The growing traffic called for ships and the colonies had extraordinary facilities for supplying them. So ship-building in the eighteenth century swelled the profits of many colonials. Tidal streams flowing from New England's hills to the sea through excellent harbors provided ideal locations for shipyards. Right at hand were the gnarled white oak and smooth white pine for keels, elbows, planks and tall, straight masts. Tar, pitch and turpentine, too, were easily obtainable and long practice bred a race of skilful shipwrights. New England seaports resounded with the noise of builders at work on hundreds of ships. The yards on the Piscataqua in New Hampshire could turn out 200 ships a year; 72 vessels were on the ways at one time at Newburyport, Massachusetts. So cheaply could vessels be built that they were ordered from abroad. Spain, Portugal and particularly England purchased eagerly and at the close of the French and Indian wars 30 per cent of English commercial vessels were of American origin.

An ally of ocean-borne commerce was the profitable fishing industry. New England vessels bore fishermen who swept the deep from Long Island to Newfoundland, where the "banks" supplied some of the richest fishing grounds in the world. Codfish, mackerel and bass were brought in by the boat load to coast stations, where they were cleaned and dried on great flakes extending over many acres. Gloucester and Marblehead were the centers for this traffic in the eighteenth century. New England alone exported 10 million pounds of fish in 1700 and the generations of hardy fishermen increased the catch as the years went on until at the close of the colonial period 665 fishing boats from New England bore 4,405 men to catch codfish and brought home hauls annually worth a million and a quarter dollars.

Yankee seamen were called far afloat by another rich treasure of the deep, for whales abounded off the New England coast and sperm oil and whalebone commanded a ready market. These giant creatures proved dangerous to hunt and prodigious to handle, but Yankee pluck and endurance were equal to the task. At first, whaling was largely an off-shore affair; when whales were sighted off the coast of Nantucket or elsewhere, the fishermen put out in small boats to harpoon them and drag them to shore to be cut up, tried out for oil and stripped for bone. By the eighteenth century regular whaling vessels were in use which scoured the seas eager for the cry: "Thar she blows!" Nantucket was the great center, New Bedford, also in Massachusetts, was developing and Sag Harbor on Long Island was busy. By the outbreak of the Revolution there was a colonial whaling fleet of 360 vessels which sailed from the Arctic circle to the Falklands and even to the shores of Africa. Truly New Englanders lived by scent of salt air and gained great profit from going down to the sea in ships.

Commerce was not confined to ships and the sea; there was money in a great inland traffic which lured much colonial and European enterprise and capital. This was the fur trade. In northern forests, particularly, the animals grew heavy pelts which could protect many a European noble or wealthy commoner from the penetrating cold of northern Europe. As European supplies were limited and giving out, there was great demand for the American furs. Beaver, mink, fox, otter, raccoon and bear were plentiful and healthy in America, so the hunt was on. As supplies along the coast were soon exhausted, hunters and trappers had to find their way through the tall forests beyond settlement and then beyond the Appalachians.

There were three divisions of this trade. The English had taken over the old Dutch traffic and Albany prospered as a depot. Here English trappers and hunters started out to rival the French woodsmen in

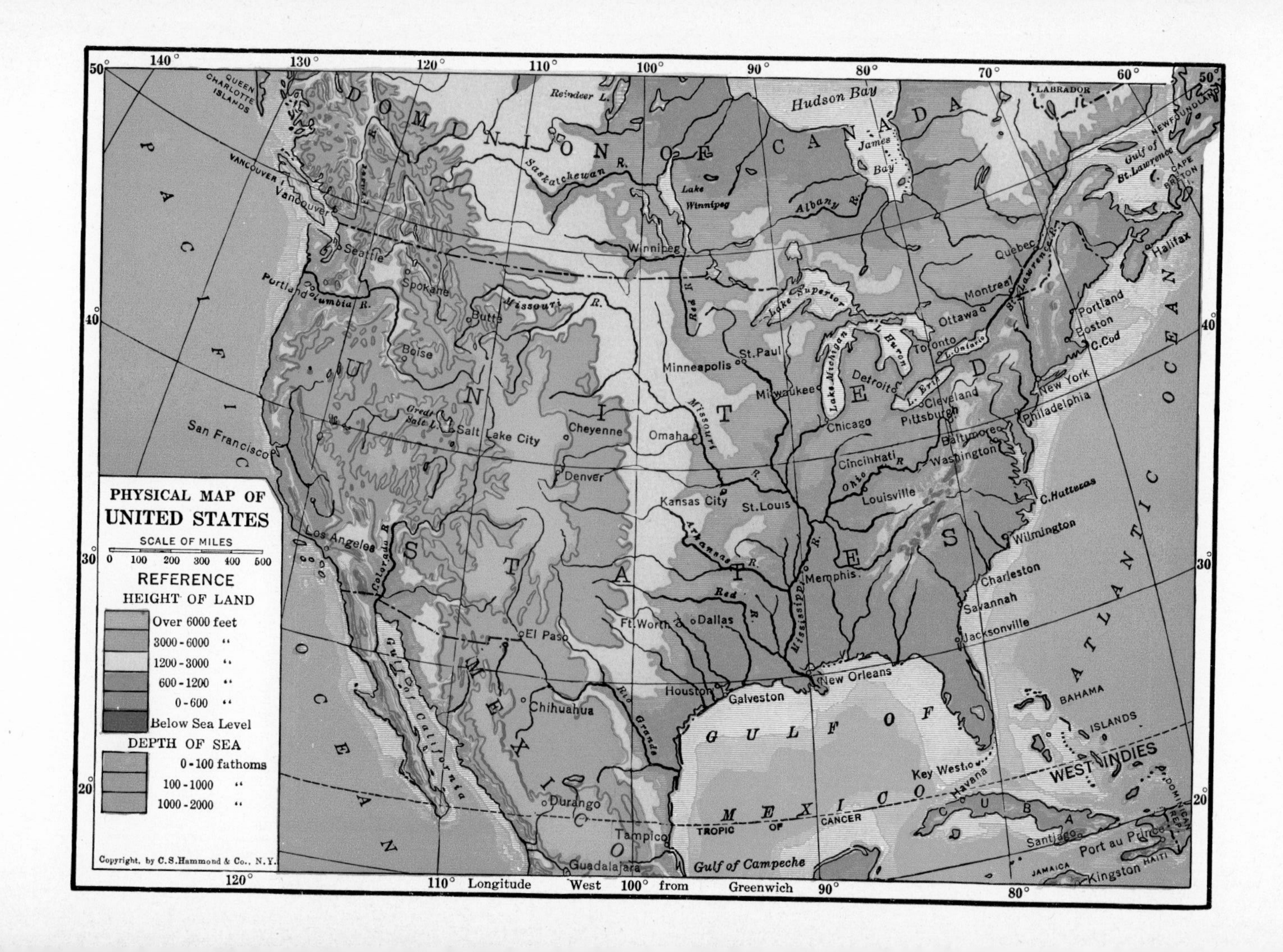
PHYSICAL MAP OF
UNITED STATES
SCALE OF MILES
0 100 200 300 400 500
REFERENCE
HEIGHT OF LAND
Over 6000 feet
3000 - 6000 "
1200 - 3000 "
600 - 1200 "
0 - 600 "
Below Sea Level
DEPTH OF SEA
0 - 100 fathoms
100 - 1000 "
1000 - 2000 "
Copyright, by C.S.Hammond & Co., N.Y.
110° Longitude West 100° from Greenwich
DOMINION OF CANADA
UNITED STATES
MEXICO
PACIFIC OCEAN
ATLANTIC OCEAN
GULF OF MEXICO
Hudson Bay
James Bay
Gulf of St. Lawrence
Gulf of California
Gulf of Campeche
TROPIC OF CANCER
WEST INDIES
BAHAMA ISLANDS
Seattle
Portland
Spokane
Butte
Boise
San Francisco
Los Angeles
Salt Lake City
Great Salt L.
Cheyenne
Denver
El Paso
Omaha
Kansas City
St. Louis
Minneapolis
St. Paul
Milwaukee
Chicago
Detroit
Cleveland
Pittsburgh
Cincinnati
Louisville
Memphis
Dallas
Ft. Worth
Houston
Galveston
New Orleans
Winnipeg
Toronto
Ottawa
Montreal
Quebec
Halifax
Portland
Boston
C. Cod
New York
Philadelphia
Baltimore
Washington
C. Hatteras
Wilmington
Charleston
Savannah
Jacksonville
Key West
Havana
Santiago
Port au Prince
Kingston
Chihuahua
Durango
Tampico
Guadalajara
Vancouver
Lake Winnipeg
Lake Superior
L. Huron
Lake Michigan
L. Erie
L. Ontario
Reindeer L.
Saskatchewan R.
Albany R.
Red R.
Missouri R.
Columbia R.
Colorado R.
Arkansas R.
Ohio R.
Mississippi R.
Rio Grande
St. Lawrence R.
LABRADOR
NEWFOUNDLAND
CAPE BRETON I.
QUEEN CHARLOTTE ISLANDS
VANCOUVER I.
CUBA
JAMAICA
HAITI
DOMINICAN REP.

tapping the great western sources. They enlisted the Iroquois as middlemen and established a series of stations to which these allies brought skins they obtained from the Indians of the Lake regions. Philadelphia was the headquarters for a trade extending via Lancaster into the Susquehanna Valley and westward under venturesome traders like George Croghan into the Ohio Valley. Charleston via Augusta was the depot for a southern trade which penetrated into the Mississippi Valley but was not operated by stations. Fur-bearing animals were much scarcer in this region, much of the traffic was really a leather trade in deerskins and individual trappers traveled literally thousands of miles gathering in the scattered peltries.

So far-flung was this fur trade that large capital and extensive operations were necessary. In the eighteenth century colonial merchants had the capital or could get it from England to organize a rich traffic extending from the Great Lakes through the southern Appalachians. Extensive supplies of "trucking" goods, like trinkets, bright cloth, hatchets, guns and particularly hard liquor, had to be assembled and distributed to agents and trappers. They scattered over thousands of miles of trail and trackless forest. They dealt with the Indians, oftentimes at great meetings where the redmen gathered with their packs. Frequently these trading periods were prolonged debauches at which the Indians were made drunk and cheated outrageously. The pelts thus traded would be loaded into boats or packed on animals and brought to the headquarters. The returns were large but so extensive a capital was needed to carry on the traffic that it was controlled by relatively few rich merchants. It did much to promote more comfortable and ostentatious living in the colonial towns.

The fur trade was much more significant than a mere series of commercial transactions. It proved to have noteworthy social and political consequences. Its influence upon the Indians and their relations with the settlers was pernicious. Not only were the aborigines corrupted by the white men's liquor, but they were outraged by the flagrant cheating. Their grievances spurred them on to revengeful raids and massacres. Also this trade placed guns, powder and iron weapons into their hands, and made them that much more dangerous. Furthermore, fur-trading stirred up rivalry and conflict between the English and their neighbors, the French and Spanish. It did much to make the colonial experience hazardous and bloody.

Even more important was the influence of this traffic in opening up the vast interior. Trappers and hunters wandering ever farther into the interior were continually blazing new trails, discovering new regions and bringing back new reports of fertile acres, convenient rivers and future homesites. The trails they blazed and the knowledge they retailed were continual invitations for settlers to follow them and enjoy the wealth they described. The fur-trader was an advance agent of the onward march of settlement.

The growth of commerce reminded eighteenth-century merchants of the need for more colonial manufacturing. Household handicrafts continued very widespread. The farmer and his family fed and clothed themselves; made and repaired tools; built their homes and outbuildings, carts and boats; manufactured furniture, tableware, candles, soap and bed linen, boxes and barrels, thread and cloth, even broadcloth. Some of these processes, such as the making of woolen and linen cloth, were complicated. All told, almost every home was a factory. Also artisans now had more shops in the towns, and hats, shoes, pottery, rope, paper and glass were made by master journeymen and apprentices. The quantity of woolen, linen and cotton cloth began to worry English manufacturers; and as American hats, stockings, shoes and other leather goods, pottery, rope, paper and glass began to make their appearance, English producers persuaded Parliament to restrict this new competition. However, ship-building and distilling, which had become the principal industries of New England, prospered, though in the case of the latter, British sugar duties threatened ruin.

Some colonial merchants were now ready to make more manufacturing advances, notably in the iron industry. In the eighteenth century the superior resources of Pennsylvania were tapped and furnaces, bloomeries, slitting mills and forges were located in the Delaware and Susquehanna valleys. Steel also was produced and scythes, axes and other edged tools were put out in quantities not yet sufficient to satisfy the colonial need. The progress of this industry brought parliamentary restriction; the colonists must learn that their function was to consume, not produce, manufactures. Parliament, however, might just as well have tried to build a bridge over the Atlantic; duties and prohibitions on manufactures were alike ignored by the independent Americans in characteristic fashion.

While much of colonial industry was still domestic and while most commerce was carried on by individual merchants, both industry and commerce needed larger capital. Companies arose, especially in the iron industry where it was convenient for local merchants to unite in organizing shareholders to invest their money in a forge or bloomery. Likewise ships were often fitted out and loaded by a group of traders who shared proportionately in the profits and risks. Fur-trading and land speculating companies such as the Hudson's Bay Company in the far north and the Susquehanna and Ohio Companies began operations. There was even a monopoly; the United Company of Spermaceti Candlers (Newport, R. I., 1702) was an intercolonial concern which controlled the industry in a manner prophetic of the future.

The growing business of the colonies was much hampered by an insufficient supply of currency. There were limited quantities of European coins, English, Spanish, French, Dutch and the like, which were used largely to settle European balances; even for this purpose the amount was hardly adequate. But where domestic business was concerned, the circulation was so limited as to make necessary a resort to substitutes. Wampum, tobacco and skins served as money and much colonial trade was carried on by barter. Massachusetts attempted a local mint but it did not produce enough to help the situation. In the effort to meet expenses incurred by participation in the first French and Indian War (1689-1697), Massachusetts began the printing of paper money. This practice was carried on so persistently and the paper depreciated so greatly that the little hard money in the colony was withdrawn from circulation and hoarded. Other colonies also yielded to the temptation to print paper currency.

As in commerce and manufacturing, so in the issue of paper the colonists felt British interference. British merchants and proprietors with creditor interests in the colonies, found their dues and rents threatened by this debauchery of the medium of exchange. Colonial governors, upon instructions from the Crown or the proprietors, vetoed the acts of the colonial assemblies authorizing paper money and in 1751 an act of Parliament prohibited the use of this currency in the New England provinces except in time of war or emergency. Its use, however, had been learned and the delights of cheap money had been tasted; a practice had been started which was to be revived repeatedly, especially in times of war or economic stress. From that time until the present, no long stretch of years has been allowed to elapse without some yielding to the temptation to expand the currency, in spite of bitter opposition from creditor interests.

The financial needs of American business called for credits as well as currency, but facilities for it were indeed slight. English merchants accepted much colonial business on a credit basis, especially with southern planters whose accounts were carried from generation to generation; but the charges for this service were very heavy. The colonies themselves were not equipped to mobilize their capital and to extend credit because funds were scattered and inadequate. The most notable attempt at banking was the Massachusetts Land Bank chartered in 1741, which issued a currency based upon land as security. This institution was suppressed by Parliament; but in the meantime, a quantity of notes had been issued, to the ruin of many who had invested in it. Not until the Revolution did a permanent banking institution emerge. Marine insurance, however, began to be written in Philadelphia as early as 1721, at a great saving from the heavy charges of British firms. Fire insurance was undertaken in the same city in 1752 by the "Philadelphia Contributionship for the Insurance of Houses from Loss by

Fire." A leaden plate, showing two clasped hands, was fastened on structures they insured, and still may be seen on old buildings there.

In the South similar tendencies toward larger operations were noticeable. The plantation system was coming into its own and was the all-engrossing enterprise of those with initiative and business ability. Tobacco flourished but its cultivation quickly exhausted the soil, warning far-sighted planters to take up large holdings. The appearance of a new labor supply removed the greatest hindrance to large operation, for the Negro slave made huge plantations possible and profitable. Negroes had been imported as early as 1619 but the supply had been limited and planters had preferred indentured servants. After British capitalists organized the Royal African Company in 1672, the traffic began to grow. When victory in a long-drawn-out war with Spain in 1713, gave British traders the contract to supply Spanish America with Negroes, a regular service was assured. Under these conditions the trade became organized and the supply abundant. The growth of both slavery and the plantation system was further encouraged by a new commodity. In the 1690's Madagascar rice was planted in the marshy coastal district of the Carolinas and since the work in the malarial rice fields was not such as white labor could stand, slaves were imported in large numbers. By 1715 more than half the population of South Carolina was of the African race.

Thus enterprise and the desire to do big things had their way in the South and large tobacco and rice plantations multiplied in Virginia and South Carolina. The planter became the dominating figure in these communities. His crops were sold to English merchants who maintained agents in the few cities and towns in the South, and he bought his supplies from the firms to whom he consigned his crops. These London firms carried the planters' accounts for years with increasingly unfavorable balances against the colonists. During the eighteenth century, in many instances, the plantation owner's tastes became more expensive and exceeded his income. Many a luxurious plantation home could not fail to remind its owner that it was a luxury which represented a growing debt, the payment of which was becoming more remote every year.

Important as were the plantation lords, they were not numerous. Many a small planter who was not successful enough to acquire a large holding, either became a tenant, or more likely moved west to the back country. Besides, a great many of the new European emigrants were going directly to the western counties, either renting or purchasing their land from the great landlords. They operated small farms and had no part in the plantation scheme except perhaps a hope of acquiring sufficient wealth some day to enter the ranks of the barons. At least 60 per cent of the farmers in the southern colonies had small holdings which could be worked without slaves or indentured labor.

The preoccupation with agriculture coupled with the new interest in big projects launched numerous real estate booms. The swelling tide of immigrants and the expansion of settlement brought into play the talents of the real estate speculator. Individuals and groups sought to anticipate or influence the tide of migration and secured land in large grants which they planned to subdivide profitably. To do so they had to attract the new-comers. In New England speculative "proprietors" secured whole townships from the legislatures and then proceeded to induce settlers to go to these outlying districts, to swell the wealth of "absentee landlords." In New York, the governors made lavish grants and enormous manors were peopled with tenants whose lot was not made happy by exactions of the landowners. In the southern colonies many a planter was a land speculator as well. Grants were easy to obtain and men like William Byrd and Lord Fairfax had princely possessions and formed companies to develop them. The Ohio Company with interests located beyond the Alleghenies was to play an historic rôle in the onward march of the nation. The disposal of land called for much of the "science" of modern real estate salesmanship, with the sale rather than the future comfort of the buyer, the main thought in the mind of the speculator.

In these various expansive projects many a venturer prospered and the earnest pursuit of wealth was given an encouraging start. The vast treasure house of America was being explored and exploited. Vested interests in land and trade were acquired by substantial men of wealth who were gaining social and political privileges and becoming jealous of any attempts to control or curtail profits. Even to those who did not succeed there remained the ever present hope that fortune would smile on the next venture. The service of mammon was not the least of the interests of the new American society.

CHAPTER V

FOUNDATIONS OF AMERICAN DEMOCRACY

The peculiar genius of the English colonists was demonstrated less by the way in which they gained a livelihood than by their ability to transplant and adapt institutions. The talent that these colonists possessed for creating "bodies politick" which could survive and in time unite into a republic was the great mark of the new American genius, and laid the foundations of American democracy.

The Practice of Self-Government

This talent was not possessed by all who planted colonies. The Spanish created their vast western empire, particularly the outlying provinces which were to become part of the United States, in the same way they had driven back the Moorish invasion. They fortified posts to house garrisons as they advanced, while the priests conducted an ardent campaign to convert the infidel. There were so few white men that, unless they held the Indians subjugated in some feudal system, they could not maintain their territorial gains. The French scheme of government was likewise feudal; a few officials and seigneurs ruled their tenants, the habitants, in ancient arbitrary fashion. Such government allowed no popular participation. The contribution of the enlightened Dutch was disappointingly slight, for Holland though a republic was more autocratic in its rule of its American posts than were Spain and France. Governors and patroons and a few influential townsmen held the government in a close grip. All told, the political institutions of the republic were to owe little to the non-English colonizers.

It was left to the Anglo-Saxons to lay the foundation of the American democracy of the future. For this task they were well equipped by experience in Britain. Here a tradition of participation in government by various groups of the populace had been growing for centuries. This experience was put to work in making plans for ordering the colonies even before the emigrants left England. In fact, the promoters of the experiments gave more thought to the organization and control of their projects than to the physical well-being of their colonists. England was in the throes of a century of political planning and changing and the colonial schemes reflected this creative activity. Each enterprise went through a preliminary stage of paper planning in England and came to

America with some sort of preconceived schedule. True, these seldom proved immediately practical and sometimes hindered more than they helped; the wilderness rather than the English imagination dictated the flexible character of these social structures.

The original plans for some of the colonies provided for extensive control to be exercised from London by proprietors who knew little or nothing about American conditions. Their instructions left scant discretion to those who were to lead the expeditions. Obviously such plans were not practical; the American shores were too far away and communication was too uncertain and too slow; a letter, if conditions were right, might receive an answer in six months. A wilderness outpost could not be administered in such fashion and self-government was inevitable, though it was not achieved without some experiments in the contrary method.

The Virginia colony was the first to obtain political responsibility. In the first plan, the King had intended to supervise the London Company through a council sitting in London. This council was to appoint a council in Virginia which was to rule strictly according to instructions received periodically from the capital. Those who were to make up the bulk of the population were considered as hired servants of the company without political privileges. Such a system did not work very well. In order to stimulate migration and to produce a better spirit in the colony itself, a measure of self-government was established in 1619, whereby representatives of the colonists were permitted to participate in legislation. The colonists entered into their new governmental responsibilities vigorously and even though in 1625 King James took over the colony and made it Crown property, he and his successors made no change in the representative system. The King's governor frequently sought to limit the functions of the assembly and tried to govern for long periods without it, but the institution remained. In Maryland, too, a legislature developed shortly after the founding which was allowed by Lord Baltimore, for he soon learned that self-government in local affairs at least was necessary to attract settlers.

In New England, self-government flourished from the beginning. The Pilgrims were a religious congregation used to some self-government and on the voyage to America they formed a "civil body politick" in the Mayflower Compact in which the power to enact just and equal laws was definitely set forth. The Massachusetts Bay colony was a corporation with a charter and government by stockholders. As outsiders came to the colony they demanded a share in the government and within four years the Company was forced to organize a legislature composed in part of the representatives of the growing number of towns. Connecticut, New Haven and Rhode Island set up their own governments and like the Massachusetts colonies elected their own officials. In these arrangements the English Crown must perforce acquiesce for there was trouble enough at home to bar any interference. Thus a fashion was set which all the later colonies followed.

Progress toward self-government was not marked solely by the creation of colonial assemblies. There were other laboratories more numerous and more fruitful which made extensive contributions to American political experiment; these were the local units within the various colonies. In 1634 Virginia established a county and parish system of local organization. Under this system which was also used in Maryland and the Carolinas, English customs were taken over bodily. Local control was vested in the hands of the more influential landowners, who as justices of the peace and vestrymen, gave direction to affairs much as the local squires did at home.

In New England, conditions were different; here the colonists had invented the local unit known as the town. The colonists in this region were mostly townsmen and also many of them had migrated in congregations. Therefore this town-church organization was naturally followed in the New World. The same people often composed town and church and they assumed to govern themselves without any particular authorization. The Massachusetts Bay Company charter had no provision for local government or the creation of towns but even as the chartered company immediately transformed itself into a self-governing colony so the local communities likewise assumed political functions. The center of the scheme was the congregational meeting which became known as the town meeting. Here all might come and speak but on most matters voting was confined to the freemen who in general must be church members. The town meeting managed town affairs, especially the common land, elected representatives to the legislature and chose local officials in large numbers. The town was also the unit in New Hampshire, Connecticut and Rhode Island. The town meeting was the seed-bed of American democracy.

When New Netherland was captured and Pennsylvania and New Jersey organized, a mixture of local institutions evolved. Community functions were divided between towns or villages and counties, but in these instances, too, localities either were granted or assumed a generous measure of authority. In such wise self-government through representative assembly and town meetings or county supervisors became a reality; but these colonies were still too near Europe to be really democratic, church membership or property-holding were among the qualifications for voting and universal manhood suffrage existed nowhere. The communities were generally controlled by small groups of those who were well-to-do. The aristocratic ideas so well recognized in England were not forgotten. Nevertheless, the germ of democracy was there.

Having gained self-government, the colonists experimented with it actively. Especially in New England, there was a strong desire to order the community along exalted spiritual lines by means of government; a holy commonwealth was to be established according to Biblical precept. Not only in the New England colonies where the professed ideal of a holy commonwealth would lead one to expect a stern measure of control, but in the southern colonies as well, the statute books provided evidence of strict ideals of human conduct. When the first Virginia legislature met in 1619 it enacted laws against Sabbath breaking, gambling, idleness and intoxication and aimed to curb extravagance in personal attire by assessing local taxes according to the clothes which a single man or a married couple possessed. Massachusetts and Connecticut were even stricter. However, no locality regulates its conduct so much by statute law as by community habit. Consequently, in the southern colonies statutes of this nature largely fell into disuse because the temper of the people was altogether contrary to the spirit of these early laws. In New England, however, such legislation fitted in more exactly with popular habit and this social approval lent force to the laws.

Compared with the legal system of England, the laws dealing with crime were humane. The death penalty was little used. Men were too scarce to be slaughtered for minor crimes; besides there was not much to steal. Death was reserved for murder, treason and rebellion, though in New England it was prescribed for heresy and witchcraft. A few examples of burning at the stake are recorded and in 1659-1660, four Quakers were hanged at Boston after they refused to be banished. Massachusetts Bay Colony had come to America to enjoy a society of its own ordering and those who disagreed with this order were not welcome, witness Roger Williams and Mrs. Anne Hutchinson, both banished for "heresy." Sometimes mutilation, such as cutting off ears or tongues, or branding were inflicted, but quite generally, ridicule was looked upon as a valuable punishing agency. Many a culprit was condemned to sit in the stocks or stand in the pillory to enjoy the jibes of his fellow citizens and an occasional application of mud, soft fruit, stale eggs or even stones. Prisons were rare, crime was scarce and the criminal legislation was largely designed to keep the indentured servants in hand.

Laws regulating economic enterprise were designed to protect the consumer by maintaining standard goods and just prices. Poverty and lack of surplus goods made colonial lawmakers seek to ensure if possible an adequate supply of staples. Embargoes were frequently laid upon the export of necessities and bounties and monopolies were granted to encourage production or manufacture. The rampant individualism and laissez-faire of a later date were foreign to seventeenth-century colonial legislation; the consumer and the needs of the community were not thought to be helped by such theories.

The colonists must needs use their self-governing powers to protect their communities from external danger. In the South there were some difficulties with Spanish neighbors, but in general the Indians were the chief menace. In the early days, Virginia suffered a good deal but after 1645 there was comparative peace. In New England conditions were reversed. After early success, misunderstandings and bloodshed developed. In 1637 the Pequot war broke out and in 1675-1676, a larger conflict, known as King Philip's War. These dangers and fear of trouble, with Dutch and French on the borders, caused an interesting experiment in colonial coöperation. After the Pequot War and a boundary dispute between Massachusetts and Plymouth, these two colonies with Connecticut and New Haven joined in 1643 to organize the United Colonies of New England. It was a loose federation with a decided guarantee of the independence of each unit; but some matters of mutual concern, especially defense, were placed under the control of joint commissioners. The organization was not very effective, the members did not easily agree and after King Philip's defeat, it became inactive. Nevertheless, it had inaugurated a precedent for intercolonial union.

The Germs of Democracy

These evidences of the desire to practise self-government were prophetic of future democracy, but the institutions created did not establish democracy immediately, for they were not based upon the idea of the participation of all adults in government. In each of the colonies there was some special interest, either religious or economic, which was in control. The legislatures were generally made up of representatives of certain groups rather than of the whole people. Even in Plymouth, Connecticut and Rhode Island where the spirit of the fundamental documents and the circumstances of the founding seemed most favorable to democracy, there was marked dominance by the churches in the first two and by landowners in the last. The day of universal suffrage and general office-holding was still afar off. Nevertheless, there were symptoms among the "bodies politick" that the germ of the spirit of democracy was there. This germ was the demand for equality and for the abolition of privilege, plus resentment at injustice and tyranny. That spirit which had led so many to leave England in search of freedom did not desert the new society, even when those who found liberty sought to assume privilege for themselves and curtail freedom in others.

Obviously, protests against arbitrary rule were not marked in the self-governing colonies of New England; they had no external authority to combat, except an occasional customs official, after 1673. Here, despite ecclesiastical and oligarchic control, the practical independence of the colonies provided a sense of self-government which did much to offset resentment at local abuses. In Massachusetts, where control by the clergy and magistrates was most intolerant, those who were dissatisfied worked peacefully and effectively to force the theocracy to make concessions. Violence was avoided. But in the royal and proprietary colonies a different spirit was manifest. Here there was an external authority, representing an absentee power, either king or proprietor. The representatives of these rulers, in the exercise of their authority, came into conflict with the settlers, a conflict which occasionally provoked violence when those who had dared the hardships of conquering the wilderness proved ready to question and resist the exercise of oppressive privilege. Dissatisfaction of this sort was frequently due to the unfortunate personalities or downright worthlessness and knavery of the political cast-offs who often were sent over as governors. But the causes were usually more general, arising out of quarrels over land distribution, quit-rents, frontier defense and other grievances due to the difficulty of social development in the untamed environment of the New World.

Virginia was the scene of one of the first manifestations of a demand for equality and justice in the matter of economic benefits. The King's governor, Sir William Berkeley, ruled arbitrarily for thirty-four years. He gathered close to him the large planters of the colony and they monopolized the government. They kept control of the assembly and in 1670 secured enactment of a law permitting only landowners to vote. This arbitrary rule was accompanied by a period of economic misfortune and the combination of trials roused a demand for redress. The chief industry of the colony was tobacco planting and this was carried on not only by large planters but also by small farmers. The business had been profitable and many small farmers had sought to expand their landholdings by borrowing money from the large planters or from merchants. But after 1660 the Dutch wars, which damaged colonial shipping, and restrictions placed upon the sale of tobacco to other than British buyers caused a long depression during which the debtor farmers found themselves in a hard place. Their debts became unpayable and many suffered foreclosure at the hands of large landholders. This procedure increased the wealth of the rich at the expense of the poor.

This farm problem was the first of a recurring series down to our own day and it was then, as ever after, to have political repercussions. The small farmers were awakened to their weakness, and to the extent to which their government was in the hands of the aristocrats. They saw how taxes were levied to the advantage of the large holders, but they had no organ of protest, for between 1661 and 1676 there had been no election of the legislature. The climax occurred when a disastrous Indian massacre ravished the frontier in 1675. Then they discovered that Berkeley would do nothing to protect the frontier; Berkeley and his rich friends, who enjoyed a monopoly of the fur trade, did not wish to endanger their profits by punishing the Indians. This was the last straw. Nathaniel Bacon, whose frontier plantation had been damaged, organized the disaffected. During more than a year there was civil war, while Berkeley tried to disperse Bacon's followers. Jamestown was captured and burned, but Bacon died of a fever (in 1677) and his followers disbanded. Berkeley exacted bloody reprisals until the news of the rebellion caused an investigation by the Crown and his recall in disgrace. His successors were somewhat less arbitrary, the legislature resumed functioning and the frontier was better cared for thereafter. Protest had not been wholly in vain, though immediate results were not startling and certain unsatisfactory aspects of aristocratic control persisted.

In the proprietary colonies, likewise, there were evidences of resentment of authority. The colony of Maryland, like Virginia, felt the tobacco depression. The citizens resented a recently enacted restriction on the suffrage. They were further discontented over quit-rents and disturbed by religious differences, for the population was largely Protestant and the proprietor Catholic. So a succession of five revolts broke out against the proprietor and in 1689 the Protestants took over the province. Two years later the Crown assumed control and retained it until 1716, when the Baltimores, now Protestant, regained it. In the Carolinas, also, and in New Jersey there was much unrest. The farmers were at feud with the proprietors and with the merchants who attempted to control their markets and crops. The language of protest was becoming well known and even in Penn's Commonwealth there were signs of dissatisfaction with the authority of even so high-minded a proprietor. He was moved to recognize Delaware in 1703 as a separate colony, to a degree independent of Pennsylvania although under the same governor.

The most violent uprising was staged in the province of New York. Here it was a fight against special privilege. When the Duke of York received this Dutch conquest he did not present it with institutions of self-government. He did not permit a legislature, partly because he enjoyed autocratic rule and partly because he was not sure of the loyalty of the Dutch population. The province was ruled by the Duke's appointees, who generally allied themselves with the wealthy landowners and merchants. The small farmers of Long Island, Westchester and the Hudson Valley, the tenants on the great estates and the small tradesmen and artisans in New York City found their interests often disregarded by the magnates. The rulers controlled prices and markets and laid down trade restrictions favorable to themselves but hard on small operators. These latter sought a means of protest but found themselves handicapped because they had no forum.

The lack of a legislature to speak and act for them was the principal grievance and the Duke of York was importuned constantly through nearly twenty years to grant one. Finally, impressed by the resistance, and particularly by the refusal of many to pay taxes, he in 1683 granted an assembly. Two years later, however, when he became king he abolished the new body and placed New York under a royal governor, and in 1688 he added it to a Dominion of New England which he had just decreed. That year was his last, for the Glorious Revolution drove him from the throne; and his deposition was the signal for the democratic group in New York to revolt. Under the leadership of a merchant of German origin, Jacob Leisler, this group seized the government, called a legislature and made Leisler governor. He maintained himself until 1691, when he turned over the government to the appointee of the new sovereigns, William and Mary. His enemies now gained the upper hand, and Leisler and his son-in-law were hanged, ostensibly for treason, but in reality as retaliation by the estate owners and merchants who had suffered the temporary destruction of their power. The assembly became a permanent institution, though elected by a very small proportion of the inhabitants. The revolt had gained some advantages and had shown the effectiveness of direct action. It was becoming more apparent that privilege, monopoly and arbitrary government would in the end be resisted and curbed, if necessary, by revolution. This determination to resist encroachment upon rights and liberties was a manifestation of the virility of that spirit, demanding equal rights and opportunity, which is the essence of American democracy.

The Stuarts could do little to curb this spirit. The most ambitious effort had been made by King James II in 1686 when he combined Massachusetts, New Hampshire, Plymouth, Connecticut and Rhode Island under one governor. Two years later, he joined New York and New Jersey to this group under a newly organized Dominion of New England. This scheme was cut short the same year when James was deposed. Ominous of future difficulty was the beginning of parliamentary interest in the colonies. To protect English merchants against Dutch rivalry Parliament had begun to experiment with navigation laws, greatly restricting the freedom of colonial trade by requiring that it be largely confined to the British empire and cut off from lucrative foreign dealings. This interference with colonial merchants in the next century was to bear unexpected fruit. In the meantime, the colonies continued their lessons in self-government. Quite unconsciously these scattered settlements were developing a self-sufficient attitude which might some day prove incompatible with British exactions upon their loyalty.

The Incubation of Independence

In the eighteenth century the colonists learned more fully the arts of independent self-government. The colonial legislatures assumed greater responsibilities and gained a stronger sense of their rights and privileges which they were ever more determined should not be interfered with by the home government. To this growing practice of independence, the home government and international wars unwittingly contributed.

After years of experimenting with committees of parliament and the privy council, a board of trade was established in 1696 to oversee colonial affairs and to advise the King and his ministers upon all matters colonial. They possessed only powers of investigation and advice, but their industry was prodigious and their influence generally potent. The duties of the board were enlarged from time to time by the gradual extension of Crown control over the proprietary colonies. The owners of New Jersey (1702), the Carolinas (1729) and Georgia (1752) found their tasks too difficult and surrendered their titles to the King. By mid-century royal governors ruled eight of the thirteen colonies and the Penns and the Baltimores had to submit the names of their appointees to the government for approval. In no case, however, was the colonial assembly abolished, and the privileges of partial self-government enjoyed under the proprietors were continued under the Crown.

One of the chief concerns of the English government in the eighteenth century was proper regulation of imperial trade. Following the prevailing theories of mercantilism, navigation laws were extended during the reign of Charles II to make certain that the profits of colonial trade were kept within the empire and concentrated as much as possible in the hands of English merchants. New restrictions were laid upon colonial freedom of trade and a band of customs officials established in the colonial ports to enforce the laws. They reported a woeful lack of respect and obedience on the part of colonists, so another statute was passed in 1696 to tighten the regulations. Courts of admiralty were organized in the colonies to handle revenue cases according to the accepted practices of admiralty law, which, unlike the English common law, made no use of juries in its procedure. To carry out these restrictions the Board of Trade gave the governors minute instructions which were supposed to be carried out to the letter in spite of the fact that they frequently harmonized neither with colonial conditions nor colonial preferences.

Despite these efforts at control, the reality of the situation was that the mother country attempted very little and left the colonists much

Death of General Wolfe

(By Benjamin West, Courtesy of National Gallery of Canada.)

to themselves. These were the years marked by "salutary neglect" and the Americans profited thereby. The thirteen colonial governments functioned effectively and lawyers, merchants, journalists and politicians developed an ever increasing independence. Political practice had not been limited exclusively to isolated colonial capitals. The years following 1689 were marked by a series of wars with the French and Indians which called forth successive intercolonial coöperative projects. Legislatures and politicians of the various colonies were called upon to contribute to the support and management of joint operations, and therein they gained experience which was to prove invaluable in the coming revolution, then hardly dreamed of.

The penetration of the French into the Mississippi and Ohio valleys and their proximity to the New England and New York border settlements had been a constant annoyance to the colonists; and French influence with the Indians made them a menace. Real estate speculation in western lands and the fur trade were hampered and endangered, and there was fear that the French might attempt conquest. In Europe the ambitions of Louis XIV to extend French control aroused general apprehension among the various powers; and England became especially concerned when he espoused the cause of the exiled Stuarts and sought to invade the island kingdoms. War broke out in 1689, 1701, 1744 and 1756; and in 1740 and 1754 warlike measures were undertaken in the colonies prior to the declaration of actual warfare in Europe. The colonial wars were reflections of European rivalries; but they were also, in a very real sense, struggles for self-defense and trade advantage, and the legislatures were called upon to arrange very active participation.

Colonial troops saw service in all of these wars. Twice they conquered French Acadia (Nova Scotia) and at length reduced the great fortress of Louisbourg on Cape Breton Island. Some of their commanders such as Sir William Phips, William Pepperrell, and George Washington rendered valiant account of themselves. Quite significantly these wars revived the idea of intercolonial coöperation. During the first of them, an intercolonial congress met in New York in May 1690 to plan for defense; while in the last, the Board of Trade in London ordered a convention of colonial representatives to meet with delegates from Indian tribes at Albany in June 1754. Not only did the latter conference place Indian affairs upon the agenda but it also took up the question of united action. Several plans were discussed; and finally a scheme of Benjamin Franklin's, to be known as the Albany Plan of Union, was adopted. Had this been carried out, it would have provided for a federal system under a British governor-general and an intercolonial parliament but it was too radical a change to gain the approval of the British government or of the colonies.

These wars came to a successful conclusion and by the final treaty signed in Paris in 1763, Great Britain acquired Canada and the eastern half of the Mississippi Valley from France, and Florida from France's ally, Spain. In return for the latter possession, Great Britain caused New Orleans and the western Mississippi Valley to be transferred to Spain, which now controlled a vast empire from the straits of Magellan to the headwaters of the Mississippi. The victory left the provincials with a distinct sense of achievement. They had organized successful armies and by coöperating among themselves they had demonstrated their own superiority over the best armies of Europe. But they also had a distinct sense of grievance.

British officers had seemed unable to recognize the merit of the militia commanders. Time and time again leading colonial soldiers, like the Virginia colonel, George Washington, had been slighted and humiliated by English officers of inferior rank. In fact, any regular officer ranked above any holder of a militia commission and even in the last campaign, which brought about the surrender of Canada, the colonial troops received what to them seemed to be studied insults. Many a colonial militia officer had unpleasant memories of slights and indignities at the hands of arrogant and stubborn English martinets.

In these years of colonial growth, a truly American society had evolved. It was no longer so English, but cosmopolitan. Its ways of life had become settled, its standard of living higher and there were signs of a cultural interest not possible in the former period. Economic life had expanded and enterprise had developed modern methods. A large and influential group of wealthy and aristocratic merchants and landowners had found in America a place of great opportunity. More than ever these colonies had been called upon to manage their own affairs and even to engage actively in affairs of international moment. They had reached the stage when they could advance their own frontiers and create new communities where the democratic spirit might flourish to offset the growing dominance of the masters of colonial wealth. This American society was prepared to undertake an even more independent rôle in the world if the occasion should arise. Though they were still, in their own opinion, loyal British subjects, circumstances had conspired to make them independent and resourceful Americans.

INDEPENDENCE

1763-1823

CHAPTER VI

THE STRUGGLE FOR LIBERTY

The wars of the eighteenth century had completed the education of the colonies for independence. They now had extensive knowledge of the indifference, the inefficiency and the short-sightedness of the home government and at the same time had discovered that they could shift for themselves. Peace brought neither relaxation nor opportunity to forget these lessons. Rather the Americans were freshly put on their mettle to protect their interests.

New Problems of Empire

Great Britain was in difficulties and the colonies shared in the common concern. A general post-war depression and debts made the burden appalling. The colonies themselves owed three-quarters of a million pounds. Presumably, had the mother country returned to her former indifference and neglect, the Americans would have set themselves to improving their financial position and their very real loyalty to the Crown would have suffered no particular strain. However, the British government was beset by difficulties which prevented such a return to old conditions.

The prolonged period of war had hoisted Britain's national debt to the staggering sum of £130,000,000. Also much new territory had been acquired and this entailed new expense. Plans for funding this debt and meeting the new costs had to be made when London capitalists were struggling with the universal financial depression. They would inevitably attempt to persuade the government to shift as much of the pressing financial burden as possible upon the colonials. It was evident, therefore, that these financial questions were bound to produce a conflict of interest which would strain to dangerous limits the loyalty of the colonies.

The colonial capitalists, merchants, planters, land speculators and fur-traders were likewise in difficulties. They needed freedom and generous policy so that they might quickly expand and regain lost ground. On the other hand, such freedom would bring them into direct competition with the London interests who wanted them to pay their debts and buy British goods rather than develop greater economic independence. In the post-war readjustments, whose interests would be regarded, those of British capital or of American enterprise? One would have to be sacrificed to the other.

The condition of the British government was such that fumbling and blundering were inevitable, for party politics was in a low state. Factions, rather than parties, squabbled among themselves, each faction out for the possession of offices and power. None of them had any policy except to stay in office as long as possible by whatever means lay nearest at hand. Statesmanship was notoriously lacking at a time when insistent problems and an economic depression called for talent of a high order. Such was the type of official which proceeded to bungle the two insistent colonial problems, of finance and administration.

The financial problem was handled in a fashion peculiarly political. The ministry wished to raise money in some manner that might not alienate the support of the wealthy landed and mercantile groups who could wield much political power; so it was certain to concoct schemes to tax the colonies. Hitherto they had escaped levies because they had supported themselves; but now that the ministry had decided to station 10,000 troops in the colonies to guard them, and to keep watchful eye upon the new French, Spanish and Indian subjects, it seemed obvious that the colonies ought to bear part of the burden of their support. Furthermore, the colonial customs service cost the Crown four times as much as the revenue it collected; and in time of economic depression, both English merchants and West Indian planters were objecting to the callous disregard with which the seaboard colonists treated the navigation laws. Evidently it was time to tighten the enforcement of the trade laws, to make them as effective and productive of revenue as possible. This decision was reached just when the colonists were suffering from post-war economic depression and were facing the task of paying their own debts by increasing local taxation.

Under such circumstances the government inaugurated a policy of increasing taxes and trade regulations. A new general customs act, passed in 1764, was the first step. It took special pains to make effective a levy which proved particularly obnoxious to the colonists, namely one on sugar and molasses. A 1733 tax of six pence per gallon on molasses had been so high that the law had been universally disregarded; under their act of 1764 the duty was reduced to three pence and specific regulations provided for its collection. Such a tax would materially reduce the profits of colonial merchants. Furthermore the government abandoned the policy hitherto followed of permitting the colonists a drawback, or partial return of import duties paid on goods which they received from foreign countries via England. Also taxes were increased upon a number of commodities, such as wine from Madeira and the Azores, which the colonists imported in large quantities. To enforce collection of these taxes, heavy bonds and elaborate certificates were required of the ship masters, to make certain that their ships carried only goods loaded in England or the colonies. The navy was ordered to enforce these acts by patrols. Colonial governors were ordered to be more strict in supervising the customs service. Penalties for violation of the law were made heavier and certain inducements were offered to encourage prosecutions for violation.

The duties under this revenue act were estimated to produce but one-seventh of the sum needed to support the colonial guard, although a "quartering" act of the same year ordered the colonies to supply the barracks and part of the food and equipment of the soldiers. To meet the deficit a second revenue scheme was devised, namely a stamp tax. This device had proved both productive of revenue and easy to collect in Great Britain and was now imposed upon the colonists by a law of 1765. Newspapers and pamphlets, dice, playing cards and all legal documents and certificates including college diplomas were to be stamped. Furthermore none of these new levies was to be eased by emission of colonial paper currency; further issue of such "legal tender" had been prohibited by an act of 1764. This untimely prohibition (from the colonials' point of view) indicated that all their small store of gold and silver would be drained off to London. In reality the government had no such immediate intention, as the tax money was actually left in the colonies to be spent there.

The second problem, hardly of less importance, was administrative. The new territory, with its alien population obtained from the French and Spanish, had to be governed and a new Indian menace guarded against. The French had been dislodged from Canada and the Mississippi Valley, and the Spanish from Florida. Great Britain's new territories literally surrounded the thirteen colonies on three sides; French, Spanish and Indians were now British subjects and the manner in which the new imperial population was to be treated could not but concern the Atlantic seaboard colonists. Hardly had the new area been acquired than it presented difficulties. An Ottawa chief, Pontiac, at the head of a federation of tribes, started a revolt in 1763; and though the uprising was put down within a year, it furnished food for thought.

Even before this revolt the British government had sought to deal more effectively with the Indians by appointing in 1761 two Indian superintendents—one for the northern and the other for the southern Indians. By 1763 the Board of Trade had come to the conclusion that until the Indians were more settled and more accustomed to the new order it would be better to segregate them and forbid fur traders, land speculators or settlers to aggravate them. To this end the Proclamation of 1763 announced the organization of three new provinces, Canada, and East and West Florida. The land between Florida and the Great

Lakes, between the Mississippi and the Appalachians, was to be set off as an Indian reservation from which white men, other than government agents, were to be barred. The prohibition of communication between Indians and whites was planned to be but temporary, though that feature was not known in the colonies. Such a policy immediately stirred up resentment, for to the Americans it destroyed a great potential source of wealth. It denied their claims to lands beyond the mountains, cut off valuable trading-grounds and ruined plans for profitable real estate speculation.

Grievance and Protest

The colonists who were now moved to protest were but following a well-established English tradition; they had ready at hand words and ideas that were current coin in this eighteenth century. The ancestors of many of them, who had left England in protest over conditions there in the preceding century, had handed down their resentments to their descendants. Thus the principles of the English Puritan revolution were well known and cherished.

These revolutions had taught the colonists the language of human rights and had particularly defined the immemorial rights of Englishmen. The Petition of Right of 1628, drafted on the eve of the Puritan migration, had brought Magna Charta up to date and had made a classic statement of these rights. Englishmen were to be free of forced loans or taxes not authorized by the people's representatives. They were protected in their persons by the privilege of the writ of habeas corpus and were thus not liable to arbitrary arrest. Neither could soldiers be quartered upon them nor could they be plagued by martial law in time of peace. These were "their rights and liberties" according to the laws and statutes of the realm. All knew that one king had been dethroned and beheaded because he refused to heed these laws and that another had fled before the consequences of his disregard of them.

In the seventeenth century philosophers and legislators had been working to formulate these principles more definitely. The experiences which England endured under Charles II and James II produced the Habeas Corpus Act of 1679 and the Bill of Rights of 1689. These laws secured the persons of Englishmen against arbitrary arrest and imprisonment and insured a fair trial by jury. They reaffirmed the points in the Petition of Rights and guaranteed the right of petition and freedom of speech and debate in Parliament.

English political philosophers were much impressed by these experiences and undertook to formulate a political theory based upon them. Thomas Hobbes, Algernon Sydney and particularly John Locke were moved to write treatises that became classics in the tradition of self-government. Locke was particularly important and his *Essay concerning Human Understanding* and his *Treatise on Civil Government* had great influence on American behavior. He developed a psychology on which he based his political science. According to Locke human beings were born with equal mental capacity, each with a mind initially a *tabula rasa* or blank sheet of paper. Individuals became what their experience dictated. Originally men lived in a state of nature endowed with natural rights of life, liberty and property but with no laws or controls save the law of nature. This liberty without law was bewildering and often led to license. So, in order to protect themselves in their rights and the enjoyment of their liberties, these inhabitants of the state of nature joined together to form a social contract. They set up government based on the consent of the governed and enjoined to protect their rights. This government should be one of divided powers; the legislative though supreme should be checked by executive and judicial branches, so that tyranny should never develop. However, if government became arbitrary and refused to consult the best interests or regard the rights of the people, then it was their privilege to revolt. Here was a theory of revolution made to order.

During the eighteenth century England's achievements, practical and theoretical, had obtained a European-wide hearing. This was the epoch of the Enlightenment, the Age of Reason. Sir Isaac Newton had discovered certain laws of physics such as the law of gravity, and his work, added to that of the astronomers who had evolved amazing formulae revealing the orderly movements of the heavenly bodies, caused an intellectual revolution. The universe, it now appeared, was not the special charge of an ever watchful and frequently intervening deity, but was a mechanism which ran according to immutable laws. These laws could be ascertained and understood by man's reason. Therefore the supreme objective was to study nature and discover natural laws. Locke had done this in the sphere of politics. Therefore his doctrines had the highest sanction.

The colonists found in Locke every justification for protest, even to the limit of revolution if a tyrannical government sought to encroach upon their natural rights. Were not the immemorial rights of Englishmen indeed "natural rights?" With the full sanction of the intellectual priests of the Age of Reason, and in harmony with the spirit of the Enlightenment, the colonials could gird their loins for resistance against Britain. When the news of the ministry's financial and administrative plans spread through the colonies, it was heard by a people armored with the tradition, language and spirit of protest.

Evidently, the British mercantile interests were to be protected at the expense of the Americans. Every aspect of the program would cost the colonists money, advantage and prospect of immediate profit.

Protest soon took definite form. A number of colonial merchant-capitalists were highly incensed, and local political leaders, trained in the colonial legislatures, were ready to make common cause with them. They set about to organize those who were disgruntled. Written petitions to the home government were prepared and in some of the New England colonies agreements were made to purchase no English goods if the obnoxious taxes and regulations were enforced. In their petitions they argued that the new revenue act would effectually ruin their already declining trade; and as a protest against the stamp tax they developed a new theory, the theory of unconstitutionality. Drawing upon their knowledge of British law and custom, they made a distinction on the one hand between external or commercial taxes, which they had accepted previously in theory at least, and on the other hand, internal or direct taxes such as the contemplated stamp tax. The latter levy they declared was a violation of the time-honored dogma that no Englishman could be taxed directly without being represented in the legislative body which laid the tax. Such petitions were received in London before the stamp law was enacted but Parliament refused to consider them.

When the news of the actual passage of the Stamp Act reached America, indignation was general. Stamps would have to be affixed to printed matter and to legal documents of all sorts; and collectors had been appointed in each of the colonies to sell them. Lawyers, clergymen, editors, business men were to have daily evidence before them of British authority; and no one could read a newspaper, make a will, pay a bill or play a game of cards without being reminded that the Crown was taxing him. Merchants who had been disturbed by new customs regulations were further exasperated by the bother and expense of affixing stamps to the great variety of their papers. Planters as well as merchants were incensed. They were always short of cash and in debt. Where would they get the money to pay the impost? George Washington feared that there was not enough actual money in the provinces to pay these new taxes. Artisans and laborers in the towns, many of whom were out of work and suffering from the depression, saw only harder times ahead.

Colonial wrath exploded. Merchants organized in local associations. Committees were formed to correspond with leaders in neighboring colonies. Local clubs, which included many in poor circumstances with a few who were better off, were formed or revived, for such groups had been a feature of colonial politics. Known as the Sons of Liberty, they could be easily roused to direct action. When the names of the stamp agents were announced, mobs formed and in some cases destroyed property. Committees, too, were active and whether persuaded by mob or local committee advice, the agents generally saw the light. When the Stamp Act went into effect in November, none of the stamp agents nor any one else could be found to handle the unpopular levy.

More formal action was also taken. The Virginia Assembly passed resolutions of protest and the Massachusetts legislature invited an intercolonial conference to meet in New York, October 1765. This body gathered at the appointed time with delegates present from nine colonies and addressed a dignified protest to the Crown, making a plea against taxation without representation. New York set an example when merchants and the public agreed not to buy British goods; and in the various colonies organizations were formed to discourage the purchase of British commodities, sometimes by force. Business was more than ever stagnant.

In England circumstances joined with the colonial petitions in urging repeal of the stamp tax. The wheel of politics had turned, another crowd of office holders had succeeded the Grenville ministry which proposed the impost. London merchants began a drive for relief so that American orders might come in once more. The new ministry seemed nothing loath to overturn the unpopular work of their predecessors and in 1766 the Stamp Act was repealed, though the politicians were careful to pass a declaratory act reasserting parliamentary authority to tax the colonies.

The colonists' victory was short-lived, however, for the budget was still unbalanced; and yet a third ministry was compelled to seek a second way to secure revenue. They could think of nothing more original than new duties to be levied on paper, glass, paint and tea, in 1767, and another attempt to make the customs service much more effective. By sticking to external taxation they hoped to soothe colonial feeling. But many new English officials were sent to America to prosecute violators of the revenue laws in the admiralty courts, where no jury trials were possible. The revised system of port regulation imposed fees and burdensome formalities to such an extent that colonial merchants suffered still more losses. Colonial governors and judges were now to be paid from the customs revenue and thus be freed from the local legislatures. From the British standpoint, on the other hand, affairs were more satisfactory; annual revenue from the colonies increased from £2,000 to £30,000 and in the seven years from 1764 to 1771 the colonials paid some £200,000 in taxes.

The British government did not confine itself to laying new duties and enforcing its customs laws; it went further and interfered with the self-governing privileges of the colonists. In 1767 the New York legislature had been disbanded because it would not bear its share in supporting troops within the borders of the colony. Next the Massachusetts legislature was threatened. Early in 1768 that body had addressed a famous circular letter to the other colonies suggesting coöperation in protest and argument. This letter angered the ministry, especially its newest member, Lord Hillsborough. The office of secretary of state for the colonies had just been created and its first occupant lost no time in ordering the Massachusetts legislature to recall this letter or be dissolved. The legislators chose to suffer the latter and were dispersed by the royal governor. Rumors also became current that the local courts were to be disregarded and colonists accused of crime were to be sent to England for trial. The hard-won privileges of self-government seemed about to be lost.

The new taxes, the renewed attempts at enforcement and the interference with colonial self-government aroused the resentment of large groups of the colonists just as the stamp tax had done. The merchants, especially in Boston, began to revive the non-importation agreements and the Sons of Liberty became restive again. So active were the patriotic organizations in Boston that the customs officials felt their authority in danger, and asked for troops to protect them and their work. Two regiments were dispatched to the New England port, and Massachusetts was required to contribute to their support. The presence of these troops was a constant source of irritation to the Boston townspeople and the less peaceable of them did what they could to make life unpleasant for the red-coats. The climax came 5 March 1770, when a few of the soldiers, much provoked by some Boston tormentors, fired on them and killed four colonists. News of this bloodshed spread throughout the colonies like wild fire and became known as the "Boston Massacre." Life as well as rights was now in danger.

Despite the increased bitterness which it produced, the violence seemed to clear the air for a time. The troops were withdrawn from the streets of Boston and by a fortunate coincidence reassuring news came from England. Before report of the massacre had reached London, still another ministry had come into power and had withdrawn all the taxes save that on tea. Peace returned and trade revived, the hard times succeeding the war were over, and as the non-importation agreements had been effective, the colonists had the balance of trade in their favor. People were more prosperous and less discontented and for a time it seemed as though the trouble would blow over.

The provincials, however, in the course of this experience had become better acquainted with ideas of rights—their rights—and of liberty. They had been schooled in the defense of self-government and to many the defiance offered to overbearing British officials had been stimulating. The populace had shaken themselves free of certain restraints of conduct and had asserted themselves. Their leaders, like Samuel Adams in Boston, had tasted the fruits of power. These lessons could not be unlearned nor these experiences forgotten. Isolated incidents of resistance to authority occurred in the years 1771-1773; and only another attempt by the British government to assert some prerogative hateful to the colonials would be needed to bring resistance to the open again. The British ministry was not long in supplying the occasion.

One of the greatest of the English corporations, the East India Company, was in financial difficulties and faced bankruptcy. To aid it the ministry decided in 1773 to grant the company the privilege of selling its tea directly to the colonies, free of all taxes, which heretofore had been collected in England; the commodity was to be subject only to the tea duty levied in America. This tax exemption meant that since the

LORD NORTH FORCING TEA DOWN THE THROAT OF AMERICA

tea could be purchased by the colonials at a price lower than any one else paid, the tea would be even cheaper than smuggled tea—then a common drink. But such a privilege meant that the tea would be sold directly to consumers and the local merchants would not handle it or make money from it. This was an ominous precedent, for if such a privilege were granted to one English corporation, a similar privilege of direct sale might be given to British dealers in other commodities and thus further harm the business of the colonials. Furthermore, it was just another example of British interference.

Had this occurred in 1763, rather than in 1773, perhaps little more than grumbling would have resulted; but much had happened in the decade and the colonists had learned the power of their protests. So the tea, it was generally agreed, would not be purchased; and in Boston some of the local enthusiasts for colonial rights disguised themselves as Indians and 16 December 1773 threw the tea, then stored on shipboard, into the harbor. Elsewhere the sale of the tea was stopped by various methods. Such defiance could not be brooked. British ministerial patience, never very abundant, was exhausted. In 1774 a series of acts was passed depriving Massachusetts of self-government and closing the port of Boston to trade.

Armed Resistance

Politicians and merchants now had common cause and the people at large knew another flagrant example of the precarious state of their rights and liberties. Something must be done to protect themselves from further tyranny. Massachusetts needed help and the necessity for renewed intercolonial coöperation advanced nationalism another step. Throughout the colonies, local committees of correspondence had been writing to one another and creating machinery for joint action. The Stamp Act congress had proved a useful precedent, and the coöperation of merchants of the various colonies in non-importation agreements had met success. The time had now come for another move toward coöperation, one that was to provide permanent machinery.

Virginia took the lead; not only was she sympathetic to Boston but she had a new grievance. The so-called Quebec Act recently passed, and certain ministerial regulations, had placed under the jurisdiction of the province of Quebec much western land which Virginia claimed. To make matters worse a British company seemed about to receive grants there, which would prevent Virginia's title from ever being revived, deprive her of future taxable assets and ruin choice speculative possibilities. In spite of the fact that the royal governor had dissolved the Virginia legislature for officially expressing sympathy with Massachusetts, its members reconvened. They passed a resolution suggesting that an annual congress of delegates from the various colonies be instituted.

The response was immediate, and at the suggestion of Massachusetts delegates from all colonies except Georgia met in Philadelphia, 5 September 1774, in what is known as the First Continental Congress. This body remained in session seven weeks and laid the basis for organized union. Besides issuing a Declaration of Rights and Grievances and petitioning the King for redress, the Congress adopted the Articles of Association, whereby they agreed not to trade with Great Britain and to abandon altogether the slave trade. Furthermore, committees to see that this agreement was enforced were to be appointed in each town and county; the committees of correspondence were charged to be even more active.

In the meantime, the people of Massachusetts were preparing to protect themselves against the British coercive measures. The legislature in spite of royal orders continued to function; the militia was newly equipped and stores and munitions collected. At various times the British commander in Boston sought to wipe out these stores by sending detachments to search for them and destroy them. On 19 April 1775 the colonists resisted an expedition of this character at Lexington and Concord, and although they lost a goodly quantity of stores, they inflicted severe punishment upon the British force. But far more significant, the King's troops had killed colonial militia and blood had been spilled. These "embattled farmers" had "fired the shot heard round the world."

Militia detachments immediately thronged the roads leading to Boston. They were marching to aid Massachusetts. Others undertook independent action, notably Ethan Allen's Vermont boys when they captured Fort Ticonderoga bloodlessly in May. The patriot militia around Boston fortified Bunker Hill, on Charlestown Neck, overlooking the city. From this threatening height the British commander determined to drive them; and 17 June he attacked their position. The colonials, short of ammunition, had instructions "not to fire till you see the whites of their eyes," as the British thrice charged up the hill. When the militia's powder gave out, the British gained the top, but not before. The bloodshed in this Battle of Bunker Hill, following that at Lexington and Concord in April, was marked by heroism among the Patriots, and further kindled the war-like spirit. More militiamen rushed to Cambridge. The dove of peace that historic summer had taken flight.

CHAPTER VII

THE DECLARATION OF INDEPENDENCE

The Second Continental Congress gathered at Philadelphia, 10 May 1775, in this atmosphere of war. It assembled at the time prescribed by its predecessor, and its members appeared with varying credentials and a variety of views. Some had been elected by the legislatures; but, as the Crown had forbidden this meeting, a number were chosen by the unofficial conventions or congresses which in several colonies illegally assumed the powers of government. Most of the delegates were determined to provide for the vigorous defense of their rights and liberties, but a substantial number still hoped for conciliation and a peaceful solution. John Hancock of Massachusetts was chosen their president.

Mobilizing

The fact of war was thrust upon the Congress within a fortnight. Massachusetts requested that the body take control of the army assembling in the vicinity of Boston and provide for its maintenance. Two days before the battle of Bunker Hill, Congress had undertaken to weld the various militia units and volunteer companies into an army. This task called for a commander. John and Samuel Adams shrewdly concluded that it would be better to find an officer outside of New England, for it would not do to give their remonstrance an exclusively New England air. They were attracted by the character, the appearance and the experience of one of the Virginia delegates, Colonel George Washington, who attended the sessions in his militia uniform. He, upon John Adams' motion, was chosen to undertake the great responsibility.

Four major-generals were likewise commissioned, as well as an adjutant-general and a series of brigadiers; officers below that rank were chosen by the colonies. Of the major-generals, the senior was Artemus Ward, to whom Massachusetts had given command of the troops at Boston. Some had expected him to be made commander-in-chief and he now was commissioned by courtesy, but he took little further part in the war. Charles Lee, second of the major-generals, had served as lieutenant-colonel in the British army during the French and Indian wars and in Poland before settling in Virginia on half-pay. He was willing to serve the colonies, flattering himself that his experience and talent entitled him, rather than Washington, to carry the honor of commander-in-chief. His pretensions made him insufferable, insubordinate and unreliable; twice he was to endanger Washington's plans seriously, but he maintained himself until 1778. The third major-general, Philip Schuyler, was a wealthy New York landowner who proved himself a good soldier; although hampered by age and ill health he faithfully served in the Patriot campaigns. Israel Putnam, the fourth major-general, was a doughty Connecticut farmer of great courage, ready for action.

For adjutant-general Congress chose Horatio Gates, another English officer who had settled in the colonies and joined their cause. He had been a major in Braddock's army; like Lee he thought of himself as a superior officer and was to lend himself to Washington's enemies. As a general his career was first crowned by good fortune, but later he failed in responsible commands and he ended his service under a cloud. The list of brigadier-generals included several who were very well chosen. Patriot troops were led effectively by such men as Nathanael Greene of Rhode Island, John Sullivan of New Hampshire and Richard Montgomery of New York. Nor did Congress forget the importance of justifying the colonial cause at home and abroad. It drew up and published a Declaration of the Causes and Necessity of Taking Up Arms. This broadside circulated widely on the seaboard and was carried across the ocean.

Meanwhile, the new commander-in-chief proceeded to New England where on the second of July he took command of the army and of the siege of Boston. This was active war-making on the Massachusetts front, but the situation was full of inconsistencies. The same Congress that was making military preparations still talked of conciliation and spoke of itself as made up of the King's loyal subjects. Its moderate faction was able to gather up a majority of votes for yet one more petition to the King, praying respectfully for a redress of their wrongs. In the colonial capitals, too, war and peace were oddly mixed. In not one of them did Lord North's conciliatory resolutions receive favorable consideration; rather was the wrath of the colonials further roused through the latest strictures imposed upon their trade by Parliament. But several colonies officially took action, protesting their lack of interest in independence. In modern parlance their attitude might be characterized as "everything short of independence."

The Congress was aware of the fact that Britain's colonies were not acting as a unit, even in resenting tyranny to the point of active resistance. In the councils of the thirteen seaboard colonies were joined neither Canada, Nova Scotia, Newfoundland, Florida nor the West Indies. In Nova Scotia and Newfoundland, particularly the former, there was some Patriot sentiment but the ruling group was well entrenched. Halifax was busy as a military depot and rendezvous for British army and navy forces, and the population was constantly augmented by those loyal to the King, the Tories who were forced to leave the thirteen colonies. Spanish Florida was too weak and indifferent to care. The West Indies did show some interest. Jamaica, for instance, appointed delegates to the Continental Congress, although they never attended, and some of the island assemblies now and again passed resolutions of sympathy and encouragement. But that was all. These islands were too isolated, too exposed to attack, too dependent upon the mother country, too near the neighboring French islands, also too indolent, to think of independent action. Then, too, they had not been so prosperous of late years and had grown to depend on English subsidy, over which their mainland neighbors had become jealous and resentful, particularly in the matter of the molasses taxes.

Altogether, Congress made a concerted effort to enlist the aid of but one of these neighboring colonies, Canada. It felt that the French Canadians would naturally be against the British and if it could make the necessary contacts the French habitants would aid. So Congress planned two military expeditions to be sent to Canada to destroy the British power and enlist the French Canadians as friends. General Philip Schuyler was in command of the first, which was to proceed up the Champlain route. His illness left affairs largely in the hands of the young Irish recruit, Richard Montgomery, who led the column into Montreal in November 1775 and then proceeded toward Quebec. To meet him there Benedict Arnold was marching through the trackless Maine forest. Their joint assault the last day of the year was a failure in spite of the brilliance and daring of the commanders. Montgomery was killed and Arnold wounded, all to no purpose. The army settled down to besiege the fortress, while Congress sent a civilian delegation consisting of Charles Carroll, the most prominent American Catholic, Benjamin Franklin and Samuel Chase, to enlist the sympathy of the French, but in vain. Some enlisted, but the apparent inability of the army to subdue the British gave the sympathizers pause. Then, too, there were the ever present differences of race, of speech and particularly of religion. Hatred bred of long-standing rivalry could not easily be forgotten. Canada was not to be the fourteenth colony.

While the Canadian campaign was in its desperate course during the winter of 1775-1776, Washington was struggling to organize an army and at the same time to maintain the siege of Boston. His was a tremendous task. His forces were composed of militia companies and volunteers, most of whom had little knowledge of military tactics and less of discipline. They had enlisted for short terms, as most of them were farmers who were bound by seedtime and harvest, and their respect for military customs was slight. There was a good deal of inde-

GENERAL GEORGE WASHINGTON

(By Charles Willson Peale, courtesy of the Pennsylvania Academy of Fine Arts.)

pendent coming and going. Absence without leave was frequent, particularly as later in the war guerilla warfare developed a type of marauder who preyed upon isolated homes in the rural regions; many a farmer-soldier felt called upon to go home to protect his family. Although the potential fighting strength of the colonies was between 250,000 and 300,000 men, there was never more than a small fraction of that number under arms. It can be ventured that 80,000 was the greatest strength at any one time. Never were there more than 18,000 men in a battle on the Patriot side and usually the number was less than 10,000. The largest encampment during the six years of active warfare was 22,000 and during the winter season the armies dwindled to a mere fraction.

Washington soon discovered that the loose militia organization and the short-term enlistments were demoralizing and he worked out with a committee of Congress a plan for a Continental army. He persuaded most of his men to reënlist in this army for a year; he could then mold his force with more authority and with more confidence in keeping it together. His task was almost insuperable, so many were the obstacles in his way. But this was a real leader—one used to responsibility. He had faced difficult situations all his life. His father had died when he was a boy and his elder brother had been sickly; so from his early youth he had been engaged in plantation management on an increasing scale. The combination of many acres, poor soil and slave labor had taught him to manage difficult enterprises with patience, diligence and infinite labor. As surveyor and militia officer in the French and Indian War he had learned the frontier and the devious arts of warfare, and his experiences had been sharpened by defeat, misunderstanding and rebuff from English military men. It was just the education needed for his later great task. He overcame treachery, cowardice, deceit and neglect and transmitted his own courage and strength to his ragged armies. Few persons could have had the combination of qualities necessary to triumph in such an uncertain and perilous venture.

While wrestling with problems of organization and discipline, Washington was in continual want of supplies. Munitions, arms, uniforms, food, shelter, all the accoutrements of war had to be gathered for the motley troops. Much of the equipment which goes with formal warfare was lacking. Uniforms were very few. Camp facilities were crude and often made on the spot from native wood and stone. Many of the soldiers provided their own guns and homemade bullets; the rest were supplied by local gunsmiths or from weapons captured from the British in battle or by privateers who intercepted supply ships on the high seas. Cannon, shot and shell were scarce. Some were captured from British fortifications like Ticonderoga; others were the spoil of battle.

The colonial iron-masters, particularly in Pennsylvania, turned to gun-casting and kept their forges busy. Later in the struggle General Henry Knox established an armory to manufacture weapons at Springfield, Massachusetts.

Most pressing of all the munition needs was that of gunpowder, which it was difficult to improvise. The colonists had used very little and had but a small supply when the conflict began. During the French and Indian wars there had been some manufacturing but this had ceased; the mills were abandoned and knowledge of the process almost lost. The colonists appropriated the royal powder supply in the magazines and were aided likewise by some lucky captures; nevertheless the supply remained very inadequate. Laws were passed to encourage an infant powder industry, but in spite of some successful efforts, notably in Pennsylvania and Massachusetts, the maximum domestic manufacture could not meet the need. American agents abroad were busy buying powder itself and also saltpeter for the colonial powder manufacturers; their purchases, amounting to several million pounds, were made from the French, the Danes, the Dutch and some even from the English merchants. The Dutch West Indian port of St. Eustatius, the French portion of the island of Haiti and the Danish islands became thriving depots where the colonials found supplies. Here they purchased also woolen cloth and stockings and a multitude of other necessities, with money loaned by French, Spanish and finally Dutch governments and bankers.

The living conditions provided for the soldiery were miserable. Lacking tents and weather-tight barracks, they generally camped in rude huts or log cabins which in winter were almost uninhabitable. Warm clothing and good shoes were scarce. Many accounts tell of the men in rags and of bloody footprints of those forced to walk barefoot in the snow. Food, too, was often scarce and inadequate. Saltmeat, firecake made of flour or meal and water, with now and then a little rum, proved a miserable diet, made none the more palatable when the soldiers knew many of their neighbors were selling food to the British.

The lack of shelter and of nourishing food, together with general unsanitary conditions, left the door wide open to disease. Dysentery, scurvy, influenza, pneumonia, rheumatism and the dread smallpox encamped with the army. The sick and wounded received barbarous treatment for lack of surgeons, of hospitals, of medicines, of food sufficiently delicate to be palatable to invalids, of instruments—in fact, of practically everything needed. Congress did not manage hospitalization well; good doctors were scarce and the pay pitiful. Few were the nurses and ignorant were many of the doctors. Some of the medical organization were thieves and grafters and appropriated money and supplies. The greatest hardships, however, came from the current lack of medical skill; operations were hideous in their torture and in their clumsy ineffectiveness; the absence of any antiseptics or anesthetics made them deadly. Many more men were cut down by disease than by bullets.

No less difficult than maintaining an army was the creation of a navy, for war vessels were expensive to build and required large sums for maintenance. So Washington struggled against this obstacle also. While he was whipping his army into shape before Boston, he enlisted naval help. The British were constantly provisioned by sea and if he could capture their supply ships he would weaken the foe while getting what his own army so much needed. The sailors of Marblehead and Gloucester were therefore organized into a naval militia by Washington and under the command of John Manly did splendid service. At the same time, Congress was considering the sea army and in November 1775 organized a navy. Esek Hopkins was made commodore and later John Paul Jones, John Barry and others were commissioned. A fleet of small vessels was collected which, like Washington's naval militia, watched for British supply boats. They also attempted an expedition and in February 1776 captured Nassau in the Bahamas. More effective were the privateers. Americans had had experience in such gainful warfare during the various French and Indian wars and its alluring profits tempted thousands. Two thousand privateer vessels, at one time or another, were commissioned to prey upon British commerce; their exploits were of the utmost value as contributions to independence. Insurance rates on British shipping went up soon and tremendously; and the consternation which continual losses created among British merchants led them initially to give only lukewarm support to the war and in later years to urge its conclusion.

Seeking Foreign Aid

While Washington was besieging Boston, Congress set about obtaining aid from Europe in solving these problems of equipment and supply. The idea of the possibility of support from England's enemies had been present in the minds of some of the colonial leaders from the start. France, humiliated by her loss of prestige after the peace made in 1763, was seeking revenge; her agents had been occasionally in America since then, observing events. The colonies had been accustomed to maintain agents in London to attend their varied interests; Franklin had served there for Pennsylvania, and numerous others for different colonies. At the time of Lexington and Concord, Arthur Lee was the agent of Massachusetts. He was much interested in the question of foreign aid and during that summer became acquainted with a talented Frenchman, Caron de Beaumarchais. This colorful figure had risen from humble circumstances to a confidential position in the French government and in his lighter moments wrote the famous *Barber of Seville* and *Marriage of Figaro*. Lee found him very responsive to the idea of aiding the fighting colonies. His enthusiasm for the cause of liberty fired him to zealous efforts to interest the French government in sending supplies to America, and he soon succeeded to the extent that they did send another observer, Bonvouloir, to travel across the sea and to make report on his observations.

Congress itself was moved to act, partly because of Lee's reports and his willingness to assume greater responsibility as their agent. They voted, 29 November 1775, to establish a committee on secret correspondence which was to keep in touch with Europe. This committee acted as an office of foreign affairs and began a correspondence with Lee and others, including a Dutch friend of Franklin's, Charles Frederick William Dumas. Lee, thus endorsed, talked further with Beaumarchais, with the result that the latter's advice was heeded. France, it was decided 2 May 1776, would give secret aid to America.

This momentous decision was influenced in part by Beaumarchais' importunities and partly by Bonvouloir's reports. No direct aid could be expected, but supplies would be forwarded through a dummy trading concern. Rodrigue Hortalez and Company was organized by Beaumarchais; and with credit and funds amounting to two million livres, half from the French government and half from the Spanish king, he set to work to prepare shipments of all sorts of war equipment, even including band instruments and music books. In the meantime, 3 March 1776, Congress had formally voted to send their own special agent to Europe to promote foreign aid, Silas Deane of Connecticut. Congress, a month later, declared the ports of the American colonies open to general trade, utterly in defiance of British navigation laws and, after the Declaration of Independence, hopefully proceeded to draw up a sample treaty of commerce for enticing the powers into aiding the United States with new trade relations. The astute Benjamin Franklin was sent that fall as additional agent at Paris; France made further subsidies amounting to another two million livres. These arrangements enabled the colonies to get numerous cargoes of supplies, although without official recognition, for these matters were arranged clandestinely. The American commissioners were now able also to set up a naval office in Paris, in January of 1777, and to seek ships. They bought several, and commissioned officers and privateers who might expect a certain amount of shelter in French ports.

While the colonials were thus exploiting European rivalries to help outfit the infant army and navy, their handicaps were further offset by Great Britain's own peculiar disadvantages. In truth, the mother country was not in a very good position to cope with such a formidable rebellion. When the war opened her army was scattered from America to India. Only 6,000 men were available in the British Isles and but 9,000 were in the American colonies. Therefore, Parliament sought to add 55,000 men to the army and to enlarge the navy from 16,000 to 28,000 men. But enlistment was slow and the transport system inefficient. It was a tremendous undertaking to get an army of any size over to America, particularly in the small boats then available. Sorely pressed to secure a force adequate to cope with the colonial militia, the King adopted the expedient of hiring soldiers. The small German princes were wont to profit by renting out the services of their conscript troops, and so George III turned to several of them, particularly the ruler of Hesse. For a price, he got numerous Hessian regiments and a few from other states. Thirty thousand men, all told, were thus secured at about seven pounds apiece and sent to quell the rebels. In the course of the entire war, the British sent over about 100,000 troops, including the Hessians, and had besides the services of some 50,000 Tories and an indeterminate number of Indians.

Further disadvantages which the British suffered arose from poor leadership. Such troops stood in peculiar need of vigorous direction but it was glaringly absent in Britain's early selections, particularly in the days of the Howes. The terrain was strange to them and difficult to master from a military standpoint. The range of the conflict was extensive and needed a much larger force than the home government was able to send over. The British were strong enough to capture important centers like New York, Philadelphia and the southern ports; but they could not hold much of the country in between. Early in the war they left New England and, in fact, after 1778 did little anywhere but in the South. They were disappointed in the response of the Loyalists; and the Hessians and even the British troops showed some slight inclination to leave the army and settle in the new country. Some were possibly driven to this idea to avoid the terror of a returning voyage, for the transports were so miserably crowded and the food and water often so bad as to make the long voyage a horrible experience. However, these disadvantages did not prevent the war from lasting a long time, and in the first winter of the conflict they failed to lighten Washington's burdens.

While Washington was struggling to keep up the siege of Boston with an ill-equipped army which the French had not yet been persuaded to outfit, the British tried to make a countermove in the South. There rousing patriotic utterances and certain Mecklenberg County resolutions, adopted at Charlotte, North Carolina, 31 May 1775, might have seemed to foreshadow independence; but the British had been given to understand that an extensive Loyalist sentiment awaited their coming. In North Carolina particularly, the Scotch Highlanders on the frontier

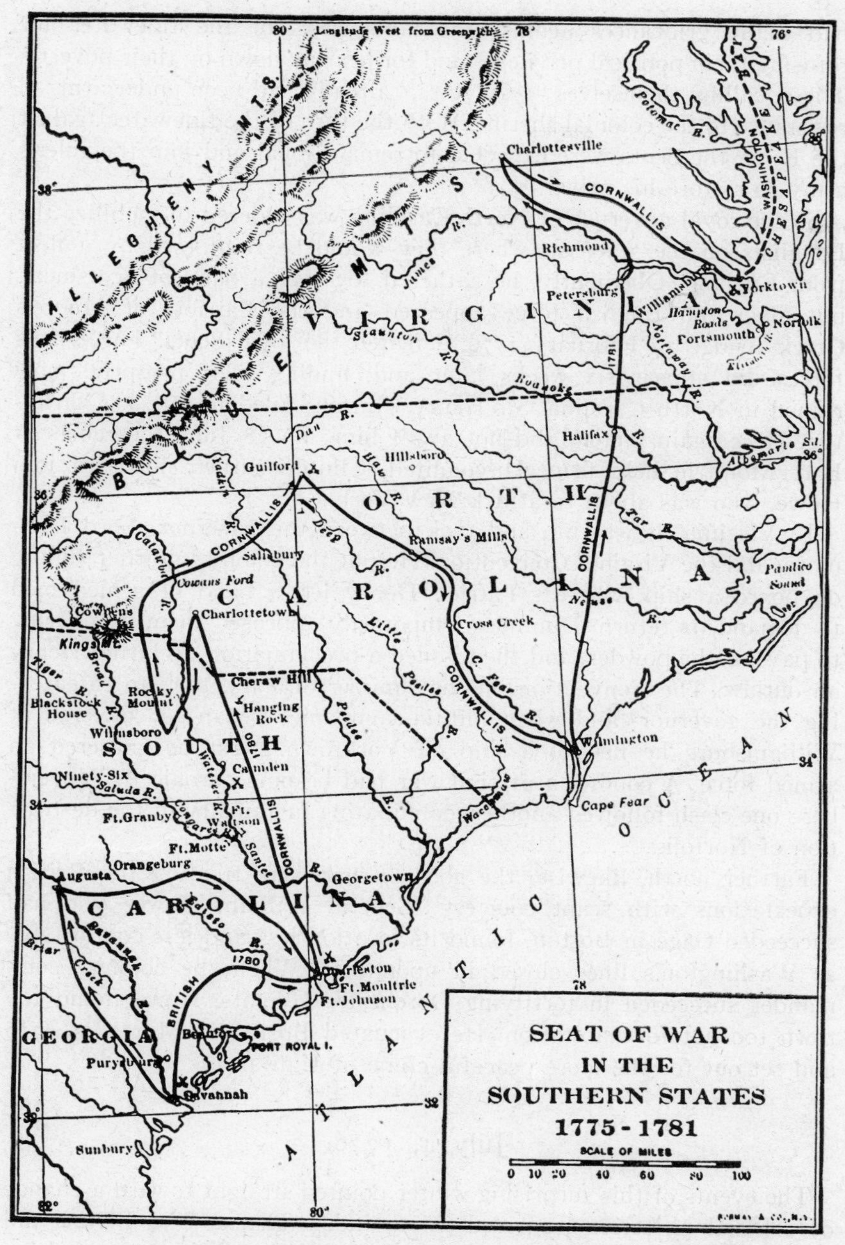

(From *The American Revolution* by Van Tyne, published by Harper and Brothers.)

had many grievances against the landowners of the tidewater for refusing them political privileges and for bearing down on their poverty. These, calling themselves "regulators," already had been under arms in resistance to the colonial sheriffs. With the turn of the tidewater against the King, the Scots were expected to remain loyal and join the ruler's army to restore his power.

So the royal governor of North Carolina was ordered to mobilize the Loyalists on the seacoast, where they would be reinforced by a fleet from England. Obediently, he gathered together a band of Scotsmen; but alack, no English force appeared and the Patriots of Moore's Creek Bridge 27 February 1776, defeated the loyal Scots. The King's forces did appear six weeks later and, finding their prospects now ruined in North Carolina, Sir Henry Clinton sailed to attack Charleston. Here again victory did not await him; on 28 June the rebels at Fort Moultrie held firm. Discomfited, Clinton turned north to join Howe, who was about to attack New York.

In Virginia, it was nip and tuck between the governor, Lord Dunmore, and the Virginia Convention. He put the colony's powder supply on board a ship, whereat Patrick Henry led a band of armed men to demand its return. Dunmore temporarily appeased them by offering to pay for the powder, and then issued a proclamation declaring Henry an outlaw. The Convention, in the summer of 1775, took to threatening the governor, and when militia companies began to converge at Williamsburg he fled to a ship off Yorktown. Next he gathered an armed force. A condition of civil war had become chronic by November; one clash followed another, culminating in January in the destruction of Norfolk.

Farther north, likewise, the gods of war were treating the British expectations with scant courtesy. General William Howe, who had succeeded Gage in Boston, found its location less and less comfortable as Washington's lines closed in upon him. When the colonial commander succeeded in fortifying Dorchester Heights, Howe found the town too hot for habitation. He evacuated Boston in March of 1776 and set out for the more peaceful clime of Halifax.

July 4, 1776

The events of this surprising winter pointed straight toward a change of colonial objective from redress to independence. The British did nothing to prevent this shift; in fact their policies could not have been better designed to ensure it. They treated the petition sent by Congress with contempt. The King refused even to receive it, on the ground that the Congress which sent it was an illegal body—which of course it technically was. At the same time (in August of 1775) he issued a proclamation declaring the colonials to be rebels. News of his attitude toward their petition and themselves was received together and as a double insult. The King's hiring of the foreign Hessians to fight them made their indignation yet more violent; and the burning of colonial towns such as Falmouth, Maine, Charlestown in Massachusetts and Norfolk in Virginia, added fuel to the flames. Finally, in January of 1776 appeared the crystallizing force which focused colonial attention on the hopelessness of further efforts at redress. A pamphlet entitled *Common Sense* opened colonial eyes.

Tom Paine, its author, was a young English ne'er-do-well who had tried his hand at many things from preaching to tax-collecting. Franklin had met him in England and sent him to Philadelphia, where he made his living by writing. Intelligent and well equipped to conduct independence propaganda, Paine produced a vigorous and appealing pamphlet which reached a wide audience. The fact of war, he argued, notwithstanding protestations of loyalty, raised a new question. Why should the colonists remain part of the British empire when it was no longer to their interests to do so? Liberty and freedom were much more attractive than subjection to the far-away British. Independence ought to be the goal. Affirmation of loyalty seemed rather hollow when the colonists were arming to resist the soldiers of the Crown. His argument reached the heights of eloquence as he concluded with the impassioned plea:

> O! ye that love mankind! Ye that dare oppose not only the tyranny but the tyrant, stand forth! Every spot of the old world is overrun with oppression. Freedom hath been hunted round the globe. Asia and Africa have long expelled her. Europe regards her like a stranger, and England hath given her warning to depart. O! receive the fugitive, and prepare in time an asylum for mankind.

The course of events supported Paine's arguments and oratory. The royal governors had attempted, in most cases as early as 1774, to curb the assemblies; they either dissolved them or refused to call them into session, or both. Their authority was openly defied and by the close of that year the various colonial leaders in all the royal and proprietary colonies, save New York, Pennsylvania and Georgia, had created provincial congresses like that of Massachusetts, which for all practical intents and purposes ruled the colonies. After the news of Lexington and Concord, New York and Georgia organized similar congresses. Even in conservative Pennsylvania, the colonial legislature and military associations began to assume a definitely independent function; the legislature conducted itself according to the usual forms but acted under the domination of a committee of safety. The governors attempted to combat this trend, particularly General Gage in Massachusetts, Dunmore in Virginia and Tryon in New York. But they proved helpless. By the beginning of 1776 all governors had given it up and retreated, except in Pennsylvania, New Jersey and Maryland.

The provincial congresses thus became in ten colonies the supreme authority, aided by committees of safety, committees of correspondence and other unofficial groups for enforcing the association and watching the Loyalists. These bodies, in some instances, began to take thought of their legal position and plan for a new fundamental law regularizing their authority. New Hampshire started it by creating a new frame of government or constitution, styled "temporary," in January 1776; in March, South Carolina, and in May, Virginia, did likewise, thus in

BRITANNIA DISMEMBERED
(A Contemporary Cartoon)

effect declaring themselves independent states. In the meantime, the Continental Congress had been considering this question; and, while Virginia was putting the finishing touches on her new constitution, advised the colonies in general to follow such procedure.

The reasoning of Paine's *Common Sense* was rapidly spreading and the logic of events was wielding a powerful influence. All these measures for fighting the home government and asserting so many forms of independent action could lead to only one end, and the colonials came to realize it. North Carolina, 12 April, blazed the trail by instructing her delegates in Congress to work for independence. Virginia a month later likewise so acted, and 7 June Richard Henry Lee of her delegation rose and offered his historic resolution: "that these united colonies are and of right ought to be, free and independent states." Thomas Jefferson, of the same colony, was made chairman of a committee to draft for Congress a Declaration of Independence.

Jefferson undertook this task with alacrity. He was a planter who had dabbled in politics and read deeply in the philosophy of the day.

He had pondered long on these questions and had definite ideas, many of them gathered from the English thinkers of the preceding century, such as John Locke. He was also a true son of the Age of Reason and had a thorough understanding of the rationalistic theories regarding man and society then current among the French Encyclopedists. Finally, he was a cogent and logical writer, although a most unengaging speaker. From his pen came a neat rationalization of the basis of American independence.

Jefferson drew upon the social theories of the philosophers of natural law. He was familiar with the social contract theory. Fortified by it Jefferson made his classic statement.

> We hold these truths to be self-evident, that all men are created equal, that they are endowed by their Creator with certain unalienable Rights, that among these are Life, Liberty and the pursuit of Happiness. That to secure these rights, Governments are instituted among Men, deriving their just powers from the consent of the governed. That whenever any Form of Government becomes destructive of these ends, it is the Right of the People to alter or to abolish it, and to institute new Government, laying its foundation on such principles and organizing its powers in such form, as to them shall seem most likely to effect their Safety and Happiness.

Having thus established the right of revolution, he showed how the colonists were justified in their contemplated act by reciting the tyrannies of the King and the vain efforts of the colonists to persuade him to respect their rights. Having failed to obtain justice by peaceful means, they were ready to declare their independence and claim and maintain for themselves "full power to levy war, conclude peace, contract alliances, establish commerce, and do all other acts and things which independent states may of right do." To this the delegates agreed and in defense of it, on 4 July 1776, they mutually pledged their lives, their fortunes and their sacred honor. The bell in the tower of Independence Hall then in truth could vigorously "Proclaim liberty throughout all the land, unto all the inhabitants thereof." The British colonies were resolved to be a nation.

CHAPTER VIII

THE WINNING OF INDEPENDENCE

The Declaration of Independence was a document which would be but empty rhetoric if it were not maintained against the inevitable attempts of Great Britain to destroy its meaning. No sooner had it been proclaimed than word came of a great expedition approaching New York to seize that vital seaport with its control of the Hudson River.

The Varying Fortunes of War

In March 1776 the British had been forced to evacuate Boston and the American commander had moved his force to New York to await a threatened British attack; for British reënforcements had been sent to Halifax and an expedition was preparing for an elaborate attempt to destroy rebellion. The British under Sir William Howe sought to capture New York and thus drive an entering wedge through the center of the colonies. In this they were all too successful. In August 1776, they captured New York City and later drove Washington through New Jersey into Pennsylvania. The Patriot general, however, turned suddenly and by a brilliant counterstroke defeated a large Hessian contingent at Trenton, on Christmas night. A few days later he won another victory at Princeton. These successes caused the British to retire to the vicinity of New York where they spent the winter while Washington encamped at Morristown.

General Howe did not campaign vigorously and seemed interested rather in seeking to conciliate and to negotiate a peace. He also enjoyed himself in comfortable colonial cities. He was furthermore confronted with difficult obstacles and his home government gave him none too generous support; the fact that he was of the opposition party in English politics perhaps contributed to his lack of energy. All these preferences and prejudices did not make him a very active general. In the spring of 1777 the war office produced a plan of conquest. An expedition was to be sent from Canada down the Hudson, which Howe was supposed to meet by moving up that stream, to perfect thereby the separation of the New England colonies from the rest. Howe on the other hand had concluded that the best way to bring peace was to capture Philadelphia, the capital of the United States, and disperse Congress.

The war office was inefficient in communicating its scheme to Howe and he went off on his own campaign.

After much delay, he took his army by sea from New York around into the Chesapeake, where he landed at the head of the bay. Washington sought to oppose him at Brandywine Creek, 11 September 1777; and when he failed to prevent the British general from entering Philadelphia, he made a second unsuccessful attempt to defeat him at Germantown, 4 October. After these disasters, Washington could do nothing but keep troubled watch from the bleak hills of Valley Forge, while Howe made merry in Philadelphia, and Congress helplessly debated at York, Pennsylvania, whether it had fled. This winter of 1777-1778 was the darkest hour of the Patriot cause but there was one bright spot. The expedition from Canada under Burgoyne had not penetrated very far into northern New York before it was defeated at Saratoga by Gen. Horatio Gates and forced to surrender en masse 14 October.

Events proved that this victory was to turn the tide. The American commissioners in Europe already had been able to direct much arms, ammunition and other equipment to the colonies. Over 90 per cent of the powder used by the Continental army during the first two years of the war had been thus obtained. When the news of the surrender of Burgoyne had been received by Congress, they decided to capitalize on it. The astute Franklin, still at Paris, was encouraged to seek recognition, which he did with renewed ardor. Success crowned his efforts; on 6 February 1778 a treaty of alliance was signed with France. The news of this great event came to Washington just as the long and dreary winter at Valley Forge was giving way to spring. Spain and the Netherlands did not join the colonies in alliance; yet they not only loaned money and gave commercial privileges but finally went to war with Great Britain and effectively diverted her attention, even if they won no spectacular victories.

The report of the French alliance was less than welcome to the British and spurred them to renewed activity. General Howe's resignation was accepted and Sir Henry Clinton made his successor. The troops were ordered to withdraw from Philadelphia, because it was feared that a French fleet might blockade the Delaware and bottle up the British forces. The presence of too many privateers in the waters of the lower Delaware and off the capes, caused the British forces to be marched overland. Washington sought to meet them and strike a decisive blow. He almost succeeded at Monmouth Court House, New Jersey, 28 June 1778, but lost most of the hoped-for advantage by the stupidity of General Charles Lee. After this disappointment, he could only march to the Hudson above New York City and await the coming of the French forces. But the united victory which Washington hoped for and which the British feared did not materialize. The

French fleet did not attack New York or capture Newport and the rest of 1778 and 1779 went by with neither side strong enough to attack the other.

Away in the West, while the armies were watching each other in the East, an empire was being won. George Rogers Clark, a major in the Virginia militia, had gone to Governor Patrick Henry with a plan to conquer the territory north of the Ohio and east of the Mississippi. With the small force that Henry could spare him, he made a well-nigh impossible march across icy swamps into that country, in the winter of 1778-1779, and was completely successful. The great area known thereafter as the Northwest Territory was captured from the British and the new nation now claimed possession of the long-coveted lands beyond the mountains.

In the meantime, the British were somewhat relieved of their apprehensions by the ineffectiveness of French aid and decided to transfer their field of activity to the South. They had enjoyed an initial success when Savannah was captured, 29 December 1778, and there was promise of much Tory support. This materialized in the capture of a second city, Charleston, in May 1780. Washington was able to do little but he sent first Gates and then General Nathanael Greene to oppose British advance under Lord Cornwallis as best they might. Their efforts were balked by several defeats; nevertheless, Cornwallis found his task difficult. While he might capture seaports and win victories he could not maintain control very far from the coast. His troops were not sufficient to guard his conquests; and, after the watchful Greene had superseded the rather ineffective Gates, he had a foe who followed him continually and constantly annoyed and endangered him. He made a long march through North Carolina, where he found little resistance and less glory. Finally Cornwallis established a base on the York River at Yorktown, Virginia, upon orders of his commander, Sir Henry Clinton, still in New York. This was to be a fatal error as events proved.

Washington in the meanwhile hoped that the French force, now much enlarged, would join him and capture New York; but the French decided that Cornwallis at Yorktown would be a more desirable prize. They took naval control of Chesapeake Bay and Washington marched to join them. Their joint siege of Yorktown ended successfully 19 October 1781 when the British commander surrendered.

Economic and Social Change

The successful resort to arms was but one phase of the revolutionary movement. The struggle profoundly affected all of colonial existence. The armies had to be fed, clothed, armed and financed, new business ventures had to be undertaken and radical changes made in the erstwhile provincial social order.

The effect of the Revolution upon economic life was particularly marked. In the regions where the armies were operating there was great demand for food, not only for the Continental troops but also for the British and French armies. In these regions agriculture was stimulated by high prices and by the gold which both British and French paid for their supplies. Also as the new state governments confiscated much land from those loyal to the Crown and then sold it, the time was opportune for farmers to enlarge their acreage. Since there was not much capital, a number of farmers borrowed money to pay for these lands, with the expectation that the high prices would last long enough to enable them to pay off their debts. However, as the fighting was restricted and transportation was bad, the great mass of farmers were slightly affected by the conflict.

Industry, however, was greatly stimulated. All British restrictions were now without effect. Clothes, arms, munitions, equipment of all sorts, and salt were much needed. There were no established manufacturers capable of producing sufficient quantities of any of this equipment. Clothing had been largely imported or manufactured in the homes. Shoes had been made to fill individual orders by local cobblers, or had been crudely put together at home. The small forges and foundries were wholly incapable of providing enough cannon and shot; facilities for making muskets and manufacturing gunpowder were likewise very limited. Manufacturing responded to the stimulus of war needs in spite of the fact that payments in Continental paper were not the best encouragement. Numerous small concerns started operations, though most of them were little more than home industries. In the iron business larger forges and foundries were built to manufacture artillery.

Business was brisk during the war period. Commerce was free now from British navigation laws; and when France allied herself to the new nation and Spain went to war with Great Britain, most of the important seaports except the English were open to American ships. Patriot privateers, too, swelled trade by their captures and the goods and money which they brought home. The warehouses of the American merchants were well stocked with European goods. Naturally, as the fortunes of the new country were in a very uncertain state, and as the currency was debauched by a flood of paper money, business profiteers were not absent; gamblers schemed to gain by the falling price of the paper money; and clandestine sales to the British, though they brought in gold, added to the uncertainty because of the risk often involved.

Many prospered during the war but unfortunately this prosperity was never shared by the Continental treasury. The finances of the government were generally in a hopeless condition, for the states could not contribute much and the Patriots had little to lend. The available coin always had been insufficient to meet the growing needs of the colonists; and for war demands, it was totally inadequate. The Continental Congress tried to borrow at home and abroad, with only moderate success. It fell back upon large issues of paper money which depreciated so rapidly that sale of produce in return for this currency amounted practically to a gift.[1] Robert Morris, the treasury's chief support, was often unable to find funds for the smallest expenses. In spite of his handicaps he made some progress toward establishing sound finance; he used a part of the gold borrowed from France to help establish the first bank, the Bank of North America, which was opened in Philadelphia in 1781.

The most significant of the changes wrought by the Revolution were social, for in the organization of society there was a revolution indeed. Neighborhoods were no longer the same, for many familiar figures were absent from the streets. Not only did the war take its toll of casualties (at least 10,000 were killed and wounded) but an important element who opposed independence was banished or in flight. There is no way of knowing how extensive that opposition was, for it varied from year to year and intensified and diminished according to the Patriot success. John Adams estimated that at least one-third of the colonists were opposed to the war and that numerous others were indifferent. Such conditions left active Patriots in the minority. Worse, when the army seemed in danger of destruction, that minority of Patriots seemed smaller than it really was.

The Loyalists, or Tories, were men of all ranks and conditions who believed that there was no justification for this treasonable rebellion against the Crown. Most important among them were large numbers of comfortable, conservative and prosperous men, who not only were loyal to the Crown, but who feared certain tendencies displayed by the more radical of the Patriots. Though there were a number of wealthy men who were heart and soul in the Patriot cause, the move in the northern colonies took on the guise of a popular uprising against a ruling class. Small tradesmen and farmers openly advocated confiscation of the land of the Tories. Many of the most influential colonial families, leaders in the provincial society which gathered around the governor and British officials, despised and feared the "rebels" and gave services and money for suppressing the rebellion. Loyalist regiments were mustered into the British army and many a Tory farmer sold supplies to the royal commissaries.

[1] $8,000,000 in specie was borrowed from abroad. Congress borrowed $67,000,000 at home and with the states issued $450,000,000 in paper money. The various states contributed $1,500,000 in specie and $54,000,000 in paper. The total cost of the war is estimated as $104,000,000 in gold values.

In the South, the conflict took on more of the aspect of a civil war than of a popular uprising. Many of the plantation owners had much the same point of view that the English country gentlemen possessed and were as loyal to the Crown as ever the cavaliers had been in the previous century. Others, just as conservative in economic and social views, felt that the politicians in the mother country were trying to gouge them and poach upon their rights; they joined the Patriots. So it was plantation owner against his neighbor; small farmer against small farmer. The strength of the Tories in the South grew during the latter part of the war when the British were actively campaigning in the region. But neither loyalty to the Crown nor the desire for independence was confined to any section or class.

Many communities in both sections were divided into bitter factions and old antagonisms and jealousies found their vent in quarrels under the guise of serving one cause or the other. In country districts neighbors often engaged in clandestine and marauding civil war, in which life and property were frequently lost and much of anxiety and hazard added to the struggle. Many a Patriot felt he must remain at home to protect his family against Tory pillagers, and the army suffered in consequence. Patriot farmers found themselves at a disadvantage, too, when their neighbors, indifferent or hostile to the patriot cause, sold their produce to British quartermasters for gold while the reward of patriotism was only depreciated paper. Such division of opinion and recompense had been more of a handicap than lack of equipment or even defeat in battle.

Naturally the Patriots sought to punish their opponents and the Tories cherished their loyalty at extreme cost to themselves. State legislatures confiscated their property and caused their imprisonment. Frequently their neighbors made it so unpleasant for them that they were forced to leave their homes, while in extreme cases tar and feathers hastened their exit. Some simply retreated to towns within the British lines, others went to England or the West Indies, and a third group settled in Canada; the latter two groups numbered somewhere between sixty and one hundred thousand persons. The property which was abandoned or confiscated, valued at £9,000,000, was kept by the state or sold to new owners. In this way some great estates were broken up; others became public land.

With the departure of the wealthy Tories, there disappeared an aristocratic ruling element in political and social circles, and in their place came a new leadership. Ambitious and energetic Patriots, adherents of republican principles, often quite humble in fortune, gained prominence through their services to the cause of liberty. They settled in the seats of the mighty. They dominated the legislatures and abolished quit-rents and primogeniture, which had done so much to maintain landed estates. Furthermore, they did what they could to encourage small holdings in fee simple, for one of the ideals of the Revolution was economic independence for the common man. This break-up of large holdings did much to make the distribution of property more democratic and to give point to the Revolutionary ideal of equality.

The cause of equality and human freedom was further advanced during the Revolution by the legislators in the states under the leadership of men like Jefferson. Religious freedom was forwarded by statutes or constitutional provisions abandoning established churches and taxation therefor. Shortly after the cessation of conflict three well-organized and independent church groups were established. The Anglican or Episcopal church broke away from English ties and secured an American bishop, Samuel Seabury, to direct its affairs. A Roman Catholic bishop, the patriotic John Carroll of Baltimore, was appointed to nourish an American church. At the same time, new Methodist congregations united in an organization and shortly adopted the episcopal system; the most notable organizer among them was Bishop Francis Asbury. These organizers had much to do, for there had been a falling away under the rationalist spirit of the Revolutionary thought and many of the religious ties had weakened. Freedom for Negro slaves was written into certain of the northern constitutions. Criminal law was made more humane. Furthermore, there was some slight evidence that a few of the leaders were thinking of education as a public responsibility. Though these were only signs, the new leadership and the new ideals, however, were facts.

The New Government

The struggle for independence made necessary many political changes. Local government, as far as towns and counties were concerned, was not much affected; but the provincial political organization had to be revised and new machinery created to meet the needs of independence. Before the Declaration the Continental Congress advised the colonies to form independent state governments, and between 1776 and 1783 this advice was followed. In Rhode Island and Connecticut, where the colonial charters had provided for independent self-government, the legislatures went no further than to reënact their charters as constitutions with but a change in title. In the other eleven colonies, however, more radical adjustments were imperative. Royal and proprietary governors could no longer be permitted to function and so an executive branch and a new judiciary had to be created.

Distrust of the executive, acquired during the colonial days when the governors represented Crown or proprietor and quarreled with the assemblies, influenced constitution makers to allow the newly created executives relatively little power. Their right of veto was sharply curbed and in some instances, generally in New England, a council was provided to share the executive responsibility with the governor. Pennsylvania in fact for a while did without one. The legislatures representing the people were to be the great repositories of power. They were composed of two houses, except in Pennsylvania, and were subject to few limitations, other than those detailed in the bills of individual rights which were to be found in most of the new constitutions.

Yet they were not altogether democratic. Some property or tax paying qualification was required for office holding and suffrage, and thus many men were denied the vote. Also the legislatures were not truly representative in many states, for the older tidewater settlements had more than their share of lawmakers and the new regions of the back country were left with much cause to complain of their lack of representation. Furthermore, religious qualifications still persisted in many of the states; and disbelievers in trinitarian Protestantism frequently found themselves disqualified, at least from office holding. In general, the makers of the new constitutions agreed that the judiciary should be somewhat more independent than had been the case in the colonies; and provision was made for the appointment of judges, either by legislature or executive, for life or during good behavior. Religious freedom was guaranteed and in some instances the emancipation of slaves begun.

The greatest problem was not, however, the reorganization of state governments, but the creation of a national government. It is extremely significant that at no time does there seem to have been any intention on the part of any of the individual states to remain separate from the rest. Independence had been declared and won together and plans for the states to join in formal confederation were concluded in the months immediately after the Declaration of Independence. On 15 November 1777 a constitution known as the Articles of Confederation was submitted to the states for ratification and in March 1781 the scheme went into effect. This plan provided for a "perpetual union" of the states in a confederation to be governed by a congress similar to the Continental Congress, consisting of one house composed of delegates from each state. In legislating each state had one vote and the agreement of nine states was necessary to pass a bill. The states jealously guarded their control of commerce and the taxing power and the Congress of the Confederation could only ask the states for what it needed. In reality, its functions were limited almost exclusively to the conduct of foreign affairs, and the administration of the common territory west of the Alleghenies.

Neither federal executive nor judiciary was provided, nor could an amendment be made except by unanimous consent of the states.

However, the basis of national citizenship was laid down by the guarantee, to citizens of one state going into another, of the privilege of citizenship in the latter. Furthermore, it was stipulated that the records and judicial proceedings of any state should be recognized in all the others and extradition of fugitives was provided for. Most of the power was retained by the states themselves and a very little was sparingly allotted to the federation. The important fact, however, was that the formal federation existed.

In this fashion a republic had been created, based upon widely distributed property and the political rights of the individual. The old order, which smacked of aristocracy, had been swept away and a new and more responsive leadership had arisen, not from any British ruling class but from the ranks of the colonists themselves. The Patriots had achieved this in coöperation, and while the states felt themselves to be independent sovereigns, they had accomplished their important task in concert, in union. Often they spoke of themselves as "Americans" and alluded to "national" projects.

Making Peace

The surrender of Cornwallis opened the way to peace. The loss of this second army was the last straw to England; reconquest was evidently impossible. The British debt had mounted up; expenses were increasing and income declining. American privateers had thrown English commerce into a sad state of demoralization aggravated by the attacks of French, Spanish and Dutch war vessels. There was but one thing to do and that was to make peace.

Benjamin Franklin, John Adams and John Jay undertook peace negotiations in 1782 at Paris. In the treaty which was finally signed, Great Britain acknowledged the independence of the thirteen united states and recognized the Mississippi as the western boundary; the Floridas were returned to Spain and Canada remained British. However, no definite, undisputed boundaries were fixed, and the seed was thus planted for later dispute and trouble. The American fishermen were to be permitted to make their catches in Canadian waters and to dry their fish on the Canadian and Newfoundland shores, while on the other hand the British were conceded free navigation of the Mississippi.

A question which caused much trouble in the conference was the status of the Loyalists. The English sought vigorously to have their civil rights and their confiscated property restored. At length, the American commissioners agreed that there should be no further confiscation of Tory property or persecution of Tory persons. They promised, further, that Congress should recommend that the states restore the confiscated property and repeal the laws which deprived Loyalists of their civil rights. Concerning the various debts owed British merchants, amounting to more than £5,000,000, the United States agreed that they should be met, while England on her part agreed to pay for slaves freed and property destroyed in her coastal raids during the war. As far as the promises of the Americans went, they were no more than gestures because Congress had no authority in these matters; and time was to show how small was the regard which the states had for the provisions of this treaty. Nevertheless, on the basis of this agreement peace was proclaimed in Paris 20 February 1783 and the last British troops left New York 25 November. The military victory was complete.

Thus in the years between 1763 and 1783, political independence had been won by thirteen sovereign and united states; but something more vital had been achieved: a group of three million people were beginning to learn that they were in fact a nation.

CHAPTER IX

CREATING THE REPUBLIC

The treaty of peace and the withdrawal of the British troops relaxed the strain of unnatural activity, intense effort and anxiety under which the people of the United States had been living for nearly a decade. The reaction brought a feeling of carelessness, a loss of unity and national feeling and an attempt to return to the petty concerns of everyday life where there was much to divert them. All was not well in the new republic but for the time being the new problems called forth no constructive handling; rather they invited further confusion.

Post-War Difficulties

Economic depression had settled down upon the business life of the nation. The expansion of agriculture and manufacturing induced by the war was no longer needed. Agricultural prices dropped but the mortgages remained to be paid. The new manufacturers were faced with a failing demand and foreign competition; only hard times and perhaps ruin seemed ahead of them. The merchants, too, were badly off, with high-priced stocks of goods bought during the wartime inflation and with ships now dumping at American ports; British surplus had accumulated while the war cut off trade. Now the British manufacturers were eager to sell their accumulations at prices with which the American merchants, with their expensive wartime stocks, could not compete. Able neither to sell their goods nor pay their debts, many faced ruin. Stirred by the danger of debtors' prisons, businessmen began to look for remedies.

The condition of the currency contributed heavily to the unstable situation. The vast quantity of paper money, Continental and state, was almost worthless and most of the small amount of specie which the country possessed was exported to pay for the flood of foreign bargains. The general government was without funds and could pay neither the principal nor interest of its large indebtedness; many who had invested their substance patriotically in government obligations were in dire straits. Besides the states were heavily in debt and some of the more thrifty were setting heavy taxes to pay their obligations; property owners were quick to groan under these burdens. Most apparent of all the ills was the prevalence of unemployment. Many a soldier, even more sailors, especially privateersmen, and some laborers were unable to find work and were on the precarious edge of starvation.

As always, the uncertainties of the economic disorganization affected the poor most directly. In spite of the destruction of the "Tory" power in society, class divisions survived, for in many cases war profiteers sought to assume the pretensions of the exiles. Most apparent was a sharp division between debtor and creditor. So many were in debt and there was so little opportunity of earning the money to satisfy creditors or to pay taxes. The holders of mortgages and notes and tax-collectors went to law and there were frequent foreclosures, especially on farms bought at wartime prices. Much land was in process of changing hands and many an independent farmer must become a tenant or migrate to the westward and make a new start.

The frequent foreclosures and dispossess actions, as well as the general hardships of the depression, told upon the nerves. People were frightened and began fumbling for a remedy. Then, as many times later, they turned to government; politicians made promises and popular agitations for new laws were set on foot. In seven of the thirteen states "radical" groups were formed to secure drastic legislation in behalf of the debtor. Their chief demand was more paper money; cheap money would be easy to get and when made legal tender would enable the debtors to free themselves from their obligations. Laws were also demanded to prevent foreclosures or court actions to collect debts. Such "stay" laws would provide a virtual moratorium until times became better.

Legislation of this character so distasteful to men of substance was very attractive to the mass; it seemed to promise security and freedom from debt. Wherever they could, political leaders of popular parties forced such laws through state legislatures. They succeeded in New York, Pennsylvania, New Jersey, Rhode Island, North Carolina, South Carolina and Georgia, where paper money was issued in larger quantities and made legal tender. Woe betide any merchant in these states who tried to refuse this rag money. The mobs which had learned violence in the preliminaries of the Revolution came forth again to threaten merchants and even the courts and their officers. Court houses were attacked, courts disbanded and in Massachusetts such an attack upon the Northampton county court led by Daniel Shays in 1786 was so threatening that 4,400 militia were called out to put down this "rebellion." Many a lover of law and order and substantial property holder became fearful of anarchy, for if the state governments "went radical," no power, certainly not the feeble Congress, existed to protect the rights of those who wished to enforce the law of contracts.

Economic disorganization induced frequent quarrels among the states. Certain of the larger commonwealths like Pennsylvania, where new industries were struggling, were trying to protect themselves from foreign competition by means of high tariffs. But other states, chiefly agricultural, were interested only in obtaining what they needed as cheaply as possible; no tariffs of theirs contained protective features. Foreign goods, therefore, flowed freely into the latter states and were easily smuggled into the protected states to the further discomfort of the hard-pressed manufacturers. As Congress had no authority over interstate or foreign commerce, no power existed which could enforce uniformity in commercial regulations. But how could the weakness of Congress be overcome?

Discontent and disorganization were almost universal and spread even beyond the Alleghenies where settlers in what were to become Kentucky and Tennessee struggled to set up local government in spite

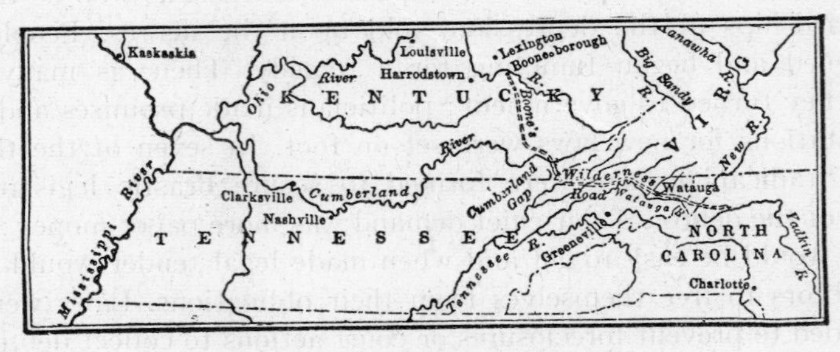

BEYOND THE APPALACHIANS

of neglect by the central government. During the Revolution, restless spirits had gone beyond the mountains. In 1769 Daniel Boone had begun to explore the Kentucky region and in the same year settlers crossed into western North Carolina to the Watauga Valley where under the leadership of James Robertson and John Sevier, an independent community was organized as the Watauga Association (1772-1778). In 1774 James Harrod made the first settlement in Kentucky at Harrodstown and in 1775 Daniel Boone, acting for Judge Richard Henderson, cut a trail up from the Cumberland Gap and established Boonesboro, Kentucky, with hardy Watauga settlers. Henderson tried to organize his Kentucky settlements as the state of Transylvania in 1775 but Virginia objected. Thereafter his agent, Robertson, in 1779 led more Wataugans into the present state of Tennessee where they established Nashville; they tried to organize the Cumberland settlements into a separate state but at length had to yield to North Carolina. After the latter state gave up her frontier lands to the federal government in 1784, John Sevier sought to organize these western settlements into the commonwealth of Franklin, and Virginia consented that Kentucky become a state. But Congress failed to act; North Carolina repealed its act of cession and resumed jurisdiction over the Tennessee region.

These western settlers felt keenly the neglect of the Congress, because of their dangerous situation. The southwestern Indians, the Cherokees, Chickasaws, Choctaws and Creeks were not pleasant neighbors, especially when urged by the Spanish to be otherwise. Congress worried about these conditions but the national army could hardly be said to exist and besides the southern states claimed this trans-Appalachian region as theirs and were jealous of even the weak interference of Congress. The westerners were further disgruntled because of Spanish restrictions on trade through the port of New Orleans. Here again Congress was powerless to help; American diplomats with no force of arms behind them could gain no concessions from the contemptuous Spanish government. So the western settlers, like their poor brethren in the East, were restive and talked of establishing their own governments, independent of the far-away and powerless East. Eastern leaders, Washington among them, feared that the West might be lost to the nation.

International troubles were not the least which beset the new republic. The federation was independent and so recognized by treaty but that did not mean that it was treated with much consideration or accorded much influence. This lack of prestige damaged American trade. Before the Revolution colonial ships had been permitted British registry and under that flag were received in the ports of the world, enjoying the privileges accorded to that symbol of power. Such protection had been destroyed by independence and the Stars and Stripes meant little to European port officers. The terms of the French alliance included commercial concessions and open ports, but even the French placed some restrictions on West Indian trade and Great Britain and Spain prohibited it altogether, thereby depriving American merchants of most important prospects. Great Britain crippled the whaling industry by high tariffs and refused to make any treaty or even send over a representative. Spain, on the other hand, dispatched Gardoqui to Philadelphia and consented to a treaty which permitted commerce with her European ports; but she barred access to her American colonies and kept the mouth of the Mississippi tightly closed. The Jay-Gardoqui plan therefore became so unpopular in the Southwest that it failed of ratification. There seemed no way to enforce diplomatic pretensions. How could a nation which didn't pay its debts, or even the interest, and whose citizens refused to pay their bills, expect any concessions from Europe?

The people were restless, the states were quarreling, westerners talked secession, foreign nations slighted the government, business was bad and state governments had "gone radical." Congress was helpless, without power, without funds, without adequate armed force, worst of all, without prestige. The politicians who now made up its membership could not deal effectively with such perplexities. In vain Congress requested funds from the states. The latter were having too hard a time raising money for their own immediate needs to permit heavier taxes for federal requisitions. Little money was sent to Philadelphia and so empty did the national treasury become that Congress in 1783 felt it wise to flee to Princeton lest they be attacked by a band of unpaid soldiers who were demanding money.

Twice Congress sought power to levy funds. They sent to the states in 1781 a proposal to permit Congress to collect an import duty of 5 per cent but it was defeated by the refusal of one state, Rhode Island, to consent. A proposition of 1783 which would have permitted duties on specified articles for twenty-five years also failed. Only one other resource seemed left to Congress, namely, the sale of the public lands.

Blueprints for the Future: Ordinances of 1785 and 1787

Jefferson in 1784 prepared a plan of government for the vast territory north of the Ohio and west of Pennsylvania which had been ceded to the Confederation by Virginia, New York, Massachusetts and Connecticut. Congress adopted this plan and in the next year ordered the region surveyed. The land, by the Ordinance of 1785, was to be laid out in townships, six miles square, made up of thirty-six sections of 640 acres each in a township. Portions were set aside for satisfying the claims of Revolutionary soldiers and one-third of any minerals found were reserved for the Confederation. There was no thought in those days of any need for conservation of natural resources.

The bulk of the land was to be sold at auction in minimum lots of 640 acres at a minimum price of one dollar per acre. The sales were to be held in the various thirteen states. Four sections in the center of each township were to be withheld to be sold later when land values had appreciated. The money received for the sale of one section in each township was to be turned over to the support of education, a provision of great future significance, for it was the basis of the elaborate systems of free education for which these states became noted. But few purchased and within three years only 73,000 acres had been sold to individuals in spite of inducements offered in the way of credit facilities. Congress therefore turned to a new policy, selling large blocks to companies and individuals at reduced prices. The most famous of these sales was made to the Ohio Company, composed principally of New England veterans who purchased 5,000,000 acres for $500,000 in 1787.

Stable government was offered as further inducement for purchase in the form of the Ordinance of 1787 which provided for an immediate, temporary government for the whole territory. A governor, three judges and a secretary were to be appointed by Congress to adapt laws to the territory and to govern it. Plans were provided for future self-government and the admission of portions as states as soon as the population was sufficient to warrant these advances. The bill of rights which this ordinance contained, for the benefit of any settlers who might seek homes in this new area, was a noteworthy statement of American ideals of social organization. Freedom of religion, of speech and of the press as well as the usual rights of individuals to be tried by jury, to petition, and to bear arms were all stipulated. Support for public education was guaranteed and slavery was forbidden in all this area. In spite of all these liberal provisions, the land did not sell and the national treasury, still empty, only emphasized the weakness of the government.

While things seemed to be at their worst, events were shaping a more auspicious future. There were signs, more apparent today than perhaps they were then, that the depression was lifting. Trade was expanding. Commercial treaties had been made with Holland, Prussia and Sweden and trading under the American flag increased in the Baltic. The British West India trade grew extensive again, in spite of English prohibitions, and importers were once more in funds. Manufacturers became more prosperous. States granted subsidies, bounties and lottery privileges. Societies were organized to promote better methods of manufacturing. These societies began to study the new machines which England was using in her industrial centers. Industry revived and emphasized a new prosperity, although the old handicraft methods were still used. The enterprising manufacturers were hampered by a lack of capital with which to try new methods. Moreover, labor was scarce because of the attractions of landowning and farming.

Plans for westward development and improved transportation facilities which might bind the sections more closely together were also signs of a new optimism and the rebirth of creative impulses. George Washington led in these plans. He had extensive holdings in western lands and was anxious to promote the building of a canal which would make the Potomac and James rivers paths of commerce and communication. He also had a project for a canal through the dismal swamp to make access to North Carolina easier. Development companies like the Ohio Company, interested in western lands, were attempting to open up town sites beyond the Alleghenies. American enterprise was reawakening.

Adopting the Constitution; the Federal System

The beginnings of prosperity sharpened the consciousness of the need of a stronger central government. The Confederation was too weak for practical men of affairs. National prestige and credit, property interests, means of livelihood and the very liberty which had cost such a struggle were in jeopardy. As need of change became more widely recognized the first steps toward effecting it were being taken. In 1785 a committee representing Virginia and Maryland met at Mt. Vernon with George Washington to discuss the question of regulating navigation on the Potomac River and Chesapeake Bay. During their deliberations they talked of the general disordered state of commercial regulation and concluded that a larger conference should be held to which representatives of the other states should be invited. Virginia called such a meeting to convene at Annapolis, Maryland, in 1786 and when delegates from only five states came those present decided to report to the states and to Congress the need for a general convention. Congress accepted the report and authorized a convention to meet in Philadelphia in May 1787. In response to this summons, delegates from all states except Rhode Island convened to consider amendments which might make the Articles of Confederation a workable document.

A remarkable group of fifty-five of the best-known Americans made up the assemblage. George Washington was its president; James Madison kept careful and voluminous notes of its proceedings. The revered Dr. Franklin, in spite of his fourscore years, was in active attendance when his health permitted. Robert Morris, Gouverneur Morris, John Dickinson, Charles Cotesworth Pinckney, Charles Pinckney, James Wilson and Alexander Hamilton were some of the others who made the convention so able a body. Only a few of the great names were absent. Some, like Patrick Henry, Samuel Adams and John Hancock, who were secure in power and influence in their own states, were suspicious of any strong central power; Rhode Island for that reason sent no delegates. Thomas Jefferson was abroad as minister to France. Practically all of the members were substantial men who believed in law and order and in the security of property, and who were opposed to the radicals who had been jeopardizing wealth in the past few years. They were agreed that the central government must be strengthened.

Though this body was commissioned only to amend the Articles of Confederation, its members boldly determined to make a new government. About most of its details they were in general agreement but there were certain differences which were to try the patience and ingenuity of the leaders in those hot summer days of 1787.

No simple government would suffice. A system had to be created which would reconcile two different powers, the powers of local control now exercised by semi-independent states and the power of a newly created central government. Members of the convention like Madison had made an intensive study of the history of governments in general and of federal governments in particular. They were well read in James Harrington, John Locke and the Baron de Montesquieu. They were prepared to create a complicated and nicely adjusted federal system which would permit the harmonious functioning of these two sets of powers and which at the same time would prevent any one interest from ever gaining control of the central government. They divided powers between the state and federal governments, attempting a rather careful definition of those of the latter. Then the mechanism of the central government was carefully constructed.

Here colonial experience and Montesquieu's idealized conception of the British government were the models. There should be three separate and distinct branches of government, each equal and coördinate with the others. The legislative branch, like the colonial legislatures and the British Parliament, was to consist of two houses. This fact made it easier to settle the fundamental quarrel between the large and small states over representation in Congress. The compromise finally adopted gave small states equal representation with large in the Senate or upper house, which was to represent the states as such. Each state legislature was to choose two senators serving for six years each. In the lower house, however, the large states secured representation by population, a principle which was to be used also in apportioning direct taxes among the states. The representatives were to serve for but two years and were to be chosen by such persons as each state permitted to vote for members of the lower house of its own legislature.

This compromise between the interests of the large and small states also involved a compromise between North and South. What status was to be accorded to Negro slaves? Were they part of the population and were southern states to have much larger representation and taxes because of their slaves? It was finally agreed to count three-fifths of the Negroes for both representation and taxes. Not until the questions as to the make up of Congress were settled was anyone confident that a new order could be achieved.

The creation of an executive was not so difficult. A president was to be chosen for a term of four years, not by the people but by electors. Some feared popular elections, but the electoral system was chosen for practical reasons. The scattered nature of the population would make concentration on any one candidate impossible and the resultant number of choices would produce only a confusion in which no one would ever get anything like the majority of the votes necessary to elect. Therefore each state was to choose as many electors as it had senators and representatives and they were to meet in their respective state capitals where each was to vote for two men. When their votes were assembled in the national Congress and counted, the man who received the largest number of votes was to be president and the next highest vice-president. The president was armed with real power. He was to be commander-in-chief of the army and navy, he could veto bills passed by Congress, his was the initiative in foreign affairs and his powers of appointment were large.

The third branch of the new government was a federal judiciary, to be composed of a supreme court and such inferior courts as Congress might create; the Constitution left large power to Congress in organizing the judiciary. The judges for these courts were to be appointed by the president, by and with the advice and consent of the Senate, to hold office during good behavior, in default of which they might be impeached and removed only by Congress. These courts were given a judicial power which should extend to all cases, in law and equity, arising under the Constitution, the laws of the United States or treaties. They were to have jurisdiction in disputes arising between any of the United States and the federal government or in quarrels between the states or their citizens. Much depended on how the proposed federal judiciary might construe their powers.

So three branches of government were created each independent and coördinate but still checked by the others. Congressional laws had to be approved by the executive who in turn had to submit his appointments and his treaties to the Senate and who himself might be impeached and removed by Congress. The judiciary was to hear all cases arising under the laws of Congress and the Constitution and must therefore interpret them, but they were appointed by the president and confirmed by the Senate; they too might be impeached by Congress. All of these branches were protected from direct influence by the public will except the lower house of Congress. Furthermore, they were chosen for a wide variety of terms and it would be impossible to effect any complete change in personnel except by revolution. Qualifications for voting for the lower house were left to the states and were thus generally hedged about by some property qualifications. The country was not yet ready for full suffrage.

These careful statesmen made certain that the central government would be strong enough to maintain social order and protect property. By five positive powers, one of which was sweeping, and by two prohibitions upon the states they forged a powerful weapon for this purpose. The power to tax granted to Congress insured the means to pay the debts so long overdue, to restore credit and to raise money for the "general welfare." Congress also was to have sole power to regulate interstate and foreign commerce, a concession which was wrung from the southern agricultural states only in return for the prohibition of export taxes and a guarantee of the continuance of the slave trade at least until 1808. This commercial power would insure uniformity of regulation and prevent quarrels between the states. The Congress furthermore had control of the public lands and the Indians and might admit new states into the union. This vast power meant control of the growth of the nation. To provide against foreign attack and domestic disturbance, the federal government possessed of tax money could organize and equip an adequate military and naval force, a bulwark of security. On the other hand, the states were forbidden to issue paper money or in any way to impair the obligation of contract. There would be no more legislation of too radical a character. Most important was the clause most famous of all whereby the federal government was granted all powers "necessary and proper" to carry out the provisions of the Constitution. What did the words "necessary and proper" mean? If they were loosely construed what might the new government not do?

In the fall of 1787 the document was signed by the members of the convention, headed by George Washington, its president, and transmitted to Congress. This body compliantly sent it to the states, although it was not the series of amendments to the "Articles" which the convention had been authorized to prepare but an entire new document proposing a revolutionary change in the structure of the government. The "Articles of Confederation" forbade amendment without unanimous consent of the states but this startling document declared itself in effect if accepted by nine of the thirteen states.

The fight for ratification began, and a fight it proved to be. Each state was to choose a convention to consider the proposal, to accept it or reject it. In the contests which marked the choice of these conventions, the friends and foes of the change marshaled their arguments and influence. It was new and proposed a major operation. Many who disliked innovation or who made up their minds slowly voted against it. Another group of opponents was composed of local politicians who were in positions of great influence in their states and mistrusted the effect of the new government upon their prestige. It was better to be first in a little Iberian village than second in Rome, so thought George Clinton of New York and Patrick Henry of Virginia and many others. They fought vigorously against the new instrument as centralizing authority and destroying the sovereignty of the states. Large numbers, particularly in the country districts, thought the new plan a device of the rich to improve their fortunes and to place the burden of taxation for the support of the new government upon the farmers' lands. Others protested that nowhere in the proposed constitution were there any provisions to safeguard the rights of individuals, no guarantees for individual liberty. The whole scheme was the plan of aristocrats to set up a strong and probably tyrannical government situated so far away from most of the people that it could safely disregard the rights of the common man.

To combat this formidable opposition the friends of the document were strategically well placed. Most important was the fact that some of the best-known men of the country were favorable; Washington's prestige was invaluable. Then there were skillful debaters among them; Madison, Hamilton and Jay wrote a series of masterly essays describing and explaining the new scheme and its expected benefits. These writings, known as the "Federalist" papers, were given thoughtful reading by influential people. The chaotic conditions prevalent in the preceding years were also a powerful argument and influenced many to support the new order. The conflict caused a renewal of party organization and as in the Revolution lines were drawn and labels became the fashion. The advocates of the adoption of the new plan called themselves "Federalists," thus emphasizing the idea of union rather than centralization, and their opponents were generally known as "Anti-Federalists."

In Delaware, Connecticut, Georgia, New Jersey, South Carolina, Pennsylvania and Maryland, the struggle was not so intense, but in Virginia, New Hampshire and Massachusetts the vote was close. In Virginia prominent politicians like Patrick Henry opposed this central government as dangerous to liberty, while in Massachusetts the farmers were afraid of the power which commercial interests might wield in the new government. New York's opposition was exceptionally bitter, and perhaps the deciding factor in the final acceptance was the knowledge that ten other states had ratified and that the new organization would be perfected without New York. As a condition of ratification some of the states had received a promise from the friends of the Constitution that amendments would be added providing for a bill of rights and when this promise was in process of fulfillment, North Carolina gave her consent in 1789. Rhode Island, however, was not brought in until the next year and then only when threatened with commercial isolation.

In such manner the Constitution was ratified. No popular vote was taken upon it, and the statistics which have survived as to votes cast for members of the ratifying conventions are fragmentary. The conflict was very bitter; the means used to overcome it sometimes savored much of modern political practice. It can be ventured that only a minority actually favored its adoption but all agreed to acquiesce and to give the new scheme a trial. The states surrendered essential parts of their sovereignty with the hope that thereby they might form a "more perfect union."

CHAPTER X

REORGANIZING UNDER THE CONSTITUTION

News of the adoption of the Constitution spread through the states in July 1788. Quick, vigorous action had secured the consent of eleven states and the new order was established—on paper. Much thought and hard work were to be required to make the plan a working reality.

Inaugurating the New Government

The old Congress and the state legislatures had the responsibility of the first steps. They must arrange for the election of the two houses of the new Congress and for the choice of a president. The old Congress notified the states that the Constitution was adopted and settled down to a prolonged debate over where the new Congress should meet and how the electoral college should be chosen. It finally agreed that New York should remain the seat of government temporarily. The electors were to be chosen, as each state should decide, on the first Wednesday in January. They should meet in their respective state capitols on the first Wednesday in February; and the new Congress was to meet to arrange for inaugurating the new government on the first Wednesday of March. Thus casually did they set 4 March as the beginning date of a new administration; the rule held from 1789 to 1937.

The state legislatures, in the meantime, arranged for the election of electors and congressmen. The electors in some instances were to be chosen by the voters; in others, by the state legislatures without reference to the voters.[1] The legislatures also elected the senators. While congressmen and senators were being chosen at various times by the several states, the program for the presidential election was carried on according to schedule. On the first Wednesday in February, the electors met and unanimously voted for George Washington. John Adams received the next highest vote and thus became vice-president. In these elections the friends of the Constitution were generally successful. Although its opponents named a few congressmen and senators, they

[1] Electors were chosen by the legislatures, in Connecticut and South Carolina. The Massachusetts legislature chose them from a list nominated by the voters. In New Jersey the governor and council made the choice while in New York, as the legislature could not agree on a method, none were selected for this election. In the remaining states the voters acted.

made no concerted campaign and no effort for the presidency. Their feeble attempt to put in Governor George Clinton of New York as vice-president netted but three votes. Consequently, the men who had devised and advocated the new system received charge of its initiation.

On 4 March 1789, the day appointed for the new government to begin its functioning, a quorum of the houses of Congress had not arrived in New York, the temporary capital. However, by April sufficient numbers had put in an appearance and on the thirtieth Washington was duly inaugurated. By fall Congress had provided revenue, had created the necessary governmental departments and had established the federal courts. Washington carefully selected friends of the Constitution to fill the numerous offices and put the executive machinery in complete operation. To assist him in his task, he chose Alexander Hamilton to fill the most responsible of all the new positions, secretary of the treasury. One old friend, General Henry Knox, was to be secretary of war; another, Edmund Randolph, attorney-general. John Jay was appointed chief justice of the Supreme Court, and meanwhile he was to continue in charge of foreign affairs until the arrival of the new secretary, Thomas Jefferson, who had been recalled from the French mission, to head the newly created Department of State. It was an able group who assumed responsibility for the success of the experiment.

Of the many difficult problems which confronted these men, by far the most important, complex and pressing was the question of financing the federal government. Congress had taken preliminary steps before the treasury was organized. It enacted a tariff on imports mainly for revenue purposes. A protective measure was demanded by Pennsylvania congressmen, then as ever after in the forefront of that movement. Although they failed to obtain a protective measure as such, the American merchant marine was fostered by a system of tonnage duties which excluded foreign ships from coastwise trade. Congress contented itself with these preliminaries and left the main burden of money-raising and fiscal policy to the new secretary.

Alexander Hamilton was a financial genius who applied himself enthusiastically to his huge task. He was well acquainted with British methods of finance and took a broad view of his problem, endeavoring to encompass in his plans devices not only for raising funds and restoring credit, but also for aiding business and stimulating general prosperity. His prophetic vision discerned the enormous potential wealth of the nation and he believed that its speedy exploitation was the key to a solvent treasury and to power in world affairs. Under this inspiration he went to work.

Hamilton's first concern was to bring order out of the confused mass of indebtedness which confronted him and to create credit. In principal and interest the United States owed about 12 millions abroad and 42 millions at home. This was a tremendous sum to raise in those days but Hamilton was by no means appalled. Far from it; his imagination leaped to assume an even greater burden. The individual states owed about 25 millions on their own account, and the Secretary conceived the audacious scheme of having the federal treasury assume that burden also. Good arguments supported him. The federal government had deprived the states of the right to levy tariffs and thus had cut off an important source of revenue. Furthermore, the states had borrowed this money to promote a common cause, the American Revolution; it was but fair for the new government to pay their debts. More particularly, it was his belief that this would bind the states in respect and loyalty to the Constitution.

To these ends, therefore, Hamilton in 1790 presented to Congress a plan to fund a debt of 80 millions by transforming all the variety of certificates of indebtedness into obligations of the new government. As these securities matured, the holders would be paid in full and in the meantime interest would be discharged at regular intervals. To meet the heavy interest and sinking fund charges, a large revenue would be required and Hamilton proposed to augment the funds obtained from the tariff by levying an excise on liquor. Such a tax would not further burden real estate or business and would rest lightly on most people, save on the frontier.

The secretary's proposals called forth heated discussion in and out of Congress. All agreed that the foreign debt should be paid in full, but that was as far as the agreement went. First of all there was objection to the full payment of the domestic debt of the Congress. Much of it had long since passed from the hands of those who had loaned to the government and had been sold for a pittance to speculators. Should such speculators reap handsome profits while the patriots who had made the sacrifice and had been forced to part with the unpaid obligations went empty handed? There was much force to this argument, but Hamilton's plan for the domestic debt was carried.

A second, greater struggle arose over the assumption of state debts. Thrifty states like New York and Virginia were unwilling to be taxed to pay the debts of their less provident neighbors. Such an assumption would too thoroughly centralize all authority and financial power in the hands of the federal government. When test votes showed that the proposal was not likely to carry, Hamilton enlisted Jefferson's aid in political bargaining. As a result the new federal capital was located in the South, on the Potomac, and enough southern votes were won to carry the assumption bill. One further struggle ensued, though it proved less difficult to combat. The liquor excise was fought by representatives of the back country, where whiskey was the chief commodity and the currency of the poverty-stricken farmers on the frontier. But on this question as on the others, Hamilton's plan triumphed.

While these plans were being put into successful operation, the Secretary turned his attention to a more elaborate and original idea, namely the founding of a Bank of the United States, to function in some respects as did the Bank of England. The country had but three banks, the Bank of North America in Philadelphia, and one each in New York and Boston; their capital was not large nor their influence important. Hamilton realized that government finances could benefit very greatly through a credit institution in close association with the treasury. The capital and deposits would provide funds for government borrowing. The note issue would provide a reliable, uniform currency such as the country sadly needed. It would have branches in the various cities where government taxes could be deposited, and bills could be paid by drafts, thus reducing the strain on the currency supply and making currency transportation less necessary. The institution would also promote business expansion by assembling capital for loan to reliable businessmen. Much hoarded money would be brought into use if there was this sound institution in which to deposit it. For these reasons, Hamilton recommended the establishment of a bank capitalized at 10 millions; the government was to subscribe one-fifth of the capital, and the rest was to be supplied by the public, who might subscribe government stock (the current term for bonds) up to three-fourths of the required amount; the charter was to run for twenty years.

Once more the opposition to Hamilton came forward. Representatives of agricultural constituencies, especially in the South, could see little good in this plan. They said it was but a scheme of city capitalists to increase their wealth; it would do nothing for country people. Their strongest argument was that the Constitution contained no provision for a government-established bank; such a proposal was clearly unconstitutional. Hamilton defended his plan with trenchant logic. Did not the Constitution give the federal government all power "necessary and proper" to carry out its provisions? Such a bank was both necessary and proper to carry out the financial responsibilities placed upon the central government by the document. The Secretary overbore congressional opposition by a narrow margin.

But Washington himself hesitated. His secretary of state, Thomas Jefferson, was now in open opposition to Hamilton and argued strongly for a strict construction of the Constitution and a veto of the bank bill. Only after Hamilton had given Washington a brilliant, written justification of the founding of the bank did the President sign the bill. There was no hesitation among the moneyed people, who eagerly subscribed to the stock. On 12 December 1791 the institution opened its doors in Philadelphia, which had been made a temporary capital until the new city of Washington, then building on the banks of the Potomac, should be ready for occupancy.

Hamilton's work was almost finished. He planned the establishment of a mint in Philadelphia to coin gold and silver money. The United States was to have a decimal system of bimetallic coinage with the unit a dollar of one hundred cents. A gold dollar was to weigh 24.75 grains and silver dollars were to be fifteen times as heavy. One further aid to government finance and business Hamilton advocated; in a report to Congress he proposed a protective tariff. This last was the only one of his suggestions which failed of immediate adoption but his arguments were to live after him. In the meantime, he had secured an adequate revenue and sound credit for a government which had possessed neither.

Creating a Foreign Policy

The second great test of the new government's mettle was foreign relations. Could it secure a decent respect from European powers? Several trying questions had been unsettled for nearly a decade and were a menace to the peace, prosperity and even stability of the new nation. First of all were border difficulties with Great Britain on the north and Spain on the west and south. Britain had refused to vacate the posts in the northwest area, still dominated the Great Lakes region and kept in close contact with the Indians. To the south Spain continued to close New Orleans and the Mississippi to American trade while she occupied portions of the southwest territory. Furthermore, not only did she intrigue with the Indians but she egged on discontented Tennesseans and Kentuckians when they talked of secession, and kept a number of American officers on her payroll. At first all efforts of Washington and Jefferson to change these conditions were vain. A European convulsion, however, came to American aid.

In 1789 a revolution had begun in France which was to shake the political world. The success of republicanism in that once absolute monarchy filled European politicians with dismay. Steps which Austria and Prussia took to aid Louis XVI finally caused France to declare war upon those two nations and upon Spain and Britain as well. By 1793 there was a general European war of which the United States could be by no means unconscious. The superior naval force of the British soon crippled the commerce of France, who turned to the American republic as the only convenient neutral with shipping adequate to carry on her necessary trade with her West Indies. England sought to throttle this new American commerce by applying the rule of 1756. In that year, England had announced that no neutral should enjoy in wartime a trade which was forbidden in time of peace. Britain's enemies had given the United States wartime privileges of trade with their colonies and Britain undertook to stop it. In enforcing this rule, formulated before the United States was thought of, the British fleet captured many an American ship and seaman, for Great Britain's navy needed men and that government ordered search to be made of neutral vessels for "British citizens," to be impressed back into her service. British and American seamen looked and acted much alike, mistakes were easy and frequent and the British navy was being recruited forcibly from the ranks of American seamen.

France in the meantime sought aid from her American ally on the basis of the treaty of 1778. She sent to obtain this aid a bumptious minister, Citizen Genêt, whose chief qualifications were enthusiasm and poor judgment. He arrived in Charleston and immediately treated America as if it were a French ally, fitting out privateers in southern ports and making enthusiastic speeches. The United States, however, was in no position to go to war; with little money, a small army and no navy such a step was preposterous. Besides, there was the argument that the treaty of alliance had been made with the French Monarchy. That no longer existed, so the United States could no longer be bound. Much to M. Genêt's disgust, Washington and even Jefferson received him coldly and in April 1793 issued a proclamation of neutrality. This was a hard blow for France.

Great Britain meanwhile continued depredations on American commerce and popular antagonism increased to such a pitch that even the British became aware of it and feared the United States might aid France. Great Britain therefore receded a little and consented in 1794 to make a treaty. In this agreement, negotiated by John Jay, Britain promised to relinquish the fur posts. All matters of monetary claims were referred to special commissions, and thereby the United States and Britain adopted that vital principle of arbitration which they were to use so often in years to come. But Jay failed utterly to obtain satisfactory commercial privileges in the West Indies, thus arousing a wave of popular antagonism to the treaty. Unsatisfactory though it was, Washington submitted it to the Senate, which ratified it by a very close vote. Thus a second war with Great Britain was avoided, for the time being at least.

Spain meanwhile viewed with alarm this friendliness with Great Britain at a time when war was about to break out between the two powers. America might easily join Britain to seize Spanish American possessions. So, to placate the United States, Spain made the treaty of 1795, which not only gave trading privileges in Europe but also opened the mouth of the Mississippi to American shipping and fixed the southern boundary favorably to American claims. From the calamities of Europe the insignificant republic gained its first advance toward international security. The United States had avoided entangling alliances;

boundaries had been more definitely settled; commercial relations had been improved. Washington had laid the foundation of a foreign policy which was to become traditional in the terms of his Farewell Address delivered in 1796. "Why, by interweaving our destiny with that of any part of Europe, entangle our peace and prosperity in the toils of European ambition, rivalship, interest, humour or caprice?"

Establishing Justice

Not the least significant of the problems facing the new government was the creation of a federal judiciary. The new nation was committed to rule by law and written constitutions; but language is of uncertain and often doubtful meaning, conditions change and much of the future of the United States must depend upon the interpretation of its fundamental documents and its statutes, state and federal. The Constitution had barely sketched a federal judiciary to wrestle with these problems of interpretations, and it devolved upon Congress to erect a court structure. Congress undertook this in its first session, enacting the famous judiciary law of 1789. A federal system of courts was to take its place beside and above the courts of the states. At its head was the Supreme Court, specified by the Constitution and consisting of a chief justice and five associate justices. As tribunals of first instance there were to be thirteen district courts, each presided over by a judge appointed by the president, allotted to the eleven states then members of the Union and the districts of Maine and Kentucky, still parts of Massachusetts and Virginia. Intermediate between these two court systems were to be three circuit courts, for the eleven states were divided into three circuits; through each of these the Supreme Court Justices would travel in pairs, meeting each district judge at a designated place in his region and sitting with him as a circuit court. The law counsel of the government was to be an attorney-general, who was expected to engage in private practice while advising and appearing for the federal government on call.

The district courts were to try most of the cases under the national jurisdiction, such as crimes against federal law and civil cases, particularly those in commerce and admiralty. A jury trial was provided in most instances. These courts were also to hear suits in which the United States was a party. The circuit courts were to try more important criminal and civil cases and hear appeals from the district courts. The Supreme Court was the court of last resort but, in addition, had some original jurisdiction in cases where one of the states was a party or where foreign representatives were involved. This court was expressly granted power to review decisions of state courts in matters involving interpretation of the Constitution or of treaties or in laws made in pursuance thereof. The chief justice of the Supreme Court was to be paid the princely sum of $4,000; the associate justices, $3,500; the district judges, salaries ranging from $1,000 to $1,800; while for the attorney-general, $1,500 was deemed sufficient.

President Washington set about selecting these officers with his usual care. John Jay of New York was named chief justice and for the associate justiceships he chose judges eminent in the states, such as John Blair of Virginia, William Cushing of Massachusetts, Robert H. Harrison of Maryland, John Rutledge of South Carolina, and James Wilson, the leader of the Pennsylvania bar. His friend Edmund Randolph was made attorney-general. As was his wont, Washington selected those who favored the new federal system. Wilson, Randolph, Jay and Rutledge had played notable parts in creating the Constitution.

The district courts began functioning in the winter of 1789-1790 with work before them. The Supreme Court gathered in New York in February for its first meeting but no cases were yet ready for it; so, after organizing and admitting qualified attorneys to practice, it adjourned. In fact, during the first three years of its existence, it had little to do as a supreme court. Its members, however, performed their duties on the circuit, and strenuous duties they were, for traveling conditions were terrible and these judges endured much of discomfort and delay. It was on the circuits that the judges began to consider questions which would be vital in the shaping of the republic. To what extent were the courts going to interfere with acts of the peoples' representatives either in state legislature or federal Congress? If the people were supreme in their right of self-government, could the courts interefere with the acts of their representatives? If the states were sovereign could federal judges overturn their acts or the decisions of their courts?

In their first two years of circuit duty, federal judges declared certain acts of state legislatures to be unconstitutional and likewise ruled that an act of Congress was out of line with the fundamental law. By 1793 cases were beginning to appear before the Supreme Court, and that body, although its decisions attracted little attention in those early days, gave signs that it would question state decisions and pass upon the constitutionality of state and federal laws. But only one of its decisions in this first decade aroused general interest. When an individual sought to bring the state of Georgia into a federal court to answer to a suit, Georgia refused to appear despite the Constitution. The Court ruled against Georgia, in Chisholm *v.* Georgia in February 1793, and ordered her to appear. This decision disturbed the states; it loosed the possibility of multitudes of suits by dispossessed Tories and others which would keep the states continually in the courts.

Times were bad, many of the state treasuries were hard pressed and these expenses might well be ruinous. So a constitutional amendment was sent to the states the next year, prohibiting suits in the federal courts against states without their consent, by citizens of other states or foreign nations; within four years it was ratified and became the eleventh amendment.

In this first decade of their existence the federal courts can not be said to have played a very important part in the life of the republic or to have attracted much attention. Membership in even the Supreme Court was not considered a very desirable elevation, primarily because of the arduous traveling which circuit duty involved. Also the membership was somewhat affected by politics. Chief Justice Jay took a long leave of absence to negotiate his treaty with England and then finally resigned to become governor of New York. John Rutledge who succeeded him was so vehement in his opposition to the Jay treaty that the Federalist Senate took its revenge by refusing to confirm him, even though he had presided over a term of the court between sessions of Congress in 1795. His successor, Oliver Ellsworth of Connecticut, remained on the bench less than four years; he, like Jay, took a recess to serve on a European diplomatic mission and then resigned so that he could remain abroad. The associate judgeships and the attorney-general's office likewise suffered frequent changes in personnel. The federal judiciary, nevertheless, became established, the caliber of its membership remained high and it was laying the foundation for an influential and significant service in maintaning the rule of law in the new republic.

The Bill of Rights

In these creative years of organizing the new government, the Congress and the states placed the capstone on the constitutional structure by adopting the first ten amendments, in fulfilment of the pledges made in some of the states to secure ratification of the Constitution. The First Congress drew up a series of twelve amendments which were duly submitted to the states. The first two provided that the House of Representatives could not be drastically reduced or enlarged in numbers and that representatives and senators might not receive an increase in pay until an election should take place after such an increase was voted. These two were not then ratified, although the latter was later adopted as a law. The remaining ten, known as the Bill of Rights, were speedily ratified and in 1791 were declared in effect.

The first of these ten was the most vital to ordered liberty; it guaranteed the freedom of religion, of speech and of the press, the right peaceably to assemble and to petition the government for "a redress of grievances." The next three wrote into the fundamental law rights which had played so important a part in the Revolution; these amendments guaranteed a militia and the right to bear arms, forbade quartering of troops in time of peace and declared the homes of citizens secure against invasion and search except by specific warrants; blank writs, such as the writs of assistance, were not to be tolerated. The next four guaranteed jury and trial procedure properly safeguarding the accused, protected citizens against arbitrary arrest or cruel and unusual punishment and declared that no person should be "deprived of life, liberty or property without due process of law" (fifth amendment). The last two amendments defined more clearly the distribution of powers between the federal government and the citizens of the states; "the enumeration in the Constitution of certain rights, shall not be construed to deny or disparage others retained by the people. . . . The powers not delegated to the United States by the Constitution, nor prohibited by it to the States, are reserved to the States respectively, or to the people."

In such manner, during the last decade of the eighteenth century, the various agencies, state and federal, worked out a new system of government. It was to be a government of law, in which the people ruled through their representatives with proper checks and safeguards, on the one hand against sudden passion and violent enthusiasm, and on the other against tyranny and the exercise of arbitrary power. It was a government in which liberty should be preserved but license banned. Would it work?

The Political Test

The new order had still to face another test. Partisan dissension was becoming bitter. Could the constitutional structure stand the strain of politics? For a time after the adoption of the Constitution the partisanship developed in the ratification struggle had subsided. It was only a matter of time before parties would form again, however, for the English two-party tradition was a strong inheritance. Washington had entered office with no discernible opposition but the policies of his administration roused bitter antagonism, especially in Congress, where Hamilton's schemes had able opponents. In Washington's own official family, there developed a deplorable lack of harmony. Jefferson and Hamilton were personally incompatible and it was not very long before the former became convinced that his rival's influence was turning Washington to aristocracy and even toward monarchy. Jefferson was a staunch republican, and in his political philosophy individual rights and the interests of the common man played a large part. He thought elaborate schemes for the benefit of the rich were dangerous. Such views made him the spokesman of the people, especially those in the country districts who were suspicious of the aristocratic tone of Washington's social life and of the capitalistic character of Hamilton's plans. The French Revolution as it progressed brought the final element needed to crystallize the growing partisanship.

When France first embraced republican ideas, much enthusiasm was felt for this great event in the United States. But when the more violent phase of the Revolution advanced and the leaders not only shed blood but also proved pronouncedly anti-religious, many of the more conservative Americans lost their enthusiasm and became hostile. Such a group applauded Washington's refusal to join France in the general European war. On the other hand, many, especially followers of Jefferson, loyal to the revolutionary principles of equality, felt that Washington and more particularly Hamilton were pro-British and had been persuaded for that reason to abandon their French ally in her time of need. The coming of Genêt caused the Francophiles to burst out in enthusiastic support. A number of societies, after the fashion of the Jacobin club of Paris, were formed and at their meetings there was extravagant praise of the glorious principles of the Revolution. In these Democratic societies, as they were called, there was much opposition to Washington and more to his associates.

Two events fed the flames. The tax on whiskey became more and more unpopular in the back country and in Pennsylvania open resistance was offered to federal collectors. Washington felt that the prestige of the new government was at stake and determined on a vigorous show of force. In 1794 an army of 15,000 militia led by Washington himself was marched against the mutineers. Such a demonstration had the desired effect of proving the ability of the government to maintain authority, but it also gave greater strength to the popular opposition to the administration. Further, when Washington accepted the unsatisfactory Jay treaty, opposition became riotous. Jefferson had resigned from the State Department in the beginning of 1794 and he was busy building up a party, called the Democratic-Republicans, to fight for republicanism and strict construction of the Constitution. Washington and his supporters adopted the name Federalists.

At first partisanship was confined to debate and congressional contests; not until 1796 did it appear in a presidential election. In 1792 Washington had been unanimously reëlected, but in spite of the importunities of his friends, he refused to consider a third term. Who was to be his successor? The Democratic-Republicans of 1796 hoped for the choice of Thomas Jefferson, while the Federalists turned to the vice-president, John Adams. The electors were pretty evenly divided but chose Adams by three votes, and Jefferson had to be satisfied with the vice-presidency. This narrow margin of defeat stimulated the

Democratic-Republicans to further effort and organization and Jefferson was not too occupied with presiding over the Senate to forget his ambitions for the chief executive's office. Events played into his hands.

France was still involved in a general European war and had never forgiven the refusal of the Americans and their acceptance of the Jay treaty with the British. Such policies, the French politicians declared, were all to Britain's advantage and their own attitude became more and more unpleasant. During Adams' administration, their government first of all refused to receive American diplomats and then suggested that only after the payment of a bribe could any business be transacted. This latter indignity was reported to Congress as the XYZ affair (from the unannounced names of those to be bribed) and the Federalists proclaimed it a war-provoking insult.

Hostility developed so strongly between the two nations that in 1798 naval battles actually occurred and formal war was narrowly averted. During this furore much abuse, stimulated somewhat by opposition politicians, was heaped upon Adams and the Federalist party; to combat it Congress passed some ill-advised laws. Among them were the Alien and Sedition Acts which gave the president and the courts arbitrary powers to punish critics of the administration policy. Nothing neater could have been provided for use by Democratic-Republican politicians; they made the most of these autocratic laws denying "free speech" and "personal rights." The legislatures of Virginia and Kentucky passed vigorous resolutions denouncing centralism and upholding the rights of individuals and of the states, even suggesting that the states, acting as the original sovereigns who had made the Constitution, had the right to nullify federal laws. Using this as a platform and exploiting popular discontent, long simmering against this aristocratic Federalist régime, the Democratic-Republicans were able to defeat Adams in the election of 1800.

This election had a broader significance than the fact that the Jeffersonians won. It provided a third test of the stability of the structure erected under the Constitution. During twelve years of political dominance by the Federalists, a strong opposition party had developed and had captured the government by orderly and constitutional means without disorder or bloodshed. On 4 March 1801 the Federalists quietly, even if ungraciously, yielded to the popular mandate and gave way to Jefferson and his partisans. Administratively, diplomatically, judicially and politically the new governmental system had proved itself a practical and satisfactory set of institutions.

CHAPTER XI

THE CONTINUING STRUGGLE FOR INDEPENDENCE

The United States might be a free and independent nation politically but there were many obvious signs that independence remained incomplete. Economically the new nation was in many respects still a colony of Europe. But of creative energy and resources there was an abundance available for the tremendous effort required to attain an independent economic organization.

Overcoming Economic Dependence

New inventions were working to promote economic independence. A drastic change had begun in Europe and was spreading to America. The industrial revolution caused by the introduction of machinery run by water power and steam had occurred in England in the decades following 1750, and the idea of utilizing the new inventions was entertained in America. England, however, forbade the exportation of them or of any models or plans which would enable any one to construct them. In the years after peace various attempts were made to circumvent these restrictions. Philadelphia capital was anxious to get these new machines and the Massachusetts legislature granted subsidies. Some units were built by mechanics brought from England for the purpose, but the first attempts to use this method were expensive and unsatisfactory. Finally in 1790 Samuel Slater, a mechanic in the cotton industry, came over to Philadelphia in response to an advertisement but was diverted by the firm of Almy and Brown of Providence, Rhode Island, to undertake a similar project for them. They provided him with a machine shop and the necessary material so that he was able to construct from memory a successful set of cotton-spinning machines. A patent act of that year offered protection to inventors who might try to promote the advance of machines. In 1793 the Scholfield brothers emigrated from Yorkshire and with the aid of Massachusetts capitalists erected a wool-spinning factory at Byfield. These early machines were operated by the abundant water power; not until 1803 when it was applied to a sawmill was steam used as power. A step significant for the future was the discovery of coal in the Lehigh valley and the organization of a mining company to produce it; hereafter coal was to be gradually accepted as fuel, first by the house owner and then by the factory operator. In Pennsylvania a veritable transportation revolution was foreshadowed when in 1787 John Fitch successfully applied steam power to water transportation. For a while in 1790 the company which backed him was able to make regular trips on the Delaware. Two decades of intermittent experiment made the steamboat an accepted mode of water travel. When Robert Fulton's *Clermont* steamed up the Hudson from New York City to Albany in 1807, the era of steam transportation really began.

Agriculture, too, was responding to mechanics, and in the South a significant change was in process. In 1793 an epoch-making invention stimulated the cultivation of short-staple cotton; in that year the problem of separating economically the seeds from the short fiber was solved. Eli Whitney, a Yale graduate who was employed as a tutor on a southern plantation, invented a machine, the cotton gin, which made the marketing of large amounts of cotton possible at a low cost. The use of the gin spread rapidly and the planting of the short staple became increasingly widespread. Climatic conditions were much less of a hindrance than in the case of the long staple. Cotton growing advanced into the upland back country or Piedmont regions, especially in Georgia and South Carolina. The belt spread over southern North Carolina, South Carolina and central Georgia, where agricultural endeavor began to be turned more and more exclusively to cotton production.

The new industry extended the plantation system. Many of the farmers were small holders with five slaves or less; but the possibility of great profits from extensive cultivation placed a premium on large units. Slaves were purchasable abroad until 1808 and in the years immediately preceding that date importations were large. In South Carolina slaves, which had made up one-fifth of the population in 1790, became one-third of it by 1810. By 1806, 80,000,000 pounds of short-staple cotton were raised annually. The cotton kingdom was in the making.

Agricultural advance was not confined to the South; in the East farming improvements tended to increase efficiency. New methods were being developed in Europe; scientific farming was emerging from the stage of experiment. To promote the knowledge and more general use of improved methods societies were formed, beginning in 1785 with the Philadelphia Society for Promoting Agriculture. These groups met and discussed the innovations, issued propaganda and offered prizes for improved results. State legislatures by grants of money sometimes subsidized experiment or rewarded achievement. In Massachusetts in 1807 was inaugurated Elkanah Watson's Berkshire plan whereby farmers in various localities organized and sponsored fairs, at which exhibits were held and prizes awarded. From this practice grew the county fair, through one hundred years a significant factor in the lives of country people.

The new science which the progressive farmers sought to spread emphasized restoration and conservation of soil fertility, rotation of crops, use of fertilizers and new tools and improvement of breeds of cattle, sheep and hogs. In regard to tools a great advance came when Charles Newbold in 1797 brought out a cast-iron plow; it proved much more effective than the ancient wooden models which were older than recorded history. Grain cradles began to be used instead of the sickle; and cast-steel shovels, forks and hoes took the place of iron ones.

Notable improvements in cattle breeding came as early as 1783 when the Patton family imported English high-grade cattle into Maryland; the idea was gradually diffused, to the great advantage of the meat and dairy industries. Hogs were penned to fatten, rather than allowed to run wild, and the enormous Poland China took the place of the smaller, tougher razor-back; thus succulent and tender pork was bred.

The most spectacular advance, however, was in the breeding of sheep. Use of machinery had increased the demand for wool, and a finer grade than could be sheared from American sheep was sought. The Spanish royal herds of Merino sheep produced the best wool known but their export was strictly prohibited. At length in 1802 the American minister, David L. Humphreys, succeeded in sending a few home and in 1808 when Napoleon invaded Spain the ban was lifted. Possession of Merino sheep became almost a craze; fabulous prices were paid for them and otherwise normal people could not be content until they became the proud possessors of a pair of these sheep. Thousands were imported, to the great improvement of the breed and the great increase in the supply of wool. Yet despite this last unusual example, progress in agriculture was slow, for farmers proved to be the most conservative of individuals, frequently disliking and distrusting change.

Commercial and Territorial Expansion

Those engaged in the new trade made possible by the war in Europe struggled against Britain's special determination to cut off the French from American supplies. Britain, using the rule of 1756, seized, as prizes for its violation, numerous carriers bound from the West Indies to Europe. France, much incensed, accused the United States of submitting tamely to Great Britain; and her allegations added to the popular enmity toward the United States inaugurated by the neutrality proclamation and the Jay treaty. To retaliate, France declared she would treat American vessels as the United States "allowed" Great

Britain to treat them and she began a similar policy of taking prizes. In less than a year 316 American vessels had been captured by the French and when in 1796 Spain entered the war as an ally of France, the privateers of that nation did the same thing; furthermore Spanish West India officials were sympathetic to French spoliation in their ports and waters. Galling as was this policy, its results, as far as profits were concerned, were the opposite of discouraging. The increased hazards made the charges heavier and as relatively few vessels were captured, the many successful voyages reaped large rewards. The volume increased steadily, as these figures show:

Value of Foreign Commerce of the United States, Both Export and Import

1790	$43,000,000	
1793	57,000,000	
1795	117,000,000	
1801	205,000,000	
1803	120,000,000	(a brief interval of peace)
1807	246,000,000	

Between 20 and 25 per cent of the trade in the peak years was re-export business developed to avoid the rule of 1756; goods from the West Indies were brought to some port in the United States and there theoretically reshipped. That is, the bills of lading were redrawn and the cargo went as from a port of the United States to one in Europe; against such traffic the rule of 1756 did not apply. Such an enormous business with its easy wealth attracted many dollars which otherwise might have been risked in new ventures, such as industries essential to economic independence. However, valuable experience and augmented capital were being accumulated, and as long as Great Britain accepted the situation profits proved satisfactory. A temporary truce between England and France, 1802 to 1803, delayed a showdown.

But agricultural as well as commercial expansion was driving the United States into conflict with European powers. The British, French and Spanish controlled her land borders and were bound ultimately to resist the press of westward-moving population. American farmers wanted new lands and a southwestern trade outlet at New Orleans.

When Spain attempted to close the port of New Orleans in 1802, conditions became intolerable and President Jefferson, although the chances seemed against it, directed James Monroe and Robert R. Livingston to broach the purchase of the city. After an initial rebuff, however, conditions became more favorable. Napoleon had been forging ahead in Europe and his plans had embraced America as well. He conceived the idea of an American empire, with a treasure house of tropical wealth in the West Indies fed from the great granary of

Louisiana. He would subdue Haiti and force Spain to cede him Louisiana. The latter was easily accomplished but the former proved impossible. His inability to hold this rich island ruined his plans, and he turned instead to Europe for the conquest of England.

His new scheme invited a British attack upon Louisiana, which he could not well defend; so, when Jefferson's ministers presented again in 1803 his offer to purchase New Orleans, they were not ignored. Instead, an astounding proposition was made; would the United States buy all of Louisiana? Hardly able to believe their ears the ministers agreed to buy the vast tract for 80,000,000 francs. When he heard of it Jefferson was disturbed by lack of express authority in the Constitution; but so much did he feel that the peace, prosperity and especially the future of the nation depended upon the purchase, that he dared to abandon consistency. Jefferson's purpose was not accomplished without opposition. New England's politicians resented the addition of this great agricultural region, which they foresaw would grow into states with opposing interests and unite with their southern neighbors to further curb the power of northeastern representatives in Congress; but Congress after a struggle voted the $15,000,000 to pay for the purchase. It was cheap at the price.

Louisiana was nearly a hundred years old, but its great area harbored only a small population of less than 50,000, clustered near the mouth of the Mississippi at New Orleans. There were a few scattered settlements northward along the river, with the most important at the mouth of the Missouri, St. Louis, a town destined to become a great city. The new territory gave another industry to American economy, sugar planting. Refugees from Haiti who had fled to the mainland in the previous decade had brought a valuable knowledge of this form of agriculture and had put it to good use. Jefferson had added greatly to the national wealth and had doubled the size of the American domain.

Hardships of a Weak Neutral

The purchase of Louisiana brought the United States a step nearer the European conflict. The contest between Great Britain and Napoleon broke out again the same year and brought American shipping increasing difficulties. In 1805 Napoleon seemed on the verge of invading England and perhaps of conquering the island. Everything must be done to hamper French power; and the English government determined to take all steps possible to prevent trade between France and her colonies. So, the British fleets were ordered to bar all territorial products from French ports, no matter whether they came technically or in reality direct from the United States to France. Direct trade, Great Britain had hitherto allowed, but now, backed by a court decision that it was contrary to the Rule of 1756, the government more aggressively seized and confiscated American ships and their French West Indian cargoes. Impressment of seamen, too, became more exasperating than ever.

During the next year, American shipping was caught between two fires. The British blockaded the European coast from Brest to the Elbe principally to close France to Danish and Dutch commerce. This blockade in itself was not so harmful but France sought to retaliate by declaring the British Isles blockaded. As the French navy had been crippled at Trafalgar such a blockade could not be effective: but it enabled French privateers and port officials, wherever Napoleon exercised control, to seize American ships suspected of trading with England.

Naturally, Great Britain retaliated in turn. In 1807 orders in council issued from London, and a further decree from Napoleon together made it impossible for an American ship to touch at a British or a continental port without being liable to seizure by either France or England. As far as financial returns went, these restrictions did not affect the total of American profit. Shippers on account of the risk raised their prices to such a point that if one cargo out of three arrived safely they made money. The commercial interests nevertheless were wroth and in 1807 talked of war.

The position of the United States as a despised neutral was an unenviable one. Were American shipping left alone, it could make fabulous profits, but the restrictions and insulting treatment cut the rewards and also hurt American pride. What was to be done to make European powers respect American neutrality? The republic was not prepared for war, and besides Jefferson had his own ideas of the proper method. During the years leading up to the Revolution, non-importation had been an effective weapon against Great Britain; might it not prove so again? In 1806, therefore, an act forbidding importation of English and French goods had been passed; but it was not put into effect, for Jefferson wanted to hold it as a reserve weapon to force Great Britain to come to some diplomatic agreement regarding impressment and neutral rights. His strategy proved unavailing and in the meantime the country was mortified and angered by a raid upon one of its war vessels by an English frigate, during which seamen were impressed from her very deck. The *Chesapeake* and *Leopard* affair, as it was called, brought war nearer. Jefferson, however, was still hopeful about peaceful coercion; and in December 1807 Congress passed an Embargo Act, at the same time putting the non-importation act into effect. Under the first no vessels could leave American ports for any foreign countries, and under the second, no goods could be brought in from England and France.

Trade stopped, ships were tied to their wharves, sailors were out of work; only those merchants whose shelves were well stocked carried on much business. The British and French, on the other hand, gave no indication of better treatment as a result of economic coercion. To many Americans it seemed that the punishing of Europe was not worth its cost. The cost was indeed heavy. In Massachusetts alone the fleet had been earning more than 15 millions annually in freight rates, not counting profits in trade. All this was stopped and the ships idled seemingly to no effect, except to cause Napoleon to issue a ludicrous decree April 1808 seizing all American ships within French reach, on the grounds that they were violating our embargo law. There seemed no limit to European insults.

Strong opposition to Jefferson's policy naturally developed in New England. A large smuggling trade sprang up in Maine and Georgia and along the northern border; ships ostensibly in the coastwise trade often found themselves hopelessly driven, by contrary winds of course, into Canadian or West Indian ports, where they disposed of their cargoes. Jefferson's port officials tried their best to compel obedience by removing sails and rigging from ships and by keeping vigilant watch. Besides, hundreds of shipowners loyally accepted the law. The result was that exports, which in 1807 had amounted to 108 millions dwindled to 22 millions in 1808.

In New England, where Federalism had been defeated of late, the old leaders seized upon this issue and condemned Jefferson for a policy so ruinous to trade and so little evocative of results. In the election of 1808 James Madison, Jefferson's chosen successor, was elected without much difficulty, but he lost all the New England states except Vermont. Pressure was so strong and European results so meagre that in March 1809 Jefferson consented to the repeal of the general features of the Embargo Act on the ground that it was more expensive than war. All trade with Great Britain and France, however, remained forbidden.

Though trade improved with the repeal of the embargo, the American diplomatic position did not. England's attitude was especially trying. First, in May 1809 she refused to ratify a treaty which her minister had negotiated agreeing to withdraw the trade restrictions of her orders in council; this was particularly embarrassing as Madison had resumed trade on the strength of the negotiation before it was ratified. He retaliated by canceling the resumption, only to be further affronted. A new British envoy, Jackson, who was sent over in July 1809 proved as unpleasant as an English minister to America in those days could be, which is saying a good deal. He added insult to injury by intriguing with Madison's political opponents; by November the President refused to deal further with him.

The regulation forbidding trade with Great Britain and France was no more popular than the embargo had been, and opposition to it became so pronounced that in May 1810 all such bans were lifted. Of Jefferson's peaceable coercion measures, none remained on the statute books except the so-called Macon Bill #2, an ill-advised offer, addressed to England and France, that in case either would withdraw its restrictions against American commerce, the United States would refuse to trade with the other. This opened the way for another diplomatic insult. In August 1810 Napoleon declared that he had accepted this offer; so Madison forbade by proclamation any trade with Great Britain; within a few months it became apparent that Napoleon had deceived him and was still enforcing his restrictions upon American shipping. At the same time Madison's minister to England left London in disgust; England would make no concessions. Thus diplomatic relations were practically severed for a time.

For six years there had been a continuous series of indignities and losses. It was apparent that the American international position was neither dignified nor potent; seemingly the rights and interests of the republic had no diplomatic weapons of protection. National pride had been wounded frequently and the futile efforts of Jefferson and Madison to gain redress peaceably had only placed the nation in positions more embarrassing. Both England and France seemed equally callous to American rights, though England was apt to be blunt and downright in her offensiveness while Napoleon was apt to profess friendship, at the same time deceiving and despoiling. New England was, of course, antagonistic to Jefferson and Madison, and captiously critical. But in general that section was in no mood for war as far as the Federalists were concerned. American exports in 1810 had recovered to the value of 66 millions. Commerce on the whole flourished.

Rather, the pressure for more vigorous resistance to the affronts of Europe came from the younger members of the party in power. Their strength was demonstrated in the congressional elections of 1810 and 1811 and when Congress met in November 1811 a large group of young men entered the House, Henry Clay, John C. Calhoun, Peter B. Porter, Langdon Cheves and others representing recklessness; and Madison in the White House and Monroe in the State Department began to feel their enthusiasm. These young men, many from the South and West, felt the urge of national pride which brooked no insults; then too, they had the land hunger of their sections and looked upon Florida and Canada with longing eyes; finally they lacked the caution of age and all unprepared had no hesitation in plunging the country into war.

Various feats of valor helped to stir the martial spirit. In 1810 Madison valiantly marched into West Florida and occupied it in the vicinity of Mobile, a desirable port, alleging that Spain was unable to maintain sovereignty and that the lawless character of the settlements made them a refuge for criminals and fugitive slaves and a menace to Mississippi Territory. In May 1811 an American frigate had a brush with a British war vessel attempting to prevent trade with France, in which the *President* worsted the *Little Belt;* this in a sense atoned for the disgrace of the *Chesapeake* by the *Leopard*. Finally, later in the same year, an Indian war broke out and at the battle of Tippecanoe, William Henry Harrison defeated the redskins and incidentally confirmed the suspicion that British encouragement had had something to do with the uprising.

Such martial events were a fitting prelude to the climax. Great Britain continued her disdainful course. Though she condescended to send another minister late in 1811, her government not only refused to revoke her orders in council but also in May 1812 scolded Madison soundly for submitting to Napoleon's deception. Thereupon Madison and Monroe lost patience; Congress eagerly acceded to the President's request for a declaration of war against Great Britain, 18 June 1812.

But why war against Britain and not France? French flouting of American dignity and disregard of American interest had been equally, if not more, high-handed. The answer is to be found presumably in revolutionary experience. Great Britain was the traditional enemy; France had been a friend. Also, Napoleon had been more polite and was a heroic and compelling figure appealing to the American imagination. England was the same old tyrant she always had been. Finally, England was at the border and a tempting possibility, especially to the statesmen of the agricultural empire. So it was to be war again with England. By an irony of fate, England's financial interests, knowing the depleted state of the treasury, influenced the ministry to withdraw the orders in council at the moment when Congress was declaring war. Had there been a cable, the news might have reached Washington in time to prevent strife, though a similar state of affairs in 1898 failed to deter the McKinley administration. At any rate, war it now was.

CHAPTER XII

THE WAR OF 1812

This war, unlike the Revolution, was precipitate. An unready nation was rushed into it headlong. It proved indeed fortunate for the United States that England was heavily preoccupied with Napoleon.

The Campaigns on Land and Sea

No preparation had been made for the conflict. The treasury was empty and unequal to the task of financing war. Owing to partisan quarreling and the jealousy of New York interests toward Philadelphia, Congress had refused in 1811 to recharter the Bank of the United States. The two or three hundred private banks lacked the means to provide the government with funds or credit and there was no banking system as such. A widespread dread of taxes hindered revenue collection.

The weapon indispensable for success—namely an adequate navy—was not at hand; the navy of about twelve effective war vessels and 5,000 sailors had far more officers than ships. The War Department, with no practice or tradition of war management, was headed by Secretary Eustis, a Boston physician; the staff consisted of aged veterans incapable of prosecuting ambitious campaigns; the ranks numbered less than 7,000. No roads adequate for transport, and no services adequate for supplies, existed. Here was one of several paradoxes. The United States set forth to win what must be a naval war, with an army emphasis. President and Congress were interested in arming the militia and bolstering the army, which were to negotiate the border expansion so dear to the war hawks.

This paradox was twin to another. This war, supposedly for free trade and sailors' rights, was most enthusiastically supported by the interior districts and most vigorously opposed by the mercantile interests of the seacoast. The latter preferred their large, though uncertain, profits to the high taxes and wholesale destruction of shipping certain in a war. The British navy would blockade their ports and the unprepared country could scarcely break the cordon. So vigorous was their opposition to the war that a combination of Federalists and disgruntled Republicans supporting De Witt Clinton of New York nearly defeated Madison when he came up for reëlection shortly after war was declared. Under such unfavorable auspices, was this war with Britain begun and, by another paradox as will be seen, won.

Clay and other ardent "war hawks" felt that Canada was so easily to be captured that its acquisition was mainly a matter of marching. Great Britain was in the midst of vigorous war-making in Europe. She could spare little aid to her Canadian forces, which were not nearly as large as those the United States was supposed to be able to bring against them, though numbers and paper armies are deceiving. With great difficulty and much confusion, militia and regular army

A Bitter Dose for Britain

(A Contemporary Cartoon Boasting of Perry's Victory.)

contingents were headed up into three expeditions to conquer Canada. They all failed during the summer of 1812. The first, under Hull, surrendered at Detroit. The second, under several generals, attempted to cross the Niagara at Queenstown, but as most of the New York militia suddenly developed scruples against serving out of the state, that attempt failed. The third, under old General Dearborn, which was expected to march on Montreal, never got started. Had it not been that vessels like the *Constitution* won several victories of a surprising character on the sea, the year of 1812 would have passed with only ignominious defeat upon its pages.

In 1813 more realistic plans developed; Americans aimed to make military operations practicable by gaining naval control of the Great Lakes. Chauncey on Lake Ontario and Perry on Lake Erie set to work to build fleets superior to those the English could muster. Perry succeeded completely and his brilliant victory on Lake Erie is one of the few bright spots in the dreary story of the Canadian campaigns. Harrison followed up this victory by securing Detroit. Chauncey on Lake Ontario was not successful in producing anything more than a deadlock and the less said about the exploits of Wilkinson, who attempted land operations, the better. The only success in that neighborhood was the capture of York (Toronto) by Dearborn and Pike. The end of the year found little actual advance made into Canada and the small American navy was in the process of being captured or blockaded by British fleets.

By 1814 Great Britain had temporarily eliminated Napoleon and despatched a number of veterans to America to take the offensive. The Canadian forces, augmented by these tried troops, stopped the last American offensive under the younger and more effective generals, Brown and Scott. However, these new troops failed in their effort to enter the United States by Lake Champlain when Captain Macdonough defeated the British fleet on that water. While these operations were proceeding, another fresh expedition appeared in the Chesapeake and easily captured the city of Washington. After burning the public buildings, the British attempted to capture Baltimore, but Fort McHenry blocked the way and the expedition left the Atlantic coast to participate in an attack on New Orleans. In this year the British blockade, which heretofore had not been applied to New England because of the opposition of that section to the war, was now extended northward and American commerce was effectually strangled.

The final operation of the war was in the Southwest. There Andrew Jackson had been conducting a vigorous campaign against the Creek Indians, who under English stimulus had been actively hostile. His operations were very successful and now he was called upon to meet a force of 10,000 veterans fresh from victorious European battle fields. To Jackson, however, British were British and 8 January 1815, he fought a vigorous battle before New Orleans and completely defeated the enemy. He did not know that his victory had been won after the war was over, for 24 December 1814 a peace treaty had been signed at Ghent.

So the war was fought. On land it had not been glorious. The army never numbered more than 30,000 effectives; 4,000 was the maximum in any battle and only 1,500 were killed in the land operations; disease proved to be more dangerous than bullets. The navy, though neglected, fared better, but beyond winning a few spectacular victories the vessels available could make little impression upon the large British navy; more effective were the 500 and more privateers which harried British commerce.

Financially too, the war had not been glorious, unpopular as it was in the section which had the most money. Of the 41 millions of bonds

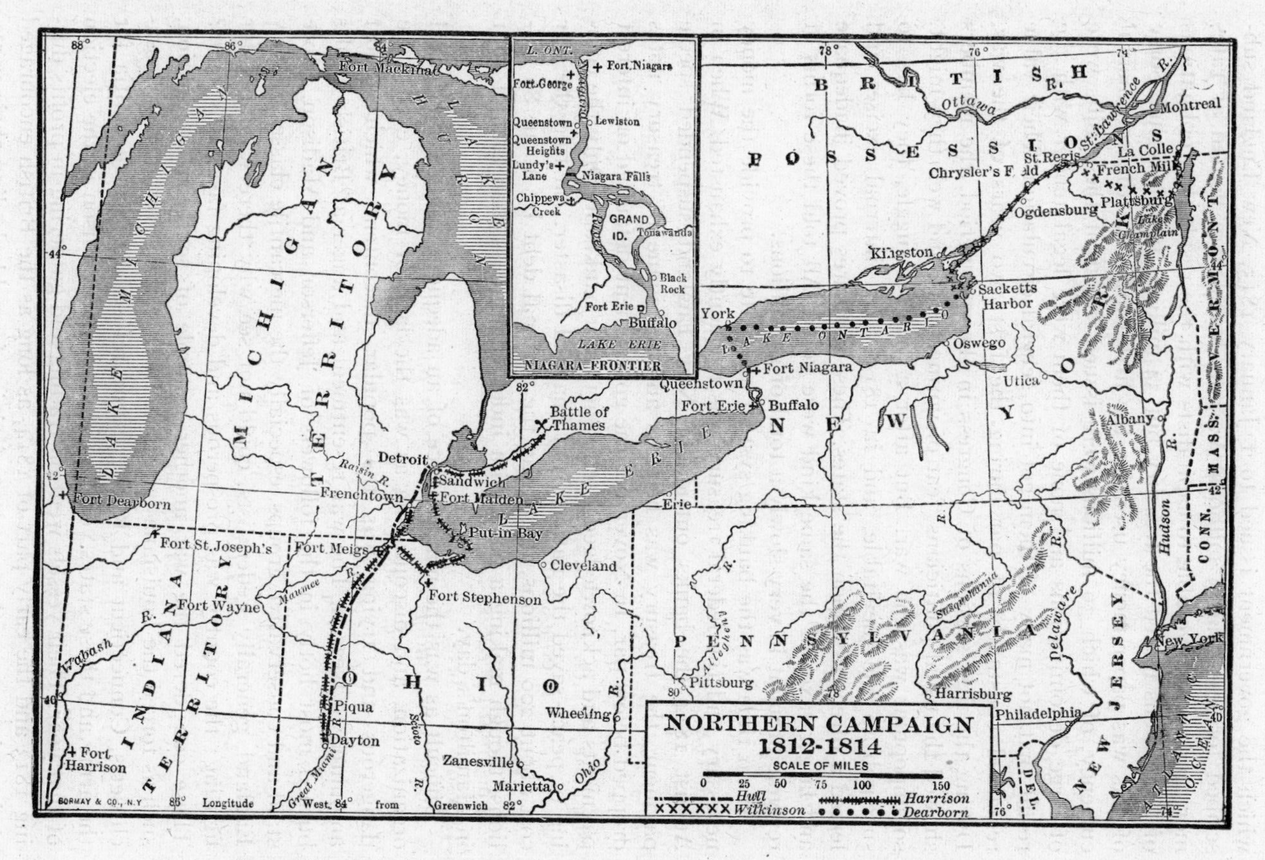

(From Kendrick, *Rise of American Nationality*, published by Harper and Brothers.)

which the government issued to 1 January 1815, New England subscribed for less than 3 millions. Various loans were floated at rates more and more favorable to capitalists with the result that obligations of 80 millions netted the treasury but 34 millions in coin value. Some of this was paper money used for the first time since the continental currency, of which 36 millions were issued. Most of these bills were of large denominations and none of them were legal tender with the result that not many of them got into general circulation. Their value remained constantly at par during the first two years of the war. During the first sessions of Congress in the war period, the members showed the usual politicians' fear of voting taxes, and well they might, so unpopular was the war. But after a year's struggle, they had to succumb to the inevitable, and in 1813 voted internal excises and levied a direct tax upon the states. These measures proved inadequate and larger taxes of the same kind were voted. All told these forms of revenue brought in very slowly a total of 25 millions.

At no time was the banking system adequate to provide the money necessary and the federal treasury was frequently exhausted. When in August 1814 the banks outside of New England suspended specie payment, the treasury was helpless and the value of treasury notes dropped below par. In November the government defaulted on interest payments and acknowledged itself practically bankrupt. Only the coming of peace saved the nation from financial disaster. All told the war cost about 200 millions, increasing the national debt by about 80 millions, though making a per capita indebtedness less than that of 1791 in Hamilton's day.

Difficult as was the maintenance of an adequate military and naval organization, and discouraging as was the lack of money, even more dangerous and trying was the popular discontent which almost amounted to treason. The war resentment and anger at British insults burned most hotly in the followers of Jefferson and Madison. More staid and conservative groups, especially the mercantile classes of New England, generally Federalists, could not see why there was need for fighting; the country was prosperous and developing fast—why fight? These considered the war another example of southern domination, such as forced the Louisiana purchase. In 1812 the governors of Massachusetts, Connecticut and Rhode Island refused to furnish militia for the army and these states voted solidly against Madison in the election of that year. Their vessels went on trading and gathering in profits during 1813 and the early part of 1814, as long as the British encouraged their resistance to the war by refraining from blockading their ports. Consequently, New England made more profits while their capitalists refused to loan these same profits to the government. Meanwhile the rest of the country was forced to buy there and this trade generally drew the country's specie into New England, to the bitter resentment of other sections.

Times were hard enough, money was scarce, prices were high, many were out of work, business in the other sections was at a standstill, farmers were in difficulties because they could not export their crops and taxes were heavy. To retaliate against New England an embargo act was passed in December 1813 forbidding any vessels to leave American ports. Worse still, when the English extended their blockade to New England in 1814 exports fell in value to less than 7 millions, although a large illegal trade was carried on unrecorded. New England, in her turn, was more embittered and resentful.

The failure of the army, the burning of Washington, the seizure of part of Maine by the British and finally the debating of a conscription act by Congress, moved these states to take positive action. Vermont had already set an example in 1813 by recalling her militia from the army to the defense of the state, and in 1814 Massachusetts and Connecticut formed state armies to defend themselves, declaring the federal government incompetent. Even New York, Maryland, Virginia, South Carolina and Kentucky followed a similar policy for defense and other states were in process when the war ended. Was the Union in danger of falling apart?

The climax of opposition and insubordination was initiated by Massachusetts. When British troops succeeded in capturing a large part of Maine, a special session of the Massachusetts legislature was called. The federal government would not aid with troops or pay the Massachusetts militia because of the state's failure to participate in the Canadian invasion, so said the leaders. They were utterly abandoned by the federal authority, they claimed; and in October 1814 they issued a call to the New England states to meet in convention at Hartford. In the meantime at the congressional elections in New England the Federalists elected 30 and the Republicans 2. The so-called Hartford convention met with delegates from all the New England states. Their purpose was to plan to gain concessions from the federal government, in the guise of amendments to the Constitution; and it was common knowledge that some of them talked of secession if these requirements were not met. Their principal demands were that acquisition of new territory must wait upon an affirmative vote in each house; presidential tenure must be limited to one term; no two presidents in succession might come from the same state; taxes and representation must be apportioned according to the free population.

Thus New England strove to break southern agricultural control of the government, acting on a theory of sectional independence which was to survive forty years longer. However, before the delegates had concluded their deliberations the Ghent treaty had been signed. When their representatives came to Washington with the proposed amendments, they were met with the news of peace.

Post-War Adjustments

Peace negotiations, in fact, had been considered almost since the beginning of the war. In 1812 the Czar had offered his services as mediator and American commissioners had been appointed to proceed abroad. England refused, however, until the first defeat of Napoleon in October 1813. Thereupon she offered to negotiate directly and commissioners met in Ghent, in the summer of 1814. Great Britain refused to make any concessions and had ambitious notions of controlling the Great Lakes and taking part of Maine. However, difficulties in Europe and the failure of Wellington's veterans to do much in Canada or at Baltimore led finally to an agreement to restore everything to the status which existed at the beginning of the war.

Thus circumstances, rather than England or the United States, won the war and defined the treaty of 24 December 1814. The United States had not conquered Canada but had fastened its hold on West Florida. The coming of peace meant there would be no immediate disregard for neutral rights or the impressment of seamen, but England officially had made no concessions. Jackson's victory at New Orleans was accepted by the people of the United States as a proper climax and, taking their cue from Madison, the public gloried in a sense of victory. The triumphant Republicans laughed to scorn New England and the Federalists. Small matter was it to them that future historians were to find little that was glorious in this unfortunate war. To the young nation it was another laurel upon its military standards; Great Britain had been taught a second lesson.

This war left a train of diplomatic adjustments to follow the inconclusive treaty of peace, for it brought the United States into a new international position. Most important were those matters at issue with Great Britain left unsettled by the peace conference, such as impressment, trade privileges and the Canadian boundary. Upon the first two Britain would make no concessions, but upon the latter she showed a willingness to yield. By the Rush-Bagot agreement of 1817, the boundary between the United States and Canada was disarmed and from then until now that three thousand mile stretch of lake, river and line has remained innocent of fortification, enjoying unbroken peace. The 49th parallel was declared by the treaty of 1818 to be the boundary between the United States and Canada from the Lake of the Woods to the Rockies and the difficult question of the possession of Oregon was postponed by the temporary expedient of arranging for joint occupation for ten years, later (1827) renewed indefinitely. No progress was made in solving the puzzle of the Maine boundary and American fishing rights in Newfoundland waters were redefined in 1818 so carelessly as to provoke a century-long dispute. Yet, in spite of a few shocks and much bellicose speech, a peace with Great Britain was inaugurated which has remained unbroken.

Spanish difficulties, too, were partly adjusted, though with little satisfaction. Spain had regained jurisdiction over Florida in 1783 but was not sufficiently strong or enterprising to do more than send a governor and a few soldiers to the several small posts which had been established. Seminole Indians and fugitive slaves roamed at will and traded with British adventurers. The acquisition of Florida had become a dream of Jefferson's when he bought Louisiana; and in 1810 and 1813 the western portion of the province was occupied. After the war of 1812 the Seminoles interfered with settlers in the Southwest and Andrew Jackson was ordered to take his Tennessee militia and punish them. He marched in vigorously, drove the Spanish out of Pensacola and St. Marks, and hanged two British whom he found aiding the Indians against him. This invasion of 1818 waked up the Spanish government and it decided it would be better to sell Florida to the United States before the latter made the formality of a sale unnecessary. In 1819 Spain agreed to transfer Florida in return for a payment of $5,000,000, to satisfy all of Spain's American creditors, and the United States agreed to the undisputed possession of Texas by the Spanish, thus abandoning a claim arising out of the indefinite provisions of the Louisiana cession treaty. The newly acquired region was largely swamp and forest which gave little promise of future popularity.

Having thus liquidated some of the questions left unsettled by the Revolution, the United States was ready for its first positive step in diplomacy. When the general peace of 1815 was finally concluded the rulers of Austria, Prussia, Russia and Great Britain signed an agreement to protect Europe from another outbreak of revolution, particularly in France. This concert of powers, known as the "Holy Alliance," interfered to stamp out signs of republicanism elsewhere in Europe. In the course of time Great Britain withdrew and in 1822 France joined the three remaining powers. After suppressing a republican revolt in Spain, this alliance took up the question of America. The Spanish American provinces had been in revolt for ten years and the home government evidently was unable to bring them back to allegiance. The European foes of democracy considered the possibility, at least, of sending an armed force across the seas. Great Britain objected; she was more interested in promoting trade with Latin America and opposed to the added power which might come to France if the latter took the lead as she seemed about to do. So Great Britain astonished America with a request that the United States join in a protest against invasion. In 1812 there had been war; in 1823 came an invitation to joint action!

President Monroe, whose easy election in 1816 had continued the "Virginia dynasty," was not unmindful of the danger which might be hovering over republicanism in America. He and his secretary of state, John Quincy Adams, son of old John Adams, had watched the struggles of the Spanish provinces with sympathy but with a reluctance to extend aid, primarily because they feared that the negotiation and ratification of the Florida treaty might be prevented thereby. After the ratified treaty was finally proclaimed (in February 1821) Monroe and Adams could be more sympathetic, and in 1822 they recognized some of the struggling states. Their natural opposition to intervention by Europe was sharpened by evidence that Russia had been seeking to extend her power down from Alaska along the Pacific Coast. Attempts to spread monarchical principles and power seemed to come from across both oceans. Assuredly Europe must be warned off—but not in Great Britain's company; that would be unpopular. There was perhaps a bolder attitude to take.

Monroe advised with two of the living ex-presidents, Jefferson and Madison, as well as with Adams and the cabinet, and the die was cast. In his annual message of 1823 the President formulated his famous doctrine. He declared that except for existing colonies, America was dedicated to republicanism and no longer open to European colonization; furthermore, the United States would consider any attempt on the part of monarchies to extend their system to America as "dangerous to our peace and safety." To quiet European fears of official republican propaganda or interference in continental revolutionary wars, Monroe declared that the United States had "never taken any part" and did not intend to. The line between republicanism and monarchy was laid down somewhere in the midst of the Atlantic. This pronouncement showed the United States still on the defensive; but in years to come the Monroe Doctrine would be amenable to many uses. Europe in 1823 was not in a position to intervene; and so the United States had the satisfaction of defying (without risk) the crowned heads of Europe.

The Approach of Economic Independence

The close of the war brought also domestic readjustments, in both politics and business. In politics, the final collapse of the old partisan rivalry became plainly evident as the conflict came to an end. The Federalists had had the misfortune to oppose a war which ended in seeming victory for American arms; the futility of their opposition turned ridicule upon them. The exigencies of the months following the war would lead the Republicans to appropriate the boasted principles of the Federalists. They would reëstablish Hamilton's bank and do many things by the loosest kind of interpretation of the Constitution. Apparently there was little left for the Federalists to cherish as their own, except a certain aristocratic aloofness which could hardly be expected to attract the votes of an increasingly democratic electorate. The Federalists' demise had been undeniably indicated by the election of 1816. Their candidate, Rufus King, carried only Massachusetts, Connecticut and Delaware; while James Monroe, choice of Madison and his friends, won the presidency almost through appointment by the outgoing administration. Four years later Monroe's reelection met no formal opposition; but one electoral vote was cast against him. The period took the name of "The Era of Good Feeling."

In spite of these seemingly conclusive indications it must not be understood that the conservative and aristocratic temper of the Federalists had disappeared from American life. In many respects it was still strong but the Federalists, themselves inept at politics and political organization, had to bide their time till a new generation more versed in the arts of popular appeal could come forward and strive to make palatable to the populace the cherished ideals of Washington and Hamilton. As yet, however, the younger generation were neither sufficiently self-confident nor wise enough to break with the older generation; and more important, there were no groups or interests of sufficient strength or in need dire enough to supply the energy and the backing so essential to a new partisan effort. When North and South again became conscious of their differences, and when economic interests began again to plan for government aid and subsidy, then a new partisanship would arise.

The most difficult of the post-war readjustments was economic. The conflict had borne most heavily upon the incomplete and unstable business system which had been unduly stimulated by the abnormal world conditions existing between 1793 and 1813. It had been jarred rudely by the hostilities, and the hope that peace would restore normal conditions proved ill founded.

American carriers, importing agents, manufacturers and merchants suffered immediately. Foreign trade had been shattered. The British naval strength had driven American freighters from the seas and shipowners could not recoup when war ceased, because neutral carriers no longer were needed. Europe could take care of trade with American ports in its own ships, no longer menaced by privateers. Almost with official word of ratification of peace terms came British vessels well laden with her wares. Her industries had piled up great surpluses during the long war period and were desperate for markets. Price was no object. So eager were British agents to sell that they abandoned the usual forms of trade. Ignoring American importers as agents of distribution, British supercargoes sold their merchandise on the docks at auction for whatever it would bring. These masses of cheap goods crowded American products out of trade, stranding manufacturers and merchants with unsold stocks. Under these circumstances it became apparent to the manufacturers at least that if they did not receive aid they would have to go out of business. When members of Congress met in December 1815 petitions for relief in the form of protective tariff duties were pressed upon their attention.

Economic organization was further disturbed by the precarious condition of the financial system. Since the closing of the First Bank of the United States in 1811, there had been no centralized, controlling banking institution of any sort. The lack gave free rein to state banks which increased in number most notably. In 1811 there had been 88; in 1813 there were 208, each one of them issuing paper money. As there were few state laws regulating the conduct of these institutions they could print money and circulate it freely, often quite beyond the range of safe banking. During the war financial difficulties had multiplied, culminating in the suspension by all banks of any attempt to redeem in coin their large emissions of paper money. The conclusion of the war therefore found business entirely dependent, for a medium of exchange, upon a depreciated paper currency, with practically no hard money in the country. As business advanced after the peace it needed an expanding, reliable currency but found none. As the months succeeded one another, there seemed to be no disposition to resume specie payment, and counterfeiting and notes of defunct banks added to the uncertainty. In this instance as in the difficulties of the manufacturers, the hope of government interference and aid grew strong and Congress found awaiting it petitions for relief from the evils of demoralized finance.

Discussion centered upon tax revision and establishment of another central bank. After prolonged debate two measures of major importance were enacted. The first of these placed the revenue upon a peacetime basis and incidentally heeded a few of the plaints of the manufacturers. Cotton cloth was to be taxed 25 per cent of its value and no cotton cloth was to be valued at less than 25¢ a yard. Such a scheme of minimum valuation was not so important at this time, as the real value of coarse cloth was about that figure; but later as the price fell, it was to prove more protective. Less fortunate were the woolen manufacturers, because raw wool as well as woolen goods was taxed, the one partly offsetting the benefits derived from the other. The iron industrialists too were not favored particularly by the duty levied on rolled or hammered iron. Whether this tariff of 1816 may properly be called protective is still a matter of debate.

Secondly, the banking question was settled by providing for another bank quite similar to that promoted by Hamilton. This institution was chartered for twenty-one years and capitalized at 35 millions, three-quarters of which was to be in government obligations and one-fourth in cash. The government was to hold one-fifth of the stock and name one-fifth of the directors; the bank might establish branches. Details of organization were completed by 1 January 1817 and the government thus once more had the advantages of a place of deposit and a financial agent. Immediately the bank announced it would do business only with specie-paying banks, thus causing by 20 February a general quick return to specie payments, unfortunately temporary. As far as policy was concerned therefore, the spirit of Hamilton had triumphed.

As a final help to American carriers, Congress passed in 1817 a navigation act imposing upon foreign vessels the restrictions which the foreign country in question imposed upon American ships. So fortified with government aid and regulation, economic conditions, it was hoped, would improve; but unfortunately such a result did not follow.

Inflation intervened. Flocks of banks were established and by 1818 there were 392, almost double the number operating in 1813. Speculation was rife, especially in the western and middle states where a multitude of real estate operators welcomed banks that would loan on easy terms; it was in this section that most of the mushroom banks sprouted. Public land sales boomed, as credit terms under the land act of 1800 were liberal and as the high price of farm products, especially cotton, drove up land values in northwest and southwest. At such a time, the policy of the United States bank should have been cautious, but it was the contrary. It joined in the policy of easy loans; its western branches sinned most outrageously, for some of their managers proved irresponsible and ignorant of sound banking. The central organization neither watched its own branches nor, after its first move toward specie, attempted any sort of control over the state banks. Under such weak leadership only disaster could be expected. As early as the winter of 1816 and 1817 there were hard times; soup kitchens had to be set up and charitable organizations sought to look after those out of work. By 1818 this distress had become widespread and in 1819 there was a panic. Banks again suspended payment, ships rotted at their wharves and factories closed their doors. Even the Bank of the United States was embarrassed and barely missed suspension.

Recovery from the panic was gradual. Little help came from the government, for Congress refused to pass a new tariff bill urged to protect the manufacturers. Many weak banks were eliminated. The Bank of the United States itself was reorganized and the new management undertook to operate along very conservative lines. Industry, twice purged, once by the influx of foreign goods and again by the financial panic, was reërected upon a new, firmer basis. None but the soundest and best managed firms had been able to survive and they now were in a position to weather any crisis. The real beginning of American industrial strength is found in these panic years.

At last economic independence had been in large part achieved. America no longer was a mere appendage of Europe, dependent on imports for the main indispensables of daily living.[1] The new nation could look forward to continuous advance along the way of self-sufficiency. The prolonged struggle for real independence had been won.

[1] Economic independence was of course not complete. The trade-balance was for years to be against the United States, owing to dependence upon Europe for loans of capital to finance new enterprise.

GROWTH AND SECTIONAL CONFLICT

1823-1865

CHAPTER XIII

THE GREAT DISPERSION: THE FRONTIER EPOCH

So long as Europe persisted in warfare, the dependent economy of the United States kept attention chained to the activities of the fighting powers. The coming of peace and the new degree of independence which the nation had attained freed American interest and made possible a release of energy. From the close of the war of 1812 to the middle 'fifties the creative power and enthusiasm of the people of the United States were free to make what they would of a tremendous opportunity.

A new nationalism, hitherto undeveloped, now pressed the people of the United States to explore and develop their share of the great continent. In this effort they were joined by ever increasing crowds of immigrants from Europe. The return to peace on that harassed continent, and friction rising when reactionary statesmen sought to stifle the liberal thought stimulated by the French Revolution, sent thousands from the Old World to enjoy the prospect of democracy and economic opportunity in the New.

Settlement of the West

Eighty per cent of the land belonging to the United States was vacant and waiting for men and women to occupy it and enjoy its fertility and wealth. This fact dominated the era.

Such an abundance of unused land could not fail to act as a lodestone and stimulate a restless desire to seize the resources. In this great and unknown western country fortune surely was to be found. Ever since the Revolutionary epoch and even before there had been signs of a great restlessness and many faces had turned westward. Wherever any one felt that he was not doing as well as he wished, there was the hope of better luck elsewhere. To many "elsewhere" meant the land beyond the Appalachians. To the majority of the European immigrants, also, the West was the chosen destination.

The so-called West for which they sought is not easy to define, for it was less a locality than a kind of living, namely, life on the frontier, and such a mode of existence in that period cannot be given a continuous boundary. Frontier conditions were still common in central New York, western Pennsylvania and Virginia, where even in 1820 large areas still had less than seven inhabitants to the square mile. In the eastern Mississippi Valley such conditions were still the rule in large measure, even after the admission of Ohio, Kentucky and Tennessee as states. Across the great river in the Louisiana Purchase there were few inhabitants except at the river's mouth in the state of Louisiana and at St. Louis. Settlers ventured into this frontier region particu-

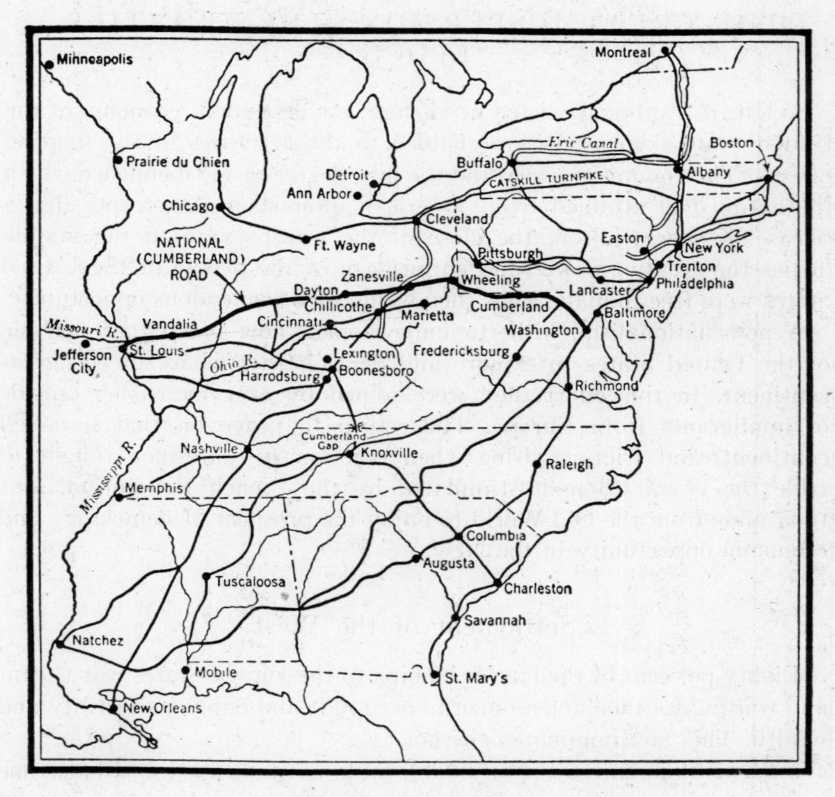

HIGHWAYS TO THE WEST

(From Clark, *The West in American History*. Copyright, 1937, by Thomas Y. Crowell Company, publishers. Reprinted by permission.)

larly in times of economic distress or war. The successive crises in the East sent waves of migration beyond the mountains, just as similar conditions had encouraged periodic migrations from Europe in the colonial period.

The decline in the fertility of New England soil led thousands to leave that region for the Northwest Territory. Original attempts to develop these lands in gross by companies had failed; myriad individuals were to accomplish this great task. The terms of the Northwest Ordinance were put into effect. The territory of Ohio emerged into a condition of partial self-government with a territorial legislature, and it was divided in 1800, when the land west of the present state of Ohio was made into the territory of Indiana. This was again subdivided as more people came in, by the establishment of Michigan territory in 1805 and Illinois territory in 1809. In 1802 Ohio had been made the first state carved from the Northwest Territory. It was the fulfillment of the promise of the Northwest Ordinance.

The process of statehood had already begun below the Ohio. The settlers from Virginia and North Carolina who had followed in the footsteps of Boone, Sevier and Henderson, had at length received their due; in 1792 Kentucky and in 1796 Tennessee had been admitted into the fellowship. And still the stream flowed on. The rich lands extending back from the Gulf between the Appalachians and the Mississippi were particularly attractive as cotton came into its own, and thither the hopeful went. To feed the gins new lands must be opened up, and the march into the southwest began. Government was needed and the territory of Mississippi was established in 1798 with its capital at Natchez. Here a New England governor ruled over a motley throng of French, Spanish and Americans. After the Louisiana Purchase, that great region was divided into two territories, and in 1812 the lower portion was made into the state of Louisiana.

In general the home-seekers moved into the new regions in parallel lines. Those from New England and the Middle States passed through the central New York river valley and the Great Lakes, or through western Pennsylvania and down the Ohio River. From the lakes or from the Ohio they could scatter into Ohio, Indiana, Michigan and Illinois. Those from the upper South went through mountain passes, like the Cumberland Gap, which were gateways into Kentucky, Tennessee, Mississippi and Louisiana, and into southern Ohio, Indiana and Illinois as well. This parallel march was to have a distinct influence upon the newly settled localities, as it projected eastern and southern social habits into the corresponding regions directly west. Thus transplanted, differences were somewhat modified, but not sufficiently to avoid the direful consequences of their existence.

These western settlers poured into the new regions in ever increasing numbers, practically doubling in some decades:

1790— 250,000 (estimate)	1810—1,078,315	1830—3,672,569
1800— 386,413	1820—2,217,474	1840—6,376,972

They reënacted many of the experiences of the colonial pioneers. Once again many a man and his family cut themselves loose from home ties and long settled associations and ventured forth into a strange country. Once again was hardship the lot of a migratory people; not so much in these days from Indians, wild animals or starvation as from exposure and disease, bad roads, dangerous streams unbridged and the weary miles of journeying by those unused to its rigors.

New European Migration: Agricultural Revolution

This advance into the western country was stimulated by restless folk from England, Scotland, Ireland and Germany. Their annual number varied but their total increase mounted. Some 1,500,000 came between 1815 and 1845, in groups ranging from 6,000 to 100,000 a year. Thereafter the rate rose; a million entered the ports of the republic, 1845-1850, and over 400,000 in the banner year of 1854.

Their reasons for coming varied; some reasons were temporary. At the close of the Napoleonic Wars the difficulties encountered by the demobilized soldiers and the distaste of youth for conscription for military service were strong motives. Periodically, especially in the late 'forties, frightful famine tortured Europe, particularly Ireland and Germany, where they depended too much upon potatoes. Also after the Revolutions of 1848 a number of liberty-loving Germans sought exile rather than to be punished for their love of independence or to witness the disappointment of their hopes.

More fundamental were long-term causes. Most significant was the great agricultural revolution that was operating in Europe, particularly in England. Since the middle of the eighteenth century the farming communities of the British Isles had been vigorously reorganized. New tools and better methods of crop raising and stock breeding had been introduced. Scientific farming was growing in prominence. Possibilities of more profits were pressing a basic change upon agriculture. Hitherto most English farming had been done on small farms, many of them worked by tenants. Now farming could be carried on more effectively in larger units. Also the growth of the new industrial cities raised the demand for meat, and consequently pasture for sheep and cattle was more needed than small fields of grain. Thus many of the small farms were bought up and their operators dispossessed. Many farmers lost their lands; they had to choose between going to city slums and working in factories, or else migrating to America where land was cheap and plentiful. Also the industrial revolution, by introducing machinery, put many hand workers, particularly weavers—both in England and on the continent—out of employment; they too began to think of America.

All these various classes of people were drawn to this new republic by its growing reputation. Travelers, promoters and those who had found happiness in the United States wrote back to Europe. Stories of its freedom, its opportunities for improvement and fortune and of the ease with which these might be realized spread far and wide. It was asserted and sometimes believed that the streets of cities in the new world were paved with gold. A horde of migrants responded.

Needs of the Frontier

The swelling tide of western migration made numerous demands upon the government and four of them proved insistent. In the first place there were thousands of Indians in the way of advance. The "civilized tribes," the Cherokees, the Choctaws and their neighbors were living settled lives in the Southwest. The Seminoles were pursuing a predatory existence in Florida. More to the westward on the prairies were nomadic tribes. They must be cleared away from the path of progress and transplanted to regions beyond the Mississippi, principally in the locality now Oklahoma. Their removal was accomplished between 1815 and 1850 with infinite difficulty which involved tedious negotiations, countless treaties, and litigation before the courts which several times went to the supreme tribunal. In some cases war was the final arbiter.

A second insistent demand was for free land. The migrants were eager for land; and the government, from the days of the Northwest Ordinance, had been eager to sell—for revenue. The revenue had not accumulated. At first sales had been limited to large lots with a section one mile square the minimum. As this had not worked well the amount was reduced in 1800 to 320, and four years later to 160, acres. The price, though maintained at a minimum of $2 an acre, could be carried on credit by making a small deposit. This system also proving unsatisfactory, and the credit scheme breaking down, the government adopted the plan of 1820 permitting plots as small as 80 acres at the reduced price of $1.25 an acre, cash. This system lasted until the Civil War except for a modification which permitted settlers to secure preemption rights, i.e., to try out land before it was put up for sale with the privilege of buying it when the government put it on the market. As years passed the western demand that the government give the land away grew more vociferous. Both eastern and southern opinion in general was opposed to such generosity, for population was leaving these regions. Thus the land question stimulated sectional rivalry.

A third demand raised by the western trek was for improved transportation. Many localities and promoters shouted for government aid to roads and canals. The federal government did undertake to build a national road from Cumberland, Maryland, over into the Northwest Territory but sectional rivalry, and the reluctance of eastern and southern representatives to vote large sums of money or quantities of land, killed other projects. It was left to states like New York and Pennsylvania to build the Erie Canal and the Pennsylvania system.

Most roads had to be financed by local taxation or by turnpike companies, which charged toll for their use.

Sectionalism

The last problem produced by the movement of people into the western country was to prove the most difficult of them all; the question of organizing these new communities into territories, and more especially into states, was to provoke a quarrel which was to end at length in the tragedy of the Civil War. Prior to 1818, the question of state organization had not troubled Congress much, except slightly in the case of Louisiana. Four states had been added to the Union in as many successive years. In 1816 Indiana had been admitted and the year following the territory of Mississippi had been divided. The western portion became the state of Mississippi and the eastern the territory of Alabama. In 1818 the territory of Illinois, reduced to her present size, was welcomed into the sisterhood of states leaving the remainder of the Northwest Territory under the jurisdiction of an enlarged Michigan. Within twelve months, Alabama ended her brief territorial experience to enter the Union. Now there were twenty-two states and it so happened that, of these twenty-two, eleven permitted Negro slavery, while the others had abolished it either at once or gradually. Politically, however, the influence of the slave and free sections had not been equal. The Democratic tenets of Jefferson's faith and his skilful organizing talents had left the aristocratic and less resourceful Federalists at a disadvantage which their opposition to the Louisiana Purchase and the War of 1812 had not removed. Jefferson, Madison and Monroe, Virginia planters representing the great mass of the agricultural and democratic Americans, seemed firmly in the saddle. The old Federalist ideal of a strong government eager to aid business enterprise and hasten development seemed dead. Then came a fire-bell in the night.

The territory of Missouri, as the region north of the state of Louisiana had been called since 1812, had been growing. Population now occupied a strip twenty miles wide along the western bank of the Mississippi, from the Arkansas to the locality some miles north of the Missouri. These people were farmers, fur-traders, boatmen and lead-miners. The traders were concentrated at St. Louis and the miners in the Ste. Genevieve region. The farming population was growing, particularly because slavery was permitted here, while it was excluded from the territories in the old Northwest. Settlers from the southern states were especially attracted and the territory doubled its population in the three years after the close of the War of 1812. Late in 1817 Missouri besought Congress for admission to the Union as a slave state, and the people to the south of the Missouri region in the

Arkansas Valley petitioned for a territorial government. These petitions pointed to the fact that the current trend of community building was producing slave states and that soon the southern interest would be greater than the northern. The slave states would outnumber the free. This prospect brought the slave issue into politics.

There was much opposition to slavery which was bound to seek political expression. A philanthropic urge to emancipate the Negroes had developed and the Quaker interest became the most active force behind it. A New Jersey Quaker, Benjamin Lundy, who had learned to hate slavery while a printer's apprentice in Wheeling, Virginia, began a militant career against the evil in 1815. Two years later a Quaker preacher, Charles Osborn, established a paper, the *Philanthropist*, at Mount Pleasant, Ohio, and devoted it to preaching temperance, peace and anti-slavery. Lundy journeyed from place to place on foot advocating the cause. His efforts spread into the South and his friend Elihu Embree, also a Quaker, began a paper, the *Emancipator*, in East Tennessee. Lundy arrived at St. Louis in 1819, just as Missouri was preparing for statehood, and he promptly joined in the effort to prevent her admission as a slave state. Other denominations were also concerned, for the Presbyterians at their General Assembly in 1818 had joined the Methodists in resolutions attacking slavery, and the Baptists likewise were girding themselves.

Opposition to slavery had taken another turn, not so drastic as abolition. Some conservatively minded people who saw no hope of persuading the South to abolish slavery thought the institution could be ameliorated if the Negroes were sent back to Africa. An organization founded in 1816 was known as the American Colonization Society and started to raise money to transport freed Negroes to Africa. They hoped that southerners, if they knew the Negroes would be carried back to Africa, would be willing to surrender them for that purpose. By 1820 they were ready to despatch their first ship but they had resources to finance the migration of only eighty-six. Truly this was to be bailing the ocean with a bucket.

The question had not been much in politics but Congress had tightened the law prohibiting the slave trade. The original act had left it to the states to determine what should be done with slaves seized as illegally imported. This had meant that they usually remained as slaves in the community, just as their importers had planned. Congress, in 1819, provided that illegal purchases should be returned to Africa, and a year later made slave-trading piracy; thenceforward slave-traders were liable to be hanged if caught. The stage was set for a sharper turn to the controversy.

Northern interests were bitterly opposed to southern domination of the federal government and sought to block the admission of more slave states. Otherwise the southern planter group would remain indefinitely in control. William H. Crawford of Georgia would succeed Monroe and where would northeastern interests be? They took advantage of the popular antipathy against permitting Negro slavery to spread into the new territory and appealed to this growing prejudice. James Tallmadge, a congressman from New York and a junior associate of the old Federalist, Rufus King, proposed to exclude slavery from Missouri. As the population of the northern states was by this time larger than that of the southern group, northern congressmen, if they voted together, could control the House of Representatives. Opposition to slavery was an excellent issue upon which to unite them against the South. Their power was apparent and southern members began to be concerned. Some adopted New England tactics and threatened secession if Missouri were denied entrance into the union as she wished to enter, namely, as a slave state. The more practical looked for a solution of the problem in compromise.

The congressional battle of 1819-1820-1821 over this question was bitter. The changes were rung on "states' rights" and the right of Missouri to have her own constitution; the North hotly condemned the sin of slavery and the crime of the southerners in owning slaves. Both sides were relieved when the so-called "Missouri Compromise" was finally enacted in 1820 after long political maneuvering. By this arrangement it was agreed that a part of Massachusetts which wished to enter the Union as the state of Maine be admitted with Missouri, one free, the other slave. This double entry would serve the purpose of keeping the balance even, twelve slave and twelve free states. So far, so good. But what of the future, what of Arkansas that would soon be coming forward? The answer to that question was found in establishing an arbitrary line, 36° 30′, dividing the remainder of the Louisiana Purchase territory so that all states entering them from the area north of the line must be free, and those coming in from the south might be slave. Arkansas itself was organized as a territory. Thus was compromise arranged and it was hoped that no such struggle would ever again occur. The question drifted off into obscurity, for no more states were destined to be made for fifteen years. But ominous arguments had been formulated and dangerous threats uttered.

Thus the settlement of the West brought out the sectional nature of the Republic. Moreover, the pioneers formed a new social grouping in these large United States. Hereafter, the term "West" was to bear a separate and distinct meaning, such as New England and the South already bore.

In many ways the people in these lands beyond the mountains were drawn together. They all had the pioneer instinct, sought new openings and welcomed new experiences, seemingly the more eagerly if risk and hardship were involved. The common interest in agriculture, too, was a bond which was strong, especially if eastern capitalists seemed to be exacting undue toll or obtaining undesirable advantages at the expense of the pioneers in the great valley. Furthermore, there was that mutual dependence between the upper and lower regions, the southern locality, with its preoccupation with cotton, depending for sustenance upon the northern fields always offering a surplus. The Ohio and the Mississippi rivers made an easy channel whereby food could be transported cheaply to the South. At the same time the mouth of the great river was the natural place of export and import for the people of the upper valley, as the other alternative, transportation over the mountains to the eastern seaboard, was too costly. So annually more flatbottomed boats floated down the great river; and with the launching of the steamboat on its waters in 1812, the possibilities of river transport were revolutionized. The foundations seemed to have been laid for a united, though enormous, inland empire dedicated to the cultivation of the soil and destined to gain fabulous wealth from its generous increase.

The empire, nevertheless, did not become homogeneous, for in it were being evolved two ways of life. The Northwest became a land of moderate-sized farms devoted to the production of food and operated by the landowners and their sons. Land was cheap, labor was scarce, each man easily became a proprietor and the new states were laid out like checkerboards in 160-acre farms. In the Southwest, on the other hand, cotton, sugar and tobacco production were most profitable when undertaken by slave labor on large plantations. So estates worked by gangs of Negroes were the ambitious hope if not the actual realization of a large portion of these farmers. Thus, while the Northwest was dedicating itself to individualism and equality, which might easily be translated into intense love of freedom, the Southwest was following the older South in building up a social order more resembling feudalism. The day was to come when the basic incompatibility would become apparent, for this great westward movement was in the end to demonstrate the inherent weakness of the United States. The far-sighted could see that there was danger. The nation was so large and its aggregation of communities so diverse that bitter intersectional rivalry might bring conflict and even dissolution. As yet, however, the great mass of enterprising Americans were interested only in advance and growth and were too preoccupied with subduing the continent to anticipate disaster.

CHAPTER XIV

CONCENTRATION OF POPULATION

The great dispersion of Americans into the western country was the most significant social force of this epoch. But there was a second tendency to migrate which, though less characteristic of the time, was to be even more significant in years to come. People were beginning to gravitate toward towns and cities, and the process of metropolitan growth was vigorously stimulated by expanding American enterprise. New business activity was hastening the concentration of population in urban communities.

New Business Conditions

The shift by the management of capital to new interests was highly significant. The old preoccupation with commerce had been much weakened by conditions in the war period which had caused large amounts of capital to be transferred to the rising industries. Nevertheless, the wharves hummed with activity, for from 1815 until 1837 foreign trade increased in value and its very size made necessary its concentration in certain seaports which became great centers of prosperity and wealth. Foreign trade, which in the decade 1790-1800 averaged 100 millions in value annually, rose to very little short of 225 millions each year of the decade 1830-1840. The balance of this trade favored Europe generally for as yet the United States had to buy much more than it could sell.

American trade embraced the entire world. The main imports were cloth, iron and other manufactured goods from Europe. But tea from China, coffee from Brazil, sugar from Cuba, cocoa from Central America, fruit from the tropics, spices from the South Sea Islands, and wine from Madeira, and the Canaries, called the ships of American merchants to all ports on the seven seas. They went out laden with domestic food stuffs, lumber and naval stores, tobacco and most particularly cotton for Europe and the rest of the world. In this traffic American merchants made millions.

In the early days of foreign trade a number of seaports located in all the maritime states had shared importance; but conditions had changed. The superior facilities and conveniences supplied by New York City tended to concentrate the bulk of trade at that depot.

Here and in Boston the merchants directed the great fleets which proudly bore the national ensign. The lumber, masts and other naval stores so generously supplied by the forests still gave American shipbuilders a splendid advantage in an age of wooden vessels. Ship-building yards continued to be scattered along the coast, notably in New England. Regular schedules of sailing to and from Europe were organized by ship "lines." The Black Ball Line, for instance, built a fleet of "packets" which sailed regularly between New York and Liverpool. In spite of new styles of building faster ships, passages could not be brought much under two weeks and a half. A beginning had been made in the use of steam for ocean travel when an American vessel, the *Savannah,* crossed in 1819 partly under steam power. Americans were not much interested in this new possibility, however, and the harbors of New York and Boston were more alive than ever with the great canvas wings of packet boats, schooners, brigs and sloops. Boston and Gloucester were busy fishing centers where fleets of boats annually brought great catches of codfish and mackerel. New Bedford, Massachusetts, rose to great prominence as a whaling center. This adventurous chase reached its peak in 1850, when 680 whalers scoured the seas in search of sperm oil and whalebone.

Sailing ships of all kinds brought wealth to their backers and concentrated capital in their home ports. Cities assumed a new importance as financial centers where the capitalists had their headquarters. John Jacob Astor of New York and Stephen Girard of Philadelphia were founding a new dynasty of magnates. The needs of capital meant that a great variety of services would be located in these centers: importing firms, brokers, insurance companies, middlemen of all sorts, transportation directors and bankers.

This increase in business activity naturally reflected itself in the expansion of banking. New York and Boston were the headquarters of powerful and long-established private banks, the Bank of the Manhattan Company and the Suffolk Bank. In Philadelphia, however, in the years 1817-1833, was located the nerve center of American finance, the Second Bank of the United States. After its early disastrous career, 1817-1820, it was saved by the strict and cautious policies of its second president, Langdon Cheves, and under its third executive, Nicholas Biddle, it became strong and prosperous. Biddle succeeded in becoming a financial power who could deal with the rare American millionaires, Girard and Astor. The Second Bank of the United States, with the advantage of government deposits and treasury coöperation, dominated the financial centers growing up in the newly important cities.

The development of strong business centers was not wholly confined to the East. Increasing trade with the western region and the growing movement to and within the West caused towns and cities to spring up in the trans-Appalachian country. Frontier trading-posts and small riverside hamlets became bustling metropolises. New roads and canals produced junction points on the Great Lakes, the Ohio and the Mississippi which soon became cities. In 1840, Cincinnati had 46,000 inhabitants, Pittsburgh 21,000 and St. Louis 16,000 at a time when only five seaboard cities had more than 90,000 population (New York, Philadelphia, Baltimore, New Orleans and Boston). At such points, the West's business activities concentrated; there goods were shipped for distribution among the inhabitants and there the produce of the region was collected to be transported east or south to the ports for Europe.

The Industrial Revolution

Most significant of all the factors which were enlarging cities was the revolution which was bringing American industry nearer the point of meeting the needs of the growing people. The United States was now ready to participate in the Industrial Revolution that had been gathering momentum in Europe. Between 1730 and 1770 machines had been invented in England which had transformed the cloth-making industry from handicraft to machine operation. English manufacturers had introduced the factory system and were running ever increasing aggregations of machines either by water power or by steam which was harnessed by engines invented at this same time. The British had sought to maintain a monopoly of these inventions, but that was impossible.

American enterprise had sought to utilize these new processes when Samuel Slater in 1790 built for his New England backers the first spinning machine in America. The time had not proved ripe, however, because the world was engrossed by the Napoleonic wars. With the coming of peace in 1815, the Industrial Revolution began an uninterrupted march. It crossed the Channel to France and Germany between 1825 and 1850; but it made its most important advance in the United States.

The American industrialists who survived the panic of 1819 were a strong lot. They were in a position to launch new ventures. The industries which transformed themselves most notably were the textile manufactures, and among them the principal advances took place in the cotton group. First of all was the introduction of the power loom. Hitherto power had been used largely for spinning thread, while the finished product had been woven on hand looms, very largely in the homes of people in the vicinity of the spinning machinery. This was all changed in the years after 1815, when spinning and weaving by power-run machinery were first combined in one factory at Waltham. Another technical change in the cotton industry between 1820 and 1830 was the manufacture of print cotton goods. Hitherto American cotton factories had confined themselves largely to the production of coarse sheetings; finer goods with patterns and colors had been either woven by hand or imported. But improved machinery made possible the weaving of finer cotton cloth so it could be sold reasonably, and the use of engraved cylinders run by power enabled manufacturers to produce goods with striking and attractive colored patterns, which gave a much finer appearance than the rather uneven pattern of home-woven goods. Favorable tariff rates helped to set the stage, in New England at least, for a very significant industrial advance.

With the introduction of these technical improvements the profits possible from large-scale production became apparent. To realize these gains it was necessary to purchase and house numerous expensive machines, and to accomplish this corporations had to be formed and factories builded. Prior to this period most American industry had been carried on by individuals or partnerships in small mills. The new ways produced the industrial revolution and a new social phenomenon in the United States, the factory town inhabited in large part by paid workers employed by a corporation and directed by a manager who was also an employee of the corporation. This was a new human relationship in American life. Heretofore most people had been either independent farmers, artisans or merchants, or if they were employees they were in immediate and frequent contact with their employer, who was a master workman or a proprietor, not a corporation. It is significant that as the developing democracy was giving the individual greater economic and political freedom in the West, the factory system of labor should be sponsoring in the East a contrary trend away from economic freedom.

This new system evolved almost exclusively in New England, although it advanced somewhat in the upper Hudson and Mohawk valleys. In New England water power at the falls of the rivers found capital also nearby. In the years following the war of 1812 the relative percentage of capital invested in foreign commerce decreased, although the absolute total grew. So the adventurous turned their hope of profit toward the new manufacturing possibilities. The Merrimack Manufacturing Company was organized in 1822, capitalized at $600,000, and in 1824 opened their first factory. They had acquired the land at the falls and began to sell water-power rights. The labor needed in their own and other Merrimac River factories developed the towns of Lowell and Lawrence, Massachusetts, and Manchester, New Hampshire; and numerous other factory towns grew up at the falls of the New England rivers. However, these corporation projects were only a part, and not a major part, of the growth of the cotton industry in the decade 1820-1830. Most of the cotton was still spun and woven in small mills managed by proprietors. Outside of northern New England the factory system developed slowly, although cotton spinning and weaving multiplied rapidly; between 1820 and 1831 the number of spindles increased four times and the number of factory looms ten times.

A slower but similar evolution can be traced in the woolen industry, on a smaller scale. The supply of raw material, unlike cotton, was never very plentiful, the process of manufacture was more complicated, the machines were more difficult to invent and required more skilled labor to operate. The household system continued and even in 1830, in New York state at least, more woolen cloth was manufactured at home than in factories. Not until 1830, when the Middlesex Company was organized at Lowell, was the day of large production in woolen goods begun, and then it proved a slow growth. The industry continued in a variety of small establishments, each carrying on one or two of its many complicated processes.

In the other important branch of American manufacturing, the metal industry, there was a steady growth closely related to the advance of mechanical civilization. It was not so much that new processes or consolidated organization were developed; the stimulus came rather from the increased demands for iron products. Stoves, steam engines and machines, water and gas-pipes, rafters for larger buildings, all made of metal, were coming into more and general use. The market therefore, called for more pig-iron, and its production area was enlarged. Discoveries of ore were made in the West and furnaces were established in Missouri, in Kentucky near the Ohio River and in Ohio northward to the Hocking Valley. The use of anthracite coal for smelting stimulated the industry greatly in the Pennsylvania river valleys, the Delaware, the Schuylkill and the Lehigh. The amount of pig-iron produced had trebled in twenty years before 1831 and had reached 191,536 tons.

Foundries for turning the pig-iron into cast-iron and steel, engine works and machine shops flourished, not only in New York, New Jersey and Pennsylvania but in the West as well where stationary engine builders were located in Steubenville and Cincinnati, Ohio, and in Louisville, Kentucky, as early as 1820. The center of the Pennsylvania rolling-mill district was at Pittsburgh, while in New England machine shops concentrated near the mills themselves. Some of the larger textile manufacturers maintained their own machine shops, but numerous ingenious individuals either invented machines themselves or bought the patents of others and ran small shops of their own. This great variety of metal manufacture was remarkable more for its increase of production that for any such industrial reorganization or social change as was characteristic of the textile group.

The social readjustments made inevitable by the advances in the textile industries were epoch-making. Labor was necessary to run the machines, and laborers had to live near the factories. This, therefore, brought a concentration of population absolutely foreign to the usual American mode of living. Previously the people, whether in country or town, had been able to command space. Even the poor were not very crowded; though their houses were small, they generally sheltered but one family and possessed a little open ground in front or rear. The ambition and reasonable expectation of a man was to become a householder, even if only a tenant. Factory-building, however, was not matched by individual house-building. Workers attracted to the factories did not find there a house for each family. Life became congested; families lived in a room or two instead of a house; tenements were built closer together in rows, with two or more stories and less open space; adequate sewage was lacking. In this early day there were unmistakable signs of the approach of slum conditions, but the process was gradual.

These unfortunate environments were in part due to the fact that industrial change had appeared suddenly in old towns not prepared for the coming of factories and their operatives. In the New England area, however, a number of communities were built to order at the falls of the rivers and in them some of the difficulties were avoided for a time. Here the tall, brick factory would be built at the river; nearby were constructed rows of small houses on regularly laid out streets which were rented to workers with families. As the mill owners were anxious to attract women operatives who had been expert in spinning and weaving at home and who would work cheaply, dormitories were provided for them with house-mothers, libraries and programs of entertainment. A church and meeting hall were sometimes furnished by the company where religious and social interests might be fostered. Also the employers operated the stores which supplied the workers and reaped profits by carefully controlling prices.

The conveniences of these new towns were strong inducements for young people to come in from the hard labor of the farms where social opportunities were few and money scarce. Cash wages, plenty of company, and even libraries, classes and lectures were eagerly sought. In fact going to a factory town to work was considered by country girls as an educational experience and an introduction to life. Travelers who visited these towns marveled at them and wrote enthusiastically about the happy, healthful and moral life led by the workers. But it was hardly a free existence; the employer dominated even though his paternalism may have seemed very benevolent.

Public safety as well as public health was necessarily of greater concern with the development of slums. Crime and disorder increased and city government was often put to it to preserve order. Day police were practically unknown and the few night watchmen were more for the purpose of detecting fires than of arresting crime. The fire forces were volunteer companies who were socially and politically active but who had none too great concern for public safety. When fires were discovered, they rushed their hand-drawn engines to the scene and quite occasionally were more interested in fighting rival companies than in putting out fires. In the late 1840's New York finally organized a uniformed police force on duty day and night. Boston and Cincinnati introduced paid fire departments. In 1852 the former city established an electric fire-alarm system and the latter metropolis in the next year began the use of steam fire-engines. Urban life was reaching a new stage in the improvement of the standard of living.

The Business Cycle

The new business conditions and the advance of industrialism, combined with the migration into new lands, caused a great era of speculation. Land prices boomed. Thousands invested in new transportation schemes. Bank credit was easy and inflationary. As the Second Bank of the United States had had to wind up its affairs when politics prevented its recharter in 1832, there was no check upon wildcat institutions. Most of the banks were issuing paper money at will.

A further strong stimulant to American business was the interest which foreign capital took in its development. Not only did Americans buy much more than they sold in Europe (the balance against them in the year 1836 was 61 millions) thus insuring active and intimate business relations with European powers, but in borrowing money for speculation the United States paid high rates of interest. So for goods and for loans American businessmen were heavily in debt, especially in England. If Europe did not need her money and in hope of high interest returns was willing to lend more, all would be well. Evidently, however, the whole financial structure was resting too exclusively upon a foundation of very insecure credit. Any slight accident might start a panic. Premonitory warnings had come in 1833-1834 when money became scarce partly because of the restriction of loans by the United States Bank as it was preparing to surrender its national charter (p. 177). In spite of a number of failures and much uncertainty, conditions righted themselves temporarily. The crash was yet to come.

In the two years before 1837 affairs had not been going very well in the business world either in America or in Europe. A bad harvest due to the devastations of the Hessian fly in 1836 caused a scarcity of food in the United States and increased purchases from Europe, making the trade balance turn more heavily against America. A fire in 1835 had burned a large part of New York City, destroying much property and many business records and had produced shortage and uncertainty. Besides, the financial plans of the government were uncertain.

Politics had destroyed the Second Bank of the United States and the funds of the government were deposited in a variety of scattered state banks. Many of these were encouraged by such deposits to emit issues of paper money very far beyond their power to redeem in coin. The administration, alarmed by the rapid expansion in wildcat currency, tried to arrest it and pushed through Congress a law designed to restore gold coins to circulation; but the measure proved ineffective. Also, the President issued an order, known as the specie circular, requiring that all payments for the public lands be made in coin. In addition to this program Congress passed a bill distributing the surplus in the treasury among the states in four installments. The specie circular and the distribution act meant that a good deal of money had to be shipped into the West as 1837 advanced and left too little money in the seaboard banking centers. All these disasters and acts of the government made the unstable credit system all the more uncertain; none of them alone or even all of them together presumably could have caused the severe crisis that was to follow.

In 1837 came a world-wide crash. European banks were alarmed; they made demands upon England. Panic ensued. English banks needed money to meet these calls and began to demand money from those who had borrowed from them. Naturally various firms sought to collect their bills to settle their accounts at the banks or to sell their securities. Many business houses in England had much money tied up in America. The trade balance, so heavily against the United States, now became a subject for British calls; British merchants had to have their money and, besides, could no longer buy cotton. American banks had to send large shipments of gold to England. The banks and foreign trading-houses could not get the money, the price of cotton tumbled, American securities were sent home in large quantities from England to be sold for what they would bring. Like a house of cards the American structure fell. The price of flour due to the shortage of wheat was so high that in February the poor rioted in the streets of New York, demanding bread. In March three important cotton firms in New Orleans which could sell no cotton in England failed and three New York firms likewise suspended, the latter involved to the extent of 9 millions. Then an avalanche of failures followed; by 11 April 128 firms had failed in New York City, thousands were out of work, business ceased. Continual runs on the banks could not be met and by 11 May most banks of the country had suspended specie payment. Neither people nor government had any money and depression was world-wide.

The finely blown and expanded bubble had broken; possessors of money had their faith in easy profits shattered and scrutinized most carefully the possibilities of any proposed purchase or investment. In the East business ceased, banks failed, imports dropped off and manufacturing concerns either stopped work or reduced their output. Many were thrown out of work and extreme poverty and distress were all too prevalent. In the South many planters failed and their lands and slaves came upon the market at ruinously low prices. Cotton was not purchased in the great quantity needed before the panic and the price fell. The West was last to experience the panic and the longest to suffer from it. Not until the demand for crops at harvest time proved to be small did the people of this section feel the full force of the crash. There was little money and no demand for the large crops. Farmers could not sell their produce nor could they pay their taxes or their debts. Even barter was resorted to because the paper of many of the banks was practically worthless. Now the ambitious schemes of state finance and public improvement seemed like great burdens, reduced tax receipts could meet neither interest nor principal charges and defaulting seemed the only way out. General business and financial stagnation had taken the place of the vigorous optimism that had previously made every risk seem to be a good one.

After a period of uncertainty lasting over a year, confidence was sufficiently restored to cause the better banks to seek an agreement for the general return to specie payments. By summer of 1838 they succeeded and there occurred a renewed outbreak of reckless speculation. Land sales doubled in a year and foreign credit, or at least buying abroad, spurted ahead. The hard times in England had so reduced the price of goods there as to attract American buyers. A shortage in the cotton crop also permitted its owners to force the price up and they hoped to profit much thereby. However, England was in such financial condition that her manufacturers would not pay the high price and much cotton lay in British warehouses unsold. In the meantime in England there had been bad harvests in 1838 and she had been compelled to buy much food from continental Europe and needed gold with which to pay for it. English business thereupon instead of taking cotton in exchange for large American purchases, refused the cotton and demanded specie. As much as 30 millions in gold had to be exported and the banks became so straitened in 1839 that by October most banks had again suspended specie payment. Business was once more in a state of collapse and financial conditions became so bad that in the next few years at least eight states defaulted on interest payments and Mississippi repudiated a bond issue on the ground that it was illegal. A temporary return to specie payment was attempted by the banks in 1841 but it was hardly undertaken before most of the institutions had to stop once more. In 1842 the sounder banks tried resumption, some under compulsion of state law, but it was not until 1844 that credit was easy and banks could deal confidently.

In the meantime while these deplorable conditions were causing much distress, there were many demands for government interference, and the political leaders of state and nation were called upon to satisfy them. Inability to meet such importunities was disastrous to many a politician. The state legislatures hastened in some instances to pass stay laws and exemption laws and other measures which would make it unnecessary for debtors to pay their obligations immediately. Bankrupt laws were enacted to make it possible for those hopelessly involved to be relieved of their debts, and in the western states, where the state debts were so tremendous, there was frequent demand for repudiation. Also laws were passed regulating banking more strictly and compelling banks which could not pay specie to go out of business. When specie payment had been so long deferred, especially in 1841-1842, a number of laws were passed to make banks resume or stop functioning. In at least one case banks were deprived of the note-issuing privilege. Simultaneously demands were made upon the government to assume the state debts, to recommence distributing the surplus revenue and to pass a general bankruptcy law. Opposition politicians began agitation for a re-charter of the national bank and the enactment of a protective tariff. Such demands focused attention upon Congress and national politics.

The President and Congress could do little to aid recovery. The time was not ripe for government aid. Politics prevented such programs from meeting real success save in raising the tariff in the act of 1842. Behind this political opposition was a belief then prevalent that conditions would right themselves if there were no government interference.

Since government action could do little to aid in the quest for recovery, the natural force of the people and the boundless resources at their command had to overcome the effects of the disaster. A new mode of transportation gave opportunity for profit and surplus labor. As early as 1815 there had been a scheme for the use of rails invented by John Stevens in New Jersey, but not until 1822 did Pennsylvania grant a railroad charter and not until 1830 was a railroad actually put into operation when the Baltimore and Ohio and the Charleston and Hamburg began the use of locomotives on their track. The development of this form of transit was slow and by 1837 only 1,500 miles had been built.

In the years following the panic, however, this mode of transportation became more popular as its utiilty was demonstrated and by 1850, some 9,000 miles had been constructed. The freight-hauling possibilities now developed by this new means, both in respect to quantity and speed, were in the course of revolutionizing internal business. The paths of commerce need no longer follow watercourses or be subject to the slow monotony of canal progress—rails could be laid almost anywhere and paths directed arbitrarily to suit the needs or whims of man. So a new interest entered business, and as its initial demands were heavy, a new mobilization of capital was called for. A new habit had to be learned by Americans, namely, rail travel, and they did not learn it easily. Early railroads were dangerous, uncomfortable and uncertain. Their early construction and equipment were often faulty and badly managed, so that accidents were all too frequent. However, the railroad had come to stay and its possibilities stimulated anew the vision of American business. When the telegraph was perfected in 1844 the annihilation of space and time can be fairly said to have begun.

The expansion of the iron industry was closely connected with railroading in stimulating business recovery. New processes made possible a greater and better output. Hot blasts, the use of coal for fuel, refining processes such as puddling and rolling were revolutionizing the technique. The use of stoves, furnaces, gas-light and plumbing continued to increase. New machines were constantly being invented; most important were those to expedite the manufacture of clothing and shoes, such as the sewing machine and pegging machines. The railroads needed locomotives and miles and miles of iron for the ever lengthening lines of tracks.

Thus while Americans were expanding their population over vast regions, they were likewise concentrating their energies in bolder enterprises which were laying the foundation for the great industrial future of the nation.

CHAPTER XV

THE ADVANCE OF DEMOCRACY

The great movements of population, expanding westward and concentrating in cities, were pointing the way to the achievement of political democracy. From the early days of colonial experience some form of self-government had been seemingly inevitable. Two hundred years and more of experiment were necessary, however, before its precise character was to take shape. By successive steps it had advancd in the direction of political democracy. First each locality had undertaken to manage its own concerns and to send representatives to participate in governing the colony. Then the colonies had undertaken to band together for independence and had organized a federal system. Throughout this evolution, the question of whether these self-governing communities were to be politically democratic, that is, whether all men were to be considered equally entitled to vote and to hold office, was left unanswered. Vestiges of old ideas of property and religious qualifications remained on into the nineteenth century. But social change directed the onward march toward a fuller realization of the implications of a democratic experiment.

The Spread of Manhood Suffrage

As people went westward and formed new states, they made new constitutions. In the western country there were few great differences in wealth; most of the pioneers were in much the same state of poverty and hope. Naturally under such conditions there was no place for political distinction; all were equally capable of bearing the responsibility of voting or governing. The new states of the days after the War of 1812, Indiana, Illinois, Alabama and Missouri, provided white manhood suffrage, though Mississippi clung to a tax provision. The tide of democracy was beginning to swell.

In the East, as well, changing conditions, especially in the growing cities, were adding their influence to the progress of political democracy. As more people flocked together in towns and cities, property became increasingly unsatisfactory as a qualification for suffrage. The large number disfranchised in the cities began to demand the vote and politicians, quick to see the advantage to them if these people were made voters, added their voice; city political leaders wanted large followings with which to defeat the rural vote. The example set by the West also was encouraging; the contest with aristocracy was on.

In 1818 conservative Connecticut made her suffrage qualifications more liberal, and two years later Massachusetts did the same, although neither went to the extent of giving the franchise to all men. The climax came when in 1821 New York state capitulated and granted universal manhood suffrage; even free Negroes were permitted to vote if they possessed property. Other states followed and male political democracy came into actual practice. No longer could aristocratic landholders and merchants retain their former influence. For all there was liberty and equality, if not fraternity. During these years the popular vote increased enormously. In round numbers a vote that had been 1,150,000 in the presidential election of 1828 had become 2,400,000 in 1840, though not all of this increase was caused by the broadening franchise, for the population itself was enlarging rapidly and swelling the number of voters.

Elections, too, became more important and interesting. When the first state constitutions were made the country was suspicious of executives; the experience with royal governors was still fresh. Consequently, most power was placed in the hands of the legislature and governors were often permitted powers purely nominal and were chosen by the legislature rather than by direct vote; to the representatives also was given the selection of the judiciary. The onrush of democracy, however, changed this procedure; legislatures, too, had been found to be fickle and unstable. As a result, there was a strengthening of the executive as a curb on the legislature and the people were entrusted with more electoral power. Not only did they choose legislators and congressmen, but they now began to elect state officers and even the judiciary. With the growing interest in elections and the increasing number of voters, political machinery had to be devised to meet the more complex conditions entering politics.

The old-fashioned personal politics was no longer possible. Communities were growing too large; candidates could no longer be known to everyone and judged on the basis of personal impression and community gossip. State-wide campaigns for gubernatorial and other offices made new machinery necessary. First of all, the choice of candidates had to be systematized. The informal method of announcing a candidacy by public notice would not suffice; state and local conventions of delegates from political subdivisions such as wards, towns or counties met together to choose candidates. Pennsylvania and Massachusetts had early developed this method and by 1835 it was in general use, usually superseding informal meetings of citizens or legislators known as caucuses. These conventions designated committees to do the work of promoting the interests of the candidates whom they had chosen, and elaborate organizations of ward, town, county and state committees came into being. This tendency to committee and convention organization was hastened by a rebirth of partisanship.

New Partisanship

The old Federalist and Democratic-Republican parties could hardly be called parties in the light of modern practice. They were too informal in their organization, and their methods were suited only to small communities and a sparse electorate. Also they had lost any true spirit of rivalry. The Federalists scarcely functioned after the War of 1812, but differences of opinion had not been abolished, nor was ambition dead. A new generation was arising which rather impatiently awaited the retirement of the fathers who had made the government. When James Monroe's term expired there was bound to be a struggle for the succession. New parties were not to be established immediately, but these rivalries were to fit in with the changing conditions of society in shaping a new political order.

These differences were in large part arising from the fact that the United States was in the grip of two great and divergent forces. As we have seen the population was dispersing into the great frontier regions, but it was also concentrating in urban centers. These two movements bred opposing interests, contrary demands upon government which constantly renewed a continuing political debate. Much thinking, writing and speaking engaged the energy of a variety of politically minded citizens. Their thoughts were generally phrased in terms of a definition of the powers of government. Those who wanted aid from the national treasury used the persuasive logic of broad federal power created by Hamilton. Those in opposition spoke in the terms of strict construction of the Constitution and the reserved rights of the states formulated by Jefferson. These issues showed that the conflict between states' rights and the new nationalism was broader than just the slavery issue.

The most controversial of these questions was the tariff. The new industrialists wanted protective duties so that they would be free from fear of competition from Europe, particularly from England. On the other hand, the agricultural states in the South knew that if such things as American cloth, which they needed to clothe their slaves, were protected, they would have to pay much higher prices than if they were free to buy at European prices, which were much cheaper. They protested vehemently, and both the industrialists and the southern planters were sufficiently influential to gain powerful support in Congress. The tariff passed in 1816 was mildly protective when passed and was not materially changed until 1824. In the meantime, Henry Clay of Kentucky had come forward as a presidential candidate. He pushed protection on the ground that it aided western farmers as well as eastern capitalists. He argued: factory workers can not raise their own food; they must buy from the farmer; therefore, the bigger the factories the bigger the home market for foodstuffs and the greater the farmer's prosperity. The bill he sponsored raised rates slightly and secured passage in 1824.

Four years later a proposal for another revision upward raised a storm of protest. The falling price of cotton in the years since 1815 had placed the southern planters in an increasingly unhappy frame of mind and in South Carolina in particular much complaint was heard against protection. By this time southern leaders, notably John C. Calhoun of South Carolina, were convinced that the increased costs imposed upon their section by these duties were a heavy charge upon their income. They made strenuous but unsuccessful efforts to defeat the tariff of 1828, which raised the protective rates above those of 1824. They made it clear that this "tariff of abominations" would be the last tariff of this type that they would tolerate. The legislature discussed a report, written by Calhoun, known as the "South Carolina Exposition" which vigorously presented the case for state sovereignty and the right of a state to protect itself against such a law by nullifying it. Despite their resistance, another measure just as distasteful was passed in 1832.

By this time political parties had been reorganized. When James Monroe's successor was to be chosen in 1824, several candidates had appeared. Three of them, Clay, Calhoun and General Andrew Jackson of Tennessee, the hero of New Orleans, were to make party history later but alike lost to a fourth, John Quincy Adams, son of President John Adams, who was elected over his nearest competitor, Andrew Jackson. Jackson and his friends immediately started to organize a party to defeat Adams in 1828. They put forward Jackson as a hero and a man of the people representing the new West. He had immense popular appeal and he easily defeated Adams in 1828. He represented the new spirit of democracy, and his party soon became known by that name, shortened from the "Democratic-Republican" used by Jefferson and his followers.

Jackson's election raised a series of controversial issues, including the tariff. Henry Clay of Kentucky, who undertook to lead the opposition to Jackson, proclaimed his belief in an "American system." He advocated government subsidies to local improvements, the re-chartering of the Bank of the United States and a protective tariff. He tried to maneuver Jackson into positions where he would have to declare himself on all of these issues. Clay and his friends secured the passage of the Maysville Road bill, which was an internal improvement measure, a bill re-chartering the Bank of the United States and the above-men-

HENRY CLAY

(By Theodore Sydney Moise, courtesy of the Metropolitan Museum of Art.)

tioned tariff of 1832. Jackson met these issues squarely. He vetoed the road bill and the Bank bill; the former because he did not think the Constitution permitted such grants and the latter because he thought the bank was interfering in politics, particularly against himself in favor of his opponents. These vetoes aroused financial and speculative interests against him, but the Bank veto was popular with the masses, who thought the Bank an oppressive institution, checking western growth. On the other hand, Jackson signed the tariff bill, partly because he and Calhoun, its chief opponent, were enemies and partly because he was indifferent on the subject. His general course won popular applause. Despite Clay's efforts to mobilize speculative and financial interests against him in a short-lived party, the National Republicans, and despite the opposition of Calhoun's southern planter interest, Jackson was triumphantly reëlected in 1832.

Then storm clouds rose in the South. The price of cotton was still low; in South Carolina there was still general indignation. In Georgia, Virginia and Mississippi, also, there had been gestures of protest. South Carolina, therefore, thought the time ripe for action. Consequently, her legislature called a convention to meet in November 1832. This convention passed a Nullification ordinance which proclaimed South Carolina's refusal to obey the law. The legislature was then reconvened and measures were passed protecting the citizens of the state from any penalties which the federal government might seek to impose for disobedience of federal law. The legislators likewise strengthened the military force.

What course would Jackson pursue? He was a soldier and used to command; never had he permitted his authority to be questioned. Now a state was attempting wholesale disobedience to a law which it was his duty to enforce; moreover the leader in the nullification was Calhoun, whom he thoroughly disliked. Less than a month therefore after the South Carolina convention the President issued a proclamation to the effect that "disunion by armed force is treason" and in the meantime sent soldiers and warships to Charleston. Thereupon he asked Congress for a "force act" to give him adequate powers. While rebellion and armed conflict were thus threatening, the politicians, notably Clay, Calhoun and Webster, were working to restore harmony by compromise.

South Carolina had found little sympathy in the other southern states, rather to her chagrin, and was in a position too uncomfortable to be maintained. Seemingly, therefore, all groups welcomed a dignified way out and the result was the enactment of a law reducing the tariff by slow stages over a period of ten years at the same time that the force act was passed. This Compromise Tariff of 1833 provided that by 1842 duties should be on a 20 per cent basis; every two years, beginning with 1834, 10 per cent of all duties in excess of 20 per cent should be removed; 1 January 1842 half of the remaining excess should be dropped and on 1 July 1842 the 20 per cent level should become general. Jackson had acted vigorously and had confounded his enemies once more. The advocates of the American system, the defenders of states' rights and Jackson's personal foes, however, were not through fighting and neither was Jackson. The Bank again became the object of the President's wrath.

Jackson's veto of the bill re-chartering the Bank and the failure of Congress to override that veto plainly informed all men that after 1836 the institution would cease to exist. Jackson, however, was not content to permit it to wind up its affairs in its own way. He became

THE BANK RACE
(An Anti-Jackson Cartoon.)

convinced that it was a wise policy to take from it all government money. The loss of this sum—about 9 millions, could not but cause the Bank to restrict its operations. Jackson decided, therefore, to cease depositing money in the Bank and gradually check out the government funds already there as the treasury needed to spend the money. His secretary of the treasury, Roger B. Taney, therefore made the order 26 September 1833, and the Bank suffered the consequences. Jackson's dominating qualities had again been demonstrated.

The politicians hopeful of Old Hickory's downfall were now ready for another attempt at organizing the rather incongruous opposition. Clay's scheme of appealing to national economic interests by organizing the National Republican party on the platform of the American system had not proved successful. Many who were in opposition to Jackson did not like the system, especially the states' rights advocates in the

South who, like Calhoun, were vigorously opposed to a tariff for protection. Some broader appeal, some more general organization, must be effected. A new issue with a more alluring program than benefits to the rich must be found if the popular imagination was to be weaned away from the people's idol. In various localities, therefore, notably in New York, in preparing for the spring elections of 1834 the opponents of Jackson made a vigorous attack upon his methods of ruling, upon his arbitrary and peculiarly Jacksonian tactics. Such policies, declared his enemies, were tyrannical, just as tyrannical as those of George III. As protest and even revolution had been necessary in 1776 to protect American rights from monarchical oppression, so now in 1834 the arbitrary rule of King Andrew I should be checked. In 1776 those who had risen to protect American liberties were called Whigs; now in 1834 a new group of Whigs must appear for the same purpose. In this manner a new party had its origin, but it was not sufficiently united to form a national group until 1839. Meanwhile, it contented itself with various local victories, and bided its time.

The defeat of Jackson's Democratic party was finally accomplished by the Whigs in 1840, through means typical of the workings of American political democracy. Jackson's hold on popular favor was so great in 1836 that he was able then to ensure the presidential nomination and election of his warm supporter and favorite, Vice-President Martin Van Buren. Unluckily for Van Buren, he struck many snags, the worst of which was the serious panic of 1837. The inability of the Democratic administration to alleviate that catastrophe encouraged a popular revolt in 1840. The mass of the voters turned to the Whig candidate, General William Henry Harrison, "Old Tippecanoe," as he was called because of his victory over the Indians. After an hilarious campaign, in which hard cider played more part than cold logic, the Whig hero was overwhelmingly elected. Since then, there has been only one instance (1876) when a ruling party has secured a presidential election after a major panic.

These contests of the so-called Jacksonian era of political partisanship and democracy had come to full flower in a fashion prophetic of future American political experience. The populace had the votes, and appeals varying from sound argument to crude emotionalism, augmented sometimes by mob coercion, bribery and the rule of bosses, all appeared in this epoch; and the desirable and undesirable features of the new era flourished side by side.

The Spirit of Reform

There was more to the quality of American democracy than the machinery of universal male political participation. The Americans

Andrew Jackson

(By Thomas Sully, courtesy of the Historical Society of Pennsylvania.)

wished to make their democracy an instrument for social betterment. Prone as Americans were to consider their institutions superior to those of the rest of the world, they were nevertheless keen to seek their improvement. Many realized that in spite of democratic progress there were many weaknesses and inequalities which could urge the altruistic to more vigorous thinking. Such thought, indeed, had become a custom; it was a colonial inheritance. Now it was intensified to a degree that was to have momentous consequences.

The strength of religious interest had much to do with these strivings for social improvement. Though the rationalism which marked the revolutionary period had somewhat undermined the strength of religion inherited from colonial days, the turn of the century brought a reaction and a quickening of religious faith. The revivals of those years following 1800 were heralds of the new interest and similar manifestations marked the period, 1825-1830.

The survival of anti-slavery zeal stemmed from religious interest and was intensified by the growing spirit of democracy and nationalism. The inconsistency between slavery and the principles of democracy had long been apparent and social disapproval had been manifest throughout the country in the first years of independence. However, the move for its abandonment was arrested by the increasing importance of cotton growing after the invention of the cotton gin; thereafter it was prized more highly and its use extended. With the advent of the reforming spirit in the 'twenties and 'thirties, the attention of many quickened consciences was fixed upon slavery as an evil to be eradicated.

The campaign against it was pushed by many. The Quaker influence remained strong, and new allies were stirred to enthusiasm as the urge was given impetus from Great Britain. There, an emancipation movement under such men as Wilberforce was growing so strong that it procured in 1833 an act of Parliament abolishing slavery in the British West Indies. In America rejuvenation of the movement had followed hard upon the Missouri Compromise. In 1821 Benjamin Lundy established in Ohio his paper, the *Genius of Universal Emancipation,* which he moved to Baltimore three years later. In 1822 the Colonization Society established on the middle coast of Africa its Negro migration settlement, appropriately named Liberia; occasionally it transported thither a few Negroes, and although the futility of such a plan became increasingly evident, the American branches of this Society by 1828 attained the respectable number of ninety-eight. Activity in anti-slavery societies generally was such that they had reached the number of 101 two years later; significantly enough, 66 of these were in northerly slave states—41 in North Carolina, 23 in Tennessee and 2 in Virginia.

The decade of the 1830's witnessed a great quickening of the movement. In the late 'twenties there had been a revival of religion, particularly in New York state; and the philanthropic capitalists, Arthur and Lewis Tappan, had supported generously an evangelist, Charles G. Finney. The Tappans, through English connections, were interested in the British Abolition Society and wished to organize one in America. They aroused Theodore D. Weld, an associate and convert of Finney's; and these four with their friends met in New York in 1831 to plan an American society. Deciding that more groundwork was essential, particularly in the Ohio Valley, they sent Weld thither to canvass and develop enthusiasm. He found the field ripe in the valley, both north and south of the river. There he met a number of men, most of them clergymen, who had been trained by anti-slavery ministers from the South, whom he was able to enlist in an enthusiastic preaching campaign against the sin of slavery. In Kentucky and in Ohio clergymen, educators and lawyers took up the work.

Most tardy of all the sections to become interested was New England. Benjamin Lundy had attempted work here but did not meet success until he enlisted a young Boston printer, William Lloyd Garrison, to accompany him to Baltimore in 1829 to help publish the *Genius of Universal Emancipation*. In the course of their experience Garrison was put in jail; released but not repentant, he went back to Boston to start a newspaper of his own, the *Liberator*. First published 1 January 1831, its career began and continued in a highly inflammatory style. It denounced slaveholders as most sinful and depraved, painted in lurid terms the sufferings of the slaves and called loudly for revolt and abolition. As Garrison sent his paper to a large number of southern editors, and as some Virginia slaves under Nat Turner at this time sought to rebel, Boston seemed all too near Richmond. The South, and some in the North, attributed the uprising to the influence of the *Liberator* and Garrison was denounced violently. No worse calamity than such an uprising could southern plantation owners picture. They knew too well what had happened under similar circumstances in the island of Haiti in the 1790's and they were fearful of a duplication of such frightful scenes of fire, murder and worse. Nat Turner's attempt failed utterly, but it awoke apprehensions that would not slumber. Hearing rumors of Garrison's violent abolition propaganda, southerners feared lest his ideas be heard and understood by the slaves and arouse them to serious attempts at rebellion. Many in the North were cool toward anti-slavery because they felt it was incendiary and violent, destructive of property.

It was just at this point that the Tappans and their friends concluded that the time was ripe for an American association. Garrison joined them, somewhat to their dismay, and in December 1833 they formed the American Anti-Slavery Society. Weld and his backers soon organized the Middle West on an even more effective basis, appointing a committee of seventy to travel and preach. Elijah P. Lovejoy started a paper in southern Illinois at Alton.

The American Anti-Slavery Society issued pamphlets and books, aided periodicals, deluged Congress with petitions and for a time grew in numbers. Abolitionists were subjected to vigorous counterattacks. They were charged with disturbing the peace, inciting to riot and promoting Negro uprisings. Their fanaticism was branded as socially dangerous, and in various places, even in the North, conservative members of society attempted to put them down by force. In Boston in 1835 Garrison was attacked by a mob and barely escaped. Even women were subject to indignity, for in 1833 Miss Prudence Crandall, who was trying to keep a school for Negroes at Canterbury, Connecticut, was put in prison.

The zeal of the opponents of slavery carried them to the point of denying the laws of property which protected slaveowners. An organized system of assisting fugitive slaves was perfected, known as the "Underground Railway." This was not a railroad, but a method of receiving slaves in private homes along the roads from the border states to Canada, hiding them by day and then carrying them to the next "station" by night. The routes ran principally through Pennsylvania, New York and Ohio and the "conductors" gave guidance, protection and transportation to many of the 2,000 slaves who annually between 1830 and 1860 broke their bonds.

Such tactics on both sides were bound to rouse resentment and divide communities. Politicians, and even clergymen, began vigorously to defend the institution as a benevolent and paternal order which brought happiness and Christian salvation to the slave, prosperity to the South and leisure to its intelligent class to ponder the great problems of democracy and culture.

Such extremes were dangerous, however, and a third group active in business and politics strove to keep the peace. Businessmen were anxious to keep the matter out of politics, and politicians like Clay and Webster were ever ready to promote compromises when flames of controversy over slavery burned too fiercely. Though the South was united in defense of its system, the North was by no means so uniform in opposition. While many were opposed to slavery and vigorously denounced any attempt to extend the system, relatively few were actual abolitionists in the sense of demanding immediate and unconditional eradication of the hated institution. On the other hand, the great mass was generally indifferent and the South had many friends who resented these bitter attacks and defended their countrymen from the charges of inhumanity. The question was constantly agitated from pulpit, press and platform during the 1830's. The northern conscience and the southern conviction both were being goaded into action.

A New Sense of Nationalism

The conflicting interests not only showed themselves in the political and reform activity of the time but had a decided influence upon the developing legal institutions of the republic. The growth of business brought a stream of cases before the Supreme Court which gave that body numerous opportunities to define the extent of federal power. What views would the federal judiciary take? Would they seek to protect contracts and federal institutions even to the extent of assuming to review the work of state legislatures and the decisions of state courts? Would they uphold the broad exercise of power by Congress or would they seek to confine it to the narrow bonds of strict construction? If wide perogative were allowed the federal government, the influence of the populous cities would be greater; whereas if the bulk of power were conceded to rest with the states, the rural districts would dominate.

The course of Marshall and the majority of his associates on the supreme bench left no doubt whatever in the minds of observers. In a series of decisions Marshall extended the functions of the federal judiciary to the limit, and beyond the express words of the Constitution. Any question embracing the constitutionality of any law, congressional or state, or any decision of a state court dealing with interpretation of the federal Constitution might be reviewed and approved or annulled by the federal judiciary. Under Chief Justice Marshall between 1809 and 1824 fourteen acts of the legislatures of eleven states were declared void, generally because they impaired the obligation of contract. Also decisions of the highest state courts, to the consternation of many states' rights advocates, were reviewed and reversed. The Chief Justice ruled in favor of loose construction and sustained the broad assumption of power by Congress. As a result of these decisions, businessmen and capitalists felt that in the federal courts there was recourse from the vagaries of popularly elected state legislatures swayed by bursts of radical opinion. They further saw in the large policies of government aid possible under a Constitution loosely construed, hope of accelerated advance and prosperity. It is of no small significance that, in a time of uncertainty as to the permanence of the Union when the agricultural demand for states rights and laissez-faire was strong, growing business was learning the increasing advantage of powerful federal government and the benefits of federal legislation and federal judicial interpretation.

Marshall's decisions were the subject of continuous controversy and the rural regions anticipated with apprehension the possibility of urban domination. They appealed vigorously to ancient pride in locality, to states' rights and sought to keep the idea of state sovereignty in vigorous circulation. But a new sense of unity was ever growing more potent. Not only was it emotionally appealing but it had a very practical source of strength. American nationality, the Union, was a valuable and effective instrument for the welfare, power, and wealth of the United States. As Daniel Webster phrased it in his reply to Calhoun's colleague, Hayne:

> It is to that Union we owe our safety at home and our consideration and dignity abroad. It is to that Union that we are chiefly indebted for whatever makes us most proud of our country. That Union we reached only by the discipline of our virtue in the severe school of adversity. It had its origin in the necessities of disordered finance, prostrate commerce, and ruined credit. Under its benign influence these great interests immediately awoke as from the dead, and sprang forth with newness of life. Every year of its duration has teemed with fresh proofs of its utility and its blessings, and although our territory has stretched out wider and wider, and our population spread farther and farther, they have not outrun its protection or its benefits. It has been to us all a copious fountain of national, social and personal happiness.... Liberty and Union, now and forever, one and inseparable.

A sense of nationality, of Union, was in the process of evolving, but it was to be of slow growth. Its perfection was to be hindered and even its existence threatened by the conflict of interests arising from the contrary forces of dispersion and concentration, but in the meantime fear of danger was hidden under the great hope of indefinite progress which was being constantly promoted.

Popular Education—The Hope of Democracy

The most fitting instrument to promote this confidence in future improvement was wider and better education. If the United States were to prove the hope of the world, the largest possible number of intelligent and educated citizens was the great goal. Universal education of at least a primary grade became a real possibility. Gradually the idea that free education was charity fit only for the poverty-stricken was dispelled, and property owners were converted to the idea of being taxed to pay for teaching other people's children. The New England states had been forerunners in this move and all but Rhode Island had some form of free education carried over from the colonial period or established shortly after independence. The new western states followed New England.

Free education was less developed in the middle states, and least of all in the South. The scattered character of the agricultural population in the latter section made district organization for free education

Daniel Webster
(Daguerreotype, courtesy of Richard H. Shryock.)

impossible at that time, so the real battle for increase in public schools was fought in the middle states. In the populous centers of these states the growth of cities, the demands of labor and the increase in the number of voters combined to enhance the strength of the advocates. In Pennsylvania a law was at length achieved in 1834, although it exempted from its provisions those communities who by popular vote refused consent. In New York, where for some time localities had been permitted to tax themselves for free schools, a general law was enacted in 1849 after a favorable referendum, only to be modified after the voters expressed themselves less favorably the next year. Thereafter the schools were partly supported by general taxes and partly by assessments on parents whose children were being educated. Not until 1867 were the schools of New York State entirely free and tax-supported. The struggle had to be continued, and on a wider front, for the laws in the New England and the Western states were not always carried out. In spite of the reverse in New York, by 1850 the idea of public schools was gaining strength and 80 per cent of the population had some sort of compulsory primary education. Though there were between 50,000 and 60,000 primary schools in session anywhere from six weeks to eight months each year, still there were at least a million illiterates. The United States had achieved an "educational consciousness," however. It was to be the bulwark of the new American democracy and the propagandist of nationalism.

CHAPTER XVI
TO THE PACIFIC

The adventurous Americans had never been content with their boundaries. To the west and southwest were Oregon, California and Texas, and American ambition stretched to the Pacific shore. Many believed that it was the "Manifest Destiny" of the United States to absorb these regions. Some force did seem pressing the United States forward. Such restlessness contributed much to the hunger for great possessions which was so openly manifest in the America of the 'forties. In all directions American eyes were turned toward the borders which might prove elastic, and there they found much to fix attention. There was some concern over Maine's northeastern boundary, which was one of the questions settled by the Webster-Ashburton treaty of 1842, but the more vital interest lay in Oregon and Texas.

Oregon and Texas

As early as 1829 it became apparent to a few, at least, that the best way to secure Oregon was to settle it with Americans. Several colonization schemes were proposed, but the missionaries to the Indians accomplished the most. The Methodist and the Presbyterian churches sent out Jason and Daniel Lee, Samuel Parker and Marcus Whitman, and their work among the aborigines was supplemented by that of a government agent sent there in 1837. In the meantime, Senator Linn of Missouri began a long campaign to persuade Congress to take action to save this territory to the nation.

The failure of the Webster-Ashburton negotiations to include Oregon led in 1843 to numerous public meetings, some quantities of resolutions and more emigrants. John C. Frémont came home with a vivid account, which was published, of his explorations in that region. The Oregon trail became a reality to a new generation of pioneers. But Oregon to the British was Hudson's Bay Company territory and American settlers found that the company's agent, Dr. John McLaughlin, was in command of the region at his post at the junction of the Columbia and Willamette rivers. The factor was an able officer, gifted with tact and a friendly disposition; therefore trouble was avoided, but it was quite apparent to the emigrants from the United States that he considered the company's position permanent. Because of his location, hardly any

Americans went beyond the Columbia river. In the meantime, Great Britain made conciliatory moves. The Oregon question might be settled amicably, though there was much bellicose talk of "protecting" American rights.

The Columbia and Willamette valleys by no means absorbed the expansive energies of the United States, for at the same time there was pressure toward the southwest as well. Even before Oregon attracted

TRAILS BEYOND THE MISSISSIPPI

popular attention, there was talk of Texas. Men with vision in the Southwest looked covetously upon the fertile soil of the river valleys in the Texan plain. After the panic of 1819 had destroyed his business, Moses Austin, then of St. Louis, sought a way to restore his wealth by settling in this portion of the Spanish Empire. Because of political friends, Spain yielded to his request and made the grant. Before he could carry out his scheme, he died, but his son Stephen took up the venture and when the Spanish government was overthrown and Mexico became independent in 1821, he obtained confirmation of the grant from the new government, which wanted the help of American settlers in maintaining its newly acquired independence. Austin therefore became the first of a number of "empresarios," as they were called. These men contracted to bring settlers who were to become Mexican and Catholic and who were to receive grants of land for their livelihood. From 1821 onward a stream of emigrants went from the United States into Mexican Texas. Most failed to become Catholic and none seemed to lose their American identity. Inevitably as they became stronger and more numerous and showed more independence, Mexico grew fearful.

In 1830 when the Mexican government inaugurated a series of restrictions, political and economic, trouble was fast on its way. New tariff regulations were put into effect to force Texans to buy in Mexico rather than over the border in Louisiana. Then Texas, in common with the other Mexican states, was stripped of power by Santa Anna when he converted the Republic into a military despotism, and Stephen Austin himself was imprisoned. Conditions were too much like those preceding 1776. These sons of the American Revolution followed the example of their fathers. In 1836 the Texans defeated Mexican armed forces led by Santa Anna and became independent. Almost immediately they sought annexation to the United States, but without success. Texas was a slaveholding area and that fact caused many in the North to oppose the acquisition of such a large addition to the southern system, so no action was taken in regard to Texas except to recognize the Lone Star republic as an independent nation. For some five years little American attention was vouchsafed the new neighbor.

In these roaring 'forties anti-British prejudices arose once more in all their venom. Great Britain recognized the independence of Texas and sent a commercial agent to California. News of these actions immediately awakened American suspicions which were further aroused when it became apparent that Great Britain was interested in Texas cotton and so was trying to arrange with Mexico to recognize Texas and to cease the intermittent warfare which was characteristic of the border. This latter move was especially unpalatable to the South because it was understood that Great Britain was urging Texas to abolish slavery in return for Mexican recognition. President John Tyler and his secretary of state, John C. Calhoun, both ardent southerners, proslavery and anti-British, finally decided to accept a renewed proffer of annexation and signed a treaty to that effect with Texas, just as the presidential nominations were being made in 1844. Enough northern senators voted against the treaty to defeat its ratification, but sentiment in various quarters for annexation had been aroused and was not to be denied.

In the maneuvering preliminary to the nominating conventions, the two most prominent candidates, Martin Van Buren, Democrat, and Henry Clay, Whig, had announced publicly their opposition to annexation. The friends of Texas, especially those in the Democratic party, consequently began to work for the defeat of Van Buren and united the question of Oregon with the Texas issue. British designs on the Columbia Valley must be defeated; the United States must have all of Oregon. The campaign efforts of these expansionists succeeded and James K. Polk, not Martin Van Buren, became the Democratic nominee. "Reoccupation (of Oregon) and Reannexation" (of Texas) became the slogan, occasionally enlivened by the more bellicose "54-40 or Fight" which indicated a determination to own all of Oregon. A vigorous campaign elected Polk over Clay by a very narrow margin and when Congress came together in December 1844 it hastened to annex Texas by joint resolution which required the approval of only a majority in Congress rather than the two-thirds vote of the Senate necessary for the ratification of a treaty. In 1845 therefore, Texas became a state.

Thus when Polk entered the White House, he found Texas on the way into the Union and Mexico so hostile that he must turn his close attention to her. No sooner was he inaugurated than the Mexican minister demanded his passport in protest and left Washington without a Mexican representative in residence. The problem then faced by Polk was four-sided. There was imminent danger that the southern republic might attempt to regain Texas by force; if she did not, she at least would insist that the southern boundary of Texas was the Nueces River, rather than the Rio Grande; she might sell or mortgage California to Great Britain; since 1843 she had made no payments on her indebtedness to the United States, acknowledged in a treaty of 1838. Polk determined upon a vigorous handling of these four problems.

First of all, he would ask Mexico to negotiate—for the recognition of the Rio Grande as the southern boundary, for settlement of the debts by territorial cessions instead of cash, and for sale of New Mexico and California. So he made inquiries as to whether his minister would be received and, when answered in the affirmative, he sent John Slidell to Mexico City. In the second place, Polk made military and naval preparations. To protect the Rio Grande as the boundary of Texas, he sent General Zachary Taylor with an army, instructed to enter as soon as Texas assented to annexation. To make certain of California, he appointed Thomas O. Larkin of Monterrey to be his confidential agent there to watch for discontent against the Mexican authority. He saw to it that an adequate fleet was off the Pacific shore with orders to seize California if war broke out. Incidentally, he permitted Frémont to undertake his third expedition, this one to explore a route to that same Mexican province. Nor did he forget Great Britain. In his annual message he warned her to stay away from California and conveniently revived the almost forgotten Monroe Doctrine.

In the meantime, this energetic President was turning his attention to Oregon. In spite of the bellicose "54-40 or Fight" platform on which he had been elected, Polk now proceeded once more to offer the 49th parallel as boundary, and once more Great Britain refused it, whereupon Polk informed her that this offer was permanently withdrawn. He secured from Congress consent to give Great Britain the required year's notice that the United States was terminating the joint occupation agreement of 1827. The implication was that at the end of that year the United States would step in and take possession. His restatement of the Monroe Doctrine might apply to Oregon as well as to California.

Over Oregon there was to be no war, for events were leading both sides to a willingness to make concessions. In England there was fear of losing American trade. By repeal of her Corn Laws and other moves, England was embarking upon a policy of free trade; she wanted American grain and cotton and American customers for her manufactured goods. Also, the Hudson's Bay Company had seen the writing on the wall; afraid of the increasing number of Americans so near its property at Fort Vancouver on the Columbia, the company decided to move its headquarters up to Vancouver Island across Puget Sound. Thereby the region between the Columbia River and the 49th parallel was partially vacated. Probably at that time there were few more than eight Americans north of the Columbia, but no one could tell when the 6,000 south of it might set up control over the whole region. Thus Britain's needs and the transfer of the principal British interest in Oregon north of the line made it easy for Aberdeen to retreat. When the British government received the American notice of termination of joint occupation, the ministry met it in conciliatory mood and offered to accept the 49th parallel. Since Polk's Mexican policy was not working well and seemed to be leading toward war, he could hardly afford to refuse conciliation. To be doubly sure, he decided to ask the advice of the Senate beforehand. That body consented and 15 June 1846 the Oregon problem was solved by a treaty accepting the proffered line.

The Mexican War

The Mexican dispute which so engrossed Polk was indeed going from bad to worse. Slidell arrived in December 1845 in Mexico City, where he met a hostile reception; the president who had agreed to receive him was so beset by his enemies that he dared not live up to his agreement. Mexico was more than ever incensed. Her offer of separate Texan recognition, made through Britain, had been spurned, and she vowed vengeance upon the people of Texas for preferring annexation to the United States. The press roared forth coarse epithets at the Yankee envoy and whipped public opinion into a fury against these robbers who had stolen Texas. The refusal to receive Slidell angered Polk, and in January he ordered Taylor to lead his army into the region between the Nueces and the Rio Grande and to establish himself at the mouth of the latter river. The Mexicans, in the meantime, had moved up to Matamoros on the other bank. Polk also stationed a fleet off Vera Cruz. He even entered into an intrigue with Santa Anna, then in exile, and decided to aid him in getting back into Mexico, believing he would help settle affairs favorably to the United States and avoid war.

During early spring Polk hoped that Mexico might reconsider and receive Slidell, but in the event he was not accepted the President was determined to go to war "to redress our wrongs." At last, in the second week in May, Slidell arrived in Washington to report his failure and Polk told his cabinet that he would ask Congress to declare war the next week. The cabinet expressed some regret that he had no specific act of aggression to report as justification for war and Polk regretted this, too. But fate was with him. That very Saturday evening (9 May) word was received from General Taylor that on 25 April Mexican soldiers had crossed the Rio Grande and engaged in a brush with a detachment from Taylor's force. "American blood had been shed on American soil." So on Monday the President asked Congress to declare war, citing this bloodshed, and war speedily became a fact.

General Taylor did not wait to hear from Washington before completing his fortifications and undertaking to drive the Mexicans south of the Rio Grande. He won several battles in quick succession and when word of his victories reached the capital Polk expected that peace might soon be a fact. Santa Anna had arrived in Mexico and the fortunes of revolution had placed him in charge. Polk, believing that he would arrange a peace if money were forthcoming, appealed to Congress for two million dollars. He failed to get it, because of congressional politics, and it became evident that Santa Anna had played Polk false. But he had other, firmer reliances. He had called out 23,000 volunteers, mostly from the southern and western states, and some of these had been sent to Taylor. General Wool was assembling a second army at San Antonio, and a third column under Colonel Stephen W. Kearney was to march on California.

Taylor's invasion of northern Mexico, begun in August, resulted in the capture of Monterrey in September; but after this victory he found his army in such a condition that he agreed to an armistice for two months. Ordered by Washington to proceed, Taylor finally reached Saltillo in November, where he was joined by Wool's army in December. After the navy captured Tampico, Taylor advanced to Victoria and by New Year's he was pretty much in control of northeastern Mexico.

Polk was dissatisfied with Taylor's advance and was particularly wroth at the Monterrey armistice. Besides, Taylor was a Whig and the victories he had won in driving the Mexicans beyond the Rio Grande had brought him forward as a presidential candidate. Polk wanted a new general. The natural choice would be Winfield Scott, but that general likewise was a Whig and hard to manage. Polk himself had the naïve idea that by commissioning any of his political friends he could make adequate generals out of them. He, in fact, appointed a number of such officers and proposed to make Senator Thomas Hart Benton a lieutenant-general, to lead an army from Vera Cruz to Mexico City. Congress, fortunately, would not consent and so Polk had to choose General Scott to command this expedition. Soldiers were found for Scott, in face of slow volunteering, by reducing Taylor's army from 10,000 to 5,000, taking most of his regular troops. Despatches containing details of this division of the army fell into Santa Anna's hands; and as soon as the veterans had left Taylor, Santa Anna attacked him, 22 February 1847, at Buena Vista. Taylor, after a desperate struggle, managed to defeat the greatly superior force and the Mexicans retreated to defend their capital. This exploit securely fastened laurels on Taylor's brow; he now had time to listen to the voice of political ambition, and his son-in-law, Colonel Bliss, continued to perfect his publicity. In spite of Polk, "Old Rough-and-Ready" was emerging as a ready-to-order presidential candidate and hero. The year 1848 was not far off.

General Scott approached Vera Cruz by sea and captured it 27 March 1847, after a siege of less than three weeks. Then he proceeded to lead a truly remarkable march inland. By 15 May he reached historic Puebla, after one noteworthy victory and some skirmishes, and thence he ascended the high plateau on which Mexico City is located. Mid-August found him advancing by a series of spectacular victories and by the 20th he had blasted his way to the immediate approaches of Mexico City. Its altitude—about 6,000 feet—is one to which people must become accustomed. Scott made an armistice with Santa Anna, to catch his breath for a couple of weeks, and for other reasons to be described. Then he recommenced, winning another series of battles which brought him by 14 September into Mexico City. The heart of Mexico was in American hands, captured by his small army of 10,000 men.

While Taylor and Scott were winning victories, the third field of operations was covered effectively. Colonel Stephen W. Kearney had set out for Santa Fé and California from Independence, Missouri, in June of 1846. He captured Santa Fé, and after ordering Colonel Doniphan with Missouri volunteers to march into northern Mexico, he proceeded toward California. Doniphan captured El Paso and the next February fought his way into Chihuahua, joining Taylor's forces in March at Saltillo.

While Kearney and Doniphan were covering their long marches, far-distant California was the scene of unauthorized but enthusiastic conquest. Frémont had arrived there in January of 1846, before the war broke out. His work disturbed the Mexican commander and nearly brought bloodshed before he diverted his march northward into Oregon. There he was overtaken by messages from home and immediately felt moved to retrace his steps southward. Finding the Americans in the Sutter's Fort region fearful that the Mexicans were going to drive them out, Frémont lent them his aid in revolting and in establishing the "Bear Flag Republic" at Sonoma. These rebels made him their commander and he marched against Sacramento. Not until then did he learn that the United States and Mexico were at war and that Commodore Sloat had captured Monterrey. San Francisco, Sutter's Fort and Sonoma, by midsummer 1847 hoisted the Stars and Stripes. Next the indefatigable Frémont went to join Sloat, who had been succeeded by Commodore Stockton, and before Christmas Kearney joined them. By New Year's Stockton, Kearney and Frémont had completed the conquest of California and had time to start quarreling among themselves.

The uniform success attending American arms on the field of battle contrasted vividly with the disastrous political results of the war at home. To say that this was an unpopular war is putting it mildly. It was started in a manner certain to make it a center of sectional and partisan conflict. The Democrats had brashly shouted for "54-40 or Fight." But they had meekly compromised northern interests by accepting from strong Great Britain the 49th parallel, while they then proceeded to fight weak Mexico to obtain everything the South wanted. Furthermore, Polk's contention that Mexico had started the war seemed far-fetched in the light of Taylor's operations in a region which Mexico claimed. The Whigs, particularly in the North, fought the President's policy at every step. But the most dangerous attack on it was made by northerners of his own party in the famous debates in which the slavery question reared its ugly head.

The unpopularity of the war was strikingly demonstrated in the enlistments. Congress authorized the calling of 50,000 volunteers and the increase of the regular army by ten new regiments. But it was found that these forces could not very readily be enlisted in northern states, particularly in New England, in spite of the fact that Polk appointed several of his Democratic followers there as brigadier-generals and colonels, and they attempted to bring loyal Democrats to the colors. In general, the bulk of the volunteering was from southern states.

The war itself could not make much of an impression upon domestic life outside of politics, for it was too brief to involve many men or much money. The total of troops was not large; the official figures, 116,587, contain duplications caused by reënlistments, and no army in the field was larger than 12,000 men. The war cost 100 million dollars in round numbers, but its financing presented no difficulties. Approximately half the outlay was met from duties, although the Walker tariff was chiefly a revenue measure. The other half was taken up by 6 per cent loan issues, which were eagerly bought. These operations, which were managed by the reëstablished independent treasury, could not cause great discomfort, for the national economy was enjoying a prosperous period.

Resistance to American arms practically ceased in October 1847, just eighteen months after the beginning of hostilities, but the peace treaty was not signed until the next February. As Polk had begun to plan for peace simultaneously with the declaration of war, he had set machinery to work as early as June 1846 to secure it. His initial efforts had been futile. Then, when he sent Scott to capture Mexico City, he undertook to make sure that the Whig general should not also capture the prestige of peace-making. So Polk sent the chief clerk of the State Department, Nicholas P. Trist, to act as his own agent, with full instructions for making a treaty. He was to secure the Rio Grande River as boundary to El Paso. For the cession of New Mexico and California, he was authorized to offer both $15,000,000 and the assumption by the United States of the $3,000,000 worth of claims held by Americans against Mexico. He was also to offer $15,000,000 for Lower California and a right of way across the Isthmus of Tehuantepec. He was entrusted with a $3,000,000 check to bind the agreement when Mexico should ratify the treaty.

Scott was not pleased at first to have this presidential agent following him; but before long he became reconciled and he and Trist became friends. He used some of his secret service money to aid Trist's negotiations and arranged the armistice before attacking Mexico City, in order to allow Trist to treat with Santa Anna. The Mexican leader wanted the $3,000,000 down-payment very much but dared not agree to land cession; and so Scott marched on the capital. As the defeated Santa Anna fled the country, it became necessary to await formation of a government which would dare to sign a treaty ceding territory to the United States. This took time.

In the meanwhile, Polk was just as much disturbed by this Scott-Trist armistice as he had been by Taylor's truce. Also victory was so complete he began to dream of taking all of Mexico, and he recalled Trist. But Scott and Trist disregarded the new orders from Washington; they had found a government ready to sign their treaty and they feared that if they waited this government might melt away. So, 2

February 1848, at the little town of Guadeloupe Hidalgo a treaty was agreed upon. Thereby the United States secured the Rio Grande as the boundary and acquired New Mexico and California at a cost of $18,250,000 in cash and claims, just as Trist's original instructions had provided. Trist carried the ratification treaty back to Polk. The President was furious at the disobedience and dismissed Trist immediately, although he accepted his treaty and sent it to the Senate for final and uneventful ratification. The United States had become the acknowledged owner of an additional area one-third as large as itself. It had at length reached the far Pacific and was now possessed of the long coast line from San Diego to Puget Sound. These acquisitions and the manner of them would prove full of meaning for the future.

The Revival of Sectionalism

While the military conflict was being waged in the Southwest, a political war broke out in Washington. The annexation of Texas and the prospective acquisition of part of Mexico presaged a great increase of slave territory, either actual or potential, and an indefinite extension of southern domination over the federal government. This prospect was particularly galling to northern representatives, who pictured themselves in perpetual subordination to southern power. So again, as at the time of the Louisiana Purchase and the admission of Missouri, northern leaders fought southern triumph. Now their resentment was more intense because of a combination of circumstances of which the acquisition of slave territory was only one. The growing nationalism would not submit to sectional domination.

The most important factor in the impending rivalry was the steadily increasing sense of insecurity which was making southern leaders apprehensive. Change had been rapid in the decade since the tariff battle of 1832-1833, and these changes had intensified feeling. The South in these years had definitely committed itself to one type of livelihood based upon the intensive cultivation by slave labor of a single crop, cotton. Socially, too, the South was very much of a unit, in that most of the population was loyal to the system which had become pervading, a system which was both feudal and democratic in spite of the seeming contradiction in terms.

The feudal character of southern society arose from its primary interest in land, cotton and slaves. Wealth was measured almost exclusively by plantation and slave property. But such property was not widely distributed. On the eve of the Civil War there were about 8,000,000 white people in the section and of these less than 25 per cent were directly connected with slavery. Less than 200,000 owned as many as ten slaves, and the large slave plantations were in the hands of 2,600 owners. These 2,600 men and their families therefore controlled the bulk of southern wealth.

The mass of the population were not large planters but small farmers who were divided into three classes. There were the yeomen farmers who owned no slaves but frequently hoped by hard work and good fortune to advance into the slaveholding group. The second group was the so-called "poor white" class which gained a precarious existence generally from marginal lands in the Piedmont. The last group lived in the isolated mountain regions and are spoken of as the "mountain whites." Socially and, to a lesser extent, politically the small aristocracy of large planters dominated these groups which were numerically so much larger, with an easy and graceful domination. The bulk of these small farmers admired and respected the planter aristocracy and loyally supported the ruling class whenever southern institutions were under attack.

One reason for this solidarity was the democratic character of the feudal system. There was nothing static about the groupings described above. The wealthy group was by no means closed or exclusively hereditary. Quite frequently new estates were created by small farmers who had been thrifty and competent. Outsiders from the North or from the border states brought in capital and entered plantation production. This was particularly true in the newer gulf region of Alabama, Mississippi and Louisiana. There was a very real sense of opportunity open for all and a species of democratic feeling arising from such a realization.

A second reason for the solidarity of the South was the presence of some three million Negro slaves. In important sections of the South there were more Negroes than whites. Some of the poorer whites had only the consciousness of their Caucasian blood to mark them as better off than the Negro slaves. If the Negroes were freed or the South abolitionized, certain regions would probably be Africanized. Therefore if white supremacy were to be maintained, Negro slavery must be supported and preserved.

Furthermore, the South was consolidated in its sentiment by outside attacks. During the period since 1830, the South had been subjected to a bombardment of continually increasing intensity. The development of anti-slavery propaganda had caused a reaction, producing a decided defense complex in the minds of the people of the South, who in 1850, numbered 40 per cent of the total population of the Union.

This self-consciousness on the part of the South was rendered most ominous by changes of an entirely different character which were taking place in the North. In the non-slaveholding states there was no such social or economic unity. Instead of uniformity there was diversity and confusion of interest. In the eastern states, population was tending to congregate in cities, where there were all sorts and kinds of business, and where no one type dominated. While the South was interested in one form of wealth, the East was engaged in the many forms of capitalism. The entrepreneurs of this region were adept in the use of money and were anxious to move forward, to try new things and to gain the satisfactions which could be obtained from increasing their wealth and power. But there was more to it than materialism. There was an idealistic desire to make a better republic by reform and "progress" in the ways of democracy.

Naturally the focus of both East and South was the emerging West. This was the most fluid and least stable region in the national aggregation. So undeveloped was it that it was a continual invitation to come and participate in the realization of its potentialities, and thither hoards of people were flocking. The West had so many needs that spelled profit to eastern capitalists. Roads, canals and railroads if built would bring greater population and trade, and if the public lands were sold cheaply or given away, new communities and large dividends to investors of capital would be the natural results. To the East, the West was a great place of opportunity if there could be proper coöperation between American enterprise and governmental power. The West should be straightway developed, new states created, new sources of wealth tapped, and a greater United States speedily achieved. Many influences in the East, therefore, joined with western promoters in working for all sorts and kinds of government subsidies.

The South, on the other hand, viewed the West with a different interest. The South was not interested in the speedy development of the new section, particularly as geographic conditions were dictating that most of it would be a free labor region unsympathetic with the institution of slavery or the southern economic and social system. Therefore if the West were quickly developed, the South realized that new free states would be created which would speedily outvote the older region and relegate it to a position of political inferiority. Consequently, when the question of organizing the new territory was brought before Congress there was bound to be a conflict. The South would be aroused to protect its interests and the question was whether it could prevent a combination of eastern and western votes from admitting the new states which would eventually deprive the South of its political power. A bitter political contest seemed inevitable and dangerous.

When the Mexican War had broken out, it was apparent that the United States would obtain some territory in the Southwest which would be convenient for slave expansion. Northern politicians opposed such acquisition from the beginning by offering the Wilmot proviso forbidding the introduction of slavery into any territory acquired from

Mexico. This measure failed to pass Congress but the Democratic party split into two factions when the followers of Martin Van Buren were defeated in an attempt to make the Proviso the official platform of the party. In 1848 Martin Van Buren ran as a Free Soil candidate for president and deprived Lewis Cass, the regular Democratic nominee, of enough votes to elect the Whig candidate General Zachary Taylor.

These signs all pointed to a fight in Congress at the slightest excuse. The struggle came when the question of governing the territory acquired from Mexico was introduced into Congress. Had the normal process of migration into this far distant region been taking its slow course the matter might not have been so fraught with peril, but an unforseen rush of circumstances intervened. In the fall of 1848 the East finally awoke to the fact that gold had really been discovered in California. By the spring of 1849 many of the adventurous and hopeful had determined to go westward to find fortunes in this far-away Eldorado. During that year at least 100,000 people entered California and overwhelmed that sleepy society of some 20,000 Spaniards and Indians with a curious motley of unorganized gold seekers. Prior to this influx of population the question of the proper government of the newly acquired territory had troubled few and the little government existing was administered according to the old Mexican local customs by the unenterprising inhabitants, with occasional exercise of authority by the small American military force.

The Compromise of 1850

So large and so tumultuous a population pouring as it did into California brought a serious social problem. There was an almost complete absence of law and order. Anarchy was imminent; life and property, especially in the vicinity of the gold fields, was subject to the caprice of individual strength or cunning. The situation was pressing and the inhabitants took the matter of government into their own hands. Among the new-comers were many politicians well versed in the forms of state government. With the approval of President Taylor a number of these new Californians organized a constitutional convention and a state government, while duly chosen senators and representatives were on their way to Washington to petition Congress for the admission of California as a state. The constitution which they carried with them prohibited slavery within the bounds of California.

There was no doubt that action must be taken in regard to California by Congress in 1850. California had decided she wanted to be a free state. This decision, quite in keeping with southern ideas of the rights of a state, complicated the question of admission because her entrance into the Union would destroy the balance between free and slave states which had been maintained in the Senate since the Missouri Compromise. The census returns showed that the North was growing much faster than the South and if the South were to be denied expansion room in the West, her inferiority and loss of power were inevitable. The great tides of industrialism and foreign migration were passing by the South and pouring wealth and population into the northern states at a much swifter rate than the South could rival them. Finally the price of cotton had fallen off and the planters felt poor and dissatisfied. With these circumstances oppressing them, southern leaders were bound to fight against any further loss of power.

The Congressional battle raged for months during 1850 and finally, after many despaired, a formula of compromise was found. California, the new territories, their government and boundaries, the return of fugitive slaves, the status of slavery in the District of Columbia, were to be disposed of so that all issues might be quieted. Southern leaders surrendered their hope of a division of the new territory by a line to the Pacific and received a stringent fugitive law to be enforced by a specially created group of federal officials independent of state aid. California was to be free as she wished and New Mexico and Utah were to have the same opportunity to choose their own way of organization. The people of the territories, not Congress, would thereafter decide the slavery issue; southern and northern sympathizers could ballot against each other at the territorial polls. New Mexico's area was left intact in spite of Texan demands for half her territory and the Lone Star State had its debts incurred during its years of independence paid by Congress as compensation. Finally, slaves could still be held in the District of Columbia but no longer could they be bought and sold there.

Thus by compromise all questions were laid aside and with secret heart burnings the prominent in both sections generally promised to abide by the result. Moves to secede which had been launched in the South suddenly subsided and, though there was much muttering about being cheated in the bargain, the southerners generally acquiesced. Ominous of the future, however, was a widely held determination phrased in resolutions passed by the Georgia legislature, to the effect that the South had made her last concessions. In the North "Union saving" meetings rejoicing in the outcome were held in many a city and town. But here again there were disquieting incidents pointing to future danger; in spite of the new fugitive slave law, the northern people were no more ready to return fugitive slaves, and a series of rescues and riots led many a southern observer to believe that the law was not worth much and that the North could not be trusted.

The excitement died down as quickly as it had flared up. Like a wave of hysteria it had passed over the political consciousness of the country. Comparing it with the situation at the time of the Missouri Compromise shows a marked and significant change. In 1820, when Missouri sought entrance as a slave state, the New England and Middle states were afraid. To them it seemed as though the southern strength was destined to be permanent, because of its hold on the Senate and the presidency. These northern states felt the sting of a consciousness of political inferiority; they demanded and wrested a compromise from the South. Now, however, it was the South which feared that the North had forged ahead and with the threat of the Wilmot proviso seemed about to deprive the South of its legislative veto sealed to it by its equality in the Senate. The South now demanded and received the compromise. Would it be as practicable for its purpose as the Missouri Compromise, still in effect in the Louisiana Purchase, had proved itself to be? Would the natural adaptability of American democracy still prove effective?

CHAPTER XVII

FAR-FLUNG INTERESTS

Though the clouds of sectional conflict might seem dark, American attention was not to be denied its far horizons. The United States sought to spread its influence, extend its trade and commerce, gain new possessions, and demonstrate its strength as a power among nations. No quarter of the globe was missed by American agents of business or diplomacy. Across Siberia, along the torrid coast of Africa, into Persia, they went. They opened the Oriental empires and trafficked in Polynesia. With zeal for commercial wealth and greater power was combined the sense of mission, the desire to preach the superiority of America's free institutions.

The Mission of Democracy

The democratic spirit, with its desire for improvement, imbued American diplomacy with a sense of mission which the buoyant spirit of the bonanza age encouraged. This was particularly true after 1848, the year of revolutions in Europe. Americans were especially interested in the fate of the revolutionists in the Hapsburg Austrian enpire. A group of youthful enthusiasts known as Young America urged the State Department to intervene and prevailed upon President Taylor to send an observer to Vienna to do what he could. Word of this got to the ears of the Austrian government, which protested this aid and comfort to their revolting subjects. Secretary of State Webster thereupon took occasion to preach Europe a sermon on democracy, in his famous "Hülsemann letter," in which he pictured the United States as a great center of republican propaganda. When the Hungarian Revolution failed, the United States government invited its leader, Louis Kossuth, to visit America and even sent a warship to bring him thither. Congress gave him a banquet and in 1852 he made a triumphal progress through various cities of the United States. The financial contributions which he was able to collect, however, disappointed him.

When the Democrats followed into power they proceeded to equal and better the record of the Whigs at republican pronunciamentos, with Secretary of State Marcy also admonishing Austria. A Hungarian exile, Martin Koszta, had come to the United States and made a declaration that he wished to become an American citizen. Then he went back to the Near East and the Austrians captured him in Smyrna. An American naval vessel was near enough to rescue him and when Austria protested Marcy turned his pen upon them in an endeavor to outdo Webster. His "Koszta letter" took its place beside Webster's Hülsemann epistle. Marcy further endeavored to preach democracy by recommending to our diplomats that they cease wearing the gold-braided coats, knee breeches and plumed hats of their European colleagues. It would better suit democratic simplicity for them to appear in the plain dress of American citizens. The luckless diplomats found that the only trouble with Marcy's dress circular was that they then could not be distinguished from the servants. Few found themselves able to obey this counsel of perfection long.

The Hülsemann and Koszta letters and the dress circular can not be dismissed as mere marginalia in American diplomacy, for the missionary sentiment which inspired and applauded them was to grow with the years. Beleaguered nations of Europe were to learn to appeal to it, and then it was to help to involve the United States in a world war far greater than the domestic cataclysm which the 'fifties brought them.

Transportation Across Central America

Emergence as a Pacific power, because of the Mexican cession, changed the international position of the United States and produced serious diplomatic complications. Hitherto the United States had been primarily interested in but one side of the sphere, that washed by the waters of the Atlantic. But the settlement of the Oregon question and the acquisition of California made the republic a Pacific power as well. Furthermore, it raised questions of transportation. The facilities for crossing the Isthmus of Panama were obviously inadequate to take care of the new demands of travel to California, and plans began to be made to meet the need. The idea of a trans-isthmian canal, which had appeared from time to time even in colonial days, was now revived. Could a canal be constructed over one of the various trans-isthmian routes, at Panama or across Nicaragua? American interests soon became involved in each of these places and usually found that British rivals were there, too.

Even before the Mexican War broke, the United States had become interested in Panama, and that almost inadvertently. The Republic of New Granada (now Colombia), which then exercised more or less nominal jurisdiction over the isthmus, had been in the habit of discriminating against American commerce, and an American diplomat was put to work to get these discriminations removed. At the same time the President of New Granada was fearful that the British had designs on the Isthmus of Panama. So in self-defense his government proposed to the United States that New Granada would grant the commercial concessions desired, as well as a right of way over the Isthmus of Panama, if the United States would agree to keep the transit open and guarantee both the neutrality of the isthmus and the rights of sovereignty of New Granada over it. The American representative, Benjamin A. Bidlack, agreed to this arrangement and signed a treaty 12 December 1846. Polk received this as the Mexican War was drawing to a close and after some hesitation submitted it to the Senate, where it was finally ratified. The United States was now possessed of "the right of way or transit across the Isthmus of Panama upon any modes of communication that now exist, or that may be hereafter constructed."

The United States had already picked out the Panama route as its official road of communication to California, and by act of Congress (3 March 1847) had arranged to let contracts for carrying the mail. These were given to a group of capitalists and politicians who incorporated two steamship companies and a railroad to take care of this service. The railroad was to be built across the isthmus to transfer the mail and passengers. These steamship companies were in service in time to transport the gold-rush crowds but the railroad was not ready until 1855 and in the interim the primitive trans-isthmian carriage had to suffice.

The route through Nicaragua was more directly complicated by Anglo-American rivalry and produced significant diplomatic consequences which were to affect American expansion for fifty years. Great Britain had gained a foothold in Central America as early as the seventeenth century, in British Honduras, which was recognized by Spain later when she granted England a concession to cut logwood. From this base Great Britain had been gradually expanding. She had settled in the Bay Islands in the Gulf of Honduras and was working down the Mosquito shore (the east coast of Nicaragua) under the guise of protecting the Mosquito Indians. By these advances Great Britain had gained possession of the approaches to the Nicaraguan isthmian route.

When she learned of the treaty between the United States and New Granada regarding Panama, and of the successful occupation of Mexico to the Rio Grande, she decided to make her possession of the Nicaraguan route sure. Therefore, in January 1848, she took the Nicaraguan town of San Juan, at the eastern terminus of a possible canal route, on the ground that it belonged to her wards, the Mosquitoes. The name of the place was changed to Greytown. Nicaragua turned to the United States and, though occupied with Mexico, Polk sent an agent, Elijah Hise, to investigate. Hise lost no time. He made a treaty with Nicaragua stronger than the Panama treaty, and gained the sole right to build a canal or railroad or both in return for the guarantee of American protection. Likewise, Cornelius Vanderbilt, an American steamship operator, had formed the American Atlantic and Pacific Ship Canal Company, for the purpose of building a canal across Nicaragua, and Hise gained a contract for it to carry out its plans.

This rivalry between American and British interests was not only exasperating but it was bound to prevent the building of any canal. Neither government was in a position to demand full control of isthmian transportation. As the Whigs were in power, and generally more friendly to the British than were the Democrats, the British ministry sent over Sir Henry Bulwer as a special envoy to work out a compromise. The result was the historic Clayton-Bulwer Treaty of 1850, whereby it was agreed that "neither government will ever obtain or maintain for itself any exclusive control over any ship canal through any part of Central America"; neither would they "colonize or assume any dominion over Central America." In other words, any canal or railroad built should be for joint use. This treaty was rather ambiguous about British interests in territory where she was already edging in, and this was to cause a good deal of trouble within the next few years. Nevertheless, the treaty remained in force for half a century and effectively prevented the United States from building a canal.

Yet it could not prevent American enterprise from organizing another trans-isthmian route. Commodore Vanderbilt failed to secure sufficient capital to dig a canal but he did not fail to transport passengers. He organized the Accessory Transit Company and developed a trans-isthmian route of an ingenious kind. He ran a steamer from Greytown up the San Juan River to Lake Nicaragua; there he established a larger steamer to carry passengers across its wide expanse; thence by stagecoach he carried them over a short wagon road, which he built, to a port on the Pacific. As he also provided steamship passage from New York to Greytown and from the Pacific port to San Francisco, Vanderbilt could carry passengers more quickly than could the Panama Company. This service began in July 1851, giving those wishing to go to California two trans-isthmian routes to select from. California was nearer than before and the transportation problem was partially solved.

Penetrating the Orient

Diplomatic efforts to open up the Orient were among the most notable achievements of this expansive period. Trade in the Far East had been going on ever since the first decade of national history, but under difficulties; it was hampered because of its irregular status. As far back as Jackson's day, efforts had been made to prevail upon the Asiatic despots to open their ports more regularly. A trader and consul, Edmund Roberts, succeeded (1833) in making treaties with Siam, and Muscat (now British) on the Gulf of Oman, but he failed with Cochin-China and never reached his final mission, Japan. Further efforts proved futile until England fought China (1839-1842) and forced her to open certain ports to English traders. When President Tyler heard of this he sent Caleb Cushing of Massachusetts to secure a similar treaty. Cushing was well received because China did not want to be confined wholly to English trade, and in 1844 the first treaty with China was signed. It granted Americans full trading rights at certain specified ports, where they might acquire land, erect buildings and enjoy extraterritorial rights. Thither the clipper ships sailed their winged way. Thus these new interests in the Orient and the new possessions, Oregon and California, gave the United States a real sense of place on the Pacific.

The lure of the Orient was the lure of profits vividly imagined but as yet quite unrealized. Japan was particularly tantalizing. To her vicinity a whaling boom was carrying Americans ships. But they dared not enter her ports, for she still kept them closed; and if shipwreck befell them their sailors met less than hospitality in their adversity. Many a tale of suffering reached the State Department. Although this tightly locked empire had repulsed several attempts at negotiations, American traders and manufacturers would not be denied their markets. They exerted such pressure that when Daniel Webster became secretary of state the last time he yielded to their importunities. Commodore M. C. Perry was despatched in 1852, with a fleet and instructions to get a treaty which should allow trading and coaling privileges. Coaling had been made important by the rising use of steam vessels.

Perry's fleet and his models of western inventions, including railroads and telegraphs, respectively amazed and impressed the Japanese. After prolonged consideration they signed a treaty, 31 March 1854, granting a few concessions; hereafter the United States might maintain one consul in Japan, her ships might enter two unimportant ports and her shipwrecked mariners would be decently cared for. A coaling base was obtained at Napa, south of Japan, through a treaty Perry made with the ruler of the then independent (now Japanese) Lew Chew Islands. The Commodore conceived of an American empire in Asia; he wished to take possession of some of these islands to serve as the foundation of United States power in the Orient. This the Pierce administration would not permit. It was not cast in the mold of McKinley's, half a century later.

The relations established in this fashion with China and Japan were bound to be unsatisfactory because so limited; efforts therefore persisted to enlarge them. Townsend Harris, the first consul-general to Japan, succeeded in 1858 in obtaining real concessions and regular diplomatic relations with that nation. Two years later Japan sent an official delegation for a visit; it was brought in state on an American warship and made an extensive and doubtless a gratifying tour of the United States. China also grew conciliatory. Out of a second war fought by the Celestial Empire, this time with England and France, there came in 1858 a new treaty which bettered trade concessions and settled various claims for damages suffered in violation of the first treaty.

Hawaii, like Japan and China, took on new importance with the occupation of the Pacific shore. American missionaries had gone there as early as the 1820's and American merchants and planters were interested in Hawaiian sugar. When it was reported that Great Britain might be planning to absorb these islands, interest grew keen. Rather than see them fall into other hands, the United States would annex them; a treaty was actually drafted in 1854 providing for that. But it provided also for immediate admission of Hawaii to the Union, something which the Pierce administration knew the Senate would not ratify. While effort was being made to modify this feature, the king who was favorable to annexation died most inconveniently. His successor was sufficiently anti-American to withdraw the treaty, an act in which the United States minister suspected that Great Britain and France took a hand. A trade reciprocity treaty was negotiated, only to fail of ratification in the Senate. Hawaiian annexation, too, was due to wait forty years.

Another quarter of the Pacific moving into the orbit of American interest was Alaska. Since 1823 Russia had made no further attempts to expand and the Russian American Company had sold out its California post to Sutter. Few Americans since had paid any attention to this far-away region. The outbreak of the Crimean War in 1854 between Russia and the allies, Great Britain and France, caused Russia to be apprehensive lest England absorb Alaska into Canada. Her minister, therefore, held conversations with William L. Marcy, Pierce's secretary of state, about selling it to the United States. No purchase was made and a dozen years were to elapse before Alaska was finally transferred. Relations with Russia were strengthened, however, and the United States was allowed to send a commercial agent to the Amoor River in Asiatic Russia. Ambitious interests typical of this bonanza period planned to penetrate the farthest portions of the earth.

Trade extension and possible territorial expansion were likewise involved in new complications over Canada. The fisheries question persisted as a bone of contention because of the ambiguous wording of a treaty of 1818. Great Britain interpreted this to mean that American fishermen could not approach the shores of the Bay of Fundy, which Americans strenuously denied. The quarrel became dangerous when warships were stationed on the fishing-grounds during the seasons of 1852 and 1853. An accident might shed blood and precipitate war. Fortunately, diplomacy intervened. There was some agitation for the annexation of Canada within the United States and Great Britain did not wish to lose the provinces. So in 1854 the Canadian Reciprocity Treaty was signed. It was agreed that, in return for more liberal fishing privileges, the United States would enter into reciprocal trade concessions with Canada whereby certain specified commodities, both manufactured goods and raw materials, should be admitted into each country with preferential rates. Ratification of this treaty in Washington, it was said, was floated through on champagne; but it was probably successful largely because southern senators preferred reciprocity to the annexation of so much free-soil territory.

The Golden Circle of the Caribbean

The great focus of interest, which the trend of manifest destiny emphasized, was the Caribbean region—a golden circle with Cuba as its center, the circumference of which extended from Panama through Central America and Mexico to the slave states of the United States. Some few dreamed of it as a great slave empire. Cuba, the Pearl of the Antilles, had been an object of continual interest to the United States. Since Jefferson's day, the republic had looked with longing upon this fair isle and had alternated between hope of acquiring it and fear that some one else would. The South was particularly concerned. Since abolitionist England had ended slavery in the British West Indies (1833) she had been urging Spain to do likewise in Cuba. Might not this encourage the great Negro population to revolt and Africanize the island in a fashion such as Haiti?

Other strong forces were drawing American interest closer to Cuba. Steamship lines, such as the United States Steamship Co., made regular stops at Havana and had developed quite a business in passengers and freight. Also it was a tubercular age and a winter in Cuba was frequently prescribed for sufferers; occasional invalids and their attendants came to know the island in this melancholy fashion. During the Mexican War, particularly on the home journey, a number of officers and men stopped off at Havana and did a little sight-seeing. Thus various Americans saw the misgovernment by the inefficient and tyrannical Spaniards and realized that Cuba was ripe for revolution, slave revolt or annexation. Spain could hardly defend it if some foreign power wished to take it.

President Polk was concerned about the fate of Cuba but could do nothing until the end of the Mexican War. Then he hurried into action. A recent debate in the British Parliament had discussed the proposal to seize Cuba for the benefit of British capitalists to whom Spain owed millions of pounds. To forestall such an unwelcome event, Polk offered Spain $100,000,000 for the island. Spanish pride, however, would not permit the sale of her last remaining possession of importance and the attempt failed.

Within Cuba itself there were men at work trying to promote union with the United States. Various of the creole families feared a slave uprising and were seeking to join the United States to ensure order and security. Their leader was Narciso López, a Venezuelan who had been a general in the Spanish army and had settled in Cuba. He plotted a revolution for June 1848 but his design was discovered and he fled to the United States. Within the haven of the northern republic he organized a Cuban junta and planned filibustering expeditions. The first was thwarted in 1849 but the year following, with the aid of certain Mexican War veterans, notably General John A. Quitman of Mississippi, he actually set sail for Cuba. The reception which his force received was so cool and discouraging that he dared not go farther and turned back to the United States. Here he found the government waiting to prosecute him for violating the neutrality law which forbade hostile expeditions to be organized in the United States against friendly powers. But López and his followers did not suffer, because sympathetic southern jurymen would not convict them. He was therefore encouraged to make one further effort and in 1851 set out with a group of adventurous southern youth. Total disaster was the end of this ill-starred attempt and López and a number of his followers were executed by Cuban authorities.

The fiasco aroused southern interest, particularly as some of the executed filibusterers were of prominent families; and it likewise quickened the hostility of Spanish officials toward Americans. Southern enthusiasts organized a secret society, the Order of the Lone Star, to promote the cause of Cuban annexation; and the Spanish authorities were on their guard. In such a situation small incidents loom large. For example, articles appeared in New York papers during the summer of 1852 describing the misrule of Cuba, and the Spanish decided the author was the purser of an American steamer, the *Crescent City,* which called at Havana. So they refused to let him land, an act which particularly annoyed the South. The State Department was urged to take action. The purser, however, swore he was not the author, the Spanish relaxed the ban and this affair died down. But a sequence of petty and disagreeable incidents continued to aggravate public opinion.

The possibilities of the situation were not lost upon Great Britain and France, who did not want the United States to have Cuba any more than the United States wanted them to own it. They, in April 1852, invited the Fillmore administration to enter a tripartite agreement guaranteeing Cuba to Spain. Answer to their proposal was delayed by Secretary Webster's fatal illness and death, and meanwhile the Democratic campaigners talked much about acquiring Cuba. So when the Whig, Edward Everett, succeeded Webster that fall he decided to take strong ground and demonstrate that the Whigs as well as the Democrats could uphold national pretensions regarding Cuba. He rejected the tripartite proposal in a high-sounding document, duly publicized. In spread-eagle language he implied that the United States wanted to be free to take Cuba if their self-defense ever should require it. More than ever, Americans were suspicious of the designs of Great Britain and France.

The Pierce administration was not long in power before more disquieting rumors and events turned its attention to Cuba. News that England was working to persuade Spain to abolish slavery reawakened southern fears of Africanization and in February 1854 another "outrage" occurred. Spanish authorities seized the cargo of an American vessel, the *Black Warrior*, at Havana, on a trumped-up charge of violation of port regulations. Pierce reported this to Congress, together with a series of such insults and losses. The administration made much of it, hoping it might help to arouse public opinion in support of a new effort to purchase Cuba. The outbreak of the Crimean War was effectually diverting British and French attention from America to the difficult task of defeating Russia and thus encouraging this new effort to influence Spain to sell the island. A curious plan had been suggested; August Belmont, Rothschild's American agent then minister to the Hague, was to work with James Buchanan, American minister at London, to persuade the leading European bankers to bring pressure upon Spain. She was hopelessly in debt to these bankers and the only way in which they could get back their money would be through assignment of a part of the 100 million the United States was willing to pay for Cuba.

Unfortunately, the American minister to Spain, Pierre Soulé, knew not the meaning of finesse. Politics had dictated the appointment of this inept and foolish diplomat who had bungled from the start and could not be entrusted with delicate negotiations. Therefore Pierce projected a secret conference, which met finally at Ostend, at which it was expected Buchanan and John Y. Mason, the American minister at Paris, would teach Soulé what to do. However, this conference was worse than a failure. Instead of being secret, it gained altogether too much publicity. Furthermore, Soulé was determined they should recommend that the United States threaten to take the island if Spain would not sell. Buchanan and Mason thought to curb such rash unwisdom. Buchanan carefully phrased a discreet report; it recommended that the United States offer $125,000,000 for Cuba direct to the Spanish Cortes or parliament, and stated the view that if Spain freed the slaves in Cuba and Africanized it, the United States would have to consider whether the law of self-preservation would not then require the seizure of the island. This Ostend report was erroneously scare-headed in the American press as a Manifesto which offered Spain the alternative of selling the island or having it seized. Thus was Buchanan's caution made of no avail. Such publicity brought forth a flood of northern anti-slavery opposition and Pierce had to drop the whole matter instantly.

When Buchanan succeeded Pierce in the White House he tried another scheme of financial pressure upon Spain. But his plan for persuading the bankrupt government to sell required a congressional appropriation of 30 million dollars, which northern members blocked. Cuba continued to interest Americans but periodically. Forty years passed before they really did anything about it.

A second attempt to extend American influence within the golden circle was made on the island of Santo Domingo. A growing steam navy set the United States hunting for coaling stations, and a study of the possibilities pointed to this island. The Pierce administration sent a special agent and an army officer to investigate. The army officer, George B. McClellan, reported that the harbor of Samana Bay was desirable. The diplomatic agent, W. L. Cazneau, reported that as the Dominican government wanted recognition by the United States and protection against England and France, it might be willing to sell or lease this harbor. Cazneau was therefore instructed in 1854 to negotiate and actually succeeded in making a treaty for a coaling station; but the Dominican congress failed to ratify it—the agent thought because of adverse French and British influence.

A great segment of the circumference of the golden circle included the Panama isthmian route which received much popular and diplomatic attention in this expansion period. Panama had proved convenient, particularly after completion of the railroad in 1855, and attracted traffic. The steamboat connections were synchronized at both ends of the railroad and the affairs of the company prospered, in no small measure encouraged by the generous mail subsidy of the United States government. However, labor troubles appeared to mar the peaceful operation of the transit monopoly. Originally, passengers had been landed at the eastern terminus, Aspinwall, by native boatmen who conveyed them from the steamer to the shore in small boats for highwaymen's prices. As this got to be a nuisance, the company provided a tug to transport people and baggage and thereby threw the local water-taximen out of work. Their resentment smoldered until in April 1856 chance presented the opportunity for a riot. A local watermelon vender accused a landing passenger of failing to pay the necessary dime for his wares and a fight started. The taximen joined in the melée and when it was over, strangely enough, much of the property of the steamship-railroad interests had been destroyed.

The State Department took it up and decided to make an issue with the government of New Granada, on the ground that Panama was so far away from the seat of central authority that Granada was unable to keep order in its distant province. American commissioners were sent down and endeavored to purchase the right to control the zone through which the railroad ran, so as to manage the affairs of the towns at each end. Thus in 1856 was anticipated by nearly fifty years the idea of a canal zone. The Granadan government refused to entertain this proposition and diplomatic relations were suspended for two years.

The segment of the golden circle adjacent to the southern states themselves was Mexico. This neighbor continued to be an object of governmental solicitude and to figure in the headlines of the popular press. Polk and his successors always regretted that more of Mexico had not been acquired by the United States. As California transportation problems grew insistent, this regret became more poignant, for Mexico had in the extreme northern provinces the Gila River valley, which was considered an excellent route for a transcontinental railroad.

The Pierce administration was decidedly interested in the railroad route and determined to attempt to purchase a large share of northern Mexico. They sent down a South Carolina railroad man, James Gadsden, who at length was able to buy from Santa Anna much less territory than Pierce hoped for. Only the Gila River valley was procured. This $10,000,000 purchase of 1853, rounded out the continental boundary of the United States as it remains today.

In the next administration Buchanan tried his best to purchase the northern provinces of Mexico and asked Congress for power to invade them, if necessary, to protect the border from marauders. But here again northern representatives would vote no money or power which might lead to the acquisition of potential slave territory. As conditions in Mexico, torn by civil war, grew worse, England, France and Spain counseled together regarding intervention. The opposition of the United States, for the time, deterred them. But if the civil conflict threatening the northern republic should break out, they would be ready to follow their original intentions. The dream of the golden circle might turn into a nightmare.

Empire at Last

Hope of imperial influence extended below the golden circle into South America. Travelers round the Horn made occasional stops at far-away ports on both the eastern and western shores of the southern continent. They gained some information regarding geographical conditions and commercial possibilities. Adventurous Americans went as far as Chile to develop steam navigation and railroading. Naval officers continued to explore in this period even more extensively than Lieutenant Charles Wilkes had done, when in 1838-1839 he visited various portions of the east and west coasts and the interior. The great Amazon was a geographic mystery which the American navy now determined to penetrate. If commercial advantages could be obtained from the free navigation of the Amazon, the State Department was interested in negotiating with Brazil for the privilege. Lieutenants William L. Herndon and Lardner Gibbon approached the exploration from the west coast, starting from Lima, Peru. Each proceeded to a separate branch of the great river and in 1851-1852 made adventurous journeys to the Atlantic coast. The information they obtained was used as the basis for negotiation with Brazil; but that empire was not then ready to yield the privilege.

A more spectacular episode arose out of American penetration into the very heart of South America. Hidden away there in those days was the country of Paraguay, which through the caprice of a dictator had been shut away from the world in the early years of its independence. In the 'forties his successor sought to develop his backward state and welcomed an American promoter, Edward A. Hopkins, to whom he gave important economic concessions. Hopkins organized a company in the United States to operate these concessions and was commissioned as American consul. However, he and the dictator had a falling-out, and in 1853 he was ordered away and his property confiscated. Just at this moment, naval Lieutenant Thomas J. Page arrived in the La Plata on an exploring expedition to study that great river system. He came to Hopkins' aid and carried the Americans in his company away in his vessel, the *Water Witch*. The rescue enraged the vindictive dictator, Carlos A. López, and when Page returned in October 1854 he interfered with his explorations and finally fired on the *Water Witch* and killed the pilot.

Negotiations over proper reparation for this outrage dragged on without satisfaction until finally in 1858 President Buchanan decided on drastic steps, unfortunately prophetic of future policy. A naval expedition was sent to Paraguay to back up the demands of a special commissioner. At the cannon's mouth such amends were granted, but with a show of strength unwarranted by the relative unimportance of the incident, and at a considerable cost to the aggressor. The notion that the exasperating Latin Americans must be dealt with severely was to attain a rank growth, leaving resentments which hampered later efforts at more intelligent diplomacy.

Commercial and agricultural developments of this period brought closer connection with Latin America and started in fact a tendency which had been seeking some place to gain expression. Soil exhausion in Virginia, Maryland and other sections of the nation made the discovery of a fertilizer a welcome event. In the 'forties began extensive use of guano, a fertilizer discovered in huge quantities on many oceanic islands used by birds as rookeries. The guano industry became most active on the Lobos Islands off the coast of Peru. There and on similar islands American guano diggers frequently came into conflict with those of other nations. As these islands were uninhabited, there was generally a question of who owned them. In order to develop an orderly procedure, Congress in 1856 passed a law providing that if Americans found guano islands and started working them they could notify the State Department; and thereafter these spots would be considered as "appertaining to the United States" and the rights of the guano workers could then be protected. So in 1858 the State Department declared that Navassa, off the island of Haiti, was in this category, and ever since has held it to be an American appurtenance. In this small way, rather than by a spectacular purchase or seizure of Cuba, the United States undertook the responsibility for its first non-contiguous possession. Most humbly the American empire had its beginning. Several other such islands were picked up around 1861 in the region of the equator, such as Jarvis and Baker's islands south of Hawaii. Aviation and Japan would give them new importance.

Thus, in this bonanza epoch, feverish diplomacy took its course, pressed in part by the spirit of the age, in part by the political situation. The Democratic administrations in power for most of the decade of the 'fifties had tried desperately to gain popular favor by diplomatic success, by the acquisition of territory and renown. Because their party believed in laissez-faire in domestic matters, and because also they saw with alarm a rising tide of northern political mobilization against southern power, they had taken refuge in diplomacy, but to little profit. The sectional conflict interfered with the congressional support necessary to attain their ends. So instead of far-flung possessions the books closed in 1860 writ small. There were inscribed some advantages in the Orient, a mere strip of Mexico, an ungracious retirement of Great Britain from a few acres in Central America, the doubtful glory of a punitive expedition against a weak neighbor and the acquisition of a few fertilizer islands. The growing precariousness of the Union almost completely hid from popular attention these slim achievements.

CHAPTER XVIII

THE IMPENDING CRISIS

The onward march of the nation was to be halted in the midst of this great period of prosperity and power. Not even national pride or love of profit and glory could protect the United States from the disasters implicit in the tightening tension. The 'fifties were to witness a series of crises pointing to the possibilty of the destruction of the democratic experiment. Could democracy survive in so large a region where such conflicting forces were at work?

The Fight for Kansas

The first crisis was political. The five territories, Minnesota, Oregon, Utah, New Mexico and Washington had not satisfied the land-hungry. Between the Pacific tier and latest midwestern communities was a vast plain, the balance of the Louisiana Purchase. Here were only roving bands of Indians, and no white man, save Indian agents, might legally enter therein. But much of the land was fertile and through it lay the path to the Pacific. It was a constant attraction to the westward-looking populace.

The discovery of gold in California had aroused a demand for overland transportation and plans for a transcontinental railroad were in the making. Furthermore, an irregular advance guard had gravitated toward this huge no-man's land, to calculate its possibilities and to pick out fertile spots which they hoped some day to possess. More and more of this type appeared at the borders, crossed over and wandered around; in Missouri and Iowa the pressure for the opening of these areas grew greater each year. Politicians of national reputation like Thomas Hart Benton of Missouri and Senator Stephen A. Douglas of Illinois began to urge the organization of the Nebraska region into a territory. Without such organization no transcontinental railroad could be built, for railroads cannot go where there are neither settlers nor property rights. The organization of a new territory was therefore a normal and necessary stage in the westward march but it was nevertheless to present a most difficult question. The spirit of sectional rivalry and jealousy was the most decisive factor in the legislative halls, and the members cast aside party allegiance to follow local or personal interest.

Western representatives were anxious to get a number of promotion measures through Congress. Without adequate capital to do big things, the West wanted the government to help. The possibility of securing river improvements to make streams more navigable, to obtain public buildings and army posts, to have roads built, to secure grants of land for local railroads, all these were the hope of western congressmen. Political contests were fought out on these lines and success or failure in reëlection often depended upon the representative's ability to bring home the fulfilment of his preëlection promises in local improvement appropriations. Also the drive for a more liberal distribution of the public land was a cherished western objective. On the other hand, the tariff was a matter of eastern interest; the protective cry needed only a slight measure of financial depression to force its renewed utterance. But southern representatives feared the speedy advance of the West and they hated high tariffs. How could they be persuaded to vote for these policies so assiduously advocated? The answer was that they could not be so persuaded without some drastic concessions to their own peculiar interests.

The southern attitude was apparent frequently and their representatives blocked many bills. Therefore when the question of organizing Nebraska arose their prejudices must be reckoned with. The territory lay above the Missouri Compromise line and was therefore free. Why should the South vote to organize free territories, eventually to become free states? The slaveholders in Missouri did not relish having a free territory so near as a convenient refuge for their runaway slaves. Their particular spokesman was Senator D. R. Atchison and he persuaded his southern colleagues to join him in a demand that if the territory were to be organized the Missouri Compromise should be repealed. Then, southern slaveholders might have a chance to go in and organize a territory where slavery would be permitted. Eventually, the new region might even become a slave state. The principal argument in favor of repeal was the claim that the northern members in refusing to extend the line 36° 30′ through the Mexican cession to the Pacific had in effect repudiated the idea of division.

Furthermore, the principle of leaving the matter of slavery to the people of the territories if desirable for the Mexican cession must be equally desirable for Nebraska. Senator Douglas who was promoting the bill for the new territory cared nothing for slavery but he cared much for western development and speculative enterprise both in railroads and real estate. When the southern senators made their demand he realized his bill could not pass unless he yielded, for they had the votes. Consequently he agreed to the repeal and convinced President Pierce that as the revised bill applied the principle of the Compromise of 1850 (popular sovereignty) it was quite in keeping with the Democratic platform, and necessary for party harmony. The result of all this politics was the sponsoring of a bill by the Democrats to organize two territories, Kansas and Nebraska, instead of one, to repeal the Missouri Compromise, and to leave the question of slavery to the inhabitants of the territories themselves. This bill became a law 30 May 1854, but it was enacted only after a bitter struggle; in fact it was the signal for a renewal of political agitation of the sectional issue which ended at length in civil war.

The time was ripe for a new political outbreak. American politics, like American business, experiences periodic cycles, each of which runs through the life of a generation. Every twenty years or so a new generation arises which seemingly must have its political enthusiasm and work out its political destiny by some new organization. Since the 'thirties, when opposition to Jackson had produced the Whigs, they had battled the Democrats with indifferent success. They were an opposition party with few principles and had not won a victory until 1840 when the voters turned away from the Democrats during the panic. Their only other success was the election of Taylor when the free-soil issue split the Democrats in 1848. The Democrats had elected James Knox Polk in 1844 and Franklin Pierce in 1852 and had maintained control of Congress most of the time since 1829. Since the Mexican war there had been a decreasing amount of partisan enthusiasm and the Whig and Democratic labels had ceased to mean very much. The Whigs, if anything, were the more conservative of the two, more responsive to demands of wealth and business. Both the Democrats and the Whigs were dominated by elder statesmen and the young and ambitious were kept in long apprenticeship. The new generation was eager to go ahead and it had at its disposal a variety of enthusiasms which it might use for party reorganization.

Today we can easily point out that the free-soil, anti-slavery enthusiasm was the most significant, but it was not clear at the time that this was so. There were two other current ideas that were also potent and which appealed to the popular imagination; one was liquor control and the other, prejudice against foreigners and Catholics. These three issues fitted very well the typical American frame of mind. In the background of national life were the old traditional English complexes. The religious interests of the Puritans deeply influenced succeeding generations, and a hatred of such sins as slavery and intemperance as well as a dislike of Catholics which dated from the days of the Reformation were natural to many Americans. The Puritans also bequeathed to the nation a zeal for reform and a blunt mode of expressing antipathies which naturally made such questions matters of public notice and discussion. Consequently these enthusiasms found their way into politics because politicians knew the value of stressing ideas or prejudices which could attract popular interest or rouse popular excitement. These three issues had long been in and out of the central focus of political attention.

There was agitation for various types of liquor legislation. Maine's enactment of a prohibition law in 1851 stimulated the drys to more active effort in other states and for the first six years of the 'fifties the issue was fought out in many a political campaign. The Democratic party was usually "wet," so its opponents saw the value of espousing the "dry" cause which was gaining such popularity. In some states "wet" and "dry" tickets were run, in others candidates of the regular parties declared or dodged about the issue and received support or failed to get votes according to the predominant sentiment in the region. Between 1851 and 1856 all the New England states, New York, Delaware, Iowa, Illinois and Nebraska went dry, although Illinois almost immediately reversed itself. Favorable votes by Wisconsin and Indiana were nullified in one way or another. Missouri, Texas, Louisiana, Mississippi and Illinois adopted local option and Ohio by various statutes was almost entirely dry. In other words, the "drys" were in the ascendant and were a political power to be reckoned with, especially as this issue appealed to the same type as were opposed to slavery. Most significant was the fact that their struggle was undermining the Democratic power in a variety of states.

The second issue which was attracting voters to organize was the "Nativist" prejudice. In the preceding twenty years an increasing number of Catholics had migrated from Ireland. These immigrants were especially conspicuous in eastern cities because they grouped themselves together in clannish settlements giving loyal adherence to the Catholic Church and to certain political leaders in the Democratic party. Furthermore they would do laborers' work for less money than native Americans and consequently cornered the unskilled labor market. Their political power caused a counter-organization and in several places, notably New York, Pennsylvania and New Jersey, "Nativist" parties appeared which, though they seldom attracted many votes outside of municipal elections, were a constantly perplexing factor.

The nativist movement revived at this time. Since 1846 a great wave of Irish immigration had been heading for America, augmented after 1848 by a German contingent. Their very numbers were a constant reminder of the old antipathy, and it began to operate in politics. The elections of 1854, especially in the East and South, witnessed the appearance of a new force, quite frequently spoken of as the "Know-Nothings," which worked in secret and attracted large numbers of super-patriotic Americans to vote for "Nativist" tickets. They carried a number of states, notably Massachusetts, and elected a score or more congressmen. It immediately appeared to politicians that if this group could be united to those opposed to the Nebraska bill, the Democrats might be universally defeated throughout the North. Events were working in that direction.

In the meantime the most significant of these three political issues also enjoyed a revival. In 1840 a few voters had supported a Liberty Party candidate for president and in 1844 this party had attracted sufficient voters from the Whigs in New York to gain for itself the credit of defeating Henry Clay. In 1848 the Free Soil party undoubtedly caused the defeat of Lewis Cass. Thus in the 'forties they had been a potent force, but the Compromise of 1850 had destroyed their issue and in 1852 the party had cut no figure though still running a ticket. However, they had a shrewd group of senators and congressmen, small in number but fertile in resource. Salmon P. Chase and Joshua Giddings of Ohio, Charles Sumner of Massachusetts and Gerrit Smith of New York were alert for an opportunity to revive their waning fortunes while ever zealous in their chosen cause of arresting the spread of slavery. Therefore as soon as the idea of repealing the Missouri Compromise was advanced they launched what proved to be a thunderbolt, "An Appeal to the Independent Democrats." The press and the pulpit took up their cry and 1854 saw a variety of combinations, coalitions and alliances. Many northern Whigs and Democrats were attracted and joined in protest. In the same year that the Know-Nothings were showing power in the East and South, there appeared this new combination, at first most potent in the West.

Enemies of the South, westerners who resented the refusal of the Democratic majority in Congress to pass promotion legislation, disgruntled politicians, old Whigs who saw a new hope in the rising power, Democrats who could not defend to northern constituencies the southern predominance in national party councils, the fighting "drys" who liked crusading against sin, and finally those who yearned for political adventure, all such heard the appeal and prepared to rally. Coalitions such as had been made occasionally since 1846 now became very popular. After earlier experiments in the spring came the notable coalition achieved at Jackson, Michigan, 4 July 1854. Here a state ticket was nominated composed of Whigs, Free Soilers and Democrats who had as their rallying cry "Restore the Missouri Compromise!" Such coalitions, sometimes called "Republican," figured successfully in the election of 1854.

The results of the Kansas-Nebraska Act provided excellent ammunition for Republican political spell-binders and press writers. As soon as the territories were opened, settlers passed in. Nothing of note occurred in Nebraska but Kansas, just west of Missouri, became the stage of an exciting drama. The Missourians had expected to settle the territory, leaving Nebraska to the northern migrants, but this was not to be. Many who resented the repeal of the Missouri Compromise were determined to make Kansas free. An organization was established in New England to aid prospective settlers by getting them cut rates on the railroads and by selling them supplies reasonably. Their existence was unduly advertised and when northerners began to appear in Kansas in the summer and fall of 1854, many in Missouri were convinced of a plot. Northern money, they said, was being used to pay people to come and vote Kansas free. The Missouri planters would not submit to this "steal" without a struggle; so when the first territorial legislature was to be elected in March 1855 a horde of Missourians went over to vote, sometimes violently. The legislature thus chosen was overwhelmingly pro-slavery. The northern settlers in turn declared they would not submit to such robbery and an incipient civil war broke out when the free state people repudiated the territorial government and established one of their own. Some blood was shed, though less than generally advertised, conditions were very much unsettled and the Republican editors and orators made the most of it. Kansas was held up as a horrible example of the results of the repeal of the time-honored Missouri Compromise.

The Republicans saw a great chance to win in 1856 and bent every effort to gaining allies. Fortunately for them, the Kansas furor caused the Know-Nothing party to split on the slavery issue and the great mass of the northern wing joined the Republicans. By this move, the great northern party feared by the South was organized in the spring of 1856. To combat this new force, the Democrats assumed a conservative rôle and chose James Buchanan, politician of long experience and "safe" views to be their leader. Their campaign was made on the issue that the conservatives must rally to save the Union from the destruction which would come if a sectional party like the Republicans should win —for then the South would surely secede. The remnant of the Whigs and the southern Know-Nothings joined to nominate ex-President Fillmore but their strength was sufficient to carry only one state, Maryland.

The Republicans entered the lists under the lead of a showy, well-advertised figure, John C. Frémont, rather romantically called the "Pathfinder" because of his western explorations. He was not burdened with past political experience or known views; his platform called for free soil and a Pacific Railroad; there were to be no new slave states under Republican rule. With such a platform no southern votes could be expected, nor were they received. Frémont captured all the northern states but six and received 114 electoral votes. Had he been able to carry Pennsylvania and either Illinois or Indiana he would have been elected. In 1852 the Republican party had never been heard of; in 1856 it was within thirty-five votes of victory. The Republicans could look forward to 1860 with high hope.

Such a political uprising taking place in the short space of two years was of the utmost significance. For the first time the growing sectional antagonism had found expression in a formidable party. The Republicans made a frank sectional appeal; they were anti-southern, pledged to stop southern advance and to decrease southern power. Many southerners now thought they saw the handwriting on the wall, gone was the old nationalism based on compromise between the sections. The North was in a numerical majority and was growing fast; northern politicians were seeking to gain the power that comes to the majority and seemed careless if not antagonistic to the rights of the minority South. Could the South afford to stay in the Union if the Republicans should win? For the time being the northern party had been defeated; perhaps it might be permanently checked. Southern leaders were going to continue the fight.

The Panic of 1857

The threat of secession voiced by southern leaders during the campaign of 1856 was ominous; the sense of relief which the fearsome enjoyed after the election was to be short-lived comfort. An economic crisis followed the political crisis. The great bonanza was about to give out. For a decade wealth had been increasing faster and faster, more and more speculative ventures had proved successful; apparently there was no end of American miracles. But the business cycle was about to complete another revolution. In 1854 certain signs appeared as warnings. A money stringency developed, the price of stocks, especially rails, fell, banks and business houses failed, industry slowed down, with a noticeable unemployment resulting. This warning was brief and disregarded and 1855 and 1856 were marked by the same feverish advance; in the latter year alone, nearly 4,000 miles of railroad were built.

During these flush years Americans had bought much abroad. The nation's exports were not large enough to pay these bills, but fortunately, so it seemed, European investors bought a great many American securities, notably railroad bonds and stocks. These purchases enabled American buyers to settle their balances on European exchanges without exporting specie to any large extent. In the spring of 1857, however, economic conditions were not prosperous in Europe, and consumers and investors stopped buying; worse, they began selling American securities and demanding cash. Such a policy not only cut heavily into American exporting business but it called for extensive shipments of coin to Europe.

In the United States, prices were high and stocks of goods were large; a great deal of money was tied up in land and in railroads and was not earning any immediate return. Therefore when heavy demands for coin were made from abroad, banks in the eastern cities were hard put to get it and began to call upon their western correspondents for loans when due. These correspondents tried to meet the calls by selling railroad securities and foreclosing mortgages, with the result that the market for stocks and lands began to sag dangerously. Western banks were in danger for some months while heavy exports of gold were worrying the bankers of the seaboard but the crash was not precipitated until 24 August when a large credit organization, the Ohio Life Insurance and Trust Company, failed. The climax came in October when the refusal of the New York banks to honor their own notes with specie meant that specie payment had ceased throughout the country. Industries as well as banks and railroads suffered. The panic, however, was not of long duration; harvests were plentiful that year and in December New York banks resumed specie payments. By 1860 economic enterprise had largely recovered its confidence. The political and psychological effects lingered on.

The shock of the disaster caused the northern industrialists to take thought about the nature of their weaknesses. The fact of foreign competition was the most easy to grasp and the remedy right at hand. If there were a protective tariff a recurrence of these conditions would be less likely. During 1858 an organized demand for protection began to be promoted by certain manufacturing interests. In 1857, several months before the panic, Congress had passed a tariff bill designed to reduce the revenue which was piling up a surplus under the revenue tariff of 1846 which the Democrats had passed. Advocates of protection now pointed to this reduction as a major cause of the panic, which of course it was not, and demanded higher duties. Naturally such agitation aroused the southern fear of the tariff, and did so at a time when southern leaders were led by the circumstances of the panic to be particularly arrogant on economic matters.

All sections had not suffered alike. Western land speculators and railroad promoters and eastern manufacturers and bankers had felt the full force of the shock but in the South the planters had continued relatively undisturbed. Cotton grew and Europe bought it; the money which the planters deposited or spent tended to bolster up northern banks and business. As a result, the southern leaders became obsessed with the idea that their section alone was stable and secure. Northern and western economic organization was weak and unreliable. The South therefore was indispensable to the economic prosperity of the nation. Moreover, the South seemingly was economically independent and could get along very well by itself. In other words cotton was king and with it the South could, if necessary, easily maintain itself independently.

John Brown's Raid

The third crisis of the 'fifties seems at first glance almost a trivial incident hardly worthy of the notice of today. But at the time it assumed catastrophic proportions and its influence was disastrous. The anti-slavery crusade found in its ranks many zealots, and of some it may be well said that their zeal outran their discretion. Such an one was John Brown. He had been actively engaged in a varied series of episodes, not all of them too creditable, trying to force Kansas to be free. But after 1858, Kansas seemed no longer to need to be freed and Brown conceived an elaborate plan of penetrating into one slave community after another, forcibly freeing some of the slaves and organizing cities of refuge to which others might flee. By this means he hoped to make slavery impossible in region after region until the South gave up the institution in despair. With less than a score of followers he attempted to put his plan into effect. Sunday night, 16 October 1859, he sought to inaugurate his scheme by capturing Harper's Ferry at the junction of the Potomac and the Shenandoah. Here he expected to seize the government arsenal and its weapons, free the slaves in the surrounding district and start a Negro republic. Harper's Ferry, all unsuspecting that sabbath evening, was easy prey to the little band but the slaves were not eager for freedom, the local militia soon gathered and by Monday evening the marines had arrived. The episode passed into history when John Brown, convicted of treason, was hanged, 2 December.

This ill-judged foray filled the South with apprehension and indignation. John Brown had received financial help at various times from prominent abolitionists, some of whom were in close touch with Republican politicians. Although there is no proof that any of them had any particular knowledge of this last scheme of Brown's, nevertheless, many in the South were convinced that the Republicans were engaging in a plot to produce a slave insurrection. The memory of the Negro uprising in Haiti in 1791 had been kept alive and now flamed up into fear of the possibility of fire, murder, and violence which would be sure to accompany such an outbreak. To emphasize the terror the governor of Virginia, when he found a number of murderous pikes among John Brown's equipment, sent one to each governor in the southern states to be exhibited as an example of what the Republicans were trying to do.

In the North, on the other hand, the hanging of John Brown was but another evidence of the barbarity of the South. When an apostle of freedom sought to save the South from its shame, that wicked section hanged him. Thoreau wrote, "Some eighteen hundred years ago, Christ was crucified, this morning John Brown was hung." Both sides held the exaggerated opinions of troublous times. Nerves were jangling, blind fears were unleashed, fanatic zeal was abroad, judgments could not be sober nor eyes clear-sighted. Jealousy had bred fear and fear begot hate. In such wise was John Brown's crazy foray a major disaster.

The Decision of 1860: Secession

As 1860 approached there were few who did not realize that the presidential election of that year was to be crucial. Upon its result probably would depend the continued existence of the Union. The South was becoming more and more apprehensive of Republican success; for after John Brown's raid, it was widely believed that the Republican party had backed Brown and that his raid was part of a plot to destroy the South by organizing a series of slave uprisings. There was no such plot but the important fact is that many people believed there was and were determined to act accordingly.

The South, therefore, strengthened in the false economic assumptions of its panic experience and frightened by the growth of the Republican party and the raid of 1859, was coming to the point where it was about ready to take a stand before the nation and make an imperious demand. The Republican party must be defeated in 1860 or the southern states would leave the Union. The only institution which could seek to enforce this demand was the Democratic party. But that party was in an harassed and distressed state and events shortly were to demonstrate that it was in no condition to cope with the Republicans. The Democratic party in power with hardly an interruption since 1828 and victorious even in 1856 was on the verge of schism and disintegration. A new power was rising.

The Republican party had made politics more complicated. Hitherto the major parties had been national, with membership drawn about equally from northern and southern states, and platforms which favored neither section widely. Now the Republican party came forward representing but one section; since it could not expect to gain any support in the South, it was free to appeal directly and completely to northern interest. Such an opponent placed the Democrats in a difficult position. They must carry states in both sections to win national elections, but how could they carry northern states if their platforms were in any sense satisfactory to the South? The Democrats had adopted the formula of "popular sovereignty" which declared neither for nor against slavery extension but left the question to the vote of the people in each new territory. Upon this platform they had won by a narrow margin in 1856. However, this doctrine had been discredited since that momentous election.

In the first place, the Supreme Court had decided, in effect, that popular sovereignty was unconstitutional. In March 1857, the tribunal rendered its decision in the Dred Scott Case. This case had been brought to the Supreme Court for political purposes by some anti-slavery men and it was used by the justices themselves in similar manner. The case could have been easily decided without much thought or the preparation of extended opinions but one of the northern justices seemed to consider it an opportunity to give a decided dissenting opinion which would benefit the Republicans. Thereupon the chief justice, Roger B. Taney of Maryland, was persuaded to write a lengthy decision. It placed in convenient form certain comforting doctrines for the South and it was hailed by their leaders as the final word. In effect Taney gave his opinion that slaves were property and could not be excluded from the territories by Congress or by popular vote because of the 5th Amendment. This not only discredited "popular sovereignty" and the demand for congressional prohibition of slavery in the territories made by the Republicans, but it encouraged extreme southern leaders now to demand protection of slaves in all territories as their "constitutional right."

When President Buchanan accepted the dictum of the Supreme Court and endeavored to put through Congress a pro-slavery constitution adopted by the southern voters in Kansas, Douglas broke with him. The outcome was a heated congressional contest which resulted in the resubmission of the constitution to all the voters of Kansas by an indirect method. The people of Kansas refused to accept the constitution and in leisurely fashion made another, prohibiting slavery.[1] This result proved to the South that "popular sovereignty" would do nothing but produce civil war and the final expulsion of slavery from any territory in the Northwest. If "popular sovereignty" continued the South could expect nothing from it.

This contest in Kansas split the Democratic party. Senator Douglas had the support of a great following of northern Democrats, while President Buchanan could rally only the southern Democrats and a minority of those in the northern states. Nevertheless Buchanan tried to "purge" Douglas and failed. Douglas after an exciting contest for re-election to the Senate with his Illinois Republican opponent, Abraham Lincoln, won a close victory. But in that same election period of 1858, the Democrats again lost the House of Representatives. They were badly split; the northern Democrats had Douglas as their leader and "popular sovereignty" as their platform, and the administration forces led by Buchanan had a group of southern senators who were trying desperately to find a platform and a candidate for 1860 which would unite the party. Could the Democratic party survive? Its success seemed vital to the continuance of the Union. For if it broke up Republican

[1] Kansas was finally admitted in January 1861 after the first southern states had seceded.

victory seemed assured and that would mean an attempt at least on the part of the South to break up the Union.

As the convention of 1860 approached a group of southern leaders were planning to demand a new platform from the Democrats calling for protection of the slaves in territories by federal power. This demand was strengthened by the fear engendered by John Brown's raid, and seemed to have the endorsement of the Supreme Court. But how could realistic national politicians accept this demand? Southern votes alone could not elect a president. Northern states must be carried, but the four-square northern appeal of the Republicans made that well-nigh impossible. Northern Democrats had one hope, namely, Douglas of Illinois. Douglas to the southern mind was unavailable because he had broken with Democratic party leaders on Kansas and still claimed that in spite of the Supreme Court, in the end, only the people of a community could decide on their institutions. If they saw fit to freeze out slavery by unfriendly local legislation it could not survive notwithstanding any constitutional interpretation of the courts. In spite of southern protests, northern Democrats were adamant in their insistence on Douglas and his doctrine as presidential nominee and platform; without him their cause in the North was lost. Whereupon the southern Democrats left the convention of 1860 and nominated candidates of their own.[1] With the Democrats split, the success of the Republicans was inevitable.

The Republicans were quick to realize their opportunity. They nominated an "available" candidate, Abraham Lincoln of Illinois, and enlarged their platform. Hitherto they had stood on a program of prohibiting the further extension of slavery and subsidizing a Pacific railroad; now they added two planks of great significance, namely, one providing for a free homestead for every citizen who wanted it and the other calling for a protective tariff. Western promoters and eastern industrialists still somewhat bruised by the late panic could not help but be attracted by these generous proposals. This clever platform was a powerful argument.

The North responded with great enthusiasm and Lincoln was elected by the electoral votes of the northern states. The South had failed to prevent the triumph of the party which they had come to believe spelled destruction to white supremacy and slave property and the loss of the political domination they had long enjoyed. It was evident when the result was announced that a crisis was at hand. During the preceding months many southern leaders had been threatening, just as they had in 1856, that if the Republicans won, the southern states would secede.

[1] The nominees of the southern Democrats were John C. Breckinridge of Kentucky and Joseph Lane of Oregon. The northern Democrats nominated Douglas and Herschel V. Johnson of Georgia. A remnant of the old Whigs formed a Constitutional Union party and nominated John Bell of Tennessee and Edward Everett of Massachusetts.

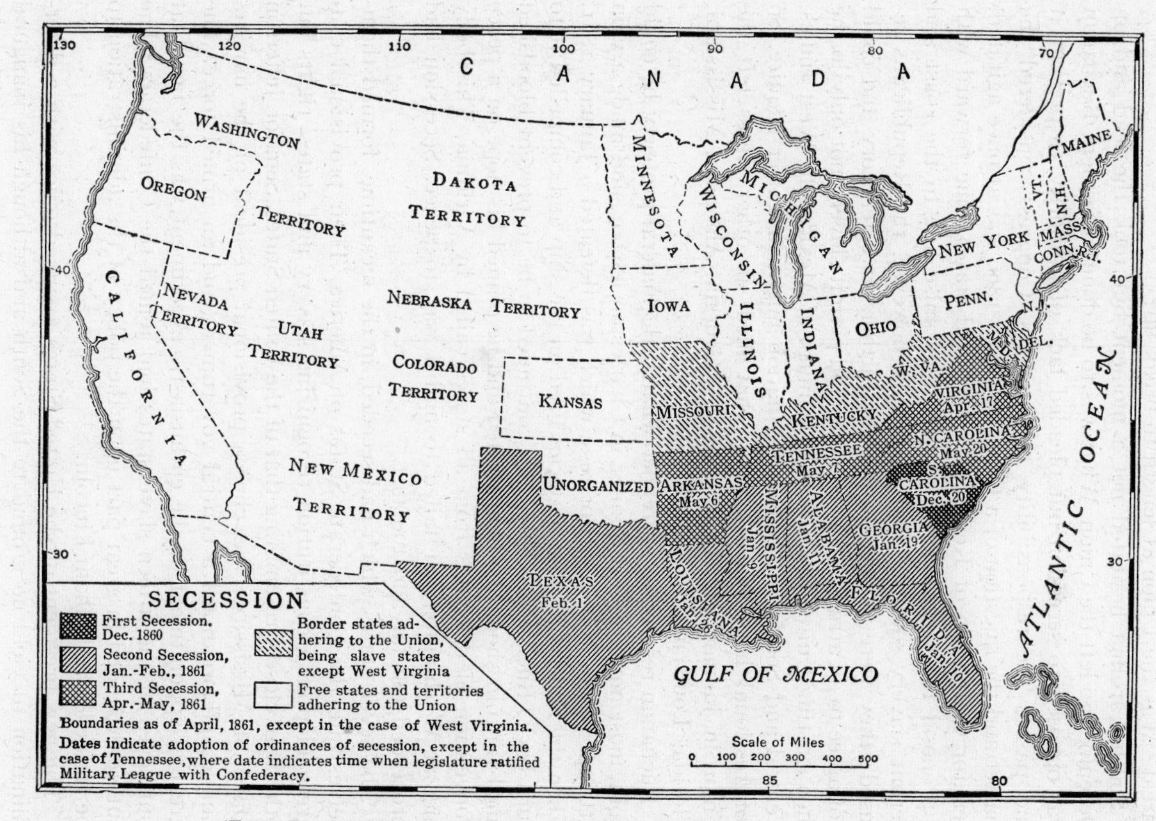

(From Randall, *The Civil War and Reconstruction*, reprinted by permission of D. C. Heath and Company, publishers.)

The question now had to be faced; was the South going to carry out its threat? Was the Union at length to break up?

South Carolina hesitated not a moment but took the lead and on December 20 left the Union. What was to be done? President Buchanan was opposed to secession but pleaded lack of authority to prevent it and passed the responsibility to Congress. Congress considered the matter and the question of a Compromise of 1860 was at once agitated. Senator Crittenden of Kentucky, Clay's old state, came forward with a proposal to extend the Missouri Compromise line to the coast and permit slavery south of that line. This, however, the Republicans refused; they were pledged to prevent further slave territory and could not agree to an arrangement which would permit slavery not only in the then existing United States but in as much of Mexico, the West Indies, Central and South America as the nation might hereafter acquire. So congressional hope faded, and as that died six other states left the Union in January and February 1861, Georgia, Alabama, Mississippi, Florida, Louisiana and Texas.

Buchanan refused to surrender what little Federal property he could hold, most notably Fort Sumter in Charleston harbor, and made a vain attempt to provision that fortress, which was defeated 9 January 1861, when the South Carolina batteries fired on the ship and compelled it to turn back. Buchanan's chief aim continued to be to prevent bloodshed until Lincoln should be inaugurated and he pinned his hope on a peace convention of delegates from all states called by Virginia. This body met at Washington but failed to find a way to peace. Secession had proceeded too far and too fast.

The seven states which had seceded, in the meantime, formed themselves into the Confederate States of America. Their provisional congress adopted a constitution recognizing slavery and states' rights but otherwise closely resembling that of the United States. Senator Jefferson Davis of Mississippi was chosen provisional president of the new republic and organized a central government and an armed force. The great disappointment of the enthusiastic experiment was the fact that but seven of the fifteen slave states had joined the Confederacy. The future depended in great part upon the policy of the administration to be formed by Abraham Lincoln.

The new president of the United States assumed office with a determination to yield no ground to the South and although his inaugural was conciliatory in its spirit, still it left little room to doubt that he would not give way to the South. But his cabinet was not a unit. Upon the morning after his inauguration an urgent call came from Fort Sumter for reënforcements, but several weeks elapsed before the cabinet agreed to the project. Seward, the secretary of state, still felt that Sumter was not worth bloodshed and if it were surrendered a plan for a war against Great Britain, France and Spain which he had devised might bring the South back to its loyalty. Lincoln felt otherwise; Sumter must be reënforced, and he notified the Confederacy that the attempt would be made. The Confederate cabinet must now decide whether they would precipitate a civil war by firing upon the approaching relief expedition or yet preserve peace. The success of their move for independence was at stake. Their sense of honor demanded that they drive the garrison from Sumter; besides they may have hoped that if they took firm action the other slave states might be rallied to join the Confederacy. So the die was cast. Sumter was bombarded and as

FIRST GUNS OF WAR: FIRING ON THE *Star of the West*

the relief expedition was too weak to render effective aid, the fort was surrendered. When President Lincoln called upon the states for volunteers to recapture Federal property, four of them refused to obey and left the Union rather than coerce their sister states. Virginia, North Carolina, Arkansas and Tennessee joined the Confederacy.[1]

The orderly procedure of American democracy had been abandoned. Rather than acknowledge the authority of a president regularly elected as prescribed in the Constitution, seven states had withdrawn from the Union. They had set up an independent government and resorted to arms to prevent the Federal authority from caring for its own property. Rather than join in reclaiming this property by force, four other states

[1] After some hesitancy and under powerful Federal pressure, military and otherwise, Maryland, Kentucky and Missouri decided not to secede. Delaware, of course, could not act unless Maryland did. Also the western counties of Virginia refused to go out of the Union and the Virginia troops which sought to hold them were driven out. In 1863 these counties became the state of West Virginia.

had likewise seceded. From the Federal point of view, these eleven states were joining in insurrection against duly constituted authority. From the Confederate point of view, they were but following the example of their Revolutionary forebears in resisting dangerous tyranny. Only force of arms could decide which was right. Democracy meanwhile must stand aside.

CHAPTER XIX

WAR

The bewildering series of events which culminated in the firing upon Fort Sumter produced an unprecedented situation. Here was the greatest republic in history, consisting of people speaking the same language and thinking in terms of much the same traditions, yet they were arming themselves and preparing to fight each other. The North was determined to prevent the southern states from destroying a great nation, and there was much talk of punishing traitors and whipping rebels; a great deal was said also of destroying the curse of slavery and there was some hope of breaking the power of the oligarchic planter class. The South, on the other hand, felt that the lives and property of its people were in danger, and that its power, and even white supremacy itself, was threatened if it remained in a country controlled by men with the ideas held by the Republican leaders. They must protect themselves by seeking independence just as their ancestors had done in the American Revolution. Each side was supremely confident of the righteousness of its cause, and as both were of the same nation and tradition, the struggle was bound to be long and disastrous. Much blood must be shed, much property destroyed, with much excitement, suffering and sorrow.

The Strength of the Opponents

Two groups, one of about 22 million people, and the other of 9 million, including 3 million Negroes, were entering each upon a tremendous community enterprise. The 22 million were to supply about 1 million men who were to devote a part at least of four years to the business of fighting, while the 9 million were to furnish about 850,000. Nearly 6 per cent of the population was to take up arms. But the remainder were by no means to be exempt from the struggle. Hardly a community or an occupation but was affected, and even the many who took no direct part could not fail to realize that they were living in times that were out of joint. All paid psychological toll of one sort or another to the conflict.

The first problem in each section was mobilizing an army. The North had the small regular army for a nucleus and the administrative system of the War Department to provide direction and equipment, while the South had only the state militia systems to build upon. The resignation from the Federal army of prominent officers and bureau chiefs such as Robert E. Lee, Joseph E. Johnston, Albert S. Johnston, Samuel Cooper, and P. G. T. Beauregard did much to help the South and to hinder the mobilization of the North. Two weeks after Lincoln's first call for 75,000 volunteers, he summoned 42,000 more; also he increased the regular army of 17,000 by enlisting 22,000 raw recruits; throughout the war the two separate services, the large volunteer force and the small regular army, had to be maintained. The Confederate Congress authorized President Davis to accept 100,000 troops and soon extended the number indefinitely. In both sections, volunteering in the first months of the war was enthusiastic and continuous, so that by the first of July, on paper at least, there were 250,000 men enlisted in the hostile armies. Most of the recruits were having their first experience with camp life and the rudiments of military drill.

Munitions and supplies in great quantity were more difficult to obtain than men. The Federal War Department was organized to supply 17,000 men and when it was called upon to equip 150,000 it failed lamentably to meet the pressing need. There was shortage or lack of even the most essential things, confusion in attempting to get them, and inefficiency in both obtaining and distributing them. But the North had money and factories and could rise to the occasion. In the South, however, there was no organization or supply of any sort to begin with; neither were there factories or money. Both sides realized that supplies, especially of cloth and munitions, could be purchased most quickly abroad, where extensive stocks were on hand, so agents were sent to Europe for that purpose. Southern representatives got there first and made contracts but in many cases were unable to pay the necessary deposits and instalments, so that the Federal agents slipped in and took the goods for ready money.

In the meantime northern industry was working feverishly to meet the demand, stimulated by the high prices offered in the contracts which the War Department distributed lavishly. There was much waste and some corruption and part of the goods delivered were shoddy and below specifications.[1] But so hurried and confused was the distribution and so insistent the demands that few except the unfortunate soldiers who suffered from the poor equipment stopped to think much about it. The great pressure stimulated invention, and new machinery, especially for sewing uniforms and making shoes, came into extensive use. The farmer also had his calls and increased his crops to meet the great need for army rations. Here, too, machines were invaluable, the reaper making extended production possible even while many a farm lad was enlisting. Lack of machines became a great handicap to the South after the

[1] The Federal War Department spent $1,184,300,000 for supplies.

tightening of the naval blockade made importation less and less possible. Southern armies had to depend upon improvised industries and their not inconsiderable captures from the North in battle; the lack of equipment was to prove well-nigh fatal.

Even more difficult was the problem of the navy. There again the North had the advantage, possessing the Federal Navy Department and most of the navy yards. Only a few war vessels, most notably the *Merrimack,* fell into the hands of the Confederates. However, the Federal fleet numbered but 90 ships, with only 29 steam vessels; these ships, manned by 9,000 officers and men, were entirely inadequate to undertake the chief naval objective of the Federal government, namely, the blockade of Confederate ports. Many of the vessels were not in condition or were at distant stations in European, Asiatic or African waters. The first task was to improvise blockading squadrons and the department went into the market for vessels of all sorts, while the navy yards began to build as fast as they could. Inventors and ship-builders began experimenting, especially in ironclads, for throughout the world naval construction was being revolutionized and wooden vessels were giving way to armored craft. During the war 313 steamers were bought and 203 were built, including 60 ironclads. The personnel of the navy was increased to 59,000 officers and men, recruited liberally from the merchant fleets. By the end of the fiscal year 1861-1862, the blockading fleets were in position and the cotton export, which in 1860-1861 had been 2 million bales, was reduced to 13,000 for the year following.

Naturally, the Confederate problem in naval matters was almost insoluble. They had no merchant marine and no shipyards; as building or chartering a navy within their bounds was impossible, their attention was turned immediately to the possibility of building abroad. Agents were despatched to make contracts, and several war vessels designed to roam the seas were built in British shipyards. Cruisers like the *Sumter, Alabama, Florida* and *Shenandoah* ravaged American commerce. Nineteen such vessels seized 258 prizes. Their work was so effective that by the end of the war they had practically driven the Stars and Stripes off the seas. At the outset, two-thirds of American foreign commerce was carried by American merchantmen; but during these dangerous years over 700 such ships transferred to British registry. Gradually the Confederate raiders were hunted down. The *Sumter* was driven to cover in January of 1862, the *Alabama* came to a most spectacular end in a naval duel with the *Kearsarge* off Cherbourg in June of 1864 and the *Florida* was seized in a Brazilian port the following October. The last of the great raiders, the *Shenandoah,* which operated particularly among the whalers on the Pacific, continued her work of destruction until June of 1865, when her captain finally learned the war was over.

At home the Confederates succeeded in getting a few war vessels in shape, such as the *Merrimack,* which was made into an ironclad, and the ram *Albemarle.* For the most part, ship construction in Confederate yards was confined to small, swift steamers, such as could be profitably employed in blockade-running. These runners succeeded quite frequently and their commerce helped to supply the Confederacy with quantities, all too inadequate, of medicines, percussion caps and a variety of other things sorely needed. The war, however, was by no means a sea struggle; even in the North the naval expenditure was but 9.3 per cent of the cost of the conflict.

The war machinery thus set going functioned with varying degrees of efficiency for four years, years of fluctuating hope and despair because until the last few months the possibility of the defeat of the Confederacy seemed often very remote. The South started with important advantages; she had the best officers of the old army and the easier position of fighting a defensive war on familiar ground. On the other hand, the North was superior in numbers and resources. Both sides, at the start, were too confident; in the North particularly did the belief prevail that one battle would decide the issue, and press and public were eager to have it over. Despite the well-grounded fear of the Federal commanders that a raw army could not be depended upon in battle, pressure was so great that in July, 1861, McDowell was ordered to march into Virginia and meet the Confederate army there assembling. The result was a Union defeat at Bull Run and the realization that this war was going to be neither brief nor one-sided.

The Diplomacy of the War

After this initial reverse, all hope of ending the war in ninety days was destroyed; both sides settled down for a long struggle. A human machine had to be trained and in the meantime increasing attention paid to diplomacy, for there is more to war than battles and this war was to be no exception. While the armies were drilling and fighting, the diplomats were carrying on a duel which at times reached spectacular limits. The Confederacy confidently expected European aid in the early days of its career and the State Department in the North feared that such help might be afforded. England needed southern cotton and the Confederates firmly believed she would recognize the seceded states to ensure her supply. As soon as the Confederate government was organized it ordered its cotton kept at home while it sent various agents abroad to secure official recognition in return for cotton. If England led the way France at least would concur and the ear of European capitalists would be obtained for loans.

Lincoln's secretary of state. Seward, as soon as he entered office, undertook to protest vigorously against any such recognition. Lincoln appointed Charles Francis Adams as minister to Great Britain, but the appointment was not made promptly and the new minister delayed starting so that events had raced ahead ere he reached his post. Great Britain realized the strength of the southern move and refused to accept the northern contention that these were rebel states unworthy of recognition even as respectable war-makers. Therefore, in realistic mood, England on 13 May recognized the Confederates as belligerents (that is, as a group of sufficient strength to be fighting under the rules of civilized warfare and not as rebels or pirates to be hanged as captured) and issued a neutrality proclamation. Although this was less than the recognition of independence which the South craved, it gave her a dignified status. Northern protest at the British action was to no avail.

Six months later a zealous northern naval officer stopped a British mail steamer and arrested the Confederate diplomats, James M. Mason and John Slidell; thereupon the two powers nearly came to blows. Lincoln, despite popular approval of this violation of international law, wisely apologized to the British and caused the diplomats to be sent on their way. In the meantime, Confederate agents secretly let contracts in British and French shipyards for war vessels and the Confederate government continued to hope for recognition of its independence, holding back cotton exports to compel favorable action.

Europe started out with sympathy for the Confederate cause. The monarchical governments had no love for the republican form and would secretly rejoice if a republic proved unable to stand. Also, the United States and England were commercial and political rivals and the mercantile and aristocratic classes of the latter realm had no love for this growing American competitor. Two nations would be easier to handle than one united people. Yet it seemed safer to delay formal recognition while giving illegal aid. So, in spite of her neutrality proclamation, Britain permitted Confederate war vessels to be built in her yards and to set forth from her shores. At length, after the *Alabama* and *Florida* had demonstrated their efficiency as destroyers of northern merchantmen, and when it seemed that three more warships were to be permitted to set sail, the crisis came. Minister Adams, in effect, threatened war if these additional ships were not detained. Britain took thought: the American navy had grown stronger and more dangerous to British commerce; announcement of Lincoln's Emancipation Proclamation was swinging liberal opinion in a northerly directly; the cotton-mill workers of the Manchester area, the class most hurt by the cotton scarcity, came out for freedom. Altogether, the British ministry, in April of 1863, were moved to put an end to this clandestine aid.

Even less friendly to the North was Napoleon III of France. A large loan was floated by the Confederates in Paris and Napoleon used American distraction as a convenient time to establish a French empire in Mexico. Spain also made an opportunity and reoccupied Santo Domingo. Only Russia seemed at all friendly, although her gesture of sending her fleet on a friendly visit to American waters was largely due to a desire to keep it safe from a possible blockade in her own ports by British and French.

Yet the Confederacy was never successful enough to command political recognition. Furthermore, that government would not offer commercial concessions to foreign powers and continued to boast of slavery. This was not a practical program in a very practical world. The Confederacy's last belated gesture in the final days of war, offering the abolition of slavery in return for recognition, came too late.

The Ebb and Flow of Battle

Long before this tortuous course of diplomacy had worked out, a desperate military conflict had raised alternate hopes and fears, as the fortunes of both armies fluctuated. After the initial reverse at Bull Run the Federal command settled down really to train the army, and George B. McClellan was chosen for that purpose. Meanwhile, a plan was devised for extended operations of conquest. One objective was to occupy the Confederate capital at Richmond. A second was to protect Kentucky, free Tennessee and gain control of the Mississippi. A third was to organize joint military and naval operations at various points along the coast and capture the seaports.

The first successes were achieved along the seaboard. Federal naval and land forces gained control of most of the North Carolina coast and commanded Pamlico and Albemarle sounds, after seizing Ocracoke and Hatteras inlets in August 1861 and Roanoke Island in the following February. A like control was gained over the South Carolina shore when Port Royal was captured in November 1861. A skilful attack on Fort Pulaski, the guardian of Savannah, placed the Georgia littoral under Federal domination the following April. Thereafter Charleston, South Carolina, and Wilmington, North Carolina, were the only Atlantic ports of importance held by the Confederates. On the Gulf coast and on the great river systems, the Union navy had much to do. Fort Pickens, off Pensacola, was all that the Union had been able to save of the extensive Gulf fortifications and preparations were made for the conquest of the area.

Success for the North was coming out of the West. There, five generals were inaugurating distinguished careers; U. S. Grant, W. T. Sherman, G. H. Thomas, Don Carlos Buell and H. W. Halleck. Their task was to prevent Confederate advance into Kentucky and to rescue

Tennessee, where eastern mountain sections contained many loyal Union men and women. The Confederate leader who skilfully opposed them was General Albert Sidney Johnston. To break his center, Grant must capture two forts on the Tennessee and Cumberland rivers—Fort Henry and Fort Donelson. Assisted by a fleet of river gunboats, commanded by Commodore Andrew H. Foote, Grant's army won these objectives in February 1862, and Grant and Buell entered Tennessee. The latter occupied Nashville and Lincoln was able thereafter to appoint Senator Andrew Johnson (later president) as military governor to bring Tennessee back into the Union. Grant proceeded up the Tennessee to enter Mississippi and Alabama, expecting Buell to join him.

Before their junction, Johnston took advantage of the separation of the two armies to attack Grant. At the battle of Pittsburgh Landing or Shiloh, 6-7 April, Grant barely saved himself and his army from defeat, and his worthy adversary, General Johnston, was killed. General Halleck, who had just been given command of all the Union troops west of the Alleghenies, now took the field. Under his direction Missouri was cleared of Confederates and a good beginning was made in Arkansas. General John Pope opened the Mississippi River almost down to Memphis, Tennessee, by capturing Island #10, and Halleck himself, after a cautious siege, captured Corinth, the vital rail junction within northern Mississippi.

The Federal successes of the spring of 1862 were completed by the navy. A joint naval and military expedition was mobilized under Commodore David G. Farragut and General Benjamin F. Butler, who engineered in April a spectacular naval attack upon the forts, and the capture of New Orleans. At the same time, Memphis fell, so that for a brief period Farragut had control of the river. He did not get the proper military support in the state of Mississippi, however, and could not prevent the Confederates from garrisoning Vicksburg and Port Hudson. They thus fastened their hold upon a stretch of river 250 miles long, and controlled the mouth of the Red River, which was the artery of communication with Texas. As long as the Texas seaports and Mobile were still in Confederate hands, they could yet give much trouble to the blockading Union squadrons in the Gulf.

Similar success did not meet Union forces in the East. McClellan's grand army was faring ill in its march upon Richmond. He had discarded McDowell's direct cross-country descent from the north, electing to approach the Confederate capital from the southeast. He would transport his army by boat to Fortress Monroe and proceed up the historic peninsula between the James and the York.

As he was preparing to embark, a startling chapter was written in the history of naval warfare. At Hampton Roads five Union frigates were stationed, guarding the approaches to Fortress Monroe and blockading Norfolk. There the Confederates had raised the frigate *Merrimack* from the spot where she had been sunk when the Union commander evacuated the Federal navy yard. Engineers had covered her with iron and fitted a ram to her prow. Renamed the *Virginia,* she steamed forth to sink the Union fleet. Their guns could not pierce her armament and 8 March she destroyed the *Cumberland* and the *Congress.* She returned to Norfolk for the night, expecting to finish the fleet the next day, a pleasant prospect but unrealized. A northern inventor, John Ericsson, had completed an ironclad for the Union navy and by chance this vessel, the *Monitor,* had just arrived at Hampton Roads. Next morning, it came to the rescue of the doomed wooden vessels and forced the *Virginia* to retire to Norfolk, her career of glory cut short. A few weeks later, when McClellan marched up the peninsula, the Confederates evacuated Norfolk and blew up their short-lived ironclad. The day of the wooden war vessel was passing; naval engineers the world over studied American experience.

Shortly after this revolutionary episode, the Army of the Potomac disembarked at Fortress Monroe, and 2 April its march began. McClellan waited a month in a needless siege of Yorktown, not knowing it was defended by wooden guns; this gave the Confederates much-needed time to complete fortification of their capital. Not until 31 May did fighting really begin at Fair Oaks, almost within sight of Richmond. Here the Union army failed to gain advantage. Hitherto McClellan had been opposed by General Joseph E. Johnston, kinsman of Albert S. Johnston, but he was severely wounded in this battle and gave place to General Robert E. Lee, the Confederacy's finest gentleman and greatest soldier. Lee was enjoying superb coöperation from another great leader of the Confederacy, General Thomas J. (Stonewall) Jackson, who had been creating a masterly diversion in the Shenandoah Valley of western Virginia. This was a natural gateway to Maryland and Washington; while McClellan was approaching Richmond, hampered by sickness and frightful roads, Jackson marched up the Shenandoah, defeated the Union forces before him and seemed headed straight for the national capital. Between 16 May and 8 June his small force of 17,000 baffled three Union commanders and thrice his numbers. Washington, in a panic, recalled from McClellan a number of troops he thought essential to his victory. Having thus hampered McClellan at a distance, Jackson turned and by another unbelievably quick march joined Lee before Richmond, in time to confront the weakened adversary in the climax of the Peninsula Campaign.

McClellan had hesitated after Fair Oaks, confounded by the various handicaps of overcaution, illness, weather and the loss of troops. His grip on Richmond, Lee was now ready to break. The two armies locked in the Seven Days' battle of 26 June-1 July, during which Lee, at great

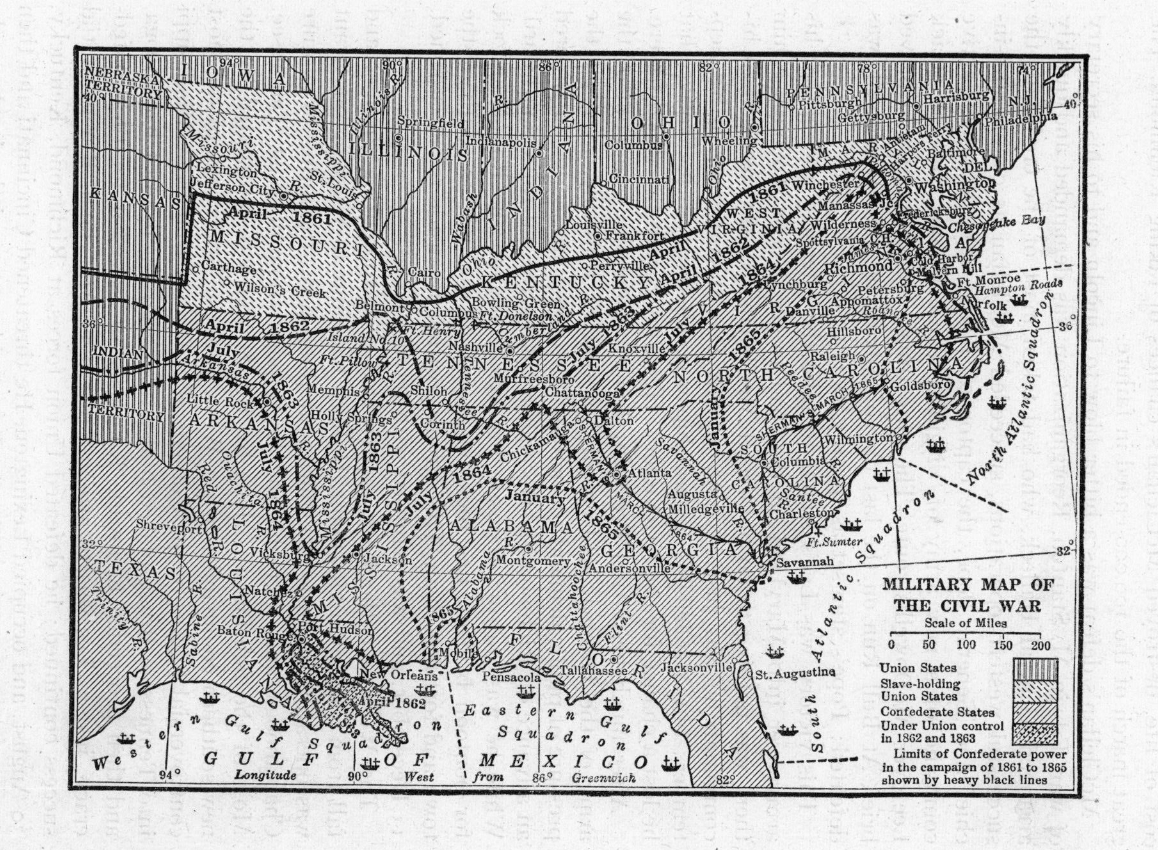

MILITARY MAP OF
THE CIVIL WAR
Scale of Miles
0 50 100 150 200
Union States
Slave-holding Union States
Confederate States
Under Union control in 1862 and 1863
Limits of Confederate power in the campaign of 1861 to 1865 shown by heavy black lines
North Atlantic Squadron
South Atlantic Squadron
Eastern Gulf Squadron
Western Gulf Squadron
GULF OF MEXICO
Longitude West from Greenwich
NEBRASKA TERRITORY
IOWA
ILLINOIS
INDIANA
OHIO
PENNSYLVANIA
N.J.
DEL.
KANSAS
MISSOURI
KENTUCKY
WEST VIRGINIA
TENNESSEE
NORTH CAROLINA
SOUTH CAROLINA
GEORGIA
ALABAMA
MISSISSIPPI
ARKANSAS
LOUISIANA
TEXAS
FLORIDA
INDIAN TERRITORY
Springfield
Indianapolis
Columbus
Wheeling
Pittsburgh
Gettysburg
Harrisburg
Philadelphia
Baltimore
Washington
Cincinnati
Lexington
Jefferson City
St. Louis
Louisville
Frankfort
Perryville
Cairo
Belmont
Bowling Green
Ft. Donelson
Ft. Henry
Island No. 10
Nashville
Knoxville
Murfreesboro
Chattanooga
Dalton
Chickamauga
Atlanta
Carthage
Wilson's Creek
Little Rock
Memphis
Holly Springs
Shiloh
Corinth
Ft. Pillow
Winchester
Manassas
Wilderness
Spottsylvania
Richmond
Lynchburg
Petersburg
Appomattox
Danville
Ft. Monroe
Hampton Roads
Norfolk
Chesapeake Bay
Hillsboro
Raleigh
Goldsboro
Wilmington
Columbia
Charleston
Ft. Sumter
Savannah
Augusta
Milledgeville
Andersonville
Montgomery
Jackson
Vicksburg
Natchez
Shreveport
Port Hudson
Baton Rouge
New Orleans
Mobile
Pensacola
Tallahassee
Jacksonville
St. Augustine
April 1861
April 1862
July 1863
July 1864
January 1865
April 1862
Mississippi R.
Ohio R.
Missouri R.
Arkansas R.
Red R.
Ouachita R.
Sabine R.
Trinity R.
Wabash R.
Tennessee R.
Cumberland R.
Savannah R.
Santee R.
Alabama R.
Chattahoochee R.
Flint R.

cost of life, destroyed McClellan's chances of taking Richmond. The great march of the 100,000 ended in failure.

McClellan's defeat was a bitter blow to Lincoln and to his secretary of war, Edwin M. Stanton. Reorganization was demanded and quickly arranged. General Halleck, who had taken most of the credit for the successful western operations, succeeded McClellan as commander-in-chief and General Pope, the captor of Island #10, obtained active command of a new army of Virginia. These legions were to attack Lee over McDowell's route. The unfortunate Pope's campaign proved brief. At Bull Run on the last day of August he, like McDowell, was defeated; Pope's star set as quickly as it rose.

This victory was Lee's signal to take the offensive and he led his army over into Maryland on the road to the North. To oppose him there was nothing to do but recall McClellan. Hastily restored to his command, he was just in time to halt Lee at Antietam, 16-17 September; but McClellan's generalship was otherwise so ineffective that he lost a chance for decisive victory. His army career ended right there.

After much hesitation President Lincoln gave the command of the army of the Potomac to General Ambrose E. Burnside, who felt the pressure of public demand for action. With some misgivings, he ordered an advance on Richmond in December, taking the old route southward. While he was waiting opposite Fredericksburg on the Rappahannock for pontoon bridges, Lee took possession of the heights south of the town and fortified them. This strong position Burnside rashly stormed, 13 December, and was repulsed with terrific losses.

The West, like the East, experienced a disappointing summer and fall from the Union viewpoint. Halleck had gone to Washington, Grant was operating against Vicksburg and Buell was attempting to capture Chattanooga and to reach the loyal population of East Tennessee. Most of the fighting was done by Buell, who was confronted by the new southern commander in the West, Braxton Bragg, one of the most controversial figures of the Confederacy. By a march from Mississippi into Tennessee, Bragg placed himself between Buell and Chattanooga, and then proceeded to invade Kentucky to "save" it for the Confederacy, just as Lee was to attempt to "save" Maryland. Bragg's initial success continued; he defeated Union forces at Richmond, Kentucky, 30 August, and occupied Lexington. He threatened Cincinnati and then proceeded toward Louisville. Buell was able to save it by hard marching and at the battle of Perryville turned Bragg back into Tennessee. But the Union government was dissatisfied with Buell's campaigning and replaced him by W. L. Rosecrans, who likewise was ordered to capture Chattanooga. Again Bragg interposed and at Stone River, as the year ended, an inconclusive engagement was fought which brought 1862 to an indecisive close.

Lincoln was almost in despair. The Union stock fell to a new low, for its armies were stopped in the West and defeated in the East. Morale was down; in the East desertion was constant and discipline lax. Perhaps there was no hope. Desperately, Lincoln sought a new commander and finally chose "Fighting Joe" Hooker, an energetic but not always dependable general. He succeeded in restoring the eastern army to something like decent order and late in April began an advance to cross the Rappahannock and Rapidan and take Richmond. At Chancellorsville, Virginia, on the border of a maze of undergrowth known as the Wilderness, he met his Waterloo. There on 3-5 May, Lee and Stonewall Jackson opposed him with a greatly inferior force; they threw tactics to the winds, took a series of desperate chances and won. Hooker seemed to lose all his power of action or ability to direct. His army collapsed. The cause of the Union seemed doomed. If this great army could get nowhere, was not Confederate success assured? Yet Lee had suffered an irreparable loss that day; Stonewall Jackson, his right arm, had been killed.

In the West the tide was turning, though very slowly. Grant had been doggedly attempting to capture Vicksburg and open the Mississippi. Operations in late 1862 and the spring of 1863 had brought many failures; not until May did results begin to favor him, with capture of Grand Gulf, a southern outpost of Vicksburg. Thereupon, he and General William T. Sherman succeeded in shutting reinforcements off from John C. Pemberton, Vicksburg's commander. They gained control of most of the state of Mississippi and proceeded to starve out the trapped Pemberton.

General Lee, in the meantime, had determined to take advantage of the Union demoralization following Chancellorsville. He began in June an invasion of the North, marching through Maryland, entering Pennsylvania and seizing Chambersburg. The Confederates reached Carlisle and some advance riders even got within gun-shot of Harrisburg. Hooker bestirred himself to protect Washington but his days were numbered. He got into a quarrel with Halleck, in a fit of anger asked to be relieved, and was taken at his word. General George G. Meade was placed in command and led the army into Pennsylvania to meet Lee at Gettysburg. Here, 1-3 July 1863, occurred the great moment of the war; when it was over, Lee was in retreat. The victory filled the North with rejoicing which became almost hysterical when it was learned that on Independence Day Vicksburg had fallen and that five days later Port Hudson had surrendered. The Father of Waters now flowed unfettered to the sea.

These victories almost had to suffice to maintain northern war enthusiasm during the remainder of 1863. Only in Tennessee was there further major campaigning. Rosecrans had begun operations in June against Chattanooga and in September finally maneuvered Bragg out of that city, while Burnside occupied Knoxville. The liberation of eastern Tennessee seemed at length accomplished. But Bragg struck back, lured a part of Rosecrans' army away from Chattanooga and then nearly overwhelmed it at the battle of Chickamauga, 18-20 September. Only the strength of General George H. Thomas, the "Rock of Chickamauga" saved the Union force. Rosecrans was now practically besieged in Chattanooga. Grant was sent to rescue him and with Sherman's aid succeeded in a series of brilliant operations, notably at Lookout Mountain, where a battle was fought above the clouds and at Missionary Ridge, 23-25 November. Bragg was driven off into Georgia and at last Tennessee was freed of Confederates.

Now that the Confederacy was broken in two and no longer figured in the border states, Lincoln, Stanton and the staff prepared for the final thrust. Grant and Sherman had emerged as the leaders to accomplish this end. Grant was made lieutenant-general and commander of the armies in February 1864. While he moved against Richmond in the East, Sherman was to enter Georgia from Tennessee and drive into the very heart of the South's communication center, to the railroad junction at Atlanta. They started simultaneously, 3 May.

Grant led a splendid army along Hooker's route down into the Wilderness. There Lee, who could only muster two-thirds as many men, attacked him 5 May in an indecisive two-day battle. Grant then sought to pass around Lee's flank. A series of desperate attacks, 12-19 May, in the vicinity of Spottsylvania Court House and again, 3 June, at Cold Harbor taught Grant that this was impossible; he had only terrific slaughter for his pains. Having failed to find a means of approach to Richmond from the north, Grant maneuvered around south of the capital. Here the city of Petersburg stood in his way, and after his direct assault was repulsed he settled down in July to besiege it. Grant had lost nearly as many men as Lee had in his entire army and was still no nearer Richmond than McClellan had been two years earlier. Was it impossible to capture Richmond? McDowell, McClellan, Pope, Burnside, Hooker and Meade had all failed. Was Grant to fail likewise?

Grant was dogged in his persistence. While his army was besieging Richmond, he worked on other ways to hamper Lee. He was particularly anxious to close the Shenandoah Valley. This inviting region had made it possible for the Confederates to threaten Washington constantly ever since Stonewall Jackson's day, and now they tried it again. In June 1864, General Jubal A. Early entered Maryland from the valley and on 11 July was within sight of Washington. Only the timely arrival of two of Grant's army corps saved the capital. The energetic Early was forced to retire but Grant was determined it should not happen again. A young cavalryman, General "Phil" Sheridan, was appointed 7 August to ravish the valley, so that "nothing should be left to invite the enemy to return." Sheridan conducted a vigorous campaign; it was climaxed by the battle of Cedar Creek, 19 October, to which he made his wild dash from Winchester "twenty miles away." Though Early then was badly defeated, Sheridan had to campaign all winter to finish the task. The southerners did not surrender easily in spite of the growing odds.

While Grant and Sheridan were meeting strenuous opposition, Sherman was marching southward into Georgia. He was opposed by the able General Joseph E. Johnston who let him take the initiative, resisting him in stubborn battle; luring him on to lose more men and to get further from his base of supplies. As Sherman continued to advance, Johnston's enemies clamored for his removal and in mid-July John B. Hood, an "attacking general," was substituted. He attempted to drive Sherman back by direct assault, failed, and 2 September Sherman captured Atlanta.

He did not pause long at the scene of his victory. He spent further force in driving Hood out of Georgia and then proposed a daring plan. He would subjugate Georgia by abandoning his communications with the North and marching to the sea, living off the country as he advanced. After some hesitation, Lincoln and Grant agreed and 16 November he started off. His march became a byword in the South. His army cut a wide swath, destroyed railroads and much other property, gathering food and carrying off anything of military value. He finally arrived at Savannah and 24 December telegraphed Lincoln, "I beg to present you as a Christmas gift the city of Savannah." Sherman had reached the sea.

His arrival on the coast enabled the navy to close the remaining active Confederate ports. It had been especially eager to close three left open after the fall of New Orleans. Union capture of the Mississippi had made the Texas ports of little use to the Confederacy but Mobile on the Gulf and Charleston and Wilmington on the Atlantic coast were much used to bring goods in past the blockade. Although Federal squadrons had been ever vigilant to end blockade-running, they had never been able to stop it completely. In April and July 1863, naval and military expeditions against Charleston had failed, but in August 1864 Farragut, in a daring exploit, had taken Mobile, and shortly after Sherman's capture of Savannah, Wilmington fell into Union hands. Charleston's fall was certain after Sherman turned northward, invading South Carolina. He occupied Columbia, 17 February, and Charleston succumbed the following day. South Carolina, the seedbed of secession, had fallen before the Union forces. Sherman proceeded on his triumphant way into North Carolina. Here for the last time he was opposed by General Joseph E. Johnston, who in mid-March suffered defeat at Bentonville.

The time now was at hand to close in on Richmond. Sheridan had finished in the valley of the Shenandoah, doing his work so thoroughly that it was said a crow, flying over that formerly fair garden spot, would have to carry his rations with him. Sherman was almost to the Virginia border. So a conference was arranged at City Point, Virginia. Here Lincoln, Grant, Sherman and Sheridan met in the last days of March to lay final plans. Lee, too, was on the move. With superb persistence he undertook to abandon Richmond, hurry to join Johnston, crush Sherman and then return with his victorious army to beat Grant. His first moves in this direction had given some slight hope of success. But Grant and Sheridan closed in on him and 1 April, Sheridan defeated him at Five Forks. Grant assaulted Petersburg and Richmond was at last evacuated. Lee reluctantly realized that a junction with Johnston was impossible. The Union cavalry was seizing his supplies and the forces closing in on him were overwhelming. Accepting generous terms proffered by Grant, he surrendered 9 April at Appomattox Court House. Johnston held out seventeen days longer, finally giving up to Sherman near Durham, North Carolina. Within a month the remaining Confederate forces in the Southwest surrendered and the war was over.

CHAPTER XX

BEHIND THE LINES

Though the military and diplomatic features of the contest were spectacular and served as a visible gage of conflicting fortunes, the real importance of the war lay in its effect upon the civilian pursuits of the sections. The conflict provided many opportunities as well as many dangers; it produced violent changes in the lives and fortunes of many who never shouldered a rifle or boasted a shoulder strap and it vitally affected the future development of the nation.

Civilian Participation

In the first place, there were four years of local civilian conflict. Many opposed the war and, by speaking and writing, voiced bitter disapproval; some northerners even went so far as to organize in secret such orders as the Knights of the Golden Circle, which discouraged enlistments, opposed the draft and spread defeatist propaganda. Confederate agents operating on the Canadian border were sometimes in touch with these disloyal orders and plotted raids and other means of hindering Union war-making, generally with slight success. The worst manifestation of opposition was in the dangerous draft riots in New York in the summer of 1863 when several hundred were killed and some property destroyed. Northern opponents of the war were generally classed as "Copperheads," and social ostracism, imprisonment and political persecution were often their portion. The Federal government took drastic steps. Lincoln early suspended the privilege of the writ of habeas corpus and in many instances arbitrarily arrested traitors; on one or two occasions the government actually suppressed newspapers.

The Confederacy had similar opposition to deal with and in some areas opponents of secession turned marauders and carried on guerrilla warfare. In both sections the draft was administered in such fashion as to emphasize the ease by which people of even moderate property might escape military service. In the North all who could pay $300 were exempt and much of the bitterness in the New York draft riots was caused by violent resentment among the poor against this glaring privilege of those who could command some money. In the South plantation owners and overseers were exempt on the theory that they were needed to control the slaves and keep up the agricultural production. There was a consciousness of class not congenial to the atmosphere of democracy.

As bitter as this opposition to the war, and even more spectacular, was the political conflict waged against the presidents of each of the governments by their partisan opponents, generally in the legislative branches. Lincoln evolved two policies in the first month of the war which brought him into conflict with a violent and determined wing of his own party. He made it clear that he held the war to be fought to preserve the Union, not to free the slaves, and furthermore he sought to gain the aid of all parties in order to ensure united effort and quick results. To Republicans of the radical type, his refusal to advocate abolition of slavery and his attempt to fraternize with the Democrats were both political heresy. Even worse in their eyes than his policies were his practices. Lincoln realized that in times of emergency action must often be taken at once to be effective and that legislative bodies were frequently ineffective and slow. Consequently, he interpreted his powers as commander-in-chief very liberally. He called for volunteers, he increased the army, he declared a state of war and a blockade, he authorized expenditures, he suspended the privilege of the writ of habeas corpus, he permitted arbitrary arrest and imprisonment without trial, he suppressed newspapers. Congress generally validated these acts after their promulgation but the President's independence of Congress gave his radical enemies many opportunities for attack.

Of all these policies and practices the one pressed by his enemies most effectively was the question of the slaves. There was continual pressure for abolition. In 1861 and 1862 Generals Frémont and Hunter tried to force the issue by ordering slaves within their lines freed; but in each case Lincoln overruled their orders, reiterating his stand that this was a war for the Union and if the Union could be saved without abolishing slavery he was ready so to restore it. Finally, however, pressure from his party, the realization of the hopelessness of peaceful reunion and the knowledge that liberal opinion in Europe was withholding support of the Union cause because he had made no move against slaves, all convinced Lincoln that the time had come to act. At a time when his enemies were attacking his arbitrary use of power and his refusal to sanction abolition he confounded them with a single act. He declared the slaves within the Confederacy emancipated, by his own proclamation as commander-in-chief. In this way he made himself stronger than ever; he had taken from his enemies their chief criticism and had increased his own power. After issuing a preliminary proclamation in September 1862, he finally decreed that on and after 1 January 1863 all slaves within the Confederacy would be free, except in parts of Louisiana and Virginia held by the Union forces.

His action was later ratified by the thirteenth amendment to the Constitution, freeing all slaves, declared in effect in December 1865.

In spite of his continued triumph over his political enemies, which was manifest in numerous ways, the lack of definitive victory to Union arms caused many to feel the war a failure. In 1864 Lincoln succeeded in reorganizing the Republican party into a Union party embracing the loyal Democrats and in renominating himself with a war Democrat, Andrew Johnson of Tennessee, as his running mate. So dark were his prospects during that summer that he himself became convinced his Democratic opponent, George B. McClellan, would be elected. Sherman's capture of Atlanta, however, is credited with turning the tide and in the November balloting Lincoln carried all states save three. Though triumphant he must nevertheless prepare for another battle, over Reconstruction. He had already started, in Louisiana, Tennessee and Arkansas, to restore the state governments by granting amnesty to those who would take an oath of allegiance and agree to accept emancipation; and he was planning to restore civil government as soon as possible. His opponents, however, thought this too easy and wanted to punish the seceded states. What the outcome would have been must ever be a mystery. Booth's pistol shot spared Lincoln the impending conflict.

In the South there was similar battle between Davis and many of the southern politicians. War must be waged by a strong central command and Davis realized it. But southern politicians had been preaching states' rights so long that their vision was blinded and they fought centralization as vigorously as they had fought northern attempts to limit slavery. Conflict then was Davis' lot and state governors like Brown of Georgia and Vance of North Carolina in the name of states' rights did much to hinder effective war-making and contributed not a little to the defeat of the Confederacy. Davis, lacking Lincoln's tact and political shrewdness, never could turn his enemies' attacks to his own advantage.

In contrast to this spirit of strife and contention there was great co-operation and self-sacrificing effort on both sides to support the troops in the field. Much civilian aid was rendered the forces. In the North it was early evident that the army medical service was inadequate and that the sick and wounded must be cared for in more effective fashion than the service could provide. In June 1861 the United States Sanitary Commission was recognized by the government. This organization functioned throughout the entire war, collected much money, procured great quantities of hospital supplies and comforts and enlisted the aid of thousands of men and women. It supervised all hospitals and worked vigorously to make them sanitary and to provide proper nursing and diet for the wounded. A great number of women went to the hospitals to act as nurses and many more made bandages and preserves at home to be sent to the front. Their task was arduous, for 318,000 were wounded in the four years in the northern forces and about 10 per cent of that army was sick throughout the war.

Another organization was the Christian Commission; it sought to provide religious worship and desirable recreation in the many hundreds of camps where temptations were by no means lacking and a moral atmosphere was sometimes difficult to maintain. This group functioned in a manner similar to the Y.M.C.A., Knights of Columbus, Salvation Army and Y.M.H.A. in later time, just as the Sanitary Commission anticipated the Red Cross. Such organizations provided an outlet for the patriotic enthusiasm of multitudes of non-combatants and gave them the satisfaction of a feeling of active participation in the cause.

The war did much to galvanize religious activities. Many a church parlor was turned into a sewing room for soldiers' supplies and surgical dressings. Women's religious organizations of all sorts did much to plan and mobilize aid, particularly for the convalescent. The pulpits, too, were forums from which to preach a holy war. Both northern and southern clergymen were fervent in blessing the arms of their young men and fast days and seasons of prayer and humiliation were proclaimed by the highest authorities. In the midst of the conflict came revivals which reached their height in 1864. Anxiety and sorrow brought many to the churches.

As the war penetrated into the enemy's country a new call was made upon philanthropy. The Negroes who fled to the Union lines or whose masters had abandoned them were in many respects in need of aid. As early as the first winter of the war, the charitably inclined in large cities like New York, Boston and Philadelphia organized Freedmen's Relief associations. In spite of much confused benevolence, relief camps and freedmen's colonies were established. Not until March 1865 did the government assume its share of the responsibility by organizing a Freedmen's Bureau.

Economic Phases

While the military and charitable energies of both sections were so mobilized by war, the economic system was submitted to tremendous strain and pressure. At the outbreak of the war, northern business was in panic. The financial structure tumbled, millions of dollars' worth of southern debts seemed lost and the future of the nation was in doubt. Public confidence in public credit was shaken, securities of all sorts declined in value and many stopped economic planning; business seemed at a standstill. But such a condition of panic was brief. Opportunities followed in amazing succession. The armies must be fed, clothed and equipped in a hurry with no questions asked about expense. Enormous sums of money had to be raised by the government and in so doing the financial system of the nation was entirely transformed.

The war was to cost in the immediate four years some 3 billions in the North and 2.7 billions in the South. Such a vast outlay was a severe strain upon the resources of both sections and placed a premium upon the financial ingenuity of financiers and politicians. Heretofore the annual expenditures of the national government had been less than 70 millions and the debt in 1861 amounted to but 75 millions. Before the war had advanced very far the Federal government was called upon to spend 2 millions a day, and extraordinary means of raising revenue had to be devised. Tax-levying was undertaken, but collection would have to be slow and besides there is always a limit to taxation. Because of the unpopularity of such imposts, politicians are apt to set this limit rather low. In the course of the war, however, a direct tax was levied upon the states according to population, as the Constitution provides. Also, an income tax was imposed. Internal revenue was collected by means of a wide variety of stamp taxes so that hardly any sale or other business transaction failed to yield some revenue. To compensate American manufacturers for this burden, high protection was placed upon manufactured goods; in fact before the war was over the manufacturers were permitted practically to write their own tariff schedules. By this great variety of means, 667 millions in taxes were raised, over 20 per cent of the money expended. Most of the remainder of the funds were borrowed. During the four years, nineteen different forms of certificates of indebtedness were issued bearing five different rates of interest. The total amount thus obtained amounted to 2.6 billions or 66 per cent of the immediate cost.

The need for such large sums in cash found the currency system of the country entirely inadequate. The coin of the nation amounted to only 160 millions and of this 28 per cent was in the South. The bulk of the business of the country was done with the unregulated and insufficiently backed notes of the 1,496 banks. In fact, the banks had but 87 millions in coin to meet note obligations amounting to 459 millions, and in December 1861 government and banks alike suspended specie payment. Gold became a commodity and the nation was faced with the use of state bank-notes of uncertain value or a resort to barter. To provide money for the extraordinary war expenses, the government in 1862 issued 150 millions worth of greenbacks or legal tender notes and required all to accept them in payment of debts. This amount was later increased to 450 millions and the government paid out these notes and then reissued them many times during the course of the struggle.

As the treasury would not redeem this fiat currency, its value fluctuated with the fortunes of the Federal armies and in one of the dark hours of the war a paper dollar fell as low in value as 39 cents in gold; never were they at par.

The instability of this currency and, as the war dragged on, the poor market performance of the bonds caused a new scheme to be devised to provide a stronger currency and a market for bonds. In 1863, 1864 and 1865 a series of acts was passed establishing a system of national banks. Hereafter any bank which bought national bonds and deposited them with the United States treasury would be given national bank-notes to the amount of 90 per cent of the market value of the bonds. Furthermore, the government taxed the state bank-notes out of existence, thus forcing banks which desired to issue currency to become national banks. This plan was not prepared in time to create an extensive national bank system under government supervision before the war closed; it grew up afterward and remained in operation until superseded in 1913 by the Federal Reserve System.

These vast financial operations and their accompanying spectacular derangement of ordinary business were paralleled by equally great demands and startling changes in the productive system. The manufacturing resources of the nation were strained to the uttermost to meet wartime needs for munitions and other equipment. In order to aid industry in its unexpected task, the government inaugurated policies which were to have lasting results. There was the protective tariff. Besides, in order to provide an adequate labor supply, a law was passed permitting the importation of contract labor from Europe. Agriculture, too, was challenged by the war and here again the government stepped in. As the southern representation was no longer present to block the move, Congress was now free to push westward expansion. So in 1862 they passed the homestead bill so long debated, giving all citizens or intended citizens 160 acres of land, and subsidized a Pacific railroad by grant of land and a bond issue. Further, a Morrill Land Grant Act gave land to each state to aid in the establishment of colleges to teach agriculture and the mechanic arts. Immigrants were attracted by these free lands and the farming areas of the West developed rapidly.

Oil was discovered and new supplies of gold and silver unearthed, so that much activity occurred in these lines, new companies sprang up hastily and their stocks began to have a ready sale. Business itself took on a feverish tone, not only because of the increase in production but also because of the unstable character of the currency. After the early months of 1862, most business was done with "greenbacks" which fluctuated violently and showed a general downward trend. Money became cheap, prices rose and speculation was the order of the day.

The possibility of combining profit with invasion was easily understood. As the armies entered the cotton district, they found thousands of cotton bales. There was a shortage in the North. Evidently, this cotton should be used. The treasury licensed certain individuals to go in and bring it out. Army officers took an interest and helped locate cotton, for a share in the proceeds. Also numerous southerners saw their opportunity and got their cotton to the Union agents in return for money and even military supplies. In fact the traffic became so large as to amount to half a million dollars a day through military lines on the Mississippi. Northern greed furnished much aid to southern armies. Equally unpleasant are the sordid tales of graft which describe Union soldiers suffering from cold and disease because contractors had supplied shoddy uniforms and pasteboard shoes and which tell of diseased horses sold for cavalry and artillery purposes, bad rifles for good, cotton blankets for wool, and many other items of like shameful practice. Profiteers fattened.

As large fortunes were being made in industry and agriculture was profitable, there was a great deal of money for investment, and speculators flourished. While the thousands were being killed or wounded on the battle-fields, the hundreds were reaping a rich reward in supplying the armies, opening up new business or agricultural enterprises, or in speculating on the chances of victory or defeat. But wages did not rise as fast as prices and the poor suffered in the midst of plenty.

Economic conditions in the South presented a different picture, for that section was but poorly equipped to meet its problems of production and had infinitely greater difficulty with finance than the North. The South at the beginning of the war had few banks and little gold; only 20 per cent of the nation's banking capital was located there and the gold supply amounted to about 40 millions. Worse, there was little industry or commerce because the greater part of the wealth of the section was invested in land and slaves and devoted almost exclusively to the raising of cotton. The South's plan to finance its war with foreign cotton sales was defeated because it withheld the cotton as a weapon to enforce recognition by the European powers. After that plan failed and southern statesmen became ready to export, the Federal blockade was too strong. Therefore the South never realized on its great crop except in a very limited way through blockade-running and more or less illicit trade with the North. With its chief resource gone, the Confederate government borrowed as much as it could and issued ever increasing amounts of paper currency. Without gold or without means of getting it, only one result was possible: the voluminous paper amounting to at least 800 millions fell to 3 cents on the dollar in the final days of the war. Taxes brought in little with the currency so valueless, and in order to keep going the Confederacy impressed supplies and levied taxes in kind to be paid in produce. The war closed with an outstanding indebtedness of nearly 1 billion, all of which was a total loss to its holders. But on both sides the cost of the conflict had only begun when the carnage ended. The amounts spent in war pensions alone in the years that followed, to say nothing of loan funding and many other expenses, made the billions of cost pile up.

As in finance, so in production the South suffered under severe handicaps. That section had developed relatively little business interest before the war and had little material from which to stimulate enterprise during the conflict. There was no immigration, no westward advance, no new mineral wealth discovered. The South continued in its agricultural state and though a great variety of small industrial attempts were made, no permanent advance was accomplished. As the currency became practically worthless, barter oftentimes took the place of regular buying and selling.

Some speculators flourished in the South. Though the blockade prevented the expected large import and export business, it was from the blockade that some profitable speculative business developed. The blockade-runners brought an uncertain and miscellaneous amount of merchandise into the country and took out an equally uncertain amount of cotton. Speculation on the precarious foreign trade facilitated some profiteering and created a few wealthy, a number of whom traded with the enemy. Most disillusioning was the failure of the South to develop more organizing talent in meeting its needs. The South had iron and fuel but it never exploited them. It devoted its whole mechanical energy to munitions and while the vital transportation system broke down, ruining chances of mobilization and supply, not a bar of railroad iron was rolled.

Social Consequences

The strain of warfare left an impression upon American life which was to last long after the guns ceased firing. For four years there had been anxiety, sorrow, enthusiasm, the satisfaction of patriotic effort, the call to duty, sacrifice, loss of health and death. On the other hand there had been profit, speculation, wealth, extravagance and dissipation. The ebb and flow of the tide of victory made all life uncertain and many sought to relieve the strain or to enjoy their newly acquired gains by an extravagant search for amusement and excitement. A crazy spirit of carnival flourished in some of the northern cities even as the newsboys hawked the black-bordered columns listing the dead and wounded. Emotions of all sorts were keyed up abnormally and the reaction was to be feared.

There was much in the life of the nation during the war to give those who looked into the future grave concern. In the North there was much that was crass and corrupt. Crime flourished. Licentiousness seemed a phase of military glory. The soldier on furlough must be amused and exhilarated; liquor, gambling, vice of all kinds pandered to this phase of warfare. Corruption and the use of money flourished when valuable contracts were to be disposed of by government. A sordid materialism which heretofore had not been so apparent now became blatant. Taste suffered, the monstrous and extravagant in display crowded out finer things, and artistically the hideous, if it were large and expensive, attracted the untutored eye of the nouveau riche.

The conflict which so disturbed and altered the lives of millions in the nation hurried on the various tendencies toward social change which already were in the process of reorganizing society. Rivalries and divisions within the North were given new causes to feed upon. After an initial shortage, the ranks of labor swelled under the wartime demand. Hordes of immigrants, contract and otherwise, came over. Negroes were also brought North. But the great reward paid to industry was not shared in large part with labor and this injustice was not unnoticed. The war contributed much to a growing class-consciousness of labor. It also changed the position of women. They took many places left by men and were never to return entirely to the home. One profession at least, school-teaching, they captured, and having made their appearance in man's public world they would not retire.

In the South there were also disquieting signs of wartime damage to the future. The South had been isolated, invaded, its fields laid waste, its property destroyed, its leaders sadly depleted by death. Worst of all, hope had died. The southerners had been forced to watch the destruction of a cherished ideal, to lose their great confidence in their own ability to stand alone, to see their power beaten down by despised northern clerks and store boys. Such a defeat was to leave wounds that only a long stretch of time could heal.

The war period aggravated the unpleasant growth of a new sectionalism. Rivalry developed between West and East. The great industrial boom in the East was much more profitable in terms of money and fortunes than the agricultural boom in the West. The eastern capitalist piled up cash reserves, while the western farmer extended his acres at the expense of mortgages. The two sections split on taxes and subsidies. To western leaders the war taxes and tariffs were one-sided. The East profited as the West paid. The railroad grants even were objects of suspicion; they were to make the western prairies vassal provinces of the East. But as yet these signs of social cleavage were hardly clear enough to attract close attention.

Most significant was the final tragedy that occurred in the midst of the dawn of peace. When news of the surrender of Lee flashed through

Copyright, M. P. Rice.

ABRAHAM LINCOLN

the North a great weight was lifted and the tension was snapped. The North entered upon a wild orgy of celebration. From Palm Sunday until Good Friday that sense of freedom was delirious. Then came John Wilkes Booth, insane avenger of the South's defeat, who assassinated President Lincoln and plunged the nation into gloom and apprehension. The great joy of the people was turned to mourning and the shouts of victory became cries for vengeance. Such a shock was not a propitious inauguration of Reconstruction. "With malice toward none and charity for all" was a sentiment driven from the northern mind by Booth's bullet.

The assassination of Lincoln had a greater significance than its immediate emotional effect. This martyrdom placed Lincoln definitely in the small group of national heroes. The struggles of the Reconstruction period might have withered his laurels, in the popular mind at least, but the manner of his death ensured his fame. More than any one else did he seem to be the epitome of the potentiality of the American. Born as he was in the humblest circumstances, he had risen to the greatest place. But so had others. His strong grip upon the popular admiration came from his rôle as the nation's spokesman in wartime. He stood first of all for humanity; he was merciful and patient, he was humble, he had a sense of humor and yet he could be ruthless and implacable in pressing the war in the face of odds and almost insurmountable obstacles. It was not by efficiency of administration but by shrewd knowledge of men and the weight of ideas that he achieved his greatest fame. For it was in his expression of the nation's thought, sensed in almost uncanny fashion, that he excelled. In his inaugurals, in his messages to Congress, in published letters and in his Gettysburg Address, he made northerners realize the righteousness of their cause and the high purpose of the struggle. Without such inspiration, victory would have been much more difficult. He was also the Great Emancipator; his fiat broke the shackles of the slaves. Finally, he was the prophet and also the personification of the democratic experiment which was to "elevate the condition of men—to lift artificial weights from all shoulders; to clear the paths of laudable pursuit for all; to afford all an unfettered start, and a fair chance in the race of life." His idealized figure was to become symbolic in the national ethics, a force for the preservation of the democratic experiment.

RECONSTRUCTION AND LARGE-SCALE ORGANIZATION

1865–1900

CHAPTER XXI

RECONSTRUCTING THE SOUTH

The end of the civil strife which came at length in 1865 marked the beginning of a new era in the history of the United States. The stress of conflict had quickened the speed of national change and affected its nature. First among the new conditions was the altered position of the South. The old South of pre-war days had been destroyed. The conflict had dragged this section from a position of power, had destroyed much of its wealth and had drastically altered its social system. The building of a new South was to be painful, for the normal processes of reconstruction were prolonged and complicated by the efforts of the Republicans controlling the federal government to punish the South for its so-called "war guilt."

Rebuilding the Economic Structure

The immediate task which the returning Confederates undertook was the rehabilitation of a wasted and devastated economy. Agriculture, the chief means of former prosperity, was well-nigh exhausted. Fields had been neglected, implements worn out, stock gone, seed scarce and poor and the general barrenness of some formerly fertile sections was so extreme that, as we have seen, it was said that a crow, flying over these regions, must carry his rations with him. The first courageous efforts to acquire cattle, horses and crops made some of the people victims of certain guerrillas and ex-soldiers, white and black, who stole and killed recklessly during the months following the peace. Comparatively few thus took advantage of the general breakdown in social restraints; nevertheless all, even the most law-abiding and industrious, lived in an atmosphere of nervous unsettlement which retarded their work, warped their point of view and jeopardized the peacefulness of community life. Under these conditions, the South turned once more to cotton. To it were still tied the fortunes and hopes of nearly everyone. Unhappily, this "cash" crop soon fastened them in the tight fetters of a "single" crop system.

The problem of rebuilding involved much more than rehabilitating agriculture. Commerce and communication had been demoralized. Foreign trade had been ruined by the blockade. River transport was risky on account of the broken-down condition of the wharves, levees, channel markers and boats. Gangs of desperadoes on some rivers lay in wait to steal cargoes and rob passengers.

Worse still was the condition of the railroads. Some important lines to the ports and toward the north, where not already dismantled by the invaders, were falling apart from lack of repair. Others, which had been reconditioned by the victors for the use of advancing northern troops, remained under the control of a federal military railroad department during several months after hostilities ceased. For return to their owners, it was required that the new management be loyal and furnish bonds guaranteeing payments to the federal government for rolling stock supplied by it. Almost none of the railroads had means to meet the obligations on these forced purchases. Large debts owed them by the Confederate government were now beyond collection, while debts they had paid the states during the war had now to be paid over again, because the courts declared payments in Confederate currency null and void. The rehabilitation of the railroads was to be expensive.

Rebuilding naturally waited upon capital, which was largely wanting. There was little money or collateral left in the South. A capital investment of nearly 2 billions had been wiped out by emancipation of slaves. Investors in bonds and notes of the Confederate states also found their holdings made worthless by defeat and repudiation. Nevertheless, the ex-citizens of these states at the same time remained liable for their personal debts, which most of them were totally unable to pay. Many a northern merchant was now known to be looking to the federal troops to collect bills long overdue. The only people with money were the few who had used the war for their own speculations and profiteering. Business concerns and productive enterprises were at a standstill where not completely killed by bankruptcy. A man's former associates were either dead or maimed, or suffering like himself from the discouraging effects of the physical and moral ruin around them. The places of 250,000 men had been vacated by death due to the hazards of warfare. A moratorium was in practical effect, where not officially declared. In sum total, there were everywhere present mortgages and debts.

But there was one obstacle to rehabilitation greater than all these—the old slave labor supply had been wiped out and a restless horde of misguided and confused freedmen had been substituted. The most tyrannous fact of southern existence became the continued presence of about 3.5 million persons recently in slavery. Obviously, all possibility of rebuilding the South on the old foundation had been destroyed. A new economy and a new social order must be devised.

Without a labor supply the South was badly handicapped in its struggle for recovery, and political interference prolonged the confusion following emancipation. Nothing had ever been done to prepare the Negro for freedom and so the former slaves were entirely unready. From the first knowledge of their freedom, many believed that they no longer need work; so they could not be prevailed upon to resume labor in the fields. Many of the Negroes wandered aimlessly in groups or else congregated in the poorer quarters of cities, endangering the health of the community. The efforts of northern agents to organize them for political purposes complicated matters.

Consternation filled the hearts of the planters. What little of civilized living the war had left them seemed to be threatened by this new "Black Terror." So desperate a situation required community action and they resolved to pass legislation which should force the labor supply to stay where there was work to be done and to do it. The ex-Confederates hurried to take the oath of loyalty and apply for pardons, in order to be in time to participate in the activities of the new state legislatures. These bodies were about to meet, because the new president, Andrew Johnson, was trying to hasten the reign of peace.

President Johnson had laid down a plan for reconstruction which was based upon Lincoln's ideas of quick restoration of repentant states. He appointed provisional governors who were to be his agents in administering the oath of loyalty to all who would take it, save the leaders in the secession move and the wealthy planters. Those who took the oath might then elect state conventions which were to repeal secession, repudiate the war debts of the states and accept Negro emancipation. If these steps were taken then state officers, legislatures and members of Congress might be chosen by the eligible voters and, as far as the President was concerned, the states would be recognized as in normal relation to the federal government.

Accordingly, under his provisional governors, the persons who had taken the oath of loyalty elected members of the constitutional conventions, and they proceeded to do the three things assigned those conventions. The membership of them was, perforce, mostly obscure persons who were eligible because they had avoided active participation in the rebellion. In the meantime, however, Johnson was enlarging the eligibility list, by pardoning large numbers of the former political and economic leaders of secession. These quickly resumed leadership in their respective communities, secured election to the new state legislatures and to the important offices, and divided much upon the old party lines into two political groups.

Assuming that the conditions of readmission to the Union, as laid down by the President, would be final and complete they undertook, after they had fulfilled them, to deal decisively with the local situation. To rescue industry and property from the "Black Terror" they devised the "Black Codes," based upon the belief that the Negro would not work unless forced to do so. These laws obligated the former masters to protect their ex-slaves to a certain extent, but they permitted them to restrict the freedmen's liberty of action and to inaugurate semi-compulsory systems of labor. In most cases the Negroes were not to be allowed military weapons or participation in court processes other than those affecting their own race; their right to hold property was restricted.

As it happened, numerous features of these codes were substantially similar to regulations laid down by an entirely different group of persons, those associated with the Freedmen's Bureau, which Congress had established on the eve of Lee's surrender to help the Negro socially and economically. In its inception it was unsympathetic to the planters, because its higher officials were northerners and its subordinates were such southerners as could take the oath that they had not been disloyal. Moreover, many of its lesser officials tended to encourage the Negro in wild dreams of land partition and ownership, thus augmenting delusion and suffering. Some ex-slaves were made chronic paupers by largesse from the Bureau and from northern philanthropists. Some of the more responsible, higher officials wrestled in good faith with the problem of metamorphosing the slaves into independent, self-supporting individuals. They dealt with them in special courts, judicial and administrative, gathered the wandering ones into camps and fed them, established hospitals and dispensaries and doctored them.

Politics Intervenes

The results of this program were disastrous. When word came north that under Johnson's plan the Negro was being put under "Black Codes" and the ex-Confederates were regaining control of the southern states, certain original Republican leaders, called Radicals, girded themselves to fight. They convinced a majority of Congress that Johnson's policy was dangerous. They then prepared a program to insure the Negro citizenship and pushed through Congress the 14th Amendment to the Constitution, highly significant then and more so later. This Amendment in substance declared: that the ex-slaves were citizens and could not be deprived of property without due process; that any state denying them the vote would have its representation reduced accordingly; that the ex-Confederate leaders could not hold office until their individual disability was removed by a two-thirds vote of Congress; and that while all Federal debts incurred during the war were to be paid in full, all of the Confederate obligations were worthless.

This overwhelming sum total of prospective disabilities challenged the political foresight of southern leadership. Tennessee ratified the amendment promptly and was readmitted to the Union without further ado; but all the other governments set up under the Johnson plan indulged in the luxury of an indignant refusal. Thereby they played directly into the hands of the Radicals, who were making an opportune use of the pending congressional elections, so manipulating the campaign that by a frantic waving of the "bloody shirt" they were able to re-arouse war prejudices and make them more venomous. Further, riots in Memphis and New Orleans in which Negroes were killed gave the extravagant warnings of the Radicals the color of reality; and when the unlucky President, in a "swing around the circle" endeavored to present matters more fairly, his malapropos speeches only dyed the Radical convictions a redder shade. Thus events conspired to place a premium upon animosity.

The outgoing Congress, accepting the popular dictum, devoted its last hours to punitive, "thorough" measures against the President and the South. They enacted the Tenure of Office law, designed to keep Johnson from ousting the Radical secretary of war, Stanton, from his cabinet. They passed the Military Reconstruction Act, designed to substitute for southern home rule a Republican patent of military control. It required the Johnson state governments to be displaced by five generals, commanding each his portion of the ten southern states, with power to replace civil officers and courts by military rule. Under such surveillance were the southerners to take their oaths of allegiance to qualify thereby, with the Negroes as registered voters, selecting as delegates to constitutional conventions such "citizens" as remained eligible after the wholesale disability imposed by the Radicals. Their new governments must favor both Negro suffrage and the 14th Amendment. When they had accepted these conditions, the reconstructed states could send representatives and senators (presumably Republicans) to sit in Congress.

Thus were the former leaders of the South thrust aside while their communities were regimented under a scheme of reconstruction compound of military law and Negro citizenry. The higher federal officials, legally in control of affairs, varied in efficiency and disinterestedness. Inevitably they could not keep within bounds the large body of underlings and hangers-on surrounding them. This latter group included two classes of opportunists destined to prove especially obnoxious—the southern white trimmers derided as "scalawags" and northern visitors aptly described as "carpetbaggers."

The legislatures set up by these persons, consisting of them and their Negro associates, complied with the congressional stipulations for securing readmission to the Union. In all states except Texas, Mississippi and Virginia they achieved readmission by fall of 1868; their struggles for recognition in the last three dragged out two years longer. However, the seating of their senators and representatives at Washington signified no approach to political stability in affairs back home. There, local government in the hands of the parvenus demonstrated how dishonest politicians can greedily utilize ignorant classes to inaugurate an era of extravagance and waste; it "went so far it left little more to steal." The grossness of most carpetbag legislation obscured meritorious efforts at public improvements, relief and education. By 1872 a burden of debt had been piled up, conservatively estimated at nearly 132 millions.

The former Confederates were not without resources to combat this new leadership. They went to work in secret and by 1867 many whites were members of a thriving secret society, the Ku Klux Klan, a brotherhood of property holders whose members donned a white-hooded uniform and operated at night. They aimed to punish carpetbaggers and frighten the Negro out of politics and back to work. Other similar societies sprang up in various parts of the South. Unfortunately, these orders became addicted to violence; and when the better class of whites attempted to disband the Klan in 1869 they were not entirely sucessful. Bands of nightriders long continued to terrorize.

The overthrow of the local carpetbag governments was destined to come from within. They were growing so heavy with corruption that they would soon "break down under their own weight." Their white members became irked by the social ostracism resultant from their Negro affiliations. The Negroes themselves became less certain that benefits were accruing to them. The leaders quarreled with each other over the diminishing spoils. The several white secret societies symbolized to the northern mind by the term "Ku Klux" craftily intimidated colored voters. In 1869 Radicals lost the legislature in Tennessee and there were unmistakable signs that other states were also on the way to home rule.

The Radicals in Congress took alarm and determined anew to ensure Republican returns in the lately rebellious states. They showed their temper by temporarily rescinding Georgia's readmission to the Union and they passed the 15th Amendment, specifically insisting that men of color should not be denied suffrage. That Amendment received enough ratifications to put it into effect the following March (1870) and Congress bolstered it with a Force Act, invoking heavy penalties against the violation of it and of the 14th Amendment. But these strenuous efforts did not prevent the Democrats from winning the legislatures of Virginia, North Carolina and Georgia during that year and the next. Before the close of 1870, therefore, all the southern states were undeniably secure in their recognition as states of the Union, after nearly six years spent in achieving that status.

Six more years elapsed before they all regained home rule and control of their own elections. Political reconstruction finally was completed in 1877, when, for the first time since the war, the Republicans had to exhaust every resource to prevent the Democrats from regaining the presidency. A mysterious Washington conference was held at which mysterious promises seem to have been made; and after the Republican, Hayes, was safely installed in the White House he saw to it that federal troops left the South. The whites then deprived the Negro of political influence by such devices as poll taxes, ballot-box stuffing, literacy tests and "grandfather clauses"; these last were various provisions so worded as to limit the franchise to persons whose grandfathers had held it, which the Negroes' grandfathers had not. With these state expedients the federal government did not interfere.

The chief result of political reconstruction had been to make the South a one-party section, a "Solid South" devoted to the Democratic party.

Toward the New South

Gradually the Negro was adapted to his free status, and as the North gave him neither a warm reception nor a speedy enfranchisement, his adaptation took place almost entirely in the South. His functioning in agriculture improved in proportion as he came to realize that he could not eat if he did not work. The more intelligent had given ear to the urgings of the better officials of the Freedmen's Bureau, like Generals Howard and Armstrong, that work was part of the lot of the free man and that one might profit by signing contracts and keeping to them. Also, the Negro improved as a workman because he became less illiterate. His eagerness for the education which had been denied him was pathetic, and teachers of his own race were made available through the establishment of normal schools and colleges open to Negroes. These institutions were supported by funds from the southern legislatures, the Freedmen's Bureau (until it was disbanded in 1869) and northern philanthropists, which funds went into the establishment of such schools as Howard, Atlanta, Berea, Straight, Shaw, Fisk and Hampton.

Through the South in general, several adverse economic factors hindered progress. The planters could not rent their land outright, because the Negroes had no cash to pay rent and no understanding of farm management. Nor could the planters hire the Negroes outright, for the planters lacked capital to pay wages and the Negroes, for their part, disliked to work steadily, day after day. They found a way out by substituting for the plantation system a system of share tenancy or "cropping," adapted to the psychological and financial handicaps of the Negroes and the planters' lack of capital. The former furnished their labor and the latter such supplies as food, tools and mules, and parcels of land from forty to eighty acres in size. The crop was apportioned between them, often in the ratio of 1 to 2, until the Negroes supplied their own food, when the division became equal. Money wages were paid chiefly to the seasonal workers—to the spring cotton-choppers and the fall pickers; but on the whole, money was seldom in evidence. Such necessities as had to be obtained from the neghborhood store were charged through winter, spring and summer, to the fall crop. When the Negro brought in his share, the value of his cotton was balanced against the total of his bill to date; and as he often was neither provident nor literate the balance frequently lay on the wrong side of the ledger.

The planter not infrequently found himself in similar fix. The bank had advanced the amounts due for machinery and supplies, and the proceeds of his share of the crop did not always meet the note. He might suggest to the banker that another year better returns would show if they tried a little diversified farming, bred more cattle or changed their methods of cultivation. But the wary banker preferred the ills of the crop he understood to those of others strange to him and his section. Thus the perpetual chain of indebtedness from Negro through planter up to banker retarded improvements in agriculture under the share-cropping system.

However, in spite of these difficulties, cotton production advanced. The planter might complain of the Negro's readiness to desert crops for campmeetings or political rallies, and the Negro might complain that the planter cheated him; yet the planters' land was at least partly in use and the Negroes were getting a living out of a relationship which was one stage advanced from slavery toward individual self-support. Moneymaking became somewhat less rare and debt less universal. All classes felt a little easier financially after the large crops of 1869 were marketed at a good price, estimated at 300 millions; and they promptly invested some of it in refurnishing their homes and improving their farm equipment.

Relatively, the large southern planter was becoming less important in the class scheme of his section, in proportion as the land which he sold or lost was divided into smaller parcels held by individual farmers. The number of individual farms increased by about 60 per cent within the decade after the war. Smaller farms meant the incursion of new classes of persons to meet the wants of those farms. Whereas the large slaveholder used to order his supplies from a distant wholesale house, the small farmer bought his from a local storekeeper. Whereas the one obtained his credit through a single "factor," the other borrowed from a village money-lender. The one sold his entire crop from his many acres to a large commission firm in a city; the other sold his to a local dealer, especially after railroad building improved transportation.

Changes in landholding and in marketing conditions helped to bring diversification in industry, a rise in the standard of living and a shift in leadership. As small farms brought into local communities merchants, money-lenders and buyers of crops, these people created a demand for more goods and more different kinds of goods than were brought in before the war. To this trade the Negroes added their moiety, for they craved to own more things than their masters used to. An emerging middle class of town dwellers pushed themselves into prominence as ambitious merchants, lawyers, and commercial people, undertaking to gain both a respectable living and recognition in public affairs. Thus actual power and wealth gradually shifted from the hands of the families who had been large landholders into the hands of an incoming middle class, unfortunately a class unused to leadership.

Industrialization came very, very slowly to the post-war South; its factories in 1860 had produced 10 per cent of the nation's manufactures, but the percentage was not recaptured until the end of the century. Considering the lack of capital and business stability, it is remarkable that there was any post-war advancement whatever, and it was chiefly due to the abundant water power, labor supply and raw materials near at hand. Northern capital experimented a little, while new mechanical industries raised their heads. Southern capital groped its way into cotton manufacture, which became substantial by 1880.

As a result of reconstruction the South became a section of small farmers still concentrating on cotton planting, with here and there the beginning of a new industrialism. Socially it was striving to solve the problem of adjusting itself and the Negro to the new relationship prescribed by emancipation. A New South was in the making.

CHAPTER XXII

TRIUMPHANT CAPITALISM

As the war had humiliated the South, it had exalted the East to a new position of dominance, particularly in economics and politics. It strode ahead rapidly while the South was in the throes of reconstruction and attained the power which the South had feared in the ante-bellum years.

Industry on the March

The East grew strong through its industrial progress, which resulted from unparalleled advantages. It now possessed both abundant man-power and inventive ability, which no longer need be diverted to war purposes; they could concentrate freely on the exploitation of the nation's rich opportunities.

A new vigor inundated the factory economy of the East. Industrialization there advanced by leaps and bounds. Workers were pouring in. The East felt the impact of a horde of immigrants, invited to America by lucrative labor contracts and by the approach of peace. Used to a lower standard of living and willing to work for lower wages, the new-comers seized the jobs of the unskilled. Having a higher birth-rate, they swelled the population. Cities and country-side of the East absorbed much of this incoming horde before the remainder scattered across the Middle West and out toward the far frontier. New-comers and natives found the air of America bracing; the talented became aware of their own creativeness and adaptability. New inventions uprooted people forcibly and speedily, taking them out of ancestral trades into new occupations overnight, stimulating their imaginations so that they could make their own contributions to this dynamic era. Persons with strong creative and acquisitive instincts were enticed by the astounding abundance of national resources. Sensing the immensity of the prospect and their exceptional opportunities, they found both greater than they had dreamed. Their quick aggrandizement canonized money-making; all classes knelt before the shrine of money and the money-getter.

The roots of a new prosperity had been growing deep in American soil and the war had fed, rather than starved, the growth. Since the day when eastern tariff advocates and western homesteaders had won the election of 1860, northern business had sung in swelling volume in the key of prosperity and more prosperity. The feel of money and use of it had become more frequent daily experiences among common folk. Many of them were handling more money of late than ever they had seen before, because of soldiers' bounties and pay, high prices and some wage increases. Although spending was enormous, savings also accumulated. The greenbacks had sharply diminished the number of bankruptcies; so many mortgages were paid off that the insurance companies had to take over government bonds to absorb their plethora of funds. Banks had multiplied and savings institutions were swollen with profits.

Into young enterprises, as well as established factory businesses, capital was poured. The people of the United States, being relatively free from inherited and over-conservative ideas, entertained toward mechanical and industrial change an attitude of enthusiastic adaptation. For example, paper manufacturing was set afloat by a concern starting in Philadelphia in 1866; and new patents in agricultural machinery absorbed much capital on the middle border, at Chicago and St. Louis. Between 1864 and 1869 there were more cotton spindles in motion, manufactures of different kinds started, lumber sawed and hewn, and houses and shops constructed, than in any previous five-year period. The same astounding activity was true of iron furnaces erected, bars rolled, steel made, coal and copper mined and gallons of petroleum collected, refined and exported.

The outstanding triumph of industrial invention was a revolutionary feat in steel-making. William Kelley of Pennsylvania had developed an air-blast process—similar to one of Henry Bessemer of England—for burning the carbon out of cast-iron, so as to convert it into steel cheaply. Kelley, a bankrupt in 1857, had sold his patent for $1,000, never regained control of it, and received altogether only about $450,000 from his great invention, while Bessemer's royalties reached approximately $10,000,000. The patents of the two inventors were combined in joint hands shortly after the war ended. Thus cheap, large-scale production of steel rails, bars and structural shapes began to affect national life. This epoch-making development spurred the use of coal, iron and petroleum—all powerful instruments of industrial advance. In a word, it lifted the United States out of the Iron, into the Steel Age.

At the outset of the Steel Age the shrinking of the globe was the investment most attractive to both the capitalist and the small investor. Communication was making vast strides. A postal money-order system and free city mail delivery became established in this period. The "Western Union" was emerging as a virtual monopoly of telegraph facilities, with its "duplex" and quadruplex instruments multiplying the number of business transactions transmissible on the wires simultaneously. The greatest advance in communication was Cyrus Field's victory over the Atlantic. He won in 1866 his heroic, twelve-year struggle to lay and finance a cable strong enough to operate over 2,000 miles of ocean, through water two miles deep. His persistence made commercial, newspaper and diplomatic contacts between the United States and Europe a matter of minutes instead of weeks.

The war had killed the merchant marine as a field for profits, but railroads were catching the public imagination and offering entrepreneurs an infinite variety of wealth-getting schemes. While transcontinental lines were being constructed in the West, little lines in the East multiplied but utilized no less than nineteen different gages, ranging from three to six feet. Gradually the four-foot, eight-and-one-half-inch "English" gage, to which the famous English locomotives were built, became standard in the United States. The first train of people traveled through without change from the Atlantic coast to Chicago in 1867, and from Chicago to the Pacific coast in 1871. Also, after much fighting and sharp practice, the principal eastern lines were assembled into four trunk line groups. With the joining of the New York Central and Hudson railways and their connections, and with the extension of the Erie, the Baltimore and Ohio and the Pennsylvania affiliations, the public and their goods could use any one of four different through routes to Chicago. No less than 24,000 miles of railroad were built during the enthusiasm of the four years (1869-1873) following completion of the transcontinental line. Manufacture of "Pullmans" and invention of the automatic air-brake and car-coupling saved the nerves and lives of passengers and crew, while expanding the field of investment in transportation.

Railroads Reach the Last Frontier

Railroads were stretching out into the Far West and aiding the promoters in developing that vast region. The Homestead Act, Morrill Land Grant College Act and Union and Central Pacific Railroad Act, all of 1862, had bestowed great gifts of land on people, states and corporations. A flood of bona-fide settlers, of speculators and corporation owners availed themselves of these gifts.

All classes felt the enthusiasm for a transcontinental railroad. Establishment of the transcontinental telegraph in 1861 had whetted the universal desire for improved transportation of goods and people. All over the United States, the tempo of life was quickening and it was generally conceded, even by people who had not the slightest chance of going west, that thirty days for a traveler to cross the continent and eighteen days for a letter by "fast" pony express were entirely too slow. Most important, would-be homesteaders wanted railroads, to carry them west and their crops east, just as the railroad managements wanted settlers, to furnish crops for paying freight. The westward push shoved everything before it.

The statutes chartering the Union Pacific and Central Pacific Railroad corporations (scheduled to construct trackage west from the 100th meridian and east from the Pacific coast) had given free rights of way, *carte blanche,* to take from nearby lands any construction material required for the work, and gifts of five alternate sections of land per mile on each side of the track, selected by the recipient from within ten miles of it. Since for each mile constructed the government agreed to loan 6 per cent federal bonds, at the rates of $16,000 across the plains, $32,000 across the plateaus, and $48,000 across the mountains (these bonds to be secured by a first mortgage on the property), the impetus to building seemed considerable; and when two years later the nation's representatives increased the alternate sections to ten, to be selected from within twenty miles of the track, and changed the government loan from a first to a second mortgage, rapid construction could not be far away.

It went forward with a rush in 1865, with both railroads in financial difficulties and competing for the lion's share of the mileage bonus. This situation made track-laying as circuitous as it was careless, especially with the Union Pacific, because of the machinations of the "Crédit Mobilier," a corporation formed by stockholders of the Union Pacific to control construction of the road so as to divert the profits of government subsidy to themselves. The Central Pacific's "Contract and Finance Company" built somewhat less hastily and dishonestly. During the winter of 1868-1869 the interest of the entire population rose to white-heat, with the competing forces employing 20,000 workmen, with the Union Pacific laying tracks on ice and snow, and the Central Pacific filing a tantalizing map registering its intention to build east of Ogden into what its rival considered its own territory. Neither side stopped to finish tunnels or spare expense, the Union Pacific sometimes paying as much as 18 per cent for loans. Defense against the Indians, and the requirement that only American iron be used, further increased costs.

Actually, the rival lines passed each other for a distance of ten miles, then turned and met near Promontory Point, Utah, 10 May 1869. The Central Pacific had annexed about three-fifths as much mileage as its opponent. Their meeting was celebrated with delight everywhere. At the meeting-place a golden spike was driven and the sound of the hammer was telegraphed across the vast, uninhabited spaces to the East and West; Chicago staged a parade miles in length; New York's Trinity chimes rang out; and Philadelphia listened to the sacred Liberty Bell.

The transcontinental railroads opened the way for settlers. Miners had already gone in to prospect for the bonanzas which were discovered in the Rocky Mountains. Gold, silver and copper made states out of Nevada and Colorado and dictated territorial organization for Montana and Idaho. On the plains herds of cattle ranged, now that the railroad had come, and ranchers and cowboys drove their stock to the railheads to send them to the slaughter-houses. This was the day of the romantic "Wild West," celebrated in song, story and the movies. But its life was short, for even before the end of reconstruction the farmers were pushing into the plains regions and the Indians were finally thrust aside. In all this campaign to conquer the last frontier, eastern money and promotion were active in taking an extravagant profit. Prodigal waste accompanied this process in a fashion to awaken apprehension later.

A New Labor Movement

As eastern capital waxed powerful, a new army of labor congregated in urban centers. The mechanical industries, moving from water-power sites in rural districts to the steam-power and labor-supply centers of the urban areas, left behind them in the country many a picturesque ruin of a deserted native village and built up around them in the city a conglomerate assortment of crowded tenements occupied by a mixture of native-born and foreign new-comers. Some rural labor the industries took with them cityward; but they did not long retain the farmers' daughters who formerly had welcomed the local factories as places to earn "pin money." These shrank before the tide of immigrants and retired into more poorly paid, if more "respectable" work, such as sewing and school-teaching. Their factory and mill places were filled from city sources, partly by native labor and partly by Negroes, Italians, Irish, Slavs and Orientals. The latter groups constituted the great horde of unskilled laborers who brought in strange tongues, lower living standards and eagerness to work at less wages and under worse conditions. Their arrival upon the American scene had been facilitated by the contract labor law of 1864.

This historic measure came up at a moment crucial to both workmen and employers. The advance of retail prices in 1861 had put nearly nine-tenths of the wage-earners in a worse position than they held in 1860; and through the next five years their situation did not materially improve, although industry lost more than a million workers through enlistment. The spread between wages and the cost of living widened, just as the demand for labor tightened. The employers, citing the loss of labor through enlistment, secured Lincoln's support for the contract labor law. It permitted business representatives to contract with prospective immigrants for control of their wages the first twelve months after arrival, in consideration for transporting them here. The manufacturers promptly began importing cheaper foreign workmen, and when the soldiers returned to look for peacetime employment they found the labor supply overabundant.

Immigration imposed a mounting handicap upon native workers in the less skilled trades, just when laborers were beginning to crave more means for entertainment and excitement. Their imaginations had been stimulated by the broadening experiences of the war; it had filled them with a restlessness which economic distress would not fail to aggravate. A few workers took the radical step of cutting loose from their familiar haunts and occupations and letting off steam in that miscalled national safety valve, the West. Others, showing skill and adaptability as tool users, met inventions and industrial changes with accommodations to division of labor, and entered new trades.

Skilled workers grew to realize labor's need for organization. They had increased the number of their local unions nearly 400 per cent between 1860 and 1865 and formed several national unions, which flourished most in the building and transportation crafts participating in the intense activity reigning toward the close of the war. These crafts included such as the carpenters and joiners, bricklayers and masons, the plasterers, painters and heaters, the ship carpenters and calkers, besides coach makers, journeymen carriers, and the Brotherhood of the Footboard, locomotive engineers.

Outstanding leaders arose urging collective bargaining. W. H. Sylvis and a few other unionists realized that their logical objective should be a national federation. Singlehanded, he had reorganized his own iron-moulders' craft; and in 1864, while industry was receiving from the war its greatest stimulus toward productivity, this young son of a poor wagonmaker of Pennsylvania had led an attempt at federation in an "Industrial Assembly of North America," convened at Louisville. Under his leadership at Baltimore two years later, trade unionists and reformers organized the "National Labor Union," in which representatives of more than half a million skilled workers at one time participated. This brought several state laws for the eight-hour day in 1867. That year an advance in money wages set in which mounted slowly through two years and then faster 1870-1871.

The year 1868 was phenomenal. It was marked by Sylvis' election as president of the young federation, his prompt appointment of a permanent Washington lobby committee to attend congressional sessions, repeal of the obnoxious contract labor law, and passage of an eight-hour law for government workers. Unluckily, ambiguity in the eight-hour law nullified it; and as the repeal did not declare contracts absolutely illegal, contract labor continued to enter, with annual immigration mounting to 400,000 by 1873, when the panic reduced it.

Worse, Sylvis, the best-known labor leader of his time, died at the height of his career in 1869, before he had reached forty-one.

A surer advance in unionization might have been won if Sylvis and his associates had concentrated their strength on strikes and other narrow means of building up solidarity in their special crafts. Instead, they strove for advancement of the mass, boldly taking the reform side on most of the political and social questions of the day. They stressed reform of society in general, by such means as producers' coöperatives, monetary legislation and a National Labor Reform Party. The labor membership of the National Labor Union eschewed such broad idealism, withdrew their support, and thus killed the union.

A different kind of nation-wide organization had been begun in 1869, identified with the name of Uriah S. Stephens, who was seven years Sylvis' senior. Stephens and associates, who had organized the Garment Cutters' Association of Philadelphia seven years earlier, now founded the "Noble Order of Knights of Labor." It had four outstanding peculiarities. Stephens was a Mason, Odd Fellow, and Knight of Pythias, and so the Knights of Labor was made a secret order; it thus remained a dozen years, until T. V. Powderly won a long fight against Stephens and his secrecy principle. Unlike the craft unions, the Knights aimed at industrial unionism—of all workers regardless of skill, occupation, color, citizenship or sex. Unlike the National Labor Union, they persistently refused to be captured by a political party, although from the outset they attempted to influence legislation. Fourthly, they worked for social and industrial reform through arbitration, rather than by strikes.

The influence of this all-labor organization was greater than that of other contemporary groups trying to offset large-scale organization of capital; but its concrete results were meagre. Claiming that labor was the sole creator of values or capital, the Knights undertook to make public opinion sympathetic to labor, to support their demands upon industrialists and politicians. They obtained establishment of several state bureaus of labor, which gathered statistics demonstrating the truth of their contention that industrialization was having a pauperizing effect. In their main objectives they failed: they did not abolish child and convict labor; nor did they secure the eight-hour day, weekly pay and mechanics' lien laws, equal pay for men and women, or legal recognition of unions. In vain they demanded government ownership of public utilities, taxation of incomes, abolition of the contract system on public works, abolition of national banks and establishment of postal savings banks, national health and safety laws and the restriction of land sales to actual settlers. In fact, only a small portion of labor was organized and the forces at the disposal of capital seemed almost too great to defeat; but labor was gaining militancy, as the panic proved.

Panic of 1873

The truth of the matter was that more fertile ground never lay fallow for the seeds of panic. The great boom period of the war and the flush times following it were closing, as the round of the business cycle approached the point of disaster, at home and abroad. Speculation, excessive and wasteful production, reckless extravagance, fluctuating prices, unsound banking, huge indebtedness—all were sowing the wind. Would America reap the whirlwind?

Europe was in no condition to save America. Europeans had bought 1.5 billions of United States securities while suffering their own strains; such as prolonged war-making, Suez canal outlays, French indemnity payments, overbuilt railways and speculative iron manufacture. The faith of foreign investors was forfeited many months before the bubble burst at home; they took warning from two storm signals—excess emissions of United States railroad and mining securities, and a notorious "Crédit Mobilier" scandal unearthed by Democrats during the 1872 campaign. When this money-making alliance between corrupt businessmen and politicians was scrutinized by a post-campaign congressional committee, prominent senators and representatives were proved to have accepted Mobilier stock. Public faith in both business and political leaders was undermined precisely when confidence was most needed. Congressional repute was still suffering from a recent "salary grab," whereby members had voted themselves a wage increase from $5,000 to $7,500. Also, fires had devastated Chicago, Boston and Portland, Maine, wiping out millions in capital.

Now did America reap the whirlwind. Jay Cooke and Company, of New York, London and Philadelphia, a supposedly invulnerable banking house, had outreached itself by banking upon future occupation, by generations yet unborn, of the area served by the Northern Pacific. On 18 October 1873 this firm closed its doors in the United States, throwing doubt on all business. Prices of securities fell so rapidly that the stock exchange was closed for ten days to stay their descent. Money was so hard to get that "clearing house certificates" were invented to take its place. Nearly every businessman proved to be in debt far beyond his capital. Speedily, marginal concerns fell into the hands of receivers, and long-established, more conservative, houses saved themselves only by amalgamation, labor displacement, and half-time operation.

To employees, the years following 1873 brought uncertainty and dread. The ground was cut from under them and their unions when employers in marginal businesses were wiped out and surviving concerns went on a half-time basis. Men, women and children who kept their jobs felt the constant pressure of unemployed thousands behind their backs, eager to step into any places they might vacate, no matter how low the wage. Long breadlines stretched before the soup kitchens month after month, waiting for business to stagger to its feet. With buying severely limited to necessities, mere maintenance of existence absorbed most energies. Money wages and the cost of living declined at about the same rate, between 1873 and 1876, but as employment steadily fell to new lows, real incomes declined seriously. Then, during the second three years of the depression, while employment was slowly rising, wages fell more rapidly than retail prices, so that work-people continued to lose ground. Misery deepened among families in such hard-hit occupations as mining and textiles.

The depression sharply affected labor organizations. In membership and effectiveness the unions suffered immense losses as the depression dragged on, with numerous strikes ending in failures as endurance diminished. In their bitterness, some laborers listened with friendly ear to various gospels of international radicalism, particularly to the theories of "economic determinism" of the German socialist, Karl Marx; he predicted that concentration of capitalist control, accompanied by increasing misery of workers, must bring decline of the middle class, destruction of capitalism and triumph of the proletariat. The vast majority, however, clung to the capitalist system; but strike failures and punishment for union membership in time shifted some unionists from the open craft unions into the secret Knights of Labor.

Transportation fell upon evil days, with railroad defaults and receiverships. As the work of rail-laying stopped, all the foundries, machine shops and steel mills dependent on construction had to close down. Firemen, brakemen and engineers, chafing under irregular work and lowered wages, resolved to strike and met some success early in the depression. Then the executives determined to crush the Brotherhood of Locomotive Engineers, and in midsummer 1877 decreed a flat 10 per cent reduction in pay, widely imposed east of the Mississippi. Workmen rose in protest all along the network of lines reaching from New York and Philadelphia far into the West. At such strategic centers as Baltimore, Pittsburgh, Buffalo, Chicago, St. Louis and San Francisco, the larger groups of trainmen participated in wide-scale disturbances. Rioting, loss of life, sympathetic strikes in other industries, and general outcry ensued. Traffic was tied up and militia called out. Federal judges committed strikers for contempt of court. Here was the labor injunction foretold, for commitment under receivers in effect was the same. The trainmen had to go back to work at a reduced wage; they had failed to force employers to recognize labor organization and collective bargaining. But the moral effect of their protests proved enormous, for public criticism was not all aimed at the rioters and labor leaders dared hope that in time they might upset the classical contentions of the businessmen.

The years of uncertainty and tribulation emphasized one continuing national attribute; hard times could not alter the youthful capacity of the nation for healthy rebound from adversity. This quality was exhibited on every hand. Inventors busily responded to the demand for improved appliances; in almost annual succession appeared the typewriter, telephone, talking machine, arc light and incandescent lamp.

Besides these helpful new fields of activity, the nation was lifted from depression by improvements in foreign trade and in domestic business atmosphere. Farmers saw the summer suns of 1878 and 1879 shine upon bumper crops in the United States, just when Europe's own food supply was failing her. Manufacturers, no longer propped by the home market, had found outlets in newly developing lands, especially for machinery. Consequently, the balance of trade turned again toward the United States. Some of the incoming gold replenished the treasury at Washington. Most of it quickly found its way into the main arteries of the industrial body, which had been drained by the violent paroxysms of deflation. Indebtedness had been erased by insolvency, and timid capital had accumulated in thriving savings banks. Rock-bottom prices had destroyed inefficient concerns and had forced surviving businesses to run without profit to keep going at all and to devise uses for waste products. The huge fatality among little partnerships had been accompanied by increasing adoption of the corporate form of business, better fitted for long life and large investments.

Indubitably, the nation was growing up to fit the clothes cut for it during the speculative boom. This justified resumption of railroad building and return of immigration. By the middle of 1879 there was employment aplenty for money and men. That subtle thing "confidence" had been restored.

CHAPTER XXIII

A NEW STRUGGLE FOR DEMOCRACY

The tone of post-war politics was lowered by the struggle over southern reconstruction and the impact of the great scramble for wealth. Worse, it was affected by the general moral relaxation which follows war. When the great conflict was over and the cause of liberty triumphant, many escaped from the tension of the struggle by excesses of one sort or another which brought carelessness and corruption to politics.

The struggle to reconstruct the South had brought the Radical Republicans into a position of dominance in Congress. They became so powerful that they brushed aside the Supreme Court and even sought to remove President Johnson and place one of their own members in the White House. They impeached the President in 1868 and brought him to trial before the Senate, where their plan failed by only one vote. As the Radicals failed in removing one president, they succeeded in making another. They controlled the Republican national convention of 1868 and nominated General U. S. Grant, who was triumphantly elected. They did more than choose the executive; they fashioned the Republican party into the political agency for the strident eastern capitalism which was making such headway in the economic affairs of the nation.

Finance and Tariff

The Civil War had sowed a crop of difficult fiscal problems. The heavy taxes, internal revenue and protective tariff which had been dictated by wartime needs proved burdensome when peace came. The war loans, staggering in sum and chaotic in organization, needed consolidation. A large mass of paper money of doubtful value had brought inflation which "sound" economists and businessmen now sought to cure.

The problem of reducing the internal revenue taxes was not as difficult as reducing the tariff. Within five years after the coming of peace, Congress repealed the obnoxious internal levies but, significantly, left untouched the high, compensatory duties based upon them. Effective opposition to retention of the high rates, which averaged 42 per cent, would have required a coalition between southern Democratic congressmen and midwestern members working together for low tariff.

As the Radicals succeeded in excluding the southerners through three vital years, 1865-1868, the manufacturers and their Republican partisans got a fine running start in their job of fortifying the protection ramparts. Opponents described this as an unholy alliance between business cupidity and political ambition. At any rate, these post-war allies stamped the lavish economic legislation (no less than the virulent Reconstruction program) with their own impress.

Effective handling of the protective tariff was prevented during the entire reconstruction period. In 1870 an act was passed which limited most of its reductions to revenue articles like coffee and tea, the only consequential protective reductions being in pig-iron; it gave considerable increases to numerous protected items, making the law as a reform measure a sham. Within two years the national exchequer overflowed because of the extravagant tariff levies, in spite of disbursements for retiring bonded indebtedness; and a new tariff law was enacted reducing duties 10 per cent. When the panic of 1873 came the next year, the tariff advocates pressed the notion that this catastrophe came because of the reduction. In 1875 the tariff was restored to the former level.

The problem of the debt and the currency were much more difficult and brought another phase of sectional politics. The western farmers found themselves in distress at the close of the war. They had increased their wartime production to a degree too great for peacetime demand. Their prices and incomes began to decline immediately after peace came, and the debts which many of them had contracted in order to buy more land remained largely unpaid. Their income shrank, but their mortgages did not; therefore they felt the need of an expanded currency. The representatives of the western debtors, however, found eastern Republicans planning contraction.

The greenback problem was solved by the Radical Republicans of House and Senate so as to fortify them with their business allies, rather than to please the debtor class. The greenbacks represented a sum in dollars greater than all the other forms of money in use put together, and this at a time when total money in circulation was greater than ever before. This most common currency, with nothing behind it but the credit of the government, was fluctuating with confidence; prices moved erratically, lenders and debtors could not forecast the value money would have when payments came due, speculators flourished and legitimate business suffered.

Should the government reduce the volume of greenbacks, it would raise their value, discourage speculation, stabilize the price structure and improve United States credit; but this would also lower prices to producers and force debtors to pay in money more valuable than they had received. Secretary of the Treasury Hugh McCulloch determined on stabilization, and business conditions improved enough to enable him to get a contraction law through Congress, over the outcry of opponents. The act of 1866 gave the Secretary authority to retire 4 millions in greenbacks monthly; it projected total retirement within about twelve years.

Similarly, the party in power solved the bond problem so as to aid bondholders. During the war this class had had to accept payments in money cheaper than they had loaned, a process which was hard on persons with fixed incomes. Now these contended they should be allowed to recoup their losses by receiving gold for government securities they had purchased with paper; they called greenback payments "repudiation." They pointed out that the credit of the United States would suffer if the nation paid its debts in greenbacks, as many cities and states were doing. After a struggle, Congress defeated bills which would have required McCulloch to pay in greenbacks, and he proceeded to use gold.

These solutions of the greenback and bond problems were soon threatened with upset, for the nation experienced a temporary depression in 1867. Congressmen heard from their humbler constituents in the West and South, and eastern debtors shared the view that contraction was nothing less than extortion. With them were allied certain optimistic business promoters who feared that contraction would hinder their schemes for exploiting the West's lands, mines and railways and the South's rebuilding needs; these entrepreneurs insisted that the natural growth of the country would soon absorb the increased currency. A plan called the "Ohio Idea" became popular. It proposed among other things payment of all debts in greenbacks (including the principal of the 5-20 government bonds) and increases in greenback issues. Thus did the greenback become the symbol of class animosities. So, the February before the campaign of 1868, Congress sharply shifted policy. It repealed the obnoxious retirement law of 1866 in an act which also left a loophole through which the Secretary might reissue the 44 millions already withdrawn. The greenbacks have never since been contracted.

The Democrats almost found here an opportunity. They were in desperate plight, because their war experience made it easy for the Republicans to label them "copperheads" and "rebels." Might they not wipe off the stain and revive and enlarge their party by taking up the cudgels for the unfortunate farmers? To this end they decided to capitalize the growing animosity toward "Wall Street" in their national platform. They inserted a plank favoring paper; but they offset this by nominating for president an eastern lawyer, ex-governor Horatio Seymour of New York, who boldly repudiated this plank. The Republicans were even less conciliatory. They and their candidate,

General Ulysses S. Grant, took a platform promising early return to the gold standard and their marshaled hosts won the election.

Thereafter, the Republicans reflected eastern dominance over their party, in a conservative bond policy, but had to pursue a more liberal greenback policy. The Republican-controlled Congress passed in 1869 a resolution declaring the intention to redeem government bonds in gold, and in 1870 a Funding Act arranging for such redemption. Businessmen, however, liked to meet their private obligations in greenbacks; and Grant coöperated after the Supreme Court in 1870 in Hepburn *v.* Griswold declared the greenbacks unconstitutional, so far as applied to contracts made before enactment of the legal tender act. Grant packed the court by adding two Republican justices, who helped reverse the decision in Knox *v.* Lee. The contest whether there should be more greenbacks or less, and whether they should be redeemable in gold, was left undecided.

The depression following 1873 strengthened the more-money side. Greenbackers gained new allies in a group of "silver" men, representing silver producers and inflation politicians; the producers wanted silver coinage to secure a market for their metal and raise its price, and the inflationists wanted it as cheap money. These allies got through Congress in 1874 a bill restoring the volume of greenbacks to 400 millions, but Grant vetoed it. Then hard times and disgust at reigning corruption helped the malcontents give the Republicans their first bad beating, in the congressional elections of 1874. Alarmed by the certainty of a Democratic House, creditor influence secured from the dying Congress another compromise—the Resumption Act of March 1875. It conceded that greenbacks in circulation were not to be further reduced but specified their redeemability in gold on and after 1 January 1879. To this extent the creditor influence had won: both bonds and greenbacks were to be paid in gold; but the debtor and western inflation urge still gave battle to the eastern capitalists.

Corruption

While these economic problems were being thrashed out in Congress and on the stump, the results of prevailing corruption began to plague the Republicans. The worst aspect of eastern domination—the careless ethics of post-war speculation and finance—engulfed political parties also, for legislative coöperation often was indispensable to economic exploitation. The nexus was best proved in railroading. As early as 1866 James Parton had satirized the situation in his *Manual for the Instruction of Rings—Railroad and Political;* but manipulators of railroads needed no schooling and those of politics learned readily.

The Erie railroad became an outstanding example of economic-political corruption. In Erie the pious Daniel Drew, the amoral stock-plungers James Fisk and Jay Gould, and the ex-ferryboat-operator "Commodore" Cornelius Vanderbilt displayed their peculiar talents. Vanderbilt, a pioneer in railroad consolidation, pieced together the Harlem, Hudson River and New York Central roads with the aid of corners in stock and sought to eliminate competition in the state by controlling Erie. "Uncle Daniel" however, had chosen Erie stock for loot to fill his own pockets. With the aid of Gould and Fisk and corrupt judges and legislators, he managed to create new Erie stock as fast as the Commodore tried to corner it. The office of the company, its stock and its officials shifted back and forth across the Hudson between New York City and Jersey, and up and down the Hudson to and from the Albany statehouse, as ingenuity dictated. Drew nearly left the resourceful Commodore "holding the bag"; but these two speculators made a secret deal for dividing the swag, to the intense anger of disappointed vote-sellers and other grafters. Through later ministrations of Gould and Fisk, Drew himself was left high and dry and the Erie irreparably damaged.

Corruption reached full flower at the national capital during Grant's eight-year term, 1869-1877. He typified his time in his reverence for the money-getter; and his credulous blindness encouraged gross malfeasance around him. His secretary of war, W. W. Belknap, and his first vice-president, Schuyler Colfax, were but two of many there lining their pockets through misuse of public office. His brother-in-law was cleverly used by Fisk and Gould to give the appearance of honesty to a corner on gold; the two sent many a broker into bankruptcy and made off with the profits before Secretary of the Treasury Boutwell awoke and dumped gold on the wild market. These developments wrote 24 September 1869 into history as "Black Friday." Grant's blind loyalty to friends undid what little there was of reform in the civil service, enabling spoilsmen to oust officeholders unfriendly to jobbery, salary grabs and frauds on the mail routes. A whisky ring, for example, reached gigantic proportions. In Philadelphia a "gas ring" fattened on public plunder. In New York "Boss" William M. Tweed, Grand Sachem of Tammany Hall, with Mayor "Elegant Oakey" Hall, Treasurer Peter B. Sweeny and Controller "Slippery Dick" Connolly directed city expenditures of continental size into their own pockets. Even Washington City had its own "Boss" Shepherd pulling the strings for puppet politicians to dance.

Attempts were made to "clean house" in city, state and nation, with reform movements gaining momentum in various areas. In New York by 1872 Thomas Nast of *Harper's Weekly* and George Jones of the *Times*, who exposed the Tweed Ring, were bringing the fleeing Tweed back from Spain to die in jail. In Missouri was General Carl Schurz,

A CARTOON BY THOMAS NAST

(In *Harper's Weekly*, August 19, 1871.)

a liberal who had escaped Germany after the 1848 Revolution, fought for the Union in the Civil War, and had become a German-language editor and speaker of such importance to the Republicans that he won the senatorship in 1869. Gathering around him a group calling themselves Liberal Republicans, he not only gained control of Missouri but spread his influence widely.

SECRETARY SCHURZ CLEANING OUT THE INDIAN BUREAU

Reform Republicans and Democrats from various sections assembled in a Cincinnati convention in May 1872 put up a ticket against Grant; it proved futile. The many disparate elements in the group enabled easterners in it to give the "Liberal Republican" nomination for president to the arch Republican protectionist, Horace Greeley, an act which angered tariff reformers and liberal Democrats. Although Greeley was officially endorsed by the June Democratic convention, and conducted a vigorous and impressive campaign, Grant's well-oiled machine ran over him. That machine functioned smoothly, in spite of damning revelations of chicanery. Evidently the majority of voters remained loyal to the hero who "crushed the Secesh." He received his second term, which proved worse than his first, with corruption traced even to his private secretary, though Grant himself was innocent. The most vicious results of southern reconstruction became apparent, while the depression added its demoralizing influence.

In 1876 the nation was tired of corruption and both parties knew it. Therefore they both made careful nominations. The Republicans presented General Rutherford B. Hayes, sometime governor of Ohio, and the Democrats chose Samuel J. Tilden, governor of New York. The election which followed proved the climax of this unfortunate epoch. It was hotly contested and the result promised to be close. Election night showed that Tilden was within one electoral vote of success. However, the carpetbag Republicans still had control of three southern states and they counted the votes to give these states to Hayes. By their handiwork he appeared to be victorious by one vote. The Democrats protested, and as they had control of the House of Representatives, they could prevent the counting of the electoral vote by refusing to go into formal session with the Senate. A plan was therefore devised to turn the question of who carried these three carpetbag states over to an electoral commission of fifteen, five from the Supreme Court, five from the Senate and five from the House.

Those who made the plan expected that this commission would consist of seven Republicans, seven Democrats and one Independent, a member of the Supreme Court. However the justice dodged the responsibility by resigning to accept a seat in the Senate and the commission was constituted of eight Republicans and seven Democrats, because there were only Republicans left on the Supreme Court. This body heard arguments of counsel for both sides but then refused to go behind the returns on the official certificates in the three states. Thus Hayes was seated, but not until his friends had agreed that he would withdraw troops from these southern states and permit them to join their fellows to make up the solid South. Thus were avoided the revolt and civil war which might have followed, lacking this compromise. Democracy had had a narrow escape.

Farmers for Democracy

The election of 1876 had presented another sign in the zodiac of American politics. There had appeared the Greenback party, representing primarily the continuing protest in the West. While Congressmen had been fighting deflation and contraction in Washington, the farmers had been learning how to organize at home to cure their grievances locally. They were not only protesting against creditor currency and gold bonds; they were in arms over railroad practices. The Greenback party had an interesting background. All the farmers except those nearest the seaboard suffered severely because of the distance products must travel to market and the lack of competitive carriers. Exorbitant rates for freight and storage took toll on everything the farmer bought or sold. Furthermore, there were few industrial shippers to second farmer demands; almost all the freight carried east by the four main line railroads out of Chicago in 1873 was farmer freight, nearly 40 per cent of it cereals and nearly 45 per cent animals and animal products. Definitely, it was the farmer who furnished the freight. After the first years of generous local subsidy to construction, and after agricultural prices fell, many decided that cruel freight rates were at the heart of their grievances. The democratic answer must be legislation establishing government supervision.

Middlemen were as obnoxious as railroads. When produce had run the gauntlet of the freight charges it fell victim to the onslaughts of the middlemen and warehouse people, who sometimes juggled the market to pay the farmer the lowest possible price and then staged a "corner" to line their own pockets. Meats were so grossly manipulated as to make the "live-stock ring" of the Chicago stockyards a generally execrated institution; and storing of grain tempted the leeches no less. Furthermore, the middlemen who sold agricultural machinery enjoyed a commission agreement with the manufacturers which gave them 20 per cent to 40 per cent as agency fees and added just that much to the farmers' costs.

Given the enlightenment, efficient organization remained essential to betterment; farmers must learn to modify their independent habits and suspicions and seek succor in coöperation. Many Germans among them had brought over to the United States the liberal concepts of the Revolution of 1848 and entertained a predilection for self-defense and leadership. But it was an Irishman, O. H. Kelley, working arduously over a period extending from 1866 to 1875, who gave the men and women of the post-frontier an opportunity for improved acquaintance, better understanding and practice in self-expression. Travel through the South had convinced this government clerk, with a background of farming life in Iowa and Minnesota, that what the farmers of the nation most needed to improve their processes and position was the intellectual stimulus derived from social intercourse.

He concluded that they could be brought together best through the medium of a secret society, of a non-political character, to which the women as well as men might swear allegiance. Its members were to be advantaged by a mutual education process. On this theory, with William Saunders of the Agricultural Department and a few other Washington associates, he organized in 1867 [1] the national "Patrons of Husbandry," better known from the designation of its local chapters as "The Grange." The founders of it offered farmers and their wives

[1] This was just a year before workmen began to find refuge in their secret society, the Knights of Labor.

the delights of membership in a "secret" society and fellowship with their neighbors.

The very nature of their grievances thrust the Grangers prominently into county and state politics, if not national. They, and farmer politicians, secured election to the lower range of offices. The railroads' money was fought with farmers' votes; they forced the state legislatures to enact (1869-1874) the so-called "Granger Laws." However, it should be noticed that the Grange and these laws were not simple cause and effect. Some of the most stringent of the acts were passed before the farmers' movement reached its full strength, and the statutes helped to a certain extent to bring the Grange from infancy to maturity. The real relationship between the Grange, allied clubs, and the "Granger laws" was one of contemporaneous interaction, the trend of events in general creating them severally and mutually.

The Grange legislatures concentrated upon the railroad grievances, especially where transportation was most in ill repute, in Illinois, Wisconsin, Minnesota, Iowa and Ohio. Into the statute books were written mandates on such subjects as passenger and freight rates, long and short haul, railroad commissions, incorporation, grain elevator rates and transportation conditions. The urgent mood of the farmers was capitally illustrated in Illinois, where as early as 1867 they forced the passage of a warehousing act forbidding railroads to refuse to deliver grain to warehouses they did not control. These canny agriculturalists, failing other legal remedy, in traditional American fashion had determined to secure "appropriate legislation." They observed with unwonted perspicacity that "nothing can be accomplished for the enforcement of our rights, and the redress of our wrongs, without an efficient organization on the well known principles that give the great corporations such tremendous power."

They rewrote the Illinois state constitution in 1870 to give the legislature the specific power of rate making, which it obediently exercised the next session by specifying maximum rates, while it also forbade discrimination in handling and storage. When the state Supreme Court declared the act unconstitutional the farmers presented themselves in convention at Springfield, so that the affrighted legislature warily enacted a yet more thorough and efficient law. At the ensuing election, some of the offending judges suffered retirement. In the van of Illinois followed Minnesota, Iowa (host to an Anti-Monopoly Convention), and Wisconsin. Fate conspired to make these laws temporary, for a panic was imminent. The farmers approached the peak of a power they were soon to lose.

The depression of 1873 turned the farmers' attention once more to money and stimulated the organization of the national Greenback party. Its tickets in the presidential election of 1876 won nearly

82,000 votes and in the congressional elections of 1878 over a million votes. In the meantime they transferred their affections from greenbacks to silver. The silver dollar had been demonetized in the United States and parts of Europe in 1873, while the metal was still too expensive to permit of coinage at the old ratio; but thereafter output continued high while the price fell until the silver content of the dollar was worth only about ninety cents in gold. The producers now demanded that free coinage be resumed at the old ratio, approximately 16:1, so that they might exchange 90 cents for $1 at the treasury until their product rose in the market. The debtors were interested in a rise, not of the price of silver but of the amount of cheap money.

The frightened politicians facing the election of 1878 determined to meet the inflationists part way, especially as the producer lobby was relentless, and as several senators were wealthy mine owners who had no compunctions against using their public office to line their private pockets. So in February Congress passed, over Hayes's veto, the Bland-Allison Act. Richard Bland was a Democratic representative from Missouri who had lost money in western mining ventures, and Senator William B. Allison of Iowa was known for his devotion to his party and place. The act directed the secretary of the treasury to purchase at the market price between 2 and 4 million dollars worth of silver monthly and to coin it at 16:1. The coin could be exchanged for silver certificates of $10 and higher. This was only a partial victory —it was a limited, not free, coinage of silver, but silver had made its début as a political issue and was to be heard from again.

It was a strange phenomenon which the Middle West farmers had shown the nation. They had interfered as a class on the side of governmental protection against oppression, imposing at least a temporary check upon those mighty entities, the public carriers. Through their attempts to deal directly with producers and manufacturers, without the aid of middlemen, they learned valuable lessons regarding the intricacy of business functions and obtained a better balanced notion of the basis of credit. The manufacturers for their part learned that organized farmers could be formidable. From the experience the farmers took some recollection of practice in coöperation and business usage, to be capitalized at a future date in the Farmers Alliance, Populism and other lineal descendants of the Grange. They had matched wits with the representatives of eastern capital, challenging eastern domination. They had won only compromises but they were to return to the struggle for justice and democracy.

CHAPTER XXIV

URBANIZATION

As the Reconstruction Era ended it became apparent that the United States was a far different nation from that which had plunged into the Civil War. The population now spread across the continent was bound together by the steel bands of the transcontinental railroads. Size and concentration were compellingly forced in this country. They were pushing Americans along toward subjection to a dominating characteristic of modern living—large-scale organization—which thoroughly permeated American life by the end of the next panic and depression period, 1893-1898. Formal acknowledgment of its sway was signalized by the growth of great cities and the organization of the giant corporations which emerged at the turn of the century. During these two decades, the correlation of growth in population with availability of natural and mechanical resources pushed leaders in all important fields of activity into schemes of monopoly. Some of these schemes had been in the making before the epoch began; others became significant only after it ended; but in the main this period was dominated by a mighty urge for organization on a national scale. That became its predominant characteristic and was carried over into succeeding epochs.

Momentum from Growing Population

The area of the United States remained the same—3,025,600 square miles—but the density of population increased greatly. With this increase other increases were involved; the whole correlated the activities of the growing nation. A few population figures suggest the momentum of growth.

Year	*Population in Millions*	*Per Cent of increase*	*Proportion of urban to total population*	*Westward movement of center of population*	*Density of population per sq. mi.*
1870	39—	23	20.9	42 miles	13.0
1880	50+	30	22.6	58 miles	16.9
1890	63—	25	29.2	48 miles	21.2
1900	76—	21	32.9	14 miles	25.6

Thus, the cities of the nation grew greater in number and size, while the farming population was appropriating new areas to the west. In fact, all over the world people were multiplying and moving.

Their closer association in cities and their survey of wider regions beyond, stimulated the most intelligent and ruthless leaders to appropriate the national resources and to exploit the human market which the growing population placed at hand. The results multiplied in geometric ratio and on a nation-wide scale: they brought the organization of economic and social groups in units crossing state boundaries; they exerted an influence more pervasive than that first conceived by the organizers themselves. Whenever large-scale organization was achieved by ruthless means, as often it was, it ultimately challenged thinking men and women to devise means whereby the national government might control forces which the states proved helpless to handle. Upon the great swell of American development the individual was swept unthinkingly, and awareness came only in extremity.

In the movement of population, native and immigrant were commingled in shifting proportions. The cities did not lose many of their workers to the country, for the cost of land, equipment and moving exceeded their slender capital. They packed into the densest area, chiefly the states of the North Atlantic Division—New England, New York, New Jersey, and Pennsylvania—14.5 million people in 162,000 square miles. To them were added those immigrants who were caught beyond release on the Atlantic seaboard.

The great fluidity was in the farming population, equipped by training and predilection for the trial of strength with nature and by 1878 in possession of almost one-third of the national area. To the native farmers was added an important percentage of farm families from northwest Europe: German, Scandinavian, English and Welsh, Scotch and Canadian. They were eagerly bid for by the federal and state governments, the railroads, steamship lines, and land companies. The national government, which still owned approximately a million square miles of land, or one-third of the nation's expanse, had legislated on the theory that the vast western area could be peopled with an independent farming population, such as already had established themselves in the Mississippi Valley, through the sale of small parcels of land on easy terms. However, the laws had been evaded with such success that much of the trans-Mississippi area was seized by absentee owners holding large units; in 1891 a federal Immigration Bureau was established, as a part of the Treasury Department. State governments, struggling to develop their unused lands, established their own immigration bureaus to furnish information, aid and inducements to prospective settlers.

The strenuous and effective immigration work done by the private corporations, with tickets and lands to sell and future freights to hope for, expanded southerly and easterly. It flourished except in those years in the 'nineties when American economic opportunity and land supply declined and conditions in western Europe improved. Their personal representatives now showered attractive literature and promises upon the peasants of all Europe. In Italy they were aided by the interests which were establishing new steamship lines from southern ports; in regions like Russia and Poland persecution of the Jews played directly into the hands of the ticket salesmen.

To all sections but one the immigration came as a valuable asset. The vast majority of the immigrants settled in the northeastern and north central states, avoiding the South with its Negro competition and low economic scale. In the western states and territories the number of foreign-born was not large, but their proportion to the total population was very heavy. As most of the immigrants had passed childhood and had not yet reached old age, the United States had a double advantage: it got people who had been reared at the expense of their home countries and who now were giving their productive years to their adopted country.

Much of the immigration had a speculative background. Many businessmen wanted cheap workers to lay railroad ties, dig ditches, and perform unskilled labor in cities and mines. The progress of invention and manufacture enlarged the market for this kind of illiterate newcomer, setting him down in his own "little Ireland," "little Italy," "little Russia," or "Chinatown," where for a time he fulfilled his destiny as a contract laborer, meanwhile unconsciously challenging efforts to assimilate him in an independent scheme of American democracy. His heavy impact upon American life is suggested by the census figures of the percentage of foreign-born in the population: in 1880, 13.3 per cent; in 1890, 14.7 per cent; in 1900, 13.6 per cent. Nearly one-third (20,676,046 persons) of the entire population by 1890 were persons whose parents were foreign-born.

This one-third exerted a pervasive influence upon national development. Living largely in sections dominated by people of their own race and tongue, they offered in the mass the maximum resistance to Americanization; they showed an unruly, undisciplined temper in the second generation in America. Also, they comprised a "selected" group, because their families had felt themselves misfits in the Old World and had dared risk what little they had on a move to the New. Many of them again would fall victim to the modern scheme of civilization. But among them must be determined leaders, daring and resourceful, who would deflect American trends into directions suiting their ambitions. As relatively few of them settled in the agricultural areas, they were affected chiefly by conditions of city life and in that fertile field sowed the seed of their influence.

The cities were growing in number, size and influence. Factory workers crowded into their slums; clerks, stenographers and the "white-collar" class lived in the modestly respectable sections and the rich built palaces in exclusive residential districts. By 1900, 32.9 per cent of the people lived in this stratified sort of environment in cities over 8,000 and were subject to the dynamics of city life. For at least twenty years the cities had been driving the nation into change in a manner sometimes brutal, sometimes beneficent, but always dynamic, for close association powerfully stimulates activity among mankind. The changes stimulated by urbanization varied in different sections of the United States; but they were most noticeable in home life, in the amount and use of leisure and in the growth of education. These things are vitally important in the history of a republic like the United States, because on their quality ultimately depends the rise or fall of democratic institutions.

The Home Urbanized

The home was the most important influence on the nation, and city home life spurred changes in such "homely" respects as marriage customs, status of children and women, food habits and furnishings.

Marriage customs could not escape change in the cities. It had been the custom, particularly in the country and small towns, for young men and women to marry early and soon to remarry after the untimely death of either of them. In the cities, with their more numerous diversions, the employment of the poorer women and advancing education for middle-class women, marriage was later, less nearly universal and less productive. Also it was less permanent; neither propaganda from the National Divorce Reform League, federal investigation of lax state laws nor tightening of those laws could prevent divorce from increasing three times as fast as the population during the 'nineties.

Children of the cities were the ones whose lives changed fastest, for their range of experience was widened by sights and sounds striking them at the city's rapid pace. Children of the middle and upper classes offered no striking problem, but children of the poor became a special charge on the nation; for republican institutions can survive only under universal, careful education, and poor children went to work instead of to school. A million boys and girls between 10 and 15 years of age were by 1880 a part of the ranks of labor; and by 1900 they had increased to one and three-quarters millions. Textile mills, stockyards, newspaper selling and sweatshops chained them. Few laws against child labor were enforced; children of Italian immigrants were sold into slavery as beggars. The spread of these slum abuses was testified by the fact that during the 'eighties societies began to be formed for the prevention of cruelty to children.

To the women of city families industrialization was bringing more wages and a feeling of independence. Women long had been in housework, factory work and teaching; now large-scale industries were multiplying openings in the telephone, publishing, typewriting, newspaper, social service, legal and medical businesses and professions. College and university experience were adding to the skills of a few, north and south. The total consequence was that employed women increased from the two and one-half millions of 1880 to five and one-third by 1900, and the higher status fostered leadership among them.

Through self-support women learned self-respect, and some inquired into their status. In most states they could now hold property, control it, keep their own earnings and make contracts of their own volition. However, they still suffered grave discrimination in such matters as control of children, divorce rights, conditions of work and (except in Colorado, Idaho, Utah and Wyoming) in suffrage.

A minority of women learned to organize, under the tireless leadership of such spirited workers as Miss Susan B. Anthony, an ex-school teacher of much executive ability, and Mrs. Elizabeth Cady Stanton, an able penwoman who was the daughter and wife of lawyers and the mother of seven children. This remarkable pair kept working together for suffrage through fifty years of discouragements which would have disheartened most men and women. Beginnings were made at voting rights for local, school, city and tax elections. Feminism obtained some support from a minority of women, a few masculine leaders and organized labor. The two wings of the movement, the National and American, in 1890 joined forces as the "National American Woman Suffrage Association." It persisted until suffrage was consummated in 1920. The first international congress of women was held at the Chicago Fair in 1893 and gave wide impetus to feminine organization.

The leaders and those opposing them were struggling to sway the indifferent majority of American women. Most were too busy with children or jobs, or too conservative, to take excursions beyond the thinking of their own male kinfolk. The majority seemed little interested in suffrage; but part of them, women of the conservative middle class—were getting the time, money and inclination to unite in clubs—art, dramatic, book, sewing, religious, musical, scientific or athletic. This trained them for broader activities in community betterment. They organized nationally in 1889 as the General Federation of Women's Clubs; and their influence became a thing to be reckoned with in social legislation affecting their households.

City folk, encouraged by cooking schools and women's pages, were branching out in variety of foods and their preparation. They provided a huge market for refrigerated fish and fruit, for "cereals," canned foods and synthetic products like oleomargerine and shortening. Adulteration was common. Large-scale manufacture and distribution so diffused responsibility and encouraged adulteration that an exposé 1,200 pages long was printed in 1887 by the chemical division of the Department of Agriculture. The manufacturers' lobbies succeeded in killing pure food legislation because the American family had yet to become constructively critical as a consumer. Vegetable, meat, and fruit growers near cities were building up a market for fresh foods. Candy and the improved, cheaper tobacco were bought more heavily than before, with cigarettes almost nine times as popular as cigars, although "respectable" women were not supposed to smoke. Shopping habits changed as department stores stocked a larger variety of goods, and as mail order and "dime" stores arose.

Home became a place less chilly, dark and smelly. The "front parlor" (especially in rural regions) remained sacred to funerals, weddings and the more important courting, if done in summertime; it cherished its marble mantel and marble-topped table crowded with china statuettes, false flowers, paintings by ambitious kin, stereoscopes and fat, plush albums of family photographs. The transformation was in the family sitting room. There a "base burner" coal stove (with the pipe enlarged into a "drum" where it passed through a bedroom above) ensured comparative wintertime comfort. The affluent boasted a hot-air furnace calculated to warm the downstairs and take the chill off the upstairs except when the wind was "wrong"; also they could abandon oil lamps for gas-lights and even for electricity in a few homes. This class was more likely, too, to have bathrooms; plumbing improvements were ousting sewer gas and zinc tub-linings at a charge—per bathroom—of eight to sixteen times the former cost.

New Uses of Leisure

Reading and other cultural pursuits were strengthened in part and in some ways hampered by the increasing leisure which a goodly portion of the population enjoyed. These hours of leisure (except for farmers, their wives and children) were now being increased—for the rich, by reason of their mounting wealth, for wage-earners through shortened hours in the work-day, for salaried persons through summer vacations. This city leisure challenged the inventive capacity of its possessors; for the most part unaware of the challenge, they hurried *en masse* to spend their spare time imitating each other's recreations, furnishing the patronage for a large-scale organization of entertainment built on the common desire to escape from a humdrum existence.

Most complete escape was found in the secret fraternal orders, of which the United States had more than all other nations. There had been only seventy-eight before 1880; but by 1901 the delight of over six million men and women in romantic ceremonials and regal robings had fostered 490 more fraternities. Other societies shifted the appeal from secret ritual to patriotic exercise. There was a great flourishing, at centennials and celebrations.

Since these various societies met but once or twice a month, they left city and townsfolk (who did not need to rise at farmer's dawn) with an amplitude of evenings for entertainment. More evenings than formerly went to reading and study, as education and publication records show; but the vast majority found diversion not at home, art institute or library, but at the many places of commercial entertainment supported on a large scale by city people. They made New York preeminent in the theatre. They increased the number of actors from five to fifteen thousand; and to meet their demands the finest dramatic productions were included in the large repertoire of talented stock companies which survived in the cities. Out from the largest centers into the hinterland, with its typical local "opera houses," went traveling companies with one "star" supported usually by much less brilliant luminaries. Audiences which were supporting the new journalism and the popular magazines, thrilled to the dime novel, western plays and metropolitan melodramas. More than half the theatre-goers were habituées of vaudeville, and many of the persons hired wintertimes for the city's 10-20-25¢ shows and dime museums went through the countryside summers appearing at amusement parks and in circuses. Circus popularity reached its peak when some forty big tents were on tour simultaneously. Barnum and Bailey joined their gigantic extravaganzas in 1881; and, like Buffalo Bill with his new Wild West Show, they took their freaks, tricksters and menageries on tour abroad, to their great profit and the amazement of curious foreigners.

In American entertainment music assumed new importance, as evanescent, popular tunes became the rage. Sentimental songs about misplaced affection were unwound on city streets by organ grinders and tooted through the land by itinerant German bands. With songs about tenement life, with jig tunes syncopated from Negro melodies and with the "ragtime" which began a long vogue in 1896, popular music entered large-scale production and consumption. Its sway was vastly extended by Edison's phonograph, which about 1878 raucously commenced its long career of recording the vagaries of American emotions, morals and manners. The polite public, beginning in 1878, delighted in light operas, such as those of the Englishmen, Gilbert and Sullivan, and in New York wealth and taste were sufficient, in 1883, to open the costly Metropolitan Opera House for "Grand Opera."

Since concert and theatre-going were confined chiefly to evening, indoor and inactive leisure, they left unsatisfied the great need of city dwellers for bodily activity out-of-doors. Realization came of the physical handicap in urban occupations and fostered indoor gymnasium work for a few people in Turnvereins, city clubs, Y.M.C.A., Y.W.C.A., colleges and schools. Basketball—an American invention of 1891—was one of the consequences.

In the great outdoors the commonalty participated, directly or as spectators, in sports; in fact was said to "have sport on the brain." Baseball, bicycling, roller-skating and football attained high popularity, reaching the proportions of professionalism and large-scale organization. In baseball the American Association, founded in 1882, joined the National League of 1876 in developing individual skill and team play, with World Series games played from 1884 to 1891. In bicycling, the new, safety-type machine, with pneumatic tires, by 1893 had a million users pedaling over automobileless roads improved through the lobby pressure of the League of American Wheelmen. Roller-skating crazes were intermittent. In football, colleges under pressure hired non-students as players and changed the game from Rugby to a much rougher spectacle; alumni and the public enthusiastically appropriated the show and made it the occasion for excited betting and unrestrained outburts of "loyalty."

Most significant was the time people spent on reading the newspapers, their interest in the affairs of locality and nation. Newspaper editors found ready to be served, the largest literate public in the world, with a reading ability approximating that of the fifth grade. There sprouted a variety of weeklies, semi-weeklies, dailies, morning and evening issues, special, extra and Sunday editions. In this era technical and industrial advance were so conjoined with large-scale organization as to make possible quick, efficient newsgathering and cheap news printing, all at a profit. Competition for this profit so challenged the ingenuity and cupidity of its creators that they all hastened to multiply and vulgarize the press. The demands they pressed upon reporters inspired the better ones to write books and influence affairs. Newspaper readers increased faster than the population; dailies were multiplying by over 200 per cent, weeklies by 50 per cent, until by 1900 the United States had more than half the world's newspapers. Their influence grew accordingly.

The news was enmeshed in large-scale organization. The Associated Press made itself temporarily dominant in newsgathering. "Patent insides" were syndicated first by S. S. McClure in 1884 and gradually a wide sale of syndicated stories, articles, serialized novels, women's and children's features, was built up. Propaganda agencies, such as the Republican National Committee in 1896, used syndicate methods to put partisan cartoons and arguments before voters as news. Large-scale newspathering and dispensing led logically to more intimate connections between papers; the Scripps brothers before 1890 had leagued together a chain of midwestern units.

City papers struck rural people with a steady, relentless impact, well defined as "urban imperialism." About one-third of the people, it has been estimated, were within a fifty-mile radius of city dailies; and although three times as many Americans were buying weekly and semi-weekly papers as bought dailies, the city papers and magazines were the stronger moving force in American journalism. Continually they impressed their large-scale contents and far-reaching practices upon country papers. City subscribers cared but little to read of agriculture —rural subscribers enviously read of "store clothes" and city excitements. This heightened the resentments which built up the Alliances, Populism and Bryan.

The editors with the greatest influence upon the masses in this period were Joseph Pulitzer and William Randolph Hearst. Pulitzer, a Hungarian immigrant, began in 1883 with the New York *World* to show how a following could be built up by appealing to the masses with sensationalism. His clever use of "human interest," cartoons, Sunday colored supplements, and evening editions; his invasion of the privacy of all and sundry; and his crusades against corruption enlarged his circulation and those of editors who complimented him with imitation. He had no serious competition until William Randolph Hearst, son of a wealthy California mine owner and senator, undertook in 1896 to outpulitzer Pulitzer, with the New York *Morning Journal*. Their titanic struggle for supremacy led to numerous inventions of the press, among them the term "yellow journalism," which grew out of their bitter lawsuits over use of the "Yellow Kid" cartoons. The reading public was enlarged if not enlightened and the damage which their sensationalism did to public taste was offset somewhat by the purgings which their exposures occasionally gave business cheats and grafting politicians.

New Rôles of Education

Upon schools, the indispensable perquisite of democratic living, the influence of the city was most beneficent. There the accumulation of taxable wealth, with the economic recovery following 1878, created funds whereby the number and kinds of free schools, their equipment and the length of their terms could all be increased. There was an outburst of enthusiasm for, and faith in, education. Americans expected it to raise the political morality of the nation and the money-earning ability of the citizenry, a typical compound of democratic idealism and practical ambition. Compulsory attendance laws by 1900 adorned the statute books of thirty-one of the states and territories in the North and West. They ordinarily included only children between eight and fourteen, and annual terms of only twelve to sixteen weeks; also they were not enforced outside the better-established states. But they were an earnest of intention, as was the fact that ten of these states invested in free textbooks by state edict. Despite the influx of immigrant children, the number of pupils cared for in the common schools increased a little faster than the population.

In urban communities, where were extremes of wealth and poverty and masses of children desperately in need of schooling, the urge for educational improvement was most felt. Advances along the line of public kindergartens, better buildings, longer school terms and higher salaries for teachers set an example for slower communities and forecast large-scale organization of education for the masses. City teachers were led to depend less on the hickory stick and more upon interesting subject-matter, to maintain discipline. Drawing, music, nature study, cooking, sewing, carpentry, commercial subjects, civics and science were introduced into the more progressive schools. There they stood stoutly against the charge that they were merely "crazes," until village schools in the next century generally followed suit.

City improvements helped to raise the professional standing of common primary school teachers. Their advance was retarded by poor wages, which sent most of the capable men into business callings and made the women (who came to compose two-thirds of the staff) regard their jobs as temporary stepping-stones to something better. When the average time in the profession was only four years, great proficiency could not be attained. Some few women obtained administrative advancement as superintendents, but the vast majority remained in the humble ranks. Their status improved as cities came to demand normal-school training, teachers organized in self-respecting associations and the number of tax-supported high schools increased. These secondary schools, by offering instruction beyond the age of fourteen, proved that property owners were accepting responsibility for the training of leadership and taking pride in the acquisition of further culture by the offspring of their class.

Immigrant education progressed amazingly and owed much to urban facilities. Those from northern Europe were accustomed to the idea of a popular education, even where they objected to using English in place of native tongues. Further, Catholics in 1884 accepted the challenge which immigration raised for them and projected a program which rapidly expanded their parochial system in industrial areas. Altogether, by 1900 American-born children of immigrants had become more literate than white children of native parents and often showed more ambition.

Country schools (and over half the population was rural) remained sadly deficient in most respects. Almost everywhere country districts clung to their poor, isolated, ungraded schools, conducted for short terms by untrained teachers paid less than farmhands. Farmers were slow to apply to their children's schooling the principles of united action and organization with which they were experimenting in the marketing of their crops. To pool their resources in consolidated schools seemed like a renunciation of their liberties. Village schools varied in primitiveness between district and city status, according to local cultural differences depending upon racial elements, nearness to a large city and sectional trends. Backward areas were enlightened by the national Bureau of Education, which under the better commissioners supplied school people with inspiration as well as information.

Particularly difficult was improvement of schooling in the South. There the higher birth-rate (for the white population was increasing much faster even than the Negro), and the large adult illiteracy made essential the enrollment of a higher percentage of the total population than in other sections. Unfortunately, the section needed time to recover from federal muddling with local affairs, was lightly supplied with taxable property, heavily supplied with children and had the extra expense of separate schools for white and colored. Alliance organization improved somewhat the facilities but southerners in general did not yet feel deeply the obligation to supply free education to the lower classes, and Congress was no longer shouldering colored problems. Negro education was advancing with the aid of private philanthropists. Negroes attending classes more than doubled between 1878 and 1898, but still about half of them had no schooling; this retarded the national advance in literacy.

Forces pulled up and down. Illiteracy declined, 1880-1900, from 17 per cent to 11 per cent, with the cities chiefly responsible; and the average of knowledge seemed so much higher than that of other nations that it won the praise of foreign observers. But literacy means no more than the ability to read and write; and the schooling of the average American had advanced but one year—to a total of five. Also the new readers with little education tended to pull the national literacy output (books, magazines and newspapers) down toward the fourth or fifth grade level of taste and understanding. However, there were the high schools, increasingly attractive to children between thirteen and eighteen years of age; and the colleges and universities more extensively attracted sons and daughters of men and women who assumed some obligation for social and intellectual leadership.

The growing faith of Americans in higher education was abundantly demonstrated between 1878 and 1898. The number of colleges and universities increased from 350 to 500 approximately and their students from 58,000 to 100,000 approximately. Ten more states of the

West and South set up their own tax-supported universities. The University of Michigan set an example in large-scale organization of higher education. High school students were invited in, under an accrediting system which dispensed with entrance examinations. In the West coeducation gained general acceptance as necessary and proper. The East still preferred separate tutelage of college women but dignified and increased their opportunities. College work of superior quality was undertaken at Bryn Mawr and Mount Holyoke, while "coördinate" schools opened at the side doors of Brown, Columbia and Harvard. At the same time the possibilities in higher education now so intrigued millionaires that they endowed whole universities, special departments and particular chairs of learning. At Harvard President Eliot popularized the elective system, trusting the students at that highly selective institution to choose from an expanded curriculum courses more closely connected than Latin and Greek with daily life. The kind of oratorical and debating opportunities provided by college societies and by intercollegiate rivalries determined the early training of such future political leaders as Beveridge, Bryan and La Follette.

Fortunately, as the stream of higher education was broadening, it was raising its level also. Mechanical experiments in industry and elective experiments in education encouraged scholars to specialize, to discover new "laws" in science and history. Technological schools expanded and improved their standards, with the East emphasizing engineering, the Far West mining and metallurgy and the South and Middle West agriculture and horticulture. Laboratory methods greatly improved. Out of agricultural difficulties had grown research at state universities. Through government and private aid, through practical utility and competitive stimulus, science branched out widely into such fertile fields as applied chemistry, mathematics, astronomy, geology and physics. American scientists coöperated with others in international undertakings.

Graduate study received its chief impetus from Germany, where during the 'eighties the number of American students doubled until they reached a total of over 2,000. They returned to permeate American scholarship with German traditions of thoroughness. The emphasis upon graduate work which Johns Hopkins had begun in 1876 was copied at Catholic University, Clark and Chicago, while the growing appeal of such work expanded it at Columbia, Cornell, Harvard, New York University, Pennsylvania, Princeton and Yale. Many a "college" became a "university."

In the universities and out, life held plenty of interest. With education taking its new rôles, with the varied uses of leisure, with the changes in home life and above all with the momentum from growing population, urban life had become a dynamic force in America.

CHAPTER XXV

THE RISE OF BIG BUSINESS

The full implication in American history of the rapid increase of population and urbanization during this period can be realized only if one stops to consider the interaction of expanding population with developing resources. The United States was not unlike a huge turkish towel, which could absorb wave on wave of immigration because it had the requisite unfilled spaces. Ten of the present states were not yet in existence in 1880 and many areas in the remaining thirty-eight were capable of supporting a larger population. The national wealth in minerals, water power, lumber, grazing lands and food-growing areas was understood just enough to create the conviction that it was boundless. Here was coal, oil, iron, gold, silver, lead and copper to mention but few of the most valuable resources—challenging the inventiveness of the engineer and scientist and the acquisitiveness of ambitious men of vision. The employment of electricity, for which stupendous resources in water power waited, was in its early infancy. On the western ranges there was yet room for more cattle and sheep to feed and clothe the incoming hordes. Billions of feet of timber still stood, awaiting conversion into houses and newsprint, and of almost all the kinds needed for industrial and domestic purposes. Even the so-called "Great American Desert" had sufficient occasional rainfall to tempt farmers on the great plains to overoptimism and their ruination.

The Needs of a Great Population

Prospects east and west amply justified an optimistic point of view, keeping Americans a nation of incurable speculators. The wealth available for use had increased in the past twenty years—despite both Civil War and depression—from a little over 16 to near 44 billion dollars. While it was most concentrated in a few heavily populated states—New York, Pennsylvania, Ohio, Illinois and Massachusetts—it was most strikingly augmented west of the Mississippi in Kansas, Nebraska, Colorado and California—concrete justification for boundless faith in resources. Even the city-bound family, which could not own land or go west to take it up, pleasantly beguiled its imagination with tales of the new discoveries. To this large class of the dissatisfied the West was a psychological, if not a physical, outlet. Possibly these gave to the nation stronger injections of optimism than did those who actually tried their fortunes beyond the "frontier line."

Back of that line was a market busily adding proof that this was indeed the "land of opportunity." The increase in population offered the farmer, builder, manufacturer and railroader progressive expansion in the demand for their goods and services—for food, clothing, houses and transportation. Outside the range of bare necessities, the providers of education, entertainment, religion, luxuries and innovations could count upon an active demand. It was the more active because much more than half of the population was under forty years of age, was still in "the age of acquisition." Moreover, they were located in an area with ample waterways and an extended coast line, convenient for commercial purposes. These expanding demands brusquely challenged America's potential leadership in every field of activity.

The economic forces which swirled around the nation aroused the cupidity and challenged the ingenuity of budding capitalists, nerving them to fabulous feats of ruthless exploitation. As the crude individualism of the frontier was rampant everywhere, they felt no inhibitions, no compulsions to moral scruples. What more convenient philosophy than that he who could seize wealth and organize production should be rewarded with special privileges at the expense of an envious, admiring, emulating public? Did not every one get ahead who deserved it and was willing to work? Were not the poor in that class for lack of brains and ability?

The far-seeing seekers for wealth developed their skill as organizers. They learned how to bring order out of the chaos of materials and men in competing industries, so that waste and competition should disappear and the market be milked efficiently. Thus they imposed their will over wide areas and millions of people. They achieved results—good and bad—which exceeded imagination. The means, ends and consequences involved in the process are best understood by examining typical cases in the major fields—in the natural resources, in transportation, finance and in manufacturing.

Oil

Large-scale organization was earliest perfected in the exploitation of natural resources. The essential tools were waiting—a large and sturdy laboring class, rich and easily preëmpted resources and a wide market. In the oil industry were these first effectively exploited. Being a product essential to this mechanical civilization, oil could form the basis of a monopoly. The industry well typified all aspects of corporate organization—the industrial, social, political and legal. The facts of its history are largely known. Its organizing genius had the originality and ruthlessness requisite to cut a pattern for beating one's competitors at their own game in modern business. Rising capitalists in other fields were duly instructed.

When John D. Rockefeller, who started business life at 16 in 1855 as a $3-a-week assistant bookkeeper, took up oil refining near Cleveland during the Civil War, the new business had graduated only recently from quack medicine and was typical of western development—speculative in nearly all its branches. The supply of oil fluctuated violently as gushers came in and wells went dry. The operators who sank the wells were gamblers; theirs was no stable industry with modest profits fairly rewarding effort, but one in which a drilling might bring a man a million or nothing. The refiners were the sharpest kind of competitors, because the cost of refining equipment was small enough to open the field to many people and the possible profits were tantalizing. Since the entire industry was speculative, prices gyrated wildly; a barrel of oil could be quoted at fifty-two cents in 1861 and at more than $8 in 1863. The only certain-sure aspect of the industry was an increase in the public demand for the product, because foreign and domestic users of kerosene for light and lubrication multiplied rapidly.

Rockefeller and his associates, foreseeing the demand, undertook to control the supply; that involved controlling all branches of the industry. The means ready to their ends had the dubious quality then current in business and in their expert hands were used quite too efficiently to meet present-day ethical standards. Ruthlessly and thoroughly they destroyed their competitors and systematized the business under their own control, cutting a pattern for trusts of all kinds. They reached their goal through four stages: first, refining; second, transportation; third, selling; and last, well-drilling and pumping; until in 1899 Standard Oil temporarily controlled them all.

The foundation for control of refining had been laid between 1862 and 1872. Rockefeller had begun with a small investment in 1862 in a Cleveland concern, a company of his own in 1865, and a Standard Oil Corporation chartered at $1,000,000 in Ohio in 1870 with such associates as H. M. Flagler and S. V. Harkness. This third company was but one of twenty-six concerns in the Cleveland area alone, which with others of Pittsburgh, New York and Philadelphia engaged in murderous competition. Efficiency, elimination of waste and improved processes could not alone cope with the industry-wide disorganization. The Rockefeller group, together with others in the four cities mentioned, therefore joined themselves in 1870 in a "South Improvement Company" which made a deal with the oil-carrying railroads, themselves competitors, to eliminate competitors. The New York Central, Erie and Pennsylvania were to raise freight charges by agreed amounts, but were to give South Improvement shippers rebates on both their own shipments and on those of their competitors, while the traffic was to be regularly apportioned. The outcry of outsiders against this discrimination forced the Pennsylvania legislature to annul the South Improvement charter in 1872; but by that time Standard Oil had acquired the property of twenty of its twenty-five Cleveland competitors and controlled 20 per cent of the refining capacity of the nation. Also, it had entered a career of regularly demanding and usually receiving secret rebates invaluable to it.

In the next decade the Standard Oil built pipe-lines, with which it forced railroads to grant more rebates, and competitors to hand over more businesses. It proved futile for the Pennsylvania Railroad or for outside refiners to try to compete by organizing their own pipe-lines. Among all competitors there was cajolery, lying, intimidation, spying, destruction of property, theft and sometimes murder. When the fight abated the Standard Oil organization had control of more companies. Forty of them, embracing control of 90 per cent of the refineries and pipe-lines of the nation, were organized under a trustee certificate plan in 1879 into the "Standard Oil Trust" which was formally created in 1882.

The trust form of organization proved so convenient for large-scale combinations that it was adopted in many fields of business and a fairly uniform procedure was devised for setting it up. First a "trust agreement" was drawn up. Then the property and assets of the various companies to be consolidated were valued. Next the stockholders of the various companies turned over their stock "in trust" to the new concern and received trust certificates, according to the proportion of the combined value of the new trust which their original shares represented. Finally operation of the trust proceeded under the management of trustees—usually nine—elected for three-year terms by the stockholders at annual meetings. In practice shareholders exercised little or no surveillance over trustees or officers. It will be seen that the trust form did three things of special importance: it greatly diminished the number of managers in control; it vastly extended their power over production and prices; and it removed them further from accountability for their policies.

While Standard Oil thus was winning control of the refining and transportation of oil, the same genius for organization was applied to oil-selling agencies. It would force merchants to sell only Standard Oil output, would keep prices at a high profit level, while occasionally cutting them drastically to eliminate other sellers, and meanwhile would build an enviable reputation for delivery of a standard quality product regularly, on time as ordered. The system effectively reached into the smallest hamlets. It contributed its quota to the maintenance of high prices at huge profits.

Control of drilling and pumping was attended to last, beginning on a large scale about 1887, and practically completed within ten years. Before 1900, therefore, large-scale organization as applied to the oil industry had placed absolute control for the nonce in the hands of Standard Oil.

This, however, could not be accomplished without ruthlessness and cruelty, violent protest, social upheaval and the enlisting of ingenious legal and legislative talents. The services which the corporation rendered the consuming public were of a high order to which they were by no means accustomed; but the approach of absolute control, coupled with high prices, brought public support to competing producers as they struggled against their ultimate fate. Men who had been eliminated filed suits at common law and attracted public attention to the evil practices of competitors.

Public interest, the United States being a democracy, had political effects. As noted, the Pennsylvania legislature annulled the charter of the South Improvement Company. A committee of Congress denounced it; the House Committee on Commerce at Washington investigated the Standard Oil Company in 1876; the Hepburn Commission in New York followed suit in 1879. The federal Anti-Trust Act of 1890 was followed the next year with trust investigations, undertaken by a commission for the New York State Senate and by the Committee on Manufactures of the national House of Representatives. In 1892 the Ohio Supreme Court ordered the Standard Oil Trust dissolved, and in 1898 an industrial commission looked further into it.

All of this had importance, as showing public disapproval of some corporation practices and public expectation of legislative and judicial remedies; but it interfered very little with oil control or profits. When the Standard Oil Trust was ordered dissolved in 1892, the charter of the company remained unimpaired. It turned out that the dissolution order could not be enforced. The men in control proceeded to perfect a new device, a holding company, with the owners of the trust certificates exchanging them for stock in a holding corporation which became the actual owner of the properties, run under consolidated management by a president and board of directors. Also Standard Oil, which had a charter from the complaisant New Jersey legislature, obtained in 1899 an amended charter highly significant in American corporate development, for it was good for almost any sort of undertaking.

As the holding company proved an effective device for evading trust disabilities, it became common in American business. The two were alike in object. They differed chiefly in that the trust operated under a comparatively informal trust agreement and the holding company under a corporate charter granted by a state. In time the holding company would prove convenient for pyramiding one company on top of another for purposes of stock manipulation and service charges, making the top-heavy structure sensitive to depression earthquakes, and likely to bury the stockholders.

Eager imitators of Standard Oil multiplied during the 'eighties and after—the cotton seed trust in 1884, linseed in 1885, in 1887 the cordage, lead and whisky trusts, in 1891 the American Sugar Refining trust. These of course remained unaffected by the Ohio decisions. The general term "trust" kept its meaning. Before January 1, 1898, eighty-two trusts, capitalized at 1,197 millions, had been organized. The cumulative force of this movement showed in the organization within the next six years of 236 trusts, with a total capitalization of 6,000 millions. Mightiest of these were Amalgamated Copper, American Smelting and Refining and the Standard Oil of 1899, Consolidated Tobacco and United States Steel in 1901 and the International Mercantile Marine of 1902, all with New Jersey charters. These consolidations were made the more easily and profitably through conditions reigning between 1898 and 1902. Then American industrial and agricultural prosperity was encouraged by the gold discoveries, increased exploitation of resources and swelling population. The world situation contributed to a trade balance favorable to the United States. The attitude of the public and of the charter-dispensing legislatures—particularly New Jersey, Delaware, West Virginia and Maine—was complaisant.

The charters were the perfect product of the nation's keenest legal lights. They found their high-paid calling in protecting private corporations from restrictions imposed by public will. The large-scale organization of business had reached the point where it undermined the government of the democracy itself. The public soon would be made aware of the fact.

Iron, Coal and Electricity

Iron and coal offered an opportunity hardly less stimulating than oil for the talents of large-scale organizers. These two natural resources could be utilized in the manufacture of steel to furnish a product indispensable to American industrial advance. In this great field Andrew Carnegie was the leading spirit and accumulated a fortune next in size to that of Rockefeller.

The United States as a "land of opportunity" found its living embodiment in Carnegie. Between 1848 and 1900 he ran the gamut from destitute child immigrant to the nation's second richest citizen. He achieved this feat by shrewd application of competitive energy, courage and optimism; persistent and unyielding, he exploited the astounding opportunities of his place and period. Carnegie's difficulties were made less because he had a personal charm and romantic temperament which could find in America a response extremely gratifying to the ego as well as to the purse.

The Civil War afforded him opportunities in telegraphy and railroading which led on into bridge building and iron manufacture. Oil dividends brought funds for investment. When he was selling American railroad bonds abroad, the vision of steel appeared to him; in Britain he grew to know Bessemer, observed his process for converting brittle iron into strong steel, and studied operations of the world's leaders in the industry. His enthusiasm was concentrated from 1873 upon smelting operations in the coal, limestone and iron area near Pittsburgh; in sixteen years (with the help of a high tariff) the United States had become the largest producer of steel in the world and Carnegie the biggest steel manufacturer in the United States. The United States and Carnegie attained these eminences bcause he and his associates as well as his competitors in steel were working at the center of American economic development.

Carnegie developed a talent for placing competitors at a disadvantage. Outside of his locale of Pittsburgh the principal producing regions were in Illinois, Tennessee, Alabama and Colorado; his three principal competitors in domestic unfinished steel therefore were the Illinois Steel Company, the Colorado Fuel and Iron Company and the Tennessee Coal, Iron and Railway Company. Also he had British competitors. He proceeded to disadvantage them through Henry Clay Frick's development of the Connellsville coke area, coke being superior to ordinary coal for smelting; he obtained for $2.50 a ton better coke than British manufacturers obtained for $4.50. Carnegie aligned Frick with him in 1882 and later yielded to the younger man's tardy urgency that he investigate the rich iron ore deposits lying practically on the surface of the shores of Lake Superior. The best of these deposits had been acquired at a cheap depression price in 1893 by Rockefeller, and from him in 1896 Carnegie leased ore lands at a price so low as to make him practically invincible against all rivals; there would be no way out for his warring competitors but large-scale combinations of their own.

All the steel manufacturers benefited by the feverish railroad building and multiplication of inventions for farms and factories. This, whether or not Carnegie realized it, was the reason why his scheme of mass production, low profits and continual expansion of output worked. Thus did transportation, agriculture, westward expansion, manufacturing in general and steel interdepend.

Being at the center of American economic development, steel making was infected by its ills—by business cycles, pitiless competition, railroad malpractice and labor unrest. The cycles, severely felt throughout the nation, moved the more violently because Carnegie set a production pace which his competitors strove to emulate, periodically glutting the market. He not only insisted that his workmen compete with rival firms, but also with each other. In depression years when weaker concerns let their equipment run down, the optimistic and far-visioned Carnegie expanded plants at minimum construction cost: he could supply the market the moment buying recommenced, at figures below those of hapless competitors with boom-time building charges. During the resulting warfare pools and other trade agreements common in railroad and oil were tried in steel, and failed on account of the same mutual suspicion. Carnegie was producing steel too cheaply to bind himself very often to an arbitrary allotment.

The competitive frenzy for tonnage, with all its evil effects, worked four great benefits. It caused quick scrapping of obsolete machinery, lightning development of inventive aspects of the industry, rapidly improved processes and lowered prices. For low-grade ores the Siemens-Martin open-hearth process was devised and by 1900 was producing more steel than the Bessemer method. Carnegie kept competitors continually trying to meet his underselling, thus giving the public the priceless boon of cheap steel.

Railroad abuses beset steel differently than oil. Because the Pennsylvania Railroad enjoyed a near monopoly at Pittsburgh, Carnegie could not secure rebates and preferences in the Rockefeller manner. He and his Pittsburgh competitors were discriminated against in favor of Chicago and Cleveland. He fought the Pennsylvania (his old employer) hard, building some trackage of his own and shipping his Lake Superior ore via Rockefeller steamships and railroads.

For labor, Carnegie felt more sympathy than many of his fellow industrialists; but his associate Frick felt less. Strained relations which had become serious by 1887 culminated in 1892 in the notorious Homestead Strike and a complete rout of the union (p. 315). Thus, in the basic industry of steel, large-scale organization of capital whipped large-scale organization of labor. This year of 1892 was the same in which various Carnegie holdings in coal, coke, limestone, iron ore, ships and railroads were combined as the Carnegie Steel Company, Limited. It was by far the strongest of the concerns producing crude and semi-finished steel.

Meanwhile, in the production of finished steel, large-scale organization was applied in almost every nook and cranny. Pitiless competition had been alternating with pools, in nearly every steel product in use; but by about 1898 J. P. Morgan of New York and William H. Moore of Chicago had engineered gigantic combinations—in wire, nails, tubes, hoops, tin plate, sheet steel, and bridge steel, to mention but a part of the products. They fortified themselves by combining into the Illinois Steel Corporation.

Then Carnegie, who now wished to retire and devote his time to charity and leisure, vigorously commenced to invade the finished steel field. Frightened, Morgan and millionaire associates, with the legal aid of E. H. Gary, bought up Carnegie's great holdings. They managed this by setting up a 1,400 million dollar corporation—United States Steel—through which they consolidated his holdings with theirs, paying to him 447 millions in bonds and to themselves large blocks of preferred and common stock. As their combined properties were conservatively estimated to be worth only about 682 millions, it was clear that they weighted down the new corporation with more than 700 millions of watered stock, based upon nothing but future hope. Fortunately for them, their dominance in steel was so complete, and American prosperity then was so pervasive, that the corporation paid dividends on its water, thus soaking it up. The water formula of large-scale organization was commonly and profitably practised by the consolidators of this period.

Incorporation of the steel trust in 1901 marked a new era in steel manufacture. Away went Carnegie's old partnership organization, wherein steel stock was owned and controlled exclusively by executives actually working in the industry, with speculation definitely ruled out. Ever since, executives have been hired and stock manipulated. More important from the standpoint of the public weal, when Carnegie departed, competition in steel departed with him. This probably had effects reaching beyond and counteracting his efforts as the incorporated philanthropist, the giver of libraries and founder of technical institutes and foundations for the advancement of knowledge.

Another natural resource, brought like oil and metals into wide use through large-scale organization, was water power. Applied to the manufacture of electricity on a large scale, for business and private consumption, it began a long career of direct influence on national life. Following 1877, dynamos and arc lights developed by C. F. Brush and John Thomson led to Thomas A. Edison's incandescent lamp of 1879, which the banking firm of Drexel-Morgan wisely financed. By 1886 George Westinghouse was ready to market alternating current, against the bitter opposition of Edison and others. Its adoption splendidly illustrates the far-reaching influence of changes in this industry. The introduction of alternating current had such significant consequences as the refinancing of electric companies, construction of municipal plants, flagrant franchise corruption, the forcing of the displaced gas companies into the heating business and the development of the huge industry of electric appliances.

The application of electricity to traction proved difficult, with Edison and Thomson advancing but slowly. Leo Daft and C. J. Van Depoele were doing somewhat better but it was not until Frank J.

Sprague succeeded at Richmond, Virginia, in constructing a traction system permitting a great many trolley cars to consume electricity at the same time, that success was assured. His company was promptly absorbed by the Edison Electric system and capitalistic control of public utilities was assured for many years. Just as there was no precedent in American experience for electric traction itself, so there was no precedent for government control of that traction; and the same thing proved true with other American electrical developments.

Vitally important in the field of electrical advance were the telegraph and telephone, which evolved in such a manner as to keep rapid communication—a vital aspect of large-scale organization—under private control. The Western Union Telegraph Company emerged from a combination of fifty companies before the Civil War; but in 1878 it entered upon a new era under the presidency of Norvin Green. Three years later its two chief competitors, the American and the Atlantic and Pacific Telegraph Companies, were absorbed by it. There followed the indispensable contracts with the railroads, which accomplished huge savings by exchanging the use of office space and telegraph wires for the sending of train despatch messages.

Meanwhile large-scale business received indispensable aid in the annihilation of distance through the efforts of entrepreneurs in the telephone business. As an avenue of wealth-getting, telephony attracted Western Union leaders who had refused to buy Alexander Bell's patent rights and launched a competing company with Elisha Gray's patents. They met their match when Theodore N. Vail assumed charge of the American Bell Telephone Company and in 1879 forced Western Union to stop infringement and retire from the field. The Bell interests in 1885 prosecuted far-reaching schemes for long-distance consolidation of companies which greatly quickened communication in American business. The telephone monopoly proved more benign than others. Many small-town units survived, although their relative importance was slight. The Bell concerns were financed conservatively, without the gross stock manipulation typical of most virgin industries. Telephony vastly increased employment, because it stimulated manufacture and distribution in innumerable fields. Successive inventions aided engineering, with such things as underground wiring, copper wiring and the fabrication of cables adapted to multiple messages over long distances.

Railroads and Manufacturing

Similar tendencies manifested themselves in the fields of railroading and manufacturing. The Northern Pacific Railroad was completed to the Pacific Coast; James J. Hill built the Great Northern; while the Southern Pacific and the Atchison Topeka and Santa Fé spanned the southwestern states and territories. In the East, William H. Vanderbilt, the old Commodore's son, labored with the financial help of J. Pierpont Morgan to build up the New York Central lines, and other financiers created the great Pennsylvania system. Convenience and monopoly here came hand in hand.

Inevitably, manufacturers resorted to large-scale methods as the needs of the nation grew. These needs became varied in kind while they swelled in total volume. They challenged inventors, capitalists and executives to fill more factories with more machines, to make more money in more different ways. Thus mechanization of the nation was quickened during the 'eighties by a manufacturing development far greater than in any previous decade. Manufacture spread westward in pursuit of raw material, usually as fast as the supply of labor, transportation and capital permitted. The number of employees increased about twice as fast as the population; capital invested in manufacturing more than doubled, as did the value of the net product of manufacturing.

But this did not mean that the number of factories and the number of employees increased as fast as the capital and the product. On the contrary, their growth was somewhat less rapid, due to the greater size of manufacturing establishments and the increased use of machinery in them. Machinery was displacing workers, at the same time as it vastly enlarged their output.

Manufacturers obtaining capital, machinery and labor in abundance, overestimated their markets. They monopolized the domestic market behind high tariff walls—walls watchfully guarded by such large-scale organizations as the American Iron and Steel Association, American Wool Manufacturers Association and the Association of American Manufacturers. They turned second to foreign buyers, expanded their plants and sharpened their wits to meet demands of the world market. This in turn made American industry more sensitive to world trade fluctuations; under the conditions of competitive machine manufacture all the great industrial nations—the United States, England, France and Germany—were likely to find themselves in a slump almost simultaneously, to the extent that local and foreign demand moved up and down together.

Thus American genius responded to the challenge of numbers and expanse. A great population spread across the continent could now be supplied through giant enterprise with the ever increasing number of commodities which the American standard of living, steadily rising, was requiring. At the same time the control of business had come into the hands of a relatively few financiers who, led by J. Pierpont Morgan and his associates in their Wall Street offices, determined the direction and character of the economic development of the nation.

CHAPTER XXVI

UNEQUAL DIVIDENDS

The benefits of this great achievement in business consolidation and efficiency did not spread uniformly over the nation's population. Some of the projects were too big. Among the results were overproduction (from the standpoint of the seller, not of the consumer), lowered prices and wages, and unemployment—the acute sufferings that go to make up a depression. These had more drastic effects than formerly because the mechanization of industry made variations more extreme, while it imposed a manner of living which left the laborers with less resource for combating unemployment. They worked ten and twelve hours for low wages; they paid high rents for an existence in squalor. During the depression of the mid-'eighties, skilled men competed for jobs paying only $1 per day, and women for fifty-cent wages. The price fall then partly compensated them for low wages, but there were too many jobless days for decent living.

Industrialization and poverty marched side by side in the United States, but most Americans tenaciously cherished the belief that theirs was still the "land of opportunity." The various forces at work by 1890 had brought 1 per cent of the families more wealth than all the other 99 per cent. Of the city population (largely foreign-born) 10 per cent then were living in poverty. Yet Andrew Carnegie in 1886 denied the existence of poverty in America. But others less blind thought poverty always was due to laziness, wastefulness, drunkenness or illiteracy. The unprosperous had but themselves to blame. It was heresy to assert that pauperism could be imposed "in the land of the free." Class fluidity did indeed remain far greater than in Europe; but it was far less than when Carnegie started to rise. To uproot such preconceptions, invalidated in fact by large-scale organization of capital, labor must perfect its own organization.

Labor Consolidation

Labor struggled for its own large-scale organization blunderingly and persistently during the 'eighties and 'nineties. Early in this period the Knights of Labor were approaching their ascendancy. They established their general assembly of 1878, on the upswing of the country's return to prosperity. The next year they abandoned secrecy and, electing T. V. Powderly as Grand Master, they entered an aggressive phase in which they abandoned their former dislike for strikes. As national and local craft unions also were very active in this period, there were, 1880-1885, over 500 strikes and lockouts annually. Union membership grew with union effectiveness and the hard times beginning in 1884 brought more radical recruits. Two years later the Knights alone had nearly 750,000 on their rolls.

With strikes and boycotts they made their mark in two fields. In industry they proved less unsuccessful than before in fighting wage reductions, forcing the eight-hour day, and securing recognition of the Knights; their most decisive victory was over the Gould railway management in 1885. In legislation their state victories brought a factory inspection act in highly industrialized Massachusetts (1879). Nationally they got exclusion of Chinese (1882) and contract labor (1885). Machinery to assist their propaganda efforts was set up within the national government in the form of a standing committee on labor in the House of Representatives (1883) and a national Bureau of Labor (1884). Their gains were insignificant compared with demands; but they made themselves a force to be reckoned with, politically and industrially.

However, 1886 brought disaster. Following a May Day movement for an eight-hour day which involved the killing of several strikers by Chicago police, a memorial mass meeting was held 4 May in Haymarket Square, Chicago. There some one, who never has been discovered, threw a bomb which killed one of the police and wounded others. The results were conviction of eight anarchists on general principles, since their direct connection with the outrage could not be proved. Many among the general public were alarmed at this evidence of the infiltration of European revolutionary ideas. Marxian doctrines from the Communist Manifesto like, "Working men of the world unite! You have nothing to lose but your chains," denied the validity of the longstanding national optimism. The bomb-throwing tactics of the Anarchists of Russia implied the end of opportunity. Labor, to the conservative and fearful, now seemed dominated by foreigners determined to destroy democracy.

The Knights of Labor endeavored to defend the accused in the Haymarket affair and were thereby discredited. But though their influence was waning, a new labor star was rising. A labor federation destined to come down into the present was being built on a narrower principle—one better calculated to succeed in the America of those years. Units of skilled craftsmen formed in 1881 a "Federation of Organized Trades and Labor Unions of the United States and Canada." Skilled craftsmen, said they, should combine solely for their own benefit. So within two years they and the Knights of Labor were at war.

After the Haymarket affair, the Federation reorganized as the "American Federation of Labor." With unaffiliated unions preferring them to the Knights of Labor, and with disaffected craftsmen coming over from the Knights, the Federation ultimately succeeded in displacing its predecessor as the strongest labor organization.

Chances of success in securing nation-wide recognition of skilled labor depended upon the quality of union leadership and membership and their skill at forging and wielding weapons. Leadership here was assumed in many cases by immigrants, who were not hampered by a belief in the perfection of existing institutions. Samuel Gompers and his associates had learned by experience that industrial warfare was a far more effective instrument than political programs and currency reform! They were imbued with the European concept of class struggle but did not attempt any basic reordering of American society. They accepted the capitalistic system and respected American traditions in self-government. That historic entity, the local union, was accepted in the Federation as a practically autonomous "city central" run democratically and frugally and tied into the national body by the familiar device of a state federation. Each national craft union kept complete autonomy, was apportioned representation in the Federation according to its membership and contributed annually to the central war chest a 3 cent per capita tax.

Their chief interest and advance was in collective bargaining. Their main constituents were local unions in railroading, mining, metal-working, building, and manufacturing which varied greatly in vision, methods and success. Union autonomy weakened unionism because locals of various crafts quarreled over jurisdiction on big jobs. The Federation worked mainly among the relatively small proportion of labor which was skilled, teaching them allegiance to the union label. They quite frequently organized effective boycotts of goods or employers who refused to use the label, particularly between 1881 and 1891. Strikes advanced beyond the limited hour-pay objective to a demand for union recognition—for the principle that industry should not be run without periodic trade agreements between capital and labor.[1] Gompers' policy of high dues and benefits enabled unions in 1893, for the first time, to pass through a panic without loss of membership. The fact that organized labor did not disintegrate, 1893-1898, against the modernized capitalistic warfare of that depression, proved its growth in strength. By 1900 the Federation had a labor press of some 500 editors and over half a million members.

Such activities in the industrial field brought forth fruit in legislation. The contract labor law was strengthened in 1891, when also federal control of immigration was established. Chinese exclusion was re-

[1] Iron molders in 1891 made the earliest trade agreement of importance.

newed in 1892. A federal law attempting the eight-hour day for government workers proved ineffective, however. Among the states, labor by 1895 had accumulated fifteen arbitration statutes. But trade unions were still illegal as corporations and therefore subject to national and state conspiracy laws; nor had labor obtained national laws satisfactory to them for cutting down the labor supply in respect to children, women, apprentices and contract immigrants.

Among the craft unions organized upon a national or international scale were important bodies which added much dignity to the cause of labor, although they held aloof from the Federation. The aristocrats among these were the Railway Brotherhoods. They had much of the paternalism of the medieval gilds; and as they were a very highly trained, selected group they had a value to their employers which the ordinary industrial worker lacked. They developed their organization cautiously, in accordance with habits inbred in them by their responsible occupation, and four conservative brotherhoods resulted—The Locomotive Engineers, the Railway Conductors, the Firemen, and the Trainmen—which finally achieved a national unity. They got little in national legislation—a railway arbitration act of 1888 proved unusable and the Erdman Act of 1898 was unpopular; but they amassed funds for accident and death benefits, and as men of resource, not easily replaced, won concessions in working conditions and wages. Outside of their ranks rose a more radical and less successful organization, the American Railway Union. It was founded by young Eugene V. Debs, former officer in the Brotherhood of Locomotive Firemen, who sought to organize all railway workers in an aggressive industrial union.

All these efforts at organization on a large scale were characteristic of labor's contribution to American development during the two final decades of the nineteenth century. Between 1881 and 1900 labor staged approximately 24,000 strikes, 1,190 annually, involving nearly a third of a million workers. The strikers won 35 per cent, compromised 17 per cent and lost 48 per cent of these engagements.

Three of these defeats illustrated vividly how large-scale organizations of capital, already achieved in key industries, could defeat large-scale organization of labor in the making. First, at Homestead, Pennsylvania, in 1892 an exceptionally strong union—the Amalgamated Association of Iron and Steel Workers of the United States—challenged Frick (and Carnegie) over reduced wages and the closed shop. In the middle of a struggle relentless on both sides, an anarchist once more damaged labor. Alexander Berkman, a Russian immigrant who had been convinced by the Haymarket affair "that America was as despotic as Russia," attempted to assassinate Frick. This deprived the Amalgamated of the sympathy of the public, and the Carnegie Corporation not only broke the strike but also wrecked the Amalgamated, postponing unionization of the industry for forty years.

Second, at Chicago in 1894 a union of Pullman car workers living in a "company town" struck against a wage reduction. The American Railway Union espoused their cause, with a boycott spreading through the Middle and Far West against handling trains to which Pullman cars were attached. To the aid of the Pullman Company came the General Managers' Association (representing the executive branches of twenty-four railroads) and the thousands of laborers grasping for any kind of a job in the depression. Also President Cleveland was a conservative on labor and Attorney-General Olney was committed to capital. When the strike involved interruption of government mails federal troops were sent (against the wishes of Governor Altgeld) to defeat the workers.

Their leaders, including Debs, were removed to jail by court action, through injunctions, a highly significant method. Labor leaders earlier had been subject to jail sentences for calling strikes, under the conspiracy laws; but in 1894 the Sherman Anti-trust Law against combinations in restraint of trade was invoked for the first time without recourse to a jury trial. Also another weapon of labor, the boycott, was declared illegal. Thus Pullman underscored the illegality of trade unions as corporations and it was a tremendous setback for labor. This was a mass defeat, with nearly 750,000 workers—even more than in 1886—involved. Added to this disaster, came the third important defeat. The United Mine Workers lost a strike in the same calamitous year. Recovery for labor must wait until the depression passed.

Thus the last two decades of the nineteenth century were marked by large-scale organization in every field of business. The economic opportunities afforded by America's growing population and abundant resources had been exploited in the mines, at the waterfalls, along the railroad lines, on Wall Street and in the factories. The profits from organization had been greatest for capital; but labor had not been entirely without advantage. A third great class lived on the American scene. Did agriculture share in the trend?

The Farmer Reaches the Last Frontier

The agriculturists inevitably became entangled in the American trend toward large-scale organization; but to them it failed to bring either a place of great power or a prosperous position, and it swept away the foundations of their thinking. The American farmer had always felt that agriculture was the great national mainstay, and that his occupation was an independent, self-sufficient, ideal manner of getting a living. In his optimism and self-reliance he had been committed to laisseztaire, like most Americans convinced that uncontrolled exploitation of the national resources by individuals without government interference was the great guarantee of his well-being. It proved his undoing. He had to call for help and fight for place.

Between 1862 and 1889 a migratory movement unequaled in world history established more than a million farms in a heretofore unpopulated region. The 'seventies had seen farm settlements in the eastern third of Kansas, Nebraska and the Dakotas; into their central and western sections and into Colorado—west of the Missouri—farming was carried during the 'eighties at a speed which within about six years covered a larger area than the thirteen original states. This was the period when agricultural migration reached its height. Some Americans were habitual migrants—the same family might settle successively in state after state, as did the Hamlin Garland family. Their hopes and those of immigrants continued to be fed by the uncensored optimism of railroad advertisements, of land companies and speculators. Also, the speculators were availing themselves more generally of a "commutation" privilege whereby land could be purchased by persons with no intention of farming or ranching.

The spurs to agricultural migration and production have varied in force in different periods of United States history. Up to 1890 the most powerful spurs were the free public lands, the low price acreage, the influx of labor to work land and (after railroads were built) the transportation which provided outlets to markets; the functioning of these agencies is a familiar historical fact and has been detailed in earlier chapters.

Almost equally important as a spur to agriculture, in the latter part of the nineteenth century, was the new machinery which then came abundantly into successful use. With farm machinery came industrial machinery adapted to farm products; together they affected city as well as country life, influencing the history of crops, enlarging the totals of indebtedness, altering the day's work of both factory employee and farm laborer. For example, oil machinery glorified the cotton seed and its by-products in the South. The cream-tester, separator and other machinery used in dairy factories of the Middle West widened the market for cheese, butter and condensed milk. Sorghum syrup machinery spurred corn growing in the Southwest.

Wheat was an agricultural product which, with its new machinery, had intimate connections with the great migration and production. New varieties of wheat and other grains were being adapted to various soils and climates over the country. Hard red spring wheat, with improvements for milling fine white flour from it, opened Minnesota and Dakota. Hard red winter wheat was destined to enjoy a boom in Kansas and thereabouts. Wheat then was the pioneer crop—with its yield of twelve bushels to the acre it belonged with cheap land, with labor scarcity, and lack of credit; and so it moved West (except where aridity barred it) close behind the frontier line. Pushed by rising land values, it spread to the Pacific coast, reaching bonanza proportions in California before 1890 and thereafter making the Columbia River basin the last wheat frontier.

Farmers on the High Plains could not realize that exceptional rainfall ruled their destines between 1877 and 1886. Even with its aid they could not have penetrated very far without the invention of barbed wire and the introduction of well drills, windmills and irrigation. In this region of scant rains and hot winds, farmers did more experimenting than on all the other farms of the United States combined. For them Europe, Asia and Africa were combed by agricultural specialists for plants to meet High Plains needs. Agriculture was "literally created" in western parts of Texas, New Mexico, Oklahoma and Kansas.

Behind wheat in its westward march followed (again, where rainfall permitted) crops repaying larger investment—corn, potatoes, diversified farming products, dairying, fruit. Planters, harvesters, huskers and shredders did for corn what threshing and mowing machinery did for grain and hay; they carried the corn belt west from Illinois into Kansas. Corn growers of the eastern and central areas adjusted themselves to competition from western growers by using 90 per cent of their corn as fodder for dairy cattle, quality beef and fat hogs, which they marketed at a profit greater than they could make by selling corn. Where dairying could follow the westward staples, it proved a more permanent type of agriculture. With the aid of cream separators introduced from Sweden in 1882, with testing machinery and the right type of foreign immigrants, Wisconsin was transformed by 1890 into a dairy state. Dairy farmers, like growers of vegetables and fruits, enjoyed a prospect of stability denied the staple farmer, for they could exploit the local scene in the coming era; they could market in the cities which now were rising nearby and demanding a more varied diet.

Another influential factor in the great migration and production was meat, responding in its way to the rising domestic and foreign demand and to the cheapening of price which followed increased production and improved transportation facilities. Beef and pork were by 1881 major factors in export trade, and until 1900 cattle increased faster than the population. Most of the cattle were raised on the small farms of the humid region, around 1880; the plains states then produced only about 15.4 per cent, Texas about 12.3 per cent and the Pacific states about 6.3 per cent. However, the vast area stretching between the 100th meridian and the mountains, from the Rio Grande to Canada, was known as the "Cattle Kingdom," and it was destined to exercise an influence upon American politics and habits out of all proportion to its economic production. It had its own peculiar problems of large-scale organization.

The depression of 1873-1878 had cheapened Texas cattle and had pushed expansion of the cattle business to the north. The trail from the Texas panhandle, bent westward by the barriers of the Kansas farmers, the Indians, and the Kansas-Missouri quarantines, found its way through the corridor of the eastern third of Colorado to the northern ranges. There mining stampedes, Custer's defeat and the military campaigns following it advertised the Yellowstone lower country and cleared the way for stockmen. The close of the 'seventies brought an end to the frontier conditions on the old Oregon trail, as the Indians had to give up nationhood and accept reservation life. As the 'eighties opened, the cattlemen were changing the mining frontier as far north as Montana into a stock frontier, with the Northern Pacific and the Union Pacific building the necessary railheads, while the national government bundled the Indians out of northern Wyoming and eastern Montana. Lands set aside for Indian reservations were opened to the whites by the Dawes Act of 1887.

When Colorado (where sheep raising was taking hold) became overstocked, Wyoming and Montana received the surplus. The demand on the northern ranges reached extreme limits. Farmers of the upper Mississippi Valley, Illinois, Wisconsin, Michigan, Iowa and Missouri, began to ship stock to western breeders. Although Texas now shipped many cattle directly east, an eager rivalry of drovers for the northern trek continued. As the cattlemen were using free the grazing land owned by the government, almost their only outlay was for stock. Exceptionally abundant rainfall and mild winters ensured easy feeding and their profits were fabulous. Railroad advertising and lurid literature on "How Cattlemen Grow Rich" encouraged an orgy of speculation. Money from the East and from England and Scotland (following Europe's tradition of profits in American land speculation) poured into cattle companies, run under absentee ownership, while the quick profits of the boom years of 1882-1883 made lucky operators "Cattle Kings" and "Cattle Queens." The growers in this area then had no great quarrel with the packing industry. Although the "big four" packers in 1880 had made a "gentlemen's agreement" for monopoly, ensuring their own economic and political power, in the early 'eighties they supported the price of beef and pork despite an export collapse.

Three other powerful spurs to the great migration and production require marked emphasis—wasteful cultivation, industrialization and the demand for exports to meet the debt payments of the United States.

Extravagant methods of cultivation, which abundance of land and scarcity of labor had fixed as national habits, were further aggravated

The Homestead Act, by offering land free, had fed the trend; and harvesting machinery (like the cotton gin) put a premium on land wastefulness. Farmers did not expect land to support one family more than twenty years; thereafter the eldest son took the old farm and the other sons went beyond the new acreage. Precautionary crop rotation and fertilization scarcely belonged in this picture; they existed to a limited extent, but only because horses and mules remained the farm motive power and required hay and oat acreage. The farmers of this period in the American West were thoughtlessly skimming the cream off agricultural resources.

Industrialization made imperious the world demand for foodstuffs in boom times. Factory workers of the United States, Britain and parts of Europe virtually commanded the farmer to feed them. Thus the flow of American wheat, corn, beef and pork facilitated the economic revolution in Europe late in the nineteenth century, as had Spanish-American gold and silver in the eighteenth.

Also Europe challenged the American farmer to maintain the debt payments of the United States. British, German and French investors in railways and other undertakings took their interest payments chiefly in food export balances. They could not take their pay in sales of their own manufactures because the United States tariff kept foreign goods out to give home manufacturers control of the domestic market. In addition, foreign producers of such daily necessities as coffee and tea, and such manufacturing essentials as dyestuffs, based their American sales on balances created through food production. The farmer met these demands so vigorously, between 1879 and 1883, as to create then a favorable "visible" balance of trade which contributed to prosperity through the entire nation.

Thus spurred—to migrate and to produce—farmers of the United States during the two decades prior to 1900 totaled a precipitous rise in food production—a rise more rapid than the increase in population. They lost their local self-sustaining powers and became dependent on sales, on commerce. Foodstuffs became much the largest element in agricultural exports, with cotton second and tobacco third, while agriculture furnished seven-tenths of all American exports. Thus important was agriculture in the national economy. Few if any of its leaders realized that by 1900 agriculture would be furnishing little more than half of total exports, and that later manufactures would preëmpt first place.

Farm Production Penalized

Many of the forces which spurred the farmer on to migrate and produce punished him for doing so.

Once the farmer took hold of machinery, it took hold of him. It put him at a special disadvantage marketwise. He still had to sell in a sharply competitive market, for he could not combine effectively to control the price of crops; but he could not buy his machinery or other necessities in the same kind of market, for competition among manufacturers was reduced. Over a hundred large machinery manufacturers competed for farmers' patronage in 1879; but by 1900 the makers of drills, harrows, harvesters and various other kinds of essential machinery had combined until there were but fourteen large concerns and these had found abroad an outlet for 12 per cent of their product. Although fewer makers of machinery did not always mean higher prices, the manufacturers enjoyed a far more independent position than the farmers to whom they sold.

Machinery put all of some farmers' eggs in one basket. It led them to substitute for diversified farming and home handicrafts the growing of staple crops adapted to machinery; their well-being they rashly entrusted to the price of staples grown in huge quantities. It increased the supply of food without a proportional increase in the number of persons to whom it afforded employment; these increased more slowly and sometimes declined. It lowered the cost of food to the consumer by making it more abundant but meanwhile increased the liabilities in farming as an occupation.

Machinery tempted the farmer to buy too much land at too high a price. Not only were machines expensive, but they called for larger farms. As the supply of good land diminished, speculation in it made acreage (rather than live stock, seed, fences, buildings and other equipment) the heaviest part of the agricultural investment. Yet at the same time capital accumulated in the impatient hands of eastern and foreign investors; western rates of 6 per cent to 12 per cent on real estate and 10 per cent to 20 per cent on chattels roused their cupidity. At first western investment companies had taken the place of timid banks in loans; then insurance companies and state banking systems came to participate with the farmer in his huge gamble on land and weather. To mortgage companies and irresponsible agents, eager easterners entrusted their funds; while the value of land and improvements temporarily skyrocketed, farmers were begged to borrow. A large part of the nation was involved in the boom, which reached its peak in California. Before drought conditions returned in 1887, more than 45 per cent of the farms in many states had been mortgaged, frequently "up to the hilt," with their village and county seat communities as heavily loaded for public improvements. This involved a ravenous increase in the proportion of crops lost to interest and taxes. The farmer could carry such liabilities only as long as values of land and of food kept correspondingly high. As values fell the farmer complained of high interest rates and taxation, of heavy renewal charges and five-year-terminal dates for mortgages. He found that low prices of land and of food spelled foreclosure.

The foreign market which cried for United States crops one day spurned them the next. By the end of the 'eighties American wheat farmers were struggling to keep their share of the world market, fighting against competition from cheaper acreage areas of Russia, India, Argentina and Canada, and against tariffs imposed upon American wheat by France, Germany, Italy and Spain. Worse, while machinery had built up the exportable surplus at a fast rate, world conditions were lowering the price at a faster one; through the 'eighties and 'nineties Americans doubled to quadrupled their output of foodstuffs and fibers against an almost continuous world fall in prices.

The American grain grower was at the mercy of international forces, because grain was a world product which had to be held until needed and he could control neither storage nor marketing. The railroads had devised a highly organized elevator system to store and handle millions of bushels of grain in bulk at large terminals. By 1880 the grain elevator business at Chicago had standardized a body of practices governing the grading, storage, transfer and sale of grain reserves so huge that their existence affected the economy of the entire nation. Uniform warehouse receipts representing these reserves expanded credit, expedited trade and made trading in futures possible. The opening up of the grain states was facilitated, routes of trade were determined, markets and whole industries were affected.

The farmer was dependent upon the primary grain markets, Milwaukee, Duluth, Minneapolis, Kansas City and St. Louis, which grew like Chicago. To these terminals came buyers who acted as brokers for the millers, eastern distributers and exporters. Chicago for a time remained the greatest grain market of the world, and the Chicago Board of Trade the outstanding exchange, with its machinery copied in many other world centers. This machinery made for grain one big world market in respect to supply, demand and price. The world price was the same, whether at Chicago, Minneapolis or Liverpool.

It was the handling charges which differed in various places and roused the farmers' wrath. The large-scale organization perfected by the buyers and traders in grain levied harshly on the grain growers; their troubles multiplied in the 'eighties when the railroads took to selling their elevators to chains. Within twenty years the chief buyers were a limited number of terminal elevator companies, enjoying special railroad favors and often operating in agreement against the growers. They paid storage to themselves and mixed bad with good grades of grain. Their futures trading decreased price fluctuations but angered growers.

Wheat growers in the mass suffered from lack of capital and a chronic tendency to act as individuals, which enabled their enemies to wield against them price-cutting, boycott and ground-leasing schemes. Their insuperable obstacle was the world-wide range of agricultural competition, which prevented growers from affecting terminal prices or restricting production. The better world crops, the worse their situation.

Bread might still be the staff of life to hungry human beings, but it was a broken reed in farm economy. Wheat well typified the plaint of agriculture—unequal dividends.

CHAPTER XXVII

LARGE-SCALE ORGANIZATION IN POLITICS

The large-scale organization, which in the 'eighties and 'nineties established its control over business, labor and agriculture, no less affected politics. The forces besetting politicians were many and mighty, making both the major parties organize on a scale unprecedented.

Gigantic Problems Facing Politicians

Political leaders now must cope with problems rising out of four currently powerful trends. The growth in population enlarged the sheer numbers of constitutents whom national officeholders must try to please. Expansion of population increased the number of states the parties must try to control. Crowding of cities multiplied the variety of voters urban bosses must try to organize. Invention of new industries raised conflicting demands, within formerly homogeneous districts, which a legislator must try to reconcile. Thus were the ears of congressmen assailed by a babel of voices, made more clamorous by loud-voiced racial and sectional demands. Politicians competed fiercely for the favor of the new economic groups, which in turn preyed upon them with organized pressure as never before.

No party which awkwardly juggled diverse elements could long retain power; therefore political organization must be perfected with consummate skill. National party lines must be maintained with an infinite variety and inconsistency of appeal, down from national into state, county, city and ward elections. Organization must be more permanent, less carelessly reassembled for recurrent campaigns. The politicians had to run machinery with two delicate systems of gears; one set adjusted to persuade the masses to continue national support, in spite of conflicting interests of sections and classes; the other capable of satisfying at least a minimum of the demands of men with more dollars than votes. It required intelligence and integration of no mean order to placate democrats and monopolists simultaneously. Failure threatened destruction.

At the same time, the rewards for those who should best perfect their national political organization loomed gigantic, for whatever party won power would possess an economic influence wholly unprecedented in range. When in control at Washington, it could direct legislation into the very nooks and crannies of the nation—into the crevices of burgeoning manufacture through tariff provisions; into the boundless store of known and dimly guessed natural resources through laws affecting exploitation of such things as coal, oil and lumber; into the bloodstream of national economic life through measures governing mighty public utilities like the transcontinental railroads, steamship combines, telephone, telegraph and electric power. Thus were politicians crowned potentates, whether they received their investiture with a sober sense of responsibility or as an opportunity for gain.

Unfortunately, the politicians who strove to perfect organizations large enough to deal with ever larger forces worked without the inspiration of generally accepted high ideals of public service. Business ideals of control for gain continued to dominate thinking in most avenues of life during this period. Blinding disparities of race, language, religion, economic and sectional interest were delaying that national likemindedness which is necessary before the general electorate can have a wide vision of the common weal. The politician, on the other hand, was a "public servant" paid but a small salary; he had the doubtful pleasure of observing how enterprise in industry won financial independence. It was therefore to be expected that a jealous or unprincipled type of politician might use his position to increase his income, either by accepting rewards for his influence or by taking advantage of his knowledge of what was to happen.

The majority of the politicians were not so much the "rascals" they were painted to be, as they were human beings, fumbling with the map and with modern problems, mixing honesty and chicanery in their objects and deeds. They subscribed to the generally accepted doctrine of "trickle" prosperity—let the rich, large organizations flourish, and prosperity must trickle down through the lower strata of society until even the grateful laborer received his mead. So they extended legislative coöperation to big business, not neglecting to levy on it to maintain their political machines. Yet they also passed such legislation as the Interstate Commerce and Anti-Trust laws, which large-scale business scarcely desired. Largely unrewarded, they were contriving somehow to preserve the practice of political compromise, which is indispensable to preservation of the democratic form of government. It sometimes made the familiar phrase "party in power" more a fiction than a fact.

The Golden Age of complete, consecutive, Republican control of Congress, which began in 1861, lasted only fourteen years; after 1875 came twenty-two years of nip and tuck, during which 80 per cent of the eligible voters were brought to the polls, an unheard-of proportion. Between 1875 and 1897 the Republicans controlled the popular branch only three Congresses, those of 1881-1883, 1889-1891 and 1895-1897.

They even lost their stronghold, the Senate, 1879-1881 and 1893-1895, and were tied with the Democrats there 1881-1883. In four out of the five presidential elections in this period the Democrats won a majority of the "popular" vote, although they took the electoral vote only twice—with the reform candidate Cleveland in 1884 and 1892. They lost the election of 1880, when General James A. Garfield of Ohio, defeated General Winfield Scott Hancock of Pennsylvania, by only 10,000 votes. There was little to choose between the major platforms that year. Altogether, shifting votes prevented either party from controlling the presidency, House and Senate more than two years at a time.

The Republicans, as the party most loyal to big business, often found the rivalry more apparent than real; but always it was worrisome. Because certain influential Democrats were as closely affiliated with big business as were the Republican managers, and because sectionalism and undisciplined individualism fomented disunity in the democracy, a Democratic victory often did not disrupt Republican projects; but the Republicans felt keenly the inconvenience and danger of legislating across party labels. Also the Irish vote worried them because Irish in cities like New York and Chicago often voted with the solid South—that South which, from the day Hayes removed northern troops from its polls, could be counted on to give its 95 electoral votes to the Democratic ticket. Irish voters cared but little about the Civil War; and so otherwise dignified Republican leaders often took to "twisting the lion's tail," for baiting England won more Irish votes than the wildest waving of the old bloody shirt.

Agitation for Reform

The assassination of President Garfield by a disappointed office seeker in 1881 called attention to political abuses and made possible some effort at reform. Levies on office holders by the political leaders had been so insistent that public offices seemed to be bought and paid for. Only those who did party work in campaigns seemed desirable as appointees and presidents and their advisers felt bound to accept only those recommended by spoils-distributing leaders. In 1881 after the assassination various local societies that had been laboring to reform these abuses joined their forces as the National Civil Service Reform League. It pressed for destruction of the nefarious system. The move was further aided by gross incompetence among political appointees and by the demand for scientific and technical work under government auspices. Gradually large cities passed civil service laws and sometimes enforced them.

Finally the Pendelton Act of 1883 forbade political assessments on federal officers. This "Magna Carta of civil-service reform" stipulated a bi-partisan National Civil Service Commission to maintain competitive examinations for filling government offices under what was called the "classified list." At first only the executive departments at Washington, the larger post offices and the customs houses were to have their new vacancies filled in this manner; but Cleveland and other presidents extended the service to other departments, and when a party was over-

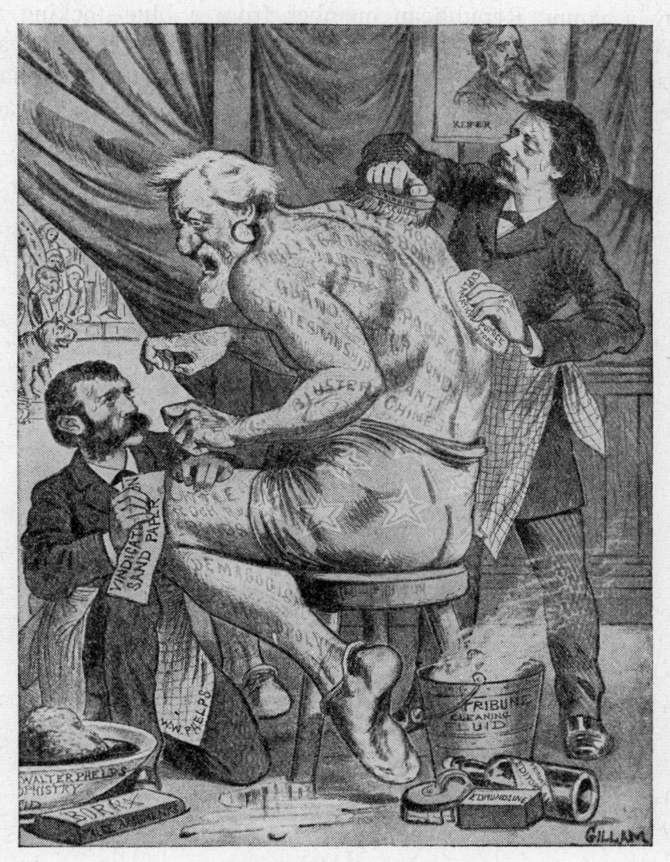

Love's Labor Lost
Trying to Scrub Blaine Clean
(Gillam in *Puck*.)

turned, the departing administration gladly enlarged the civil service to establish its recent appointees.

Although these were scarcely worthy motives for good acts, and although state and local salaries continued to finance many of the lesser elections, the spoils system was kept almost continuously on the defensive. New York and Massachusetts legislated for the merit system in 1883 and 1884; and the old open ballot which was so easy a device for the purchase of votes began to be displaced by the secret "Australian" ballot, which forced the purchaser of a vote to trust the honesty of the man whom he was paying to be dishonest. Louisville, Kentucky, established the secret ballot in 1888, Massachusetts soon made it state-wide and New York took refuge in secrecy between 1889 and 1895. Meanwhile, the federal Civil Service Commission was actively advertised by a young Republican member from a blue-stocking area of New York, one Theodore Roosevelt, who had a yet more actively advertised career ahead of him. Before 1900 the merit system had some legal recognition in such important centers as Chicago, Philadelphia and New Orleans.

President Cleveland and a Running Mate

The reform movement and large-scale organization put the party machine to added expense; and, since its purse could no longer be refilled regularly by patronage and assessments of the spoils, the managers turned anew to corporations and the rich to refill it. Thus major parties became increasingly subservient to wealth. This was strikingly demonstrated in campaigns and economic legislation, as will be seen.

The strength and limitations of large-scale organization in politics were capitally demonstrated by the 1884 campaign, the only canvass between 1864 and 1896 in which little voters became intensely interested. Their interest arose not over party principles—both major groups confined their planks to threadbare, pussyfooting platitudes—but over personalities. The Republicans nominated James G. Blaine, the glamorous "plumed knight," as his admirers described him, who was the perfect product of large-scale organization; unfortunately he was vulnerable to charges of corruption. The Democrats nominated Grover Cleveland, reform governor of New York who was elected by the closest possible margin. A plurality of the voters had rebelled against Republican machine domination and had elected a man with reform leanings.

The Farmer Militant

Agitation for reform was not confined to those who wanted the merit system in the civil service and honest candidates in public office. There were those who had much more searching questions to ask and more sweeping reforms to demand. From the prairies and plains, the demands first uttered by the Grangers were now heard more plainly in the campaigns.

The gap between farm income and farm debts was blamed by farmers upon the monopolistic influences obviously at work in America —in landownership, transportation and finance. They did not blame increased production or clearly appreciate the fact that agricultural depression was world-wide. It was monopoly that was immoral, because it was unfair. A moral crusade for restoration of competition would restore their status. Theirs was no attack upon the capitalistic system at its foundation, for they either owned property or hoped to own it and expected to make money on it. Their program was merely palliative, not revolutionary.

The farmers would invoke government aid to enjoin laissez-faire, but only so far as it was victimizing them. They would equalize railroad rates either through government ownership or operation; check collusion in the middleman's purchase of farm products and in the manufacturer's sale of farm supplies; shift the burden of taxation from real estate to cash income; ease credit by lowering interest rates and expanding the currency with the population. These were the principal alterations which the farmers of the 'eighties and 'nineties wished to make in the American manner of living. They expressed their demands in a variety of terms, of course, and exerted their influence through various channels.

As the Grange lost influence, and as the Knights of Labor became in most areas little more than an agricultural social group, cudgels for the farmer were grasped by an "Alliance" movement. It rose after the comparative prosperity of 1879-1882 had temporarily quieted farmer agitation. Alliances originally had much the same appeal as the Granges, emphasizing coöperative enterprise and social betterment and suffered from much the same difficulties; but they usually had new leadership and eventually proved more aggressive and sophisticated in attitude toward national finance and politics. They had the strength and the weakness of all movements which spring spontaneously direct from the soil.

A Southern Alliance was built up. Texas farmers as early as 1875 were forming a secret county organization which first emerged in 1878 as a Grand State Alliance. It expanded into adjoining states under the direction of C. W. Macune, who with his *National Economist* exhorted cotton raisers to ape, in their own defense, the national trend toward organization. It joined with the Farmers' Union, which originated in Louisiana, to form the "National Farmers Alliance and Coöperative Union." It annexed an "Agricultural Wheel" which had started rolling in Arkansas, and other societies and clubs; the whole came to be spoken of ordinarily as the "Southern Alliance," which Macune pushed as a "strictly white man's non-political, secret, business association." By 1890 it claimed a million members.

Meanwhile, near Chicago, Milton George was promoting with his *Western Rural* another group which, vitalized by a Kansas Alliance and by recurrent hard times, grew into the "National Farmers' Union," generally distinguished as the "Northwestern Alliance." It engaged in coöperative enterprises somewhat less than the Southern Alliance and in politics much more. It stressed railroad and land reforms; the southerners, finance.

These organizations had been gathering strength which brought results in Cleveland's administration. They made effort against almost insuperable odds to spread the application of democratic theories over the strategic fields of transportation, trusts, the currency and the tariff. In these fields, strong economic, political and sectional forces were inextricably tangled, certain to resist reordering.

The momentum behind federal regulation of railroads had been accumulating through two decades, while the farmers, joined by eastern manufacturers and merchants, collected sufficient pressure to push back the very powerful railroad lobby. Its members were past masters in the art of corrupting local, state and national legislators. They long violated the traditions of democracy with impunity, but their political activities were so deeply resented, South as well as West, that the railroad interests preceded the trusts as the best-hated foe of the commonalty. It was said that no passengers paid fares except those who could not well afford to pay.

Faced by the imperious facts of transcontinental lines and widespread railroad systems, the agitators quit advocating competition and turned to fight discrimination and rebates. These last particularly incensed eastern manufacturers, who through their tariff lobbies had acquired a skill at intimidating lawmakers greater than that of the railroad representatives. Grangers and Alliance men had their own techniques, perfected by practice on state legislatures. So at Washington from 1874 on, a series of committee investigations—especially those under Senators William Windom of Minnesota and Shelby M. Cullom of Illinois—of bills—especially in the House—and of presidential recommendations—especially a message from Arthur—pointed in the direction of federal regulation.

The attitude of the judiciary, particularly the Supreme Court, was also making federal legislation inevitable, for the highest tribunal had changed its views on state regulation. At first it had upheld state efforts to restrain railroads. In two decisions of 1876, Munn *v.* Illinois and Peik *v.* Chicago and Northwestern Railway Company, it had gone so far as to allow state regulation of interstate commerce in the absence of federal law. Operators who found compulsory rates to be confiscatory must appeal to the people at the polls, said the decisions; they must gain a new legislature to repeal the laws, for the remedy did not rest with the bar.

Within a decade, however, the Supreme Court was assuming broader responsibility. Astute railroad attorneys were pressing upon the tribunal a special constitutional argument based on the 14th Amendment. It contained the clause, "nor shall any State deprive any person of life, liberty, or property, without due process of law." The railroad attorneys asserted that their clients were "persons" within the intent of the Amendment and that the state regulation was depriving them of property—fair profits—without due process of law. Originally, in the Slaughter Houses cases of 1873, the highest tribunal had held that the Amendment applied only to Negroes; but thereafter two members of the Joint Committee of Fifteen on Reconstruction which had formulated the Amendment—John Bingham of Ohio and Roscoe Conkling of New York—asserted that the Committee had intended to place corporations as well as individuals under its protection. The majority of the Court accepted this contention in the Wabash case of 1886, wherein they ruled also that interstate commerce was a federal matter to be regulated only by federal law. As few railroads were confined within the boundaries of one state, the decision made most of them subject to the national government, both legislatively and judicially.

The unworkableness of state regulation already had been proved to the discerning by the ineffectiveness of state laws and commissions; the state courts had often balked the legislatures, which could scarcely keep within their purview business crossing state lines. Furthermore many other corporations besides the public carriers were grown greater than states. American industry and agriculture were traversing many state lines. Since the public temper was most irate at the railroads at this time, congressional action on them became inevitable. The terms of the law would amount to the lowest common denominator of congressional compromise under the circumstances, a compromise reached by the legislators while they were being pushed to the left by aroused public opinion and to the right by carrier interests.

There resulted the historic Interstate Commerce Act of 1887, a measure which read nicely but enforced badly. It forbade pooling, traffic agreements and rebates; all charges should be "reasonable" and no more should be charged for a short haul than a long one, under "substantially similar circumstances and conditions." Uniform accounting and filing of tariffs were required, and annual reports. However, the Commission had to appeal to the courts to uphold its decisions and the courts gave the law a narrower interpretation than the apparent intent of the legislators. The railroad lobby proved able to keep the Commission from obtaining real authority over them and continually checkmated proposals from agricultural shippers. Abolition of pooling spurred consolidation—through purchase, lease and stock control—almost continuously until 1904; resulting gains in efficiency were offset by loss of competition.

Bargains of 1890

A stronger attack upon monopoly was staged in 1890 in the three fields of the trusts, silver and the tariff, because events long had been building up a triple mandate for action. In 1887 Cleveland had become alarmed at a growing surplus which was piling up in the Treasury and was drawing money from circulation. He wished to put his party on record for the lower rates which he believed would both increase the circulation and lower the cost of living and devoted his annual message to a strong argument for tariff reductions. The Republicans hastened to make this the campaign issue of 1888 and nominated Benjamin Harrison on a protectionist platform. They charged the Democrats with attempting to destroy the nation's prosperity by destroying protection. They appealed to manufacturers and workingmen alike to vote for the Republicans to protect the "American standard of living." Cleveland, running for reëlection, was defeated. For the first time, however, a national contest had been fought on issues arising from the great economic and social changes of the epoch.

When the Republicans regained their power in 1888 they were expected to pass a protective tariff with higher rates. However, they were in danger of proving unable to deliver the increased rates, for they had an advantage of but seven sure in the House and two in the Senate. A few of their more extreme and short-sighted members strove to secure Democratic votes by the threat of a "Force Bill" which would reëstablish federal control of southern elections; but wiser members realized that tariff increases had to be explained to farmers and that anti-trust and cheap money promises were better bait with farmers, debtors and large elements of the population. Out of this delicate situation during the session before the congressional election of 1890 emerged three acts highly important in the history of the United States —the "Sherman" Anti-Trust, the "Sherman" Silver Purchase, and the "McKinley" tariff laws. It is significant that these were all technically sponsored from Ohio, a state narrowly divided between Republicans and Democrats.

First to complete passage was the Anti-Trust measure of 2 July. Anti-monopoly legislation had been gathering momentum throughout the country, because of the flagrant habit of large-scale organization to take toll of the unorganized. Both major parties and two minor ones of 1888 adopted planks demanding either the regulation or the abolition of trusts. A House committee submitted testimony on the practices of the American Sugar Refining Company and the Standard Oil Corporation which further galvanized public sentiment. By 1890 fourteen states and territories had anti-monopoly provisions in their constitutions; thirteen had anti-trust laws. The public realized the need for a national law. Finally, three eastern senators (George F. Edmunds of Vermont, William M. Evarts of New York and George F. Hoar of Massachusetts) revamped a Sherman bill and it passed with but one dissenting vote.

The act feebly responded to the popular demand; it declared the common law principle that trusts or other combinations in restraint of trade were illegal. Congress, however, could not destroy trusts by declaring them illegal; and the terms of the act were left too loose to apply with accuracy. The law provided no precise definition of "trust" or "restraint" and did not specify whether it applied to combinations of labor as well as capital. In reality Congress was afraid to handle this big issue and deliberately left such vital questions for the courts to decide. However, the act had real importance as an effort to regulate private property in the public interest; it forced trust makers to adjust their devices somewhat to aroused public opinion.

Secondly, Congress produced the Silver Purchase Act of 14 July, also considered an attack upon monopoly, the banking monopoly of money and credit. Three classes were most prominent in securing this law—farmers, silver producers and debtors in general. The so-called "Sherman Silver Purchase Act" increased the fixed amount of silver money, or the paper representatives of silver, which the treasury was forced to inject into the channels of national life. It enlarged purchases from a minimum of $2,000,000 and a maximum of $4,000,000 monthly to a flat monthly amount of 4,500,000 ounces, calculated to absorb all the national production of the metal. Two million ounces of this must be coined monthly until 1 July 1891. More important, these purchases must be paid for with "treasury notes," redeemable in "coin" on demand, reissuable after redemption, and legal tender for both public and private debts; and the treasury was advised to follow such a policy of redemption in "coin" as should maintain gold and silver on a parity. This the treasury interpreted as forcing the repeated redemption of the notes in gold, whenever demanded, because redemption in silver would destroy the parity.

The "McKinley" tariff law—the third significant measure revealing the disparity between effective organization in business and ineffective organization in farming—was enacted just on the eve of the election, 1 October 1890. It gave big business a vast enlargement of the protective principle; restrictive duties should not be abolished when businesses became firmly established but should remain into the far future, giving domestic manufacturers leave to set their own prices regardless of world prices.

To watchful farmers and other ordinary consumers such provisions opened an alarming prospect; the increases required sugar coating. So duties were raised on the farmers' wool, barley, hemp, and flax; and wheat, corn, potatoes and eggs were given petty levies, although these could have no important effect. To please consumers and the sugar-refining trust, raw sugar was made free; to compensate sugar cane and beet planters, who produced but one-tenth of the sugar Americans consumed, a bounty of two cents per pound went on their products. A curious Blaine provision for backhanded reciprocity provided that if any countries exporting sugar, molasses, tea, coffee, or hides into the United States (where they could enter free) dared to impose unreasonable duties upon United States exports, the president could promptly retaliate with duties on the five products. This was supposed to enlarge the South American demand for United States grain, flour, provisions, and manufactures.

In this fashion the large-scale political organizations had begun to take account of the social needs of a nation so large and diverse as the United States. The result was the first feeble steps away from the time-honored doctrine of laissez-faire in the direction of social control.

CHAPTER XXVIII

THE ISSUE JOINED

The road toward genuine social control was still a long one. The Interstate Commerce Act, the Anti-Trust Law and additional silver purchases were not going to do much for a nation already afflicted with hardship and a sense of injustice and about to descend into a severe depression.

Rise of the Populists

The farmers were uniting for political war. After years of independent existence and unsuccessful attempts at coöperation the Southern and Western Alliances met in the same city, St. Louis, in December 1889. This meeting had threefold importance. First, because they failed to fuse: sectional prejudices, northern fear of southern dominance, and diversities of interest and attitudes toward rebels, Negroes, secrecy and third parties prevented fusion; the number of agricultural societies was not diminished greatly then or later. Second, despite failure to fuse, both memberships nevertheless presented a united front as a class; they demonstrated their sympathy one with another upon the vital issues of monopoly, money supply, railroad control and landownership. Both denounced trusts, national banks and trading in grain futures; both demanded inflation, free coinage, government ownership or operation of the railroads and landownership restricted to Americans.

Third, at St. Louis the Southern Alliance endorsed a significant commodity credit scheme for freeing the farmer from the tyranny of gold prices, bank credit and fall sales. This was to be managed through a "subtreasury plan." Under it the government would store the grain crop in federal warehouses, giving the farmer a warehouse receipt for it and also a loan of greenbacks specially issued for a part of the crop's value. These greenbacks would carry the farmer over until spring, when the government would sell his grain at a price above the fall level and then pay the farmer the balance over the loan. Forty years later part of this commodity credit program would be inaugurated from Washington. Dissension over it, between 1890 and 1891, almost split the Southern Alliance in two. Nevertheless, the superior organization and leadership in the southern group was attracting more than two and one-half times the northern membership. They joined from as far west as the Pacific coast and as far east as Ohio, Pennsylvania and New York. Kansas and Dakota Alliances virtually seceded from the Northwestern to join the Southern Alliance; and some northerners supported the subtreasury scheme "more or less" to win southern support for government ownership of railroads.

Although Alliance men failed to merge their organizations, and although financial and political difficulties were rising which were destined to send the Alliance movement into its decline, before that unhappy day its basic principles were winning enough popular support to compel Congress to act. Land laws devised for easier individual ownership had been obtained. More important, farmer influence had contributed no small part to the pressure which had forced from Congress the three significant concessions of 1887-1890, the laws relating to railroads, money and trusts. The land laws had proved disappointing in their effects because, although they dealt with a somewhat less complicated set of factors, the complications yet proved too intricate for congressional mastery. The interstate commerce, anti-trust, and silver legislation of 1887-1890 would prove yet more intricate and disappointing.

Unrest was abroad in the land beyond the Mississippi as the "heartbreaking 'nineties" began. The frontier, by its imperious mandates, had forced the frontiersman to became an innovator, and economic ills were inspiring his children to concoct radical remedies. Thence came, to South and North, "the Alliance summer of 1890." This movement was native, mobilized close to the soil; it expressed two resentments. One was against economic inferiority—against a fall in total return on farm produce at a time when manufacturing groups were enjoying a degree of relative prosperity. The other was against psychological inferiority; sons and daughters were deserting to the city, attracted by its cash return; even the new immigrants, agriculturalists born and bred from southern and eastern Europe, were becoming urban in the United States. Agriculture no longer was the occupation of greatest recognized value. These farmer resentments were accompanied naturally by a greater toleration for lawlessness and a greater susceptibility to demagoguery, which attracted also some urban workers incensed by the McKinley tariff of that summer.

Western Alliance men and women were angered anew by a United States Supreme Court decision invalidating a Minnesota railroad rate law; they had worked so hard to improve upon the earlier Grange statutes. They became impatient to influence the 1890 election with their own political party. Their orators had had a rigorous training in frontier experience and in lecturing before sharp-witted Alliance audiences at schoolhouses, public squares and exciting picnics. Ignatius Donnelly of Minnesota and James B. Weaver of Iowa were long-practised at marshaling the arguments of discontent. The sweep of oratory and song that summer was cyclonic, especially in the central third of Kansas. Deflated land values made it the stronghold of a new political enthusiasm called the "People's Party" or Populism. There intense and purposeful evangelists like Mrs. Mary Elizabeth Lease exhorted the farmers to "raise less corn and more HELL"; while "Sockless" Jerry Simpson, an habitual third-party heretic, and long-whiskered, inflexible William A. Peffer preached in a pentecost of politics.

They made 2 November a Judgment Day indeed. The Kansas "People's Party" sent Simpson to the House of Representatives and Peffer to the Senate and elected also four other congressional representatives and a majority of the state legislature. South Dakota's "Independent Party" elected Reverend James H. Kyle to the Senate while obtaining the balance of power in the legislature; and Nebraska's "People's Independent Party," working in a formerly solid Republican state, won a majority of the legislature and one of the congressional seats. In Minnesota, Michigan and Indiana, Alliance politics diverted 1890 victory from Republicans to Democrats. Eight westerners frankly carried the Populist or Independent label to the national House, besides old-party men who modified their behavior, if not their labels.

In the South, fear of aiding Republicans deterred Alliance men from forming third parties, and so they undertook to pledge Democrats to Alliance policies. The capable and ambitious president of the Southern Alliance, L. L. Polk, led the North Carolina Alliance men in placing four of their members in Democratic congressional seats. The wrathful, one-eyed Ben Tillman, as South Carolina's gubernatorial candidate, won the Democratic nomination for himself and for his entire ticket. The suspicious and combative Thomas E. Watson led a hot Georgia campaign which gave Alliance men the governorship, a majority of the state legislature and six of the state's congressional districts. Also they affected events in Alabama, Florida, Kentucky, Mississippi, Missouri, Tennessee and Virginia. Altogether, they won three governorships and legislative control of eight states and sent to Washington two senators and forty-four representatives pledged to Alliance policies.

How were the mighty fallen! Alliance and Populist inroads had upset the Washington balance of power in 1890, defeating enough Republicans to give the Democrats a huge House majority and putting the fear of God in the hearts of certain western senators. The Republicans had thought to sew up for long their Senate power by hurriedly admitting North and South Dakota, Montana and Washington in 1889 and Idaho and Wyoming in 1890. The political leaders of the no-man's land of western disaffection bedeviled rather than blessed their benefactors.

Southern leaders, encouraged especially by third-party advocates, flocked to Ocala, Florida, in December 1890, to attempt again a united political organization of farmers. There delegates from Southern Alliances, from the Farmers' Mutual Benefit Association and from the Colored Farmers' Alliance met simultaneously. Again they reaffirmed the familiar principles, with some widening of the scope of their reform planks; but again southern reluctance to abandon a war-bred Democratic label prevented their united participation in the formation of a national third party. Also the actual achievements of the Alliance legislatures were proving meagre.

However, the third-party trend could not be stopped in the West. Alliance and Knights of Labor members, with a majority hailing from Illinois, Indiana, Kansas, Nebraska and Ohio, convened at Cincinnati 19 May 1891 and put forth a platform enlarged to attract non-agricultural voters, such as veterans, laborers and liberals in general. The action at Cincinnati pleased all radicals and "let in on the ground floor" of this new movement the professional third-party men who chronically, according to their critics, "don't know what they want and will never be satisfied until they get it." They got "surprisingly slender results" in the elections of that year but professed satisfaction. The next step was a Washington's Birthday Convention at St. Louis in 1892 which launched, with some Southern Alliance support, a "People's Party of America"; and the job of organizing was completed with a July convention at Omaha which nominated James B. Weaver of Iowa for president of the People's Party ticket.

The ferment in the hinterland continued, carrying its momentum into the 1892 campaign. President Harrison faced an impossible situation; he could satisfy neither farmers, laborers nor Republican bosses, but he was able to force his own renomination in 1892. Conversely, Cleveland's popularity compelled the Democratic bosses to accept his renomination. Neither of the major parties offered platforms which impressed the extreme malcontents; among them, the Prohibitionists polled their largest total in history, 262,000 votes, depriving Harrison of the endorsement of his own state of Indiana, and the Populists, with help from silverites, obtained 22 electoral votes. This left Cleveland for the third time with a popular plurality rather than a majority. However, as he won 132 more electoral votes than Harrison, he returned to Washington in 1893 to try to mitigate the consequences of the ill-advised tariff and currency legislation of 1890.

Panic of 1893

As world trade conditions were taking a bad turn, Cleveland was assured of the heaviest obstacles. Panic struck the stock exchange in May 1893 and a five-year depression dragged its weary length into American experience, exposing the harsh outlines of ill-balanced industry and agriculture, and putting the political sense of the democracy to severe test.

The first thought of the second Cleveland administration was to protect the disappearing gold supply of the treasury, on which national credit rested. At a hot special session of 1893 Cleveland drove through repeal of the purchase provision of the Sherman silver act after a terrific struggle with the silver senators. This left his store of patronage persuasion very inadequate for his tariff reduction project, especially as the manufacturers' lobby was the strongest then in Washington and industrialization was proceeding apace in the Middle West and South. Genuine reductions by the House were transformed into near-Republican rates by a bipartisan Senate protective combination using Louisiana's "sugar senators" particularly. To obtain votes for the high levies, there was added an income-tax provision—one of the foremost Populist demands—as a levy on the rich. Thus the Wilson-Gorman bill was shouldered through, a travesty on tariff reform. Cleveland allowed it to become law without his signature.

From the abyss of the depression, in 1894, the silver issue was springing to new life. The way had been well prepared by the farmers' attempts to organize and by the silver producers. The 1893 repeal had not sufficed to kill the movement, for it had been sired from strong stock. The extremely able Republican senator, John P. Jones of Nevada (where silver-mining practically ceased from 1890 to 1900), had elaborated useful arguments back in 1876—arguments which the silverites had burnished with continual restatement. An effective propaganda organization for silver had been maintained since 1889 by the American Bimetallic League. The League first battened on the drought condition in the West and then upon the nation-wide depression.

That depression was exploited most astutely by one of its victims, William H. Harvey, who had lost what he had saved at ranching and prospecting in Montana and had failed as a journalist in Chicago. In 1894 he sprang to fame with a graphically illustrated paper-bound book, *Coin's Financial School,* in which he presented with consummate cleverness the arguments for free coinage. They were seized upon as gospel by hundreds of thousands of dissatisfied people. Politicians fed with their oratory an inflation sentiment which silver producers gratefully helped to finance. They had no notion that forty years would elapse before their subsidy would be restored, and under a Democratic president. By the fall of 1895 it was obvious that Cleveland's party had deserted him for the debtor position, and silver producers seemed justified in optimistic expectations.

The leaders of the free silver movement had little to fear from sober second thought upon the long-time effects of a silver standard, for among the groups to whom they appealed the immediate advantage to the debtor was obvious, and future evil was optimistically exorcised. Typical was the psychology of Nebraska, which bred three of the great apostles to the farmers in this period—W. E. Smythe and H. W. Campbell, working miracles in irrigation and dry farming, and William Jennings Bryan, painting a new heaven and a new earth, made new by "free and unlimited" coinage of silver.

Bryan

The tall, handsome, black-haired young Bryan (born in 1860) was a "natural." He had caught some radical contagion from an apprenticeship in the Chicago law office of the very independent-spirited Judge Lyman Trumbull. Two terms as a Nebraska representative at Washington during the turgid years of 1891-1895 and an editorial connection with the Omaha *World-Herald* had taught Bryan and his wife Mary that the tariff and kindred issues were but poor stepping-stones to fame compared with free coinage—a philosophy nicely fitting their temperaments, talents, environment and personal situation.

Evidently they were not disturbed over the conflicting objectives of silvermen; it gave them no pause that the mine owners expected free coinage to make the metal more expensive, that the debtors expected it to bring cheaper money and the Populists expected it to pave the way for a fiat currency of paper. The point was its popularity. From lecture platforms in every section they looked down upon audiences which gave indubitable evidence of the magic and power in Bryan's free silver oratory. Had not silver made the widest appeal of all the Populist planks, rising to domination of that party? They could observe that some southern Democrats were afraid to oppose free silver lest they lose control of the South and that southern and western silverites were planning to control the Democratic party. A silver convention at Memphis in June of 1895 had made this doubly clear.

The Republican party, however, was not subject to silver capture. Its capitalist supporters could not tolerate silver and their position was endorsed by bankers, investors, treasury leaders, Cleveland, and others of all classes and conditions, who saw personal and national ruin in a depreciated standard. When the Republicans convened at St. Louis, 16 June 1896, they were forced to abandon equivocation; such anxious gold emissaries as Senator Henry Cabot Lodge of Massachusetts and

Senator Joseph B. Foraker of Ohio were there to thwart any pussyfooting. They were particularly excited because a Cleveland iron manufacturer and capitalist, Marcus A. Hanna, was collecting votes for his friend William McKinley for the presidential nomination, and McKinley had straddled. As an Ohio representative and governor, he had left seaboard capitalists with much uncertainty as to his "soundness"; but not Hanna. That astute Warwick pretended to be reluctant to give up an evasive currency plank, in order to trade for support for McKinley.

YOUNG BRYAN

When the various eager platform-makers had done with their real and fancied phrase-making, they had accepted McKinley as their standard-bearer (with banker Garrett A. Hobart of New Jersey as running mate) and had flatly declared their party "unalterably opposed" to currency depreciation. There could be no free coinage of silver "except by international agreement with the leading commercial nations of the world, which we pledge ourself to promote." Except for planks which promised free homesteads and vague benefits from the tariff and reciprocity, the Republican platform ignored the farmers' distress.

When the Democrats convened at Chicago, 7 July, they were ready to throw the words of the Republicans in their teeth. They declared themselves "unalterably opposed" to the gold standard and demanded free coinage at 16 to 1 "without waiting for the aid or consent of any other nation." They offered the disaffected farmer and laboring classes planks against interest-bearing government bonds, national banks, high tariff, lavish appropriation, injunctions and high railroad rates. In scathing terms they denounced the Cleveland administration. They rose to a state of exultation when they heard Bryan make the reply to the Republicans which he had practiced before many another smaller and less important audience:

> "Having behind us the producing masses of the nation and the world, the laboring interests and the toilers everywhere, we will answer their demand for a gold standard by saying to them: "You shall not press down upon the brow of labor this crown of thorns—you shall not crucify mankind upon a cross of gold!"

The convention wildly acclaimed Bryan as standard-bearer, taking the precaution at the same time to name an eastern banker and railroad director who espoused silver, Arthur Sewall of Maine, as their vice-presidential nominee.

The Democratic nominees were endorsed three weeks later at St. Louis by two groups. The smaller of these, calling itself the "Silver Party" and led by producers of and dealers in the metal, hailed this "patriotic" fruition of their persistent propaganda. The larger was the Populists, who had allowed free silver to overshadow their major program. When they convened, too late, at St. Louis 22 July, they were faced by an accomplished fact. The Democrats had stolen their thunder; a Populist candidate against Bryan might divide and possibly defeat that free coinage which Populists no less than Democrats demanded. Republicans were on hand lobbying against such a fusion and Democrats for it. It was resisted particularly by southern Populists, who had burned their bridges in their fight against the old-line Democratic Bourbons, and "middle of the road" members who feared party death; these were defeated by the fusionists.

For nominee they passed over their long-time leaders and named Bryan, although they substituted the Georgia Populist, Thomas E. Watson, for Sewall. The platform became chiefly a face-saving device; first they reiterated the program for the social and economic well-being of the people which long had held their loyalty (much of which today is on the statute books) and promised to maintain their organization for the vindication of those principles. Second, they acknowledged that "the pressing issue" was financial; wherefore, "we cordially invite the aid and coöperation of all organizations and citizens agreeing with us upon this vital question." Thus feebly they attempted to describe the Democratic party as a tail to the Populist kite and committed party suicide.

Upon so vital an issue as inflation no nation-wide party could hold all classes of its membership. From the gold-standard Republican convention departed thirty-four silverites under the leadership of Senator Henry M. Teller of Colorado, declaring for free coinage. After the Democratic convention, gold-standard members organized the "National Democratic" party to endorse the Cleveland Administration and nominate gold Democrats, John M. Palmer of Illinois and Simon B. Buckner of Kentucky. Even the Prohibition party, which never obtained enough votes to be represented in the electoral column, sent off seceders who as a "National" party endorsed free coinage. Only the "Socialist-Labor" party, almost equally obscure, managed to avoid both a pronouncement on silver and a split over it.

The politicians who insisted upon free coinage platforms and candidates counted on the panacea to attract many sorts of discontented voters. Particularly they were after the millions of farmers discouraged by the panic and depression, and the laboring class embittered by the Homestead and Pullman strikes. Also resentment was running high against recent decisions of the Supreme Court which seemed to kill all hope of curbing private wealth by governmental instruments.

The highest tribunal was giving much ammunition to those who were attacking it as reactionary. In 1895 it rendered three decisions which particularly aroused popular disfavor. The first of these scuttled the Sherman Anti-Trust Law, for the court ruled that a monopoly in manufacture was not controllable under federal power over interstate commerce. The law which was thus vitiated had been dearly held by the common people as their protection against exorbitant prices for the necessities of life. A second decision invalidated the income tax provision of the Wilson-Gorman Tariff Act on the ground that direct taxes could be levied only in proportion to population; this verdict, interpreted as a victory of the rich over the poor, added to discontent during the depression. Thirdly, the Supreme Court upheld the use of the injunction against labor organizations in strikes by refusing to reverse the sentence of Debs to prison; to the more radical of the working class it appeared that they had no rights which the courts were bound to respect. Altogether, there was much discussion of the rights of rich and poor, and many of the poor believed that the balance could be redressed in their favor by free coinage.

Thus the United States in 1896 presented the novel spectacle of a whole people intensely engrossed in serious debate on money. Free coinage had the best of the argument through the summer, with the desperate gold Republicans unable to divert public interest from the currency to the tariff and the "full dinner pail." Hanna, chairman of their national committee, levied systematically on frightened creditor interests for sinews of war, demanding from leading banks, for example, contributions equal to one-fourth of one per cent of their combined capital and surplus. Industrial workers were terrorized into abandoning Bryan by the warning that if he won, factory doors would be closed the day after election. Democratic levies upon silver producers apparently netted less than might have been expected; and for terrorism they had to depend upon bad crop prospects.

Finally the weather turned gold standard; fall crops came out better than expected. The former Grange states of the Old Northwest, with Iowa, Minnesota and North Dakota, were not sufficiently unprosperous to follow their Populist leadership. With the farm market as well as the big money against him, no amount of special combinations between Populists and Democrats, or Populists and Silver Republicans, could save the eloquent and indefatigable Bryan. He lost five states west of the Mississippi and four south of the Mason and Dixon line which he needed to offset McKinley's lead east of the Mississippi and north of the Ohio. Of nearly 14 million votes silver got about 6.25 million and gold about 7.1 million, with the electoral votes divided 176 to 271. McKinley thus became the only president elected in this period who obtained a majority of the popular vote. There was free silver versus sandwiches and coffee; and the coffee won.

Republican Triumph

Unfortunately, business did not at once endorse Hanna's victory; some factories, opened on faith in the gold standard, had shortly to close again. During the winter of 1896-1897 political promises again succumbed to economic forces. The tactful McKinley, uneasy and well versed in the political uncertainties of the hinterland, hoisted water to both shoulders. He at once sent Senator Edward O. Wolcott of Colorado on a futile European mission to investigate that elusive agreement for international bimetallism which the Republican platform had pledged him to promote. Second, in his inaugural address he stated that he considered his election a mandate (not from certain campaign contributors but from the electorate) for immediate tariff legislation; he promptly called Congress in special session, 15 March, to fulfill this pressing obligation.

Some of the party's leaders did not wish to ignore the fact that the country at large supposed the election had been fought over the currency. They had made pledges against extreme protection to gold Democrats who helped elect McKinley but opposed high tariff. Meanwhile Chairman Dingley of the Ways and Means Committee and Speaker Reed, both of Maine, used the majority machinery of the House during the short session to prepare a tariff for quick enactment. They set rates little above the McKinley law.

However, the economic and political set-up made inevitable stiff boosts in the Senate. The fiscal situation, with the federal treasury's deficit mounting annually since 1893, lent to upward rates the appearance of budget necessity, a necessity quickly ignored in setting prohibitive rates. Business interests, especially manufacturers, were impatient to collect on their political investments, although Hanna returned an unused portion after victory. Exporters wanted renewal of negotiations for reciprocity to enlarge their foreign markets and clamored for tariff action. With Democratic opposition thoroughly discredited by that party's increases in the Wilson-Gorman Act and by Bryan's dramatic defeat over silver, little chance remained for effective resistance to an arrogant attitude. Also the fourteen senators from the high plains and mountain areas of the West would not be outsmarted in the art of pressure politics; they would force concessions far beyond the reach of their paltry House membership.

In 1897 the United States system for determining rates by committee hearings of interested parties and by trades between senators was for the first time thoroughly applied to the vast, conglomerate reaches of the nation. The map proved the method ridiculous. This was best demonstrated by vital schedules of clothing and food. In the wool schedules, sheepmen of Ohio, Michigan and Pennsylvania obtained increases on combing and clothing wools; the herdsmen of Montana, Wyoming and Idaho (natural competitors of the other states) received increases on carpet wools; and the woolen manufacturers of the East and elsewhere were "compensated" with increases on their finished products. Similarly with shoes; cattle interests obtained a duty of 15 per cent on hides, which had been free since 1872, and manufacturers using leather received "compensation." The sugar schedule was a group of compromises arranged to satisfy the conflicting interests of western beet-growers, Louisiana cane-growers and the American Sugar Refining Company, which enjoyed a near-monopoly of refining in the United States. Thus did the producing and manufacturing interests of varied sections impose double levies on 75,000,000 consumers.

The metal schedules gave the West restoration of the 1890 duties on lead and lead ores. There was little boosting by iron and steel manufacturers, however, because earlier favors and improved mechanical processes had placed them in an easy position to meet British competition.

Campaign pledges for reciprocity were met in part by three provisions. One stipulated, in effect, that if Latin American countries discriminated against American goods their tea, coffee, tonka beans and vanilla beans would be taken off the free list; this led to treaties favorable to the United States. Another authorized the president to reward concessions with reductions on such things as brandy, wine, pictures and statuary; this brought agreements with France, Germany, Italy, Holland, Portugal, Switzerland, Spain and Bulgaria. A third empowered the president to make treaties—with Senate approval—for reductions up to 20 per cent on all articles; but when some eleven treaties thus negotiated had been rejected by the Senate, it became clear that reciprocity sentiment could not prevail against Senate backscratching. The Republican party's "backhanded reciprocity" was a temporary response to demands for world markets, rather than a permanent success in obtaining those markets. As finally enacted, the Dingley tariff of 24 July 1897 raised the average level to a new high of approximately 50 per cent.

Business stubbornly refused to leap into emphatic prosperity at the touch of the Dingley rates, and early in 1898 some Republican politicians felt concern over those fall elections which from the further distance of 24 July 1897 had seemed so safe. Tariff prosperity, like Bryan-defeat prosperity, failed to come up to expectations. Early in 1898 silver senators, their power strengthened by six Populist victories in 1896 and by the slow recovery, made another showing; they put through the Senate a resolution that the government had the option to pay its bonds in silver dollars and that to do so was no violation of public faith; also with the help of twenty-five third-party men elected to the House in 1896, they forced into the war revenue act a provision directing the treasury to coin monthly not less than one and one-half million silver dollars out of the bullion accumulated under the Sherman Act. Boss Brayton of Rhode Island sent Senator Aldrich, who with great men of business was opposing needless interference in Cuba, an earnest plea for a war to save the fall elections. He did not persuade the Senator, but other conditions ensured hostilities and by the time the war had reached its quick and successful conclusion trade was definitely acknowledged to be better, and the Republicans won the 1898 campaign.

The difficult job of recovery was being accomplished mainly by natural resources. Gold discoveries in Australia, the Klondike, and Nome areas of Alaska, and the Rand section of Africa proceeded to inject enough new activity into lagging world business to hasten prosperity in the United States. To agriculturists rains and good crops brought comfort. To the fagged nation at large emotional and moral stimulus was provided by the Spanish War.

The sense of national well-being was reflected in a victory by banking and commercial interests after the 1898 election. By making concessions valued by the small fry among bankers, they obtained the so-called Gold Standard Act of 14 March 1900, which was supposed to administer the *coup de grâce* to silver agitation for all time. This law declared the gold dollar the standard of value (as indeed it had been since 1834) and provided for redemption of paper in gold without special legislation by Congress. It stipulated a minimum treasury reserve of 100 millions—granting the secretary of the treasury authority to sell short-term bonds whenever ordinary gold receipts should be inadequate to hold the reserve at that figure—and gave permission for a reserve of 150 millions. Small bankers were gratified by a reduction, from 50 thousands to 25 thousands, in the capital necessary for establishing a national bank, and the profits of all bankers were raised by an expansion in the permissible bank note issue from 90 per cent to 100 per cent of the government bonds purchased to secure the privilege of note issue. It appeared that the currency had been settled permanently; although politics is a kaleidoscopic profession, lawmakers, being human, fool themselves with static hopes.

Thus at the close of the century the Republican party, representing the new tendencies toward large-scale organization, business dominance and centralized control, was back in power. The collective cupidity, cowardice and short-sightedness shown in the politics of 1878-1900 are easy to decry. But such judgment is hardly fair. The politicians who had to formulate policies to meet the unfamiliar emergencies of this age, with its new sectionalism and its preoccupation with large-scale organization, probably were no more unintelligent or grasping, in the long run, than the voters who elected them or the corporation directors who so frequently dictated to them. In their United States the new sectionalism was breeding new interests and antagonisms, and the all-pervasive urge to organize in a big way was setting up aggregations of wealth and power which in the last analysis victimized their creators. The history of the democracy during these years is the history of the swift creation of these forces and the slow realization of the need for their control.

CHAPTER XXIX
AMERICA'S APPROACH TO IMPERIALISM

The nature and extent of America's excursions into the field of foreign relations, between the Civil War and the end of the century, were determined in the main by two influences—the nation's economic status and the attitude of her people. England, France and Germany, during the last third of the century, were engaged in an outburst of rival imperialistic ventures, reaching out for supplies and markets. The United States, however, was slow to join them. Her doubling population had ample room at home and ensured an expanding domestic market for her products. Her resources provided abundant raw materials. Her exploitation of the great trans-Mississippi domain ran parallel in many respects to the new European imperialism. Her phenomenal development brought tempting opportunities for internal investment of her savings. Witness her production of huge surplus crops and her development of large-scale manufactures behind tariff walls. The urge for national prestige found much satisfaction in safe, domestic achievements.

Liquidation of War Issues

The popular attitude of aloofness was endorsed by a highly preferential position which gave Americans a considerable sense of security and superiority. Safe remoteness from attack and dangerous alliances seemed guaranteed by two oceans. In fact this was a period when there was maintained among the European governments a balance of power which took little account of the United States and left her largely unbesought. Economic independence was underwritten by that wealth of agricultural and metallic resources which gave the United States richer prospects of prosperity than any other nation then could anticipate. Political superiority was attested by a Union victory which had demonstrated conclusively that the American experiment in democracy could withstand even the acid test of prolonged civil war. The sense of pride in America, which was the heritage of her revolutionary descent, burned the fiercer in the immigrants who had fled from a worse to a better situation. Economic facilities and national attitudes ultimately would develop into influences toward war on a grand scale, but before 1890 they on the whole continued to insulate.

America's regular international relations remained mostly routine, non-political and little appreciated. She participated in agreements concerning the Red Cross, weights and measures, patents and trademarks, the slave trade, exchange of publications and publication of tariff schedules, submarine cables and protection of industrial property. She coöperated in polar exploration, famine relief, a meridian conference and some peace, missionary and arbitration movements. The turn of fortune in successive administrations frequently made the State Department govern its policy by domestic, political opportunism, but by each foreign engagement ties with Europe were drawn a little closer, for American economic growth pointed toward a leading political rôle among world powers of the future. In their more conspicuous negotiations prior to 1898, America's officials usually cultivated her prestige and economic gains—which are the chief concerns of international policy—along lines projected during earlier administrations.

First came liquidation of war issues. In 1863 the French Emperor, Napoleon III, had ventured into Latin America for political purposes. Against a waning prestige he schemed to win over both the clerical and republican parties by establishing French influence in Mexico which should glorify him as the protector of church property and the provider of opportunities for trade and investment. He essayed to set up Archduke Maximilian, brother of the Austrian emperor, as emperor of Mexico, counting on American preoccupation with fratricidal strife. Officials high in the French government who were speculators in repudiated Mexican bonds applauded Napoleon's purpose. But Appomattox freed Seward to protest to the French government, while President Johnson resisted the temptation to strengthen his own political position by diverting popular attention to a war-like venture. Abroad, the movement for German unity and other European miscalculations forced Napoleon III to abandon the Mexican project. This left the Archduke to die in Mexico and raised American prestige through Latin America.

Next in importance came settlement of the wartime dispute with Britain, where lay through this period the most serious and numerous conflicts. Although Britain's ministerial rule was something of an approximation to the American ideal of self-government, the traditions of Anglophobia nourished by the Revolution, the War of 1812, trade disputes, fishery quarrels and Celtic immigrants, made it profitable for hard-pressed politicians recurrently to twist the lion's tail. Yet the two powers managed to continue that policy of mutual conciliation which since 1815 has permitted the settlement of all Anglo-American disputes either by arbitration or (in the case of the Isthmian and Panama Canal questions) by diplomacy.

Americans of 1865 and after resented not only the accumulated prewar differences but also the losses inflicted upon the Union cause and the merchant marine by the Confederate cruisers—the *Alabama*, *Flor-*

ida, Shenandoah and other vessels—built, equipped and manned in British territory. The damages, according to Senator Charles Sumner of Massachusetts, chairman of the Senate Committee on Foreign Relations and persistent schemer for Canadian annexation, were huge. For her part Great Britain was faced by serious complications in Europe and the Far East; she well realized her need to destroy the bad precedent she had created, for she was bound to suffer if the United States should perform a like service for Britain's enemies. Therefore she listened sympathetically to Secretary of State Fish when President Grant's obsession with a Santo Domingo scheme left the Secretary relatively free to urge a reasonable settlement. He asked that Britain express regret, make an acceptable declaration of the principles of international law involved and pay the claims for the vessels' depredations.

Britain duly expressed her regret for failure to exercise "due diligence"[1] in the great arbitral convention of 1871 known as the Treaty of Washington. This treaty, floated through the Senate by a flow of champagne, registered the sensible determination of both governments to settle peaceably accumulated differences. It announced reciprocal agreements on fishing privileges, use of rivers and canals and bonding of goods; more important, it entrusted other issues to arbitrators. Under it the German emperor determined the Puget Sound boundary favorably to the United States and a commission of five—an American, a Brazilian, Briton, Italian and Swiss—conducted the famous "Geneva Arbitration." That court (with the British member dissenting) awarded the United States 15.5 millions for the Confederate cruiser damages, while a general claims commission and a Halifax fisheries commission, sitting under the same treaty, allotted Britain approximately 7.5 millions in counterclaims. Thus did Britain invest some 8 millions in American good-will; it paid her high dividends. The two nations, drawn together by racial and economic ties, established an invaluable habit of compromise which repeatedly hurdled serious obstacles to cordial relations.

Expansion Continued

Expansion had ever been a strong characteristic of the American people, but the war between the states had wiped out the two classes—slaveholders and merchant shippers—who might have pressed for acquisitions off the mainland. Not until after the supply of rich, free land gave out and the source of immigration shifted from northern to southern Europe (both about 1890) and investments abroad grew considerable (about 1898) would the tempo of acquisition greatly accelerate. Meanwhile, Americans were content with simple protection of modest

[1] America expected the rules of due diligence would be included in an international code, but they were not so accepted until the Second Hague Conference of 1907.

commercial interests and expansion proceeded very slowly along lines earlier suggested.

Secretary Seward and Senator Sumner particularly led those who clung to the long-standing hope for annexation of Canada. Any co-operation of the Canadians to this end, however, was sacrificed when Fenians raided Canada and Congress tried to force her to come in by terminating a reciprocity trade agreement. Britain cleverly countered by encouraging the plan for Canadian union which materialized in 1867 in the establishment of the Dominion, which has continued into the present.

Beyond Canada lay the territory of Alaska. Russia knew she could not defend it in case of war and that it would be a buffer state between her Asiatic holdings and British possessions if it were United States property. Therefore, although only a few Americans, such as those interested in fishing and fur-trading, had any desire for Alaska, Russia cleverly brought the negotiations to a sudden head in 1867. She capitalized her record of friendliness to the Union during the Civil War, she attended to a few mysterious gratuities and she received a purchase price of 7.2 millions for a territory which since that time has paid for itself more than 100 to 1.

Thereafter Alaska furnished two fields for Anglo-American mutual conciliation—the fur seals and the boundary. To protect the seals from complete destruction by rival fishermen the two powers agreed to the arbitral convention of 29 February 1892 which denied Blaine's legal claims but endorsed his objective by prescribing fishing restrictions. As this still left the seals to be decimated by other nationals, it was not until Russia and Japan joined in the quadruple sealing convention of 1911 that the herd was saved from ultimate destruction, by international regulation and profit-sharing in this industry. Seals fall easy prey to marauding fishermen.

The Alaskan boundary became important through the discovery of gold in the Klondike area, which led to the hectic gold rush of 1898. Canada moved Britain to claim the line cut across the fiords instead of lying ten leagues within the coast line around the inlets. As this claim was not consistent with the maps of long standing, the United States was unwilling to accept a British proposal for arbitration and suggested instead a commission. The matter dragged along from June 1898 until 1903, when President Theodore Roosevelt consented to an ostensible arbitration by a Boundary Commission of six members, with a majority of four to decide the issue. That majority was carefully picked to ensure defeat of the unjustifiable Canadian demands and so the American position was upheld.

Successive American secretaries of state attempted to seal Anglo-American friendship with a general arbitration treaty pledging postponement of any hostilities pending action by a tribunal or mediation by friendly powers. Parliament proved willing, but the Senate was loath to give up the right to pass on particular disputes as they came up. So the treaty failed. Inconsistently enough, the United States ratified without reservation three conventions agreed on at the first Hague conference of 1899 and ten years later entrusted to the Permanent Court of Arbitration at The Hague the settlement of the long-standing and harassing dispute over the North Atlantic fisheries. In like spirit of comity, the two powers in 1914 signed one of Bryan's cooling-off "Treaties for the Advancement of Peace."

Meanwhile Seward's and Grant's expansionist activities proceeded elsewhere without benefit of public interest. At the same time that Seward was closing the Alaska bargain before Americans were scarcely aware of it, he was advancing another step toward Asia by raising the American flag upon the uninhabited Midway Islands. At this point his annexationist proclivities were definitely discouraged by the complete lack of public interest and by an economical phase in Congress. With difficulty he secured the appropriation to pay Russia. The Senate blocked plans for Caribbean purchases—Seward's for the Danish West Indies as a naval coaling site, and Grant's for Santo Domingo, which a speculative clique urged upon him. Hostility to expansion in the Pacific was gradually overcome in the case of Samoa and of Hawaii.

The Samoan Islands, another Pacific ambition of Seward's, are as important in the southern Pacific as Hawaii in the northern, because they cover the water approaches to the British Antipodes. They possibly could have been acquired, up to about 1875, without serious objections from Germany or Great Britain; but American opinion remained unready. The Hayes administration, however, obtained control of the fine harbor of Pago Pago, on the island of Tutuila, second only to Pearl Harbor and Manila Bay. Next, rivalries with Britain and Germany over concessions and dummy native kingships were resolved by the tripartite protectorate arranged at the Berlin Conference of 1889. A decade later, when Britain withdrew, taking compensation from Germany elsewhere, American interest had been raised by the victory over Spain. So, the islands were divided between Germany[1] and the United States, which obtained Tutuila and all the islets east of it.

Expansion to Hawaii neatly illustrated the imperial thrust of successive missionaries, traders, investors and militarists against popular indifference and opposition. Hawaii's location on the sea lanes of the North Pacific assisted the strategists. Since as early as 1840 Honolulu had been quite familiar with New England merchandise and ministers, for traders in sandalwood and whalers followed the missionaries; Secretary of State Marcy nearly accomplished annexation, but that waited

[1] The New Zealanders obtained Germany's share during the First World War.

until the sugar crop tied the island to the United States. Here again, executives went faster than the electorate; five successive adminstrations took steps to ensure that Hawaii should not become the perquisite of any other power, while other nations showed comparatively little desire to challenge American interests.

Hawaii's white population, largely descendants of American missionaries and traders, was led by a few planters who acquired ownership of about three-fourths of the private plantation lands. They manipulated the native rulers into pledges of an exchange of special trade privileges with the United States and a guarantee that no third power should infringe Hawaiian sovereignty. The Senate finally (1875) ratified such a treaty. Garfield's secretary of state, James G. Blaine, perpetuated this policy and Arthur's administration obtained (1884) exclusive right to a fortified naval base at the splendid location of Pearl Harbor. Cleveland's secretary of state, Thomas F. Bayard, managed to sidestep a Franco-British proposal for guarantee of Hawaiian independence.

Reciprocity brought prosperity to the sugar growers through near-free trade with the United States, which by 1890 bought 99 per cent of Hawaii's exports. The growers tired of their continual struggle to protect their monopoly of the island's resources from the political ambitions of native rulers sensitive to the aspirations of natives, white laborers and coolies. The McKinley tariff deprived Hawaiian sugar of its preferred position and the next year Queen Liliuokalani ascended the throne with the firm intention of breaking American ties. Soon the United States minister, John L. Stevens, was conniving with the growers, who deposed "Queen Lil" and prepared a treaty of annexation which Secretary of State Foster signed. Then Harrison lost the election to Cleveland, who exposed the scheme, withdrew the treaty and tried to reëstablish the somewhat bloodthirsty queen. She tactlessly refused to promise to spare the heads of the conspirators and they set up a new republic under a constitution authorizing annexation when practicable. They made their republic a going concern, forcing recognition from Cleveland's administration and thereafter from other governments, while waiting a change of party at Washington.

Senator Lodge and other annexationists stressed the importance of Hawaii to a future isthmian canal and the danger of Japanese control until McKinley, 17 June 1897, hurried a new treaty of annexation to the Senate. But that body was so uncertain on outright imperialism and far-flung naval stations that a ratification majority of two-thirds did not appear. Not until the Spanish War and Hawaii's eager tender of her facilities for a naval base did they achieve their object. Even then they accomplished it, 7 July 1898, only by using a joint resolution of annexation, patterned after the Texas example, requiring only straight majority votes. Two years later Hawaii was made a full-fledged territory eligible for statehood, with its polyglot population, largely Malaysian but including Orientals also, made citizens of the United States.

Supporting the Monroe Doctrine

Toward Latin America the basic policy remained normally one of peace. Through many years most of the republics to the south were for all practical purposes farther from the United States than was all Europe. As the United States grew in economic and political importance she assumed bolder leadership and promoted commercial relationships, but her investment stake was not yet large enough to attach a severely dictatorial amendment to the Monroe Doctrine. The only approach to war with a South American republic came when an Irish-American minister to Chile, Patrick Egan, allowed his anti-British sentiments to place him on the minority side in a Chilean revolution of 1891 which enjoyed British support. The victorious revolutionaries, incensed at Egan, attacked sailors ashore from the U.S.S. *Baltimore,* inflicting a few casualties. Secretary of State Blaine, fortunately, exercised restraint and the *Baltimore* was called home. After investigation, apology and reparations were demanded of Chile; she tendered them upon a change in the personnel of her government.

The gratifying rôle of arbitrator came readily and frequently. The United States helped to bring to a legal end in 1871 Spain's prolonged war with the Pacific coast republics of Bolivia, Chile, Ecuador and Peru. President Hayes acted as arbitrator on the Argentine-Paraguay boundary, President Cleveland on that of Argentine-Brazil, W. I. Buchanan (American minister to the Argentine) on Argentine-Chile, and the controversy over Tacna-Arica, which from 1883 divided Chile and Peru, was finally settled some forty-six years later through the good offices of the United States.

The more vigorous rôle of sponsor of western democracy as against European autocracy well suited the government which had proclaimed the Monroe Doctrine. The rôle was best glorified in the Brazilian incident. When a bloodless revolution in 1889 overthrew that Empire, the United States was the first government outside Latin America to recognize the new republic. European powers, however, extended aid four years later to the monarchists, who seized the Brazilian navy and undertook to reëstablish themselves. Cleveland refused to recognize them and United States manufacturers despatched munitions for the republican forces. Germany had many nationals in southern Brazil, did not realize how rapidly the population was being welded into one nation and particularly feared the republican government might displace German with United States influence. British battleships joined hers in a blockade to prevent delivery of munitions to the republicans. Thereupon the American admiral took a firm stand and prepared to attack; the English ships withdrew rather than antagonize the United States and the German vessels, left alone, retired. This signalized defeat of the monarchists; it won for the United States the friendship of Brazil and a higher respect abroad for the Monroe Doctrine.

Not so glorious was the exploitation of the Monroe Doctrine in Venezuela. When gold discoveries during Cleveland's second administration made the line between Venezuela and British Guiana important, Britain claimed a boundary which would have increased Guiana's area about 40 per cent, and Venezuela counterclaimed at least half of Guiana. Britain was not particularly moved when Venezuela broke off relations and Cleveland recommended arbitration. But during Cleveland's second administration domestic discord tempted him (as it did other presidents) to seek compensation abroad, especially as British seizure of the Nicaraguan customs to secure payment of a claim had aroused resentment. A joint congressional resolution of April 1894 supported Cleveland in another plea for arbitration. A year later, while a declaration of war (which would much embarrass the United States) by Venezuela against Britain threatened, the President permitted Secretary of State Olney to make an extremely brusque demand for arbitration, with the assertion that the Monroe Doctrine was involved. Olney rashly declared it had become a "doctrine of American public law. Today the United States is practically sovereign on this continent and its fiat is law upon the subjects to which it confines its interposition."

To this undiplomatic language and far-fetched assertion Britain waited for months before making reply that the imposition of arbitration by the United States was unreasonable and unjustified by international law. Thereupon Cleveland, with congressional support and confident that British consent was near, created a fact-finding commission whether Britain would or no. A few sensible leaders on both sides opposed war, but jingo sentiment was strong. At this strained juncture came the Jameson raid into Boer territory, and an aggressive congratulatory telegram from the German Kaiser to the Boer leader, Kruger, revealed German hostility to British colonial expansion. London was moved to conciliate Washington with an arbitration tribunal; it decided mainly in Britain's favor.

Olney's assertion that the United States was "sovereign" over the continent harmed such beginnings of cordial relations with Latin republics as had been cultivated. Primarily interested in export markets, Blaine had sought to check the infiltration of European influence into Latin American trade and politics, by inter-American treaties of reciprocity and arbitration. But the delegates of the seventeen Latin powers who accepted invitations to the first Pan-American conference, convened at Washington in 1889, would not ratify Blaine's propositions except to agree to establishment of an information center, the International Union of Latin American Republics. It became the Pan-American Union, which Andrew Carnegie housed in a palatial structure in Washington. Pan-Americanism proved a tender plant, easily wilted by southern fear of northern aggression.

The ease with which United States exploiters secured control of Mexico's resources from the eagerly coöperative President Diaz (in office thirty years) was bound to add to Latin suspicions; nor did trade expand sufficiently to allay them. Between 1860 and 1900 the percentage of total United States imports from South America grew from 9 per cent to 11 per cent but exports to South America fell from 4 per cent to 2 per cent. Reciprocity treaties negotiated under the tariffs of 1890 and 1897 were blasted by protectionist influence in the Senate lobby. British and German salesmen proved better than Americans at studying the southern temperament. Most important, the period closed with a dramatic expansion of northern political power down into the Caribbean, verifying the suspicion that the United States now took, from the fact of her widely separated coast lines, a command to acquire a protective sphere of domination to the south.

The New Navy

When the Civil War closed the United States possessed a great navy, but with the passing of the crisis public interest had turned elsewhere. The navy was not kept in good trim. Vessels were held in a condition of minimum usefulness and personnel was allowed to shrink. World naval improvements were not followed.

The American navy, which at the end of the Civil War had numbered 700 ships, had been allowed to decline until in 1881 there were but 37 cruising vessels. Even more amazing is the fact that, in a day of steel and iron construction, these were all of wood save four which had iron hulls. Nor did these ships have one high-powered gun. During the Garfield-Arthur administration the Navy Department started a crusade to secure a new navy. An advisory committee made a report and in 1883 four steel vessels were authorized. They were tiny when measured by modern standards, as the largest was only 4,500 tons, and they were otherwise unsatisfactory; but they were a beginning proudly referred to as the "Great White Fleet."

During the Cleveland administration construction was carried further. An armored cruiser, the *New York* of 8,000 tons, carried six 8-inch guns. Two second-class battleships including the to-be-famous *Maine* were of 6,000 tons burden and carried 10 and 12-inch guns. Another famous ship was one of six protected cruisers, the *Olympia* of 6,000 tons, which had 8-inch and 5-inch guns and six torpedo tubes. Gunboats and torpedo-boats likewise were constructed. In the Harrison administration 10,000-ton first class battleships were introduced, including another historic ship, the *Oregon,* which was equipped with 13-inch guns.

In the course of this construction differences of opinion arose. One group of experts was determined to concentrate on swift cruisers, while others urged battleships with heavy armor and batteries. Experts also experimented with "dynamite cruisers" and at length a submarine was authorized. Vessels grew larger and better fortified; the 11,300-ton battleship *Kearsarge* of the second Cleveland administration was equipped with improved fighting turrets. After fourteen years of effort, 1883-1897, the Great White Fleet numbered 42 ships with 33 more under construction. Battleships and torpedo-boats were to be the principal classes. The United States had risen from twelfth to fifth among the naval powers of the world. The few Americans who realized this fact took pride in it; some of them were ready to wager that, if put to use, the new navy would acquit itself second to none.

CHAPTER XXX

THE UNITED STATES A WORLD POWER

As the nineteenth century drew to a close, Americans were restive. They had been engrossed in filling up the West, building railroads, exploiting resources, developing great industries, meeting demands of the domestic market and struggling with a depression. Now the frontier was gone. There was some weight of boredom with matters mundane. Without realizing exactly why, people were eager for post-panic emotional outlets. Bright young men were full of activity. New York City Police Commissioner Theodore Roosevelt, Senators Henry Cabot Lodge and Albert J. Beveridge and other ambitious Republicans, Democrats and Populists were unwilling to rest under Bryan's youthful challenge. There was a new navy the efficiency of which the staff was eager to demonstrate, and the public which had gaped at the U.S.S. *Illinois* at the Columbian Exposition was growing navy conscious. Altogether here was a psychological ripeness which clever politicians could richly harvest. Trade, too, pointed sharply outward. Since 1876 exports regularly had exceeded imports every year except 1888, 1889 and 1893. Moreover, the increase in exports was more marked among manufactured articles than among foodstuffs, although the latter continued to overshadow the former; and manufacturers were more skilful than farmers at pointing out such matters to presidents.

The Spanish War

The direction which venturesomeness should take already had been determined upon by eager expansionists. Such men as Lodge, Roosevelt, Minister John Hay in London, Whitelaw Reid, editor of the New York *Tribune,* and Albert Shaw, editor of the *American Review of Reviews,* pressed forward the arguments of the naval historian, Captain A. T. Mahan. He preached that United States coastal defense, trade prestige and power required a big navy, an isthmian canal, control of the Caribbean and acquisition of Hawaii and Samoa. Each need seemed inseparable from the others, with Caribbean openings wide to the eye. Sidelong glances they cast toward the Philippines and trade with the Orient. From some outstanding professors of history, sociology and economics came endorsement of these views. In magazines, public speeches and private communications they were pressed. No less able, if less exciting, were the more sober arguments of the anti-imperialists who also included topnotch leaders in the professions and politics, besides wealthy men of affairs.

A Cuban situation was ready at hand. That unhappy island had experienced an exhausting contest with the mother country, Spain; during their crisis of 1868-1878 Secretary Fish had been hard put to it to prevent President Grant from following Congress in recognition of Cuban belligerency. Filibusters, conveniently led by naturalized American citizens, had wrongfully flown the American flag at the masthead of vessels operating in aid and comfort to the Cubans. The summary execution of the crew and passengers of one of these vessels, the *Virginius,* had aroused a great deal of excitement in 1873 and easily could have brought war. Then the United States was in a position to have waged it with some ease and without European intervention, but public interest did not reach fever heat and Fish was able to avoid war. Exhaustion ended the revolt in 1878; they were contending against a depression greater than that behind the American Revolution. Ex-filibuster politicians found a restless refuge in New York, Florida and Louisiana, whence they established some tradition of popular interest in Cuba whilst lobbying in Washington, selling bonds and outfitting expeditions. American investors proceeded to acquire in eighteen years a direct property interest of 50 millions, mostly in sugar, iron and tobacco; but their stake was small compared to British, German and French holders and they evidently preferred the profits of peace to the hazards of war. Their distaste for jingoism appears to have been shared by commercial interests—the shippers, manufacturers, exporters and importers whose trade connections reached the annual amount of 103 millions in 1893.

By 1895 the Cubans were revolting again; to the burden of Spanish misrule and exploitation were added a serious depression with a crisis in the sugar industry. The export trade was smashed by the hard times in the United States and by the end of reciprocity, for the Wilson-Gorman tariff reimposed the 40 per cent sugar duties and Spanish schedules retaliated. Tobacco had not recovered from an increased duty in the McKinley tariff. The Cuban-American trade dropped to 63 millions in 1895, while all kinds of property on the island were wrecked by the insurgents, who ended work operation by terrorism and levied assessments on planters. The owners hated the thought of an American intervention which should turn them over defenseless to native control, and Secretary Olney was fully apprised of their attitude, particularly through E. A. Atkins, prominent American sugar planter.

To crush the guerrillas, the Spanish General Weyler, called "Butcher Weyler," restorted to "reconcentration," placing all non-combatants—men, women and children—in a few camps and treating the remainder of the population as insurrectionists. Reconcentration later was practised by Britain in South Africa and the United States in the Philippines, but Spain lacked foodstuffs and sanitation adequate to keep alive all the *reconcentrados.*

Also in 1895 William R. Hearst and Joseph Pulitzer began their journalistic rivalry. The color, emotion and cruelty in the Cuban situation had high news value and lent themselves readily to vivid picturization, manipulation and untruth while the *Journal* and the *World* madly competed for circulation. The sales of lesser editors who bought their stuff also jumped, while other editors took up the cry on the basis of its popularity and the Associated Press lent its influence to sensationalism. Americans proceeded enthusiastically to confuse their pride in expansion with their altruistic emotions. Did not the poor Cubans need deliverance from the Spanish yoke? Would not the western hemisphere, including the United States, be better off with the Spaniards out? Thus did the yellow press come to the aid of the ardent expansionists while the public went to the aid of the Cubans.

Against this muddy current Cleveland set himself. Considerable care and funds were expended to stop filibuster use of numerous Atlantic ports. He and Olney followed the precedent established by Grant and Fish, insisting upon protection of the treaty rights of American citizens and tendering mediatory services. Disavowing any designs against Spanish sovereignty, they proposed mediation toward a peace based on home rule. The congressional majority, however, was less defiant of mass missionary sentiment in an election year; they passed the concurrent resolution of 6 April 1896 proclaiming their opinion that the belligerents should be recognized and that American mediation should look toward Cuban independence. As theirs was not a joint resolution it neither required the president's signature nor had the force of law, but Madrid knew that Cleveland had lost political influence, that Republicans were less tolerant of Spanish rule and that politicians of both parties might see advantage in a foreign diversion.

Many of the Spanish people were intransigent, knew not the weakness of their navy and threatened to unseat the government if they should compromise too hastily. Late in 1897 a Conservative was followed by a Liberal ministry which finally offered the Cubans liberal propositions approximating autonomy. The gesture came too late; loyal Spaniards in Cuba opposed autonomy as giving the Cubans control over them; the revolutionists rejected autonomy because now they had high hopes of United States intervention and independence.

Intervention took great impetus from February events. Hearst published in the New York *Journal,* 9 February, a stolen letter written by the Spanish minister, Enrique Dupuy de Lôme to a Cuban friend: "McKinley is weak and a bidder for the admiration of the crowd, besides being a would-be politician who tries to leave a door open behind himself while keeping on good terms with the jingoes of his party." This was not likely to stiffen the presidential spine against a Spanish war. Six days later the United States battleship *Maine,* which had been stationed at Havana harbor for reasons never made clear, was blown up, killing 260 men. Regrets of the Spanish government over this disaster, for which it apparently had no responsibility, could scarce be heard against the hysterical American cry, "Remember the Maine!"

The Madrid government, desiring peace, belatedly revoked the reconcentration orders, granted suspension of hostilities and urged the Pope to save their prestige by pleading for peace. They promised Washington to go in this direction "as far and as fast" as their public opinion permitted. But the Cubans wanted no peace, and the missionary-minded American public unlike Wall Street, the Republican high command and investors in Cuba was eager for a war of liberation. McKinley, fearful for his party leadership, reported the Spanish capitulation to Congress very sketchily, and left the decision to the popular body. It passed the war resolutions of 19 April 1898, the Senate by a vote of 42-35, the House by 311-6. Congress hesitated only long enough to include the famous self-denying ordinance of Senator Teller, which reflected the missionary mood of the moment; it disclaimed any intention to annex Cuba. Thus did the leading democracy of the New World go to war against Spain as the symbol of all Old World autocracy. Only the few expansionist schemers intended the war should embark the United States upon an imperialistic policy.

The conflict proved short and decisive. With plenty of martial spirit the sea and land forces, the latter after some delay, were ranged against those of Spain in and about Cuba, Puerto Rico and the Philippines. The United States navy had a skill and aggressiveness which made it vastly superior to the Spanish armada, even with half the North Atlantic fleet left to guard the little-fortified Atlantic seaboard. The small United States army had to contend against politician-management in Washington but showed abundant courage and resource and was aided by the failure of the Spanish Captain-General to send more than a fraction of his troops to oppose their advance. A more than adequate contingent of newspaper correspondents kept American readers fully informed of the real and fancied exploits of their forces against a weak and discouraged enemy.

Theodore Roosevelt, lately become assistant secretary of the navy, had been busily laying the groundwork for just such an eventuality. He had written *The Naval War of 1812*—in 1882—and had become an ardent expansionist. He had seized the occasion, when Secretary Long was absent one afternoon from the Department, to station Admiral Dewey at Hongkong in readiness for a run to Manila. Previously he had managed to place Dewey in command of the Pacific fleet and had done much to place both the Atlantic and Pacific fleets on a war footing.

For his part, Dewey had established at Hongkong friendly relations with an exiled insurrectionist, Emilio Aguinaldo, who understood that the Admiral was pledged to Philippine independence. Aguinaldo happily coöperated with Dewey and General Merritt, commander of the land forces in that area, to defeat the Spanish. Dewey also enjoyed the conspicuous friendliness of the British Captain Chichester, who was on the scene as an observer. Dewey with ease destroyed the Spanish squadron in Manila Bay, 1 May, and ten weeks later a combined attack by American naval and land forces and Aguinaldo's insurgents forced surrender of the city of Manila. These victories on the other side of the world were completed 13 August, one day after the signing of an armistice at Washington. Also the vacant Wake Island and the Spanish island of Guam had been occupied by American forces en route to the Philippines.

Americans had taken comparatively little note at the moment of the unaccountable Pacific excursion. They had been excited over the war around the Caribbean. There Admirals Schley and Sampson were blockading Cuba, while the Spanish fleet under Admiral Cervera took refuge in Santiago harbor. The daring Lieutenant Hobson was sinking the *Merrimac* in the harbor in an effort to "bottle up" Cervera. The fleet was waiting overlong for the delayed army to help capture Santiago. The three-hundred-pound General Shafter was struggling to move troops ailing from the ill effects of winter clothing and poor food and medicine issued for summer use in subtropical territory! Colonel Roosevelt was gaily leading his "horseless Rough Riders." The army was capturing three heights overlooking Santiago—San Juan Hill, Kettle Hill and El Caney—within twelve hours of fighting. Cervera was escaping from the harbor only to suffer destruction of his fleet in the four-hour battle of 3 July, which made for a Glorious Fourth! General Miles was making joyful progress through Puerto Rico to the huzzas of the natives.

An armistice was signed 12 August. The truce had saved the lives of numerous Spanish soldiers, Cuban insurrectos and civilians who would have died during a dragging civil war. The war is estimated to have cost, eventually, the lives of about 5,500 Americans (many dead of disease, not bullets) and a total of more than 1,300 millions in expense, including pensions. But these sacrifices were readily entered upon, for American expansion in the Caribbean was a logical trend, dictated by geography, and there lay public interest.

Oriental Entanglements: New Frontiers

The terms of the armistice suggested, however, a hand pointing toward Far Eastern expansion, for in addition to certain expected Caribbean terms it specified that the United States was to hold Manila until a peace conference settled the status of the Philippines. The imperialists planned to inject American influence far eastward of its natural limits and some business men dreamed of profits in the China trade. Britain was encouraging American interest in the Far East in order to prevent the excessive growth of German and Japanese interests there. When Britain had secretly invited the United States in March 1898 to join in keeping these powers from advancing in China, she was repeating history. In 1823 she had urged the United States to aid in maintaining the balance of power in the Caribbean; now she was seeking the same end in the Far East.

McKinley declined this invitation but his interest in the Philippines grew. The fact that Great Britain, Germany and Japan were all known to be interested in the archipelago gave it an attractiveness which was enhanced by the enthusiasm of victory. How would the President instruct the delegates of the United States, waiting upon his decision at Paris? They had been well-chosen, unlike the Paris peace commission of 1919, for their strategic influence at home. Chairmanship was entrusted to William R. Day, who had resigned as secretary of state for this purpose; the other Republican members were the chairman of the Senate Committee on Foreign Relations, C. K. Davis, the Senate's president *pro tempore,* W. P. Frye, and New York's most influential Republican editor, Whitelaw Reid. Senate opposition was scantily recognized by inclusion of a lone Democrat, George Gray of Delaware.

Upon the well-intentioned McKinley the imperialists concentrated their arguments, stressing civilization, morality and trade—although the Spanish government was both civilized and Christian. On these grounds he painfully reconciled himself to instructing the delegates to demand all of the Philippine Islands. Consequently when the Treaty of Paris finally was signed, 10 December 1898, Spain ceded all of these. With them she gave up to the United States the island of Guam near Hawaii, and the expected Caribbean areas—Puerto Rico and all of the other Spanish West Indies except Cuba, over which she simply renounced sovereignty. Also she was forced to assume the Cuban debt of 400 millions. She received from the United States consolation money amounting to 20 millions, ostensibly for a speedy departure from the islands.

Such a treaty posed the new and fundamental question of American imperialism. Would the Senate ratify? The Anti-Imperialist League, led by Senator Hoar of Massachusetts and supported by prominent persons from all the different occupations and parties, questioned the value of the insular possessions. Why subject Americans to competition with cheap agriculture (as in beet-sugar and tobacco), with cheap Oriental labor and with madly extravagant imperialistic powers? The Philippines would be difficult, if not impossible to defend, would saddle the United States with a heavy liability and would involve the government in the unfamiliar mazes of Far Eastern diplomacy. To seize the Philippines was contrary to the ideals of the Declaration of Independence, would violate moral obligations to the Filipinos and ensure the ill-will of Aguinaldo and his Independence Party. Indeed, they already were fighting the perfidious Merritt, as they regarded him.

The anxieties of Senator Hoar and of the interested and disinterested backers of the League were shared by enough members of the Senate to make it possible for a Democratic leadership to deprive the Republicans of their necessary two-thirds vote. A confused Democratic leader was Bryan. He disapproved of imperialism and wanted the nation to have an opportunity to defeat it in 1900. Like many another American politician, he did not ascribe to foreign relations an importance which would debar their use as a football in domestic politics. His oratory and understanding had been spent earnestly but fruitlessly on the currency issue in 1896. Might not a crusade against imperialism save America in 1900? With the help of his advice, not yet fully explained or measured, enough Democrats voted for ratification, 6 February 1899, to save the treaty by a margin of one vote.

Adjusting Democracy to Imperialism

The war with Spain had swept into the orbit of American influence the polyglot of yellow, brown and black people chiefly inhabiting Hawaii, the Philippines, Puerto Rico, Cuba and most of the other Caribbean areas. Their social and political institutions had not been designed after the Anglo-Saxon pattern from which had been fashioned the United States experiment in democracy. Their economic resources of raw material and manpower would partly complement, partly compete with, the American economy. Thus they added their quota of diversities to that sum total of differences which had made the history of the United States a long series of compromises. This basic fact was but little weighed at first.

No less diverse was the reaction of Americans to the allotments of the Peace of Paris. Improvement was a prominent objective among beneficent persons, whose enthusiasm moved from freeing the oppressed of Spain to establishing sanitation, education, transportation and orderliness among backward peoples. Protection was the object of military strategists, who drew the defense line from Alaska to Hawaii (some said the Philippines) through an isthmian canal and into a dominated Caribbean. Prestige was the object of those who proclaimed that the United States had "come of age" as an acknowledged world power and thenceforth must steam across the seas to council tables in either hemisphere. Profit was the object of producers and investors. With these objectives others became entangled, heterogeneous, opportunistic. Clashes quickly developed between parties at interest. The steps toward imperialism were to run contrary to some American ideals.

Inasmuch as pursuit of the various objectives quickly carried American policy beyond accepted boundaries, the need soon arose for a judicial assignment of rights, privileges, and immunities. If Puerto Rico and the Philippines enjoyed the status of all previously acquired areas, they were en route to statehood; their people were citizens of the United States, and they could market on the mainland free of duty, to the inconvenience of sugar, tobacco, and other producers previously protected against them by the Dingley tariff. Could they not rather be given a classification new to United States experience—as dependencies? Americans hated to adopt the term "colonies."

Dispute raged furiously; did the Constitution follow the flag? It became evident that while protectionist sentiment temporarily was strong enough to insist upon its profitable perquisites, yet the American public persistently cherished the theory of inalienable rights. The Supreme Court majority by various and close decisions in "insular cases" of 1901-1917 accommodated themselves to this situation. They decided that the dependencies were not foreign countries, but that their people were not necessarily citizens of the United States. They lived in "unincorporated" rather than "incorporated" territories. The "fundamental" rights of the Constitution, such as life, liberty and property, applied to them, but not the "formal" rights of grand and petit jury practice; and Congress could decide how far the Constitution and the statutes applied to them. Congress proceeded to regulate duties on insular products and for political pattern turned, after periods of military rule, to British colonial experience. Government of the Philippines and Puerto Rico was assigned to an appointed governor and a legislature composed of an appointive, executive council and an elected lower house, with the governor—unlike the American colonial officials—empowered to continue appropriations when the assembly proved recalcitrant. Such arrangements made the political and economic (and consequently the social) status of the colonies dependent upon the ebb and flow of pressures on Congress.

For good or ill the United States had undertaken to maintain her influence in the eastern hemisphere, 7,000 miles from her Pacific coast and neighbor to an awakening yellow race. A new era was acknowledged in foreign relations.

and the Philippines [illegible] an isthmian canal and into a [illegible] Caribbean [illegible] who proclaimed that the United States had "come of age" [illegible] acknowledged world power and [illegible] across the sea to commit [illegible] in other hemispheres. Trade was the object of producers and investors. [illegible] others became [illegible] China [illegible] at interest. [illegible] to some American ideals.

Inasmuch as pursuit of the [illegible] contradicted American policy [illegible] guarantees [illegible] of rights, [illegible] and immunities. In Puerto Rico and the Philippines [illegible] their people were citizens of the United States and they could not [illegible] of duty [illegible] of sugar, tobacco, and other products [illegible] tariff [illegible] United States [illegible] Americans [illegible].

[illegible] did the Constitution follow the flag? It [illegible] that, while [illegible] Constitution [illegible] cases of 1901 [illegible] the Constitution. They decided that the [illegible] were not [illegible] and that their people were not necessarily citizens of the United States. [illegible] "unincorporated" [illegible] "incorporated" territories. [illegible] such as the [illegible] applied to them, but not [illegible] rights [illegible] products [illegible] Philippines and Puerto Rico [illegible] latter composed of [illegible] lower house, [illegible] governor [illegible] power [illegible] appropriations [illegible] political [illegible] of the colonies dependent upon the [illegible] of Congress.

[illegible] United States [illegible] from her Pacific coast [illegible] in foreign relations.

PERFECTION OF DEMOCRACY

1900–1919

CHAPTER XXXI

THE MIGHTY FORCE OF PROGRESS

The Progressive Era was the period in which the people of the United States undertook to fuse their sense of knowledge with their sense of power. Always this nation had been conscious of progress and confident of its continuance, for they had had enough security to make them expect more. The peculiarity of this era was the pervasive interest in directing the course of progress along lines of public welfare. Americans felt greatly enlightened. Cherishing their historic theory of democracy, they worked for its realization in fact as never before. Could there be any limit to further achievement? Such an attitude is by no means common in world history; it can stimulate an entire people as nothing else can. The United States during the first decade and a half of the twentieth century luxuriated in that kind of era.

The Sense of Power

The sense of power rose partly from heavier use of water, coal, steam, electricity and gasoline, which were more securely chained to do service in settled places and to annihilate farther distances on the earth's surface, underground and in the air. The more intensive exploitation of physical resources and manpower stimulated production, revolutionized industry and made intercommunication vastly easier and home life far more convenient. As it changed habits and spread ideas, it so heightened the tempo of life as to work effects beyond measure.

One of the sharpest impulses came from electricity; the possibilities in it now began to be more fully realized. Nicola Tesla's researches after his immigration from Austria, and those of his successors, had lengthened transmission wires to more than 150 miles. At Niagara by 1900 and Keokuk, Iowa, by 1914 vast hydroelectric plants were setting a pace for hundreds of others at less favorable sites. The 2,000 power stations of 1898 grew in number by 1914 to 5,000, delivering current to homes as well as factories, meeting continual demands for more electricity. Unfortunately the general resourcefulness shown in producing current was not matched by intelligence in dispensing it. Experiments of twenty years had cheapened production but the huge profits were not used to lower charges so as to expand the market and the profits to the outer limits of potential consumption. A nation which long had practised private ownership and control of national resources would be slow to require a sharing of the gains from them.

Nevertheless, electric lights and telephones moved out of the class of luxuries. They became necessities for business and the middle class, increasing the output of work and multiplying the uses of leisure. Thanks to the inventive and managerial abilities of Alexander G. Bell and Theodore N. Vail, Americans by 1900 were using more than 700,000 telephones (more than twice as many as in all Europe) and by 1915 about 6,000,000. Long-distance communication reached its farthest range in direct connections between New York and San Francisco by overhead wires in 1915. Meanwhile, along the Atlantic seaboard, underground wires beneath the Hudson and between the largest cities were ensuring continuous service in bad weather and in spite of natural obstacles. Wireless telegraphy was proved practical over the Atlantic by 1901 and all large ships had this equipment inside of half a dozen years. An American, Lee De Forest, contributed much to this improvement.

As the delivery of current was perfected, the largest users became the trolleys and elevated railroads. They aroused the enthusiasm of the riding public in the cities and between towns and attracted the genius of engineers, financiers and executives. Electric trains displaced steam railroads on the elevated lines of New York, Chicago and Boston, beginning in 1901; and American subway construction, imitating London, came to Boston, New York, Brooklyn and New Jersey (1898-1908). The enthusiasm for trolleys built them between most of the towns in the heavily populated areas and threatened the fare schedules of the steam railways so that some of the latter purchased the trolley lines and electrified their own railroads.

The steam railroads continued to expand their annual mileage construction until 1907, when interurban competition and declining profits resulting from watered stock and mismanagement cut down construction. Most of the new tracks were built to unite existing lines; only the Los Angeles-Salt Lake line of 1905 reached out to tap new areas—important mineral deposits. As this line also cut twenty-four hours from the time of express trains carrying fruit from California to eastern tables, it modified national diet habits. Railroads continued to reflect the ingenuity, imagination and aspiration of Americans in many ways. One symbol was pride in stations. At Boston, Washington, Chicago and Kansas City huge structures rose, while the Pennsylvania Station and Grand Central Terminal at New York (1910 and 1913) outshone all others in combining beauty, immensity and usefulness.

Most influential was the automobile, for it was becoming a practical adjunct of daily life. On "horseless carriages" many minds, especially European, had been working during the past 150 years. Since

1879, when George B. Selden of Rochester had applied for his first patent for a gasoline vehicle, numerous American mechanics had experimented with electricity, gasoline, steam, compressed air, carbonic acid gas and alcohol as motive power. A gasoline car contrived by Henry Ford of Detroit during the 1893 panic made twenty-five miles an hour and many fundamental principles were embodied in a vehicle patented by Selden two years later. With the lightening of the depression in 1897 came various successful demonstrations by Ford, C. E. Duryea, Elwood Haynes and R. E. Olds, and by the end of the century some eight thousand automobiles were registered, with electricity and steam about equally popular as motive power.

The hard-won Selden patent of 1895 had embodied so many fundamental principles that manufacturers who, unlike Selden, had capital to venture, agreed to pay him a modest royalty and organized an exclusive Association of Licensed Automobile Manufacturers to protect their patent. They successfully sued Ford and other independents for infringement. But the latter group fought the decisions up from the lower courts until in 1911 the Federal Circuit Court of Appeals decided that they were not infringing the patent in the test cases. Thus American automobile manufacture was less retarded by patent monopoly.

Keen competition for profits drove rival manufacturers to breakneck speed in devising such mechanical improvements and cheapened production as should bring cars within the reach of ordinary citizens who had neither mechanical training nor large means. The low speed and narrow range of the electrics and the explosive propensities of steam automobiles swung manufacturers toward gasoline. Jerky, "one-lung" motors evolved into smoother-running "fours," "sixes" and "eights." By moving the engine from beneath the car to in front of it and by equipping it with a self-starter (1913-1914), looks and convenience were doubly served. As air-filled tires displaced hard rubber and as roads were paved motion became smooth and rapid.

American manufacturers were applying to the underlying inventions of other nationals a standardization of process which cheapened production and converted the automobile from a plaything of the wealthy to an indispensable of business and a pleasure necessity of the middle class. Ford, who had been charging from $850 to above $2,000, in 1908 began progressive reductions; there came a general tendency for the manufacture of cheaper cars to increase. Total registration of business and pleasure vehicles in the United States jumped from 8,000 in 1900 to 2,500,000 by 1915. Rural isolation was becoming impossible in many areas and suburban development was powerfully stimulated.

Production and purchase of automobiles repainted the industrial landscape. Capital invested in them multiplied about seventy times.

They were bought so rapidly as to surpass the increase in other manufactures and diverted interest from some. They created a tremendous amount of work. Jobs in manufacturing the car itself, plus jobs in all the industries which feed automobile manufacture (such as copper, oil and steel) helped to keep the United States free of wide panic between 1898 and 1929, for capital was being created at least as fast as the increase in population. More than any other invention since the Civil War, probably, the automobile has changed the situation and behavior, the daily life, of our people.

Alteration of daily living through the use of airplanes, however, waited while French, English and American inventors experimented with them as instruments of war. Samuel P. Langley, secretary of the Smithsonian Institution in Washington, devised models which in 1898 won a War Department appropriation of $50,000 for a man-sized experiment. He just missed success in the fall of 1903, only a few days before two Dayton bicycle mechanics who had been experimenting with gliders—Orville and Wilbur Wright—made successful flights of twelve and fifty-nine seconds' duration in North Carolina. On this encouragement Americans and Europeans set to work anew, with the latter making most of the advances during the next decade. G. E. Curtis in 1911 made an American contribution in a successful hydroplane flight over the Hudson, and an airplane flight across the Atlantic was in preparation when in 1914 war intervened.

The Sense of Well-Being

Another great service which mechanized power did for the democracy was its elevation of living standards, rural and urban. To farmers came a new degree of self-confidence and hope inspired by returning prosperity and widening opportunities. Few of them now had to live in sod houses on the prairies, for the majority, except in the South, had substantial houses of wood or brick, capacious barns, new equipment and improved roads. The prospering ex-Populist enjoyed an expansive mood as he rode in a spring buggy, sat on upholstered furniture, read the daily paper—brought by rural free delivery—by gas or electricity, telephoned his neighbors—or heard them telephoning—over the "party" line, listened to his gramophone and heard his daughter practise on the piano. Of his outside contacts he and his associates were daily conscious, for in addition to their better roads they acquired more frequent train service and, quite gradually, automobiles.

It was this class of the more fortunate farm folk, and the villagers who shared their economy, who furnished the backbone of what became the progressive movement in the Middle West. That movement could not have held sway, however, without considerable support from the urban population, because of the growing proportion of the voters who lived in towns and because city folk had their own sense of progress. Seven-tenths of the 16 million increase in population between 1900 and 1910 was urban; that is, 70 per cent flowed into towns over 2,500 in population. Most of the influx was foreign but approximately 3 million hailed from the country.

Every state except Montana and Wyoming between 1900 and 1910 found its towns growing faster than its country districts. This meant more cities in farming states as well as spectacular expansion in industrial states. Immigration and the overflow from centers like New York, Boston and Philadelphia built up far-flung suburban areas in neighboring states. Expanding markets for iron developed cities like Birmingham; automobiles built up Michigan and Ohio cities, and electricity, Schenectady. California and Florida enjoyed the triple stimuli of citrus fruit, well-to-do winter visitors and a large, permanent influx from other states. Over 20 per cent of Americans in 1910 had moved outside of the states of their birth, a slight increase over the mobility of 1880-1900. The main stream still faced west, with southern Negroes continuing to move north and west; their "talented tenth" joined their manual element in this trek, chiefly to the colored districts of the great northern cities.

Urban dwellers experienced many changes which they considered "progress," both in diet and home furnishings. Apartment buildings in the larger cities increased in size and height, with the servicing of electric elevators from street conduits, and individual apartments grew smaller. Among things effectively crowded out of small apartments was storage space for family lares and penates; this encouraged junking of family records.

In the home and out, at leisure or employed, all but the poorest wives and daughters of this period were groping for new avenues of self-expression in personal improvement and community service. Inroads upon higher education opened many avenues and a few won popularity and wealth as authors. While fewer women were lawyers and ministers than formerly and physicians did not multiply greatly, women entered an increased number of professions and in teaching continually enlarged their percentage. Into home economics, industrial studies, athletics, social welfare, patriotic projects, club activities and any number of "movements," women plunged. Leadership from Jane Addams in settlement work heightened their interest in public affairs. Membership in groups affiliated with the General Federation of Women's Clubs grew from 50,000 in 1898 to 1,000,000 in 1914. Since women's clubs often were the only community organizations pressing for civic improvement, they made a large and immeasurable contribution to the Progressive Era.

Because active women of the Progressive Era were increasing their importance in the scheme of daily living, the legal status of the sex could be raised, though unevenly, and in the South very slowly. They made sufficient progress in winning control of their own earnings, equal control of their children and admission to the bar, to convince militant feminists that they should concentrate upon equal suffrage. For it a few women had been agitating through three-quarters of a century, but only four states, Colorado, Idaho, Utah and Wyoming (where women were at a premium) had granted full suffrage by 1898. Progressive advances between 1910 and 1914 added Washington, California, Oregon, Kansas, Arizona, Montana and Nevada, but only Illinois farther east. Passive indifference from most women and men, with active hostility from a minority of women, corrupt political groups and liquor interests proved the main obstructions to suffrage through state legislation.

When the militant faction decided to concentrate upon a federal amendment as a short-cut and revived the Susan B. Anthony amendment which had been pending since 1878, Congress, Roosevelt, Taft and Wilson successively sidestepped. The year 1912, however, brought Roosevelt a change of heart and Wilson's inauguration gave publicity as well as abuse to suffrage paraders led by a new, more aggressive technician, Alice Paul. As her preference for militant English tactics was not shared by Dr. Anna Howard Shaw and other leaders of the majority of the National American Woman Suffrage Association, Miss Paul organized her own "Congressional Union" and later the National Woman's Party which did much to force Congress to its final surrender on an equal suffrage amendment in 1919.

Very influential was the sense of release through recreation, which now was generally recognized to have its own importance. Feeling the need to forget their workaday environment, city dwellers now used automobiles, as well as trolleys and bicycles, to transport them away from it. Propaganda for exercise as a means of efficiency roused both public officials and private citizens. Cities marked this era with wide extensions of play areas, creating park belts and systems in and near cities, while state and national governments provided "reservations" at a distance.

In exercise itself American interest grew almost to "an athletic renaissance" because of wide participation by all classes, either directly or as onlookers, in "championship" contests. Public interest in sports was both a cause and effect of press publicity given them. Professional baseball, with players' salaries at new highs, became more commercialized throughout. To the old National League, formerly successful in killing promising competition, the new American League gave a challenge which in 1903 forced compromise and stabilized the industry for the next decade. Thenceforward the public watched through the summer while Chicago or New York usually won the National pennant and Philadelphia or Detroit the American, then cheered and bet through the World Series in the fall.

The middle-aged of the middle class now had the leisure to transform golf from a "dude" fad to an inexpensive obsession enjoyed on public links. It and motoring were the most notable additions to outdoor life of the era. By 1914 more adults were said to be playing golf than any other outdoor sport, its popularity enhanced by publicity given the "open golf championship." "International Davis Cup" contests were helping tennis to regain the popularity of which bicycling earlier deprived it, and American victory in international yacht competition with Sir Thomas Lipton sustained public interest in a sport open only to the wealthy.

Professionalism in college football, and play so strenuous as to cause fatalities, drew attention to the harm football was doing. Some smaller colleges depended upon it for support; others took funds badly needed for education and erected monster stadiums to please sporting alumni. The National Collegiate Athletic Association, formed in 1906, began a long series of efforts to revise the rules to save life and education. The reformers hoped athletic coaches could be absorbed into the faculty and the mass of the student body could be made to share in intramural sports. They built huge gymnasiums to house basketball and track teams, which broke records and won laurels at the Olympics in 1896, 1900 and 1904.

A new recreation, destined to became one of the greatest national industries, gradually was growing from the crude, animated films which during the 'nineties had been shown in makeshift quarters for 5 cents admission. These curiosities had reached even the small towns, as traveling exhibitions. In 1905 Edison set up a rude studio for indoor picture-making and within the next five years money was invested in elaborate studios where outdoor pictures, especially ranch plots and slapstick comedy, were manufactured for sale to a rapidly multiplying number of theatres patronized by ever larger audiences. Movies took theatrical entertainment to places formerly without it and brought to third and fourth-rate areas a rise in theatrical standards. Movies became a part of the very popular vaudeville performances.

National diversion included a rage for expositions, in imitation of Chicago. Local pride, sectional rivalry, commercialism and propaganda achieved amazing things with the aid of electricity. A Trans-Mississippi Exposition at Omaha in 1898 was followed in 1901 by the Pan American Exposition at Buffalo and the Interstate Exposition at Charleston, South Carolina. In rapid succession St. Louis, Portland (Oregon), Hampton Roads (Virginia), Seattle, San Francisco and San Diego offered their own Expositions. Most of them involved financial losses to the host communities, but the educational gain was tremendous, for Americans will save during part of the year for the sake of travel at vacation time. The Expositions helped the Progressive Era because they weakened resistance to change and strengthened faith in betterment.

Impetus from Education

The responsibility of the schools in this period was heavier than ever, because almost all people came to consider education indispensable to progress for individuals and for the nation. An everyday remark in thousands of households was, "I want my child to have what I ain't got." The forward urge necessarily recognized youth as the future reliance of the republic. So the public financed, built and organized expanding school systems, and the more thoughtful educators devised new curricula and methods. Thus the period possessed the leadership and the following for a strong educational impetus.

Some educators now sought to make the schools a powerful instrument for progress. Endeavoring to connect the schools more closely with actual life, they and their followers developed a new philosophy of education. They believed in pragmatism and empiricism, that is, that the value of an idea depended upon how well it worked and that one must arbitrarily select ideas for trial. The object of democratic education must be social efficiency and its method must be coöperation in work and play. Schools must never lose sight of the actual conditions around them. The practical effect was considerable. When the desirability of tying education to life was admitted, school surveys looking to improvements were made by some educational leaders (mostly city-connected), by numerous cities and several states. Progressive elementary schools paid enthusiastic attention to music, drawing, domestic science and manual and physical training. In some high schools college preparatory courses began to be shifted from prominence and vocational training—in agriculture, industry, trade and commerce—was added.

These adjustments recognized the basic fact that 90 per cent of the children never reached high school. The very largest group included those who went only up to the tenth grade; for them curricula in large cities (beginning about 1910) were broadened to allow for individual differences by making the seventh, eighth and ninth grades into a junior high school with courses taught by special and departmental instructors. For the next stage came the senior high school, and beyond, the junior college.

Quantitatively, educational expansion set new highs. The number of pupils in elementary schools was increasing, 1898-1914, more than 25 per cent; in high schools more than 100 per cent. A new public high school was established for each day of the year from 1890 to 1918. Southern states, with a rising income, could now respond to the pervasive educational movement by acceptance of the high school as a part of the state system, by strengthening educational features of their laws, by doubling or trebling their school funds, by greatly expanding their white enrollment. Rural communities in a few progressive states began to pool their resources to finance better buildings, instruction and grade division, and transportation of children by the new school buses, for which they had to improve their roads. Even in the old, one-room, ungraded schools, they somewhat improved the teaching by raising requirements slightly; teacher-training courses in high schools aimed to help. Among the normal schools, growth in number and enrollments stimulated some increase in understanding.

Assuming that the majority were fitted for college and would profit by the experience, Americans between 1893 and 1916 multiplied by five their contributions to colleges, and trebled the number of students they sent, until by 1914 at least one person in every twenty-five between the ages of 19 and 23 was in college. On a similar assumption state universities undertook to carry higher education beyond the campus, providing study centers, lecture and correspondence courses, traveling libraries and exhibits. A few of the smallest colleges passed out of existence, while the largest ones established professional schools of education, journalism and business which transformed them into departmentalized universities. Although public taxation assumed much of the burden of the expansion, multimillionaire endowments continued. The multiplication of departments and application of business methods to universities tended to make them "degree factories." In the hinterland small colleges multiplied and were anything but degree factories. Their environment and personnel tended to make them the breeding grounds for progressives who would be likely to lead the struggle to loosen the dominance of special privilege over American life.

The boldest of progressive leaders must have cried down the wind in vain—but for the practical economics taught adults of America outside of formal schools and colleges. A combination of Redpath lectures, lyceums and Chautauqua features now brought light and learning even to snowbound villages, painlessly administering instruction with entertainment and not infrequently propagating liberal ideas. Summertime Chautauqua reached its "golden age" in these years of the Progressive Era, when its programs improved, it maintained an International Alliance and its small offspring flourished in the hinterland. To hundreds of local centers for a week every summer folk flocked to hear music, see plays and listen to discussions of current affairs. Chautauqua shared a belief in community of interest, equality of understanding and educability of the nation; they were peculiarly responsive to liberals who proceeded upon the same assumptions. A favorite with Chautauqua and lyceum audiences was R. M. La Follette's lecture, "Dangers Threatening Representative Government."

Adult education was popularized all along the line, with group study in women's clubs, with forums, corespondence schools, schools for immigrants and with broadening of library functions. Libraries increased in numbers and equipment, expanding from routine circulation of books to an aggressive effort to meet public needs and improve public taste. Libraries of more than 5,000 volumes increased approximately from 1,700 to 3,000, while the New York Public Library alone threw out sixty-five branches.

The Urge of the Press

Millions of people who never entered libraries participated in the progressive urge through popular newspapers and magazines, which both reflected and affected the movement. On the newspaper level, editors profited from further improvements on such earlier inventions as the speedy power press, linotype, typewriter and telegraph; newly come to their aid were the wireless, printing telephoto machine and motor-truck. To the existing newsgathering agencies Hearst added his International News Service. Sunday editions were swollen with feature articles, special departments, and the rotogravure introduced by the New York *Times*.

The great loss to newspapers came through standardization and degradation. Syndication of articles, joint use of press services, dominance of editorial policy by economic and political views of stockholders and single ownership of many papers destroyed most of the remaining individuality. To the earlier Scripps-McRae chains were added transcontinental purchases by Hearst and Munsey, who were interested in controlling the field, not in editing. A few papers kept their identity through strong personalities.

In many localities the press was losing the confidence of the public because it was believed to be venal and subservient to advertisers. News was tainted at its source, according to those who accused the Associated Press of ultraconservatism and the United Press of ultraradicalism. Gross frauds, perpetrated through advertisers' dictation of press policy, became matter of such common belief that Scripps-McRae established their own censorship (1903) and the Associated Advertising Clubs of America set up a vigilance committee (1913). Public attention was fixed upon it largely through exposures of patent medicines. State and federal legislators passed laws on truth in advertising and on libel; the courts attempted to suppress sensationalism and the post office tried to prevent delivery of mail to fraudulent concerns. The campaign for truth brought political attacks upon the freedom of the press; President Theodore Roosevelt forced the federal government to sue the critical Indianapolis *News* but lost the decision. The New York *World* was sued for exposing the seizure of Panama.

The reform legislation of the progressive period would not have been possible without the publicity given to abuses by some magazines. During the 'nineties two periodicals, the *Arena* and *Forum,* had prospered by what might be called a pre-muckrake policy. As the twentieth century opened, the huge task of exposing the cankers in the democracy was deliberately shouldered by Samuel S. McClure, one of the most significant editors in American history, he who in 1884 had founded the first newspaper syndicate and in 1893 had established *McClure's Magazine.* He was convinced that consolidation had become the biggest fact of American life. His determination to expose it had far-reaching results.

He undertook to finance an investigation of various forms of consolidation, trying to do it thoroughly, dispassionately and factually. The process educated the public and lined McClure's pockets simultaneously. He put Ida Tarbell, daughter of a competitor of Rockefeller, on research in the field of Standard Oil, Lincoln Steffens on city government—beginning with St. Louis—and on state government, and Ray Stannard Baker on the railroads and the Negro problem. The public grew interested and excited and the articles reappeared in book form as *The History of the Standard Oil* (1904), *The Shame of the Cities* (1904), and *The Struggle for Self-Government* (1906).

In 1904 Baker, Steffens and Tarbell took over the *American Magazine* and infused it with the spirit of their articles. The exposure field was entered by the *Cosmopolitan, Everybody's* (a significant title), *Hampton's, Munsey's* and *Pierson's.* Life insurance graft was bared in articles by Burton J. Hendrick, frauds in patent medicines and other advertising by Samuel Hopkins Adams, vice conditions in New York and Chicago by G. K. Turner and Alfred Henry Lewis. Judge Ben Lindsey wrote of injustices in juvenile laws. Charles Edward Russell described the beef trust and the tie-up between the Southern Pacific and the California state government. These articles attacked along a very broad and vulnerable front. As presented by McClure and his early staff, they usually avoided overstatement and meant thorough investigation. The fact that neither the magazines nor the authors lost important suits for libel based on these articles added to their impressiveness and influence.

Crass sensationalism entered the field when *Everybody's* published Lawson's "Frenzied Finance," an exposé of Wall Street, and Hearst published Phillips' "Treason of the Senate," in the *Cosmopolitan*. The last threw so lurid a light on Senate control by big business, especially in the person of Senator Chauncey Depew, chairman of the board of directors of the New York Central, that it frightened President Roosevelt, who felt keenly the necessity of Senate coöperation if he was to complete his executive program. Therefore at a gridiron dinner, 17 March 1906, he referred to the exposurists as "muckrakers." The label thus applied at an unreported affair spread by word of mouth and proved so popular that Roosevelt characteristically determined to announce his authorship publicly. He seized the occasion of the dedication of the House Office Building, 14 April following, to attack both big business and the "lunatic fringe" of muckrakers. The title stuck to all the exposurists, McClure's as well as Hearst's, and to the era as well, but differences must not be overlooked. The factual Steffens, unlike Lawson and his tribe, was supplying home truth which was sadly lacking in current texts on American government. With him it was special privilege, whether applied to big business or little business, which was the basic evil. Muckraking had done an inestimable service by demonstrating the need for protection from special privilege. Throughout the nation the religious outlook inherited from Puritan forebears was still strong, even with many who no longer acknowledged its influence. There was still an instinctive dislike of sin and injustice, still sensitive consciences to urge people on to reform.

The urge to reform was thus reinforced, in this period, by the many dynamic, compelling influences in the environment—by the sense of power, the sense of well-being, the schools and the press; altogether these made of progress a mighty force; they made of this period the Progressive Era.

CHAPTER XXXII

IMPLEMENTING FAITH IN DEMOCRACY

Many Americans around 1900 were inclined to a critical appraisal of their environment. Things were looking up now, but the nation had been under the long strains of the falling price era of the 'eighties and 'nineties and of the passing of the idea of free land. Faith in the limitlessness of resources and opportunities had been sufficiently shaken to raise doubts as to the perpetual benevolence of the American scheme of things. Looking about, private citizens and public servants found themselves confronting special privilege as a dominating factor in American life, giving strength to capital and weakness to consumers. They found it to be an integral part of that large-scale organization which had given speed and pervasiveness to change. They came to realize that while the resources, capital and manpower of a rich nation lay open for exploitation in a period of invention, the social conscience had not functioned very effectively. They said that this had placed a premium upon ruthless application of the principles of laissez-faire, regardless of heavy costs to humanity, that it had bred a race of aggressive, talented and greedy captains of industry whose competition eliminated the least ably ferocious. Large-scale organization had evolved into combinations of combinations—into the trusts. As the nation gradually awakened to changes which only a minority formerly had perceived, they took an active hand in politics for the purpose of maintaining progress. In this they were not without foreign example and inspiration, for in England, France and Germany also there was rising a quest for social justice.

Reforming Local Government

This struggle for progress through reform began not on the national political stage but in the hinterland, under city and state leadership. There, liberals had been bred for the struggle by some of the colleges. In the decades closing the nineteenth century small colleges, often hardly more than large academies, abounded in Ohio and other states of the Mississippi Valley, and their students were but a generation or two removed from the vital experience of pioneer coöperation. These colleges but recently had been chiefly training ground for ministers, but the secular trend had been vastly accelerated by the Morrill Land

Grant Act. Its emphasis upon training in agriculture and mechanic arts had invited a new type of student and stirred the hopes of farm parents for sending their sons, if not their daughters, to get a new kind of college education.

The hard struggles of these families to keep one member at college gave the rising generation a personal experience in coöperation for the common good—an experience which emphasized and underscored community traditions of coöperation. Such boys and girls absorbed a belief in the educability of common citizens, and a faith in their ability to cure old maladjustments, which made the Progressive Era possible. This type of college contacts injected some potential leaders with a concentrated solution of such faiths and beliefs; it gave them a high resistance to corporate poisons, equipping them as donors of democratic blood to the monopoly-ridden republic.

Many of the persons who, at the turn of the century out in the provinces, were lighting the fires of the political movement against special privilege, had been influenced—as young people—by three practising liberal theorists of the 'seventies, 'eighties and 'nineties—by Henry D. Lloyd, Edward Bellamy and Henry George. All three had a pronounced religious upbringing; Lloyd and George worked actively in local reform politics and Bellamy and George knew from bitter experience the distress of abject poverty. The breadth of their influence can be gathered from their contacts. Bellamy, son of a Baptist minister, had over a million purchasers for *Looking Backward,* his argument, published in 1888 in fiction form, that Americans in enlightened self-interest should profit under a socialistic form of government. Lloyd, son of a rigid, Calvinist pastor, descended on both sides from long lines of pioneer, dissenting forebears, had reached thousands of readers through the Chicago *Tribune,* of which he was an editor, and through magazines. His "Story of a Great Monopoly," published in the *Atlantic Monthly* in 1881, described the ramifications of large-scale organization. In *Wealth against Commonwealth* (1894) he again exposed various monopolies, with emphasis upon Standard Oil, in the hope that a popular uprising against privilege might follow. Henry George, son of a publisher of religious books whose wife was also extremely religious, long knew direst poverty and whilst so situated evolved a scheme for curing the inequitable distribution of wealth by laying taxes on land only. His gospel, circulated in pamphlet form as *Our Land Policy* (1871), was elaborated in his most notable book, *Progress and Poverty* (1880). George became a leader of reform politics in California and New York.

At the University of Wisconsin a liberal philosopher with a background of poverty and Puritanism, John Bascom, was president from 1874 to 1887, when he left because of differences with the state Republican boss, who also bossed the university regents. Bascom taught the philosophy course which all seniors took and ever stressed the importance of moral victory, urging action on conviction and emphasizing the obligations of citizenship. Among the many students acknowledging their educational indebtedness to Bascom were Charles R. Van Hise, Belle Case and Robert M. La Follette, three graduates of 1879. Van Hise stayed at the University as a science teacher with many outside contacts until 1903, when he became its president, so remaining until his death. He conceived of a state university as the servant of the citizenry and therefore aggressively developed the extension department and other means for making the institution useful for state purposes; also he served the nation in the fields of conservation and trust control.

Young La Follette

(Courtesy Miss Fola La Follette.)

Van Hise and the La Follettes developed the "Wisconsin Idea." It included the direct primary, tax reform, railroad control and commissions of experts to protect the public interest in technical fields. President Van Hise and the La Follettes correlated the best talents of the University and of the La Follette followers to advance the progressive program in the state, particularly during La Follette's governorship, 1900-1906. This success had widespread influence.

The beliefs and faiths stirring in Wisconsin liberals were important because they were not unique. The young insurgents rising in several states in revolt against arrogant machines were led by men and aided by women with the social imagination and political ingenuity to feed and use resentment against corruption. Some encouragement they had from the old Mugwumps. Revolt came first in cities, where democratic government can be its worst and where uprisings stand the quickest chance of success. As mayors were infected, so were governors. The progressivism of these ambitious leaders was sharpened by their desperate conflict with relentless opponents. Their real enemy was entrenched business, which pulled the strings for puppet politicians to dance.

In the practice of the new leadership during the 'nineties there were other active personalities. In Illinois the Democratic governor J. P. Altgeld, the iconoclastic attorney and legislator, Clarence Darrow, and Judge E. F. Dunne, helped to keep Chicago the most radical large city in the United States. In Texas, Governor James S. Hogg was securing a state railway commission and was checking security issues, city extravagances and gigantic landholding companies. In Ohio Sam Jones at Toledo and Tom Johnson at Cleveland were preparing to inject honesty into that most graft-ridden of political and social entities, the United States city.

"Golden Rule" Jones (a Welshman), like Altgeld, was a successful manufacturer who once was worth half a million, but he became convinced that government should be by the Golden Rule and as one of the first "Henry George mayors," he tried to bring to Toledo freedom from domination by the street railway and electric lighting corporations. His agitation from 1897 to 1904 made it possible for his satellite, Brand Whitlock (mayor for four succeeding terms) to obtain a new charter providing for the initiative, referendum, recall, and direct nomination. At Cleveland Mayor Tom Johnson, who also was a wealthy manufacturer converted by Henry George, undertook to fight for public ownership of utilities. He helped Mayor Dunne in Chicago and Henry George in New York; and among his aides was Newton D. Baker, who secured the mayoralty two years after Johnson's 1909 defeat and saved much of the Johnson program. Meanwhile other cities obtained mayors with courage to oppose boss control in spite of opposition from pulpit, press and chambers of commerce. St. Louis had Joseph W. Folk, 1900-1904. The Ames Ring at Minneapolis was uncovered by Hovey C. Clarke as grand jury foreman in 1902. Denver's boss rule was fought by Judge Lindsey of the Children's Court. Jersey City's control by railroad and trolley interests was fought by Mark Fagan. In New York the reformer Seth Low, president of Columbia University, was elected mayor in 1901. Texas established an effective pattern in municipal efficiency by the commission form of government, which the tidal wave disaster of 1900 forced on Galveston; the commission form slowly spread thereafter. Employment of a city manager became not uncommon, to substitute business-like efficiency for glaring waste; and the largest cities forced state legislatures to allow them "home rule." A more radical departure was made in Milwaukee in 1910 with the election of Emil Seidel, the Socialist mayor.

The fight against control by utilities and bosses widened out from the circle of cities into state governments. In Oregon a private citizen, William S. U'ren, between 1891 and 1910 typified the progressives' faith in the ultimate wisdom of the electorate. He engineered adoption there of most of the progressives' political devices and although they were adopted in numerous other states, especially in the Middle and Far

West, they were popularly called the "Oregon System." They included the Australian ballot, registration of voters, initiative and referendum, direct primary, recall and corrupt practices acts. Each was supposed to fill a special function in cleansing democracy of corrupt devices. The Australian ballot ensured a secret vote, thus lessening opportunities for intimidation. Registration of voters lessened repeat and non-resident voting. The initiative and referendum permitted the electorate to initiate laws and vote upon them, thereby forcing a legislature to act. The direct primary enabled party members to state by secret ballot at the polls their preferences for nominees to offices, thus weakening control by the party machine. The recall permitted voters to oust officials from office by secret ballot, making officeholders more responsive to popular will. The corrupt practices acts restricted campaign contributions and political favoritism, thus making it harder for the old corrupt machines to maintain themselves and easier for persons outside the machine to influence affairs.

All these opportunities for participation in running political machinery were supposed to enlist citizens in perpetual watchfulness over government. If citizens were to remain continuously watchful they needed watchful governors. The most outstanding were La Follette in Wisconsin, 1900-1906, Folk in Missouri, 1905-1909, Cummins in Iowa, 1902-1908, Hughes in New York, 1906-1910, and Wilson in New Jersey, 1910-1912. The wide scattering of city and state reform movements from Oregon to New York indicates the reach of progressive influence and backing. In each state reforms became possible only after severe struggles by disinterested citizens and disappointed office-seekers, backed by a few capitalists of generous instincts and by brilliant journalists.

Essential to progressive purposes was a sympathetic press, which utility control of most newspapers put almost out of reach. For this purpose the Scripps family proved invaluable in the daily newspaper field because they then showed political independence, sympathy toward unions and liberality of view. Edward W. Scripps had been born in Illinois in 1854, the year of the birth of Joseph Fels and Tom Johnson, the year before La Follette and Debs were born. Edward, with his half-brothers James and George and his half-sister Ellen, had had the imagination to start cheap and popular evening newspapers designed for the "95 per cent" of the population. They established them in Detroit, Cleveland, St. Louis, Cincinnati and elsewhere, the first daily newspaper chain in the United States. Subsequently E. W. Scripps and M. A. McRae organized the independent gathering of news for a league of papers which led finally into the United Press news service. Their press in Cleveland supported Tom Johnson and permitted some latitude to Bob Paine in his reporting of the Wisconsin undertakings at a time when other papers were almost universally hostile. Scripps papers supported progressive presidential candidates—Roosevelt in 1912 and La Follette in 1924.

The progressive leaders owed much to the muckrakers and to personal attacks on the bosses. The bold fight of a few persons against the boss system helped to create a demand for muckraking articles and by the same token the articles helped to embolden the politicians. Exposure of dishonest advertising, filthy meat packing, impure food and drugs and corrupt insurance practices gave courage to politicians to defy boss control. The boss could be featured with tremendous effect as a devil; his name, appearance, disposition, income and all manner of personal details fed public curiosity and stiffened opposition to him. The general electorate would respond to the call to oust malefactors because they were concrete symbols, but the time had not yet come when many voters could be throughly aroused against the ideas back of the malefactors, against that worship of individual success and of laissez-faire which were jeopardizing the republic. Consequently the minority of progressives who fought against the system as such (rather than simply against bosses) could not carry reforms down deep to underlying causes. They did, however, obtain a temporary redirection of political thought and action into public welfare legislation. A more radical program came in with F. D. Roosevelt.

A special technique, extremely arduous, had to be practised by those who defied the reigning bosses. Men and women of conviction who were effective speakers and prodigal of their strength, by unremitting toil instructed local conventions and caucuses in the principles of the new democracy. They liberalized the personnel of the local, district and state conventions until they were able to force progressive planks into state platforms. At the same time they pushed the process of public education in campaign periods by taking the stump when they had but little chance of nomination or election, clinging desperately meanwhile to the party labels which held the loyalties of most voters. By this process they so spread their influence within the major parties that by the turn of the century the electorate in many states was showing a new independence of the old party managers. The results were seen in party planks, in the membership of state legislatures and in choices for governors. There was, of course, nothing unusual about adoption of liberal planks for decorative purposes. But the new legislators were often young men who had not lost their sympathy for change and were not yet firmly tied to organized business. Some were congenital progressives and others entertained a willingness to challenge the reigning machine in direct ratio to their thwarted ambition to be a part of it. Both the new politicians and the old knew that youth held the key to the fate of both parties.

This tide of progressive legislation was most concerned with the reform of elections and the protection of voters in expressing their will. There were certain questions of social and economic justice to which they gave little direct heed. These problems were more the concern of the leaders of labor.

Labor Seeks Economic Democracy

The labor movement of the early twentieth century attempted to urge the cause of social justice just as emphatically as the "progressives," but in a different way. They were working under handicaps. Most important of these was their ill repute arising from the violence of certain strikes of the 'eighties, 'nineties and the next decade.

A further disability suffered by labor was the fact that workers remained too abundant and their position too unstable, on the whole, for effective bargaining with their employers. The progress of mechanical invention repeatedly reduced the number of skilled jobs, substituting unskilled work at machinery, and when new inventions fostered new skills, the Federation had to work hard and long to organize and affiliate the latest type of skilled workmen. Nor did benefits commensurate to industrial expansion come to the unskilled, for immigration put too sharp an edge on competition for jobs.

The total of immigrants reached a new high—at least 700,000 in every year but two between 1902 and 1914, and more than a million annually in 1905-1907, 1910, 1913 and 1914. Their proportion to the entire population became greater than at any time since the 1840's. Poverty-stricken peasants of Southeast Europe, Austro-Hungarian Slavs and persecuted Russian Jews eagerly believed the optimistic tales of agents of steamship companies, land-grant railroads and labor contractors. Settling most heavily in New England and the Middle Atlantic states, by 1910 they had made the majority of the population there either foreign-born white or native whites of foreign or mixed parentage.

These non-Teutonic Europeans proved hard to assimilate. The prospect of competition with them increasingly deterred from immigration the workmen and peasants of England, Ireland and Germany, especially as broad social legislation, improved agrarian policies and industrial expansion were alleviating the situation there. Approximately one-fourth of these newest immigrants planned to return to their home-lands. Mainly segregated in their own sections in the cities, slow to intermarry with the earlier strains, they very gradually injected into the United States stock an influence making for a shorter, swarthier and more temperamental population—one representative of all Europe, rather than only of its western part.

American labor leaders agitating for restriction of immigration met a stubborn obstacle in the personal experience and national tradition of the United States as a land of opportunity for the poor and oppressed, who could be absorbed without disadvantage, a concept fostered by employers and transportation agencies. Restrictionists obtained, in statutes of 1903 and 1907, exclusion of the diseased, immoral, anarchistic and imbecile and those whose passage was paid by some corporation, association or government, but evasion was frequent. Restrictionists turned to accomplish their objectives through a literacy test, since 25 per cent of adult immigrants were illiterate, as were about half of the largest single group—the Italians. Literacy planks were placed in Republican and Democratic platforms. An Immigration Commission was obtained and it demonstrated—in 41 volumes—the illiteracy and other serious problems involved. Congress twice was persuaded to put up bars against illiterates, but Taft and Wilson (like Cleveland) tore them down with vetoes.

Absolute exclusion was obtained against a small group only, and that through the aid of the color line. Japanese were increasing from 24,000 to 72,000, 1900-1910, mostly in California; their extremely low living standards and industrious habits made them serious competitors of white labor and landowners wherever they intruded. An Asiatic Exclusion League, formed under labor auspices in 1905, fomented propaganda which led the San Francisco School Board to segregate some ninety-eight Japanese children in a separate school. The circle of agitation widened into diplomatic interchanges until the "gentleman's agreement" of 1907 between Secretary of War Elihu Root and Ambassador Takahira; Japan agreed not to issue passports to skilled and unskilled laborers wishing to go to the United States, if only she would not be insulted by legislation aimed at her nationals. Still the California legislature showed truculence, until federal laws of 1913 and 1920 barred Japanese from owning or leasing agricultural or other real property.

Under these circumstances labor's fight for social justice brought mixed results. Certain spectacular developments became the focus of public attention, with the efforts of the United Mine Workers Union particularly noticed. In the Pennsylvania anthracite field a mine-railroad-capitalist combine, amounting practically to a trust, controlled about two-thirds of the output and prevented recognition. The miners turned to political weapons—the United States being a republic—and staged strikes in the presidential and congressional campaigns of 1900 and 1902. This frightened Mark Hanna and Theodore Roosevelt into mediating between J. P. Morgan's capitalist group and John Mitchell (president of the United Mine Workers) with his 100,000 to 150,000 miners. The operators in 1902 expected Roosevelt to follow Cleveland's example at Pullman by sending troops to end the strike as a violation of the Sherman Anti-Trust Law; instead he threatened government operation and suggested Cleveland as head of an arbitral commission. Such devices won the miners wage increases, a nine-hour instead of a ten-hour day, abandonment of the sliding scale, and a union man to check weights. Thus much had the politico-industrial climate moderated in favor of labor between 1894 and 1902.

Still, 1902 had not brought union recognition, and the Board of Conciliation which adjusted difficulties for the next decade was unable to prevent a strike in the high-progressive campaign of 1912. Again a partial success—a four-year contract for higher pay without union recognition. During the next two years, despite the sweep of social legislation, the United Mine Workers suffered disastrous defeat; the Colorado Fuel and Iron Company, using machine guns, private troops and dynamite, broke a strike waged there on behalf of 30,000 immigrants who labored under unspeakable conditions. Arbitration proposals from President Wilson did not win acceptance. The crushing of this strike demonstrated the narrow limits of progressive influence. The Miners' Union, building up membership meanwhile, had to wait for wartime markets to bring them recognition.

Worse blows than the Colorado defeat of immigrants and semi-skilled workers were struck at organized labor in the hat and stove-making trades on the Atlantic coast, by a hostile judiciary. It specialized in invoking the anti-trust law against unions and declared injunctions against boycotts. A fourteen-year fight between the Danbury Hatters Union and the D. E. Lowe Company ended with a decision that a secondary boycott was illegal as contrary to the Sherman Law and that the members of the union were subject to a fine of $235,000. In the Buck Stove and Range case officers and members of the A. F. of L. were enjoined from listing the stove company's products in the "we don't patronize" column of their official periodical and from mentioning the dispute in print or conversation. Gompers, Mitchell and Frank Morrison, secretary of the A. F. of L., were sentenced to prison. The Supreme Court finally dismissed the action as outlawed by the statute of limitations, but the court avoided the fundamental issue of constitutional guarantees of free speech, free press and peaceable assemblage.

Such abuses were meanwhile arousing sympathy for labor among the thoughtful of the middle class who cherished liberal traditions. Among other outrages, they resented the clubbing of strikers by state police, which had been almost unknown before 1900. The Pennsylvania constabulary in particular was hateful to labor because called in regularly from other duties in time of strike to protect capital investment, and it had a reputation for cruelty toward strikers. Sympathetic liberals, of the American Association for Labor Legislation, founded in 1906, the National Consumers League, Civic Federation and Child Labor Committee variously urged state and national legislation recognizing the trade agreement and collective bargaining, while they were espousing other broader legislation more in the progressive field of action. Support from such typical progressives helped labor to persuade state legislatures and Congress to pass palliative measures and thereby kept the main body of labor from falling into the hands of extremists.

State legislatures did not always disappoint the laboring electorate; they passed laws on child labor, women's work, sweating, minimum wages, hazards and physical conditions of employment in an amount far exceeding all other periods. For a time there was some fear that the Supreme Court might interfere in these efforts, notably after the decision of the Lockner case in 1905. New York had enacted a law for a sixty-hour week in the baking business to safeguard the workers' health. This the Supreme Court declared unconstitutional on the ground that it interfered with the "right of contract between the employer and employees, concerning the number of hours in which the latter may labor in the bakery." However, this view of the court was contrary to the new spirit of the day, and three years later an Oregon statute regulating women's hours was upheld, as was a California eight-hour law in 1915.

In workmen's compensation the United States was the last great power to accept the principle that the industry rather than the individual was responsible for occupational accidents, of which this country had an exceptional number. The state laws in this field were soon declared unconstitutional; but more carefully framed measures and constitutional amendments by 1921 had placed in effect, in all but six states and the District of Columbia, employers' liability acts. The imperfections of the laws and court decisions adverse to them could not end the effort to enact them. There ensued action in such fields as old age and mothers' pensions, sick and unemployment insurance and labor exchanges, where again America was extremely slow to follow Europe's example.

In the federal field labor gained also. The Commissioner of Labor, who since 1888 had headed an independent department without cabinet rank, was in 1903 made head of a bureau in the newly created Department of Commerce and Labor. A separate Department of Labor was set up in 1913 as a cabinet unit, with a most important Bureau of Labor Statistics in it. Federal employees obtained a compensation act in 1908 and an eight-hour day was set for workers on government contracts in 1912. Most important was labor's gain by the Clayton Act of 1914. This measure exempted unions—as well as farm groups—from prosecution under the Anti-Trust laws. It limited use of injunctions in labor disputes, prescribed jury trial in most contempt cases and declared strikes, picketing, boycotts, peaceable assemblage and the collection of strike benefits as not in violation of federal law. Unluckily for labor, this so-called "Magna Charta" of trade unionism did not long deter justices in issuing injunctions, as will be seen later. Meanwhile the war brought the La Follette law of 1915 for decent working conditions for seamen and a year later the Adamson eight-hour law for railroad workers.

Congress gathered momentum on child labor slowly. Senator Albert J. Beveridge of Indiana in 1906 urged in vain a constitutional amendment restricting it. Congress in 1907 appropriated $150,000 for an investigation and report and 1912 saw a Children's Bureau set up in the Department of Commerce and Labor. Finally in 1916 an act went through Congress barring the products of child labor from interstate commerce. This measure of course would be tested in the courts, but no decision was delivered prior to the entrance of the United States into the First World War.

The fact was that the public interest lay less in economic than in political reforms. In the latter the state winnings of the progressives pointed to possible success in the national field. First came victories in national political platforms, when the major parties were forced to take on planks which only the minor parties previously had dared to endorse. These planks were of three main types—first, those which gave the voter a more direct influence in the choice of candidates and the subject matter of legislation by means of direct primaries, direct election of senators, the recall, and the initiative and referendum; second, those which challenged that control over legislation which long had been exercised by the manufacturing and transportation lobbies; third, those aiming at more equable taxation.

Next came enactment of legislation more or less in fulfilment of the planks. This process continued through the administrations of Theodore Roosevelt, Taft and Wilson. The resulting body of welfare legislation fell short, it is true, of destroying the foundations of special privilege erected on the ruins of the Civil War. For such a purpose there was not sufficient resentment against dominance by wealth, not enough starving and unhappy people. These were years of economic and social unrest, but also years of a rising price level which confounded the more radical reformers with prosperity and optimism. Nevertheless, in spite of these limits, the progressive legislation had long-range repercussions reaching far forward into the present. Those laws, and the dramatic political struggles inseparable from them, marked a significant step in national development. Americans were striving to implement their faith in democracy.

CHAPTER XXXIII

NATIONAL REFORM

The progressive era in national politics was introduced by the accidental accession of Theodore Roosevelt to the presidency in 1901. The new chief executive had risen as a liberal to be governor of New York and vice-president under the second McKinley administration. When his chief was assassinated he found himself in the White House at a time when reform was gathering momentum.

Trust-Busting

Theodore Roosevelt's most spectacular activity concerned his denunciation of trusts and monopolies. They were very popular targets. Trusts ramified through all important aspects of life in the republic; they could be approached from such divers angles as the railroads, labor, Wall Street, the courts and food manufacture. In some of these could not the president lead, and would not others follow?

The time was crucial, for by the end of 1903 that large-scale organization which has been traced in detail earlier was reaching a peak, with the process of capital investment moving at unprecedented pace. That process was familiar: profits made in fortunate concerns had been reinvested in additional businesses, with each successive depression throwing more weak concerns into the hands of men with capital to spare, who created more capital by issuing watered stock on their mergers. They, in the perpetual search for places to invest, accumulated funds, continually broadened the reach of their influence, continually became directors on more boards, meeting thereon their fellow financiers with whom they formed "interlocking directorates" which brought unified control. Out from industry into other fields such as transportation and insurance went the excess funds seeking investment, until consolidated capital held control of every major facility of modern life.

The extent of the control is illustrated in industrial statistics. By the end of 1903 approximately 5,300 plants with capitalization above 7 billions had been merged into 318 "greater" or "lesser" trusts. Through the Progressive Era consolidations continued (although at reduced speed after 1903) until by 1914 over three-fourths of the wage-workers were employed by less than one-eighth of the existing industrial establishments, which in turn produced in value over four-fifths of the products. Between 1890 and 1913 national wealth had increased 188 per cent, the aggregate income of wage-earners in the basic industries of manufacturing, mining and transportation had risen 95 per cent and the population to be fed, clothed and sheltered had increased approximately 50 per cent.

Some statisticians asserted that 80 per cent of the population lived a marginal existence, while the wealth was held by the remaining 20 per cent; others reported a much wider gap. In fact, as has been noted, wealth distribution was broader in the United States than anywhere else then or earlier; but this did not mean content. The great mass of Americans, 1900-1914, were in the peculiar position of a people whose total wealth was increasing and whose consumer tastes were rising, while their purchasing power—their real wages—suffered a slight fall. The evidence of prosperity near them encouraged the demand for further sharing of it.

Any plan to curb consolidation had to face the fact that the courts interpreted regulatory laws narrowly, and the final arbiter, the Supreme Court, repeatedly declared them unconstitutional. Federal regulation was vitiated whenever the Supreme Court ruled that the individual states, not Congress, had jurisdiction. State regulation was vitiated when a state attempted to coerce a corporation operating in many states. This left a twilight zone in which corporations could operate without restriction. Liberal legislation frequently had to depend for its endorsement upon whether the Court would admit that an act came under the "general welfare" clause of the Constitution, which was a part of Section 8 of Article I.

The Court had fully accepted the doctrine that corporations were "persons" entitled to protection under the 14th Amendment and had undertaken to review acts of state and federal bodies to determine whether corporations were being deprived of property without "due process of law." While this use of the doctrine effectively weakened state efforts at regulation of big business, it had most far-reaching influence in the fields of federal regulation essayed under the Interstate Commerce Law of 1887 and the Anti-Trust Law of 1890. Efforts to put teeth in the Anti-Trust Act lapsed in 1895 with the Knight case; here the Court declared that a manufacturing monopoly was not prohibited under the law, on the ground that production and manufacture are not a part of interstate commerce, to which congressional authority is limited.

Regulation of railroad rates by the Interstate Commerce Commission also was made practically impossible; the Court repeatedly insisted that "due process" requires provision for judicial review and that rates must be high enough to yield "a fair return" on a fair valuation of property. A method for determining a rate and valuation fair both to the public and the companies had thus far eluded the justices. In the Maximum Freight Rate case of 1896 and the Alabama Midland case they had destroyed any semblance of power the federal commission might have exercised. The state commissions and legislatures were not better sustained. In the Minnesota Rate case of 1889 the Court had set side as "unfair" a rate set for the Chicago, Milwaukee and St. Paul by that state's railroad commission; by 1897 it had established its willingness to thrust aside rates set by state legislatures. It became indubitably clear that the Supreme Court, a conservative body, was willing to pass judgment on any state or federal regulatory action.

Roosevelt chose the railroads as his springboard for attack upon monopoly. At this moment they were affording a prime illustration of the workings of the "money trust." A Northern Securities Company, a holding corporation, was formed in 1901 by E. H. Harriman, J. P. Morgan and Jacob Schiff to integrate the lines—the Northern Pacific, Great Northern and Chicago, Burlington and Quincy—serving the area between Lake Michigan and Puget Sound; the management might even synchronize with that of the Union Pacific and Southern Pacific. To these plans James J. Hill, builder of the Great Northern and reorganizer of the Northern Pacific, raised such stout resistance that the stock was briefly pushed to $1,000 a share and the stock market suffered a disturbance which would have been worse if there had not been abundant crops and a good foreign market for them. The struggle was the more notorious because the securities market during the early 1900's was booming, well-nigh as reckless and unscrupulous as in the Grant era. Bold stock swindling, railroad wrecking, security inflation and legislative corruption prevailed. Into this scene in March of 1902 Roosevelt shot a government suit for the dissolution of the Northern Securities Company!

The suit pended through the congressional campaign of that year, with Roosevelt employing a speaking tour in attacks on trusts and with the issue sharply pointed by the struggle between the striking coal miners and the railroad-mine operators. The strike overshadowed the tariff issue raised in the Middle West, and the settlement negotiated by Roosevelt helped to keep the Republicans in control of Congress, although their majority was reduced.

As the Northern Securities suit languished, Congress passed the Expedition Act of 11 February 1903 to grease the ways for government suits under the Interstate Commerce and Anti-Trust Acts. This enabled the Court to report in March 1904, well before the presidential campaign. The Court decided, 5 to 4, that the Northern Securities Corporation was a "combination in restraint of trade" and must be dissolved. This outcome was hailed as indicating that prosecutions under the Anti-Trust Act might again prove successful. Little notice was taken of the fact that the dissolution order was so worded as to leave intact the bond issue floated against the Great Northern and Northern Pacific, and that this enabled Hill to squeeze Harriman out of the control of the latter. Other railroads, including the New Haven and Union Pacific, also were ordered by the Court to relinquish some of their holdings. Such orders, however, were easy to nullify; by interlocking directorates and management agreements the trusts freed themselves from the pains of dissolution. Roosevelt later came to recognize their immunity; he turned from dissolution to regulation, declaring "good" trusts should be let alone, "bad" ones prosecuted.

Meanwhile the Old Guard, all within two weeks of that historic February, had been forced to allow the taking of three other steps designed to help restrict monopoly: the Commerce and Labor Act of 14 February, a special appropriation of 25 February and the Elkins law of 19 February. The first, as already noted, added a ninth member to Roosevelt's official family—a secretary of commerce and labor—in which place Roosevelt installed his secretary and warm personal admirer, George B. Cortelyou. Establishment of this new executive department was fought by the conservatives because it included a Bureau of Corporations designed to investigate diligently "the organization, conduct and management of corporations." The appropriation item allowed $500,000 for improved enforcement of the Interstate Commerce and Anti-Trust laws.

The Elkins Act had a comparatively easy passage because it aimed to eliminate rebating, an abuse which victimized the management as well as the shippers. This practice, contrary to the spirit of the Interstate Commerce Act, had been perpetuated by the violent competition between both railroads and shippers. The act forbade variation from published rates and the receiving and giving of rebates. Guilty corporations and their agents were both declared punishable, with fines from $1,000 to $20,000. Enforcement was facilitated by clauses permitting injunction proceedings to restrain violations and declaring variations from published tariff rates to be *prima facie* evidence of violations. Conviction was made easier by removal of the penalty of imprisonment.

That year the anti-monopoly issue received further impetus from a stock market panic. Consolidation was overreaching itself, with daily sales of securities on the exchange declining from 4 million to between 2 and 3 millions. This "rich men's panic," so called, was not long felt far from Wall Street. It served somewhat to facilitate further mergers, through purchase of bankrupt properties by bigger capitalists, and to afford them opportunity to charge Roosevelt with evil designs on legitimate business. The rate of consolidation slowed down thenceforward, probably more affected by overspeculation and the overissue of "indigestible" securities than by the President's fulminations against "malefactors of great wealth." After the Northern Securities decision the following March, he was firmly established in the public mind as a "trust-buster." During his administration a total of 16 civil and 18 criminal suits were instituted to enforce the Sherman law; and those suits were much better publicized than the fact that consolidation continued.

The food trust was another "person" prominent in the preëlection picture of 1904. The rising cost of living and the tireless activities of Dr. H. W. Wiley, chief chemist of the Department of Agriculture and most implacable foe of adulteration, had been drawing attention to price and quality in food manufacture. A Wiley "poison squad" of twelve men working in 1902 definitely proved conscienceless adulteration of food and drugs, and the next year a bill was pressed in Congress to impose fine and imprisonment upon every one who offered for sale adulterated canned goods. The bill was killed in the Senate by the united efforts of the distillers' lobby, food manufacturers and critics who deplored placing the onus on the corner grocer; but during the campaign excitements of 1904 the new commissioner of corporations busily investigated food from the angle of price and sued a branch of the "beef trust." He charged that 60 per cent of the dealers in fresh meat had agreed not to compete with each other in the live-stock markets, a policy which lowered farmers' incomes; that they had agreed to raise prices by restricting output, which raised consumers' expenses; that they kept a blacklist, which lowered wages through discouragement of union organization; and that they got railroad rebates, which infuriated all other shippers. The Supreme Court, following the election returns, in January 1905 ordered dissolution of the trust.

Controlling the Railroads

Despite the hostility of the conservatives Roosevelt had no difficulty in securing renomination and reëlection in 1904. He had caught the popular imagination and in company with other progressives achieved notable success. In Wisconsin the Republican La Follette won reëlection as governor, a liberal majority in both houses and election (to succeed the conservative Senator Quarles) as Spooner's colleague in the United States Senate; he postponed his departure for Washington through 1905, while he and his followers expanded their state program and the Wisconsin movement won national attention. In four other states, which gave their electoral votes to the "trust-busting" Republican president, Democratic governors were elected, and for reasons sufficient. Missouri chose Joseph W. Folk for his anti-boodle record; Massachusetts, William L. Douglas for his reciprocity, anti-trust platform; Colorado,

Alva Adams in resentment against the anti-labor policy of his predecessor; Minnesota, John A. Johnson, who had risen from abject poverty.

Roosevelt took his victory as a mandate for action; he had before him four years and three months in which to get legislation on the statute books. None knew better the power of the Old Guard to block congressional machinery when action was distasteful, but he counted upon the majority of the rank and file of newly elected members to feel something of what he felt—the rising popular demand for economic and social legislation. With their help he could force the standpatters to yield enough ground to permit moderate, not drastic legislation.

This counsel of compromise for immediate results ill suited the governor of Wisconsin, who did not feel pressed to accept halfway legislation. He was only about to commence his national career and believed that by unremitting persistence progressives ultimately (after temporary defeat) could force Congress to take the "full step" for effective legislation. This difference in their attitude toward time cut a chasm between the governor-senator and president, making for mutual distrust between these two outstanding leaders, with fateful results to their party.

The incoming Congress adopted the Roosevelt doctrine. They convened 4 December 1905, and before they had to face the 1906 campaign they passed anti-monopoly legislation in such popular important fields as transportation and foodstuffs.

Lawmaking on railroads was first in interest and importance because they were completely identified with the bad as well as the good developments in American economic life. Just as their central position in national economy had kept them the object of capitalistic rivalries, the victim of manipulation and the symbol of special privilege, so they had remained acutely sensitive to the ebbs and flows of prosperity and politics. The phenomenal expansion era, in which long-distance transportation was projected far ahead of income from freight, thus raising the national wealth in real estate and other values far in advance of population growth, was closing. Consolidation, however, continued very rapidly, reaching the point in 1906 where approximately 77 per cent of total mileage was divided among seventeen systems. Of these the most influential were the five interlocked in the Morgan, Vanderbilt, Hill, Gould and Pennsylvania groups.

The issue was not simple, for the public was accessory to railroad sinning. On the one hand, violent fluctuations in personality of railroad control, in prices of rail securities and in rates for freight and passengers had aroused shippers and the using public over the means by which a few great railroad fortunes had been amassed through speculation, gross mismanagement, amalgamation and rate tyranny. On the other hand, most legislators were accustomed to riding on a pass, most railroads paid only minimum taxes, hectic pursuit of prosperity hurried many persons into acceptance of extortion and frequently blackmailers introduced anti-railroad legislation for the sole purpose of being paid to kill it. Thus the need for stronger railroad regulation was well known, while firmly established legislative and legal practices blocked it. This was demonstrated when the Elkins Act of 1903 was confined to rebates, leaving untouched the basic problems of rate-making, valuation and monopoly control.

The problem of giving the Interstate Commerce Commission responsibility and power over rates was foremost. So complicated were the factors affecting rates, with and without justification, that a fair understanding of regulation eluded most of the electorate who demanded it and most of the legislators who were forced to acknowledge the demand. Fragmentary and fumbling approaches to the problem therefore were usual, with the tactical advantage on the side of the railroads' lawyer lobbyists. State railroad commissions had been numerous for twenty years. Their existence in Illinois and Iowa had brought somewhat lowered schedules. Minnesota and Wisconsin investigated and uncovered railroad earnings heretofore hidden from tax assessors, and 1906-1907 was notable for the number of railroad and tax laws passed in the Middle West and South. Continued state activity inspired national action, and La Follette came to the Senate 1 January 1906 eager for physical valuation as a nation-wide basis for rates. Although he was inclined to overlook other factors affecting rates, this valuation principle was the closest approximation to rate reality of that period.

After a bitter struggle, in which the railroad lobby killed the valuation proposition, Congress enacted a compromise—the so-called "Hepburn" railroad law of 1906. It did not give the Interstate Commerce Commission the power to set original rates. It could merely reduce those it found unreasonable after complaint by shippers; furthermore orders and schedules set by the Commission could be suspended pending judicial review, and court sympathy for railroad contentions had been habitual. The act, nevertheless, applied enough principles of social control in the vitally important field of transportation to bolster American democracy against advancing plutocracy.

Its great influence and significance as the outstanding economic legislation of the Roosevelt administration require a full listing of its provisions. It brought within the scope of Commission regulations express, sleeping-car, pipe-line, bridge, ferry and terminal companies and transportation which was part rail and part water. It gave the commission, now enlarged from five to seven to handle the load, power to standardize accounting procedure—vital for taxation and rate-making. It placed the burden of proof upon the carrier rather than the

Commission, thus lessening court interference. It declared illegal those hoary devices for securing special favors—midnight tariffs and passes for non-employees. It attempted to push transportation companies out of mining and other businesses by forbidding carriers to transport commodities they produced (except timber) unless needed for the operation of the carrier; but the court practically nullified the commodity clause by declaring that it required railroad companies merely to transfer their coal stock to separately organized corporations.

In spite of the limitations of the Hepburn Act, shippers gave abundant proof of their faith in it. They had filed less than 900 former complaints in the two decades since 1887, but now proceeded to file 1,500 within the next two years. Within five years the Commission had halved approximately 194,000 of the rates existing in 1906, and the Supreme Court had upheld the constitutionality of the anti-rebating and commodity clauses and had recognized the right of Congress to lay down operating principles for the Commission. The carriers had to prove confiscation "beyond any just or reasonable doubt" to get relief from the courts, and a decision of 1913 reaffirmed with finality the right of the Commission both to regulate rates and to intervene in internal administration of railway companies.

While the Interstate Commerce Commission held the center of the stage, Congress passed two laws on behalf of organized railroad workers. Their Erdman Act of 1898 had fallen afoul of the Supreme Court for not specifying interstate employees. The interest in labor legislation was general, as shown by the large number of state measures to regulate and improve employment conditions for men, women and children. Maryland in 1902 had started experimenting with employers' liability (or workmen's compensation as it often is termed), and constitutional amendments and improvements in drafting gradually ushered such laws past the courts, in fact, between 1911 and 1921, forty-two states had them. Meanwhile, in 1906 Congress passed an interstate liability act applicable to common carriers, and in 1908 met court criticism of it by a better drafted law. Also, in 1907 Congress set standards of safety and hours for common carriers. The current attitudes toward monopolistic railroad practices were reflected in the action of Judge Kenesaw Mountain Landis, who in April following fined the Standard Oil Company of New Jersey $29,240,000 for getting rebates from the Chicago and Alton Railroad, a sentence reversed on appeal.

Purifying Food and Finance

Scarcely less interesting to the commonalty than railroads, was purity in foods and drugs; but here advance was laggard. The earlier agitation was reinforced, 1904-1906, by the popular magazines. *The Ladies*

Home Journal and *Collier's Weekly* exposed patent medicine frauds, and *Everybody's* published a carefully documented series of articles by Russell on the food preparation practices of Armour, Swift and others, under the title "The Greatest Trust in the World." Upton Sinclair followed early in 1906 with his dramatic novel of the Chicago Stockyards, *The Jungle*. Forthwith, Roosevelt detailed James B. Reynolds and Charles P. Neill to investigate meat packing, while Senator Beveridge introduced a bill for effective inspection of packing houses. Loathsome disclosures made by partial publication of the Neill-Reynolds report strengthened the hands of the department chemists, physicians, humanitarians and progressives who were pushing a pure food and drug bill.

The manufacturers' lobby undertook to counter the movement. The result was a law which was supposed to prevent manufacture, sale or transportation of adulterated, misbranded or poisonous foods, drugs and liquors; but its provisions were left weak. Also it purported to leave a wide field of discretionary policy to the Bureau of Chemistry of the Department of Agriculture, but the President and the courts tended to limit the chemists' activity. A 1911 amendment, prohibiting the use of misleading labels, failed of great effect because the public buys attractive-looking goods, in spite of adulterated contents, almost as quickly as they buy falsely labeled articles. Deceptive advertising which does the worst damage, was left to flourish. The meat provisions of the Department of Agriculture Appropriation bill better met their object; they extended inspection beyond the class of export products, specified since 1891, to cover meat in interstate commerce.

Aggressive action relating to monopoly in food received further endorsement in 1907, by disclosure of the fact that the American Sugar Refining Company, which virtually controlled the nation's sugar supply, had been cheating the federal treasury by wholesale tampering with the scales which weighed their imported raw sugar. They could not convincingly deny their guilt when the government proved able to recover some $4,000,000 in damages and to secure conviction of several officials and employees as criminals. Such disclosures ensured further anti-trust suits.

The money trust also took the limelight in this exciting 1907, with a "silent" panic in March and a "bankers' " or "Wall Street" panic in October. Almost all the railroads, shipping lines and public utilities bore the scars of the titanic rivalries which had left burdens of watered stock, wasteful construction and weak morale. Speculation again overreached itself. The October panic was touched off when Wall Street speculation in copper brought revelations discreditable to the president and directors of the Mercantile National Bank, which in turn exposed weakness in interlocking directorates of the system. Country banks, alarmed, undertook to withdraw reserves from city institutions and these in turn from their correspondents in New York. There thirteen banking institutions closed and the stringency sent a number of manipulated railroads into receiverships. The government stepped into the breach between 29 and 31 October with emergency deposits of $36,000,000, and the clearing house issued temporary certificates. But speculators responsible for the panic ultimately were shown to have been guilty of criminal practices; some suffered prison sentences as well as loss of wealth. Workers were penalized with depressed wages, unemployment and suffering.

The more astute financiers used the panic to climb to higher eminence, with U. S. Steel profiting most. J. P. Morgan visited Roosevelt to state that the best way to stabilize the money-market would be to assure the steel corporation of immunity from anti-trust suit, if it should absorb its only important surviving competitor, the Tennessee Coal and Iron Company. The President, disturbed by a charge that he was blamable for the stringency, gave tacit consent. Thus depression again spurred consolidation.

The 1907 stringency had one excellent effect, for it attracted attention to weaknesses in the currency and banking system, pointing the way to monetary reform. By now the bankers as well as poor folk were interested in the volume of the currency, although their points of view never jibe.

Bankers and businessmen became leading advocates of currency expansion in the progressive era, for then large crops, heavy exports and business activity convinced them that the money supply was inadequate for full profit-taking. The system devised when the government was floating heavy issues of wartime bonds seemed too rigid for peacetime business expanding under rising prices. Farmers and rural businessmen also complained. Farming now required larger capital investment and credit facilities; lack of funds inconvenienced movement of fall crops and the hinterland had to wait impatiently upon the East for credits. The various classes clamoring for greater currency elasticity and fluidity of reserves scarcely reflected that activity might be too great or that the real lack might be a central bank, holding larger reserves.

The panics of 1907 upset business enough to alarm conservatives, and their influence expedited the passage of stop-gap legislation, the Aldrich-Vreeland Act of June, 1908. This measure aimed to provide currency elasticity in emergency. It empowered national banks to issue notes upon bonds of approved states, counties and municipalities—these bonds being stock-in-trade of eastern banks—and upon four-months' commercial paper—heavily held by western institutions. The notes were to be severely limited and taxed to confine them to emergency use.

Also the act provided for a National Monetary Commission to investigate and report a scheme of reform.

The debate on this measure demonstrated a rise in Middle West influence in two particulars. The section won some recognition of its special banking needs, as indicated, and its outstanding progressive, La Follette, so behaved as to hasten the launching of the outstanding conservative, Aldrich, upon immediate consideration of monetary reform. La Follette prepared a detailed, factual statement on consolidated railroad control, thereby forcing the withdrawal of an Aldrich proposal for including railroad bonds among the securities usable for emergency note issue. The statement increased his ultimate following, although he won only two supporters for his futile filibuster against this bill. Furthermore, he contended that the measure was designed to prevent basic overhauling of the banking system—a contention which challenged Senator Aldrich, who was already greatly concerned over the problem. When the National Monetary Commission was stipulated, Aldrich took the chairmanship himself and began, personally, an exhaustive survey of banking practice and theory at home and abroad.

The eight years from 1901 to 1909 saw the tide of reform overflow from the localities on to the national scene. The insurgents in Congress and President Theodore Roosevelt had made the perfection of the democratic process a political "must."

CHAPTER XXXIV

COMING OF THE PROGRESSIVE PARTY

When Roosevelt was reëlected in 1904 he had publicly and hastily disclaimed any idea of running again and in 1908 undertook to choose his successor. So great was his hold on the popular imagination that the Republican machine had to accord him this privilege. His final choice was his secretary of war, William Howard Taft of Ohio, a progressive associate. In the election of 1908 Taft had no difficulty in defeating William J. Bryan, for a third time candidate of the Democrats. On Taft's inauguration day Roosevelt departed on a hunting trip to darkest Africa.

Taft's Achievements

Taft settled down to carry on Roosevelt's policies, with a Congress in which the progressive group had been strengthened by new recruits. Promptly they enacted further measures embodying progressive principles; they concerned transportation, the trusts, express companies, banks and political practices.

Government regulation of transportation was strengthened by the Mann-Elkins Act of 1910; shippers and courts had treated the Hepburn law with considerable respect, but its limitations had kept the issue alive. The 1910 law enlarged the Commission's jurisdiction to embrace telegraph, telephone, cable and wireless companies, empowered it to suspend a new schedule ten months, pending examination of its reasonableness, eliminated obscure language of the 1887 act on long and short hauls and set up a special Commerce Court to hear appeals against Commission rulings. However, the Court seemed too sympathetic to corporations; after one justice was impeached it was abolished in 1912 by the same Congress which empowered the Interstate Commerce Commission to study the physical valuation of railroads with the ultimate view of basing rates thereon. Meanwhile the Commerce and Labor Department was divided into two, and safety appliances on railroads received further attention.

In anti-trust suits the Taft administration doubled the number brought by its predecessor. Also the President proposed establishment of a federal Corporation Commission to license and supervise interstate corporations, and legislation to end both stockwatering and the creation of holding companies. The United States Circuit Court of

Appeals in 1907 had set aside as confiscatory the $29,240,000 fine against the Standard Oil Company of Indiana; in 1911 court decisions ordered dissolution of the unpopular Standard Oil and American Tobacco corporations, but here an *obiter dictum* was issued declaring that a "rule of reason" required that the anti-trust law should be applied only to *unreasonable* restraint of trade.

PRESIDENT ROOSEVELT AND HIS HEIR,
PRESIDENT TAFT

(Courtesy of Harris and Ewing and Roosevelt House.)

Furious objections from the lobbies of the banks and express companies could not prevent legislation putting the government post office in the banking and parcel-carrying business. The postal-savings law of 1910 was designed to encourage poor people to save and to assure them of safety from bank failures. The bank lobby succeeded in setting the interest at 2 per cent on a full year's deposits—a return so low as to discourage deposits during boom years of high interest. In times of depression and low bank rates, however, small investors flocked to the post office, further attracted by the privilege of exchanging their postal savings certificates for small, tax-exempt, postal savings bonds bearing interest at 2½ per cent. Bankers also grew to like the system after the government came to deposit some of the postal savings funds in the banks. With this law, as with the Federal Reserve Act later, bankers as a class won comparatively favorable terms from the progressive movement. The express companies for, lo, these many years had forestalled legislation by transporting free many a lawmaker's goods and even live stock; but the proven success of Europe's parcel post brought a law for such a system here in 1913. The innovation proved so useful for domestic and business purposes, especially for mail-order retailing to rural people, that it soon had wide support sufficient to prevent repeal.

The Progressive Era was one which developed acute interest in expenditures for political and public purposes. Laws of 1910 and 1911 limited the funds a candidate for the House and Senate might spend and required publication of all receipts and expenditures before and after primaries and elections.[1] Congress in 1912 proposed the 17th Amendment, stipulating that senators be elected by popular vote instead of by state legislatures; it was ratified by sufficient states to make it law in 1913. Within his official family Taft encouraged efforts toward governmental efficiency. His appointment of an economy and efficiency commission to investigate waste in administrative departments was one of the first steps toward a federal budget.

Republican Schism

While the long view of history perceives that the Taft administration made important contributions to progress, the contemporary view saw him as a reactionary because he did not accommodate his party to the progressive urge. Perhaps no Republican president could have made a political success under the conditions of 1909-1913. Certainly Taft lacked appropriate equipment for this emergency. His best traits were his unclouded integrity, broad sympathies, excellent judicial mind and great administrative talent. His worst traits were vacillation, irritation, inability to lead and political ineptitude. Unlike Roosevelt, he interpreted the Constitution narrowly, believing the president and Congress could exercise only the powers expressly granted them; for more, amendments must be made. That process, however, seemed too slow in this period of impatience, and the rush of events left Taft lagging behind, while the battle front was occupied by conservatives and progressives of his party who were past masters at political warfare.

[1] The Supreme Court in 1921 declared the provision unconstitutional as applied to senatorial primary expenditures, in Newberry *v.* U.S.

His deplorable predicament was best summarized in his own words: "Politics makes me sick."

President Taft, who never had been elected to an office in the usual sense, since the many he held prior to his presidency were all by appointment and Roosevelt's endorsement in 1908 amounted almost to the same thing, may not have realized that the tariff was political dynamite. He did know that the times demanded a revision of the tariff not attempted since 1897 and that his party had made rather ambiguous promises to revise it during his campaign for election, promises important in the Midwest. At any rate he was not a timid man and did not shrink from conflict. He pressed the Committee on Ways and Means of the outgoing Congress to begin preparation of new schedules immediately, and when Congress met 15 March 1909, in special session at his call, the House version of the tariff was almost ready to be introduced. Twelve insurgent Republican congressmen, for their part, were quite ready to use the tariff issue and Democratic aid to unseat Speaker Cannon. This proved unsuccessful because eastern Democrats were scarcely less conservative than the Republican Old Guard and because Taft (as Roosevelt had cautioned him) saw that if he aided the hybrid group he would destroy all chance of fulfilment of his administration's program by the Republican majority. Therefore Cannon again was elected Speaker and Chairman Payne of the Committee on Ways and Means received the commission to see the tariff bill through the House. The House bill carried an inheritance tax advocated by Taft, and the rates were a revision downward, because the Chairman and the House both fought jokers and secret increases and the progressive contingent was active. The job was completed after three weeks of "debate" because every one knew that the real political battle over the tariff would be fought in the Senate.

There the progressives had been scheming to discredit the work of the Senate Finance Committee, which remained in conservative control under the chairmanship of Senator Aldrich. The La Follettes were trying to weld House and Senate progressives into a closer personal and political understanding. Also, in 1909 their weekly organ, *La Follette's Magazine,* was established with talented contributors. The deep personal resentment which senators felt toward La Follette, because he read Senate roll-calls on the stump, required that other progressives should play the more conspicuous part; in fact he habitually pushed them forward, realizing that his purposes could be accomplished only through careful teamwork. This fed their egos and scarcely diminished his influence upon legislation.

The tariff bill, as it reached the Senate from the Finance Committee, had become a capital example of logrolling. Its atrocities (which went further than Aldrich himself preferred) were the perfection of political practices long hallowed by use among senators of both parties. Certain increases in the cotton, woolen, silk, rubber and some other schedules particularly showed how special interests were entrenched behind the tariff. These increases played into the hands of the insurgent senators, who apportioned them among themselves for denunciation; each at night amassed data on his assignment to expose a schedule the next day on the Senate floor. The evil social implications of exorbitant rates were aired thoroughly over the nation by the various devices of the insurgents, by some Democrats and by such magazine writers as Ida Tarbell and David Graham Phillips, who wrote human interest stories on the schedules. The insurgents won much popularity in home districts.

Outside applause, however, did not break the hold of protection lobbyists upon senators of both parties and therefore the Payne-Aldrich tariff of 1909 in its final form showed that the insurgents had introduced no essential change into the United States tariff system, although they had attached a bad odor to the extreme protectionists. The obnoxious schedules withstood attack in the main; the reductions were mostly on unimportant items and the act expressly repealed all reciprocity arrangements. Yet the President and the insurgents had accomplished something. Taft intervened little until Senate and House conferees appeared in deadlock, when he succeeded in enlarging the free list to include hides; also he welcomed establishment of a Tariff Commission, the first attempt at scientific investigation of rates, and the act included it. The insurgents fenced the extreme protectionists into a defensive position, so that the act also contained a corporation tax, an income tax amendment and a few reductions important enough to lower the average below the Dingley rates. The income tax was conceived as a levy upon wealth and secured such endorsement that it was proclaimed as the 16th Amendment to the Constitution in 1913. On the whole, the most important economic effect of the progressive tariff fight was that at this point in American history it stopped the upward tide.

When Congress adjourned, 5 August, after a hot, exhausting and bitter session, the insurgents were free to go up and down the countryside pointing out that this tariff was a gross and inequitable assumption of special privilege by entrenched interests. They convinced the Middle Border that Taft's administration was at the service of Cannon, Aldrich and all their cohorts. Against their outcry it was of no avail that the *Outlook,* with which Roosevelt was to be connected, pronounced the Payne-Aldrich law "by far the most enlightened protectionist measure ever enacted," nor for Roosevelt to tell *Outlook* readers that it was better than Dingley's. It was the height of political folly for President Taft to tell an audience at Winona, Minnesota, that this tariff was on the whole the best the country ever had had. The President did improve it to the extent that he declined to superimpose 25 per cent retaliatory, maximum rates, which it put in his control; but that could not metamorphose the work of the Senate into a law in tune with the highly vocal sentiment of that moment.

The tariff mistake raised only half the din, for the Ballinger-Pinchot controversy raged at the same time. It grew out of the fact that water-power sites in Montana and Wyoming withdrawn from sale by Roosevelt and Pinchot were quickly reopened by Taft and Ballinger. The latter two, unlike the former, had legal scruples and wished to wait for specific, enabling legislation; also Ballinger hailed from Washington, and the West was none too enthusiastic about postponing state development. The action of the Secretary of the Interior and Taft fanned the flames of animosity and rivalry for prestige which had burned between the Interior and Agriculture departments ever since Roosevelt took the administration of the forest reserves away from the Interior and gave it to Agriculture. Pinchot, the crusader, still chief forester in the Agriculture Department, became apprehensive for his beloved conservation program. He publicly drew attention to the fact that the power trust was seizing water power and hinted that Ballinger was implicated.

Into this breach jumped Louis R. Glavis, investigator for the Department of the Interior, and widened it. He had been examining claims made by a Cunningham corporation to valuable Alaskan coal lands, and Ballinger had withdrawn him from the task. Guggenheim and Morgan interests were operating in the territory. Glavis now announced that their claims were fraudulent and that the group pressing them were personal friends of Ballinger, their former counsel. Pinchot, ignoring the rule that departmental subordinates must not take up issues with congressmen over the heads of their superiors, wrote Senator Dolliver a hot letter endorsing Glavis. Taft, as chief executive, upheld Ballinger, dismissed Glavis and also (most unwillingly) Roosevelt's friend, Pinchot.

In a Congress in the process of disruption over the tariff, the Ballinger-Pinchot controversy proved a high explosive. As conservation cut deeply across the system of special privilege, it ceased to be merely a symbol of prudent land use, became a symbol of progressive principles in general and widened the split in the Republican party. Although a congressional committee of investigation essayed to "exonerate" Ballinger, his intolerable position forced his resignation in March of 1911. Protection of national resources in Alaska and elsewhere became a recognized test of honest administration, and legislation in the field became an obligation of thoughtful lawmakers. Taft himself made three important contributions to conservation, although little credited for them. He obtained a law legalizing land withdrawals in the public interest and another act modernizing the land laws so as to separate undersurface titles from surface titles and to substitute leasing for selling of coal and other mineral lands. A Bureau of Mines was established. Also he withdrew oil lands from sale. Congress in addition enacted the Appalachian Forest Reserve law, appropriating $2,000,000 annually (until 30 June 1915) for purchase and maintenance of areas around the heads of navigable streams.

As political devices the fights over the tariff and conservation did their perfect work, fomenting personal hatreds which rankled and cut deeply, hatreds which in times of stress become the most active agents in determining the course of legislation. Those Republican progressives who invaded the bailiwicks of the Old Guard, reading the record of their votes and interpreting that record in terms of unfaithfulness to American democratic ideals, were adopting the only effective means for ousting the old leaders from their pathway. They attacked with imagination and energy. While firmly insisting upon their Republication affiliation, they asked Republicans in general to question their habitual assumption that the old party managers managed well enough. The movement, as is usual in politics, gained its greatest momentum from attacks on personalities. The electorate shows more interest in persons than in principles.

UNCLE JOE HIMSELF

An outstanding legislative symbol of the old régime, of that philosophy of government for the privileged which had flowered luxuriantly since the Civil War, was Speaker Cannon. Early in his career he had carefully created an impression of homespun common sense. However, by March 1910 Cannon was so entirely a product of his twenty-seven years of intimate connection with the direction of Republican legislation that he became the foremost target for progressive fire. He was serving his fourth speakership, with a record of coöperation with the dominant senators in their resistance to the social legislation of the 1900's. He had appointed the House committees and run the Rules Committee to suit the Old Guard. With the small group of representatives who shared with him membership on the Committee on Rules and held the chairmanships of the other significant committees, Ways and Means, and Banking and Currency, he had often bent the majority against their will and modified legislation to please special interests and party managers.

That March nearly forty members of the House, led by George W. Norris of Nebraska, determined to be cogs in the Cannon machine no longer. Taft, remembering the counsel from Roosevelt that an administration without coöperation from a party machine is wrecked, gave them no help, but they joined with the Democrats, who had not elected a Speaker of their own since 1893, to pass a Norris resolution changing the rules. It debarred the speaker from membership on the Committee on Rules and made it elective by the House. Cannon offered to resign, but the Sixty-First Congress was willing to keep Samson now that he was shorn of part of his strength. The next Congress, which had a Democratic majority and speaker, assigned to the Ways and Means Committee the duties of a Committee on Committees and made all committees elective. Thus was the speakership shorn of its two great powers and reduced to a mere presiding office.

This left an important question unanswered. Where was House leadership to rest? Who would marshal congressmen behind legislation? An answer seemed immaterial in the first flush of freedom from dictation, when party loyalties were become a fault, rather than a virtue. Altogether, it was evident that the fight over the tariff and conservation had split the Republican party wide open and was sending its conservative faction into retreat.

The Three-Cornered Campaign of 1912

If its progressive wing was going to control the Republican party, who would be the leader? La Follette? Roosevelt? Could any one reunite the party in time for a 1912 victory? The national urge for progress was not yet satisfied and no party could win which did not inspire the majority with faith in its liberal intentions. Between June 1910 and November 1912 the nation was largely occupied with the question of choosing the political instrument to carry out its social will.

In June of 1910 Theodore Roosevelt was on his way home from Africa. He had been met at the upper waters of the Nile, when his political genius was suffering from a year's inactivity, by the angry and eloquent Gifford Pinchot. After a number of weeks given to a triumphal progress through Europe, Roosevelt reached New York, where La Follette and other progressives unburdened themselves to him. Plunging into the mêlée, he won a contest for temporary chairmanship of the New York State Republican convention, endorsement of the direct primary and choice of a gubernatorial nominee; but his candidate, Henry L. Stimson, lost to the Democrat.

That summer and autumn Roosevelt took the pulse of the country from western and southern platforms; he found that it was quickened by his version of progressive principles, which he later labeled the "New Nationalism." He found the old stand-pat organization, with which he had coöperated on most essentials during his presidency, on the defensive, insurgents of his party capturing the applause and the primaries, and the Democrats making loud music with the tariff, Cannonism and the high cost of living. He himself at times endorsed and at times impugned his own anointed, President Taft, whose administration was bringing worse than no acclaim to his patron. Taft soon was engulfed in a cloud of obscurity wrapped about him by the conspicuous popularity of his predecessor.

That fall Roosevelt observed that Democrats won the governorships in many states, several in the West of course—including Ohio and Oregon—but surprisingly in Maine, Massachusetts, Connecticut, New Jersey and New York. The eastern defections were hardest to bear. In the total situation there was more than enough to wound the tender pride of the ex-president. He burned for active leadership. The membership of the United States Senate was slipping from the party which had been in titular control there since 1897. Nine state legislatures which were due to elect senators were made Democratic by the 1910 voting. The new Senate would have forty-two Democrats, and of its forty-nine Republicans, too many were insurgents to permit party harmony. Cannon had been defeated for the House; to it had been elected a Socialist and 228 Democrats, who with the insurgents among the 162 Republicans evidently would prove responsive to progressivism.

President Taft cast about clumsily for means to establish his own leadership over Republicans. Hoping to make the nation understand that he was the moderate reformer—which indeed he had become—he again laid awkward hands upon the tariff. Overestimating American interest in development of international trade, underestimating the instant resistance of sectional lobbies to measures for the general welfare, he demanded of his expiring Republican majority in Congress a measure for reciprocity with Canada. It was calculated to bring free trade in many raw materials and some food products, with reductions in tariffs on some manufactured goods. Endorsement might fairly be expected from the American Newspaper Publishers' Association because the agreement proposed duty-free newsprint; from James J. Hill's railroad interests because they would haul the goods of the expanding trade, and from Minnesota millers who wanted Canada's hard wheat to blend with American softer wheat.

Bitter opposition, however, came from manufacturers of lumber and

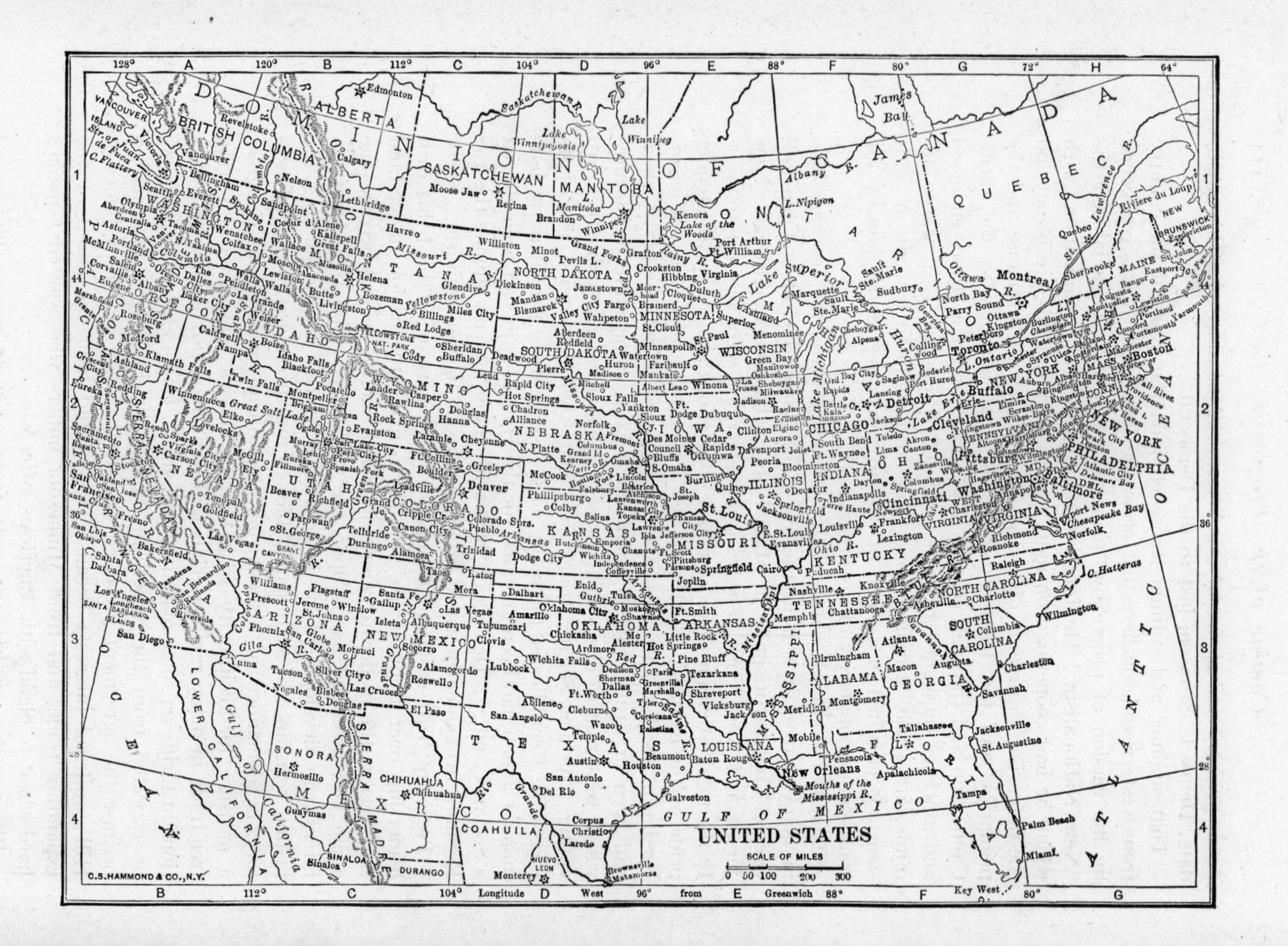
UNITED STATES
SCALE OF MILES
0 50 100 200 300
C.S.HAMMOND & CO., N.Y.
Longitude West from Greenwich
DOMINION OF CANADA
BRITISH COLUMBIA
ALBERTA
SASKATCHEWAN
MANITOBA
ONTARIO
QUEBEC
NEW BRUNSWICK
WASHINGTON
OREGON
CALIFORNIA
NEVADA
IDAHO
UTAH
ARIZONA
NEW MEXICO
COLORADO
WYOMING
NORTH DAKOTA
SOUTH DAKOTA
NEBRASKA
KANSAS
OKLAHOMA
TEXAS
MINNESOTA
IOWA
MISSOURI
ARKANSAS
LOUISIANA
WISCONSIN
ILLINOIS
INDIANA
OHIO
KENTUCKY
TENNESSEE
MISSISSIPPI
ALABAMA
GEORGIA
FLORIDA
SOUTH CAROLINA
NORTH CAROLINA
VIRGINIA
WEST VIRGINIA
NEW YORK
MAINE
LOWER CALIFORNIA
SONORA
CHIHUAHUA
COAHUILA
SINALOA
DURANGO
NUEVO LEON
MEXICO
GULF OF MEXICO
ATLANTIC OCEAN
PACIFIC OCEAN
Lake Superior
Lake Michigan
L. Huron
L. Erie
L. Ontario
Lake Winnipeg
James Bay
Gulf of California
SIERRA NEVADA
SIERRA MADRE
Mouths of the Mississippi R.
C. Hatteras
Chesapeake Bay
CHICAGO
NEW YORK
PHILADELPHIA
Boston
Washington
Baltimore
Pittsburg
Cleveland
Detroit
Buffalo
Cincinnati
St. Louis
New Orleans
Denver
San Francisco
Los Angeles
Montreal
Toronto

paper and from farmers who feared Canadian competition. Interests opposed to any weakening of the protective principle supplied copious propaganda against reciprocity to the farm press. Some progressives of North Dakota for example, held the proposed reciprocity to be rankly discriminatory. Again Taft appeared as the farmers' enemy. He managed to obtain a large congressional majority for the agreement, but only after fierce internecine warfare with Republicans. These pyrotechnics fed into Canadian politics, and the agreement was killed at Ottawa.

The new Democratic majority went through the motions of passing what were called "pop" bills, which were proposals for reducing the rates on a few of the items which had great political significance—sugar, steel, chemicals, wool, and cotton. There was no pretense that this was a scientific way to approach the tariff but it was generally agreed that it was clever politics. Taft vetoed the "pop" bills and the Democrats gleefully used this to strengthen their 1912 campaign.

While Roosevelt, Taft and the Democrats were each trying to handle the situation, La Follette had not been idle. At his home in Washington, 21 January 1911, was formed the National Progressive Republican League, with Senator Bourne as president. La Follette and Bristow led the van of senators, Irvine Lenroot of Wisconsin the congressmen; Bourne gave indispensable funds and Brandeis invaluable counsel. Their "Declaration of Principles" proposed to preserve honesty in democracy and to establish moral standards in business practice by the direct participation of voters in the most important political processes —by popular election of senators, direct primaries for nomination of elective officials, direct election of delegates to national conventions, with opportunity for the voter to express his choice for president and vice-president, by the initiative, referendum and recall and by a thorough corrupt practices act. What leader would the League choose to stand on this platform?

The ex-president was watching, fearful lest the League shrink into a small group far ahead of public sentiment, desirous that it delay nomination of a candidate against Taft. Within four months the inner group had agreed to settle upon an anti-Taft candidate and several, including friends of Roosevelt, had assured La Follette that they and Roosevelt would favor him. He announced his candidacy in June and asked Roosevelt for open endorsement, but although Roosevelt aided the candidacy in various ways, he would not actually commit himself to it. Nevertheless, at a Chicago conference in October, La Follette progressives overbore counsels for delay and secured League endorsement of the Senator.

By January of 1912 the La Follette boom was expiring, because Roosevelt was reaching the determination to lead the progressive movement himself. The administration had wounded his self-esteem terribly by a suit against the United States Steel Corporation in which aspersions were thrown upon his wisdom in coöperating on the Tennessee Coal and Iron acquisition. Roosevelt knew that an anti-Taft movement probably would give the Democrats the election, but he burned to lead it. Already the state of his emotions had drawn him into denunciation of Taft for pushing principles of arbitration and reciprocity which he earlier had espoused. Now he became obsessed with the belief that it was his duty to "sacrifice" himself to a progressive campaign.

The Roosevelt following demanded that La Follette retire in favor of the more popular candidate, who was more likely to obtain the party's nomination. La Follette perhaps was the ablest, most persistent and far-seeing of the progressive leadership, but his stubborn addiction to relatively drastic reforms and his tendency to reject compromises marred his availability as a candidate of a movement which perforce included many members devoted to the immediate main chance. Roosevelt, on the other hand, repeatedly had accepted compromises in order to get immediate action, and this had not destroyed the general belief that he was the living embodiment of "the square deal." Most important, his popular following was greater than that of any other person thus far in United States history.

Luckily for Roosevelt, at this juncture La Follette was exhausting his strength and judgment by an inhumanly heavy speaking schedule and by worries over the serious illness of a daughter and over Roosevelt's attitude. Most of his following and financial backers were only waiting an occasion to announce their shift to the more highly magnetic and available ex-president. La Follette provided the occasion. When the Periodical Publishers Association included him in their list of after-dinner speakers at a Philadelphia banquet, 12 February 1912, he inflicted upon a tired, uninterested and not entirely sober throng of publicity men a very long and critical speech. By contrast, a fellow guest named Woodrow Wilson had advantaged himself with a very brief, felicitous talk. Next morning, the press loudly proclaimed the appreciation and the resentment respectively earned.

Promptly Gifford Pinchot, whom La Follette had understood to have pledged that Roosevelt would not be a candidate, announced that La Follette was too ill to assume such a responsibility. Roosevelt seized the cue 21 February with a ringing speech to a Columbus, Ohio, audience, proclaiming the progressive principles which La Follette had done more than any other one man to advance and adding thereto the far more extreme propositions of recall of judges and of judicial decisions. Three days later he planned a formal request for his own candidacy; it was obediently presented to him by seven western governors in attendance at Oyster Bay, and he acceded to their "importunity." La Follette had been outmaneuvered.

During the four months preceding the Republican Convention at Chicago, 18 June, the new progressive leader staged a series of platform appearances over the United States, dramatizing his candidacy for the Republican nomination by a shrill attack upon his unfortunate heir in the White House and on the tariff he had praised. Taft had responded to the progressive urge with considerable liberal legislation, but that now availed him nought. Had he not failed properly to apply "my" policies? Had he not discarded the advice of Roosevelt's friends? The fact that Taft's cabinet included Roosevelt's Attorney General Knox as secretary of state, Roosevelt's Postmaster General Meyer as secretary of the navy and Roosevelt's Secretary of Agriculture Wilson in the same capacity, seemed immaterial. Roosevelt's Secretary of the Interior Garfield had been replaced by Ballinger; worse, Pinchot had been dismissed. Roosevelt earlier had conceded Taft's right to appoint his own cabinet, and Pinchot's successor was the former head of the Yale School of Forestry, who pushed conservation. Again, this was immaterial.

Taft tried, unskilfully, pitifully, to reply to Roosevelt in kind, and the electorate, pleasurably excited, cared not at all that the campaign descended quite completely from principles to personalities. They were enjoying the favorite quadrennial sport of Americans, heightened by a most dramatic fight for the Republican nomination.

The states which had established presidential primaries registered their preference for Roosevelt, who was the majority choice of the Republican rank and file; but that did not give him the clear majority of the convention delegates, to which he declared himself entitled. In the remaining thirty-four states Republican conventions managed under the old system endorsed Taft. Some two hundred "doubtful" delegates at the National Convention were the result. The National Committee, following customary precedents and usual patronage methods, especially with southern delegates, gave the contested seats to Taft's friends and thus renominated him. The platform soft-pedaled factional issues and advocated regulation of the trusts by a federal commission, monetary reform and "readjustment" of the tariff with the help of a board of experts.

Exceeding wroth at the use of nomination devices which he himself had employed in 1904 and 1908, Roosevelt protested the "theft" of eighty or ninety delegates, instructed his following to participate neither in the platform nor the nominations of their party and prepared to secure his own nomination at a convention of bolters. The Republican party which had battled so continuously for power since 1856 had been split by the rise of a new and youthful enthusiasm.

CHAPTER XXXV

THE NEW FREEDOM

The schism in the Republican party insured the formation of a new third party, wholeheartedly devoted to the ideals of the Progressive Era. Two thousand progressive Republicans, each paying his or her own expenses, converged at Chicago from all the states of the Union, 5 August, in at atmosphere of deep religious fervor. Hymns, sermons, Biblical quotations, tears and solemnity attested their sincere conviction that they were engaged in a holy cause. Taking the formal title, the Progressive party, they nominated Roosevelt for president and made Hiram W. Johnson of California—one of the abler reform politicians, who in 1910 had stepped out of the obscurity, where the Old Guard had tried to keep him, and into the governorship—his running mate. Popularly, theirs was known as the "Bull Moose Party," for Roosevelt had always liked to say, "I feel as strong as a bull moose."

Wilson's Triumph

Presumably a few progressives believed that "Teddy's" primary success and personal popularity had some chance of winning for him a plurality of the votes in November. Politicians of experience, however, knew that the Republican split presaged Democratic victory. Critical liberals read on the roster of Roosevelt's campaign backers the names of millionaires like George W. Perkins of the J. P. Morgan firm, Frank A. Munsey, owner of the New York *Press,* and the Pinchot brothers. Such backers scarcely could be expected to favor too literal an application of the new party's platform. Its makers described it as "a contract with the people" and summed up its principles as "The New Nationalism." By that they meant a new paternalism, a grant of enlarged powers to the national government in order to protect the people against the tyranny of special privilege. They emphasized the executive power in the government. Outside of the tariff, most of their planks were not very different from those chosen by the Democrats five weeks earlier, because both groups banked on progressive capital—upon the liberal doctrines for which sentiment had been built up through the past dozen years. But to the familiar proposals for initiative, referendum and recall Roosevelt added recall of judicial decisions. This really radical proposition turned many of his old lawyer friends, like Root, completely against him.

Meanwhile the Democrats had assembled at Baltimore 25 June with much the same notion as to what kind of contract the people wanted, and Woodrow Wilson later summed up their principles as "the New Freedom." Their platform stressed the popular devices for mitigating the evils of trust control; Congress, said they, could so legislate as to substitute for interlocking directorates a restored competition. Their emphasis lay on the voter who should win freedom, rather than upon paternalistic government which should give it to him. Herein the Democrats contrasted with the Progressives. The two in spirit reflected the age-old difference between the Jeffersonian and the Hamiltonian party traditions. Among the many specific fields in which the Democrats promised to force wealth to have regard for social welfare were the railroads whose rates were to be based on valuation, the banks which were to provide elastic credit, and the courts which were not to kill strikes by injunctions. The passing of the Spanish War fervor was suggested by a plank promising the Philippines independence as soon as a stable government was established.

The veteran liberal of the democracy, Bryan, had the experience of determining the candidate. The Democrats had watched the Republican split with keen delight, certain that it meant victory for them; and so their conservative faction, which had dictated the nomination but once since 1892—in 1904—made a futile attempt to recapture the party organization, which soon would have loaves and fishes to distribute. Rivalries among Democrats who had won office in 1910 as reform governors simmered down to a contest between Wilson of New Jersey and Speaker Clark of Missouri.

Wilson (1856-1924), who was the son of a southern Presbyterian minister, had taken a Ph.D. in history and government at Johns Hopkins, writing a notable dissertation on *Congressional Government* and following it later with other writing, of which the best concerned politics. After teaching at Bryn Mawr and Wesleyan he became professor, and then president, at Princeton. There his efforts to democratize the instruction and social life of an institution which he thought dominated by caste failed, and when Boss James Smith offered him the Democratic nomination for governor in 1910 he accepted and his liberal reputation helped to bring the party victory. His thinking had evolved into a Rooseveltian conviction—that a political executive must exert all the leadership of which he is capable; and so the governor insisted upon being his own man, not Smith's. He shifted the United States senatorship to one James Martine, rather than Smith, because Martine had the primary nomination. He forced through the legislature progressive measures promised by his party's platform, for ballot reform and against corrupt practices, for utilities control and employers' liability. Outstanding were the "seven sisters" laws for ending the notoriously easy incorporation situation. This liberal governor who was making a success in a boss-ridden state had been taken up by a Texas Warwick, Colonel Edward M. House, and had been widely and favorably publicized.

Speaker Champ Clark had come to prominence by a different route. In Congress since 1893, except for 1895-1897, he had long service on the Ways and Means and Foreign Affairs committees. Trusted lieutenant of John Sharp Williams, Democratic minority leader, he succeeded to that place when Williams went to the Senate in 1907. He had led the Democrats in their fight to unseat Cannon.

When Tammany braves wheeled into position behind the Clark banner, Bryan detected signs of "Wall Street" support and although his 1896 campaign had been generously underwritten by that section of Wall Street which placed its investments in silver, he gave Tammany support as the reason for preferring Wilson. Some said Bryan wanted to maneuver the convention into his own nomination. At any rate Wilson was named on the forty-sixth ballot. Governor Thomas R. Marshall of Indiana was nominated vice-president. The New Jersey governor, who was a master of the spoken and written word, proceeded to spend a summer in the profitable campaign business of assuring the voters that his "New Freedom" embraced all of the economic, political and social devices which the liberal electorate were inclined to consider a guarantee of a reformed America. It was a campaign in terms of Utopias.

Setting aside the conservative Republicans who were bound to Taft either by economic affiliation or loyalty to his label, the contest developed into one between Wilson and Roosevelt. Taft himself, in July, privately and candidly admitted the probability of his defeat, but his supporters found much solace in keeping their party machinery out of Progressive control. In November nearly 3,500,000 people cast their votes for Taft, probably well aware that in the ordinary sense they were "wasting" their suffrage. More than 4,125,000 voters cast Roosevelt ballots, registering thereby the height of liberal feeling, for they were sufficiently stirred by their faith in the New Nationalism to wrench their traditional Republican ties. Wilson received approximately 6,280,000 votes, less than any of Bryan's totals, but enough in this three-cornered fight to give him 435 electoral votes and the election. Roosevelt won 88 and Taft 8, those of Utah and Vermont; Senate and House went Democratic, as did many states, while the Progressive ticket lost out in local and state contests.

Most of Wilson's voters were old-line Democrats whose support of the New Freedom involved no grand gesture of renunciation of an inherited label. Not less significant is the fact that nearly one million Americans were sure that liberal leaders had not invented devices which could prove successful in safeguarding public welfare against the overwhelming fact of large-scale organization; they voted for the Socialist Debs, and their total was more than twice as great as in 1908. Thus they, too, reflected the rising surge for reform.

Reform Reaches the Tariff

Wilson and his Democratic Senate and House proceeded to discharge their obligations to Democratic, Progressive and Socialist malcontents by legislating in the five major fields of the tariff, trusts, finance, transportation, agriculture and labor.

The tariff of 1913 was somewhat less dominated by political considerations than were preceding tariffs; since the Progressive as well as the Democratic platform and candidates had admitted the necessity for reductions, revision downward was a certainty. The so-called "Underwood-Simmons" tariff was the first item on the Wilson agenda and he in person, one month after his inauguration, called upon Congress to restore "effective competition" between American and foreign manufactures. As Underwood's Ways and Means Committee, according to precedent, had been engaged on a bill through the previous session, a measure passed the House at the end of a month, and by a strict party vote. The lobbies undertook to elevate the schedules with Senate aid, but the insurgent attitude of the nation made it possible for Wilson to prevent the degree of rewriting which had been done in the administrations of Harrison, Cleveland and Taft.

This was the first tariff measure since the Civil War that aimed to benefit the nation as a whole. Logrolling was kept at such a minimum that the average rate of duty was lowered from the 36.86 per cent of the 1909 act to 26.67 per cent in 1913. Instead of choking off all foreign competition, it aimed at moderate protection, with plain and relatively simple *ad-valorem* duties instead of the old specific rates which had been perfected as devices to raise rates secretly. Duties on chemicals and some other products went up, but farmers and the consuming public were pleased by its large free list of common daily necessities, and groups who had risen in revolt against extremes of wealth were gratified by its program for increasing revenue with the aid of income taxes.

While the passage of such a law would not have been possible without the previous progressive agitation, the reductions were due in part to the fact that heavy and unfinished steel products already were being produced by American manufacturers more cheaply than by Europeans. Iron and steel went on the free list. Also, that principle of "compensation" which had elevated the rates in 1897 and 1909 now could be worked in the opposite direction, owing to the weight of public opinion. Since raw wool was free, the compensating specific duties could be taken from woolen manufactures. Rates on these and cotton goods were heavily reduced; since nitrate of soda, boots, shoes, agricultural implements and certain other items of foreign use were put on the free list, that list could also include corn, wheat, rye, eggs, meat, cattle, sheep and like items.

Manufacturing interests could find some solace. The act contained an anti-dumping section and penalties against bounty-supported imports. While the president was empowered to negotiate reciprocity agreements, their acceptance was made dependent upon Congress. Furthermore, the tariff board was not reëstablished and exports to Cuba and the Philippines were encouraged by a reciprocity agreement with the one and complete free trade with the other.

The 1913 tariff was a significant advance in the social, economic and political development of the American nation because of its income tax features. The states had taken nearly four years to ratify the 16th Amendment to the Constitution which Secretary of State Knox had proclaimed 25 February 1913. The Underwood Tariff seized upon the income tax to destroy the deficit created by the lowered schedules; all net incomes over $3,000 were to pay 1 per cent, except that married men were allowed an exemption of $1,000; all net incomes above $20,000 were subject to an additional tax, called a surtax, starting at 1 per cent and reaching 6 per cent on incomes above $500,000. Also corporations must continue to pay 1 per cent on net incomes above $5,000. These provisions weakened the historic excuse for tariff increases, the deficit. They also meant that accumulated, invisible wealth had lost its tax immunity; it must supply funds which in part had formerly been collected from the poor in the form of tariff duties. Such provisions were an earnest of future taxes on competence and special privilege. This epoch-making tariff marks a high point in the stream of progressive accomplishment before it was engulfed in the flood of a World War.

Regulation of Business and Finance

Another high point was the so-called "Pujo Committee," sponsored by the House Committee on Banking and Currency and empowered by the Sixty-Second Congress to ascertain the facts regarding the "money trust." The committee accumulated evidence showing that capital consolidation had reached a point where money and credit were largely monopolized by three banks: J. P. Morgan and Company, the First National Bank of New York and the National City Bank (a Rockefeller institution). These, through seven subsidiary banks, controlled approximately 2 billions of capital; four allied institutions of New York City held 341 directorships in various concerns with resources aggregating 22.2 billions. Rivalry between these often was abandoned for profitable cross investments and interlocking directorates. They obtained control over trust companies, in which insurance companies could invest under most state laws. Morgan came to dominate in the "Big Three" of the insurance world: the Equitable, Mutual and New York Life. Billions of dollars in savings thus became available for speculative and monopolistic purposes.

Evidence abounded that the money trust was the core of the trust system of non-competitive consolidation in control of American production, that the little competitive businesses (which numbered over 75 per cent of American concerns) had sunk to insignificance in the scheme of labor policy, output, price and all the other aspects of business affecting general prosperity. Welfare hung upon the judgment of the few individuals in economic control of the nation. Chairman Pujo asked one of these, George F. Baker (banking associate of J. P. Morgan), if he considered this "a comfortable situation for a great country to be in." Baker answered "not entirely."

A remedy for this parlous state was obligatory to the first Wilson Congress, then riding the crest of the progressive wave and led by a president who recently had stiffened New Jersey's notoriously lax corporation laws. Congress responded in 1914 with two statutes intended to regulate trusts and preserve competition. The Federal Trade Commission Act, designed primarily for trust regulation, wiped out the Bureau of Corporations, which as a part of the Department of Commerce had proved flaccid in its trust supervision, and set up a bipartisan commission of five, empowered with investigative and regulatory duties. Within their purview came all corporations engaged in interstate commerce (except common carriers and banks) and subject to anti-trust laws and court decrees. They could make public such reports as they thought best and investigate trade relations with foreign countries. They could issue certain "cease and desist orders" in cases of unfair competition and their findings as to fact were to be held as conclusive.

In other words, the Federal Trade Commission was set up as an agency for establishing the fact of dishonest practices in business; these once proved by it, the Sherman law as amplified by the Clayton law was to be employed to reëstablish "effective competition." The Clayton Act, another law of this Congress, attacked some of the competition-throttling devices which had been perfected during the twenty-four years since 1890: price discrimination, interlocking directorates and tied contracts. Some practices it prohibited, certain remedies it prescribed and (as already noted) since farmers' organizations and labor unions thus far had proved ineffective against trusts, the law expressly exempted these two groups from prosecution as conspiracies in restraint of trade.

The same Congress registered popular resentment against some of the most flagrant stock manipulation in transportation—particularly the ruin of the New Haven under Morgan and Rockefeller. It formulated the "Rayburn" bill for giving the Interstate Commerce Commission power to pass on securities of common carriers before issuance. The outbreak of war postponed further legislation in this field for two decades.

Also in Wilson's first Congress culminated the second great effort (Bryan's had been the first) to vest control of the nation's monetary system in the federal government. The National Monetary Commission, headed by Senator Aldrich, had made extensive investigations but had not submitted a formal plan until January 1912, after the progressive tide had washed out Aldrich and his régime. The Aldrich plan incorporated some European practices adjusted to American conditions, with extensions of domestic clearing-house machinery. It was prepared by him with the aid of H. P. Davison, F. A. Vanderlip, P. M. Warburg and J. B. Forgan—bankers representing the dominant eastern banking houses of Morgan, Rockefeller, and Kuhn, Loeb and Company, and Chicago's leader, the First National. The regulatory institution which they proposed to set up was to operate under private control centered in New York.

Any plan was bound to be modified by a Democratic-progressive coalition in a direction toward decentralization and political supervision, and there emerged the Glass-Owen Federal Reserve Act of 1913. It acknowledged the obligation of the government to supervise banking while safeguarding sectional, agricultural and commercial interests therein. It modified the out-grown, fifty-year-old national bank system with a Federal Reserve establishment to which all national banks were to belong, participating in ownership of stock in regional Federal Reserve Banks. One-third of the boards of these banks, and all members of the central Federal Reserve Board, must be nominated by political influence (the president)—a Bryan requirement supposed to prevent Wall Street control.

Twelve regional reserve banks, designed to be subsidiary to the Federal Reserve Board, were to meet currency needs of their respective sections, taking the rôle of bankers' banks, granting them loans and buying and selling domestic and foreign exchange. They could rediscount agricultural paper for six months, commercial for three; and on the basis of this paper they could issue the new, more elastic, currency, named "federal reserve notes," up to any amount, provided a 40 per cent reserve was kept in gold. As they could not rediscount paper issued for the purpose of trading in stocks and bonds, speculation was supposed to be debarred from enjoying the currency-expansion privileges of industry and agriculture. The old, inelastic, national bank-notes, dependent upon government bonds, were to be retired.

The Federal Reserve Act encountered bitter resistance from bankers opposing regimentation of their operations, but the large institutions entered the system, which within fifteen years embraced more than four-fifths of the nation's bank resources. Many disputes arose over management, political manipulation and influence exerted by the New York Reserve Bank. After the Progressive Era closed, legislative amendments and administrative policy moved the system further away from the democratic objectives of some of its sponsors and toward private control. The system served, however, to increase money in circulation and the total sum in the country, and it forwarded three of the major demands of monetary reformers: currency expansion, mobilization of reserves and control for national, rather than personal, ends.

This legislation was enacted against a background of political uneasiness, with the newly installed Democrats anxious for more security. Their liberal leader, President Wilson, had received in 1912 less than 42 per cent of the popular vote, although his party had rolled up a majority of 145 in the House and 6 in the Senate. In fact, no Democratic presidential candidate had received a popular majority since 1852 except Tilden, whose victory was made an empty one. Democratic insecurity helps to account for their remarkably fine legislative record, achieved in spite of the distractions of the Mexican Revolution, the Panama Canal Tolls dispute and the outbreak of the First World War, which are to be described in the following chapters. Early in the spring of 1914 the Democratic National Committee issued a review of their record; it indicated that legislation asked for by progressives, of all shades regardless of party label, had been passed by the ambitious Democratic majority in Congress under Wilson's urging. Adjournment came 24 October 1914, after the longest consecutive session to that date.

Would this work be recognized at the elections a fortnight later? The straight Democratic majority in the House was then pared down from 145 to 30, although the Senate majority was raised from 6 to 16. The war unsettlements, conservative resistance to liberal legislation and the usual tendency to a congressional shift in a presidential midterm canvass account for the change. More significant was the fact that the Progressive party, as a separate political entity, gave evidence of disintegrating; this election reduced the number of members carrying independent labels into the House from 18 to 8, leaving the Senate, with its 1, unchanged. Thus once again in United States history a protest party was defeated by its success; as the Progressive party's principles won endorsement under Wilson's New Freedom, that party's continued existence became impossible.

The return to old labels did not mean, however, a return to the pre-1900 conservatism. In spite of ever more recurrent wartime interruptions, the Sixty-Fourth Congress found time to enact the liberal measures of 1915-1917. Agriculture and labor were particularly recognized—agriculture with the Federal Farm Loan and Good Roads Acts of 1916 and the Smith-Hughes Vocational Education Law of 1917. Labor obtained the La Follette Seamen's Act of 1915, the Keating-Owen Child Labor Law and Adamson Eight Hour Railroad Act of 1916. No verdict on these measures ever was registered at the polls, for the First World War became the background for the election of 1916, to be described shortly. Just how much farther along the road of social reform the Wilson administration might have been carried by the momentum of public interest and political ambition will never be known. The war which broke out in Europe in August of 1914 both diverted public interest from domestic welfare and divided the Democrats on war policy.

Altogether, legislation typical of the Progressive Era—whether touching transportation, trusts, finance, labor or agriculture—had consisted of a series of devices in the democratic tradition, invented to safeguard freedom under modern capitalism. Americans of the early twentieth century recognized as dangerous the control of practically all major activities by a handful of persons who ran supercombinations known as trusts; but in the main they indignantly repudiated the notion of substituting for this a scheme of general control by the masses. They cherished their faith in individualism, and although it had become monopolistic, they distrusted people in the mass. The capitalistic system, not collectivism, remained the preferred vehicle for carrying on the nation in free living.

So the people of the United States had gone on fighting graft, demanding the "common honesty" which had sufficed in the old agricultural régime and failing to realize how modern living strains to the breaking point the homely virtues. They had thought to safeguard their interests adequately by passing laws "against" big business and special privilege. This effort defined the Progressive Era. From it their attention was violently diverted by the prospect of participation in a struggle to save democracy abroad.

CHAPTER XXXVI

EXPANDING IMPERIALISM

Public attention during the Progressive Era was not completely absorbed in domestic concerns. While the struggle for purer democracy and social betterment was waged, the international position of the United States was changing.

The United States in Foreign Markets

The majority of Americans who welcomed the Treaty of Paris were confident of profits from the undertaking. Whitelaw Reid pictured the Pacific become an "American Lake," and many were certain that at least the Caribbean would become such a placid sheet. The fact that only the latter of these ambitions was achieved did not mean that American trade and investment affected foreign relations only in that confined precinct. Their ramifications require some notice.

The nation's accrued debts held by European investors kept the United States a net debtor in international payments until 1914, but in trade and investment Americans were making such strides as to have reached the creditor position even if there had been no World War. Between 1881 and 1897—a period of falling prices—they had increased the volume of their exports sufficiently at least to keep the total value of them comparatively stable; then in 1897 the export trend veered upward sharply, reaching 2.5 billions in 1913. European manufacturers fearing for their markets protested against the "invasion." Furthermore, American investments abroad, which totaled only 635 millions in 1897, quintupled to 3,314 millions by 1 July 1914. This activity of traders and investors followed lines patterned by competing capitalists of all the highly industrialized nations.

First, as to trade; foreign sales organizations sprouted. Standard Oil by 1911 had sixteen subsidiaries; International Harvester by 1912 had fifty-three foreign branch houses; United States Steel by 1913 had 268 agencies scattered over about sixty countries; National Cash Register by 1914 was assigning one-third of its output to foreign dispersion. Foreign areas were thoroughly penetrated also by other machinery, by meats, shoes and soap. Foreign transportation facilities, storehouses and warehouses were required for use. Branch banks, however, were so restricted under American law that exporters and investors had to depend for facilities largely upon British, French, German and Dutch branches.

Second, as to investments, some 1,000 millions in securities of foreign governments and foreign-controlled corporations found purchasers in the United States between 1897 and 1914. Vastly more influential, in the imperial situation, were the direct investments in American-controlled ventures abroad as the United States contingent in the world scramble for control of natural resources became, with government aid, very active. They invested most heavily in those minerals closely integrated with modern industrial production—oil,[1] copper, aluminum, lead, nickel, tin, zinc, iron—and such non-metallic minerals as nitrates, coal, asbestos, gypsum and sulphur; in these they invested eight times as much as in gold and silver mines.

Capital for agriculture went principally into tropical products needed by a nation located in a temperate clime: sugar plantations and mills in the Philippines, Cuba, Puerto Rico and Hawaii attracted the larger part; second came fruit (especially bananas in the Caribbean area) and other tropical foodstuffs like cocoanuts, cacao, chicle, coffee, tea and spices; most of the remainder went into rubber plantations and Mexican and Canadian ranches and farms. Sisal, jute and hemp had some attractions.

Capital for branch factories had begun to engage Americans as soon as the factory came to the United States, and by 1914 most outstanding concerns had foreign factories; their stake rose from perhaps 100 millions in 1910 to about 500 millions in 1914, distributed about 220 in Canada, 200 in Europe, and almost 60 in Latin America and the rest of the world. In foreign railways, chiefly Caribbean, American investment rose from 143 millions in 1897 to 350 millions in 1924.

Thus, to this wide extent, were Americans locating their fortunes outside their native land. Their progress in this risky business is indicated by the figures of the aggregate value of American-controlled enterprises abroad—in 1897, 655 millions; in 1914, 2.7 billions; in 1929, 7.6 billions. But no less significant than the aggregate is the fact that it includes, besides investment of new money, subsidies given by foreign governments as concessions, unearned increments, appreciation and reinvestments. The getting of all of these, and the manner of it, largely determined the social, economic, and political dynamics of imperialism.

In the dependencies and protectorates, pursuit of profits brought with it United States government-financed improvements in the environment of work, producing roads, sanitation, disease control and

[1] Oil was particularly important because the United States came to produce and use about three-fourths of the world consumption and other nationals shut her out of foreign fields; the government obtained a share for United States interests in Turkey and the East Indies.

some modicum of modern education and conveniences. Similarly, order and stability were firmly imposed upon regions of chronic revolution and change. There the dictatorship was assumed by economic forces, which dispossessed the inefficient and small land and property owners, using them as employees in the large, one or two-crop systems—such as tobacco and sugar—with which the great corporations earned dividends from huge plantations. The agricultural classes of Cuba, Puerto Rico and the Philippines became landless employees of absentee landlords, virtually peons; so did the workers in Mexico and other Caribbean areas where foreign capital took over the main economic processes.

These were some of the more powerful economic processes of the developing imperialistic foreign policy. As they operated in various locales, they worked different effects. Around the Caribbean, United States imperialism reached its height in dependencies and protectorates; in Mexico and Venezuela exploitation was curbed by native sovereignty; in the Orient neither trade nor influence reached expectations; in Europe and Africa came occasional coöperation along lines of peace. To these various ventures the public reacted according to individual opinions as to the military necessity and humanity of the policies.

Around the Caribbean

Around the Caribbean appeared dependencies and protectorates in Cuba, Puerto Rico, Panama, Santo Domingo, Haiti, Nicaragua and the Virgin Islands. The background of the picture in this region revealed elements present also in almost every other Latin American area—elements persistently affecting relations with the United States and therefore essential to be kept in mind. First in importance was the continual expansion of investment and trade. Secondly, all European competitors here held dear one common objective: to foster anti-United States feeling. Thirdly, to offset their hostile influence and to protect the preferential position actually won by American capital, Washington had to invent "Pan Americanism" and had to struggle through the years to give it something other than a domineering connotation.

Cuba became a virtual protectorate. There United States military rule continued four years after peace. The military did much for the social and political reconstruction of the island, substituting order for complete chaos, establishing the beginnings of self-government and sound finance, cleaning up Havana and discovering (with the sacrifice of the lives of Dr. James Carroll and Dr. Jesse Lazear) that the yellow fever scourge could be stamped out by mosquito control. Withdrawal of the troops was a foregone conclusion; the conditions of that withdrawal, in view of American interests, were the issue. The pledge of the

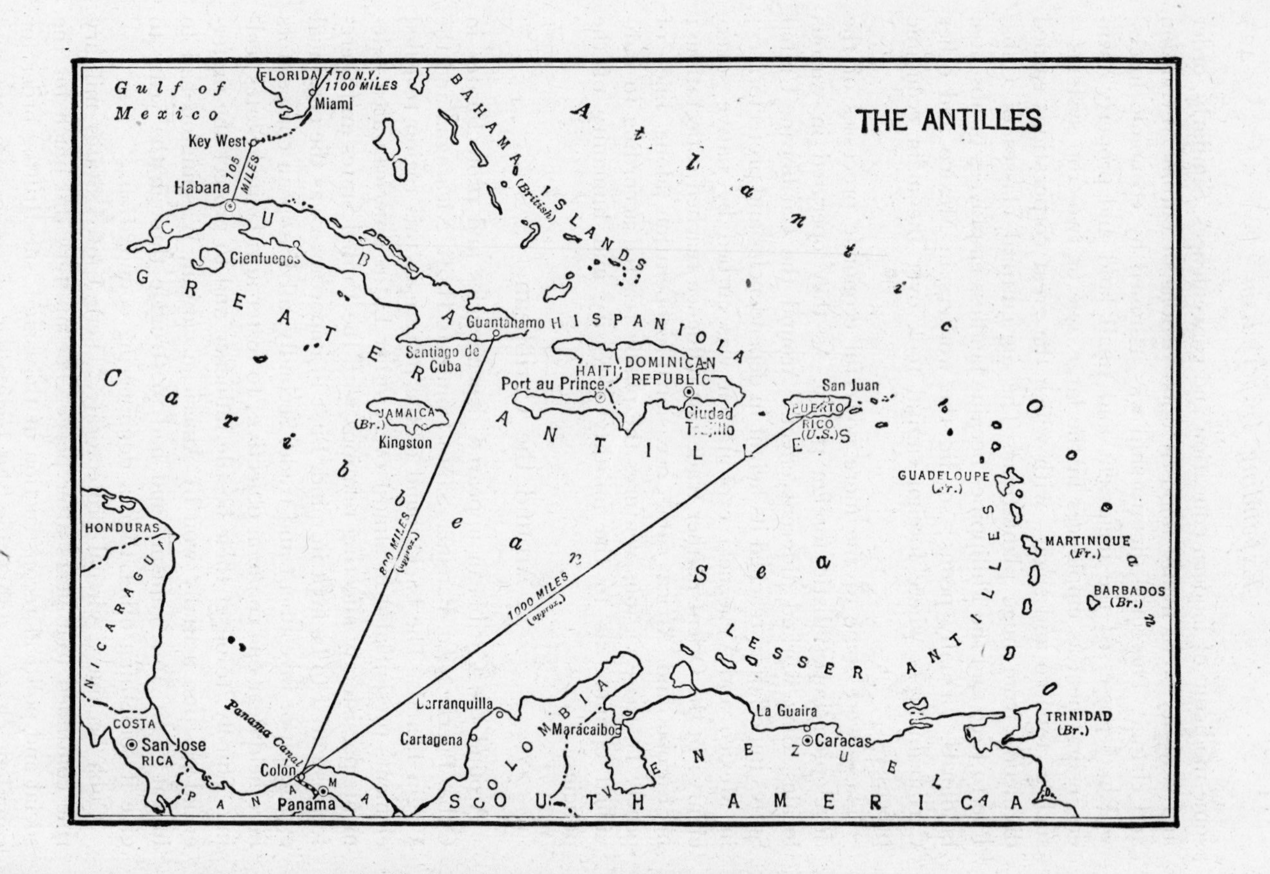

THE ANTILLES
Gulf of Mexico
FLORIDA
TO N.Y. 1100 MILES
Miami
Key West
105 MILES
Habana
CUBA
Cienfuegos
GREATER ANTILLES
BAHAMA ISLANDS (British)
Atlantic Ocean
Guantanamo
Santiago de Cuba
HISPANIOLA
HAITI
DOMINICAN REPUBLIC
Port au Prince
Ciudad Trujillo
JAMAICA (Br.)
Kingston
San Juan
PUERTO RICO (U.S.)
Caribbean Sea
800 MILES (approx.)
1000 MILES (approx.)
GUADELOUPE (Fr.)
MARTINIQUE (Fr.)
BARBADOS (Br.)
LESSER ANTILLES
TRINIDAD (Br.)
HONDURAS
NICARAGUA
COSTA RICA
San Jose
Panama Canal
Colon
Panama
PANAMA
Cartagena
Maracaibo
COLOMBIA
La Guaira
Caracas
VENEZUELA
SOUTH AMERICA

Teller amendment, that Cuba should be left to the Cubans, had been made during the excitement of declaring war with Spain, but the pledge conformed to historic, popular, democratic ideals and stubbornly resisted the schemes of General Wood and divers expansionists to displace it with annexation.

Secretary of War Root, thoroughly committed to the maintenance of United States interests, military and economic, public and private, undertook to protect them. A so-called "Platt Amendment" to the army appropriation bill of 1901 made military withdrawal dependent upon Cuba's acceptance of a treaty embodying significant pledges: Cuba was to ratify all the acts of the United States military régime, continue the sanitation program and eschew extraordinary indebtedness; she was not to jeopardize her "independence" (nor the influence of the United States) in compacts with other nations; naval and coaling stations were to be available for United States lease or purchase; most important, Cuba was to admit the right of the United States to intervene for the preservation of Cuban independence, the maintenance of a government adequate for the protection of life, liberty and property, and the discharge of obligations under the Treaty of Paris. The right of intervention spelled annexation to the Cubans, but Root reassured them and they signed the treaty, incorporated its provisions in a new constitution as per directions and thus in 1902 temporarily rid themselves of American troops.

Economic prosperity was undertaken through reciprocity treaties which since 1903 have maintained for Cuban exports to the United States a 20 per cent preference over products from other nations; American exports to Cuba obtained preferences ranging from 20 per cent to 40 per cent. These arrangements aided the sugar-producing companies, American sugar refiners and American exporters, to the disadvantage of consumers. The World War carried Cuba to the side of the Allies within twenty-four hours after the United States joined them; but it so overstimulated sugar production that post-war bankruptcy resulted; American and Canadian banks holding sugar paper took over financial control. Economic domination from United States sources became obvious and complete.

Political independence proved impossible to maintain in financial stringencies. Furthermore rival political factions frequently tried to ride into power on the tails of American intervention, sometimes engaging in violent disorder to bring it about and then campaigning against the "American ogre." American troops and control returned, for stays varying from three years to a few months, in 1906, 1912, 1917 and 1920. During the 'twenties, however, nationalism strengthened in Cuba while imperialism weakened in the United States, and when the depression of 1929 coincided with a revolution against the terroristic

Machado, the United States did not follow the old pattern. For military intervention was substituted a careful easing out of Machado, and a treaty of "general relations" in 1934 recognized a new régime. Under executive agreement (which neatly avoided ratification by the United States Senate) new reciprocal tariffs were granted which aimed to benefit Cuba as well as the United States; the Platt amendment and the right of intervention were abandoned, and thus the protectorate was nearly abolished. Only the naval station of Guantanamo was retained. This left Cuba free to feel assured of the right to maintain her own government, except, perhaps, if other powers should attempt to intervene. As the United States came to adopt liberal expedients likewise in other areas embraced in her Panama policy, she improved upon Europe's example in imperialism.

Puerto Rico became a colony. It well illustrated how much easier it is to grant the forms of political democracy than to establish the facts of general well-being. Under congressional acts of 1900 and 1917 the government approached a territorial status and Puerto Ricans, although lacking the complete home rule many desired, attained United States citizenship. These political advances were possible largely because of stable characteristics of the inhabitants. Some social advance came with attention to education, sanitation, transportation and public works. Trade and wealth expanded with the exploitation of abundant cheap labor in the production of sugar, tobacco, fruit, coffee and manufactured goods. But these could not lift the masses out of a dependence so extreme that in the depression year of 1930 more than 60 per cent of them lacked full-time employment. Since 1902 they have been inside the United States tariff system, which means free trade between them and the mainland but extension of the American high price structure over their poor purchasing power. Their overcrowded situation, their liability to hookworm and their overdependence upon the American sugar market help to push them deeper into peonization.

Panama Policy

Panama became a virtual protectorate, by a devious route. The two-month voyage of the battleship *Oregon* in 1898, from the coast of Washington 14,000 miles around the Cape of Good Hope to Florida, had indicated that an isthmian canal was essential to coast-line defense. Also the canal idea was part of the expansionists' program and appealed to western farmers as a freight-lowering device. The United States, unfortunately, had agreed in the Clayton-Bulwer treaty of 1850 that any isthmian canal should be internationalized and neutralized. To build under that treaty would mean construction at American expense of an unfortified canal, controlled equally by Britain and shared, as to facilities, equally by all nations. This was not to the interest of the United States; secretaries Blaine and Frelinghuysen had tried to change it, and party platforms demanded abrogation of the old treaty. The series of canal negotiations undertaken at the turn of the century came to involve questions of America's policy as a world power in both hemispheres. So closely connected are decisions near and far.

Great Britain at this juncture was prepared to make concessions. Desiring an Anglo-American alliance, needing American support for her far-eastern program, she hoped that for canal concessions she might be compensated on the Alaskan boundary and realized that her interest lay in leaving control of the Caribbean to the United States. As events proved, the Senate would not tolerate the alliance, nor would the Roosevelt administration yield on Alaska (p. 351); but meanwhile Britain instructed her ambassador at Washington, Lord Pauncefote, to follow up a first, unpopular treaty which the Senate had killed, with a second Hay-Pauncefote treaty of 21 February 1902, which the Senate accepted.

What this treaty did not concede openly it conceded tacitly by omission. It declared the Clayton-Bulwer treaty superseded; it did not prohibit fortification by the United States nor provide for the adherence of other nations. Although its rules for neutralization prohibited any act of war within the canal, Great Britain during the negotiations admitted the right of the United States to fortify and defend it; and Britain followed ratification by virtually withdrawing from the Caribbean, removing her principal naval forces and reducing her permanent garrisons. Fortifications subsequently erected there by the United States became the key to America's defense policy.

With Great Britain out of the way, canal routing could proceed; and as French and American companies attempting private construction had gone into bankruptcy, it was clearly a task for the government. Routing could cross either Colombian or Nicaraguan territory, as transit rights had been secured long since from Colombia (then New Granada) in 1846 and from Nicaragua in 1867. Three official American commissions declared for Nicaragua, where one American company had buried capital before the 1893 panic and another now held a speculative concession; and the House of Representatives in 1902 passed a bill for construction there.

On the other hand, a French company headed by the Suez engineer, DeLesseps, in the 'eighties had squandered some 400 millions on a ditch in the Panama section of Colombia; by 1901 American speculators had taken over the wreckage. Ably managed by the J. P. Morgan banking company, by a New York attorney-lobbyist, W. N. Cromwell, and by a versatile ex-engineer, Bunau-Varilla, they undertook to salvage their investment with government aid before their franchise expired in 1904.

A timely volcanic eruption in Nicaragua helped them. They pared their sale price to 40 millions, convinced President Roosevelt and Senator Hanna that Panama was best and lobbied through the Senate a Spooner amendment to the House bill, authorizing purchase of the Panama property if Colombia acceded.

Secretary Hay and Colombian Minister Herran proceeded to negotiate a treaty authorizing the Panama Company to sell to the United States, granting the latter full control over a strip of land six miles wide and allotting to Colombia immediate payment of 10 millions and after nine years annual payments of $250,000. These figures were generally considered fair, but the Colombian Senate delayed, possibly for higher figures and expiration of the company rights.

The none-too-patient Roosevelt, consulting Secretary of War Root, was assured that the treaty of 1846 could be interpreted to justify intervention, if to prevent interruption of transit through "domestic disturbances." [1] All apparently required for the intervention was the disturbance. So a quiet "revolution" against Colombia was staged at Panama 3 November 1903, a few hours later than expected in Washington and while United States warships hovered conveniently near to prevent landing of Colombian troops. Inside of three days Colombia offered to accept the Hay-Herran treaty if her isthmus sovereignty were protected, but the United States recognized the *de facto* government on the 6th and other powers quickly followed.

Bunau-Varilla, now accredited Panamanian plenipotentiary, signed with Hay the treaty of 18 November giving Panama the 10 millions in gold and the $250,000 annually. Panama tendered the right to build and fortify a canal and to possess a zone ten miles wide across the isthmus. The United States promised to maintain Panama's independence but received other rights which virtually made Panama a protectorate. Canal construction was turned over, after some initial bad appointments, to Colonel Gorgas and Colonel Goethals, who respectively made a malaria and yellow fever-ridden region healthy, and an almost impossible engineering dream an accomplished fact.

Thus Theodore Roosevelt "took" the canal. That was his own description and it is history's verdict. American attitudes in foreign relations were then so casual as to tolerate such a performance. The seizure antagonized not only Colombia, which is the only government refusing today to recognize Panama, but all Latin America. It burdened the United States with a heavy moral liability. Root in vain offered Colombia three treaties tendering 2.5 millions of Panama's annuities in exchange for recognition. Next, the Wilson administration negotiated a Bryan treaty which offered an apology and an indemnity of 25 mil-

[1] The Hay-Pauncefote treaty provided that no change in the territorial sovereignty of the canal would alter the obligation of the signatories.

lions; this was defeated in the Senate by friends of ex-President Roosevelt. Meanwhile, Britain was objecting strenuously because Congress by a 1912 law had exempted coastwise shipping from tolls; she indicated that the Hay-Pauncefote treaty stipulated equal treatment for vessels of all nations. Perhaps the United States had a case for arbitration, but Wilson had a tacit bargain with the British for support of his Mexican policy (p. 437); so the exemption law was repealed in mid-1914, shortly before the canal was opened to commercial traffic.

Finally in 1921 Colombia balked at petroleum concessions to American interests, and a treaty resulted which omitted the Bryan apology but paid the 25 millions; after seventeen years more, amity between the two governments reached the point where they raised their legations to embassies. When the second Roosevelt was liquidating as much as possible of the Caribbean liabilities, needing and cultivating Latin friendship, a treaty was signed looking toward the end of the protectorate over Panama. Two facts, however, remained unchanged: Latin America could not forget the seizure and the United States could not dispense with the canal.

The assumption of canal responsibilities brought a keener interest in the affairs of the Latin American Republics in the Caribbean. Many of them were under heavy financial obligations to European powers, and often they failed to pay their debts. Some European powers threatened to intervene to force the collection of these debts and incidentally to control a landing place or naval station near the canal. The United States could not look with equanimity on such practice. Therefore in 1902 when Germany, Britain and Italy jointly blockaded defaulting Venezuela, bombarded two ports and seized several gunboats, President Theodore Roosevelt supported Venezuela's insistence on arbitration. Germany also took note of the fact that Admiral Dewey's fleet was wintering off Puerto Rico. Arbitration was therefore agreed upon as a substitute for intervention. The incident led to adoption (in modified form) at The Hague conference of 1907 of the so-called Drago Doctrine; [1] it outlawed collection of contract debts by force if the debtor agreed to arbitrate, and served as an international supplement to the Monroe Doctrine.

The United States further undertook financial protectorates to forestall intervention. In 1904 Santo Domingo got into similar difficulties, and again Roosevelt acted. He conveniently invented what became known as the "Roosevelt corollary" to the Monroe Doctrine; according to it, since the United States could not allow Europe to collect western debts, she must collect them herself.[2] He arranged a treaty under which

[1] Named for its proposer, Dr. Luis Drago, Argentine Minister of Foreign Affairs.

[2] He based this assumption upon a larger one:—that in case of flagrant disregard of international obligations the United States had the right to intervene in Latin America, under the "international police power."

an American receiver would collect Dominican customs, apportioning 55 per cent of the revenue to creditors and the remainder to the island government. When the Senate refused to accept either corollary or treaty, he proceeded to collect the debts anyhow under a *modus vivendi* until the Senate two years later ratified a new treaty with new loans. By an outburst of revolutions between 1911 and 1916 the Dominicans jeopardized payments on loans floated by Kuhn, Loeb and the National City Bank. President Wilson ended the disorder by an armed intervention which continued until a Dominican constitution of 1924 established a financial protectorate—significant because a terminal date was set for it.

Haiti, Santo Domingo's neighbor on the western half of the island, contended with similar difficulties. Secretary of State Knox forced an entrance to the republic for American capital. Political conditions became chaotic by 1915, and although President Wilson disclaimed any designs upon Haiti's political or territorial integrity he sent down the marines. Germany, rumor said, sought a naval base there for use in the current war. Under a treaty ratified by a puppet government exploitation was facilitated; a protectorate broader than Santo Domingo's was set up, with most functions supervised by United States advisers under marine protection. Some few instances of atrocities helped to arouse public opinion against a too inclusive and brutal occupation, and so the marines were withdrawn in 1934 and financial dictation was modified the next year by placing revenue collection under the Haitian National Bank.

Nicaragua was the Central American country of greatest concern to the United States government, because of her closeness to Panama, her possession of territory usable for a second canal and her chronic political and financial difficulties. When these difficulties became too severe and American lives and property were endangered, the Taft Administration despatched marines in 1912 to remain in Nicaragua most of the time for twenty years, and Brown Brothers and J. and W. Seligman made loan agreements without benefit of treaties. The bankers firmly thrust development and exchequer control upon the little countries, nominating customs receivers, after consultation with and approval by the State Department. Thus the United States avoided official guarantees but encouraged numerous arrangements for protecting investments. President Taft gave the policy the accurate but odorous description of "dollar diplomacy."

The Wilson administration continued it, putting through the Bryan-Chamorro treaty paying Nicaragua 3 millions for a lease of the Great Corn and Little Corn islands and of a naval base on the Gulf of Fonseca. This was calculated to protect canal rights but was denounced by the Central American Court of International Justice, a miniature league of nations sponsored in 1906-1907 by the United States and Mexico, as an infringement of sovereignty. When revolutionists busied the marines with guerrilla warfare, the United States extended her policy of embargoes on arms to revolutionists, particularly in Nicaragua, Honduras and Cuba. The great importance of Central American order to the United States led to an effort, in 1922-1923, to strengthen the Central American Court; treaties were signed for "cooling off" before going to war, and for refusing recognition to revolutionary governments. This proved no bar, however, to further revolt in Nicaragua and a reoccupation by marines. Evacuation of Nicaragua was not completed until 1933.

As the 'twenties wore on, it became increasingly clear that the United States had few fears remaining of European threat to the Panama region and that continual intervention was impractical, costly and bad for trade. Therefore, in one country after another intervention had been tapered off, to the delight of those Americans who thought it wholly commercial in origin. In 1929 the Department of State published the so-called "Clark Memorandum" which in effect cut from the Monroe Doctrine the Roosevelt corollary. This left non-American intervention still taboo but removed the pledge of United States intervention. A capstone on this new policy was placed by the Montevideo treaty of 1935 which conceded that "no state has the right to intervene in the internal or external affairs of another."

The only other area considered necessary to round out the Panama policy was the Danish West Indies, the three little, poverty-stricken and undeveloped islands which the Senate had refused Seward. Enthusiastic expansionists of 1898, in the days before oil-burning ships, had committed the Republican party to their purchase. The Senate in 1902 agreed to give 5 millions for them; they were only a liability to Denmark, but her Rigsdag rejected that treaty by one vote. In 1917 the German admiral, Von Tirpitz, was understood to covet these Virgin Islands, as they had come to be called, and the United States, in wartime enthusiasm, paid 25 millions, an exorbitant sum. Thus United States imperialism expanded around the Caribbean; and as the shadow of European rivalries grew deeper the nation was ever more vigilant, lest the spirit of the Monroe Doctrine be violated.

CHAPTER XXXVII

IN WORLD POLITICS

The watchfulness of the United States was further sharpened by the trend of events very near home.

Over the Border

Mexico has posed a most delicate problem in neighborhood diplomacy, complicated by rich resources, heavy investment, frequent revolutions, extreme differences in culture and temperament and the memory of 1848. Officially, the United States since then has shown forbearance, displaying force seldom and briefly; but Mexican politicians and people read private, foreign expropriation between the lines of every diplomatic document, and Latin Americans generally measure the sincerity of the words of the United States by her actions in Mexico. Capital from the United States and other nations got a sixty-year head start of the Mexicans in the exploitation of their country. The process was such as to ensure a violent reaction when the Mexican nation awakened to the fact.

Dictator Porfirio Diaz, who was tremendously interested in rapid exploitation of resources and totally illiterate in human values, kept political control from 1877 to 1910, while he lavishly dispensed concessions, chiefly to foreigners. They invested about 2 billions—one-half of it from the United States—in agricultural lands, electric power, mines, oil, rubber and railroads. Diaz's absolute dictatorship had the support of the landed aristocracy, the Creoles, that tenth of the population who absorbed whatever profits did not leave Mexico for foreign pockets. The other nine-tenths of the population, deprived of the lands they had worked on the communal system, became worse off than the slaves in the United States had been. Of Indian, Negro and other mixed blood, they sank into a condition of peonage, desperately poor, ignorant, superstitious and diseased. Of education, sanitation and public welfare there was none. No middle-class group, with the wish and power to implement representative government, existed to preserve for the nation its just share of the profits from exploitation, as the middle class in the United States had done throughout the long years of foreign investment.

Popular resentment accumulated in huge volume, not against Creoles or European investors so much as against the "gringoes" from the north.

This concentrated hatred became tremendously important in Mexican emotional, cultural and political life. No politician could ignore it; all would be tempted to use it. The overturn of Diaz by more liberal forces (apparently aided by American oil interests resentful of concessions to Englishmen) began a decade of revolution during which successive leaders fought for control. While Mexico painfully moved in the direction of constitutional liberties and social regeneration, the northern democracy showed remarkable sympathy and forbearance.

National traditions and population characteristics made impossible anything like the orderly fighting of the United States Civil War. Pillage, outrage, slaughter, insurrection, deceit and guerrilla warfare generally characterized Mexico's struggles. Bandits and honest citizens alike voiced their rivalries and discontent in terms of violent hatred of the United States whenever a more precise statement of objectives taxed ingenuity. In a decade of revolutions, between 40,000 and 50,000 citizens of the United States abandoned their property and suffered damage estimated at 170 millions (Mexican); nearly 800 lost their lives. Three perennial problems faced Presidents Taft and Wilson: protection of lives and property, recognition of revolutionary governments and chastisement for outrages. Always there was the painful decision: should forceful intervention be used for these purposes.

President Wilson sympathized with the agrarian reform program planned by Madero (president of Mexico from 1910 until murdered in 1913) and undertook—against the wishes of powerful foreign capitalists—to unseat his reactionary successor, Huerta. Clumsy efforts to block arms shipments into Mexico led to shelling of Vera Cruz by United States guns, but Wilson generally handled the situation with such restraint that South America began to pay him dividends on his moderation. Argentina, Brazil and Chile offered to mediate—an innovation—and the "A.B.C. Conference" at Niagara Falls exonerated him of aggression and set up the salutary principle of an inter-American guarantee of mutual independence. Meanwhile, Wilson had reached an agreement with Britain for concessions on Panama tolls in exchange for support in unseating Huerta. Huerta finally departed.

Wilson anxiously adopted a policy of "watchful waiting," as he called it, which only American traditions of democracy enabled him to maintain. He recognized a new president, Carranza, who was favored by South American powers, and accepted his promise to punish a troublesome bandit, Pancho Villa. Villa was committing murders on both sides of the international boundary in the effort to provoke armed invasion, exploit Mexican hatred of gringoes, destroy Carranza and elevate himself. Although Congress passed a resolution for armed intervention and Theodore Roosevelt and investors in Mexican holdings shouted for the scalps of both Carranza and Villa, Wilson limited himself to mobilization of militia on the border and despatch of General Pershing in pursuit of the bandit.

Villa was not captured, nor would Carranza recognize the foreign right of intervention, nor pledge protection to foreign citizens and property. These guarantees he probably could not give, and Wilson in January of 1917 ordered withdrawal of troops without them. Wilson wanted no Mexican war on the eve of entrance into the European struggle.

Carranza soon secured election by the Mexican Congress, which demonstrated its prejudices by hissing Ambassador Henry P. Fletcher and applauding the German ambassador. At the moment, Germany's scheme for a joint attack by Japan and Mexico upon Texas, California and the states between had just been published. Although Wilson's self-restraint had cost Mexico's respect, it had gained him the good-will of Latin America and prevented war. It left uncertain the property rights of foreigners, their claims for damages to person and property, for expropriated farm and mineral lands and for defaulted bonds.

Mexico's crucial problem remained the recovery of her resources for the benefit of her people. To solve it a new constitution in 1917 provided for the protection of labor from capitalistic domination, for the nationalization of church property and secularization of schools and for an end to foreign concessions. The famous "Article 27" declared all lands, waters and mineral deposits the property of the nation, which could determine conditions of private holdings and could expropriate them in the public interest; oil, formerly allowed to lie in private ownership, was to be brought into fifty-year leaseholds under state ownership. A "Calvo clause" required foreign concessionaires not to call on their governments for support of title against the Mexican government.

Alarmed American investors, particularly oil interests aided by Senator Fall, exhausted every expedient during the next decade to secure agreement that the reforms should not be retroactive, as indeed the 1917 constitution said they could not. Intervention was demanded by American Catholics also. War nearly came in 1919, and there were no diplomatic relations, 1920-1923; but Secretaries Hughes and Kellogg found that the American public preferred patient negotiation. American demands were tempered to Mexican political realities in a series of agreements known as the "Bucareli Conferences," and satisfaction was expressed in reassuring amendments to the Mexican code.

The Mexicans gradually achieved political stability under more liberal presidents. They passed Petroleum and Alien Land Laws in 1925 to implement the 1917 reform, hitherto applied only in temporary decrees. Finally Dwight W. Morrow, a liberal member of the J. P. Morgan firm, was sent down as ambassador. By exceptional tact and understanding he obtained compromises on the moot points of titles, the

Calvo clause, the church and land claims. Amicable relations were assisted not a little by the rising interest of American tourists and intellectuals in Mexico's culture and history, and by "good-will flights" begun by C. A. Lindbergh, who met in Mexico his future wife, Anne Morrow. Strained relations did not return until Calles' successor, Cardenas, confronted the F. D. Roosevelt administration with another effort to apply the constitution of 1917 to land distribution.

Oriental Excursions

The reaction of the American people to possession of the Philippines demonstrated that imperialism came unnaturally, made them uncomfortable and could not be maintained according to the European pattern. Although Bryan met defeat in the 1900 campaign on imperialism, the treaty with Spain had been ratified with difficulty, the Senate came within a vice-president's vote of pledging Filipinos speedy independence and from the outset Congress reiterated the intention to let them go. Maintenance of this colony, which Congress labeled an "unincorporated territory," with its 7,000,000 people multiplying to 12,000,000 "citizens of the Philippines," violated democratic mores. It put Americans on the defensive, an unwonted rôle since 1865, and gave them three disconcerting surprises.

The Filipinos would not admit that possession by the beneficent, well-intentioned United States was a privilege. They put up a bitter, three-year fight for independence against the odds of 60,000 United States troops, relentlessly captained. They demonstrated that their vast majority was not uncivilized, unintelligent, unchristian or incapable of political organization. Facts surprising to Americans were revealed by commissions sent out to learn what manner of people were being subjugated and instructed. Some well-meaning patriots suffered discomfiture.

No less surprising was the failure of the Philippines to prove a gold mine. Their acquisition did not convert the Pacific into an "American lake." The islands proved neither a phenomenal outlet for American products nor a convenient reëxport depot for the China trade, which fell rather than rose. Tariff adjustments failed to remedy this situation: in 1902 Congress tried a 25 per cent reduction from Dingley domestic schedules; in 1909 they tried free trade in everything except certain products, like sugar, tobacco, and hemp, competing with American production; in 1913 they established nearly complete free trade. Yet the Filipinos proceeded to sell Americans more than 30 per cent more than they bought; and their biggest export crop, sugar, which was produced by non-American capital, competed with American-financed sugar of Cuba, Puerto Rico, Hawaii and the mainland. Nor did capitalists find

Philippine investments attractive; they confined their modest outlays chiefly to railways, public utilities and government obligations.

A third surprise was that the Philippines proved a distinct liability. With lack of abundant private profits went heavy public outlays. As elsewhere, American governors with hearty approval from home spent lavishly to establish facilities considered indispensable for intelligent, progressive living; imperialism should be justified by paternalism. The Filipinos eagerly used the facilities, with little expense to themselves and heavy outlay to the United States Treasury, but were not too grateful to want to be free. Moreover some American naval experts were sure that islands 6,200 miles distant could not be defended and that the United States was in an exposed position, to which prestige and moral obligations chained her!

Whatever the solution, it quickly became evident that military rule would not long be maintained without a vestige of native participation. Three Filipinos shortly were given places on the Taft Commission which established civil government in 1901; the Philippines (Foraker) Act of 1902 provided that an elective, lower house should be established after census taking, and it met in 1907. Next, the Democrats, committed to independence since 1900, added an elective senate under the Jones Act of 1916, authorized native reorganization of the government and formally promised future withdrawal. Wilson's gubernatorial appointee, General Francis B. Harrison, wisely prepared the islands for self-rule, encouraging native civil servants and state control of island development. Wilson asked Congress to make them independent.

The Republicans took no such mandate and Harding's appointee, General Wood, undid Harrison's reforms; but his successor, Stimson, practiced conciliation. The independence party received strong reënforcements from American competition with Filipino goods and labor and from the return of the Democrats to power. They rejected an independence act of 1932 as too unfair but accepted a 1934 law. It provided for independence after a ten-year probationary period, with the United States keeping naval privileges, barring Filipino immigration (which had been worrying California white labor) and shutting out Filipino goods.

The price of independence, apparently, would be economic collapse, for in 1935, 80 per cent of the islands' exports went to the United States, and they could ill compete with cheaper markets to the East. Moreover, Japanese imperialism effectively confused American oriental policy, threatening to substitute for self-rule under American paternalism an economic and political subjection under Nipponese militarism. Aguinaldo himself took second thought on the blessings of independence, as the years of "probation" wore on.

Pacific-mindedness carried America into the "backyard of European politics"—China—where the modern powers were scrambling for the spoils. There the United States aided them, more than herself, by a policy of benevolence mixed with impracticality in which missionary zeal far outstripped investments. Perry's push against the closed door of Japanese trade in 1853 had helped to awaken Japan to modern aggressiveness. Next, the United States (which had insisted upon equal trading privileges in China since 1844) obtained in 1883 a trade agreement with Korea and stumbled into a most delicate situation, for Japan and China had been contending there for dominance through three hundred years, and Korea, as a buffer state between China, Japan and Russia, had become the "touchstone" of Far Eastern diplomacy. The Arthur administration obtained the Korean treaty by giving her more considerate terms than other governments would have offered, and the latter hastily copied them to obtain like privileges.

The agreement also avoided reference to Korea as a dependency of China, which advantaged Japan. She was bound to exploit the scramble of the western powers over China so as to get the opportunity to expel occidental influence and substitute her own. She exposed China's weakness in the war of 1894-1895 by which Japan won Formosa and domination of Korea; this inspired France, Germany, Italy and Russia to follow Britain's example in seizing port leases and railroad concessions.

When Britain "went shopping for allies" to counter her rivalries, she proposed that the United States join her in insistence upon the "open door" in China. Secretary of State Hay was very sympathetic toward England,[1] American interest in eastern trade was forward and capitalists had no desire to throw away the Spanish victory; but joint action would seem to suggest an "entangling alliance." Therefore Hay made in 1899 an independent appeal to the powers to guarantee, in their respective Chinese spheres of influence, equality of trade opportunity, so that merchants of all nations would pay the same tariffs, port dues and railroad charges. Only Britain formally seconded Hay's doctrine, but he announced that it had become established. Britain, gratified, facilitated subsequently the canal and Alaskan settlements (pp. 351, 431).

When patriotic Chinese formed a secret organization called the Boxers and proceeded in 1900 to stage an outbreak against foreign concessionaires, the United States sent troops to help rescue the whites. Hay announced in explanation that America's Asiatic policy included preservation of China's territorial and administrative entity. This amazing assumption of responsibility, without compensating advantages and impossible to fulfill, was consented to by the other powers to placate America, and Hay was able to soften somewhat the onerous pen-

[1] He leaned on an American friend, W. W. Rockhill, who leaned on a shrewd Englishman, Alfred Hippesley.

alties imposed upon China for the uprising.[1] The United States had won the friendship of China at a cost of aggravating occidental powers.

The rising Asiatic power, Japan, also was provoked. When she went to war in 1904 to drive Russia out of Manchuria, so as to clear her own way into China, American sympathies lay with her because she had not shown Russia's contempt for the open door. Indeed, Roosevelt mediated for a peace at a juncture more favorable to Japan than to Russia, though both were well-nigh exhausted. Under arrangements made by him the negotiators consummated a peace at Portsmouth, New Hampshire, in 1905 under his friendly eye, thus giving the United States a unique experience as host. Afterward the Japanese blamed Roosevelt for their failure to obtain an indemnity and the whole (instead of one-half) of Sakhalin island, and they turned his portrait to the wall. This resentment would be one of many. They disliked immigration bars erected in Hawaii and the Philippines. They were angered by restrictions upon Japanese immigration, schooling and landownership in America, including areas outside the United States; the Senate in 1912 interposed the Monroe Doctrine against Japanese leases on the Mexican coast. Nor would California permit the federal government to tolerate equal treatment of persons of Japanese birth, for they offered too much competition as farmers and laborers.

Roosevelt salved Japan's pride temporarily in 1907 by the "gentlemen's agreement" which put Japan on her honor to issue no passports for entry into the United States by skilled or unskilled labor. Events proved that the substitution by the treaty of Portsmouth of Japan for Russia in Manchuria did not bring the open door there and did give Japan recognition as a world power, which she in time would use to close the door to China.

Roosevelt pursued his oriental excursions through careful avoidance of treaty-making, which would have revealed that neither Senate nor nation acquiesced. After Portsmouth he made two personal agreements with Japan. By the Taft-Katsura memorandum and the Root-Takahira agreement America endorsed the Anglo-Japanese alliance and approved a free hand for Japan in Korea, while Japan disavowed aggressive designs on the Philippines and made pious pledges on Chinese independence and the open door. Both knew, however, that the status quo to which they pledged themselves was transitory and that the door was closing. The United States navy made an ostentatious visit to Japanese waters while Japan seized some more of Manchuria and continued her practice of working with European capitalists, particularly English, to hinder American profit-sharing in Chinese exploitation.

[1] Of the 333 millions of reparations the United States claimed only about 25 millions and later remitted about three-fourths of that. The Chinese allocated nearly 11 millions of the remission to a fund for educating their youth in the United States.

President Taft and Secretary of State Knox first proposed that the powers renounce the special railroad concessions which were destroying China's integrity and subscribe to a joint loan whereby China either could buy foreign-held lines or construct a competing, neutral line; coöperation did not come. Then Taft and Knox tried to open the door for United States capitalists, the former in the notion that such beneficent influence would prevent Chinese bankruptcy and dismemberment, the latter as a business-like application of dollar diplomacy. They helped American bankers to participation in a four-power railroad loan; but their project for a share in a six-power "consortium," planned for financing reorganization after China's 1911 revolution, was killed by President Wilson, and the bankers did not get into China again until 1920. Wilson was not unaware that America's stake in China was small, and he was acutely conscious of the fact that forced loans undermined Chinese independence and violated the American democratic principle also.

The World War freed Japan to penetrate unhindered; she made "Twenty-one Demands" on China which victimized her, and by the Lansing-Ishii agreement of 1917 the United States recognized that Japan had special interests and Japan secretly agreed to spare the rights of friendly powers. Japan obtained Germany's concessions and practically ignored the open door while elevating herself to primacy as the imperial power of the East. The occidental powers could make little official headway against this trend.

The disarmament movement of the early 'twenties gave the United States an opening for a graceful retreat from Asiatic imperialism. At a Nine-Power Conference convened at Washington in 1921 at the invitation of the Harding administration, Japan publicly gave the pledge secretly made in 1917. The old British-Japanese alliance was ended by a "four-power treaty" in which Britain, France, Japan, and the United States agreed to respect each other's rights in the Pacific and to handle differences through diplomacy. These four, with Belgium, China, Holland, Italy and Portugal, signed the "nine-power treaty," which among other things guaranteed China's integrity and the open door. Thus the United States shifted onto nine shoulders the burden she formerly had assumed to carry alone.

The same treaty, however, presaged future strained relations with Japan. It set a naval building program of 5-5-3 for Britain, the United States and Japan respectively; and a London conference of 1930 kept Japan in the same minor position, although it accorded her parity with the United States in submarines. Shortly she was destroying Chinese sovereignty in larger areas and further invalidating the open door. By 1934 she was ready to demand complete parity, and the London conference of 1936 was wrecked on the same demand. She managed to turn to her own advantage the purchase of Chinese silver by the United States and prevented some American capital from fleeing the country for safety. Her cheaply made goods, offered as barter, invaded United States markets in some parts of the American hemisphere. Across the Pacific she confronted the F. D. Roosevelt administration with the fait accompli of her own Monroe Doctrine in Asia; its corollary was a closed door.

Africa and Europe

While the European struggle of competing governments to maintain and to upset their "balance of power" was hastening the partition of China, it operated likewise in Africa and kept the European continent on tenterhooks. In these areas, as in China, American public opinion resisted involvement, the Theodore Roosevelt administration marked an interfering phase, and small, isolated incidents led tenuously toward entanglement.

American philanthropists in 1822 had founded Liberia as a haven for freed slaves, but the United States steadfastly refused to assume a protectorate and in 1847 acknowledged its independence. When the powers in 1885 established the Congo Free State President Cleveland refused to involve his people.

In the badly managed sultanate of Morocco, however, the powers in 1880 had made a definition of extra-territorial protection to which the Hayes administration had subscribed; and in that troubled area the T. Roosevelt administration figured thrice. It connived in payment of $65,000 in 1901 to ransom from bandits an American missionary, Miss Stone. It demanded and secured in 1904 the release from bandits of Jon Perdicaris, an alleged American. Roosevelt knew he was not a citizen, but caused publication (the Republican national convention was just meeting) of the rousing part of a cablegram to Morocco: "We want Perdicaris alive or Raisuli [the bandit leader] dead." The unpublished part of the telegram instructed the Americans not to land marines. Perdicaris was released, and the convention applauded.

Shortly thereafter German domestic troubles required the Kaiser to demand that France and Britain consult Germany before settling the matter of control over Morocco, and the Kaiser appealed to Roosevelt. There was no real United States interest in the Morocco business, but the President readily persuaded himself he could figure as one who prevented a European war; he urged France to admit Germany to conference. As the resulting Algeciras convention of 1906 gave Germany recognition and gave France a preferred position in Morocco, both sides (unlike the parties to the Portsmouth treaty) were pleased. Roosevelt was highly gratified.

The United States Senate, however, was apprehensive. While ratifying the treaty, they pinned to it a protective reservation which from 1899 they attached to all multi-lateral treaties having the slightest political significance. They disavowed United States concern in anything other than the lives, property and commerce of her citizens and the peace of the world. They reiterated that she had no purpose to abandon her traditional aloofness from European political settlements.

The other treaties negotiated with European powers between 1898 and 1914 concerned social betterment and disarmament. Sixteen non-political instruments dealt with sanitation, public health, hospitals, drug formulas, the white slave traffic, an international institute of agriculture, war wounded and importation of liquor into Africa. On disarmament the first Hague conference in 1899 reached no agreement, but the United States subscribed to three compacts: that neutral powers could tender peace offices, that an involved nation could call for a Commission of Inquiry and that there should be a permanent Court of Arbitration.

With five other powers America in 1904 signed conventions for submitting all but vital disagreements to the Hague tribunal, arrangements amended by the Senate in 1908. At the second Hague conference in 1907 an international prize court was set up and provision made for the London Naval Conference of 1908. Secretary Knox sought in 1911 to extent the field of arbitration, but the Senate refused. The high water mark in peace coöperation was Bryan's negotiation of "cooling-off" treaties with thirty powers in 1913 and 1914. This was the most important undertaking which Wilson allowed his first secretary of state. Being an ardent pacifist, Bryan worked hard to persuade the powers to agree to submit "every otherwise insoluble dispute," without exception, to permanent investigating commissions. Wars were to wait, presumably a year, pending recommendations from the commissions, the theory being that whatever the recommendation and whether or not the government accepted it, the interval of delay would effectually discourage war-making. Twenty-two of the thirty treaties actually went into effect, and, although the "grape juice diplomacy" of this teetotaler secretary was ridiculed by the press, it proved significant. Apparently the lack of such a treaty with Germany affected American entrance into the First World War, and demonstrably Bryan's projects affected the post-war peace set-up.

In spite of dollar diplomacy, armed intervention and the calculating character of much of American diplomacy, it was not all out of line with the aspirations of the Progressive Era. There developed a somewhat belated desire to treat Latin American neighbors as equals; laudable efforts were made to promote fair dealing in the Orient; and there was hope of insuring lasting peace. The American democracy as of old had a sense of world responsibility which could rise above rivalry for gain.

CHAPTER XXXVIII

TOWARD WAR

In the second decade of the twentieth century, as the United States reached a climax in democratic advance under Wilson's New Freedom, world events were conspiring to open a new era for the American republic. World war—a symptom of the great revolution of the twentieth century—was speeding up the reordering of the condition of mankind; and the United States was to be forced into a new testing of the democratic experiment. Few Americans foresaw such a possibility as the storm broke in 1914.

Europe Goes to War

Most Americans in that midsummer of 1914 were engrossed in domestic affairs. Those who enjoyed foreign contacts and information usually apportioned their regard and admiration among outstanding persons and institutions of various nationalities, without particular thought of any one power as threatening peace and democracy. The Progressive Era had reënforced a long-standing assumption that mankind might continually advance toward some "bigger and better" scheme of existence. Cosmic-minded citizens dreamed of European coöperation in steps toward the common good; President Wilson in May had despatched Colonel E. M. House to interest England, France and Germany in international disarmament, a clean-up of the tropics and development of waste areas—worthy, peacetime objectives.

In Europe, however, France, Russia and England as a Triple Entente stood ranged against Austria, Germany and Italy as a Triple Alliance, in a delicate "balance of power." Imperial rivalries over trade and natural resources, secret treaties, armaments, rampant nationalism, clashing ideologies and race hatreds had set the world stage for war. Through forty-three years—ever since the Franco-Prussian War—each recurrent crisis had been deflected from becoming a major conflict; but war machinery had been perfected, while the will—and probably the power—to avoid war diminished. Finally resentments between Serb Nationalists and Austro-Hungarian Imperialists, and between Pan-Slavs and Pan-Germans, caused the murder by a Bosnian Serb, 28 June 1914, of Archduke Ferdinand, heir to Austria's throne, and his wife, while visiting Sarajevo, Bosnia.

This assassination touched the match. Germany endorsed Austria in plans for rigorous punishment of Serbia; Russia went to the aid of this diminutive Slav state; France joined Russia against Germany, which promptly declared war, 1-3 August 1914, on both and quickly marched troops across neutral Belgium toward Paris. England, vulnerably located just across the channel, joined the anti-German group, hereafter called the "Allies," on 5 August. Japan, allied with Britain since 1902, soon came in. Of the Balkan states, Greece and Rumania joined the Serbs on the side of the Allies; Bulgaria and Turkey went with Germany and Austria, these four comprising what came to be called the "Central Powers." Italy, however, could and did refuse to take fire until the Allies later tendered big bargains in territorial pledges. Only minor Iberian and Baltic powers out on Europe's margins—Spain, Holland, Denmark, Sweden and Norway—contrived, like Switzerland, to preserve neutrality in a war which engaged 28 "allied" nations against the 4 "Central Powers."

Early Neutrality

The outbreak of the war found the people of the United States little aware of its significance. They thought it small concern of theirs and President Wilson spoke the common wish when, on 4 August, he proclaimed that the United States government was adopting the position of neutrality. He called upon the nation to be "neutral in fact as well as in name," to be "impartial in thought as well as in action." However, neutrality was not in fact a status fortified by frequent practice down through the ages. It was a delicate relationship, as between warring powers, which governments had been able to assume occasionally only within the past two centuries.

When the news came that Belgium had been invaded, and further word of that country's heroic resistance, indignation and admiration blazed up. Early in the war, Americans began to speak of Germans as Huns. The nation that would violate its word, speak of a solemn treaty as a mere "scrap of paper" and murder and torture Belgian women and children ought to be beaten. Most Americans definitely sympathized with the Allies from the start.

President Wilson ventured prompt offices for peace, only to be rebuffed. Congress was in session, still legislating under progressive impetus, and it soon took a hand. American exporters, of cotton especially, were hurt by Allied blockade of the Central Powers and by conversion of Allied freight vessels into troop transports. Also federal revenues were suffering through a falling off of $100,000,000 worth in dutiable imports. So Congress took time in an election year for emergency laws, providing for a Bureau of War Risk Insurance, for transfer of cargo ships from belligerent flags to American registry, and for special excises to restore revenues. In the congressional campaign the Democrats were stressing America's freedom from war, but domestic factors proved mainly responsible for leaving Wilson a majority in both houses.

In the meantime President Wilson, Secretary of State Bryan, Robert Lansing (counsellor of the State Department), Walter Hines Page, (ambassador to Great Britain), James W. Gerard (ambassador to Germany), and the President's intimate friend, Edward M. House, were plunged into ever more complicated diplomatic negotiations with the principal governments of the Allies and the Central European powers. It was to become apparent that the United States was to be dominated largely by external influences and was only slowly to comprehend the realities of the nation's position. To meet the difficulties of the hour her statesmen and diplomats were either ill prepared or emotionally committed to take sides. Page, Lansing and House were frankly pro-Ally. The President was aloof from the country, given to self-communing and to formulating policies alone. These characteristics plus the ardent pro-Ally views of his few close friends were unconsciously forming his opinions despite an honest effort to be neutral. He maintained a high moral tone and exercised occasional firmness and sagacity, but he satisfied himself with general statements of principles rather than with shrewd trading negotiations, for he never realized the strength of his bargaining power.

The techniques of business deals rather than the precepts of international law were pertinent to this situation, for the United States was a great neutral trader, and self-interest dictated watchful safeguarding of that gainful position. She must champion neutral rights. The world long since had learned that England, as mistress of the seas, defined the law of the sea to suit her needs; blockades to be legal had to be effective; contraband carried by neutrals was liable to seizure. The United States when a weak neutral at the time of the Napoleonic wars had upheld the doctrine of neutral rights, and as she grew stronger she had enlarged it somewhat. Then came the Civil War and a change; to starve the South she restricted neutral rights, extending her definition of a blockade to ban goods bound to a neutral port when destined for an enemy. Britain had accepted this doctrine of "ultimate destination" with an eye to the future. The future arrived in 1914.

During the first decade of the twentieth century the European balance of power had become so precarious that the governments sought to safeguard themselves with various treaties. In 1909 representatives of the principal world powers had drawn up the Declaration of London which dealt with neutral rights. It validated the Civil War contention as to munitions but protected neutral commerce in "conditional contraband," such as food and certain supplies used by noncombatants, when bound to a neutral. Germany of course accepted this Declaration as likely to replenish supplies; Britain vetoed it because of its probable usefulness to Germany; the United States accepted it, but Taft withheld ratification after the British veto. The Declaration had little chance of fulfilment, at best, in a world-wide conflict. International law thus had remained vague on controversial matters as between neutral and belligerent rights and was of course silent on the vital problem of submarines.

Two days after the American proclamation of neutrality, the State Department suggested that the warring powers accept the rules of the Declaration of London. Germany and Austria agreed, as they expected to profit greatly by neutral trade. Great Britain, however, would not concede such an advantage to her enemies. Some attempts were made to find a formula to insure Britain's adherence. During October of 1914, despatches passed between Wilson and Lansing, Page and Lord Grey, the British foreign minister, which in effect proposed that Britain declare the Declaration of London to be in force while she proceeded to do as she pleased regarding actual enforcement. Thus instructed, Britain could discount official protests long before United States investments and exports were firmly tied to the Allied cause. Official as well as public sentiment thus preceded economic interests in preventing vigorous retaliation for British violation of neutral rights. After such rather feeble efforts to get Great Britain to modify her policy, the State Department acquiesced in her refusal and 22 October announced that it would protect American trading rights "as defined by the existing rules of international law and the treaties of the United States."

Great Britain undertook to make some concessions to American trade in her contraband schedules. Also she permitted the United States to have certain imperial products, such as rubber, wool and manganese, export of which was generally forbidden. A working agreement was concluded between the two powers which went into effect early in 1915 whereby, in return for needed products from Britain, the United States placed manufacturers using such raw materials practically under British control as far as their foreign trade was concerned.

This did not work too well. Britain applied the rule of final destination to conditional contraband as well as to munitions. Treating wheat and flour as contraband, even when consigned to neutrals, would starve out the Central Powers. Declaring the North Sea a "military zone" for searching and seizing ships enroute to neutral feeders of Germany, she subjected rich American cargoes to costly interference. Extending the right of search, she dragged neutral cargoes into British ports for leisurely examination for British-defined contraband. Her warships hovered close to American territorial waters. British and French commanders seized "suspicious" characters from American ships. Mail between the United States and neutrals was wantonly molested; German goods needed for American industries were intercepted; some United States firms were blacklisted, others cut off from neutral customers so that British traders might annex business.

American interests, incensed, demanded protests from the State Department. These were couched in vigorous language but not backed up by pressure. Britain delayed her replies, yielded nothing of her position and gave the United States the minimum of satisfaction. In fact the British Foreign Office cited precedents from the American Civil War which showed that then the American blockaders had done everything against which the United States now protested; and American court decisions of that period now supplied Britain with her logic. Nevertheless, American sympathy and interest were so wedded to Britain that the United States did nothing to back up its claims.

On the other hand, Germany was increasingly aware of British power over neutral shipping. At first the German government protested vigorously and scored the United States for failing to protect neutral rights against Great Britain. This soon proved quite useless, so she took more vigorous measures. She had a small fleet of a new weapon, the submarine, and she proceeded to use it.

To offset blockade with blockade, Germany, 4 February 1915, declared the waters surrounding Great Britain a war zone and ships entering it liable to submarine attack. Also, since submarines had no carrying facilities and were highly vulnerable, their commanders would not follow the old rule of international law requiring that passengers and crew be placed in safety before a ship was sunk. As Britain freely used neutral flags (a war device of long standing) it was clear that Germany would sink neutral as well as enemy ships. This she did. Thus were the warring powers undertaking to prevent neutral aid from reaching the enemy. In the meantime emotions were being stirred up and new interests created by the conflict.

Economic and Emotional Interests Intervene

To business the war brought relief, reversing a downward trend begun in 1913; federal rate-making, wage-regulating, prosecutions and anti-trust laws had been met with a slowing down in industry and a practical stoppage of railway construction. The stock exchange had closed 31 July 1914, not to resume wholly unrestricted trading until April following, but industrial and agricultural production after five months registered a tremendous spurt. Munitions factories, some spurred by British ownership of majority stock and control of production, raised munitions exports from 40 millions in 1914 to 1,290 millions in 1916. The United States became the base of military supplies for England. Metal and lumber industries expanded to supply the machinery of death, houses to shelter workers who made it and ships to carry it. All manpower diverted to destructive manufacturing still had to be fed. Although many goods and services were not paid for in gold, the gold in the federal treasury, approximately 1,250 millions 1 July 1914, had doubled by April 1917. By the end of the war, the United States had become a strong creditor nation.

Payments for Allied purchases came to be made increasingly from loans of money and credit obtained in the United States. Secretary of State Bryan, who had been devoting much effort to negotiation of "cooling-off" treaties, by which war-inclined powers agreed to postpone open hostilities twelve months, saw that war loans must imperil neutrality. He desired official discouragement of such loans, although he defended munitions exports. The Administration early warned against loans but soon tolerated credit loans and, when Bryan later resigned, withdrew what remained of opposition. Business and political pressure, exerted through Secretary of State Lansing and Secretary of the Treasury McAdoo, facilitated loans.

J. P. Morgan, who was intimately connected with banking houses in Paris and London as well as New York, became central purchasing agent of the Allies in the United States and obtained practically a free hand to engineer purchases sometimes amounting to 10 millions daily. Eager domestic investors absorbed 250 millions in American securities unloaded by Europeans and bought so many English and French securities that in mid-November 1916 the Federal Reserve Board issued a warning that too many American funds were traveling beyond the reach of American businessmen. By the time the United States became an "associate" of the Allies, Americans held at least 1,500 millions in Allied paper; their German holdings then were down to about 27 millions.

Emotional complexes, as well as economic interests, affected the relationship of the American nation to the war abroad. Social and political influences were powerful. On the one hand, America's heterogeneous population, of which one-third was either foreign-born or of foreign parentage, included about 9 million persons who had at least one German parent; the Irish element also ranged against England's side, contributing its share to what was called "hyphenism." On the other hand, a very great many Americans felt drawn to Britain by ties of language, literature, ideology and institutions. Thence stemmed most of their constitutional, legal and political customs. Revolutionary resentments had died out. In the Spanish war, Britain had shown herself friendly at Manila Bay while Germany seemed hostile, although she had complied with a request to search a vessel suspected of carrying war supplies from Hamburg to Spain. Subsequent contacts had encouraged the feeling that Germany was a militaristic power rather than a friendly democracy, especially when she had refused a "cooling-off" treaty. For France, Americans entertained a feeling of gratitude which the compatriots of Lafayette were not slow to exploit.

The best instincts of many Americans made them extremely susceptible. They had entered the twentieth century righteously interested in reform of their own institutions and of those of other nations. The progressive movement had developed their uplift urge to a very high point. The war administered a series of severe shocks, making them peculiarly responsive to proposals for transforming the struggle into a benefit to mankind. They had scant accurate information on the causes of the war and knew not the territorial bargains among the Allies. Ready to believe that Britain and France were busy saving the world from barbarism, they and many of their outstanding leaders accepted British accounts of German "atrocities," therein following the example of America's notable friend, Lord Bryce.

The British adroitly appealed to American sympathies, prejudices and idealism. Their efficient publicity expert in America, Sir Gilbert Parker, supplied weekly war reviews to hundreds of newspapers, inspired pro-Ally articles under the authorship, usually, of native Americans and watched over the movies. Personal contacts between Englishmen and leaders of American thought and politics helped to make speeches, debates and lectures friendly. British interception of international mails and control of cables, which were strictly censored, left only the wireless for transmission to the public of Central Power information and propaganda. The British Intelligence service unhesitatingly eavesdropped on informative ciphers passing between the United States government and her emissaries abroad. The gospel of Allied innocence and German infamy classified questioners as "Huns."

German propaganda was inept, blundering. Slow to follow the British "White Paper" with one of their own in October of 1914, they gave many Americans the impression that Germany alone was responsible for the war. Their frank references to the Belgian neutrality treaty as "just a scrap of paper" were more realistic than American ears liked. Their purchase of the New York *Evening Mail,* and other subsidizing by them became known so quickly as to defeat their objectives. The British were more effective with their Providence *Journal.* The Austrian ambassador, Dumba, with German military and naval attachés Von Papen and Boy-Ed, through sabotage of munitions plants discredited their cause. The U-boats were soon to underscore suspicions of infamy aroused by the German invasion of Belgium.

The anti-German cause was taken up by highly influential Republicans, the most important of whom was "T. R." His dislike of Wilson had developed after the spring of 1914, when Wilson had recommended the $25,000,000 payment to Colombia in apology for Roosevelt's coup at Panama; and the ex-President long had had pro-British leanings, althought he (like Taft) had preached German virility and efficiency to Americans. He had close personal friendships with Spring-Rice, Lord Bryce and other English notables. Also, as president he had had a secret understanding with England and Japan regarding the Orient and had assured Edward VII, through Senator Lodge, that the United States intended working with England. His pro-British leanings then had given color to rumors of a secret pledge of United States aid to England and France against Pan-Germanism. Immediately after the rape of Belgium he came out for neutrality, but many weeks had not passed before he was thoroughly committed to the Allies. Thenceforward, as long as Wilson was understood to be trying to maintain neutrality, Roosevelt denounced him to the nation. Through innumerable public pronouncements, active correspondence and in the columns of the *Outlook,* he effectively undermined the respectability of peace.

Although predisposed to the Allies, the American people were not quick to abandon their national tradition of isolation so far as to fight Germany. Their history showed them averse to pacifism, but they steadfastly regarded themselves as peace-lovers. The arbitration treaties and Hague conferences in which recent administrations had participated (see Chapter XXXVII) attested loyalty to the peace ideal in many walks of life, especially in the Middle West. An American League to Limit Armaments, a Union against Militarism and a Women's Peace Party were very earnest. Henry Ford transported some of their membership to Europe in December 1915, filled with the hopeful but futile ambition to "get the boys out of the trenches by Christmas." Germans and Irish-Americans organized, pressed for an embargo and took such attractive titles as the Friends of Peace, American Independence Union, Labor's National Peace Council and the American Humanity League. Numerous peace-lovers found distinguished leadership in the League to Enforce Peace launched at Independence Hall, 15 June 1915, under the guidance of such notable persons as Jane Addams, ex-President Taft, President Lowell of Harvard and Hamilton Holt, editor of the *Independent;* they sought to combine realism and idealism in an international league. Such factors, emotional and economic, worked upon the so-called "neutral" nation, making it impossible to follow Wilson's initial counsel to be "impartial in thought as well as in action."

CHAPTER XXXIX

THE TORPEDOING OF NEUTRALITY

Neutrality indeed was on the way to be sunk by a torpedo from a submarine, submarines having been non-existent when international neutrality laws first were formulated. Germany's announcement of 4 February 1915, that she would torpedo *without warning* neutral vessels headed for British ports, raised an outcry in the United States. To sink a neutral ship without warning was a violation of international law. Germany in reply pointed out that a submarine could not stop ships and search them without too great chance that the submarine might be sunk. This challenged United States interests, and six days later a note was dispatched to Germany saying that the American government would hold her to "strict accountability" if American life and property were harmed. Great Britain, for her part, announced she would seize any ships she thought might be carrying goods to Germany.

Submarine Peril

Not all United States opinion favored continuance of trade in munitions and other contraband under these circumstances. Some believed that the United States should follow European neutral example and impose embargoes against war materials. The farmers and planters of the Middle West and South found themselves suffering because the Allies blocked wheat and cotton exports to Germany; the Eastern interests, meanwhile, fattened on munitions sales to the Allies. Their representatives denounced this munitions business as a patent violation of neutrality. Senators Hitchcock of Nebraska and Stone of Missouri tried to place senators on record against shipments of contraband; the Speaker and Majority Leader, Champ Clark of Missouri and Claude Kitchin of North Carolina, boldly urged an embargo and a warning against such shipments. Was not an embargo the strongest weapon a neutral nation could wield? Would it not probably reduce the likelihood of a neutral entering a war?

The embargo advocates, however, were easily pushed on the defensive by the combined force of economic interest, popular sentiment and the possibility of Allied defeat. The business lobbies were militant; was not the war trade helping to remove the possibility of an economic depression, which had seemed to threaten the nation in 1914? Were not the war profiteers but a small part of the total situation? Nor did the administration, which had captured the White House only through a three-cornered fight, have political resources adequate to redirect the popular trend, if it had wished to try. Only leadership with extraordinary influence could have swung any embargo program, with its jeopardizing of immediate profits for possible future non-involvement in the war, when such embargo would have hurt those belligerents for whom the President and the majority of the people had the greater natural sympathy. Many suggested what later evidence indicated as possible, that a munitions embargo any time after the middle of 1915 would have ended Allied belligerency.

Great Britain, unlike Germany and Austria, was dependent upon the United States for munitions and vulnerable to an embargo; therefore she took some care, in maintaining the Allied blockade of Germany early in the war, not to carry violations of neutral trading rights to the point of driving America into an embargo. She did not at first include in her classification of "conditional contraband" such products as cotton, tobacco, resin and turpentine, for such action would infuriate powerful interests shipping these to Central Powers. She delayed somewhat her use of war excuses for weakening American competition in areas her own commercial interests hoped to control. Extreme measures came mainly after United States prosperity was firmly tied to Allied purchases, after predominant sentiment was definitely anti-German and after Allied victory was in reasonable doubt. Such was the background against which the Wilson administration was pressed to frame a policy.

The President felt the need of direct information on the European situation and sent his close friend, Colonel Edward M. House, abroad in the spring of 1915 as a private emissary of peace. House, who was two years Wilson's junior, was a wealthy owner of Texas cotton and railroad properties who had been concerned in the rejuvenation of the Democratic party ever since Cleveland's day. After Bryan's third defeat he had pinned his faith to Wilson, made his acquaintance and thereafter seldom left his side for long until they broke in 1918. Rarely has a president had a more intimate, trusted counselor, but his mission to Europe did not bring peace or solve the problem of the submarine, with which international lawyers and publicists all were wrestling.

The people of the United States resented the ruthless use of the submarine, an American invention. All their moralists but not all navy men denounced it. Their government asserted that a modern war machine could not modify international law and suggested a *modus vivendi.* Germany should renounce mine laying and submarine attacks, while Britain restricted use of neutral flags and permitted transport of foodstuffs to Germany's civilian population. The replies of both revealed their indifference to peace. The Allies replied that Germany could not be trusted to keep a bargain; Germany insisted that raw materials, including those applicable to army use, should be classified with foodstuffs as non-contraband and safe from blockade. Each equally eager for starvation and economic strangulation of the other, neither paid any more respect to international law than self-interest dictated. Their notes to the United States regularly made a pretext of being forced into desperate retaliation by the inhuman conduct of

COLONEL HOUSE AND PRESIDENT WOODROW WILSON
(Courtesy of Charles Seymour and Houghton Mifflin Co.)

others; it really was a race in inhumanity. The inhumanity at first lay chiefly at the door of Germany for her use of U-boats; later at the door of the Allies for their long blockade of foodstuffs for civilians continued even after the armistice.

Submarine ruthlessness culminated 7 May 1915 in the sinking of the *Lusitania*. This giant passenger liner had been making frequent trips across the Atlantic, on occasion carrying military supplies. Germany was preparing to sink vessels carrying contraband where possible but in this case took the extraordinary precaution to publish, adjacent to the sailing notice in the New York newspapers, a notice warning Americans that they boarded Allied ships at their own risk. Undaunted 197 Americans set sail on the vessel which also carried 4,200 cases of cartridges and other contraband. Her captain disobeyed instructions to outwit submarines by following a zigzag course; he followed a straight course; his ship was sighted off the Irish coast by a submarine and was torpedoed without warning, sinking in eighteen minutes. The death toll of 1,198 persons included 128 citizens of the United States.

The *Lusitania* sinking increased pro-Ally sympathy tremendously, for violations of international law by British blockades affected chiefly inanimate cargoes, while submarine sinkings destroyed also many passengers and crews; material loss paled into insignificance compared with destruction of human life. Wilson and the American people were generally horrified and angered by this brutal deed, but the President did not consider it a cause for war. He was sincerely devoted to maintaining peace and shortly after the sinking he declared in a public address, "There is such a thing as a man being too proud to fight. There is such a thing as a nation being so right that it does not need to convince others by force that it is right." Nevertheless, he began a series of bellicose notes to Germany which led to a break with Secretary of State Bryan. Bryan sensed in the situation an opportunity to bargain between Great Britain and Germany for maintenance of the laws of war; he thought a serious threat of an embargo might bring both belligerents to terms. The President could not accept Bryan's plans for counterbalancing England and Germany in United States diplomacy, nor could he agree with Bryan that loans to belligerents and travel by Americans on armed vessels should be discouraged. Such opposite views could not be reconciled.

The submarine prevented Wilson and most of the populace from treating Britain and Germany alike. He demanded an end to submarine ruthlessness, warning that repetition would be considered "deliberately unfriendly"; he ordered naval and war secretaries to prepare defense plans. The peace-loving Bryan resigned his place to Robert Lansing, 9 June. Lansing believed the Allies were fighting the cause of Democracy versus Autocracy; his instincts assured him that submarines would turn the scale in their favor, and his policy was to send the British "wordy fleabites" instead of bringing them to book. Though Germany gave Wilson no formal satisfaction, she stopped sinking liners, and for a while no American lives were lost.

The issue reopened 19 August 1915 when the *Arabic*, an English passenger vessel, was torpedoed in violation of orders, and two United States citizens were lost. This renewed the interchange of notes and the consideration of a break in relations. Germany apologized for the *Arabic*, and her ambassador, Count von Bernstorff, notified the White

House, 1 September, that she agreed no liner should be sunk without warning and that she would provide safety for noncombatants, except where the liner resisted or tried to resist. The Berlin government at that time was hopeful of winning the war before supplies ran too low, was uncertain whether her fleet of twenty-eight submarines could starve England and hesitated to risk the effect of ruthlessness upon American sentiment.

Germany's disavowal was followed by six months without the loss of American lives through submarine activities, months marked (as events later proved) by tightening of Wilson's attitude. He clung longer than any other leader in the United States to the determination to maintain neutrality and to aid peace, but by the end of 1915 he had been driven to the Allied side, while the people likewise were losing neutrality although craving peace. He knew that none of the various belligerents was especially righteous and that Britain's interests particularly were primarily commercial and imperialistic; but apparently he reasoned that the type of industrial imperialism to which Germany wished to subject Europe was a threat to American civilization no less than to Europe's. He concluded he ought to shift his line of attack from domestic, industrial abuses to greater tyrannies on a world scale. His abhorrence of methods dominating European diplomacy flowered into an unshakable determination to inject liberalism into world relationships. So his initial lack of confidence in his own ability to handle foreign relations was transformed into an assumption that the powers could be moved to higher ground and that he could move them. If he took America into the war would not he be in a position to write into the peace treaty provisions for an end to all war?

Wilson again sent House to Europe early in 1916 to promote his peace proposals. As a result of his conferences House filed with the Allies, 22 February, the House Memorandum. It proposed that the United States offer to organize a peace conference whenever the English and French might desire it; then if the Allies accepted and Germany refused, the United States would "probably" join the Allies. Britain, not yet apprehensive of defeat, and bound by secret treaties with Russia, Italy and Japan, rebuffed this overture. Then Wilson took another tack. He sounded Democratic congressional leaders on American participation in behalf of civilization, but to the southern and middle western leaders of his party he sounded bellicose.

Just at this time came Germany's announcement of 8 February that after the 29th all armed enemy merchantmen would be treated as ships of war; this meant renewal of her submarine campaign and immediately aroused the adherents of neutrality. Representative Atkins J. McLemore of Texas and the blind Senator Thomas P. Gore of Oklahoma introduced into House and Senate resolutions which asked

Wilson to warn Americans that if they traveled in the war zone they did so at their own risk. This tacit withdrawal of official protection from traveling Americans had support among both parties and probably would have passed if the President had not actively opposed it. The vote to table the McLemore resolution stood 182 Democrats and 93 Republicans for, and 33 Democrats and 102 Republicans against; Gore's resolution was kept from a vote.

It was not long before the results of Germany's renewed submarine activity became apparent. A French steamer, the *Sussex,* was sunk 24 March 1916, killing three Americans. Wilson moved decisively. He addressed a bristling note to Germany and read it to a joint session of Congress on the anniversary of the Battle of Lexington. In this he threatened to sever relations, which drew from Germany another proposition certain of non-acceptance. She promised to abide by the rules of visitation and search—to give warning and to put passengers and crews in safety—provided that merchant ships cease carrying contraband and remain unarmed and that the United States hold England, also, to strict accountability. A submarine truce ensued, lasting about nine months, well past the presidential campaign with its preparedness legislation and its slogan—"He kept us out of war." The nation, Wilson wrote, "seems to demand two inconsistent things, firmness and the avoidance of war."

The President in the meantime had become concerned about armament. He realized when writing his notes about the *Lusitania* that he might have to back them up and therefore ordered the War and Navy departments to supply him with facts and figures. In rearmament he had a divided country to deal with, but support was growing as preparedness groups urging American entrance into the war were struggling for control of public opinion. A National Security League demanded fighting equipment, an offshoot called the American Defense Society demanded American entrance following the *Lusitania* sinking, and an American Rights Committee, from December 1915, fought for immediate participation. By that time the war-minded groups had given the peace societies such ill-repute that most of them were left in control of pacifists whose preachments increased the fervor of the militarists.

Campaigning in Wartime

While Wilson was waiting and public sentiment was crystallizing, the approaching presidential campaign of 1916 was affecting legislation. Progressive and neutrality issues were curiously mixed, with neutrality bothering Democrats and progressivism the Republicans. The Democrats knew the din an interventionist minority could raise, and events were weakening their resistance to additional military preparations.

Fearing vociferous Republican charges of inadequate defense, the Democrats passed four important preparedness laws before election. A National Defense Act projected within three years an army of 175,000 men and a national guard of 450,000 and provided for training of reserve officers and permanent establishment of a training camp, which had been under way experimentally at Plattsburg, New York; compulsory military service, however, was not included. The Naval Act of 1916 projected a three-year construction program of 10 dreadnoughts, 16 cruisers and 140 minor vessels at a cost of $500,000,000—the largest naval appropriation on record to that date.

A third law provided for a Council of National Defense to design "the coördination of industries and resources," in other words to plan industrial mobilization in case war came; its board was to consist of six cabinet officers and seven experts from outside government, serving without pay. Under the fourth measure a United States Shipping Board was established to see that the nation built or bought adequate merchant fleets and to safeguard commercial profits under neutrality, a difficult task.

There was also a votive offering to non-interventionists. Wilson in September 1916 obtained from Congress authority to prohibit loans and restrict exports to the Allies if they did not alter their "intolerable course." Also some of his supporters made much use of the slogan, "He kept us out of war."

For their part, Republicans dared not ignore pro-German or progressive voters. They tried to convince Irish and German-Americans that Republicans who clamored for preparedness aimed to aid the Central Powers thereby; at the same time they alienated peace groups by criticising and ridiculing Wilson's moderation toward European belligerents and Mexico. Eagerly they welcomed Progressives back into the Grand Old Party, including Roosevelt, who threw all his strength to them, refusing the Progressives' nomination and thereby destroying their ticket. Reunited, the Republicans nominated Charles E. Hughes, who in 1907 had become New York's reform governor as a consequence of legal work in exposing insurance scandals, and who, while associate justice of the United States Supreme Court 1910-1916, had proved fairly conservative.

The Republicans were aided somewhat by Democratic eagerness to clinch the labor vote and by Wilson's opposition to woman suffrage. The market for labor had tightened, owing to the boom in munitions manufacturing and allied war industries, and as wages rose and unions prospered, strikes increased. The rising cost of living was penalizing persons of fixed incomes, but factory workers, before the war ended, had obtained higher real wages than ever before. One branch of labor particularly saw an advantage during the campaign and took it. Railroad workers threatened to strike unless Congress passed a law granting them an eight-hour day. Rather than suffer a nation-wide tie-up, the Democratic leaders yielded and stipulated eight hours in the Adamson Act of September. Many persons denounced this as a hold-up and turned to Hughes; their attacks, however, alienated most of whatever labor support his ticket might have gained. The Republicans gained other votes by endorsing national woman's suffrage, which Wilson had labeled a state question. These advantages were offset, however, by certain political accidents. For instance, in California Hughes failed to meet Senator Hiram Johnson, the state's favorite son and outstanding Progressive Republican. His friends were deeply offended. At the end the finish was very close. Hughes carried New York and the usually pivotal states, and most people went to bed election night believing him elected. Then in the morning came more returns from the Far West. After four days it was certain that Californians had reëlected Johnson but had given their electoral majority to Wilson.

When the shouting and confusion ended, Wilson had won on both the progressive and neutrality issues. His 9 million popular votes as against Hughes' 8.5 millions were so distributed as to give him 277 electoral votes against Hughes' 254. While all the industrial and financial, high-tariff sections of the North and East except New Hampshire and Ohio had voted for Hughes and against the "New Freedom," every state in the trans-Mississippi area except Minnesota, Oregon and South Dakota had joined Maryland, Kentucky and the solid South in support of Wilson. A liberal legislative record attractive to foes of capitalistic imperialism, joined with frequent party use of Bryan's slogan, "He kept us out of war," had overcome the handicap of a relatively small campaign fund.[1] Through raising his 1912 total by 3 million votes, the Executive gained the satisfaction of ceasing to be a minority president. The public did not know that peace and progressivism already were defeated, that Wilson no longer believed he could keep the United States neutral and that as war president he would be given more power than any other ruler in the world.

Entering the War

The campaign of 1916 with its endorsement of peace was based on a false hope. The influences drawing the United States into war were growing stronger. Germany was in the ascendant at the moment but beginning to weaken. She expected some advantage from a negotiated peace, and knowing that Wilson had been endeavoring to organize a peace conference she on 12 December 1916 asked him to inform the

[1] The Democrats had about $1,800,000 as compared with $2,500,000 of acknowledged Republican funds.

powers that she was willing to negotiate. On his part, Wilson had already learned through European observers that peace propositions might be welcome, and he had planned to ask the various belligerents for a formal statement of peace objectives. The German request, therefore, put him in the embarrassing position of seeming to act on their initiative rather than his own; nevertheless he transmitted the German note to the Allies. A few days later, 20 December, he issued his own call for the war aims of the belligerents. Among the Allies his call lost force because it came after the German proposal. Furthermore the Allies now saw so many indications of American assistance in the near future that they visioned something more advantageous than a negotiated peace. True, their food and credit status was troubling their loan agent in the United States, but they decided to gamble on the future. Their reply to Wilson stipulated peace terms so drastic as to indicate they preferred a decisive victory to a compromise peace.

The President felt he must try to advocate a more lasting peace formula than the mere transfer of territory; helped by House, he was phrasing his own formula and announced it to Congress and the world 22 January 1917. It called for a "peace without victory" which should stabilize those international relations which had been so uncertain and provocative of war. His peace would guarantee to all nations large and small their rights: to government by consent of the governed, to independence, to sea outlets, to freedom of the oceans and to peace by international agreement. This program was to reappear later.

The Germans, like the British, entertained a cynicism foreign to the President. After vaguely expressing willingness to negotiate, they made specifications indicating no more eagerness for peace than the Allies; and against the advice of Ambassador Bernstorff they repudiated the *Sussex* pledge and announced resumption of unrestricted submarine warfare 1 February 1917. By now they had a fleet of more than 100 submarines which they estimated could cut British imports by about 40 per cent and end the war within six months, before their own manpower and resources were exhausted. Calculating that American participation would not enlarge the current stream of credit and supplies reaching the Allies and would not add manpower, they decided they could afford to alienate the United States.

Wilson promptly severed diplomatic relations; he and the majority of his people found submarine warfare intolerable. Yet so many Americans were uneager for war that the President received an unexpected set-back when he asked Congress to grant authority to arm merchant ships. A bill for that purpose passed the House with little opposition, but in the Senate were twelve members who apprehended that arming ships would immediately cause an overt act and drag the nation into war; they filibustered until the session expired on the eve of Wilson's second inauguration, 4 March 1917. The bill expired with it. Wilson bitterly denounced the filibusterers as "twelve wilful men who represent no opinion but their own," and he went ahead to arm the ships, anyway, under an old law of 1797 never repealed. Merchantmen were now to fire at submarines on sight.

The British Intelligence Service was intervening to galvanize opinion, particularly in the hesitant Southwest. They handed the State Department a month-old message filched by them from cables passing between the German Foreign office and its Washington Embassy over American wires. On 1 March Wilson had handed it to the press. The public thus learned that Foreign Secretary Zimmerman had instructed Ambassador Bernstorff that if the United States joined the Allies he should approach Mexico on a possible partition of American territory. Mexico was to be promised Texas, New Mexico and Arizona, a sort of *Mexico irridenta;* Japan might be offered Pacific Coast areas.

Zimmerman's note galvanized sentiment. American resentment flamed up against Germany just when a Russian Revolution substituted a liberal for an autocratic régime and strengthened the belief that the Allies were waging a war for democracy. British emissaries came, reporting that England had grain enough for only six weeks and could not possibly hold out beyond 1 November. Munitions manufacturers, merchants and other creditors of the Allies worried over possible losses from a stalemate or an Allied defeat. Some peace-lovers concluded that rich old England as victor would prove more peaceful than young, ambitious Germany. Thus, mixed sentiments of patriotism, gain and philanthropy helped to carry America toward war.

When German submarines during February and March sank six United States ships, three carrying her citizens, they forced Wilson to go to war or be inconsistent. After taking thirteen days to prepare a message, the President finally, 2 April 1917, asked Congress to declare war "to make the world safe for democracy." Some of the "wilful twelve," including Senators Stone of Missouri and La Follette of Wisconsin, objected that the Allies in many respects were more autocratic than democratic and that the United States had not protested German and British violations of neutral rights impartially. The people, they argued, did not want war; and, in fact, the rigorous conscription and espionage laws passed soon after the United States did go to war indicated something less than a unanimous desire to enter it. The majority in Congress, however, was convinced of the necessity, and after the war resolution had been carefully drafted so as to describe the United States as "associated" rather than "allied" with the Allies, the Senate (4 April, 86-6) and the House (6 April, 373-50) passed a resolution declaring that a state of war with Germany existed.

A mighty combination of factors—among them, democratic traditions, propaganda, profit-seeking, weak peace forces, inexpert statesmanship, altruism, anger at German ruthlessness and belief that German victory would endanger the existence of the Republic—had drawn in the United States. As the problem of neutrality had not been solved, intervention had proved unavoidable. America's entrance would not only determine the outcome of the war but would alter greatly the course of world history.

CHAPTER XL

THE UNITED STATES IN THE FIRST WORLD WAR

With general enthusiasm the American people turned to the perilous and nerve-wearing task of war-making. With comparatively little objection they accepted minute supervision over what had been their private affairs, demonstrating their faith in the cause, and the contagion of war fervor. War entrance released pent-up feelings and abundant energies, encouraging feverish activity. The emergency taught individuals new modes of behavior while placing them in a new relation to the state. Nearly every man and woman was made to realize that he or she was part of the largest mass movement in history.

Military and Naval Mobilization

To assist the Allies the entire nation was mobilized, though only about 2 million soldiers went overseas. Immediately upon American entrance the Allies asked for manpower. The popular French general, Joseph Joffre, and the astute English politician, Arthur J. Balfour, headed missions which came over at once to explain the extent of Allied exhaustion and to ask for 500,000 troops. The extremely able secretary of war, Newton D. Baker, superintended a badly needed military reorganization and within eighteen months created a force of 4 million men of whom about half went abroad and 1.4 million fought in the trenches. This achievement was effected through a draft under a Selective Service Act.

The decision to abandon the time-honored volunteer system was enacted into law over strong opposition. Some declared conscription to be un-American, and Bryan had spoken of a million men volunteering for the colors in time of need. Also the friends of Theodore Roosevelt wished to leave the way open for him to lead a "Roosevelt Division" of picked cavalry volunteers. However, the War Department's plan prevailed, and 17 May 1917 the Selective Service Act was passed. Under it all men between the ages of twenty-one and thirty inclusive were enrolled; the limits were later extended to eighteen and forty-five. These age groups were registered by civilians at the polling places with complete good order and in the spirit of patriotism. Registration and the entire administration of the Act moved smoothly in contrast to the draft riots of the Civil War. Altogether about 24,225,000 registered and 2,800,000 were called from the lists. Voluntary enlistments also were accepted in the regular army, navy, national guard and marines. Propaganda machinery used in other war activities found its counterpart in recruiting, with service flags hung in windows of houses and offices to proclaim patriotism. The drafted men revealed disturbing deficiencies in the physical fitness of American youth. Native whites from the country proved better endowed than alien born, colored, or city youths; boys from the Middle West extending from Texas to North Dakota were 70 to 80 per cent fit, while those from the Far West and some of the industrial states rated little above 50 per cent.

The soldiers were trained at thirty-two camps of about 48,000 men each, where they experienced a regimentation wholly new to most of them, under reserve officers hastily trained for the emergency. The army was provisioned chiefly by domestic products, except for English and French supplies and arms made necessary by the speed with which soldiers were sent overseas and by the inadequacy of American artillery and aircraft manufacture.

The navy assumed its due responsibilities. Admiral Sims had been sent to England in March, and the navy ultimately contributed its quota to check the submarine menace. It contributed eighty destroyers to the Allied forces in European waters and laid 56,000 mines in the North Sea blockade of Germany. It convoyed four-fifths of America's troop ships and prevented any of them from being torpedoed. By the end of the war over 300 United States war vessels and 75,000 sailors were in European waters, and Germany had lost almost half of her U-boats.

American soldiers and sailors received more consideration than those of any other nation. Their pay already was highest and was raised still further, and the government paid part of it to families where desired. Government insurance was provided at low rates in a vain effort to avoid post-war pension drives. Social service organizations supplied entertainment, smokes, and delicacies and generally concerned themselves for the comfort and well-being of the forces in the effort to lighten the strain of soldiering.

Originally the administration planned to wait despatch of troops until March 1918, but upon Allied insistence Wilson sent General John J. Pershing, his excellent choice of a commander, to France in the spring of 1917. Ports and railroads were equipped to land the troops and carry them toward the battle line. Pershing and Wilson, against strong pressure from France and Britain, insisted upon the principle that their soldiers should remain a separate entity instead of being scattered to fill in depleted regiments of the Allies. American pride, the morale of the soldiers themselves and the need for continued enthusiasm in the United States dictated this course. Troops landed in September 1917 and received a course of hardening before entering the trenches. Assigned at first to quiet sectors, they exerted more moral than military effect.

Mobilization on the Home Front

Behind the military forces was a great army of civilian effort. Approximately 11.5 million took up war jobs, and all learned that modern warfare enlists everybody. Clad in a uniform, even an insignificant person attracted attention—from both sexes. Every woman who took a man's former job found a sense of broadening power; women did practically everything except enter the trenches. Americans expected to contribute food, supplies, transportation and money rather than men, whom they at first supposed would not be needed in large numbers, or if needed could not be transported. For war purposes Congress, temporarily as in the Civil War, gave the President broad, unconstitutional powers; and the citizenry tolerated assumption of still wider functions, until he was exercising the widest powers of all occidental rulers.

Domestic mobilization was achieved at amazing speed though at high cost. Americans, accustomed to large-scale organization, loyally yielded the resources, leadership and following for the most colossal regimentation the world ever had witnessed. The Council of National Defense, set up in imitation of European practice in 1916 under the supervision of the secretaries of the treasury, war, navy, interior, commerce and labor, assisted by the seven civilian experts, was expanded and patterned after in the states, until war boards were supervising every major activity and many minor ones. A highly perfected technique of large-scale organization was readily invented and applied in each major field.

Food control was particularly important in order to conserve supplies for the Allies, and in April congressional approval was asked for the Lever Food and Fuel Control bill. It aroused stout opposition because of the deep-seated fear among progressives of monopoly in the United States. Only after repeated emphasis upon the legislation as essential to majority welfare was the bill finally passed in August 1917.

Food regimentation, however, was by that time well under way. The Council for National Defense had had a food committee at work, and in May Herbert Hoover, a wealthy mining engineer turned philanthropist, who had done a splendid job at distributing American food to starving Belgian children, became head of a voluntary food administration. Upon passage of the Lever Act he became head of the official Food Administration, and under its aegis a Grain Corporation and a Sugar Equalization Board eventually were set up to supervise sale and distribution of these particularly vital crops. A wheat price of $2.20 per bushel was guaranteed (a figure too low in view of other prices), and special emphasis was laid on reduced consumption of sugar. "Food will win the war" was Hoover's slogan, for this was a slogan war; and so everyone learned about how to "hooverize," that is, to increase production and decrease consumption. Through local food committees, war gardens, enthusiastic women's clubs, wheatless and meatless days, sugar limitation, pledge cards, etc., Americans so rapidly decreased consumption and increased production of breadstuffs, meats and sugar that they were enabled to export in 1918 three times their normal bulk of those commodities.

Agriculture was encouraged to finance expansion beyond the bounds of profitable peacetime farming, although the total physical output of agriculture (1917-1919) increased but slightly. In the excitement speculation raised land prices, while erosion and lack of fertilization depleted the soil. The soil of the semi-arid plains was plowed up for grain-growing, preparing the day for devastating dust storms. There was much farm operation at a loss.

In industrial life, also, diversion of production to war needs and acceleration of certain outputs progressed under close supervision. Congress created a War Industries Board, 28 July 1917, succeeding a short-lived General Munitions Board, and early in the next year the headship of it was given to Bernard Baruch, a stock exchange operator who had notably expanded his talents as adviser to the Council of National Defense. He helped to bring order out of a chaos of competing wartime production and allocation. The Board had complete control over manufacturing and purchasing, could tell manufacturers what they must produce and the Allies what they might have. With coöperation from the nation's Chamber of Commerce organizations, more than 500 war service committees functioned, handling relations between various industries and the government; manufacturers were forced to stop non-war activities unless approved by the War Industries Board, and the nature of industries was in some cases arbitrarily changed. The total physical output of mines and factories (1917-1919) declined. Leaders in industry gave an amazing degree of coöperation; they submitted to arbitrary fixing of contracts, prices, material distribution and the priority in which orders should be filled. Some businessmen who had spent their lives engrossed in their own plants volunteered as "dollar a year" men at Washington. The amount of voluntary cooperation which businessmen and women contributed in this compulsory situation made it something less than an industrial dictatorship.

Many industrialists profited during regimentation. Competitive bidding by purchasers representing various Allies made prices fantastic until a United States government and inter-Allied war council set up joint purchasing agencies which reduced somewhat this type of abuse. A few American entrepreneurs were rewarded with control of valuable alien property, such as the German dye privileges. War fortunes reached heights far beyond those obtained by profiteers of the 'sixties.

The relations between capital and labor came under the supervision of a War Labor Conference Board, and machinery for arbitration of disputes was provided in a National War Labor Board headed by ex-President Taft (at this time a Yale law professor) and Frank P. Walsh, a liberal Kansas attorney and publisher with experience in arbitration. Disputes were conciliated the more easily because public disapproval would focus on dissentients.

Organized labor both coöperated and profited, with Gompers and lesser Federation leaders conciliated by the government and enthusiastic in support of it. The war gave a tremendous impetus to their organizing activities and government influence. They exploited the labor shortage created by a 50 per cent fall in immigration and a diversion of 4.8 million men to army and navy occupations. A. F. of L. membership increased 37 per cent. Given places on the Labor Conference Board and elsewhere, leaders agreed to removal of some working restrictions on the understanding that the government would not permit a fall in labor standards. Their official position was "Work or Fight." A government employment service placed nearly as many men as the recruiting service. Housing problems obtained attention. While the cost of living rose faster than wages for consumers in general, organized labor managed to obtain an increase in real wages. Their greatest triumph was a law won over Wilson's veto imposing a literacy test on immigrants.

It was as vital to control fuel as it was food and industry, and so under the Lever Act the Fuel Administration was set up with Harry A. Garfield, president of Williams College, as chairman. Under his direction every effort was made to get fuel for vital industrial and transportation activities. Home and automobile owners were emphatically urged to conserve in every way possible. Coal, oil and gasoline were thus controlled and rationed. Some non-essential factories were put on a five-day week by a series of "heatless Mondays." "Daylight saving" was inaugurated by the Fuel Administration throughout the country.

The nation's railroad systems broke down early in the emergency, with full cars choking some eastern ports, depriving the production areas of the empty cars they desperately needed. The railroads attempted to solve this problem coöperatively by a Railroads War Board after getting assurance that this would not lay them open to prosecution under the Sherman Act, but the problem was too big. So in December 1917 Wilson issued a proclamation for government operation, and Congress three months later legislated for it. The secretary of the treasury, William G. McAdoo, became director-general of railroads in charge of the Railroad Administration. The railroads were now operated from Washington and were paid high rentals under guarantees of adequate compensation to owners. As the government kept freights low and spent heavily to modernize the railroads, the cost climbed to a total of $714,000,000. This outlay was denounced by those who forgot that government operation brought order out of chaos and made for some unwonted efficiencies.

Troops and supplies likewise depended upon shipping. Germany's submarine campaign was making heavy inroads upon Allied shipping, sometimes sinking as many as sixty in a week, making it clear that ships, like food, would "Win the War." The Shipping Board (originally established in 1916) therefore undertook to offset these losses. As the "farmer-labor-planter" group would not consent to subsidize private enterprise, an Emergency Fleet Corporation was set up to build a government merchant marine. Commanded by Charles M. Schwab, in private life chairman of the board of the Bethlehem Steel Company, and Edward N. Hurley, a prominent Chicago Democrat, it undertook to build a "bridge of ships" to France. It raised available tonnage from 1 million to 10 million tons and made it possible for all of the military supplies and 80 per cent of the troops sent abroad to be carried on American ships. Here, too, costs were enormous, raised further by a "cost plus" system. This system was devised so that a contractor was guaranteed a price made up of the cost of his output plus 10 per cent. His profits rose by uneconomical operation and made him indifferent to high prices for raw materials and over-time pay for labor.

The sixth of the war boards was the War Trade Board. This was organized to prevent any commerce which would interfere with the war, particularly trading with the enemy. All trading was licensed and non-essential exporting and importing were limited drastically. Vance McCormick, a Pittsburgh newspaper publisher who was chairman of the Democratic National Committee in 1916, headed this board and acted under authority granted by an Espionage Act and a Trading-with-the-Enemy Act. Under the latter law vigorous effort was made to discover and take over all business owned by enemy aliens. When discovered, these were operated under the direction of an alien property custodian, in which office Wilson placed a Democratic ex-congressman from Pennsylvania, A. Mitchell Palmer.

By the creation of these various boards and corporations the functions of the United States government were enlarged to insure an "all-out" effort under centralized, efficient administration. President Wilson assembled and organized the heads of the Food, War Industries, Fuel, Railroad, Shipping and War Trade boards into a second cabinet; he met with them regularly in the final months of the war.

War Financing and Public Support

Costs of this military and economic mobilization were tremendous, and to finance them the nation's money and credit had likewise to be mobilized. To meet the outlays the Democrats had to depend almost wholly on new taxes and bond issues, for tariff increases violated their traditions. The progressive element—Socialists, agrarians and middle westerners—disliked bond issues and opposed burdening unborn generations with past wars. Taxation alone could not finance the war, with $10,000,000,000 loaned to the Allies and associates, $26,000,000,000 spent at home and $6,000,000,000 in indirect outlays adding up to $42,000,000,000. About one-third of the total was raised by taxes, an amount which compared favorably with earlier war practice. Congress laid progressive levies on incomes and inheritances, with heavy rates on excess profits of corporations and partnerships. Increased excises and amusement and luxury taxes did not rouse violent protest. Although some levies were avoided by stock dividends, income from taxes increased almost sixfold over 1916 and reached an amount heavier than any other war power levied.

The remaining two-thirds of war cost was charged to the oncoming generations by issuing notes and bonds to be repaid later. Secretary of the Treasury McAdoo employed a "continuous" revenue system, with treasury estimates of expenditures far exceeding actuality and with government finance on a "boom" basis. Every two weeks he issued short term notes in turn taken up by proceeds from long term bonds. Four "Liberty" loans and one "Victory" loan, issued at interest of only 3½, 4, 4¼ and 4¾ per cent (only the first of which was wholly tax exempt) brought in about $21,500,000,000. Over 65 million persons contributed, for employers coöperated with the government in strenuous drives for oversubscriptions; the treasury artificially supported the market; and the Federal Reserve Banks encouraged people to borrow money to buy bonds. Liberty loan window cards, service buttons, vaudeville entertainers and popular speakers persuaded and enticed on every hand. From persons of low income $1,000,000,000 was collected through twenty-five cent savings stamps and five-dollar war savings certificates. All these issues were sold direct to the people over the counter instead of through syndicates as in the Civil War. They made the entire nation security-conscious, a state of mind which would contribute greatly to the wild stock market boom before the crash of 1929. Also the Federal Reserve was riveting its hold on commercial banking, which would affect future prosperity.

The deep reservoir of American funds and enthusiasm was tapped eagerly by the Allies. Their clamorous competition for loans belatedly forced the United States to establish an American Purchasing Commission, and with the aid of the Interallied Finance Council, which functioned under an American chairman, it managed to lessen the misallocation of loans. Repayment was not then of concern.

The bond campaigns were perhaps the most effective agencies for sustaining war morale, but nearly every war activity created an enthusiasm which communicated itself to another activity. Their total force became well-nigh irresistible.

As vital as military and economic mobilization was the mobilizing of the nation's morale. Of first importance was unity of public opinion. Patriotism in its best, truest sense burned for Wilsonian ideals, for spreading over the world the progressive spirit. A war "for humanity," "to end wars," to punish autocratic German rulers but not the German people and "to make the world safe for democracy" justified the highest zeal.

There was present also, human nature being what it is, the pseudo-patriotism which is completely engrossed in intolerant emotionalism. Separation from the scene of conflict had spared Americans that acute suffering which chastens the emotions, so that naturally many ordinarily democratic citizens now were tempted to abandon all restraint, to bedeck intolerance with the American flag. Congress passed espionage and sedition acts 15 June 1917 and 16 May 1918, the latter with such unanimity that only twenty-four Republicans and two Democrats voted against it. Although editorial influence kept out of these laws that censorship of the press which the Department of Justice tried to put in, the administration found means to badger the press under the general terms of the acts.

The acts were occasionally used. Socialists, like Debs, Stokes and Berger, were sent to prison alongside some 450 military objectors; La Follette's enemies tried to have him expelled from the Senate. Expression of an unenthusiastic viewpoint invited bitter persecution and relentless ostracism in all walks of life. The Department of Justice organized a volunteer American Protective League of approximately 250,000 indiscriminate enrollees to report evidence of disloyalty. This afforded some types a fine chance to vent personal spleen or succumb to neurotic fears. The courts and intelligence offices of the State, War and Navy Departments made complete the country-wide search for German spies and Bolsheviks. Terms of ten to twenty years were imposed. However, such was the basic loyalty of Americans that no first-class spy or revolutionist was found in all this fine network over the nation.

In mobilizing public opinion the United States far outdid the Allies through a Committee on Public Information set up under the efficient George Creel, who had had eighteen years' experience as a newspaper editor in Kansas and Colorado and who had written *Wilson and the*

Wednesday

30

APRIL

1952

MARCH						
S	M	T	W	T	F	S
						1
2	3	4	5	6	7	8
9	10	11	12	13	14	15
16	17	18	19	20	21	22
23	24	25	26	27	28	29
30	31					

APRIL						
S	M	T	W	T	F	S
		1	2	3	4	5
6	7	8	9	10	11	12
13	14	15	16	17	18	19
20	21	22	23	24	25	26
27	28	29	30			

MAY						
S	M	T	W	T	F	S
				1	2	3
4	5	6	7	8	9	10
11	12	13	14	15	16	17
18	19	20	21	22	23	24
25	26	27	28	29	30	31

MEMO

Issues to assist his reëlection. He "advertised America," as he put it, by spreading information over North and South America, and even into Europe and the Orient. The output of such printed literature in many languages was simply stupendous. Also the Committee used orators continually. To the playhouses, movies, concert halls and other places of entertainment were sent "four-minute" speakers selected for their eloquence and endurance. Across country were sent prominent persons to make lecture tours, as did ex-President Roosevelt, who inveighed bitterly against the non-conformists. The committee had the coöperation of all manner of institutions. The churches gave pulpit testimony, putting aside the gospel of peace to preach "a war to end war." The colleges gave required courses in "war aims," and some faculty members took responsible positions in the Creel organization.

The Creel Committee demonstrated the usefulness of efficient propaganda in modern warfare, when public opinion is perhaps the most valuable of all war arms. By its very nature it was inevitable that it should resort to extremes intolerable in peacetime. The public was asked to believe, and accepted, stories of enemy atrocities as violent as modern warfare could invent. It systematically discredited nonconformists; when a few pacifistic persons calling themselves "The People's Council for Democracy and Terms of Peace" sallied forth toward a Minneapolis convention, they were trailed across country and efficiently discredited by a group of government emissaries calling themselves "The American Alliance for Labor and Democracy." To expect a war weapon to be tolerant is to deny its character.

The schools were enlisted with the rest. Through the grade-school teachers and their pupils every family was quickly informed of the coöperation in saving which the Food and Fuel Administrations and the Treasury Department expected of them. The colleges at first were little affected except as courses on the background of the war were introduced, greater emphasis was placed on engineering and medical training and younger members of the teaching staffs left for war service. However, when the draft age was lowered from twenty-one to eighteen many colleges and universities were threatened with a ruinous loss of students. So the government set up a Student Army Training Corps to teach youth military tactics in college. Organized in most colleges in September 1918, it uniformed and supported the boys of draft age while they studied "war aims" and other streamlined courses and drilled under army officers.

Patriotism thus mobilized assumed responsibility for many private aids and services for the enlisted personnel. Thus was gained support in enthusiasm and money for the Red Cross, the Y.M.C.A., Y.W.C.A., Knights of Columbus, Y.M.H.A., Y.W.H.A. and the Salvation Army.

At first these various organizations sought funds independently, but shortly their needs were pooled and combined drives like Liberty Loan drives were conducted, netting hundreds of millions of dollars. Multitudes of organizations and private individuals gave their aid, contributing money, making surgical dressings, knitting and otherwise proving their desire to "do their bit." Refusal could not be tolerated.

CHAPTER XLI

VICTORY

While mobilization at home was progressing in such gigantic fashion, its purpose was being fulfilled abroad. American troops were on the fighting line.

Winning the War

Shortly after they reached France in September 1917 disasters occurred which made their valor all the more essential. In October the Italian line broke; in November Bolshevik Communists overthrew the liberal Kerensky régime in Russia; and in March they accepted from Germany the harsh peace treaty of Brest-Litovsk. These combined disasters forced the Allies to spare for the Italian frontier troops badly needed to the west just when 500,000 Germans were being freed from eastern fighting for western assault. There by spring the Germans had a numerical superiority and prepared to take Paris and win the war.

Furthermore, Allied prestige had suffered serious discredit. Wilson had been proclaiming that the real object of the Allies was "to make the world safe for Democracy," but in December 1917 the Bolsheviki published secret treaties which they had found in the archives of the Imperial Government. These treaties proved that at least the European and Asiatic allies were fighting not for democracy but for territorial aggrandizement. Such exposures disaffected the long-suffering populaces. Desertions among French and other soldiers and restiveness among British and other laborers turned the Allies toward Wilson for a convincing proclamation that theirs was the cause of humanity. Subsequent evidence has indicated that he had known of the secret treaties; but his world program was at stake.

Wilson promptly, 8 January 1918, addressed Congress and the world on the terms of a just peace. He projected a peace embodying "fourteen points": five, for the general good, specified open diplomacy, freedom of the seas, removal of trade barriers, reduction of armaments and fair colonial adjustments; eight specified territorial adjustments conforming to racial differences; the fourteenth proposed an association of nations guaranteeing political independence and territorial integrity to big and little powers alike. Allied diplomats accepted these points in principle but not specifically and made no protest against them as long as victory remained uncertain. As the military situation shifted, they issued peace pronouncements vaguely referring to the Fourteen Points, which they found particularly effective as propaganda published in their own press and dropped over Germany's entire country-side.

Meanwhile American forces had entered the trenches in October 1917, but their first battle had been postponed until the following spring. Then they were called upon to take active, and what proved heroic, part in stopping a great German drive. Heavy enemy assaults between 2 March and 18 July 1918 forced the Allies to establish the unified command under Marshal Foch which the United States had been urging. A Supreme War Council and Naval, Maritime, and Munitions Councils were set up. Pershing and Wilson agreed to a temporary scattering of United States troops among beleaguered salients. There they proved well their mettle. On 28 May they captured Cantigny, and

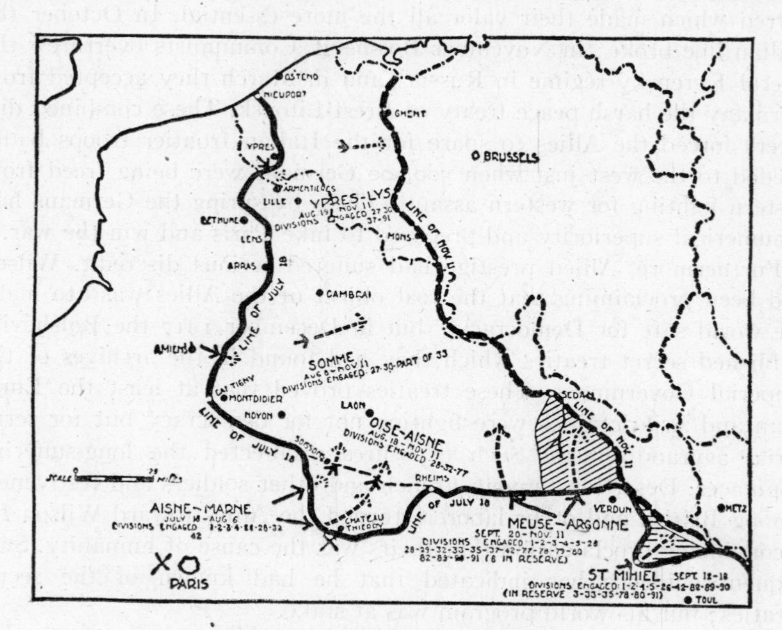

Where Americans Fought

in June they distinguished themselves in Belleau Woods and at Château Thierry. That month the prime ministers of England, France and Italy cabled for 300,000 Yankee troops monthly; the war machine promptly filled the quota and so continued until November.

American aid by mid-July was turning the tide, and Foch under Pershing's urgency launched a counteroffensive by the combined Allied armies. In August the American army was enabled to resume separate status, and Pershing organized eighteen divisions into the "First

American Army"; supported by a few outside troops and British and French tanks and airplanes it took over nearly one-fourth of the line. It undertook to drive the Germans out of the Saint-Mihiel salient to the south and east of Verdun. This was accomplished by brilliant fighting early in September, and Pershing was ready to push eastward into Germany. However, the Allied generals vetoed this. Instead the Americans were turned north into the battle of the Meuse-Argonne directed against Sedan. This offensive was articulated with three others directed by the Allies designed to break the Hindenburg line and sweep the Germans out of France.

American soldiers were sent not only to France but also to Belgium, Italy and Russia. The United States like the Allies resented the Bolshevik withdrawal from the war and the cancellation of Russia's war debt. Therefore she coöperated in sending troops to aid the White Russians, anti-communists who were trying to oust the Bolshevik régime with the aid of outside capital and military forces. One American contingent of 10,000 served in Eastern Siberia, and another of half the size did some fighting near Archangel. These troops remained in Russia until after the peace, some staying in Siberia until 1920.

Meanwhile events of the fall of 1918 were hurrying on. Relentlessly the Allied armies drove against Turkey, Bulgaria and Austria with uniform success, while a crushing offensive against Germany irreparably damaged her fighting power also. Each month saw an enemy crushed. September saw Bulgaria out; October, Turkey; and early November, Austria; while the Allies continually pressed the German retirement from France and Belgium.

At the same time events behind the military front among the home people of the Central Powers were rushing toward peace faster than the Allied armies against the Hindenberg line. There morale was undermined by the triple onslaught of undernourishment, military defeat and the gospel of the Fourteen Points. New political forces were daring to raise their heads, to demand that control be taken from the hands of reigning autocrats. Revolutions were breaking out and thrones were falling by late October, when sailors of Germany's own fleet were in mutiny, some of her soldiers were refusing to fight further and Independent Socialists were preaching revolution to her civilian population. The military leaders themselves were privately urging the civil rulers to make peace while the army yet remained intact, fighting hard. Emperor William was promising wide democratic reforms, and a new, more liberal German chancellor—Prince Maximilian of Baden, who had been installed early in October—was asking Wilson for peace on the basis of the Fourteen Points. He so assured the Reichstag.

Yet peace on that basis could not be obtained, nor was the fighting immediately ended, although Germany had begun negotiations with the United States 5 October. Austria's surrender came 3 November but the armistice with Germany was delayed until the 11th. Wilson could not at first believe that the Chancellor's plea was sincere and representative of the German people, and he would not transfer the negotiations to Foch until he was thoroughly assured. Furthermore Britain and France were forcing him to leave out of the armistice agreement two cardinal elements of the Fourteen Points: they would not include freedom of the seas, and they would insist on full reparations. Germany must be forced to pay for all the damage wrought by her invasion of Allied domain. Wilson finally agreed and 5 November told the Germans that they would conclude the armistice with Foch and must accept the two amendments to the Fourteen Points. Four days later the Kaiser fled into Holland. On 11 November at five o'clock in the morning representatives of a new German government accepted the Allies' terms, the armistice was signed and the guns were silenced.

Losing the Peace

One of the most vital factors which had influenced Wilson to go to war was his belief that only by American participation could lasting peace be made along lines of better world order. This idea had never been absent from his mind in the course of war-making. Apparently he had not always taken advantage of opportunities to promote his purpose. When the Allied missions early in 1917 so eagerly sought the immediate despatch of armies to Europe, he had neglected an opportunity to have a clear understanding with them as to their acceptance of his peace plan.

Also, in August 1917 he and the Allies brushed aside a plan of the Pope for a peace based on mutual restoration of territory and disarmament which might have kept Americans out of the trenches. The Allies then were too confident for peace-making; they even forbade attendance of their citizens upon an International Conference of Socialists convened in September at Stockholm. On the American side, to a certain extent the momentum acquired in erecting a leviathan of a war machine propelled its confident makers on into a demonstration of its running power. Also Wilson felt that only by destruction of German autocracy could a better world order be assured. He proclaimed that the Allies were not fighting the German people but their leaders and that their real objective was "to make the world safe for Democracy." This thesis was accepted in the United States, where the laboring and socialistic groups became committed to the war and did much to help unite the nation behind it.

If the American nation was convinced that they had won the war, the President felt no less confident that the victory was his. Determined to vindicate American entrance by ending all warfare, he made meticulous preparations for a plan for a League of Nations which should be made a part of the peace treaty and should ensure permanent peace. He wrote a draft of a league plan and Colonel House and Dr. D. Hunter Miller of the State Department also worked out one. It was the last-named who with Sir Cecil Hurst of Britain finally drafted the league plan. A host of experts labored months on details. Wilson assumed, with much reason, that his doctrines had effective support. A reorganized Republican party, in which Theodore Roosevelt participated actively, had somewhat discredited Wilson in the 1918 election, defeating his plea for a sweeping Democratic victory in endorsement of his projects. Nevertheless millions of people at home and abroad were enthusiastically acclaiming his hope for a sane peace.

About 150 peace societies existed in the western world in 1914, with the World Peace Foundation at Boston rich enough to afford lavish publicity. Less influential but no less earnest were the Women's Peace Party, the American Union against Militarism and the American League to Limit Armaments. A League to Enforce Peace, organized under non-partisan auspices, had enjoyed bipartisan support when Wilson and Lodge addressed it from the same platform in 1916. Ex-President Taft, President Butler of Columbia University and President Lowell of Harvard had prepared drafts for an international league, as had some British and French groups during 1917. Objections to a League as impractical were not current before 1917, when Senator Lodge appeared as the only prominent dissenter.

Thereafter, however, Mr. Creel's committee had immersed Americans in a heavy bath of hate. Acquiescing in suppression of liberalism, many had given themselves up to vindictiveness or greed. These, like millions abroad, still burned with hatreds propaganda had lighted, a fact Wilson forgot, though partly responsible for it. Forced to qualify his doctrines, he still expected to overcome foreign and domestic opposition to a just peace, believing he could successfully pit his idealism against crafty, European statesmanship. Not realizing how a citizenry can become more uncompromising than its diplomats, he determined to attend the peace conference and there protect the peoples of the world from their leaders.

Wilson minimized his domestic problem, assuming that Republican support outside Congress would offset Republican opposition within. Forgetting that his bargaining position might be stronger if treaty makers had to appeal to him, as well as to the Senate, from across the ocean, he went in person to the peace conference, 4 December 1918. He took a thousand experts and the plan of a treaty. For official associates he took Colonel House, General T. H. Bliss of the army, Secretary of

State Robert Lansing and Henry White, a Republican career diplomat who had had no official status since 1909 when President Taft removed him from the position of ambassador to France. This selection was unfortunate as lacking a representative Republican, a member of the Senate foreign relations committee and an American of outstanding international repute.

Politics and psychology together destroyed the Fourteen Points. The disembarking President found imperialistic editors prepared to discount him from the outset; they taunted him with the fact that the Republicans victorious in the congressional campaign of 1918 had found among the voters some support for a savage peace and against a league treaty. English and French candidates were campaigning on slogans of hate and retaliation: although the masses acclaimed Wilson, on a triumphal tour, as the apostle of forgiveness and magnanimity, Lloyd George found nothing magnanimous in England's "Khaki election," nor Clemenceau in relentless French nationalism. The European electorates voted with their war resentments, and the bourgeois capitalist class, afraid of Bolshevism, feared to be liberal. Lloyd George and Clemenceau were not the premiers to challenge the popular resentment, the demand for security and insistence upon territorial gains, which were rife in England, France and Germany. In so jingoistic an atmosphere the only leader interested in a just peace was the American President, and he could not implement his high aspirations with political and diplomatic astuteness.

The decisions awaiting the peace-makers seemed the most portentous in history. Any peace at all was a feat. The business mainly lay with the three premiers and Wilson, logical heirs of a pre-armistice council of Lloyd George, Clemenceau, Orlando and House. They barred the doors of discussion to the defeated powers (an innovation in modern practice) and listened little to lesser Allies. After secret negotiations lasting until 28 June 1919 their treaty was signed. It showed that Wilson had not been defeated on all issues. He had prevented charging Germany with the entire cost of the war, although he failed to make the sum of reparations either definite or reasonable in prospect. Also he somewhat reduced territorial spoils obtained by Italy, Japan, France and Poland, although in the main, except for Russia, the bribes of the secret treaties were paid. Thirdly, he forced the League into the treaty itself.

The grand object of the League was a world peace to be obtained by arbitration and arms reduction administered through League machinery. All nations were invited to participate, each with an equal vote, in a popular lower house called the Assembly. Executive functions were allotted to a council of nine composed of five permanent members representing England, France, Italy, Japan and the United States and temporary elective members from four other powers. Their duty was to wipe out political friction by planning arms reduction, publicizing treaties, exercising mandates and investigating disputes submitted to them. Legal frictions were to be handled by a permanent Court of International Justice sitting at The Hague. A permanent League Secretariat and International Labor Bureau were to function from Geneva. All member nations pledged themselves to respect and preserve three basic principles: territorial integrity, political independence and arbitral practices; they would avoid war with nations accepting League awards, impose sanctions on recalcitrant powers, arbitrate disputes and delay war three months while negotiations were going on.

In order to make the Covenant of the League an integral part of the treaty with Germany, Wilson yielded on the vital moral question of blame. The treaty laid all the blame on Germany, contrary to the spirit of the Fourteen Points. Her economic ruin was predicated upon reparations imposed beyond ability to pay, upon a gold penalty of 33 billions and upon loss of areas producing coal, iron, potash and other materials essential to strength. She seemed unlikely to reënter competition for world markets after losing Alsace-Lorraine to France and other strategic economic areas to Poland, Belgium and Denmark. Reduction of her army to 100,000 men and a fifteen-year occupation of the Rhineland by the Allies capped her punishment.

While these terms were formulating at Paris, American politicians and publicists worried over Wilson's commitments. They made him aware of a responsible American demand that the League should recognize the Monroe Doctrine and exclude domestic concerns from its interference. Unanimity of voting in the Council and withdrawal of members at will also were pressed. The urgencies of charitable critics, who included Taft, Hughes and Root, persuaded Wilson to secure reservations on the Monroe Doctrine and on withdrawals from the League. But he did not obtain specifications that the United States was not to pledge sanctions, nor get that exclusion of domestic matters which would have conciliated senators interested in controlling immigration and the tariff.

During a month's interlude in the United States (14 February-14 March) Wilson gave a White House dinner to Senate and House foreign relations committeemen and made public comments; but he neither invited official Senate suggestions nor outmaneuvered politicians inspired by political and personal animosities. Thirty-nine senators and senators-elect determined to defy the President. Led on the left by La Follette, Borah, Johnson and Poindexter, and on the right by Brandegee, Hitchcock, Knox, Lodge, McCormick, Moses and Sherman, the thirty-nine signed a round-robin 2 March 1919 declaring that the League must wait until after peace. No less defiant, Wilson proclaimed the Covenant would be in the treaty, inseparable from it.

Before Wilson returned again to the United States, a newspaper friend favored Borah with an advance draft of the Covenant, which he read into the *Congressional Record*. Thus the pact was exposed to criticism a month before Wilson officially presented it to the Senate. Objections tended to concentrate on Article X, which pledged members of the new league to respect and preserve, as against external aggression, the territorial integrity and existing political independence of all other members. This the opposition asserted would continually compel the United States to send armed forces to adjust European disputes.

Republican senators had filibustered against appropriation bills to make sure of an early meeting of the Sixty-Sixth Congress, which had an anti-Wilson majority because the elections of 1918 had turned against him. Wilson had to call a special session of Congress 19 May 1919. The Senate was controlled by the Republicans by one vote, and they organized the committees. Thus anti-League sentiment held triumphant sway over the vital Foreign Relations Committee, and its majority installed the implacable Senator Henry Cabot Lodge as chairman. In the Senate itself there developed two main groups opposing the treaty, one group unalterably opposed who were called "Irreconcilables," and the other who would compromise and accept the League with "reservations." Had the President been willing to accept certain of the latter, such as one which would have declared that United States forces could be used under Article X only with the consent of Congress, he perhaps might have been able to outwit the committee strategists. As it was he had both the Irreconcilables and the reservationists against him.

Realizing that public opinion strongly favored the League, the Irreconcilables had recourse to delay, to interminable hearings held publicly contrary to current custom and promptly published and to long drawn out amendments and reservations. Some forty-five amendments to the treaty and four reservations, designed to protect American sovereignty and to separate the United States from execution of the treaty, were gradually accumulated for Senate voting. Alexander Frick and Andrew Mellon of Pittsburgh, outstanding leaders in the manufacture of steel and aluminum respectively, contributed lavishly of funds to help turn public opinion against the League.

The President, who had made broad concessions to foreigners to place the League Covenant in the treaty, could not be persuaded by Colonel House or Viscount Edward Grey, British Ambassador, to make concessions to the Senate. His type of mind plus physical exhaustion ill equipped him to strike a balance between Versailles and Washington, if indeed it could have been struck. He undertook a tour into the home states of the Irreconcilables to turn the flank of the opposition, but they dogged his platforms, denying his assertions. In Colorado 27 September he suffered a physical collapse culminating in a paralytic stroke after his return to Washington. There intervened about four months of almost complete incapacity just at the crucial stage in his Covenant fortunes. Through these dark days Mrs. Wilson and his devoted personal secretary, Joseph P. Tumulty, undertook to act as channels for indispensable contacts between the outside world and the sickroom. Meanwhile Secretary of State Robert Lansing ventured unofficial cabinet meetings but his dismissal at the end of this period of most severe illness indicated that Wilson disapproved of them.

The President's health improved somewhat, but as he remained largely prisoner to poor health, his Covenant became a hostage to fate. Without his vigorous defense of it the Irreconcilables were able to defeat the treaty in three Senate votes of 19 November 1919, to the amazement of the people of the United States and of the world. These votes did not convince adherents or satisfy the public generally.

A second Senate poll had to be taken, but it was delayed four months. Meanwhile political capital was being made against Wilson and many citizens were becoming engrossed in domestic and private affairs and were tiring of world idealism. Arguments that the League meant British dominance, American entanglement in European wars and perpetuation of injustice gained weight. More than three-fourths of the Senate remained ready to accept League membership with modifications, but those modifications were unacceptable to the President. On 19 March 1920 Wilson's Covenant again failed of a two-thirds endorsement in the Senate: a switch of seven votes would have saved it.

Officially the United States was still at war, an embarrassing situation requiring relief. On 27 May 1920 a prominent Republican reservationist, P. C. Knox of Pennsylvania, Taft's secretary of state, secured passage of a resolution which, by repealing the declaration of war, admitted that the war was over. Wilson, however, would admit nothing of peace without the League. He vetoed the resolution and asked the nation to make the approaching election "a great and solemn referendum" on the issue. As will be seen, the majority would not heed his wishes. The President who had risked everything for a war to end wars left office 4 March 1921 without the Covenant which was to have justified his sacrifice and that of the nation.

BETWEEN WORLD WARS

1919-1939

CHAPTER XLII

BACK TO PEACE AND PROSPERITY

The decade between the armistice and the depression offers a striking contrast to the Progressive Era preceding it and to the New Deal following it. The nation during this post-war period felt much more cynicism and indifference than interest in reform. Pressure-groups could be relied upon to lobby for their own advantage, but the general welfare was no longer a rousing political issue. Pursuit of prosperity seemed more real than politics and largely separate from it. Public interest, thus diverted, left the average politician, business-men and lesser folk relatively free to follow their individual devices without regulatory discipline. This trend was shown particularly in four respects: in the congressional arrangements for demobilization, in the civilian lack of "time to care" about preservation of law and freedom of expression, in the retention of Republican rule despite gigantic scandals and in the persistent attempt to shunt Europe to the background.

Demobilization in a Hurry

The international conflict had taken the entire nation into its toils in one way or another, and the armistice was no sooner signed than men and women impatiently demanded release from the gigantic war machine. Individuals and corporations alike were anxious to slough off government control and pursue peacetime vocations as they willed. Other governments had been studying demobilization ever since early in the war in order to cushion the shock of the end of the conflict, but the Wilson administration had been so engrossed in the League objective that the armistice came without due preparation, and few of the populace stopped to think that some war boards could help the peace set-up.

The military machine was suddenly halted. Congress hastily repealed war legislation, abolishing emergency powers and boards without regard to the possible usefulness of some of them to post-war America. Most of the guidance government had given industry and labor was summarily withdrawn, notably the United States employment service in July 1919, just when a tremendous field of usefulness was opening up before it. Contracts for goods were canceled, manufacturers reimbursed for contract losses, and millions of dollars worth of excess, government-owned materials were sold, largely in France, at mere fractions of cost. Factory production and employment were left to wrench themselves back to peacetime markets with little government aid. After some delay the human element in the military machine, the 4 million soldiers and sailors and the 11.4 million civilian workers were dumped on the domestic labor market, mostly to fend for themselves.

The veterans were in no mood for summary treatment. Their benefits began with a discharge bonus of $256,000,000 and were vastly increased by establishment of their own lobbies. A few American officers and men in Paris early in 1919 determined that they should not get off to the slow start of the G.A.R. after the Civil War and that the current low state of soldier morale should not lead to a radical organization. From a St. Louis convention of May 1920 emerged the American Legion, destined to become one of the strongest influences in American politics; other ex-soldiers formed the less aggressive Veterans of Foreign Wars. These groups at first placed their emphasis on compensation for the disabled; for them Congress in 1921 set up the Veterans Bureau to spend liberal appropriations on pensions allowed dependents, on hospitalization and vocational training, as well as to administer the insurance allowed all soldiers on enlistment. The work of this bureau was to expand constantly.

Before long the ex-soldiers were demanding aid for those who had not been disabled. Some on reaching home had found their jobs held by other persons, who had received wages as high as $10 a day while the draftees were getting $30 a month. Thousands were eagerly organized behind a movement for "adjusted" compensation, popularly called the "bonus." They demanded that the difference in recompense be made up to them, and some seventeen state legislatures appropriated modest funds for this purpose. These varied betwen $10 and $30 for each month of service. The pressure for bigger grants on a national scale put through Congress in 1922 a bill for a $50 federal grant which died when Harding vetoed it. Two years more and they had the influence to override a Coolidge veto of a larger grant. The "adjusted service certificate" law of 1924 allowed every veteran an insurance policy amounting to $1.25 a day for overseas service and $1 a day for home service; it was payable in 1945, and one could borrow on it up to 22½ per cent of its face value. This measure made 3.5 million men eligible for a gift averaging $1,000 but made no provision for funds with which to pay it. Next came a demand for immediate cashing of the policies—in greenbacks if nothing else; this proposition was so patently inflationary that they could not get it through; but they did get allowances for disabilities unconnected with the war and further easing of restrictions. The depression would bring them more later.

Transportation also received quick post-war attention, for the far-flung nation was dependent upon it. First came the railroads, still the main reliance for transporting people and freight, comprising one-tenth the national wealth and with their stocks and bonds still the most important single group of American securities. It was common knowledge that wartime costs, competition from trolleys and government-aided canals and restrictions imposed by government and labor had cut net profits. Worst was the competition from trucks and buses, for congressional appropriations helped build and maintain the heavy-traffic, cross-continental roads which local taxing bodies alone could not support. It was not universally recognized that railroad mileage had reached the saturation point, with more miles abandoned than built since 1916, and that changing conditions dictated drastic reorganization. Many people assumed that mere return to private control would restore prosperity and that government methods were solely responsible for recently increased deficits. The railroad brotherhoods and the A. F. of L., however, endorsed a "Plumb Plan" for government purchase, with lease to a management composed equally of workers, railroad officials and presidential appointees. The operators, fearing public ownership, offered to accept more supervision. President Wilson opposed a peacetime trial of government operation and set 1 March 1920 as the date for return to private ownership.

Congress, thus pressed, enacted the Esch-Cummins law of 1920, which completely satisfied neither the unions, the operators, nor the administration. The act returned the railroads to private ownership and control and granted a temporary guarantee of 6 per cent net profits, but half of any profits over 6 per cent was to go into a revolving fund for the benefit of weak lines, a provision known as the "recapture" clause. The act gave the workers a Railway Labor Board to arrange agreements and gave the Interstate Commerce Commission expanded powers over rates, service, traffic, trackage, profits, finance and consolidation.

As applied by the Commission and courts the new law most favored the operators. The Commission granted increase in rates from 25 per cent to 50 per cent and in wages about 22 per cent. The Railway Labor Board failed to prevent a shopmen's strike of 1922, proved ineffective and was replaced in 1926 by a Federal Mediation Board which could intervene only when a disputant so requested. The recapture clause would not work and was repealed. On the question of the basis for estimating net profits, the Commission argued for 1914 reproduction costs; the operators demanded 1920 figures, which would help care for watered stock; the Supreme Court, in St. Louis and

O'Fallon Railway Co. *v.* US (1929), adopted the latter. Both Commission and courts reversed the trend of the Northern Securities decision. They encouraged, even urged, consolidation of lines and systems to a point beyond the then desires of the operators themselves. By 1928 6,000 lines had been reduced to about 800. By 1930 the railroad operators were proposing consolidation of all northeastern lines into four systems: the Pennsylvania, Baltimore and Ohio, New York Central and Cheseapeake and Ohio; but the depression prevented it.

Of almost equal interest was the merchant marine, for the war had shown the need for a permanent merchant fleet auxiliary to the navy. It had taught the farmers their dependence upon merchantmen, moderating their ancient antipathy to subsidies. After bitter dispute Congress decided to sponsor both public and private ownership and operation. So the Jones Merchant Marine Act of 1920 authorized the Shipping Board (1) to sell government-owned vessels to private corporations controlled by American citizens, (2) to loan money to companies following new trade routes marked out by the Board and (3) to operate unsold ships. Various ancient and dubious devices such as mail-carrying subsidies, preferential tariffs patterned after a 1789 act and colonial carrying restrictions in imitation of eighteenth century mercantilism also were authorized. The government guaranteed to cover losses on new routes. The Shipping Board sold many vessels at 2.5 per cent of their cost, and its annual deficit averaged over $142,000,000. Yet in eight years the United States' percentage of total world commerce fell from 42.7 to 32.2.

Considerable sentiment rose for a government-owned marine, but Congress returned to the more familiar practice of subsidy to private capital, passing various measures authorizing aid, including the Jones-White law of 1928. Under it the government was lavish. It paid for water mail-carrying at more than sixty times estimated actual costs, gave generous construction loans at low interest for displacing outmoded vessels with Diesel-driven ships and paid half the salary of naval officers serving in the merchant marine. One-half the crew now could be foreigners, ineligible for the higher wages compulsory under the La Follette Act. The government engaged to operate unprofitable lines until they paid and then to turn them over to private companies. In spite of all this, marine subsidy was more than offset by a trade-killing tariff policy and proved a pitiable failure.

Subsidy to aviation also became an accepted policy. The war had reminded Americans of the military uses of planes while exposing their deficiencies in construction and personnel. The public imagination was caught by various pioneer trans-oceanic flights: the first across the Atlantic in 1919 by John Alcock and Arthur W. Brown, that of Admiral Byrd and Floyd Bennett to the North Pole in 1926 and

Charles A. Lindbergh's solo flight to Paris in 1927. A warship was detailed to bring Lindbergh back, the recipient of the greatest honors America ever had given a person who was neither a politician nor a military hero. That year a few others, some civilians and some in government service, flew to Europe, and the Pacific was spanned as far as Hawaii. Four years later another civilian, Wiley Post—an oil-driller who had lost one eye in an accident and had used the $2,000 award to buy a second-hand plane—flew around the world with Harold Gatty in less than nine days.

The airplane industry was bound to expand. Municipalities eagerly assumed costs of airport construction. Private capital became interested as the industry entered the phase of profitable commercial development and obtained in 1925 a law authorizing transfer of air mail to private lines. The sympathy of the Hoover administration for subsidies and for elimination of competition helped both legitimate and illegitimate promoters of aviation, who gratefully contributed to Republican campaigns. However the freezing out of small concerns helped the favored ones to develop large-scale efficiency and resistance to depression strains. Also, Hoover's postmaster general, Walter F. Brown, so phrased air mail contracts as to encourage use of larger planes capable of passenger service; this helped to lay the basis for the remarkable trans-continental mail, express and passenger service developed in the United States during the 'thirties. Exposure of gross abuses waited until the next depression sharpened the public conscience. Finally in 1934 a congressional investigating committee exposed exorbitant mail-carrying fees paid aviation companies. President Roosevelt canceled the contracts, gave the mail to army fliers; the latter, ill equipped and inexperienced as mail-carriers, cracked up under bad flying conditions. A special investigation of army aviation ensued while mail-carrying was returned to private companies—although under a chastened scale of bidding.

Thus with aviation as with shipping, railroads and veterans, Congress legislated hurriedly in the post-war decade and then was forced by ensuing difficulties to reconsider problems. Long range planning repeatedly proved itself contrary to the spirit of the period.

Financial Demobilization

Somewhere, somehow, the United States had to find new, peacetime money and credit, or else it could not liquidate the expenses of the foreign war or finance such expanding domestic obligations as subsidies to agriculture, transportation and the veterans. Added to these were new local costs born of the changing national economy and unloaded upon the federal shoulders because too unwieldy for cities, counties and states to handle. The heaviest tribute went to wars, past and future, covering army, navy, World War debts and veterans; but spending for constructive, social objects also increased. A car-conscious people multiplied their outlays on highways four thousand times between 1916 and 1930. They trebled their educational expenditure over the nation in the two decades following 1916. They inaugurated costly programs of flood control, dams and waterways. Their income never overtook their outgo: per capita debt in America stood at $9.88 in 1914; $228 at the war's close; $134 by 1930; $368.74 by 1941. Behind those violent fluctuations is an interesting story.

As the world's post-war emphasis upon national self-sufficiency was making the customs income grossly inadequate and as prohibition destroyed income from liquor, voters with a progressive heritage struggled to shift the burdens and benefits of new taxes. The battle raged over reductions from the wartime levies on wealth and competence; over surtaxes and taxes on excess profits, corporation income, estates, gifts and inheritances; over exemptions on basic income, earned income, income from government securities and salaries; over exemption of income of religious, charitable, scientific, literary, educational, and labor groups and agricultural coöperatives; over taxation of the poor through nuisance and sales taxes; over evasions and publication of tax returns.

The war had furnished a powerful impetus to multiplication of levies, and some old Progressives argued that high income taxes should be retained, because Europe ultimately would default on her indebtedness to the United States and leave Americans to make up the money she owed. Domestic tax legislation of the 'twenties was predicated upon the assumption that the foreign debt would be paid. This made it easier to get through Congress laws for reduction of income taxes. Consequently, although incomes rose between 1920 and 1929 to fantastic figures, the federal receipts from income taxes fell from 4 billions to 2.3 billions. Less than 40 per cent of the corporations reporting in 1930 paid taxes. Outstanding federal indebtedness meanwhile was reduced from 24 billions to 17 billions. Such a record might have amazed John Sherman and other treasury secretaries who together liquidated the Civil War in twenty years, but Secretary Mellon, more than they, had won assurance and optimism from phenomenal success. His rules of safe practice were those acquired in the game of corporation finance as played most successfully early in the twentieth century.

Tax legislation and litigation of 1921-1929 proceeded largely upon Mellon's comfortable assumptions. In 1921 although the corporate income tax was increased, the surtax was reduced and the excess profits levy repealed. In 1923 the Supreme Court ruled that stock dividends were not taxable; this helped to halve income tax receipts. In 1924 the low-exemption levels were raised, the normal tax and surtax were reduced and earned income partly rebated; the same Congress, however, raised the tax on estates and invented a new levy on money gifts—which last the Supreme Court invalidated.

Full congressional acceptance of the Mellon thesis was indicated two years later in much wider relief for wealth on surtax and estate levies, in another rise of the exemption level, and in a retroactive repeal of the gift tax. Such policies were further pursued in 1928 and 1929, when taxable wealth was at its highest level in American history. The freed funds poured into the stock market, to contribute to a mad orgy of speculation.

Attempts at sanity on debts and taxation were not wholly lacking. An economy and efficiency commission under Taft had urged the budgeting of national expenditures. Wilson, Harding and Coolidge regularly discussed injection of business methods into governmental practice. Finally in 1921 the business recession made it possible to pass a Budget and Accounting Act designed to restrict expenditures to funds in hand, with the aid of a Budget Bureau in the Treasury Department. The president was to submit annually to Congress a budget of receipts and expenditures for the previous, the present and ensuing year; and the Budget Bureau was to receive requests for funds. Its first director was Charles G. Dawes, a Chicago banker, whose Republican work went back to McKinley's pre-nomination days, and he soon showed the value of the Bureau. Lawmakers of 1923 and 1930, struggling for businesslike efficiency, established a Personnel Classification Board and made the Director of the Budget its chairman.

Another outstanding proof of congressional misunderstanding of post-war conditions was the tariff, for the extreme protectionism of recent Republican policy conflicted with America's new status as the great, international creditor. Foreign nationals, lacking gold, asked to pay their obligations in the only coin they had—goods; and Wilson repeatedly told Congress in substance, "If we want to sell, we must be prepared to buy." But American labor and manufacturers naturally took fright at the first signs of European payment in imports. What dire things might not happen to domestic industry if Europe dumped her goods?

Against this alarm the arguments of the creditor interests, who here broke their long-standing alliance with manufacturers' lobbies, did not carry weight. A congressional majority of protectionists from both parties passed an emergency tariff to dam the flood early in 1921, and Wilson vetoed it. Not so Harding; he promptly sent a special message, "It is our purpose to prosper America first," and signed the controverted measure. It had been repassed with the connivance of the farm lobby, after they received agricultural increases which committed them to protection without, as the event proved, enabling them to dispose of their surplus.

The emergency tariff of 1921 raised rates on wheat (to cut Canadian competition), on corn, meat, sugar, wool and other agrarian items; it also embargoed German dyestuffs and prohibited dumping. The next year the agrarians contributed votes for a "permanent" schedule—the Fordney-McCumber Tariff, built even higher than the Payne-Aldrich Law—in the effort to shut out the increasingly clamorous foreigner. The rates were made excessive, but apparently to mitigate them the drafters inserted a "flexibility" feature based on the familiar doctrine of "difference in cost of production." It empowered the President, upon advice from the Tariff Commission, to raise or lower rates by as much as 50 per cent to equalize such differences. This resulted chiefly in increases. Also the tariff bars were the more firmly fastened by recodification and tightening of the rules governing tariff administration. Hereafter either the American or the foreign valuation could be used as the basis for ad valorem duties, whichever was the higher.

Additional increases in agricultural duties were granted before the elections of 1924 and 1926, but these, like the extreme protective principle generally, failed "to prosper America first." Foreign debtors defaulted, and trade diminished in both directions. Surplus food and manufactured goods could not be absorbed at home, and foreign governments found ways to keep them out. In so far as the rates encouraged monopoly, they penalized domestic consumers. These combined consequences raised doubts among economists, international bankers and some labor leaders as to the sacrosanct nature of extreme protection. There were serious losses in the Canadian and Latin American trade, which were very important to the United States.

Nevertheless President Hoover's first Congress in 1930 enacted the highest tariff in United States history, the Hawley-Smoot Law. Hoover had given western agrarians a campaign promise of higher rates on their products, and industrialists had no mind, they said, to let Congress forget that they had given money to Hoover's campaign fund. With every lobbyist and every member of Congress engaged in the scramble to "protect" his product or his constituency, the rate average was shoved about 20 per cent above the 1922 high. Over 1,000 economists sent Hoover a protect against the bill, pointing out its bad foreign and domestic effects: it would hurt debt, investment and trade relations besides hoisting the cost of living at home. He sought solace in plans to correct gross inequities by use of the "flexibility" powers of the president, and signed the bill. The Hawley-Smoot rates tightened the strain between the United States and other powers and increased the international tension in a world already far too tense. Foreign governments retaliated quickly and sharply, raising high barriers to American goods. Great Britain became thoroughly protectionist, shutting tightly the free trade book she had long since started to close. Some manufacturers like Ford and Remington established foreign branches to escape retaliation, but the farmers lacked this release. The law was characteristic of the lack of foresighted statesmanship in the period. Politicis, too, was at a low ebb.

CHAPTER XLIII

POST-WAR POLITICS

The process of military and economic demobilization was accompanied by a moral demobilization which is ever the dread of a post-war period. Just as after the Civil War there was the Grant régime, so after the First World War came the days of Harding.

Return to Normalcy

Throughout the decade between the First World War and the depression, 1919-1929, the Republican party remained the chosen political instrument of the majority of the people of the United States. After the last previous congressional campaign, that of 1918, they had held a majority of thirty-nine in the House and half the Senate seats. Through the elections of 1920, 1922, 1924, 1926 and 1928, they thrice elected their presidential nominee, retained control of the House, and but once (1926) fell as low as half the places in the Senate. Of course the Republican label continued to mean very different things in different parts of the country, but at least the Democratic label could not regain a majority. The reigning party kept their grasp on the presidency twelve years, 1921-1933, which was eight less than their record following the end of the War Between the States.

This tenure was due to significant factors. At the outset probably the strongest feeling was war fatigue, the wish to be rid of the party immediately identified with wartime strains. Also post-war readjustments to peace were accompanied by an economic recession, moderate in business but severe in agriculture, which began in 1920 and continued through 1922; it sharpened the focus upon prosperity as a major objective and upon the party popularly associated with it. The victorious Republicans capitalized the backward look—back to the prosperous days of McKinley and Hanna, to taking government out of business and putting more business in government. However, such business gains, such elimination of competition as twenty years had brought, must be preserved. Let the government abandon supervision and control and hold fast to its higher duty of subsidy. Since four years of war had created more new millionaires than an entire decade of peace, pressure for the doctrines of rugged individualism and laissez-faire was amply reinforced. Perhaps they scarcely needed reinforcement for apparently the majority of little folk were as committed to the backward look as was big business. This attitude could be cherished as long as there was neither severe depression nor war to shake the faith in the historic set-up.

Outstanding political leadership was no necessity to a nation in this static state of mind. Was not Wilson a dangerous dictator who led the nation along untried paths? Was not political experiment risky? So political leadership to many minds became a thing suspect. Of the three presidents, Harding was incapable of leadership, Congress prevented Coolidge from exercising it in the few instances he wished to assume it, and Hoover was unable to gather a following when he strove to lead. The war had liberated the imaginations of the people without giving them a chart; they floundered about, directionless, in many fields, especially politics. Those who were not prosperous, and who therefore sought new leaders, were confused by the world of economic unreality in which they were living; they split off from both major parties into factions. Congressional leadership was assumed largely by lobbies for special groups. Thus comparatively few felt burdened by a sense of responsibility, and few were seriously held accountable.

Altogether, party performance in such a period could not attain a very high level. An average of mediocrity—if not less—was recorded by the three presidential campaigns and the successive administrations.

In the campaign of 1920, with its post-war problems, both the major parties picked inconspicuous candidates and hedging platforms, although the Republicans were fairly sure of catching the voters on their post-war rebound. The Republican convention, meeting in Chicago 8 June, was controlled by machine politicians loyal to the old alliance with the manufacturers and not above turning a political penny in oil. They picked an affable, obscure and obliging cog in the Ohio party machine, Senator Warren G. Harding, a newspaper editor sent into the Senate in 1915, who had nominated Taft against Roosevelt in the 1912 conclave, was permanent chairman in that of 1916 and was a "Lodge reservationist." His running mate, Governor Calvin Coolidge of Massachusetts, was chosen by the delegates themselves.

The Republican platform took the safe domestic ground of advocating relief for the farmers, economy in government and prosperity for the nation. On foreign affairs it questioned the League of Nations, but in terms conveniently cautious; Johnson argued they meant isolation and Harding vaguely endorsed "an association of nations," which thirty-one prominent Republicans (including Hoover, Hughes, Root and Taft) advertised as meaning the League. One writer neatly defined this as "the league to elect Harding."

The Democrats, meeting in San Francisco 28 June, could not play quite so safe. They nominated, on the forty-fourth ballot, another Ohio newspaper editor, James M. Cox, who had been in the House of Representatives 1909-1913 and now held his third term as governor. He was untainted by Wilsonianism but was given the assistant secretary of the navy, Franklin D. Roosevelt, as running mate. Also they had to run on a platform which endorsed the administration of Wilson and his League and which he required them to take seriously. This handicap could not be overcome by other platform promises adjusted to farm voters or by A. F. of L. official support.

The majority of the electorate in 1920, including the majority of the women enfranchised by proclamation of the 19th Amendment 2 August, were determined to vote anti-Wilson; they were not pro-Harding as such. Big business had hated Wilson's "New Freedom"; liberals hated the red-baiting of Palmer and Postmaster General Burleson; some internationalists hated the ruthless aspects of the Versailles Treaty; and many voters were vaguely nervous over the uncertain economic situation and possible European entanglements. Thus they put the Republicans back in power, but far from unanimously. Thirty-four per cent supported Wilson, League and all. Over 900,000 dared vote for the Socialist candidate, Eugene Debs, still in Atlanta Penitentiary; and over 250,000 backed Parley P. Christiansen, candidate of a "Farmer-Labor" party which will be described in the discussion of the plight of agriculture.

Although the Republicans had hedged against making the election an out-and-out referendum on the League, Wilson's earlier insistence that the vote was to be a verdict enabled the Irreconcilables to interpret his defeat as a mandate against United States membership. Harding, once inaugurated, pronounced against it. Wilson, it will be recalled, had refused to accept peace without the League, and the United States therefore had yet to make official declaration that the war was over. The new administration hence enacted the joint resolution of 2 July 1921, a modified version of the earlier Knox resolution. It declared the war ended and reserved to the United States all of the rights which would have accrued to her if she had joined the Allies in signing the Versailles, St. Germain and Trianon treaties by which they had made peace with Germany, Austria and Hungary. Also it stipulated that until those powers signed separate treaties with the United States agreeing to satisfy our war-damage claims, our government should keep the enemy property seized in wartime. In August the treaties were forthcoming, and later mixed commissions adjudicated the claims on both sides.

Thus did the United States keep herself free to watch the League experiment without obligating herself to coöperate in it. Without her the member nations gradually proved unwilling to yield practical concessions toward a peace ideal, and the League failed as a weapon of permanent defense for England and France against Germany. None can know, but many will venture to assert, how the League would have fared if the United States had joined it.

The League was disposed of as a matter of politics, not statesmanship, and politics ruled the Harding roost. He interpreted his election as a mandate for return to what he labeled "normalcy." The president installed by the machine had spent thirty-six of his fifty-five years of life as editor of the Marion *Star,* the newspaper of that central Ohio town of about 18,000 population; local concerns had been interrupted by four years as state senator, two years as lieutenant governor and election as United States Senator in 1914. Politically he had run with an "Ohio Gang" of amoral, stand-pat partisans, and socially he had best enjoyed a lively, convivial evening at cards. To this easy-going, reactionary, party-regular, party duty had consisted of obliging Republican friends and distributing the loaves and fishes among the loyal. Friendly and weak, self-indulgent and undisciplined, unintelligent and unassuming, Harding entered the presidency handicapped by the loyal henchman's life-long habit of letting things and people "ride along."

The only high notables he named to his cabinet were his Secretary of State, Charles E. Hughes, formerly of the Supreme Court and Republican standard-bearer in 1916, and his Secretary of Commerce, Herbert Hoover of Belgian Relief and Food Administration fame. The treasury went to the aluminum-made multimillionaire, Andrew W. Mellon, whose belief in "trickle" prosperity excused tax evasions and inspired tax reductions for the wealthy.

Harding left a free hand to other intimates whose grafting lifted him and them from obscurity to odious notoriety, and the worst scandals developed in the diversion to commercial profiteering of oil reserved for the U. S. Navy. To head the important Department of the Interior, which is obligated to conserve natural resources, Harding selected a senate crony, Albert B. Fall of New Mexico, a lawyer long interested in mining, lumber and ranch properties. Fall, with the passive assent of Secretary of the Navy Edwin Denby, a Michigan lawyer who had been in the House from 1905-1910, leased the Navy's Elk Hill oil reserve in California to E. L. Doheny. He was a big oil producer who had been a member of the subcommittee on oil of the Council of National Defense. The Teapot Dome naval oil reserve in Wyoming was leased to H. F. Sinclair, another ex-committee member who was president of the large Sinclair Consolidated Oil Corporation and was a liberal contributor to the Republican chest. For this generosity the government received some storage tanks in Hawaii at Pearl Harbor, and Fall "borrowed" at least $100,000 from Doheny and $300,000 from Sinclair.

The peculiar situation was called to the attention of a Democratic senator from Montana, Thomas J. Walsh, who ably led an investigation which forced Fall to resign in 1923 and Denby in 1924. Eventually Fall and Sinclair went to prison and the oil leases were canceled. The extent of the malpractice in oil, of which the United States was the world's greatest consumer, was proved to have exceeded the wildest imagination.

A like devotion to his private purse was discovered in Harding's director of the Veterans Bureau, Col. Charles R. Forbes, in his custodian of alien property, Col. Thomas W. Miller (an ex-congressman from Delaware) and in his attorney general, Harry Daugherty, kingpin of the reigning "Ohio Gang." The courts placed Forbes in the penitentiary for corruption involving losses above $200,000,000 in handling contracts. Miller was convicted of criminal conspiracy for selling cheaply some valuable German chemical patents. Daugherty was tried but never convicted; the testimony tended to show that the U. S. Department of Justice had been prostituted by the worst of the "Ohio Gang," with corruption determining decisions.

The grafting of Harding's intimates brought him no financial gain and some political loss. Failing in health and repute because of loose personal habits and a dawning realization of friendship betrayed, he sought recuperation in a trip to Alaska, never before visited by a president. At San Francisco en route home he died, 2 August 1923, in time to be spared the full exposure of his disreputable entourage, which was laid bare by zealous enemies of the Republican party in the next year. Alive, he would have sunk his ticket in 1924. Dead, there was opportunity for campaign devices to break the moral force of the revelations, especially as his successor was one of the "moralest" men ever to rise in politics.

Prosperity in Politics

Harding's death elevated to the presidency a Massachusetts lawyer of provincial mentality whose cautious policy as a machine politician had made him governor of Massachusetts in 1919 and vice-president in 1921. Calvin Coolidge took the presidential oath from his father by the light of a kerosene lamp in a Vermont farmhouse. Since he was personally abstemious and parsimonious, he seemed, to people who did not know the historic idealism of New England, "a sound Yankee." They trusted him to avoid personal scandal and to restore the "good old days" of democratic, confident, practical Americanism. His and their confidence is understandable because prosperity came in before him and departed behind him. He remained popular with the middle and wealthy classes and with all who did not perceive that America faced problems demanding positive, executive ability—an attribute foreign to Coolidge's negative philosophy. His more significant negatives included opposition to reforms, to taxation of wealth, to subsidy for farmers and to bonuses for veterans.

The question posed by 1924 was whether the Harding scandals, like those in the Grant administration, would fail to unseat the party in power. The Democrats, split wide on religious, economic and prohibition issues, shared much of the general insensitivity to corruption and lacked leadership capable of uniting them on reform. Their convention meeting 24 June at New York was one of the longest and stormiest on record. Here William Jennings Bryan made his last convention appearance crusading in support of prohibition, opposing the nomination of the outstanding wet of his party, Governor Alfred E. Smith of New York. A young man on crutches recovering from a serious attack of infantile paralysis, Franklin D. Roosevelt, nominated Smith. The drys wanted Wilson's Protestant secretary of the treasury, McAdoo, who had Klan support. Finally, on the one hundred and third ballot, the fight was settled by nominating John W. Davis, who had been solicitor general in Wilson's cabinet, ambassador to Great Britain and head of a prosperous New York law firm. To counterbalance his conservative affiliations, Governor Charles W. Bryan of Nebraska, brother of the Great Commoner, was named vice-presidential candidate. The platform veered slightly in the direction of lowering the tariff, made promises to the farmers, advocated a League referendum and upbraided the Republicans for their inefficiency and frauds.

The Republicans, unabashed, had confidently met at Cleveland, 10 June, nominating Coolidge and naming the wealthy Chicago banker and reparations commissioner, Charles G. Dawes, as running mate. Their platform cited the return to prosperity, movements by the administration toward peace without the League, and reductions in taxes and in appropriations.

Coolidge rested comfortably in the belief that Theodore Roosevelt had destroyed special privilege and nothing further need be done about it, but there were some labor, farmer and middle-class reform groups of a less sanguine opinion. They now endorsed Senator Robert M. La Follette as an independent candidate who had conclusively demonstrated that special privilege was more active than heretofore. He wrote the "Progressive" ticket, choosing as running mate a Democratic senator, Burton K. Wheeler of Montana, who had been active in exposing the Harding scandals. They ran on a clear-cut reform platform, calling for redress in agricultural, labor, tax, tariff and utility legislation, besides a constitutional amendment for a congressional veto of Supreme Court decisions. The candidates and their platform received the support of the A.F. of L. and many state and national federations of labor, the Socialists and the Farmer-Labor party. This proved that there was a background of ferment even during Coolidge prosperity.

The election proved that the majority was not excited over honesty in government. Lawlessness was flourishing. Homicides were reaching the world's highest total. All classes were speculating on the main chance; to win it the Republicans warned them they must "Keep Cool with Coolidge" and eschew such dangerous doctrine as was preached by that Communist-Socialist-generally-evil reform party. La Follette could not divert the nation from money-making to deep-seated social problems. He got a little more than half as many votes as Davis, who got a little more than half as many as Coolidge. Only about 52 per cent of the electorate bothered to vote.

The Coolidge administration's objective was prosperity, but as its definition of the term was not broad enough to embrace the unskilled masses and as it stressed urban at the expense of rural needs, it satisfied neither labor nor agriculture. Those groups fostered a degree of insurgency in Congress which threatened to give their lobbyists the balance of power. This soon forced the Republicans to restore the La Follette faction to party standing and patronage privileges, in the effort to become the actual as well as the titular controlling party. The political balance remained artificial, with economic realities continually breaking party lines. Coolidge often was disregarded by Congress, and "normalcy" legislation was mitigated to pacify dissentients, as will be revealed in the description of legislation on agriculture and industry. There occurred an unprecedented increase in national wealth and a phenomenal rise in the standard of living.

Assuming full credit for this, the Republicans planned their 1928 campaign on a prosperity keynote. They wished to renominate their curious symbol of lush, vociferous prosperity, the abstemious, frugal and reputedly taciturn Coolidge. The President sagely took a vacation in 1927 in the bracing air of the Black Hills, and on 2 August there was delivered at his headquarters, Rapid City, South Dakota, a cryptic announcement, "I do not choose to run." This astounded his party and opened the way for Herbert Hoover. As secretary of commerce under Harding and Coolidge he had adapted departmental machinery to the needs and ambitions of big business whilst also perfecting a personal organization. His success record, including his early career as a prosperous mining engineer in the United States, China and Africa, had earned him the admiring respect of that large body of Americans who shared the ideals of Horatio Alger's heroes. The Republican convention meeting at Kansas City 12 June gave him the presidential nomination and chose as running mate Charles Curtis of Kansas, part Indian, and senator since 1907. Their platform pledged further government aid to industry and endorsed prohibition. It was proclaimed that Hoover, who had once put Americans on wartime rations, would guarantee now "two chickens in every pot and a car in every garage."

The Democrats, meeting at Houston, Texas, 26 June abandoned their traditional line of approach and nominated Governor Smith who, although a Tammany man, had followed the counsel of a liberal group in giving New York state eight years of progressive leadership. His record of honest government and his rise from the sidewalks of the Bowery gave him much popular appeal in the East. To offset his Roman Catholic faith, his Tammany connections and his frankly wet position, he was given as running mate Joseph T. Robinson, Senator from Arkansas since 1913, a dry, a Protestant, and a conservative. Their platform was dry in spite of Smith's well-known opposition to prohibition.

The 1928 campaign was not a contest over political principles, however. Both the major parties enjoyed financial support from big business, especially as Smith denied low tariff sympathies and was known by his closest intimates to be untainted with radicalism. The contest descended to personalities. The Ku Klux Klan still had vast political power in the South and West. As it had helped to prevent Smith's nomination in 1924, it now helped to divert attention from serious problems to a "whispering campaign" against him. Also his humble origin, unpolished manners, Tammany connections and his frankly wet position alienated voters outside urban areas of the Northeast. The excitement brought to the polls about 34 per cent more voters than in 1924 and enabled Hoover to take the North and West and break into the solid South, carrying Virginia, North Carolina, Florida, Texas and Tennessee,[1] leaving Smith only six southern states and Massachusetts and Rhode Island. The Republican Senate majority rose to fifteen, that in the House to 101. Little notice was taken of significant victories by independent candidates in Minnesota, Nebraska, New Mexico, North Dakota, Washington and Wisconsin.

President Hoover set out to advance the prosperity principle with more humanitarianism and less frugality than his popular predecessor. He subscribed to the conservative Republican doctrine that each American citizen remains pretty well able to look after himself as an individual but that national welfare occasionally requires government to extend a helping hand to organized industry. Congress also acted on the principle that it need attend to aiding but a few elements in the nation. These politicos little thought a panic might wreck their hopes and self-assurance.

[1] Tennessee had gone Republican in 1920, also.

Breakdown of Law Enforcement

This period of public laxity was marked by two great challenges to two principles essential to democracy: obedience to law and the maintenance of civil liberty. Even the majority who kept the law in that period seemed not sufficiently interested to demand drastic punishment for those who broke it. Thus the post-war thug, whether he operated around alleys, on the highways, among politicians or in Wall Street, had respectable connivance in working his old rackets and in establishing new ones. Political scandals under Harding exceeded those under Grant; stockjobbery before the panic of 1929 surpassed the frenzied finance before the Exchange fright of 1907 and highwaymanship under national prohibition reached an undreamed perfection of technique.

Post-war lawlessness has been perhaps too largely laid to prohibition, yet its responsibility remains extremely heavy, for the circumstances of its establishment were such as to make it an encouragement to lawbreaking from the start. The 18th Amendment, forbidding the manufacture, sale or transportation "of intoxicating liquors," had passed Congress during the uprush of war idealism in December 1917, when two-thirds of the nation were living under local prohibition and the other third knew severe wartime restrictions on drinking. Pending ratification, Congress in October 1919 had passed over Wilson's veto a bill partly sponsored by Representative Andrew J. Volstead of Minnesota which made stringent provision for enforcement of prohibition and defined as intoxicating all beverages containing one-half of one per cent of alcohol. The following January three-fourths of the states had ratified the 18th Amendment and it was proclaimed in force; all but two, Connecticut and Rhode Island, finally ratified. These measures were the fruition, at a favoring moment, of ten decades of temperance agitation. The pleas of church and women's organizations were strengthened by corrupt practices of liquor interests, by the desire of southern whites to keep alcohol from Negroes, by automobile risks, by German control of breweries and by the efficient pressure politics of the Anti-Saloon League. However, the amendment and law were rural mid-west in concept, taking no account of the fixed habits of many urban dwellers, particularly of recent immigrant stock. Also they violated the United States tradition that strictly personal habits are no affair of government. Without sustaining public support, could prohibition be enforced?

The effort was made and certain gains ensued. Pauperism diminished greatly; teachers in poor school districts noticed that pupils were better fed and wore new shoes. Savings and other workingmen's investments rose. Such businesses as soft drinks and candy-selling, movies and theatres profited. Total alcoholic consumption fell, and people took to eating at coffee-shops.

On the other hand, a large proportion of the population flouted the law more or less openly. Expensive drinking at speakeasies and road-houses became highly fashionable; even high school youngsters proudly took to carrying hip flasks; others drank to show their contempt for the law. Drinking in public by women became respectable, and both sexes and all ages weakened in their respect for law in general. Home-brewers blossomed forth as liberty-loving patriots, whether their product was bathtub gin or weak wine. A taste was cultivated for "hard" liquor rather than the light beer and wines formerly popular. Habitual drunkards among the poor sometimes were sold industrial alcohol from which so little of the denaturing element had been removed that the drinker was blinded or died. Rumrunners found that high-speed boats and trucks made it not too difficult to elude the coast guard and customs officers. Enforcement was in the hands of the Prohibition Bureau, which until 1927 was not under Civil Service and had mostly an indifferent political personnel; it started without experience, while the bootleggers had been trained in the states which had established prohibition earlier. Moreover the Bureau had to deal with forty-eight uncertainties in state coöperation; some urban states removed the local props from under the Volstead Act.

Easy profits filled the capacious pockets of bootleggers, speakeasy operators and corrupt government agents, supporting a new and highly organized kingdom of violence ruled by gangsters, hi-jackers and racketeers. As their business was illegal, the competing "big shots" had no recourse to the courts in their disputes; rather it was bludgeoning, bullets and dumping dead bodies into the bay that decided arguments. Becoming expert at terrorism, they branched out into narcotics, hockey, prize-fighting and racing. They ran great distilleries, breweries and printing-plants twenty-four hours a day turning out counterfeit booze and labels. They operated hotels and restaurants and backed Broadway shows. Their excesses helped to bring repeal of the measures on which their sudden wealth depended.

Prohibition became a delicate political issue, and so it remained until its repeal. The most persistent attack was based on the ground of personal liberty. Some repealists stressed economic arguments: that it caused unemployment, withheld tax revenues and closed an important sugar and cereal outlet to American farmers. In 1924 the issue helped to split the Democratic National Convention into William G. McAdoo (dry) and Alfred E. Smith (wet) factions, with neither getting the nomination. In 1928 it helped to nominate Smith, although neither the Democratic nor the Republican platform then dared to abandon official endorsement of enforcement. Republicans, fearful of alienating their rural vote, then gave the louder lip service to prohibition. The prevalence of lawlessness of all kinds in 1929 forced Hoover to appoint the George W. Wickersham Commission. It officially opposed repeal yet showed that enforcement had proved a failure. In 1932 the Republicans adopted in substance a Smith proposition of 1928 for a revised scheme of state regulation, while the Democrats advocated outright repeal. As a Democratic landslide ensued, Hoover's last Congress arranged for a 21st Amendment to repeal the 18th; state conventions, instead of the usual legislatures, were specified to vote on it. Within ten months it was ratified. Each state proceeded to handle liquor-selling its own way. Repeal was part of the general depression urge to get out of all kinds of bad fixes, many of them highly complicated.

Thus ended the "noble experiment," but the lawlessness did not end. The old saloon had corrupted politics; now gangsters trained in the bootlegging business widened their sphere into bank burglaries, kidnaping, which became the "snatch racket," and corruption of legitimate businesses. When one big-shot tried to "muscle in" on another's racket, the stronger would "rub out" the other. Fortunately, gangsterism did not remain a paying business. The big-shots could not keep either their money or their freedom. Two years after Charles A. Lindbergh's small son was kidnaped and killed in 1932, Congress passed crime laws to make kidnaping and some other offenses subject to federal punishment where the perpetrators crossed state lines; also some gangsters were put in the penitentiary for violating the federal income tax laws. The Federal Bureau of Investigation, headed by J. Edgar Hoover and charged with the elimination of gangsterism, became known and feared for its efficiency.

Dangers to Civil Liberty

The same citizenry that so long tolerated lawlessness was meanwhile indifferent to the preservation of the right of freedom of expression, to the sanctity of civil liberty. The people of the United States were become victims of standardization. Every small town throughout the land boasted a Main Street, commercial association, country club and church set-up basically on the pattern of the others. Violation of this pattern was not tolerated. Any nation recently regimented by war stress readily suspects independent thought and action. Fearing idealism, suspecting liberals, and hating radicals, many persons tended to denounce any bold critic of the status quo as a heretic or a "red." Leaders in national and local governments and in societies joined the baiting, and dangerous discretionary power was entrusted to ordinary police officials. Some of the federal and state law-enforcing agencies, some of the American Legion, church fundamentalists, demagogues and persons with an axe to grind, were found bursting forth into flagrant violation of constitutional rights. According to their situation and locale they selected groups to persecute—whether Socialists, aliens, Communists, free-thinkers, scientists, Catholics, Negroes or Jews—and they then indiscriminately and erratically denied to them freedom of speech, press or assemblage, sometimes even of liberty or life.

Scores of illegal imprisonments and lawless lynchings, some deportations and hundreds of terroristic intimidations and raids were countenanced by the nation-wide surge of intolerance. Post-war nationalism and Communist propaganda from Soviet Russia roused fear of "Red" influence, especially after left-wing Socialists here formed a Communist or Workers' Party in 1919, and a Wall Street bomb in 1920 injured hundreds and killed thirty-eight. At Washington Wilson's and Harding's attorneys general, Palmer and Daugherty, set the staffs of the Department of Justice at red-baiting, jailing and deporting. In Massachusetts two Italians, Nicola Sacco and Bartolomeo Vanzetti, were tried for the murder of a factory paymaster and guard; and after it was learned that they were atheists, draft-dodgers and "philosophical-anarchists," seven years (1920-1927) of public protest could not save them from eventual execution. In New York the 1920 state legislature ousted five Socialist members, with as conservative a party leader as Charles E. Hughes denouncing the outrage. Thirty-two states enacted criminal syndicalist laws. In San Francisco two labor leaders, Thomas Mooney and Warren K. Billings, were convicted of a preparedness day bomb-throwing in 1916, although evidence accumulated that their conviction was arranged through perjury; no governor dared face the political risk of pardoning them until 1939.

Intolerance beat against the schools. In a last-ditch stand against evolution, the legislatures of Arkansas, Mississippi and Tennessee made the teaching of evolution illegal. Further, no less than twenty-one states between 1917 and 1935 singled out teachers as a class who must take oaths to prove their loyalty. Textbooks, as well as novels, plays, movies and works of art were dissected with morbid criticism.

An outstanding example of intolerance was the new Ku Klux Klan, a "100 per cent American" secret society founded in 1915 and nationally known by 1920. It used the implements of the earlier Ku Klux: the masks, white robes, fiery crosses, threats, tar and feathering and sometimes murder; but it had a far broader base. It was native, white, fundamentalist and Protestant in belief, opposing any increase in the national importance of Negroes, Jews, Catholics or immigrants. These prejudices in time led it to oppose such things as repeal of prohibition, birth-control, the League of Nations and pacifism. An exposé of its methods by the New York *World* in 1921 and a congressional investigation could not stop its growth. Politicians of the South, Southwest and Middle West had to trim their sails to its violent tempests, for in some states during the middle 'twenties it held the balance of power, enrolling then and there not less than 4 million members, irrespective of political parties. The Democrats, however, were most inconvenienced by it, because nearly all its principles were a challenge to their northern, urban membership. Their 1924 convention was held in session for 103 ballots because the Klan set up the dry, Protestant, William G. McAdoo as candidate and the New York Democrats insisted upon the wet, Catholic Alfred E. Smith. Both had to lose, and John W. Davis, unconnected with the fight, carried the limp Democratic banner that year for a hopelessly divided party.

All during these trying years there was fortunately continuous effort to protect civil liberty. Various organizations were formed, like the American Civil Liberties Union; and liberal weeklies like the *Nation*, the *New Republic* and the *Freeman* joined the labor press in the fight. A few notable lawyers devoted themselves to the struggle. Two justices of the Supreme Court, Oliver Wendell Holmes, Jr., and Louis D. Brandeis, rendered famous opinions [1] which, though representing the minority view, later became the basis for more successful legal action. Not until the 'thirties was the balance once more restored. Then the Supreme Court concurred in opinions written by Chief Justice Hughes reaffirming the liberties of speech and the press.[2] By this time the period of moral demobilization was gone and a new era of social awareness had taken its place.

[1] Abrams *v.* U.S., Gilbert *v.* Minnesota, Gitlow *v.* People of New York.
[2] Near *v.* Minnesota, De Jonge *v.* Oregon.

CHAPTER XLIV

DIFFICULTIES OF AGRICULTURE AND LABOR

"Normalcy" did not save the farmer from deflation, nor could it bring much that gave to labor a real sense of security.

Agricultural Deflation

Agriculture was descending from its position as chief occupation in the United States. It had always known chronic instability, chronic speculation, individualism and waste; now its distress became chronic, notably in the North Central States which had known steady well-being. The 'twenties saw a decrease in the number of farmowners, farms, farm animals, total value of farm lands and acres in cultivation. The 'twenties saw an increase in the number of non-producing (absentee) land owners and renters, in the size of farms, freight and tax loads and in outstanding mortgage debts. Readjustments demanded by changing dress and food habits were painful; wool and cotton lost ground to silk and rayon; meat, potatoes and grain to fruit, milk and sugar. From 1910 to 1920 the value of farm property rose 90 per cent then declined over 26 per cent from 1920 to 1930 and by 1933 reached a level under that of 1910.

The overhead in interest payments, machinery prices, freights and wages kept up, while crop prices fluctuated (usually downward), swelling the portion of farm return which went to non-farmers, destroying the margin between income and outgo. At the same time the farmers wanted to advance their standard of living in line with that of city dwellers. Debts incurred lightly to "tide over" one bad year could not be discharged under the heavier conditions of the next, even with the aid of special concessions under the Federal Reserve Law. The federal farm loan banks, provided under the 1916 law, held only a tiny percentage of the mortgages. Farmers' local banks, state institutions in small towns, went down with them.

To this unhappy situation many powerful factors contributed. Most of them may be grouped under (1) overemphasis upon productive efficiency and (2) neglect of marketing efficiency.

Mechanization—meaning use of such things as tractors, trucks, automobiles, improved planting machinery, combined harvesters, stationary gas-engines and electric power—had encouraged a technical efficiency which defeated its own object, benefiting consumers and middlemen while jeopardizing the producer. The machinery which the farmer found so useful raised competition against him: it released for human food production perhaps 30 million acres formerly needed to feed draft horses and mules; it enticed distant areas into production by bringing them closer to railheads and marketing centers; it encouraged experiments in tilling uncertain regions ill adapted by soil and climate to tillage; it destroyed fertility in a mad rush for immediate profits. Also entire families—fathers, mothers and children—competed enthusiastically in meat, milk and egg production campaigns. The war accentuated their preoccupation with production; it removed the last vestiges of caution against raising their capital investment and obligations too far above their normal carrying power.

On the other hand, their marketing inefficiency had not received adequate attention. The Department of Agriculture's Bureau of Markets had continued its spadework; the farmers' coöperatives had grown strong enough to secure exemption from the anti-trust restrictions of the Clayton Act of 1914; and under the Webb-Pomerene Act of 1918, permission had been granted farmers (as well as manufacturers) to form export trade associations. But control in agriculture remained absent.

The ending of the war opened their eyes. Farmers found their power of production had outstripped peacetime consumption. With machine aid they had increased their crops and reduced farm jobs, only to see the demand for American foodstuffs fall and the demand for jobs rise. America in 1870 required two workers out of every four to produce food; in 1920 but one. All governments were entering upon stricter regulation of commerce, thereby reducing world trade. Nationalism was rampant and so governments pushed self-sufficiency programs, substituting barter and "managed" money for international trade under the old gold standard. Retaliatory tariffs, manipulated currencies, new discriminatory devices and monopolies were revolutionizing world economy. United States agriculture and industry would require drastic readjustment. The necessity came first to agriculture and proved a hard one. Sharing prostration, could farmers unite for prosperity? Could they control farming?

Those agrarians who studied marketing from the narrow angle of domestic prices and who realized that the United States was following the world trend toward economic nationalism, sought control through crop reduction. This principle made headway fastest in the cotton country. There expanding acreage tended to depress prices whenever the boll weevil and bad weather did not intervene; prosperity often eluded the planter, whether the crop yields were good or poor. Slumps were worst when other factors, such as the outbreak of war in 1914 and the post-war deflation in 1920, helped to lower prices.

Leadership in the search for relief originated among specialists, local, state and federal, familiar with areas hardest hit. Some suggested reviving compulsory devices of crop reduction used in the Confederacy, but they could not move a large following. The day of a South-wide plan for compulsory acreage reduction was not yet. Even "voluntary" acreage reduction was obtainable only at times and in spots, as for example when credit was withheld for that purpose by bankers and merchants, or when campaigns of education and house-to-house canvasses for pledges were conducted much after the manner of the Liberty Loan drives.

Such voluntary efforts, when seconded by acute lack of funds for planting and by erratic weather, effected reduced yields, Acreage reductions of approximately 14 per cent and 15 per cent helped improve planter status in 1915 and 1921. It was a Coolidge-appointed Cotton Emergency Committee which formulated the Intermediate Credits Act of 1923. In 1926 a South-wide conference for reduction was achieved, with fourteen states drawn into varying degrees of coöperation; other conferences followed. There was a broadening in the makeup of state and local committees and in their fields of effort. Besides farmers, state agricultural officials and county bureau agents, the committees included bankers, merchants, chamber of commerce leaders and superintendents of education. Fields of coöperative agitation widened to include such things as diversified feed and money crops and compulsory school attendance, for children had been producing and gathering 25 per cent of the cotton crop. Patently, cotton difficulties were taking the leaders of the most conservative agricultural section of the United States along radical paths. A marked change was coming in the southern planters' concept of governmental functions.

Farmer Lobby Achievements

Meanwhile, in the broad field of nation-wide agriculture, farm leadership was reaching the point where it would consciously undertake to make agriculture a united, national force with lobby influence commensurate to that of industry and labor, potent to devise a program and legislate it into existence.

The machinery for this important purpose was at hand in the farm bureaus, which had an interesting history. The war had stimulated the agricultural colleges and the federal Department of Agriculture to integrate their extension activities through organization of farm bureaus, clubs of farmers united in local groups, for education in improved production. The bureaus could demand public and private contributions in a manner impossible to the older farm groups, the Grange, Equity, and Farmers' Union, for the latter were secret, class and commercial organizations ineligible for tax money and weighted down by accumulated jealousies and personal, sectional and religious connotations. The bureaus lacked those handicaps. So they had received help from federal and state funds under the Smith-Lever Act of 1914 and further appropriations under the Smith-Hughes Emergency Food Production Act of 1917. The funds enabled them to strengthen their personnel and program. In each county the farm bureau agent became a familiar and influential figure and the bureau became the local medium for farmers' social and economic activities. Formation of state federations followed, and finally with a national organization, the American Farm Bureau Federation founded in 1919, the educational extension program of the Department of Agriculture appeared to have come into full flower. Out in the states, meanwhile, approximately 6,000 coöperative organizations had gone into efficient operation, dealing successfully in dairy products, fruit, grain, live stock and vegetables.

The political approach to agrarian problems also was tried. Since 1915 a National Nonpartisan League, founded by the ex-Socialist Arthur C. Townley and designed to eliminate middlemen by the familiar populistic devices, had won a brief control in North Dakota and much influence in neighboring areas. It failed to capture the Republican machines of the Northwest, but it united with labor and with a progressive "Committee of 48" to form the Farmer-Labor party of 1920 and helped to weaken the Republicans in 1922. It survived to cooperate in 1924 with the Committee for Progressive Political Action which nominated La Follette, and its chief importance was its encouragement of liberal action by United States senators from that area which was decidedly vocal.

When the hard times had come in 1920, farmers losing foreign purchasers of their surplus became vitally concerned in debt-servicing, distribution, limitation of production and enlargement of legislative influence. The Farm Bureau Federation, against the wishes of a minority, shifted emphasis from education for efficient production to legislation for restoring profits. It soon became spokesman for the farmers' economic interests in dealing with other groups and with the government. It set up its own permanent secretariat in Washington, where three other farm organizations already had established lobbies as an outgrowth of the war. These were the National Board of Farm Organizations, set up there in 1917; the left-wing Farmers' National Council, set up in 1918; and the National Grange, organized in 1919. The existence of their Washington offices tended to focalize the work of the executive committees of the four organizations. They conferred and formulated individual and joint programs for congressional action.

The Washington office of the Federation hatched farm blocs in both House and Senate, the latter at one time consisting of fourteen Republicans and twelve Democrats. They were energized by polls of constituent opinion, sent through the local bureaus.

The Department of Agriculture during the 'twenties carried much responsibility for further developments. Its States Relation Service circulated *Document 65* on how to organize a farm bureau, and county bureaus multiplied rapidly. Most of the states of the East and Middle West and a few of the Far West established bureaus under various patterns. They expanded their functions from education into coöperative buying and selling. Meanwhile at Washington the Department increased its economic usefulness by consolidating (1 July 1922) its marketing, crop-estimating, farm management and farm economics functions into one Bureau of Agricultural Economics. The Department could well use the friendly offices of the Federation, for constant lobby watchfulness was essential to maintenance of departmental functions. Its major work was not carried on under legal authorization of permanent laws but depended for continuance upon annual appropriations affecting especially agricultural experiments, education and investigation; and such appropriations are continually subject to mutilation.

The ranks of farm lobbyists were strengthened by the energetic county agents, trained in the nip and tuck of local farm bureau work, close to the earth and to human nature. They helped to give agricultural influence on Capitol Hill a continuity and force never previously maintained. Thus "organized agriculture" became a reality on the federal, law-making scene.

The objectives, strength and mode of operation of the farm lobby of course varied from time to time. The farm bloc first emphasized marketing and credit curatives, employing the filibuster as a weapon. Congress was persuaded in 1921 to reëstablish the War Finance Corporation as an aid to credits and exports, besides inserting some agrarian items in the tariffs of that year and the next. President Harding had to promise far-reaching legislation to Gray Silver, chief Federation representative in Washington, before the Senate farm bloc would permit Congress to adjourn that year. The farm bloc, with the help of a progressive remnant, was blocking Republican plans for normalcy, lessening the size of ship subsidies and hindering reduction of taxes on opulence, while insisting that small incomes get some reductions. Harding's promises materialized as a Packer and Stockyards Act (1921), a Grain Futures Trading Act (1921), the Capper-Volstead Act (1922), an intermediate Credits Act (1923) and amendments to the federal Farm Loan Law. The first two laws prohibited unfair and deceptive practices by packers, commission merchants and brokers. The Capper-

Volstead measure freed coöperative associations in interstate commerce from anti-trust prosecution, while detailing the Secretary of Agriculture to watch against their becoming monopolies. The credits acts aimed to stabilize the market by adjusting short-term credit facilities to turnover in crops and live-stock production. It set up intermediate credit banks, one in each federal land bank district, to provide credits between the short-term (commercial) loans and long-term (land mortgage) loans; it also authorized national agricultural credit corporations, liberalized the agricultural functions of the Federal Reserve System and prolonged the life of the War Finance Corporation. Congress was constantly legislating on agriculture.

These domestic devices, however, could not bring prosperity to farmers raising surpluses which the world would not buy at American prices; the tariff was useless for that 85 per cent of farm production which raised surpluses. A big manufacturer, President George N. Peek of the Moline Plow Company, decided that the government must restore the farmer's purchasing power by compensating for export losses. He proposed a government corporation to buy the most important surpluses and sell them abroad at world prices, the cost to be met by a levy (called an "equalization fee") against the commodities thus marketed. This device was supposed to keep prices up and make the tariff effective.

The equalization plan was embodied in four McNary-Haugen bills. Two of these were passed by Congress, only to be killed by Coolidge's veto, and Hoover vetoed another version of this subsidy. The reduced-purchasing-power aspect of the farm problem so impressed President Hoover, however, that he urged erection of a Federal Farm Board. Congress established one under an Agricultural Marketing Act passed in special session June 1929, and it bought, sold and fixed prices of grain, cotton, live stock and other things through coöperatives and stabilization corporations. It strenuously urged voluntary crop reduction while spending hundreds of millions in a contradictory emphasis upon credit and further production. Whatever chance this law might have had for success was offset by the atrocious tariff of 1930, which was first proposed as a measure limited to agricultural relief but ultimately emerged as an effective instrument for destruction of trade. Against it a new "foreign agricultural service," also part of the 1930 legislation, could make slight headway.

Then followed the 1930 drought, reducing corn, hay and other yields (wheat slightly) but leaving the accumulated surplus still too large for notable price increases. Congress continued at cross-purposes, making lavish appropriations the next year for more production and for voluntary crop reduction, and added to these some additional credits under the 1932 Reconstruction Finance Corporation. Still agriculture could not rise and prosper. Organized capital and labor at home kept their power to raise the domestic price of what farmers had to buy; abroad new areas of cultivation and programs for national self-sufficiency further reduced the market and price for what farmers had to sell nearly everywhere.

Their reserve resources against the impact of panic and depression had been pretty thoroughly destroyed before the rest of the nation became aware of the impermanence of prosperity. Then between 1929 and 1933 their share of the national income shrank from 15 per cent to 7 per cent, and their purchasing power, in terms of their own products, fell nearly 40 per cent. When the F. D. Roosevelt administration came in, it found the farm surplus an acknowledged government obligation; dumped on its doorstep was the terrific problem of balancing farm production with world consumption.

Divisions Among Organized Labor

While the farmer was organizing to secure protection against his declining fortunes, labor leaders were endeavoring to combat unfortunate trends which were victimizing their followers. Organized labor was ill equipped to see and combat these trends. The aristocratic faction in labor, organized under the A.F. of L., obtained enough wage rises, while prices were going down, to markedly increase their real wages. They had officially supported the war and otherwise so strengthened their position that their membership grew from 1.6 million in 1910 to about 4 million in 1920, in the midst of an aggressive campaign of strikes. Possessed of property and relatively permanent jobs, their membership as a whole did not care to jeopardize their savings and their influence by close association with the masses of unskilled laborers. Organization of women and children, Negroes and recent immigrants still appeared unprofitable and was long resisted.

Immigration and child labor were in process of reduction, but women workers were increasing until by 1930 over one-fifth of all wage-earners were women, with approximately 3 per cent of them estimated as organized. State minimum wage laws helped to raise both the general level of women's wages and the proportion of women getting above minimum wages, but women remained largely employed in low-wage industries under conditions of exploitation where organization was particularly difficult. Negroes—nearly 3 million of them—were moved northward by the post-war agricultural depression and industrial activity. There they acquired the lowest-paid jobs, formerly held by non-voting immigrants, and the ballot. Poor, unlettered, debarred from the A.F. of L., which might have been unable to organize them if it had tried, they naturally followed radical leadership in labor and politics.

They secured the balance of political power in various localities, and some became Communists.

While the unskilled massed outside the Federation gates, its leaders clung tenaciously to their narrow craft definition of unionization, a relic from the era of hand labor. Machinery, however, now was making it possible for employers to use an ever increasing proportion of unskilled workers in great industries such as automobiles, oil and steel. Workers there could be organized effectively only as industries—horizontally regardless of particular function—rather than in competing craft groups. Yet the old notions continued to control the A.F. of L., which permitted warring crafts to quarrel within industries; they could not see that if they broadened their sympathies they might save their skins with less difficulty.

This aided company executives and radical groups. Capital long since had testified to their fear of expanding unionization, and by now many managers were successfully floating the device of "company unions," especially in the textile and coal industries. The company union gave labor the appearance without the reality of bargaining power. Companies set up unions under employee officers, paid by if not chosen by them; this diverted the natural leaders among employees to managerial functions and sympathies. Isolation was the weapon against solidarity. Just as the feudalistic company town, with its corporation-controlled houses, stores, churches, schools, clubs and (oftentimes) courts kept employees physically isolated from workers in other crafts, so the company union safeguarded ideological isolation—kept their workers from contact with fellow-craftsmen under other employers. Spy systems and strict rules against fraternization were maintained to preserve the isolation, which the workers themselves tightened by their suspicion of outside help; southern labor was especially suspicious of northern organizers.

The unskilled barricaded behind the company unions aroused little sympathy from the A.F. of L. but attracted the interest of more radical leaders of the unskilled. Ever since the Socialists withdrew (in 1895) from the A.F. of L., leaders like Daniel De Leon, Eugene Debs, John P. St. John, W. E. Trautman and Wm. Z. Foster had been sponsoring various organizations based on the horizontal or industrial union principle. The doctrines of the Socialist Trade and Labor Alliance, the I.W.W., the Western Federation of Miners, the Workers' International Industrial Union, etc. ranged all the long way from Socialism to Anarchism. Frequently they stressed overthrow of the capitalistic system through sympathetic strikes and sabotage spread across all industry.

Gompers' technique remained relatively peaceful; it embraced big strike funds and benefits to finance long, strategic strikes to force employers into making binding agreements for increasing labor's share of the profits. The radicals usually wanted not industrial peace, expensive strikes or binding agreements, but destruction of capitalism itself. Neither was consistent politically. Gompers abandoned his traditional opposition to party affiliation by supporting La Follette in 1924. The Communists, after disrupting the Socialist party in 1919, formed groups of their own and then determined to bore into the A.F. of L. from within. For this purpose Foster and his following formed the "Trade Union Educational League" to bend the less conservative organized workers in the A.F. of L. toward revolution. Upon the various Communist groups the Communist International of Russia forced a united program.

The post-war reversion to ultra-conservatism made the 'twenties an anti-labor period, with the government relaxing control and the employers driving for an open shop. Consequently the continuing fight between the A.F. of L. and the industrial unions was accompanied by the fight of both against capital and against unfriendly public sentiment. Among the more important strikes was a Seattle traction outbreak in February of 1919 when all the city's functions fell into strikers' control and they demonstrated solidarity and capacity for order. That fall began the third effort of the A.F. of L. to unionize steel. This titanic struggle began with radical and conservative labor coöperating. Then labor divided. Negro strike-breakers were brought in, and charges of Communism completed the defeat. Conferences of capital and labor arranged by Wilson failed to reach a solution.

The post-war misfortune continued to pursue the unions. President Wilson went so far in October 1919 as to declare a United Mine Workers strike illegal, on the ground that the United States was still at war. Furthermore the Supreme Court was restricting the application of the Clayton Anti-Trust Law to industrial disputes. In decisions of 1920 and 1921 the court's majority stripped from labor's Magna Charta most of the safeguards earlier thought to be firmly attached to it (p. 421). There was left little except the right of jury trial for strikers accused of contempt of court in injunction cases. The use of injunctions spread. Harding's attorney general, Daugherty, killed a railway shopmen's strike of 1922 with an extraordinarily sweeping injunction. Other big strikes of 1921 and 1922 involved the International Typographical Union and the United Mine Workers. Defeat and ill-repute together reduced Federation membership drastically before Gompers' death, 13 December 1924.

The Communist influence grew more important in trade-union affairs. An outstanding Communist, Albert Weisbord, had organized the unskilled of the Botany textile mills at Passaic in the first strike under such leadership; and in 1926, following withdrawal by Weisbord, the A.F. of L. under the leadership of Gompers' successor, William Green, admitted to membership a union organized by Communists on an industrial basis. Communists of the Trade Union Educational League, reorganized as the Trade Union Unity League, sponsored between 1925 and 1932 eleven independent unions. The Communists and also the A.F. of L. undertook strikes in various southern textile fields. Their desperate struggles at Gastonia, North Carolina, Elizabeth, Tennessee, and Danville, Virginia at least made southern workers and public aware of the existence of the problem. In the Illinois coal-fields during 1931 Communist and Federation factions worked at cross-purposes. Mass demonstrations and hunger-marches on Washington, more alarming to conservatives than dangerous, marked the Communist depression technique.

Defeat seemed the most frequent reward for both craft and industrial union agitation between the First World War and the depression, but there were some gains of note. More states paid more attention to workmen's compensation acts and enforced protection against disaster. A Federal Industrial Rehabilitation Law of 1920 provided government funds to be contributed to states to help those injured in industrial accidents to return to employment. A year later federal money was appropriated to aid in reducing child-birth mortality. Seventeen states by 1930 had adopted old-age pensions. The effort of the steel workers to get the closed shop moved the Inter-Church World Movement to investigate conditions, and their revelations shocked the middle class. An eight-hour day, despite Gary's contention it must ruin steel, came to be successfully substituted for the twelve-hour day. The effort of the coal-miners to get a guarantee of permanent employment caused Congress to enlarge the powers of the Interstate Commerce Commission, with the idea of lowering unjust prices and controlling shipments in emergencies; it provided a federal coal director and created an investigating agency which reported that mining was properly regulated by the federal government. Broad use of injunctions and contempt-of-court proceedings to break strikes finally brought in 1932 the Norris-La Guardia Act, which aimed at preferential treatment for labor, to prevent such court abuses.

Court opposition undermined federal legislation on child labor. Congress had attempted to prohibit child labor by the law of 1916, which had forbidden interstate shipment of products made by child labor, but in 1918 the Supreme Court had ruled that labor conditions were the concern of the states and could not be regulated under the federal power over interstate commerce. Thereupon Congress promptly attacked the problem from another angle, passing in 1919 a law levying a tax upon such products as entered interstate commerce. This likewise was tossed aside by the Supreme Court, on the ground that it attempted to use taxation to exercise a power not belonging to the federal government. So Congress in 1924 passed a resolution for a constitutional amendment which gave Congress the power to "limit, regulate, and prohibit the labor of persons under eighteen"; over eighteen years have passed without enough state ratifications to validate this.

Furthermore court opposition destroyed state legislation on minimum wages. Legislation of this character had been enacted by fifteen states when the Supreme Court in 1923 declared a District of Columbia law for women and minors unconstitutional. A wave of repeals and adverse decisions ensued, with the minimum wage too often converted into the maximum figure. As workers found themselves displaced, their earnings sacrificed and their social scale fallen, an increasing proportion of them ceased to share the middle-class conviction that they were their own economic masters. These became aware that classes no longer were fluid; they turned from proletarian individualism toward a mass movement. This change had been retarded by the industrial and agricultural opportunities of a frontier era, which stretched the transition from a mercantile to an industrial economy over most of the nineteenth century. Machinery destroyed all that. It proved that individual proletarianism could no longer work; it established class lines, laying the foundation for a labor movement beyond the imagination of Samuel Gompers.

CHAPTER XLV

PROSPERITY AND DEPRESSION

The policies followed toward agriculture and labor en route to the great depression were in large measure shaped by the imperious mandates of machine civilization. Machinery was working a fundamental change in American business following the First World War. Economic relationships in nearly all industries were revolutionized and their interdependence sharply revealed, but the revelation went almost unheeded—until the depression.

New Strains in Industry

Americans were living in an age of mass production, with nearly 30 per cent of the workers engaged in industrial occupations and by 1930 with over one-third of the national income industrial in origin. A market for goods was the continuing necessity for workers, managers, investors and for all who sold to any of these. Therefore anything which stopped factory wheels would jeopardize indirectly the food, clothing and shelter of almost everybody. During the 'twenties forces were at work to undermine that market, to diminish the purchasing power of the farmers and city people who bought most of the goods and of the foreigners who took the remainder. Trade was being hurt by speculative psychology and a bad tariff policy.

Additional serious strain was put upon industry by several less obvious but no less important factors. Among these were the strain of supporting new classes of unemployables, owing to a decline in the increase in the birth-rate, a trek from the country to the city, and a fall in immigration. Between 1920 and 1930 all but about 2.5 million of the 17 million increase in population was urban. Ambitious country youth transplanted their energies to city activities. The striding influence of the cities would be realized after a reapportionment law of 1929, which based representation upon the 1930 census.

Urban industry formerly had not had to pay for the rearing of labor or for the maintenance of the aged, for they had been left behind, in Europe and in the farming communities, when workers flocked over to American factories. In the 'twenties, however, industry had to shoulder more of the cost of supporting unemployables, for reduced immigration lowered the percentage of the population which was in its working prime. The war had aroused apprehension of a post-war influx of foreign labor which might glut the market for it and also might introduce radical European political ideas, such as Russian Communism. Two years after Wilson vetoed the literacy immigration bill of 1915, Congress had succeeded in passing over his veto a bill requiring that all immigrants over sixteen be able to read. Subsequent laws of 1921, 1922 and 1924, sponsored by labor in self-protection and, to some extent, by "100 per cent American" sentiment, had set quota limits which were in fact long overdue.

A 1921 Emergency Immigration Act limited new-comers from Europe and Africa to a quota of 3 per cent of the nationals of those respective countries resident in the United States in 1910; this was amended the next year to make aliens, already resident, subject to quota requirements until they had lived here five years. Next, the Johnson Act of 1924 reduced the quota to 2 per cent of the nationals of 1890. Further, by that law, the total number of annual immigrants was limited to 150,000 after 1 July 1927; the respective quotas were not to change the relative racial "composition" of the United States as it had been in 1920—a difficult thing to figure out and not applied until 1929. Still further, this law barred the Japanese entirely, for it made inadmissible all aliens who were ineligible for citizenship. None of these restrictions, however, applied to native Latin Americans or Canadians; and so immigration inspectors took to debarring Mexicans (who had flooded into illiterate, manual jobs) by declaring them likely to become public charges. The clear effect of these laws upon immigration from Europe was to favor that from the northern section and greatly restrict that from the southern area. The total of new-comers fell from the 1901-1910 annual average of about 880,000 to about 411,000 for 1921-1930, and only 35,500 for the depression year of 1932.

Since industry now had to shoulder more of the cost of supporting unemployables, the expanding profits of this decade were required to carry the higher wage scales needed to maintain infants and oldsters. Unfortunately, the former bounding rate of expansion in profits could not be kept up indefinitely; the market ultimately must contract to the slowing down of population increase and to the decline of farmers' purchasing power.

Furthermore, industry suffered from two drastic kinds of displacement: displacement of goods and of people. Displacement of goods destroyed the value of the holdings of all persons engaged in producing those goods. They now suffered by an increase in the substitution of one thing for another and by change of locale. Hay and oats were displaced in part by automotive power, coal in part by oil, water and gas, cotton by silk and rayon, iron by scrap, etc. Industries migrated within and without the United States. Investments in houses, land, equipment, schools, factories and churches lost their value when busy industries were silenced and whole towns were abandoned for new sites. Serious displacement in American extractive industries came through foreign competition, particularly noticeable in Russian anthracite and Latin American copper and oil. By 1930 imports of copper reached 98 per cent of exports, of crude oil 70 per cent of exports, with agricultural imports passing exports by $300,000,000.

Displacement of people was even more serious. By 1920 it was clear that in manufactures and minerals machine-use had so raised output and reduced jobs that far more was produced than would-be consumers had the money to buy. Thus "excess" production, from the sellers' viewpoint, resulted. Machinery raised the productive power of workers and displaced them, particularly in coal, steel, railroading, electric lamp making, clothing and foodstuffs. For example, a steamshovel displaced 199 men out of 200 diggers; a sewing-machine, 24 out of 25 clothing makers; a bread-wrapper, 19 out of 20 wrappers; one bricklayer, 725. Some of the victims of this "technological unemployment" found places in mechanized automobile manufacture or in new industries born of the electric stimulus, for electricity spurred invention, investment and a rising standard of living. Use of power was growing three and three-quarters faster than the population. But as electricity multiplied the use of machines and the output of individuals, it too displaced workers.

Only a very few leaders appreciated the facts that mass production requires widening of the domestic market if a foreign market fails and that a loss in agricultural purchasing power must be compensated for among urban buyers, who are becoming the most important market for American producers. In their study of how to safeguard their profits, the captains of industry had concentrated upon their rivals and their wage bills, to the neglect of their customers; they invented means for keeping prices up and wages down through elimination of competition and defeat of unions but gave only superficial study to volume of sales. They were not compelled; national expansion had provided them with a spreading market, postponing a sharp realization that an employee is a consumer. So they poured profits back into plant expansion for more production instead of into wages and lower prices for more consumption.

Stock-watering forced production managers who hoped to pay dividends on common stock either to raise prices or lower wages, and a raise in prices was preferable; but post-war conditions vetoed it. The end of the war brought a decline in business and in national income, but war prices largely were retained until European demand failed. Europe could not buy American products at the high prices asked. Her own harvests had increased so that American grain was not needed. Also the United States tariff set prices above Europe's reach. Unless the United States continued its generous loans, Europe would not have the dollar exchange with which to shop.

In the United States, also, there was price resistance in 1920. It came to a head in buyers' strikes and boycotts, reducing food and clothing prices. Business failures in 1920 passed 8,000 and in 1921 were more than twice that number. Unemployment mounted to nearly 3.5 million workers. With depreciated inventories came wage reductions, countered by an epidemic of strikes. Prices seemed generally adjusted to a lower level by 1924, except in agriculture and a few other directions, but neither capital nor labor could be content with this readjustment or with subsequent, irregular rises. They floundered while a new economic set-up was revolutionizing their status.

Prosperity requires that consumption and production expand simultaneously, but between 1919 and 1929 the gap between them widened ominously. While manufacturing output was increasing about 42 per cent real wages in manufacturing were increasing about 15 per cent. The income of the masses was rising less rapidly than that of the rich, until by 1929 the one-tenth per cent of American families at the top of the social scale were receiving approximately as much income as the 42 per cent of the families at the bottom of that scale. The latter numbered approximately 12 million families, and their annual incomes stood below $1,500. If they could have fulfilled their desires, they would have absorbed an output many times the peak productive output of 1929, for the United States has not yet attained a productive capacity to equal what Americans would like to consume.

Moreover, since approximately 2 million persons and sometimes 4 million remained unemployed during the height of "prosperity," the problem of finding buyers to keep factories operating must become acute. When the unemployed reached 15 million, as some estimators counted it in 1932, there would exist a market for perhaps less than half of the potential output of existing establishments. Thus was the process of economic progress retarded by impediments in wealth diffusion. A panic would reveal the desperate need for readjustments between production and consumption. The direct, material loss, staggering as it was, would prove less than the almost irreparable destruction of human values.

Monopoly and Speculation at Their Peak

Labor was struggling to adjust itself to the hydro-electric age which the twentieth century had become. As electricity developed into an indispensable servant of modern existence, it also gave the mastery to those who controlled the supply of electricity. American carelessness with water resources, upon which cheap electricity depends, had permitted them to fall into private hands at strategic points, without adequate regulation. Electric power touched closely many social and economic issues and symbolized the greatest American problem of the twentieth century—the challenge of monopoly.

High prices for power led post-war communities into further experiments in municipal power plants and made senators James Couzens and G. W. Norris lead movements for government regulation and operation. The power combine organized the efficient National Electric Light Association to fight the trend; its clever publicity was fed to governors and legislators, teachers and pupils, clergy and congregations, publishers, writers and readers, speakers and listeners. This helped pull some of the teeth from the legislation of 1920 and 1930 which established first a part-time and then a full-time Federal Power Commission to license and regulate power companies. Muscle Shoals came to symbolize the contest over public control of natural resources, as private interests repeatedly tried to get control of that plant and defeated legislation for government development of it. Throughout the decade they waged a hot and usually successful fight against the Norris program. He got bills through Congress in 1928 and 1931, but Coolidge and Hoover vetoed them.

The power interest, like all the other moving parts of the American economic machine, was geared to mass production for a rapidly expanding market under monopoly management. Monopoly now was monopolized. The interlocking directorates, against which La Follette long had fulminated, had blossomed into holding companies, which in turn were controlled by banker giants who manipulated assets and directorates according to their ideas of profit.

One-half the corporate wealth was controlled by 200 corporations, in turn controlled by a handful of men. Their hold upon natural resources and manufacturing processes stretched across land and sea. In addition to hydro-electricity their dominant control over vital parts of mechanized existence included such indispensable modern products as copper, iron, nickel, bauxite (the basis of aluminum), anthracite and oil.

These men who directed the machinery which ran American manufacture, mining, finance, transportation, utilities and trade, had been trained chiefly to safeguard profitable production. Consumption seemed to them, even in the 'twenties, mostly a problem of advertising, because instalment selling appeared successful and foreign markets had not yet been too painfully restricted by economic nationalism. Few of the giants in business stopped to reflect seriously upon the possible necessity, for their market, of a broad rise in the actual purchasing power of the lower classes. They could scarcely be expected to show vision in a field which was closed to the minds of presidents of this great nation.

President Coolidge could not ponder the larger aspects of trust control as long as he rested serene in the conviction that the "Big Stick" had destroyed special privilege. President Hoover thought of competition chiefly in terms of its wastefulness. He wished to eliminate what remained of it in important fields. As secretary of commerce he had hurried to encourage formation of "trade associations." Over 400 were sponsored; they pooled information and reached profitable agreements —until the Supreme Court found them in violation of the Sherman Anti-Trust Act. That law had been written in a state of fear at the mysterious rapidity of our growth; in so far as it embodied the politico-economic notions swaying Congress in 1890, it could scarcely fit the situation forty years later.

The resourceful secretary thereupon made his Department the clearing-house for information; over 200 "codes of fair practice" were drawn up, some of them destined to be copied by the NRA. The Federal Trade Commission found next that the Commerce Department had become an instrumentality for open price-fixing; but the Supreme Court declared for the codes. In effect, the courts and the Interstate Commerce Commission suspended efforts to put teeth into the anti-trust law. Thus what the tariff and the executives had left undone to encourage monopoly, the courts did.

Americans on the whole felt slight concern over the tightening grip of monopoly or the other little-noticed forces working to grind them between the gears of modern machinery. Between the outbreak of the First World War and 1929 the total national income jumped from 34 to 83 billions. A less encouraging fact, that wealth distribution was not improving proportionately, that 60 per cent of the national wealth was accruing to 2 per cent of the population, went little noticed as long as the "average" person knew some rise in standards of living.

Egged on by instalment selling, by speculative fervor and by the sense of insecurity and change natural to a post-war period, people spent their past, present and future earnings. They bought an increasing variety of attractive, electric timesavers such as washing-machines, mixers and refrigerators; they went in for radios, automobiles, travel and habitual movie attendance. They allowed themselves the luxuries of speculation and college courses for their children. The figures tell a vivid story. Radio receiving sets jumped from zero in 1920, when the first broadcasting station was erected, to 10 million in 1930. In the decade automobile ownership grew from 8 to 26.5 million, weekly movie attendance from 30 to 100 million, college and university attendance from 355 to 970 thousand.

Tax evasion flourished, fostered by the speculation rampant in Wall Street and the overcapitalization in industry. Made ingenious by cupidity, people secured tax exemption by giving land to tax-free religious institutions in exchange for annuities; others invested heavily in tax-free securities, set up foreign or "dummy" corporations, made evasive "joint" returns and "wash sales" to relatives. Exemption and evasion together ruined the effectiveness of the income tax, drove capital out of productive functions and induced extravagance.

Even the poorest classes indulged an optimistic belief in mounting prosperity and in the all-importance of larger incomes. Few of these were acquiring bank accounts or buying homes, but they felt less poor. They were advantaged by public outlays of tax money and by private benefactions. So much was done for them by schools, hospitals and social-minded foundations that the national average was raised in longevity, health, education and other indices of well-being.

The trouble lay in the fact that the attitudes toward wealth, production and use did not change as fast as economic processes. Nearly every one clung to a mental pose which no longer fitted his or her actual environment. They cherished the war-profiteering spirit, kept the notion that one can "get something for nothing," anything in fact, which one can "get away with." There was confidence that inflation was permanent, an idea encouraged by the gold influx; and as population shifted from the country to urban centers people forgot the lesson of the soil—that one must produce to live—and became infected with stock-market phraseology. Use of modern inventions gave mankind a sense of mastery: of miracles they would make no end.

It seemed natural and sensible, during the 'twenties, to buy relatively less food and clothing—20 per cent less of it—and more "durable" goods: automobiles, electrical appliances, heaters, radios, lights and refrigerators—70 per cent more of them. This that they called the higher standard of living was raised by the joint push of mechanization and credit. Credit had become one of the mightiest instruments of modern capitalism without people learning how to control instead of abuse it. People grew contemptuous of self-denial, oblivious to the fact that instalment contracts usually are mortgages, dependent on the maintenance of values. It seemed the clever mortgages and instalment financing could endlessly expand one's comforts and pleasures. Did not the government, in wartime and peace, issue money on obligations? The more charge accounts a family carried, the higher seemed its credit status. Therefore Americans accelerated their growth in indebtedness faster than their expansion in wealth, raising the debt by 1930 up to one-third the wealth.

More than 21 million Americans had developed familiarity with paper investments by purchase of Liberty Loan securities; newspaper headlines had told them of huge profits in stock "war brides." The number of stock owners, 4 million in 1900, multiplied five times by

1930. Speculation, rather than investment, motivated perhaps 90 per cent of the purchasers as erstwhile conservative bondholders moved over to stocks, "unlisted" and "over the counter" paper. Gambling on margin involved at least 1 million persons in the 'twenties, hoisting brokers' loans nearly 250 per cent in two years, raising stock prices out of all connection with dividends, and giving 1929 the unprecedented stock average of 4 million shares daily. Profits from both speculation and "legitimate" business were attracted into the market instead of to consumption, at the fatal juncture that consumption was suffering from the plowing back of business profits into producing plant and surpluses instead of into distribution as salaries and wages.

Wide distribution of stock ownership must ultimately mean wide sharing of disastrous deflation, but during the period of "benevolent anarchy" all but the poorest groups were caught by the net. Women, reputedly the more conservative sex, blindly believed the men's assurances of a perpetual boom; their rise in economic power gave their faith importance, as percentages of insurance paid to them, estates inherited and individual wealth held by them increased greatly. They long had been the chief buyers of goods; now they comprised the majority of stockholders in certain corporations, without directing policy. Like the men, they had become used to colossal figures, were eager to make money for themselves and sceptical of social control.

All classes sought to emulate the example of financiers whose "ability" they worshiped. Financiers, nothing loath, floated new securities—$11.6 billion worth in 1929 alone. Promoters of giant combinations paid themselves in watered common stock, unloaded it upon a gullible public, and set up "investment trusts" to woo the savings of the timid but trustful. The less gullible had their savings quietly misappropriated by trust "fund" managers who displaced bonds and preferred stocks of conservative businesses with common stocks representing no par value and incapable of producing income. The area to be victimized was widened by foreign investors' interest in the American market. Likewise American investors plunged into foreign governmental and private loans, sinking around 12 billions in the same hole where more than 10 billions of American war loans had already disappeared. As long as quotations climbed nearly everybody cheered, for most business indices seemed buoyant and President Hoover breathed supreme confidence.

Unfortunately, these easy assumptions of invincible prosperity assured its end, for leaders stayed blind and deaf to portents of change. In fact the "prosperity" of 1922-1929 was raising storm signals in many areas. At least one-fifth of the banks, more than 6,000 of them, were failing, and chiefly in farm communities. Vital industries like coal, railroad equipment, textiles, and leather suffered severely from technological changes. Unemployment was seldom less than 2 million and often much more. By 1928 building, automobile and steel trades had begun to lag; the oil market was deluged. Defaults on private debts were increasing, while international repayments continued only because America supplied further loans.

Down into the Depression

During midsummer, 1929, a few well-informed Americans and Europeans cashed in on their stock profits. The two great creditor nations—England and the United States—undertook to withdraw their support from the topheavy structure of foreign and domestic debt. A sag in stocks became noticeable 21 October 1929. Complete rout came to Wall Street within the next eight days. Every cog in America's delicate economic machinery was jammed by the collapse of speculation, catching in a vise farmers and factory hands, builders and mortgagors, bankers and tax delinquents. No help was to be had from elsewhere, for the stringency was world-wide. Not counting foreign losses, American speculators had dissipated approximately 25 billions in savings; and thus stripped they entered the depression.

Yet national arrogance died hard. Incredulous businessmen and politicians insisted, "Recovery is just around the corner," and "We shall muddle through somehow, as we have before." Thus three painful years dragged by before realities of the situation came home. Agriculture and industry found their surpluses unexportable. Railroad revenue from freight and passengers fell 50 per cent, with about 16 per cent of mileage practically in receivership. Falling prices indicated "overproduction" of necessities, although "one-third of a nation" went ill fed, ill clothed, and ill housed. Wages those three years fell 55 per cent, although dividends and interest fell relatively little. Industries which had been lagging before the collapse by 1930 furnished 90 per cent of the workpeople on strike. Scant impression could strikers make, however, with between 12 and 15 million unemployed. Organized capital entrenched itself behind court injunctions and price control and swallowed distressed, independent producers. Some banks saved themselves at the expense of public welfare; more than 5,000 fell. Morale was lost with jobs, businesses and deposits.

President Hoover realized the need of strenuous effort to avert a general crash of banks, insurance companies and railroads. He called upon businessmen to sacrifice in order to retain employees and wage rolls. Otherwise unemployment would cut purchasing power down to a dangerously low point. Private efforts were made to cushion the depression by a "spread" in work through reduction of hours, to give more people opportunity to earn at least a partial wage. Private charity also sought to help those in need and made heroic attempts to collect more money.

The national Treasury was ill-equipped for the emergency. The same policy which had heightened tariff walls, to keep out goods with which the foreigners might have paid some of their debts, cut the customs income available for national support. Duties had fallen from nearly half the revenue in 1903 to less than 15 per cent of it in 1928. War debt payments collapsed in 1931. The income tax failed miserably as a depression source of funds, although Congress in 1930 and 1932 tightened some of the restrictions it had loosened earlier. It abolished exemption on earned income in 1930; in 1932 it raised estate and surtaxes and lowered the figure for normal exemption.

All taxing units turned, as in wartime, to common aspects of everyday life for tax funds. They applied nuisance and sales levies to amusements, bank checks, club dues, furs, gifts and stock sales; to automobiles, lubricating oils and tires; to electricity, matches, refrigerators and toilet articles. But through all these taxes restless America paid less than through the one tax on gasoline, applied at first to maintain roads for a nation on the move, and later diverted to a multiplicity of crying needs. By such means the tax officials reached the poorest citizen, and oftener than Mellon would have dreamed. The proportion of the taxes levied indirectly—on all persons regardless of ability to pay—rose from 27 per cent in 1920 to 58 per cent in 1933. Thus, among the issues challenging the incoming administration was the fundamental question: should the poor constitute the principal support of the government?

During prosperity the rich seemed to come off best in the shifting struggle with the poor over incidence of taxation. The depression violently upset all calculations. Little and big governments proved incapable of cutting outgo as low as income. Although local and state units had continued to depend principally upon property taxes until real estate values collapsed in 1930, twenty of them had tapped incomes. Some had levied on tobacco, chain stores and sales; all were adopting inheritance and estate levies. The loss of liquor taxes, due to prohibition, had encouraged experimental taxation, and the growing complexity of the problem turned towns, cities and counties to the state for a share of its tax returns. The depression brought all these subsidiary units as well as private persons and businesses to the federal government for succor.

It became painfully evident that government must do more than advise. State legislatures, to the number of at least twenty-two, experimented with relief and pension laws, besides attempting to lighten the situation by various measures on injunctions and shorter hours. The Congress elected in 1930, made more sensitive by a shift of control to a coalition of Democrats and progressive Republicans, essayed the Wagner unemployment law, which would have enlisted federal functioning. This President Hoover vetoed, insisting that relief was a local matter. He set up a voluntary Emergency Relief Organization to encourage state and private relief, but the latter soon proved so totally inadequate that federal aid became imperative. At length wheat and cotton held by the Federal Farm Board were turned over to the ERO to be used to aid the distressed, and Congress appropriated $300,000,000 to be loaned to states no longer able to provide for their poor.

President Hoover sought to start public works, so that money expended and men employed on them would "prime the pump" and stimulate spending and producing. All told over $2,250,000,000 were spent during his administration on a variety of public works. The most elaborate of these was a gigantic dam across the Colorado River, known first as Hoover Dam but renamed by his successor, Boulder Dam. It would furnish irrigation and power in several states, besides ensuring safety from floods for California's Imperial Valley and an adequate water supply for her greatest metropolis, Los Angeles.

These undertakings and other lesser ones revealed that the stern facts of the depression were carrying the conservative Republican administration far beyond its preferred range of activities. Although it is scarcely admitted in some quarters, the Hoover administration pointed the direction for a number of palliatives mainly credited to the New Deal.

President Hoover and his intimate associates knew much about European finance, and after a period in which they trusted that the depression would prove a temporary stock-market affair curable by "return of confidence," they concluded that a large part of America's ills could be laid at Europe's doors. This idea was strengthened when French politics contributed in May 1931 to banking collapse in Austria and Germany. Hoover took decisive action. On 20 June he declared a moratorium on Europe's obligations to the United States. Unfortunately this proved of permanent help on neither side of the ocean, and Britain had to abandon the gold standard the following September. Gold, indeed, had lost all place as a gage of international payments and had become the plaything of panic unreason.

To American businessmen, however, gold had been sacrosanct since Bryan's defeat, and they resented Britain's action. They wanted to believe that this depression like earlier ones could work off through deflation under the gold standard. But the old, swift liquidation was prevented by control of one-half the business wealth by two hundred corporations, each strong enough to prevent and withstand price reductions over a long period. Nor could the water be squeezed out of the railroads; they were now too closely held by insurance and banking corporations whose bankruptcy would wipe out small as well as large savings.

Faced by these problems, by the possibility of direct relief over his veto, and by his own desire for reëlection, President Hoover asked for the "Reconstruction Finance Corporation" law of January 1932 and broad extensions of it in July. Through these the government would loan relief funds, but not to individuals as such: to bank, railroad, trust, mortgage, insurance, and industrial corporations and to states, agricultural boards and self-liquidating construction projects. Struggling to end the depression by credit inflation, Congress made appropriations for a Federal Home Loan banking system and broadened Federal Reserve powers. The Federal Reserve now could use government bonds as collateral for Federal Reserve notes, could lend to individuals and sometimes could omit collateral for member bank loans. A slight rise in the weekly business index occurred. Such measures improved the outlook in so far as they bolstered the sense of security among the relatively conservative groups which received the credit.

This was not as broad a kind of security as the rank and file of voters wanted in 1932. They demanded social security, meaning steady work, paying crops, homes and farms safe from foreclosure, and pensions for old age. In substance they challenged the politicians to preserve these things. The Republicans, popularly identified with the depression and loaded down with Bourbon traditions and backing, could scarcely be sanguine.

The Republicans convened at Chicago, 14 June, with administration henchmen very numerous, and put on the best possible face, renominating Hoover and Curtis and lauding the administration. Their platform could not promise much more than public works, drought relief, Farm Board aid and local charity; on prohibition they pledged themselves to submit a repeal amendment on which members could act as they chose. The party was in desperate straits, although big employers, including Henry Ford, urged their workmen to vote for Hoover.

The Democratic prospects were rosy when they met at Chicago, 27 June, with no dearth of presidential aspirants. Those foremost included John Nance Garner, Texas member of Congress since 1903 and Speaker since the Democrats took control of the House in 1931; Wilson's secretary of war, Newton D. Baker; and three governors, Albert C. Ritchie of Maryland and the previous and present New York governors, Smith and Franklin D. Roosevelt. Roosevelt had been put far in the lead by the labor of James A. Farley, a New York building-supply executive who proved one of the most expert of the many political experts given the American nation by the talented Irish race. Although Smith opposed the nomination of the man who had nominated him in 1924 and who had run for governor at his request in 1928, and although conservatives fought it, a ticket of Roosevelt and Garner was put through on the fourth ballot. Governor Roosevelt was a country gentleman of liberal leanings and record, a leader of amazing skill, and Speaker Garner knew intimately the ways of Democratic legislators in Washington. Their party platform of course blistered the record of the Republicans, held them responsible for the depression and promised to relieve it. Not only would the farmer and unemployed laborer have more assistance and relief, but the nation as a whole would be helped, by reducing government expenditures, by stock-exchange regulation, banking reform, reciprocal trading agreements, a "competitive" revenue tariff and immediate prohibition repeal.

Roosevelt went to the country with infectious optimism and not too much definiteness; he admitted domestic causes for the depression and gave the platform a personal significance to most of his listeners. Millions were assured that rescue would come through new measures and men, a "New Deal." This gospel was as manna to the unemployed in the great factory centers. His attacks upon the Hoover régime were so scorching and convincing that he persuaded millions of Republicans to cast their first Democratic votes. As he appeared to be the chosen instrument for preserving democracy under the capitalistic system, the liberal Republicans led by Senators Cutting of New Mexico, Johnson of California, La Follette of Wisconsin and Norris of Nebraska turned to him.

Following business recession during October, approximately 23 million citizens went to the polls and cast their votes for the "New Deal." Hoover's 1932 defeat reached the proportions of his 1928 victory. Only six states, and they among the most conservative in the country—Maine, Vermont, New Hampshire, Connecticut, Pennsylvania and Delaware—gave their electoral votes to Hoover; and only eight Republican governors managed to get elected. Stalwart Republican senators went down, and the Democrats won the House, three to one.

Thus did the Democratic leadership receive a mandate to free Americans from the toils of a world-wide, but little understood, depression. They did not then think of it as more than a passing problem, one calling for but a temporary change in the details of democratic government. They were spared the foreknowledge that their democracy, like others in Europe, was to be put on trial for its life.

CHAPTER XLVI

ESTABLISHING THE NEW DEAL

The mid-depression election of 1932 was an act of faith—faith in the essential soundness of the American economic system and in the efficacy of a political shift to help lift the depression. This was in line with national tradition. Always, except in dealing with slavery, political parties had furnished an outlet for discontent over the workings of the system. Vocal minorities, by persistent pressure, had moved major parties to modify institutions, albeit haphazardly. Even postwar disillusionment, with twelve years of cynical reactions in politics, government and business practice and with mounting evidence that mechanization and large-scale organization were attacking democracy at its roots, could not destroy faith in the familiar institutions. Through three years of deepening depression, fears had been accumulating, but the nation in general remained more stunned by the shock to its optimism than aroused to violent disorder. In 1932 they cast ballots, not bombs.

Under New Leadership

Intimate personal experience with struggle, defeat and victory had given superior equipment to the shrewd and able politician to whom 57 per cent of the voters had turned to lead them out of the depression. Franklin D. Roosevelt was a scion of the same wealthy, New York patrician family as Theodore, who was his "fifth" cousin and who had come up to New York from Washington in 1905 to "give away" his niece, Eleanor Roosevelt, to her distant cousin, Franklin. He had studied at Groton, Harvard and Columbia Law School among members of his own class, but political ambitions soon widened his contacts. He won a fight against Tammany in the state senate, worked hard as assistant secretary of the navy in Wilson's liberal administration and experienced a vigorous vice-presidential campaign and overwhelming defeat with Cox in 1920. An onslaught of infantile paralysis in 1921 had struck him down at thirty-nine.

An amazing feat of rehabilitation followed. He did endless special exercises. He read widely and corresponded actively, gaining a wide view of national problems and a growing influence in the Democratic party. This work of rehabilitation had unfailing encouragement from three strong personalities, his wife, his secretary, Louis M. Howe, and the governor of New York, Alfred E. Smith. There developed a personality with the imagination, daring and optimism which come to one who wins against a living death and has no more to fear.

The Franklin D. Roosevelt who emerged after three years made an extraordinary political comeback. At the Democratic National Convention of 1924 he tried vigorously to make Smith presidential nominee. In 1928 he was himself elected governor of New York, although Smith (now nominee) was defeated for the presidency. Reëlected in 1930, he developed a popular depression-policy of a 100 per cent increase in state income taxes to secure funds for direct relief. Upon his own presidential nomination in 1932, his nation-wide campaign tour demonstrated his conquest over paralysis and advertised his promise of a "New Deal" for the "forgotten man." Not only should there be prohibition repeal, lowered tariffs and judiciary reform, but also betterments for consumers, farmers, electricity users, investors, railroads, taxpayers and the unemployed. Depression, said he, must yield to a program for the common good.

His leadership would be boldly experimental along liberal lines. The men and women with whom Roosevelt mainly consulted, in handling the immediate emergency and projecting a "planned economy" thereafter, were popularly designated, and in some quarters derided, as "the brain trust." Most of them were of liberal bent. An administration with this slant would rely upon the democratic heritage of the nation to support it in reappraisal and experiment. It would accept leadership with an eager boldness totally foreign to Harding, Coolidge or Hoover, employing the radio and press to interpret and strengthen that leadership.

Roosevelt underscored his position as leader of both his party and the nation. He appeared in person before the 1932 and 1936 conventions to "accept" the nominations, traveling by airplane on the former occasion. He spoke to the people directly and informally, broadcasting projects and personality in "fireside chats" over the radio and delivering important messages to Congress over nation-wide hook-ups. He wrote and inspired others to write books and magazine articles explaining and defending current policies. No daily paper could deny emphasis upon his leadership, for he established press interviews on an oral-question basis, with permissive direct quotation and free indirect quotation except on "off the record" information.

Congress eagerly abdicated leadership in favor of the executive. The late winter of 1932-1933 was a nightmare of bank closings, and the fear and confusion of the populace found ample expression in congressmen. Then and thereafter was confirmed in most of them a trend long fostered by the rapid onslaught of machine-age problems, a disinclination toward responsibility. The electorate of the democ-

Franklin Delano Roosevelt
(Photograph by U.S. Army Signal Corps.)

racy did not look to their local representatives but to the executive to handle emergency problems which were wider and more intricate than those of any single state and which overflowed the mystic area of no-man's land between federal and state prerogatives.

Without adequate thought as to means for the safe, temporary delegation of powers, Congress participated in a shift of functions from the legislature to the executive. The principles to be embodied in legislation were formulated by the President and his "brain trust," to be submitted one or two at a time; the phraseology was written by a few expert, executive drafters; authorship was ascribed to the sympathetic senators and congressmen who shepherded the measures through congressional amendment en route to passage; and the resultant statutes usually enhanced the power of the executive at the expense of the legislature.

They expanded the bureaucracy by an unprecedented increase in the numbers and functions of the commissions, with a National Emergency Council as coördinator. They gave bureaucratic orders the effect of laws for the sake of quick action and coördination in highly specialized fields. Such measures were based on the belief that a republic could assemble in its bureaus a corps of specialists fitted by training and temperament to discharge impartially the vital, regulatory powers delegated to them. In response an unprecedented number of experts left business, commercial and professional callings from time to time to work with and for the federal government. Political opponents and representatives of interests resentful of regulation rang the welkin with denunciation of Roosevelt's political ambition and of his machine, which was run by Postmaster-General James A. Farley from 1933 to 1940 with efficient distribution of the loaves and fishes. The number of employees in the executive department, 1933-1941, increased from 565,432 to 1,358,150.

The trend further away from laissez-faire toward governmental control was less by design than by force of circumstances. The majority of the nation were basically conservative, loyal to historic institutions; but they faced the problem of implementing their government to protect them and their industrial system from the abuses which were undermining both, and the job had to be tackled in an international atmosphere of unpredictable cross-currents. They and their government felt their way from day to day in the dark murk of a stubborn, world-wide depression. It was not in the American tradition to let millions of people suffer cold and hunger, and if private charity could not succor them the government must; so the depression forced Americans to envisage relief for anyone, anywhere, at public expense. Furthermore, recovery from the depression and reform of the evils contributory to it were also conceived of as government jobs. With the three difficult tasks of relief, recovery and reform all placed on government shoulders, centralization of power at Washington would develop with extreme rapidity.

Expanding Money and Credit

To perform its triple tasks the government required money and credit, but no considerable supply of either was inherited from the previous administration. During the interregnum between Hoover's defeat and Roosevelt's accession, Hoover had tried vainly to commit his successor to a modified form of the old laissez-faire pattern for recovery: deflation and economy, wage-cutting and bankruptcy. But that pattern had not sufficed to reinforce the weakening money and credit institutions during three years of depression, and Roosevelt determined not to bind himself.

The United States was the only country suffering a crisis in the first quarter of 1933; the unsound banking system, political hysteria and sudden enthusiasm for moratoria had brought rapid deterioration to the whole business set-up. The RFC, instead of following the practice of German and Italian RFC's (also set up in 1932) of taking over banks' bad assets and giving them government bonds to rely upon, had chosen to take the best assets, leaving American banks their weakest securities for use in stress. Public apprehension panicked into terror; gold was hoarded and exported; and practically all banks and every security and commodity exchange were closed on inauguration day. Many were fearful that Monday might find the banking system prostrate.

Reassurance was the keynote of the Saturday inaugural. "The only thing we have to fear is fear," said the President as he moved to allay anxiety as quickly as possible. Monday an executive proclamation placed an embargo on withdrawal and transfer of gold and silver and closed all banks for ninety-six hours. The administration was convinced that the load of public and private debt had been made unsupportable by the fall in prices. Hurriedly it plunged into efforts to lighten debts, raise prices and increase the volume and circulation of money and credit.

Congress convened Thursday, 9 March, and passed that day the administration's Emergency Banking and Gold Control law; it provided for bank reopenings under treasury supervision, RFC subscriptions to bank and trust company stock, an increase in the volume of Federal Reserve notes and Federal Reserve loans to persons and corporations on government bond security. Other measures soon carried still further the participation of government in banking and credit; commercial and investment banking were divorced; a Federal Deposit Insurance Corporation, FDIC, was set up to insure deposits: and the Federal Reserve system was expanded to embrace more banks, make more loans and to enlarge its authority over the volume and kind of credit. Easier credit was among the objects of a Federal Farm Mortgage Corporation, FFMC, and a Home Owners' Loan Corporation, HOLC. Wide concessions were made to corporations, municipalities and farmers for easier bankruptcy. A Senate Subcommittee on Stock Exchange Practice, with the aid of Ferdinand Pecora as counsel, so thoroughly uncovered stock-exchange practices that a Federal Securities and Exchange Commission was established in 1934 to license and regulate stock exchanges.

To raise prices while expanding the currency and relieving the federal treasury, the administration obtained a few "blanket" laws under which it could develop its currency policy by frequent "executive orders." It quickly forbade the hoarding of gold and the use of it to pay indebtedness; gold exports were prohibited, and every one was ordered to exchange his gold for paper money, at the old valuation of $20.67 an ounce. Gold certificates were called in by the Secretary of the treasury, also. The government took over the purchase of all gold which was produced in the United States or might be offered to it from abroad, hoping to raise prices. This failing, the price was set at $35 under the Gold Reserve Act of 31 January 1934. The "gold content" of the dollar was lowered from 25.8 grains to 15 5/21 grains, thus depreciating it to 59.06 per cent of its former gold content. Two billions of the "gain" which the treasury made by revaluing its stock at $35 was allotted to the Secretary for use as a "Stabilization Fund"; this enabled him to practice the secret purchase and sale of exchange, so as to manipulate the international value of the dollar when desired to offset trade balances or speculative and foreign forces.

Senators and congressmen from silver-producing states, or with debtor constituencies, exploited this opportunity; the first wanted dear silver and the second wanted more abundant currency. They joined forces and were supported in part by manufacturers desirous of a cheap dollar to undersell competitors abroad. These persistent allies secured legislation, in May 1933, in June 1934 and in July 1939, which established government silver-buying on a scale which would have made the old silver crowd green with envy. Under their pressure the administration agreed to nationalize silver and to buy it at home and abroad until either silver holdings equalled in value one-third of gold holdings, or silver reached $1.29 an ounce in world markets. The government jacked up the purchase price from 28¢ to as high as 80¢ before settling down to a 35¢ level for foreign silver and a 71.11¢ level for domestic silver. It accepted $98,000,000 worth of foreign silver, at 50¢ an ounce, on war debt payments. It issued more than 1.5 billions in silver certificates for domestic circulation. After all this, silver remains today far from the announced objective.

The best effect of the gold and silver purchases was their stimulation of American exports, for there was cutthroat competition for the relatively few remaining world markets. Their worst effect was to concentrate over 22 billions of gold—about 80 per cent of the world's known supply—in the United States, to the detriment of trade and other international relations. They could not achieve the desired rise in the American price level or in the world price of silver. They contributed to a badly unbalanced budget at the same time that they furnished some metallic backing for the currency which was paid out for the bonus and for the relief-recovery-reform expenditures.

Some of America's trade competitors had fondly hoped that the United States would accept their currency devaluations without retaliation, and a London Economic Conference had been planned to arrange international economic relations on that basis. Roosevelt had astounded the conferees 2 July 1933 by cabling refusal to agree to the perpetuation of the current ratio, although he acceded to a scheme of Senator Pittman of Nevada whereby the United States shouldered the heaviest load in the silver market.

The subsequent entrance of the United States into world competition in currency depreciation led to an international agreement, for the gold and silver experiments alarmed trade competitors and seriously affected the economy of those nations whose currency was overvalued by the American policy. To make the general uncertainty less intolerable, England, France and the United States (with Belgium acceding) made a "Tripartite Agreement" 25 September 1936, under which each promised not to abandon the then current ratio without due notice to the others. Thus currency control as a weapon of international economic warfare became a secret, day-to-day affair among these powers, a mystery to the average citizen.

The banking and credit legislation furnished other illustrations of complicated consequences. RFC loans saved insolvent bankers and ill-managed railroads as well as the solvent and well managed. Inflation aided some wealthy corporations as well as many poor debtors, and it increased prices to consumers as well as for producers. These were all parts of the effort to make captive capitalism work.

Providing Work, Subsistence and a Future

As world trade under the international gold standard was thus set aside for "national self-sufficiency" under "managed currency," the market for goods and labor contracted, forcing America to desperate expedients for finding her own nationals a job and a living. The urgent emergency compelled hasty action, which was taken at first in confident expectation of quick recovery, as was natural to a people with the background and resources of optimistic America. Direct, minimum monetary relief, as in the English "dole" system, was used in part, but it was opposed by the majority of the nation as unproductive and destructive to morale, on the assumption that Americans would prefer work to idleness.

So the more costly "work relief," in part at "prevailing hourly rates," was stressed. Jobs were created by setting up federal projects and also by part-financing, with federal funds, projects of state and local governments, for which standards of execution were set by federal authorities. President and Congress rapidly established special agencies, variously naming them administrations, authorities, boards, commissions, companies and corporations; and the public designated them by their first letters, so that they were described as "government by alphabet." They usually were independent of existing departments but often worked with and through the latter. Only the most significant aspects of their work can here be noted.

Neglected youth and women received work relief. Industry had no jobs to offer the 500,000 youth annually finishing school, and many thousands took to roaming the country aimlessly. A Civilian Conservation Corps, CCC, established in 1933, absorbed first 200,000 then about 300,000 persons—unmarried young men of seventeen to twenty-three and war veterans on relief—placing them in camps to work on reforestation, trails, pest-control, drainage, erosion, floods and fire-fighting. This effort at conservation of human and natural resources illustrated interdepartmental coöperation, with the War, Interior and Agriculture Departments and the Veterans Administration participating. A National Youth Administration, NYA, of 1933, furnished part-time employment to students. A few camps to give occupational education to women opened in 1934, and a vast number of work projects—sewing, canning, household aid, nursing and school-lunch activities—subsequently materialized. A United States Employment Service was set up within the Department of Labor. Funds were supplied to exhausted state relief agencies through a Federal Emergency Relief Administration, FERA, also of 1933. To help the 15 million unemployed through the desperate winter of 1933-1934 a Civil Works Administration, CWA, financed work relief on a great variety of civic projects.

Relief plans broadened with need and experience, for by the close of 1934 more than 15 per cent of the population was on relief. Many of the errors and abuses which inevitably entered the first experiments were eliminated in May 1935 by coördinating work relief in a Works Progress Administration, WPA, established on a more permanent basis. It made possible the construction and rehabilitation of all kinds of public property, and hundreds of kinds of white-collar activity. Five

WPA federal "arts" projects in historical records, painting and sculpture, drama, music and writing furnished employment and spread culture. The benefits were broadened as numerous local projects in household economics, health, recreation, education, libraries and research were integrated into a federal program.

In the meantime a special relief program was devised to rehabilitate the heavy industries vital to both capital and labor. Symptomatic of the sad state of these industries was that of building. Between 1928 and 1933 house-repair had fallen 90 per cent, residential construction 95 per cent and all construction 73 per cent. Workers in a multitude of interdependent trades, such as the production of steel, iron, copper, lead, wood, brick, plumbing and electrical equipment, shared unemployment and loss of purchasing power. Mining, machinery and transportation were depressed together.

A Public Works Administration, PWA, first set up in 1933 under Secretary of the Interior Harold L. Ickes, stimulated private employment of machinery and non-relief labor, as distinguished from the WPA emphasis on heavy construction. The United States Housing Authority was established in 1937 and given an initial grant of 800 millions to use in slum clearance and replacement with decent modern housing. Much of its work was loaning money to communities for that purpose. People of small means were aided in building and buying houses by the Home Owners' Loan Corporation, the Federal Housing Administration and Federal Savings and Loan Associations. These organizations loaned money obtained from the federal government or from local sources at attractive terms. Country subsistence homesteads and suburban housing for city workers were sponsored by the Resettlement Administration.

The New Deal's relief and recovery program met stiff resistance from vested interests determined to stigmatize it thoroughly; charges of inefficiency were aimed particularly at WPA. Undeniably waste and error intervened, working evil effects on national morale and economy. Not all of the projects were needed on the elaborate scales selected, nor was a method of finally paying for them worked out. Yet neither is it possible to estimate the disasters which might have befallen democracy if the administration had acted on the assumption of its severest critics that the distressed classes would have endured a ruthless, unrelieved deflation.

The underlying democratic objective, enhancement of the common good, was achieved in an amazing number of constructive undertakings. The program brought new schools and college buildings; libraries, guide-books, bibliographies and historical, cultural and economic surveys; concerts, plays, art exhibitions and mural decorations; health services, hospitals, playgrounds and slum clearance; sewage, waterworks, grade-crossing elimination and road building; reforestation and conservation; federal, state and municipal buildings; airports, irrigation projects, "yardstick" power plants and flood-control. All these the depression must have denied the nation without government aid.

The AAA

No less pressing than unemployment was the farm problem. The farmers' plight was particularly dangerous, for without their well-being America never could recover permanent prosperity. In 1933 farmers were crushed by surpluses unsalable at prices below cost of production. Roused out of their natural conservatism, they resentfully destroyed milk supplies in Iowa, Minnesota and Wisconsin, sponsored some old inflation panaceas and everywhere demanded further government aid to restore their buying power. Their congressmen received political support from implement manufacturers and others aware of the penalties of lost farm-purchasing.

The Roosevelt administration decided to approach the problem from a nationalistic point of view. World markets having disappointed American farmers, salvation must lie in domestic markets. Security might be attained through an "ever-normal granary," an idea as old as Confucius. This program rested on faith that America could maintain farm prices above the world level (as she had maintained manufacturing prices), could surmount climatic vagaries and could substitute for ingrained, unrestricted agricultural competition a habit of coöperation in restriction.

So the "Agricultural Adjustment Act," the AAA, of 12 May 1933, and subsequent amendments thereto launched a scheme of reduced crops for higher prices. Prices should be raised to "parity," to their estimated fair exchange value with other commodities, estimated with due regard to the nation's total purchasing power. To restore the purchasing power of 1909-1914, farmers were voluntarily to restrict production of important staples.

The government was to assure them compensation by "processing taxes" collected at the points of processing, such as meat-packing houses, cotton-gins and flour mills; the amount of the tax was to be governed by the difference between "parity" and current farm prices. Recalcitrant farmers exceeding some allotments were to be punished by prohibitive taxes on their excess. Thus far had agricultural philosophy progressed from the old notion that Uncle Sam could remain a Santa Claus without becoming a dictator. These laws, aided by inflationary measures and the severe drought of 1934 (the worst in forty years), raised farm purchasing power as of 1934 20 per cent above that of 1932. During the next two years, unfortunately, the drought laid a heavy scourge upon a region embracing some 6 million acres on the western plains, an area of marginal acres ill fitted to continual cultivation under the old methods. The dry topsoil, overworked and unprotected by windbreaks, blew before the wind, engulfing the farmsteads in a desolate Dust Bowl. By 1939, however, only 1 million acres remained thus victimized, for increased rainfall was accompanied by government measures of conservation. Planting of clover crops, and three "shelter belts," with contour cultivation brought relief to the devastated region.

Other laws and policies aimed to coördinate the agricultural situation with the national relief problem and with international trade. For relief, a Federal Surplus Relief Corporation, FSRC, was set up to receive from the AAA donations of products for distribution; from 1935 it functioned as a commodities corporation to remove surpluses from market channels. To help trade, Secretary of State Hull reversed the traditional practice of devoting trade agreements to industrial interests, and under a "Reciprocal Trade Agreement Act" of 1934 (extended in 1937, 1940 and 1942), he undertook to emphasize reciprocity for agriculture. The act permitted lowering or raising rates by 50 per cent, without congressional interference.

It marked a significant improvement upon traditional tariff procedure, in six respects. It permitted each product to be considered individually; some classes of the same product could be treated differently from others; duties could be reduced during a part of a year; reductions could be made on limited quantities; concessions by the United States could be made contingent upon reciprocal advantages to American exports; and finally action could be taken quickly and effectually as emergencies arose. All this placed Hull in a strong diplomatic position. He achieved, in spite of some farm criticism, numerous executive agreements, increasing trade in various agricultural and industrial products. A federal Export-Import Bank further facilitated trade by special loans for export use.

Farmers crushed by debt received special assistance in getting out from under the fixed-cost, inflated debt load which was cutting farm profits to the point of requiring relief. The farm credit system was extended until each of the twelve farm credit districts had one each of four kinds of banks: land banks for mortgage loans, production credit corporations for production loans, intermediate credit banks for intermediate term discounts and banks for loans to coöperatives. Farm bankruptcies decreased. The RFC organized a Commodity Credit Corporation to hold crops accepted as security for cash loans. Millions of bushels were thus accumulated.

Localities differed. Some areas stressed the long-term, farm-purchase credit facilities of the Farm Credit Administration, FCA, and of a

Frazier-Lemke five-year mortgage moratorium law passed and then repassed to meet Supreme Court objections. In other areas the nationwide trend toward tenantry and migratory farm labor could be arrested only by revolutionary changes in farming practices.

The work of reorganizing and improving rural living conditions was started by the FERA and then turned over to the specially created Resettlement Administration, RA. The object was to move farmers from poor land to good and to return the bad land to forest or grazing fields. Various experiments were tried, one of which was the development of a farming community in the Matanuska Valley in Alaska. In some instances the RA tried to develop a new mode of life, to organize suburban industrial communities in which men could work in factories part of the time and cultivate vegetable gardens for subsistence, as well. These experiments were difficult because it was hard to get the farmers, no matter how badly off, to move, and the expense was tremendous. In 1937 the RA became the Farm Security Administration, FSA, chiefly engaged in loaning money to enterprising farmers to improve their status. Furthermore it aided coöperative farm efforts like that at Matanuska. A Rural Electrification Administration was created to aid in extending the use of electricity and electric equipment.

Meanwhile the AAA program was proving inadequate for many reasons. It was not unaffected by climatic, economic and political trends in many foreign countries. These trends, combined with the AAA, tended to reduce further our farm export market, to increase an already acute unemployment problem and to rouse resentment. By 1935 there was an estimated reduction of 1 million man-hours in farm work. Dairymen and poultrymen complained of costlier feed bills, and consumers, of dearer milk, butter and eggs. The proletariat felt the pinch most severely in the price of meats, which was affected by the drought. Some economists declared that the act simply gave temporary relief to agriculture at the expense of consumers. In the midst of the struggle for improved farm purchasing power, suits were brought by processors, and 6 January 1936 the Supreme Court, 6 to 3, held the processing tax and production control features of the AAA unconstitutional.

Undaunted the administration eliminated the pressure for invalidation by shifting to the federal treasury the direct burden of paying for the farmers' program, with emphasis shifted from production control to "soil conservation" in the "Soil Conservation and Domestic Allotment Act" of 1936. After two years without effective crop control came the new AAA Act of 1938. Like its predecessors this act planned to reduce the surplus of crops by authorizing payments to farmers who reduced their plantings. Also loans were to be made on crops in storage to keep them off the market, thus bolstering up the price. Against drought, flood and insects, the wheat-farmers were offered insurance by a Federal Crop Insurance Corporation. Following Canada's lead the government provided export subsidies to facilitate dumping wheat abroad, a practice formerly denounced in America and now made useless by imitation. Benefit payments to growers coöperating in "soil conservation" were widened on some crops to the point where non-coöperating farmers no longer could hold off. Cash farm income, down to approximately 4 billions in 1932, passed 9 billions in 1940.

Yet the twin spectres of good weather and bad business increased production and decreased consumption, relentlessly defeating "economy of scarcity." The predicament of cotton, which had accounted for about 25 per cent of American exports since 1820, and which ultimately affected national welfare outside the South as well as in it, became most alarming. World consumption went up, but consumption of United States cotton went down, assisted by the high import tariffs which discouraged exchange for American exports generally. In 1932-1933, the last season of unrestricted cotton output, American growers sold about 60 per cent of world consumption and 45 per cent of consumption outside the United States; in 1936-1937 they sold only 42 per cent and 23 per cent respectively; and in five years American taxpayers footed a direct bill of about $750,000,000 in benefit payments to growers, exclusive of other heavy cotton outlays. Despite reduced acreage, 1937 brought an unprecedented American crop of 19 million bales, and an average price of only 8.4¢ per pound. The government shouldered more than one-fourth of it as loan collateral, and 1938 acreage was cut 22 per cent lower.

Other important staples also failed to prosper. The wheat crop of 1938 was two-thirds planted before the new AAA Act, and record surpluses met an average world price in August 1938 of about 51¢ a bushel compared with a parity price of $1.12, a 1937 price of 96¢ and government loans around 60¢. Dairy products, especially butter, potatoes and some fruits struggled with surpluses unsalable at asked prices. Farmer sentiment ran toward price-fixing, often proved ineffective, and toward a two-price system wherein the farmer would produce all he wished and accept the world price only on exported and relief-use crops, with other prices subsidized by the government.

In 1939 the agricultural surplus was attacked from a different angle with considerable success. Seasonal surpluses were put to use by a "food stamp plan"; under it low-income families in selected areas received from the government stamps good for free purchase of certain surplus foods important to health. This improved the condition of the ill nourished at the same time as it expanded the farmers' domestic market, and made jobs for people who processed and distributed the food. The plan became popular and was used until severe war shortages ended it. Until the United States entered the Second World War, agricultural supplies stubbornly remained far in excess of demand at current prices; shrinking acreage and expanding crop loans could not stop the world price fall. World political and financial conditions—quite unamenable to control by America—now complicate the agricultural, as well as the banking and relief problems of the United States.

CHAPTER XLVII

REËNFORCING THE NEW DEAL

The New Deal's vigorous attack upon banking, relief and agricultural problems was matched by equally energetic efforts in the fields of industry and labor, resources and business, politics and the judiciary.

The NRA

The difficult problem of industrial security was complicated by conflicting interests of capital, labor and consumer. Chaotic conditions, revealed and emphasized by the depression, inspired a desire for balance and orderliness, which American industry never had known. Employer and employee suffered from the bitter resistance of the former to collective bargaining by the latter, from violent elimination of competitors and from a chronic succession of business spurts and depressions. The nation generally assumed that it would not be too difficult to recover competition and to establish enlightened self-government by industry.

Congress hurriedly passed the National Industrial Recovery Act of 16 June 1933 as an enabling act; it provided that industry should draw up "codes of fair competition" for its own governance, under the executive supervision of a National Recovery Administration, NRA. There were a compliance board, to supervise enforcement, and advisory boards for industry, labor and consumers. A vague section, number 7a, purported to guarantee labor the right of collective bargaining under unions of labor's own choosing. Goods manufactured in compliance with NRA standards were to be endorsed by a "blue eagle" label.

In application the act failed of its broad purpose. Big industrial executives thought the situation called for two kinds of concessions. In return for concessions by executives to labor on such moot points as minimum pay, shorter hours, better working conditions and abolition of child labor, the government should concede suspension of the antitrust laws. So the executives transplanted the essential provisions of their trade agreements of Hoover days into the NRA codes, openly inserting price-fixing into more than half of them, and through their Industrial Recovery Board they advised an enforcement of the codes which little regarded the interests of small business, consumers and labor. The codes restricted the opportunities of little, local firms to compete against large, national corporations. The Labor Advisory Board proved ineffective, and the Consumers Advisory Board vainly struggled for the knowledge, skill and opportunity to offset monopolistic trends.

A less ineffective labor agency, the National Labor Board, was provided by a separate act of 5 August 1933 which also eliminated some cutthroat practices. But neither the new board nor the National Labor Relations Board which followed it in 1934 could secure enforcement of Section 7a. The NRA succeeded in raising labor standards in some industries and brought a temporary ban on child labor under sixteen, but on the whole it proved too crude an instrument for meeting the complex industrial needs of the far-flung nation. Its good and bad features alike fell on 27 May 1935 when the Supreme Court unanimously decided that it was an unconstitutional delegation of the lawmaking power to the executive and a federal invasion of intrastate commerce.

As the great body of American judicial practice and law had been built up around the employers' contention that collective bargaining was an unfair practice when done by labor, Congress now undertook to erect a solid structure of congressional policy for legal and property rights of that class. Firm foundations for this structure had been laid between 1926 and 1934. The strong, well-organized and relatively conservative railway workers had obtained the Railway Labor Act of 1926, which partially protected their particular right to organize; the Supreme Court four years later upheld the law. Next, the Norris-La Guardia Act of 1932 declared the right of other kinds of workers to be free from employer influence in their organizational activities, although this law did not provide enforcement for the declaration. The railworkers obtained in 1934 amendments to their labor law which gave their group the wanted machinery for enforcement but left employees in other interstate occupations unprotected.

This gap Congress filled by the historic Wagner National Labor Relations Act of 1935, the first exclusively pro-labor law in United States history. The NRA had paved the way for it. It included a rephrased section guaranteeing labor the broad rights of self-organization, collective bargaining and "concerted activities for other mutual aid." It listed five types of practices which it prohibited to employers as being unfair to labor. It proclaimed the principle of selection of bargaining representatives by the majority of employees in a unit. It provided a new National Labor Relations Board to administer the act.

The congressional prescription that the workers involved in a dispute with employers should choose their bargaining agent by the democratic method of free, secret balloting presupposed a fair degree of labor unity. In fact, disunity became rife in the labor movement at this crucial juncture, greatly hindering progress out of the depression. The long-standing rivalry between craft and industrial unions came to a head in 1935, when for the first time A.F. of L. dominance over organized labor was seriously threatened. Although the A.F. of L. had admitted some industrial unions, it had refused to tolerate unrestricted chartering of unions on the vertical plan in such large fields as aluminum, automobiles, cement, rubber, utilities and steel.

The industrial faction led by John L. Lewis, ex-miner and now president of the powerful United Mine Workers union, defied the A.F. of L. with a competing group, at first the Committee, then the Congress for Industrial Organizations—the CIO. It proceeded to unite ten strong unions under the vertical plan and made a powerful drive to unionize steel, automobile and airplane workers. By 1941 it had organized more than three-fourths of steel and the major part of the automobile industry. Rival recruiting by the A.F. of L. and the CIO approximately double total union membership, with the A.F. of L. exceeding in 1940 its 4 million record of 1920 and the CIO reporting a gross membership of 4 millions.

The inter-union warfare victimized the nation. In so far as the CIO adopted the reduced hour and restricted output philosophy of some of the craft unions and the "economy of scarcity" device of some of the New Dealers, it appeared to defeat its own objects, for it forbade technology to bring that increased output at lowered prices on which improvements in consumption and mass income depend. The general public suffered also through the costly boycotts by rival unions of goods handled by each other, and small business was victimized when CIO members picketed shops which had made arrangements with A.F. of L., and vice versa.

The labor split resisted healing despite peace negotiations intermittent since October 1937. Communistic domination of four of the CIO unions weakened it in public opinion, confused issues and caused revolts among its membership. For a time strikes increased in number, scope and violence, with tear-gas a common resort on both sides. The more radical elements turned to the drastic "general strike" at San Francisco and to the sit-down strike in many areas, which devices cost the sympathy of some moderate liberals. Capital, no less intransigent, frequently smashed the strikes, using injunctions, armed police, militia, vigilantes, spies, intimidation and back-to-work propaganda.

Gradually friction appeared for a time to be easing off; American capital and labor, admonished by Supreme Court verdicts which generally upheld the decisions of the NLRB and the constitutionality of the Wage-Hour Law, seemed to be reluctantly accepting government jurisdiction. The Wagner Act was changing the face of industrial relations as the Supreme Court gradually built up a body of definitions as to what constitutes unfair labor practices. While the CIO and

A.F. of L. were no closer to real harmony than before, they nevertheless showed some inclination to coöperate on non-controversial matters and to reduce jurisdictional disputes.

Labor urged other measures than the enforcement of collective bargaining. Their pressure for a legal floor under wages and a ceiling over hours led Congress to pass the Fair Labor Standards Act of 1938. It prescribed for employees engaged in interstate commerce or in the production of goods for interstate commerce a sliding wage and hour scale which eventually should reach a minimum wage rate of not less than 40¢ an hour and a maximum weekly hour base of forty hours, with time-and-a-half for over-time. It also set up industry committees for fixing a minimum higher than that in the law. Also, high labor standards were required of all firms receiving government contracts, under the Walsh-Healy Act of 1936. The general level of state-labor legislation was raised by coöperation between federal and state agencies, which coördinated programs. All in all, labor has status today as never before, and that status carries with it responsibility to reach an accord in the interest of labor, employer and public.

These efforts, however, strenuous as they were, did not touch the subsistence problems of the unfortunate, the unemployed and the aged poor, for whose provision America had lagged far behind other nations. A few states, such as New York, Ohio and Wisconsin, had recognized this kind of responsibility and had emphasized the need for national social security legislation.

After it was realized that America had continuously at least 5 million unemployed, the Social Security Act of 1935 was passed. It undertook to coördinate a federal and state program of old age and unemployment insurance and old age assistance and to aid the states on child and maternity welfare, the blind, public health and vocational rehabilitation; but all farm and domestic laborers were specifically excluded from its benefits. It was freely predicted that the Supreme Court must invalidate the act, because its theories did not meet earlier court positions. Yet practically all the states within two years complied with federal stipulations, and 24 May 1937 a majority of the Supreme Court proved its adaptability by sustaining the pensions clause 7-2, and job-insurance 5-4.

The act has come to epitomize the social philosophy behind the New Deal, for it admits the right of every one—the idle as well as the earning—to the bare essentials of food, clothing and shelter; and it suggests the right to health and a modest happiness also. Social security funds pushed the states into active and intelligent disease prevention. In innumerable ways the act instructed the nation in well-being.

Control of Resources and of Business

National well-being was a strong New Deal tenet and President Roosevelt believed that relief and recovery could be made permanent only if there were reforms in the control of resources and of business. Permanent security—for all—could only be insured if natural resources were properly protected and their use planned for. It was a problem of conservation in the broadest sense. His definition of conservation had three parts. It included the traditional notion of conservation, which emphasized increased production and future use, with irrigation of submarginal lands and withholding from sale of unappropriated resources. It included also the ideas of recapturing control of resources from such corporations as used them unfairly, and of imposing drastic corporation taxes as a lever in shifting control and in paying the costs of the shift. The President had fought the power trusts in New York and was determined to make the New Deal definition effective throughout the nation.

The necessary coöperation from the electorate was forthcoming during the next six years, because a long-lasting depression, marked by droughts, dust-storms, floods, hurricanes and revelations of chicanery, awakened realization of the need for a planned economy. People in general concluded that there must be an improved use of privately owned resources and that the monopolists in control of them would not make the public welfare their intimate, daily concern. This reasoning led to general acceptance of federal control of public utilities and government oversight of many other businesses "vested with a public interest." The people did not mean to renounce capitalism; probably the majority shared Roosevelt's announced conviction that their distress was due more to short-sighted, individual capitalists than to the institution of capitalism; but they did endorse an administration which made the greatest drive in history for the control of national resources.

Every agency at work upon relief, recovery, reform or national security became involved. The CCC, RA, PWA, WPA and flood-control units included in their programs the preservation of soils and forests, storing of waters and combating of droughts, floods and forest fires. They and a host of other agencies engaged in broader experiments in resource control. Most significant of these experiments was that conducted by the Tennessee Valley Authority, established in 1933 to enhance "the general social and economic well-being of the Valley." The TVA proceeded to operate Muscle Shoals and other dams to serve the seven southern states of Alabama, Georgia, Kentucky, Mississippi, North Carolina, Tennessee and Virginia, a region where outside capital had been skimming the cream off southern resources.

Its people began to find their daily life revolutionized by the broadest social service agency ever implemented, by flood control, navigation improvement, nitrate manufacture, vocational education, reforestation, subsistence homesteads, scientific agriculture, community life and the generation and cheap sale of electric power. An Electric Farm and Home Authority facilitated purchase of appliances. PWA loans and the Rural Electrification Administration enabled municipalities and rural coöperatives to use cheap public current rather than the more expensive service of privately capitalized companies. Federal funds were sent to Bonneville and Grand Coulee to develop dams for the Columbia River basin. The private power companies neglected no court device to upset this program, but the Supreme Court did not declare the TVA unconstitutional. A series of joint purchases of private utilities by the TVA and public bodies ensued.

Federal intervention ranged up and down the utility field. The powers of the FTC, FPC and SEC were broadened, under the Wheeler-Rayburn Utility Act of 1935 and the Robinson-Patman Act of 1936, to cover regulation of interstate gas and electric rates and to end the pyramided, holding-company system which was held responsible for the worst utility abuses. The ICC, FCC, Maritime Commission and NLRB also regulated utilities. Between these and the congressional investigations, the utilities were thoroughly put on the defensive; many made heavy outlays of stockholders' funds for legal defense, lowered rates and cleaned house. The administration and New York Power Authority locked horns with the utilities over the St. Lawrence Waterway treaty. Some non-profit utilities were allowed to merge.

The state of many railroads was financially pitiable, and there was much talk of government ownership. The Roosevelt administration wished to avoid this and sponsored the Emergency Railroad Transportation Act of 1933, which provided for a federal coördinator to eliminate waste and to direct refinancing. The government aided grade-crossing elimination, electrification and other technical improvements. Congress adjusted railway employees' pension plans to meet Supreme Court objections. Some effort was made to regulate competition of buses and trucks, which were placed under the Interstate Commerce Commission. This Commission also was entrusted with larger functions and not only put fares and freight rates up and down but also passed upon railroad purchase projects. Air transportation became a matter of concern, and in 1938 the Civil Aeronautics Authority was created to supervise it and to encourage commercial aviation.

Federal intervention was used to aid business as well as to regulate it. The NIRA principle was also applied to the chaotic soft-coal industry. The Guffey-Snyder Act of 1935 sought to regulate it by establishing codes of fair practices and was sometimes called the "little

NIRA." This, like the NIRA Act, was voided by the Supreme Court, but Congress passed a modified version, the Guffey-Vinson Act of 1937, which imposed a penalty tax upon coal operators not subscribing to the code and which survived.

In other relations with business, also, the government moved far beyond the old anti-monopoly objective of protecting competitors into the limitless field of protecting consumers. Federal regulatory bodies struck out against monopoly in directions as various as bakers and buckles, electric machinery and milk. Money was lavished by government and corporations upon investigations, prosecutions and defense of such industrial giants as the aluminum, automobile, oil, telegraph and telephone industries. Although little businessmen won against consumers in enactment of the Robinson-Patman anti-chain-store bill of 1936, other laws showed more solicitude for buyers. Heavy responsibilities were laid on the FTC by the Wheeler-Lea Act, of March 1938, to regulate advertising, a major American industry. A livelier conscience was given the food, drug and cosmetic industries by a 1938 federal food and drug law which somewhat tightened restrictions on adulteration and deceit and was taken as a pattern for state acts passed in various parts of the nation. By such means the New Deal undertook to control resources and business in the public interest.

Wielding the Tax Weapon

Although the New Deal measures for relief, recovery and reform proved so expensive as to require increased taxation, the administration did not find this a disadvantage; taxation could be so imposed as to advance the New Deal principles. The ideal of a balanced budget was expressed at the outset but did not long remain of much concern. The World War veterans helped somewhat to unbalance it. They secured in 1936, after two Roosevelt vetoes, a bonus law which paid them their cherished bonus in bonds which might be redeemed in cash. This was but one of innumerable extraordinary expenditures of the period. Deficits rose the faster because the mass of the electorate remained insensitive to them, as long as they were not taxed. Nor did the mounting deficit worry the treasury by causing a weak market for government bonds. There were too many would-be buyers. The depression and regimentation contracted the outlets for savings in private business; foreign funds fled from European uncertainties; and the treasury so controlled currency and credit as to keep money easy for the government to get.

Since government could proceed largely by loan, tax policies could be experimental. Transformation of the federal tax system was largely completed during the calendar years 1932-1933. They brought liquor, gift and nuisance taxes, 3¢ postage, the first federal automobile and gas taxes and AAA processing taxes. They also brought income levies second only to 1918 and doubled estate rates. This was due to the fact that the new philosophy called for a wider distribution of wealth, and since outright distribution conflicted with historic patterns, redistribution through taxation was the current solution. The years 1934-1936 brought redoubling on estate rates, rises in surtaxes, double taxation of corporation dividends and taxation of corporations' undistributed profits, besides a projected levy of 9 per cent on payrolls for social security. By various devices tax receipts of 1933 were almost trebled by 1937. Long continuance of the depression gradually brought taxation closer to the masses, but the mounting debt had not troubled the majority of the electorate as long as expenditures seemed to save them.

Keeping Political Dominance

Unfortunately the various expeditures were not rewarded with permanent prosperity and therefore raised a serious challenge to New Deal policy. The recession beginning in 1937 drew attention to the fact that the industrial production of the United States had fallen further than that of any other important world power, except Germany, and had recovered the least. Big business blamed the administration and labor, insisting that permanent recovery for capitalism could not be founded upon irresponsible unionism, expanding taxation, close regulation and competition with tax-supported agencies. The administration blamed the recession on industrial sabotage, insisting that prices were made high and profits low by overhead costs of idle machinery kept idle by high prices. Both sides rushed to the radio to try to swing public opinion.

The Democratic leadership had to face also a threat from the left because of the growth of independent organizations. The most spectacular was the "Share the Wealth" host assembled by Senator Huey P. Long. Born in 1893 the son of a poor farmer, he had risen from a job as traveling salesman to a lawyer's practice. He built up a machine in his native Louisiana which made him governor, and then dictator, of that state. Then he sought a broader following, sending organizers into other southern states to preach the gospel of the abolition of high incomes and the establishment of wealth-sharing. Elected to the United States Senate in 1932, he so used that rostrum that he came to claim 3 million followers and announced that he would seek the presidency in 1936. His meteoric rise and dramatic appeal made him a formidable rival. What might have happened will be forever a mystery, for he was assassinated by an outraged Louisianian in 1935.

A more venerable Messiah to the poor was Dr. Francis E. Townsend of Los Angeles. He pressed a plan to pay old people comfortable pensions through a scheme of constant spending. He persuaded some six million to pay dues to "Old Age Revolving Pensions Limited." Likewise Father Charles E. Coughlin, popular Michigan radio priest, attracted 8 million adherents to a "National Union for Social Justice" which he mobilized occasionally to attack President Roosevelt. Most of the millions in these organizations would have voted for Roosevelt otherwise, and the question was whether his political fortunes could survive their defection.

His managers officially ignored the danger and held a great convention opening at Philadelphia 23 June 1936 to renominate him. Here the radio was employed effectively, with all important speeches made over the evening, nation-wide hookups. Looking to the future, the managers took this occasion to abolish the 104-year-old two-thirds rule for nominations. Hereafter a simple majority would suffice, and southern delegations could not block the will of the majority. It took five nights to adopt a platform endorsing the New Deal and to renominate Roosevelt and Garner by acclamation. The climax came when Roosevelt accepted the nomination at a vast open-air session in Franklin Field. Almost in the shadow of Independence Hall he called upon the nation in 1936 to defeat the "economic royalists" as their ancestors had done in 1776.

The Republicans were not in very good shape to challenge Roosevelt. In 1934 and since, they had lost ground because of support given them by a group of wealthy people who organized the American Liberty League to rally property holders against the New Deal. This movement was too conservative for the majority of the electorate and weakened Republican prestige. The party strove to recapture the farm vote, which before 1932 had often given them an East-Middle West alliance strong enough to defeat the Solid South. They adopted a "grab-bag" platform tolerant of relief and named a ticket headed by Alfred M. Landon of Kansas and Frank Knox, respectively the only Republican governor reëlected in 1934 and the editor of the Chicago *Daily News*. When the polls closed, the Republicans had 36.4 per cent of the popular vote, so distributed as to furnish them only eight electoral votes: Maine's five and Vermont's three. Roosevelt and Garner had 60.7 per cent, with 523 electoral votes. Also the Democrats won all but six of the governorship contests. Democratic victory was due partly to improving economic conditions which encouraged a majority to believe that Roosevelt's program, reaffirmed and enlarged in campaign promises, would implement permanent prosperity under the American system.

After his triumphant reëlection in 1936, President Roosevelt made a good-will voyage to Buenos Aires and Rio de Janeiro, where he was hailed by thousands of enthusiastic Latin Americans, and he returned in time for an early inauguration. Under the 20th Amendment, which had gone into effect during his administration, his term expired 20 January instead of 4 March.[1]

The President now searched for further means to insure the permanence of New Deal reforms and to advance its boundaries. He and his intimates knew that progressive enthusiasms subside; they hurried to use the high tide of his popularity to make governmental machinery more responsive to their concept of the needs of the nation. They assumed that with the Republicans eclipsed nationally and locally the President need placate Congress less and could command it more; but there remained a third branch of the government—the judiciary—which had persistently defied the New Deal. The next step must be judiciary reform.

Judicial Reform

The main object of judiciary reform was to place in a minority that majority of Supreme Court judges who by 5 to 4 decisions had ruled against the government in about half the cases of the 1935-1936 term, blocking the New Deal approach to social welfare. Here F. D. Roosevelt faced the same sort of problem as Jefferson, Jackson, Lincoln and Theodore Roosevelt, all of whom had vigorously protested when the Supreme Court's work ran counter to their wishes on fundamental question of policy. Through the years this "super-legislature" had continued its assumption of legislative functions, substituting for democracy "government by lawsuit." In their nullification of the New Deal the conservative five, holding to laissez-faire, had interpreted the Constitution so as to limit powers of national and state governments narrowly while enlarging those of private interests. On such issues as the NRA, AAA and Guffey coal law, they had insisted that manufacture, agriculture and mining were local activities beyond the scope of federal regulation.

The conservative five also perpetuated the wide twilight zone, where neither federal nor state governments could intervene to protect public from private interest. Problems as diverse as corporation taxes, hydroelectric power, industrial relations, crime, crops, relief, traffic, liquor, milk and water supply and health had crossed state boundaries. The crisscross caused establishment of an "American Legislators' Associa-

[1] Largely through the efforts of Senator George W. Norris, this amendment had been submitted to the states in 1932. It was designed primarily to abolish the old "lame duck" session of Congress heretofore held December to March after elections. In these sessions Senators and Representatives who had been defeated by their constituents in November frequently returned to continue for three months longer the work which had been repudiated.

tion," which grew into a "Council of State Governments" and secured much functional coördination among states. Some of the resulting interstate compacts had been specifically approved by Congress, and sometimes states joined the national government in defending, before federal courts, federal legislation of concern to them. The conservative five, however, were erecting judicial barriers against this current trend toward interstate coöperation in executive and legislative functioning.

Furthermore, the court system as a whole hampered federal interests in various ways: for example, appeals on constitutional questions dragged through a number of lesser courts before finally reaching the Supreme Court, and judges issued injunctions against enforcement of congressional acts without hearing federal attorneys. The need for changes on some of these matters had been widely admitted, and a "clarifying" amendment to the Constitution had been frequently proposed as the method. That would be slow and could not be compulsory, since the court-system had evolved under the direction not of the Constitution but of Congress; but it suited American preconceptions, for the doctrine of judicial supremacy had been accepted through ninety years.

The New Deal group decided that the depression dictated a quicker method of change, that of a congressional act; and Roosevelt, apparently without consulting his party's congressional leaders, sent Congress 5 February 1937 a call for court reform. He demanded principally an increase in Supreme Court justices from nine to a maximum of fifteen if those reaching seventy-five declined to retire. Whereas Taft had named five, Wilson three, Harding four, and Hoover three, Roosevelt had as yet named none and six of the court were past seventy, and five were not confirmed liberals. His proposal also included a total increase of not more than fifty judges in all classes of federal courts, despatch of appeals on constitutional questions direct from lower courts to the Supreme tribunal, and a required hearing of federal attorneys before any lower court issued an injunction against an enforcement of a congressional act.

The proposal to enlarge the court, reminiscent of Grant's expedient in 1869, aroused bitter opposition; special interests objected because its end was implementation of the New Deal, and political conservatives objected because its means were expansion of executive powers. Its opponents proved resourceful. Congress undermined it by quickly passing the Supreme Court Retirement Act of 1 March, which permitted voluntary retirement of the justices on full pay at seventy; conservative seventy-eight-year-old Justice Van Devanter neatly put the capstone to this by announcing his own intention to resign. The court itself fought the bill briskly by taking a more liberal attitude in March, April and May. In 5-4 decisions it upheld abrogation of gold payments and reversed earlier reasoning against state regulation of women's wages. It unanimously upheld the Frazier-Lemke Farm Mortgage Moratorium Act and significant provisions of the Railway Labor Act. In one case unanimously and in four instances by 5-4 decisions it upheld the Wagner National Labor Relations Act to such effect as to admit manufacturing to classification as an interstate activity subject to congressional regulation; this suggested ultimate inclusion of mining and agriculture. It approved by 5-4 and 7-2 decisions the unemployment insurance and old age pensions sections of the Social Security Act.

Meanwhile the Senate and the country fiercely debated the bill's constitutionality and its threat to the "independence" of the judiciary. Some widely influential Democrats broke sharply with the President, openly acknowledging the schism which long had been cutting deeply beneath the party surface. Certain House Democrats joined senators in revolt, and Senator Joseph T. Robinson succumbed to heart disease while struggling in hot weather to hold his party in line. After Death joined the opposition and lesser factors complicated the issue, defeat befell Roosevelt's main proposition. The Judicial Procedure Reform Law enacted 25 August did not touch tenure; it principally facilitated participation by the federal Department of Justice in cases involving constitutional interpretation. The nation had witnessed the bitterest debate since the League of Nations struggle, and its effects were long-lasting. It left political sores which festered through the lifetime of some participants. Worse, it hobbled the democracy all the more tightly with the thongs of judicial supremacy.

The court had saved its privilege; yet a quasi-victory for Roosevelt was soon attained with the help of Father Time. Within six years following introduction of the ill-fated bill, Roosevelt filled eight places on the Supreme bench. He practically remade the court.

Decisions became increasingly liberal, as indicated by the term following the fight: in 1937-1938 the government won 92 out of 114 cases argued and decided on the merits, or approximately 80 per cent. Among subsequent significant endorsements of New Deal policies were decisions of 8 and 29 April 1940 tending to uphold the National Labor Relations Act and the Walsh-Healy Act as applied to "little steel," and of 3 February 1941 upholding the Federal Wage and Hour Law as applied to southern lumber workers. The last-named decision specifically overruled the 1918 verdict invalidating the Federal Child Labor Law. Thus does the politics of the Supreme Court reflect the canons of selection used by the appointing executive. Judicially the New Deal was safe. It was fortified administratively, also. Although the voters in the congressional elections of 1938 denied Roosevelt's demand that they punish all the opponents of court reform, the next Congress expanded the executive's functions. It granted him broad powers to reorganize some administrative departments and agencies by issuing his own executive orders, which were to go into effect within sixty days after issuance *unless* meanwhile revoked by concurrent congressional action. These powers could be so used as to further apply the New Deal pattern to national life.

CHAPTER XLVIII

THE PROBLEM OF ISOLATION

While the people of the United States were feeling their way toward economic and political security, other nations were facing that problem, too; desperate struggles had them all hopelessly involved by the end of the 'thirties, during which most Americans stood aloof as long as possible, determinedly seeking safety in isolation. Yet neither the political death of the League of Nations in the Senate nor frantic and fervent expression by most Americans of their distaste for European entanglements could isolate the United States.

Struggling to Maintain Isolation

A confusion of ideal and practical considerations kept the United States in close contact with Europe. The democratic missionary zeal which had animated Wilson reached too far down into America's spiritual heritage to be uprooted. Also the modern age had woven transoceanic ties, economic, social and cultural, too strong for war and politics to kill. Lovers of world peace and militarists with surplus energies, bankers and industrialists with surplus funds and goods and farmers with surplus crops each sought their particular objects; all were caught by a common result: world contacts. The concept of isolation remained, but like American war debt policy, as will be seen shortly, it was not based on reality. Popular interest lay in the positive aspects of disarmament and peace. The government, however, awoke also to negative imperatives: the United States as a "have" nation might be affected by rearmament by the "have nots"; she could not remain unaffected by the struggle between her erstwhile allies and the defeated powers over whether victory should be static or upset by a return of the vanquished to power and glory. The sequence of events since 1920 vividly shows how this great nation continually has become more involved in European arrangements.

Americans ardently hoped for disarmament. At Washington was convened the World Disarmament Conference of 1921-1922, when the United States with Great Britain, Japan, France and Italy agreed to scrap all but a certain number of battleships and to limit for ten years new battleship construction to the respective proportionate ratios of 5-5-3-1.7-1.7. Significantly, they failed to regulate the auxiliary ship-building so important in swift modern warfare: submarines, destroyers, etc. This "Five Power Treaty" proved no more successful and no less significant than the Four and Nine Power treaties on eastern affairs reached at the same Washington Conference. In fact they gave Japan two strategic advantages. Her share in the naval ratio made it possible for her to build a navy altogether too large for British and American comfort in the Pacific. The non-fortification agreements, which Japan did not carry out, caused the United States to build no protection west of Hawaii while Japan heavily fortified in the vicinity of the Philippines, Guam, Hong Kong and the Southwest Pacific Islands. She thus used islands obtained under the Versailles treaty.

Nothing seemingly could be done to overcome Senate fear of United States membership in world judicial and political bodies. Determined efforts were made to secure American adherence to the World Court. This body had been established at The Hague in 1922 as a League adjunct for aiding peace through judicial decisions on international law, obligations and treaties. It was founded on rules which Elihu Root had helped to formulate, and it regularly kept one American jurist on its bench. It both interested and repelled Americans. Although both parties pledged membership, although Europe virtually accepted United States reservations and although each succeeding president tried to overcome Senate opposition to membership, none succeeded. The broad scope of early League activities attracted "unofficial observers" from Washington to Geneva, and the existence of the League finally was officially recognized in 1923. Official American delegations attended League gatherings after 1924, safeguarding American interests, coöperating on non-political matters and encouraging some public and private financial support. They observed and reported the failure of the League, whether regarded as an implement for peace or for preventing reapportionment of the spoils divided in 1919. Although the United States never entered the League proper, she latterly maintained a secretariat at its doors. Some of her leaders hoped to mobilize world peace opinion as a substitute for the League's scheme of collective security and economic boycott.

The peace ideal remained strong in theory but weak in performance. In Europe it had sponsored the Locarno Pact of 1925 by which France, Belgium and Germany agreed always to settle disputes by arbitration rather than war; but when President Coolidge, pressed by American disarmament hopes, two years later tried to implement peace through further naval limitation, he failed, to the gratification of international armament interests which fought the conference. Hoover joined Secretary of State Kellogg and France's premier, Aristide Briand, in proffering the 1928 Pact of Paris renouncing war and agreeing to settle disputes solely by peaceful means. Fifteen powers signed forthwith and forty-seven lesser governments followed suit. Washington showed its good faith by pushing a series of bilateral agreements, based on foundations laid by Root and Bryan, for arbitration and investigation of disputes.

President Hoover pursued the effort further in 1930, coöperating when London became host to the signatories of the "Five Power Treaty" of 1922. The 1930 treaty extended the battleship "holiday" to 1936 and included auxiliary vessels within the ratio limitations but raised the ratio to 10-10-7. Britain admitted Japan to submarine parity with her, and these two with the United States sought safety in an "escalator" clause permitting any signatory to disregard limitations if threatened by the building program of any non-signatory. However since France and Italy failed to ratify, and Japan was scarcely quiescent under her subsidiary status, the peace conference of 1930 chiefly admitted progress in preparation for war.

As long as the American majority remained strongly isolationist, congressional coöperation with Europe stayed at a minimum. It is true that American ideology, moral support and financial assistance virtually predominated in most of the two hundred and more international associations working in the field of public administration, but it was only a small group of ardent internationalists who made this a fact. Although Congress accepted affiliation with the International Labor Office (1934) and allowed officials to give the first United States ratification of an international labor convention (1938), in broader fields involvement was avoided.

Debt Controversy

The tendency to isolation was strengthened by unpaid Allied debts to the United States. These obligations amounted to approximately 10.5 billions, over 7 billions loaned the Allies for war purposes after America entered the struggle, and some 3.25 billions loaned for reconstruction purposes after the armistice to various governments, new and old, including erstwhile enemies.

The victorious Allies undertook to find the money to pay the United States in Germany, levying against her an overwhelming reparations fine of 33 billions on the theory that she was solely to blame for the war and that an impoverished and disabled nation could pay a staggering debt. From her they in time collected about three times as much as they repaid to the United States. Badly confused by post-war economic readjustments, all the powers were blindly rushing into extreme, nationalistic devices, rearming and erecting tariff and exchange barriers which strangled the international trade they needed to revive. The debtors felt slight moral obligation to pay America, insisting that

"Uncle Shylock" ought to forgive the debts and certainly could expect only fractional payment.

Americans divided. Capitalists who wished to profit by new reconstruction flotation of foreign securities, industrialists and exporters eager for trade, protected industries fearful of payment in competing goods and some humanitarians and economists conversant with the economic realities of the situation were among the classes tolerant of cancelation. The citizenry by and large, however, agreed with Coolidge that "they hired the money, didn't they?" and insisted that political platforms and congressional policy should stick to the theory of payment. They felt no responsibility for making payment practically possible either by lowering tariff barriers (for that would have increased unemployment), or by expanding marine use of foreign facilities (instead they further subsidized their own), or by encouraging, instead of practically ending, immigration. American investors did, however, buy lavishly of foreign securities with government encouragement until 1929, so that thus long some payments continued, and the assumption persisted that the debts would be paid. Their purchases in German securities, private and public, were greater than the total of reparations Germany paid to all the powers.

In the effort to collect, Congress established a World War Foreign Debt Commission which between 1922 and 1930 made agreements with fifteen of the twenty debtor nations for payments, over a sixty-two year period, at interest varying, with supposed ability to pay, from .4 per cent to 3.3 per cent. But America admitted no connection between reparations and debts owed her, and after France in 1923 made a futile effort to secure unobtainable reparations by reoccupation of the Ruhr, Europe established two successive bodies under American chairmanship, the Dawes Commission of 1924 and the Owen D. Young Commission of 1928, to amortize payments. Both pared them down; neither plan worked; and the unofficial suggestion of the latter commission, that reparations be scaled down in relation to reduction of the debt owed America, was politically unacceptable at home. Hopes of payment died hard.

The depression, however, forced President Hoover to declare in 1931 the one-year moratorium, applied to both debts and reparations, and to call on Europe to devise a new expedient. At Lausanne the next year Belgium, Britain, France, Italy and Japan agreed with Germany to reduce her reparations to 2 per cent of the original sum and to accept that small payment in German bonds. The United States Congress could not follow suit, and therefore, after a few "token" payments, by December of 1933 all governments except Finland were in default. A resentful Congress responded with the Johnson Act embargoing further loans to defaulting nations.

REPARATIONS PAYMENTS AND DEBT PAYMENTS

Compared in Relation to Foreign Loans to Germany
(at time of stoppage of payments in 1931)

Total reparations paid by Germany, official figures of Reparations Commission	$4,470,300,000.00
Total amount paid by Allies to U.S. on war debts account	$2,606,340,012.48
	$1,863,959,987.52
Amounts loaned by private capital to Germany	
Estimated from U.S.	$2,475,000,000
Estimated from other nations	$3,809,000,000
	$6,284,000,000

Rise of Dictators: Bolshevism, Fascism, Nazism

During these years of attempted isolation American diplomats and men of affairs heard of a new Europe with new frictions and dangers. Forces hostile to democracy were spreading over the continent, discarding honor and fair dealing in preference for gangster methods.

The legacy of economic instability left by the First World War helped new, aggressive groups to rise to power. In Russia, even before the peace, the revolutionary spirit had transformed the Empire of the Czars into the Russian Socialist Federated Soviet Republic. This new order was dedicated to the destruction of capitalism and the development of a state which should own and control all instruments of production; in religion it was atheistic. The new government was managed by the political faction of the Communist party known as the "Bolshevik" or majority. The Bolshevik executive committee governed through local party organizations or soviets, established throughout Russia in all the federated states. The ambitious plans of Lenin and Trotsky included active promotion of their system throughout the world and in 1919 they organized a propaganda agency, the Third International or Comintern.

The Russian experiment proceeded, at the expense of much modification, to march along the difficult road to success. Its steps were marked by compromise with capitalism. In 1921 it restored trade in agricultural produce and the use of money. After the death of Lenin and the accession of Stalin to power (1924) even more attention was given to organization than heretofore. The leaders summoned world experts in science and technology to teach Russia how to use its great resources to become a self-sufficient state. In 1928 a strenuous Five Year Plan was adopted, followed by a second in 1933. These were great blueprints of social and economic planning which embraced everything from industrialization to the promotion of education and the arts. A numerous corps of governmental and social scientists worked for the Bolshevik's State Planning Commission. At the same time a tremendous army was created. Despite capitalistic predictions based on wishful thinking that the régime would collapse, it attained a success which the world is now beginning to realize.

During the 'twenties and 'thirties the words *Russia* and *Communism* became symbols of European unrest and fear. When workers endeavored to improve their position or to gain power they frequently unfurled the "Red" flag, sang the "Internationale" and invoked the doctrines of Communism; those doctrines threatened both private property and religious faiths. So, the workers' parties of Europe were fought by capitalistic and religious interests. As most post-war governments there were endeavoring to operate on parliamentary, or republican, principles, with frequent elections and the paraphernalia of partisan debate, the Communists had ample occasion to expound their doctrines. Bitter political controversy, superimposed upon economic distress, produced dire results, particularly in Italy and Germany.

Italy had been bitterly disappointed by the peace; hardly any of her territorial ambitions had been realized. The war had disrupted her economic system, and her politics were notoriously divisive and corrupt. Returned soldiers and workers were uneasy and from 1919 through 1922 there was a series of strikes. The government seemed powerless to improve economic conditions or to carry on effective diplomacy. Out of the chaos came a new régime. Some ex-soldiers and Socialists formed a Fascist group in 1919, aiming to make Italy efficient and aggressive. They put much emphasis upon discipline, wore black shirts as their regalia and were patronized by those property holders and industrialists who feared that labor unrest would produce Communism. By 1921 they numbered some 250,000 and organized as a political party.

The Fascists now made a drive under their leader, Benito Mussolini, to take over the government. They abandoned most of their Socialist pretensions and as conservatives, foes of Communism, they organized squads to carry on by violence. In 1922 they smashed an attempt at a general strike and then marched on Rome. Led by Mussolini some 50,000 presented themselves to the King of Italy that October and forced him to make Mussolini premier.

At first Mussolini kept the old, parliamentary forms, slightly disguising his dictatorship. He set about to restore order, to introduce efficiency and to extend Italy's sway. He made his peace with the Pope, setting up the Vatican as a state. Temporarily he tolerated opposition, but in 1924 came violent suppression, dictatorship open and undisguised. In 1928 he made Italy into a "corporative state"; industry, agriculture, labor and business were organized into a series of associations or occupational groups, each of which was to send members to a new kind of parliament, an assembly of corporations. Whatever this may have looked like on paper, Mussolini was supreme dictator and his chief interest became expansion of Italy into a restored Roman Empire. The Mediterranean must become *Mare Nostrum,* an Italian Lake. When he should begin to interfere in the Balkans and North Africa, he naturally would come up against British, French and Russian interests.

Meanwhile, Germany was about to produce a third undemocratic ideology. The Allied governments had made over the German Empire into the Weimar Republic, a middle-class government. It struggled to bear the burden of reparations and to protect itself from possible Russian aggression with the paltry armament left by the Versailles Treaty. The load was crushing; hard times, unemployment and unrest mounted. Communists appeared. Strikes and violence became common. Various local groups sought to organize secessions from the Republic. One of these, a "brown shirt" movement in Bavaria, enlisted the aid of a National Socialist Workers' Party; the latter had been organized along military lines by a group which included an ex-soldier, now an emotional fanatic, Adolf Hitler. Hitler in 1923 rushed the Bavarian movement into a premature outbreak, or "Putsch," at Munich. The result was a fiasco and his imprisonment for a year, during which he wrote his blueprint, *Mein Kampf.*

Germany's economic situation approached hopelessness in 1930. The weight of reparations and the world depression made it impossible to finance the Republic. The National Socialist Party, popularly called the Nazis, presented a program of economic reorganization based on discipline and regulation of enterprise. It became less socialistic and made overtures to capitalism. Furthermore it played up the fear of Communism and denounced international bankers and Jews as the source of Germany's woes. In the presidential election of 1932 this party of 900,000 members influenced 13,000,000 to vote for Hitler. Old Field Marshal Von Hindenburg won a second term but the Nazi rise was prophetic. The Republic tried to disband this armed organization, but it was too strong. The government was bankrupt, economic conditions were horrible and Germany was prostrate. Fear of Communism and economic chaos evidently brought some important industrialists to believe that Hitler's Nazis could save the situation. In 1933 Von Hindenburg, aged and of impaired health, was persuaded to make Hitler chancellor.

Hitler and his intimate associates, Hermann Goering and Paul Joseph Goebbels, like the Fascists almost immediately raised the Communist bogey and when the Reichstag building was burned, charged it to a Communist plot. The Reichstag was persuaded, in April 1933, to vest its power in Hitler and reëstablish the German *Reich* or Empire.

Armed with this authorization Hitler and his brown shirts assumed complete control. The Gestapo, or secret police, penetrated everywhere and a series of cruel campaigns purged the *Reich* of Communists and Jews, appropriating their property. The Nazis instituted a cult of Aryanism; only those free from the taint of Jewish blood were true Germans. Jews were ousted from business, the professions, the universities and all desirable situations; they were sent to concentration camps, tortured and murdered. When Von Hindenburg died in 1934 the office of president was not filled. Hitler as *Führer* became supreme.

The German *Reich* now became a totalitarian state, like Italy; the Nazi party was to rule through the representation of various occupational groups. However, the Nazis, unlike the Fascists, made no peace with religion; they attacked Christianity and tried to restore paganism. They set out to educate the children in a paganism exalting efficiency, power and the use of force. Various disciplined groups of youths were drilled to bow to the will of the state and to follow the *Führer* implicitly. The Germans secretly began to rearm in violation of the Versailles Treaty, while Hitler undertook to follow the *Mein Kampf* blueprint. This called for restoration of the Empire, including within it all Germans. Austria, Czechoslovakia, Poland and France beware! Such was Europe in 1935.

Threats in the Far East

In the Far East, also, war clouds gathered. China had been endeavoring, since 1916, to transform an ancient empire into a republic, an effort eyed itchingly by Soviet Russia and, especially, Japan. China lay divided, unorganized, exposed to exploitation and encroachment. At first the republicans tried to secure Russian aid to build up military strength against Japanese aggression. The republican leader was a young soldier, Chiang Kai-shek. With his wife, Soong Mei-ling, a Wellesley graduate, he undertook to unite China; their campaign by 1930 showed some success. They were extending Chinese power into Manchuria and the neighborhood of Shantung, the center of Japanese interests. A most effective weapon was the boycott of Japanese goods; also they cast loose from Russian influence and vigorously promoted Chinese nationalism.

Japan meanwhile was suffering from the world depression, viewed with hatred China's rise and felt the pinch of the boycott. Japan had extensive interests in Manchuria and Shantung and needed materials which China could supply. A militaristic clique made capital against the ruling, somewhat liberal, ministry, charging it with inability to protect Japanese interests. The militarists surmised that the depression probably would prevent interference from the United States or Great

Britain and noted that Russia was herself fighting Chinese nationalists in Manchuria and probably would not object to a Japanese diversion. So Japan in 1931 invaded Manchuria. President Hoover's secretary of state, Henry L. Stimson, tried to enlist international protest but Great Britain would not coöperate. Nor did he receive much backing in the United States.

Although both Oriental and European signposts were pointing toward war, the majority of Americans would not look where they pointed. A few were preaching "collective security"; that is, joint action by the governments to prevent forcible overturn of the balance of power set up after the First World War. The joint action should consist of the imposition of "sanctions"; that is, penalties, against any nation trying to upset the balance. Collective security and sanctions, however, could scarcely attract a people recently victimized by defaults on war debts and by bitter trade rivalry. Moreover a munitions investigating committee led by Senator Gerald P. Nye of North Dakota, 1934-1936, uncovered munitions graft, bankers' profiteering and propaganda aspects of the War to Save Democracy, while novelists and playwrights with dread realism stripped military service of its glamour. The people of the United States felt cheated and disillusioned.

Dictators on the March

While they were in this mood the march of aggression quickened across the sea. Mussolini in 1934 moved on the African salient of his cherished Roman Empire; he seized Abyssinia, thereafter to be known as Ethiopia. In 1936 Italy's King assumed the title of Emperor. Also in 1936 Hitler marched into the demilitarized Rhineland, in violation of the Versailles Treaty and the Locarno Pact: and he and Mussolini formed the Rome-Berlin Axis. Germany then signed a treaty with Japan against Communism and the next year Italy added her signature. This "Axis" made a sinister grouping; the three proceeded to give military aid to Fascist General Franco of Spain, who was leading a revolt against the Republic there. Russia thereupon aided the republicans, and thus these powers rehearsed for a greater war. After three years of this, the Republic was destroyed and Franco established a Fascist rule in Spain. Most alarming was the continued advance of Hitler. In March of 1938 he took over Austria and soon revealed his intention to seize the Sudetenland section of Czechoslovakia.

Great Britain and France had viewed these advances with anxiety but did not intervene actively. France imagined that her elaborate eastern fortifications, the Maginot line, could bar Germany. Great Britain was unready, too vulnerable to interfere. They resorted to appeasement. Britain's Premier Chamberlain, umbrella over his arm, flew to Munich to postpone the deluge; there he signed with Hitler in September 1938 the Munich Pact, wherein Britain acceded to Hitler's rape of Czechoslovakia in exchange for Hitler's pledge to end his seizures and to enforce "peace in our time." American interventionists shouted to the isolationists, in Biblical phrase, "They cry peace, peace, but there is no peace."

CHAPTER XLIX

ISOLATION DESTROYED

However slim the chances for peace abroad, the majority of the people of the United States held to a firm resolve: "We'll not be drawn into the European mess *this* time."

Protecting Neutrality

As the dictators proceeded to alter the political map of Europe and Asia, they confirmed the people of the United States in their suspicion of collective security and their preference for isolation. Congress observed that England and France either failed to invoke sanctions against the aggressors or did it ineffectively, and so undertook legislation to keep America out of the next great war. Remembering how heavy exports and credits to the Allies had preceded American entrance into the First World War, Congress planned to restrict trade to peaceful channels but acceded to executive supervision in this. By successive neutrality acts of August 1935, February 1936 and May 1937 it advanced to the stage of empowering the President to proclaim the existence of a "state of war," whereupon he *must* forbid Americans to export munitions to belligerents, transport munitions to them, travel on their ships, purchase their securities, or arm American merchantmen. Also he *could* bar our port facilities to foreign submarines, belligerent warships and armed merchantmen, forbid American transport of *any* commodities to belligerents, and (for two years) could require the latter to pay cash before taking goods away—the "cash and carry" provision. However, these terms were declared inapplicable to wars between Latin American powers and nations outside this hemisphere.

By this drastic legislation of 1937 the United States abandoned its historic, precious principle of freedom of the seas. It tied strings to diplomatic policy and ignored the possibility that equal treatment of warring powers, as to embargoes on arms, credits and loans, might harm American interests and help enemies of democracy. The national determination to avoid war simply would not be gainsaid. In 1938 it nearly made law of the Ludlow resolution which required that, except in case of invasion, a war declaration must wait upon a popular referendum; Roosevelt defeated this only through patronage deals arranged by Farley.

The national distaste for war and the congressional suspicion of war-making by the executive were demonstrated also in relations with Japan. She was of peculiar concern because she wished to control the Far East, including the Philippines, which the United States might find it difficult if not impossible to defend, and the East Indies, whence came vital supplies of rubber and tin. The Ludlow resolution had been inspired by congressional apprehension of overt action by the executive against Japan. Six years earlier a Hoover appointee had sat with a League Commission which censured Japan for invading Manchuria. After Japan in 1934 served notice that she would not be bound by her subsidiary naval status beyond 1936, Roosevelt appointees participated with French and British in the futile London Conference of 1935; they set naval limitations supposedly good until 1942 but were careful to make them qualitative, not quantitative; and of course the dictators were conspicuously absent and non-participating.

After Japan began (August 1937) her undeclared war of invasion of China, Roosevelt became more urgent. He exhorted the nation in October to help other powers "quarantine" aggressors, but the next week public opinion forced him to deny a Brussels conference (attended by nineteen powers) a pledge of concrete coöperation and American initiative in support of the Nine Power Pact of 1922 (p. 561) which Britain particularly had desired. Two months later American newsreels focused sharply upon Japanese deliberate sinking of the United States gunboat *Panay,* but the public was content peaceably to accept apologies and indemnities; they had heard that less than 1 per cent of their foreign investments lay in China. The stake there soon became negligible.

Trade with Japan was far more important, in both directions; but Japan was ready to sacrifice it to her campaign for the domination of Asia and adjacent islands. In 1937 she was the third largest source of imports to the United States and the third largest foreign buyer of American goods, but within a year the one fell 37 per cent and the other 30.5 per cent. American disapproval of Japan's conquests caused considerable boycott of her goods, but further conquests and trade controls over China enabled her to proclaim in 1938 the closing of the Open Door, an act much more detrimental to British than to American economy. The Roosevelt administration, like its predecessors traditionally committed to the Open Door, now repeatedly demanded that it reopen in compliance with the Nine Power Pact and hit back in three ways. Using the fact that Japan had not made an official declaration of war against China, Roosevelt avoided applying the neutrality laws, which otherwise would have deprived China of United States munitions. He discouraged munitions shipments to Japan, although he allowed the scrap-iron trade to boom, and although he purchased Japanese-seized

Chinese silver to the advantage of Japan's war-chest. He gave China renewed gold credits, based on purchases of her silver, and Export-Import Bank loans for importing trucks and other supplies. She must not be left too much a prey to Japan.

President Roosevelt, who seemed more interested in trans-Atlantic than trans-Pacific events, wanted freedom to act as the world's leader in democracy; but until 1939 the majority of the nation and Congress held him back. Straining at the congressional leash, he sometimes dodged equal application of the neutrality laws in order to favor victim, non-aggressor nations like China. Continually he fought isolation with "educational" propaganda for United States participation in collective security and in sanctions, but Congress long repudiated his assumptions. It refused in 1933 to endorse a pledge which Roosevelt's personal ambassador-at-large, Norman Davis, gave the League that the United States would not hinder collective security. It declined in 1935 to change the neutrality laws to allow coöperation in League sanctions against Italian seizure of Ethiopia. It secured in 1936 withdrawal of American warships from Spanish waters; aloofness here was a compromise, for some few Americans sent funds to the republican Loyalists or enlisted on their side, while partial support of Loyalists by Russia alienated other Americans. Spain was a case where equal application of neutrality laws withheld American munitions from defenders of democracy, while totalitarian aid was pouring in to the Fascist insurgents.

While the majority of the people of the United States continued to shun collective security as applied to political wars and to Europe, they tried its application to trade and to South America. In these two fields they followed the leadership of Secretary of State Hull and President Roosevelt. Hull believed that free-flowing international trade was indispensable to world peace, that nations aiming at economic self-sufficiency make war on their neighbors. Also he believed that American prosperity required recapture of the foreign markets which formerly absorbed 10 per cent of her production. However, when he became secretary, managed currency, barter and quota systems already were being employed by hostile powers aiming at national self-sufficiency; and within four months his own president, abandoning the gold standard and adopting managed currency as a trade weapon, had pressed a broad program of national self-sufficiency. The world trend toward trade restrictions developed so fast that by 1938 some 380 bilateral, special agreements were known to exist which excluded United States products.

Against this trend Hull meanwhile made a determined stand. He pushed unconditional, most-favored-nation treaties of reciprocity, under which the signatories agreed to give each others' goods treatment as favorable as those signatories granted to any country. This of course was the direct opposite of the bilateral agreements which limit special favors to two powers only. Hull pressed his diplomatic advantage under the Trade Agreements Act of 12 June 1934 which permitted him to raise or lower rates as much as 50 per cent. The extension of that law in 1937 and 1940 by Congress, against bitter opposition from the old protection group, attested the growing weight given international affairs.

Relations with Latin America

Latin America became the busy scene of efforts by Hull and Roosevelt to gain rich trade, understanding and political likemindedness. They preached an All-American collective security which was called "hemispheric solidarity." Hoover's conciliation program was perfected into what the Roosevelt administration termed its "Good Neighbor" policy. Caribbean imperialism was liquidated by complete withdrawal of marines from Haiti and abrogation of the Platt amendment concerning Cuba in 1934, by relinquishment of the right to intervention in Panama in 1936 and by ending the Dominican customs receivership in 1940.

The difference between dollar diplomacy and the Good Neighbor policy was strikingly demonstrated in the case of Mexico, when the Cardenas administration appropriated valuable farm and mining lands owned in part by United States capitalists. The Roosevelt administration appreciated that Cardenas was trying to steer a middle course between Communists and Fascist elements and needed lands to placate landless peasants. Yet this most recent outbreak of expropriations raised a most delicate issue because of the contagion in the Mexican example, because the oil was sold to foreign dictatorships and because the expropriation was financed largely through funds obtained from United States purchases of silver mined in Mexico on property held by Americans. Instead of bluster, a long and delicate negotiation was begun, aimed at recovery of at least the actual cash outlay of the companies.

Great effort was made to replace suspicion with friendliness throughout Latin America. Differences with various republics over defaulted bonds were negotiated cautiously. Armed intervention was renounced officially at the Seventh Pan American Conference meeting at Montevideo in 1933 and attended by Hull. At an Inter-American Peace Conference assembled in Buenos Aires upon Roosevelt's suggestion in 1936 and attended by him, the Americas signed treaties of non-aggression, binding themselves not to war over boundaries, or to recognize war-made boundaries or interfere in each other's internal affairs. At the Eighth Pan American Conference meeting at Lima in December 1938 Hull reasserted those conciliatory pledges of non-interference, equality of status and coöperation which the United States had given at Montevideo and Buenos Aires.

The Lima conference, however, was complicated by an accession of Nazi strength. A strenuous German campaign to bind Latin America to her own economic system and political ideology was threatening Hull's reciprocal trade agreement program. On the economic side, Germany, and to a lesser extent Italy and Japan, offered a natural market for Latin raw materials, many of which the United States would not buy because she produced them herself. On the political side, the Latins were more accustomed to dictatorships (albeit not the kind that destroyed almost all personal liberty) than they were to representative democracy like that in the United States, and their cultural ties bound them less closely to the United States than to Europe.

The Nazis were skilfully dovetailing their economic and political programs to advance their world ambitions. They paid for goods with barter credits, which gave them the triple advantage of unloading their own products, closing markets to competitors and protecting their scant reserve of foreign exchange. Their various ingenious devices could be ruthlessly applied because of government control. Increasingly Nazi purchases of Latin surpluses were conditioned upon acceptance of Nazi political dogma, as when foreign export houses were required to dismiss Jewish employees and give influential places to Nazi agents. Britain lost more trade than did the United States, relatively, but the latter became the pet target of anti-democratic, radio attacks of Nazi origin and could not fight back by totalitarian methods. Congress in 1938 refused a special broadcast appropriation, but the administration used the Departments of State, Agriculture, Commerce and Interior, the Maritime Commission and the Export-Import Bank to encourage two-way trade. Also the United States had the advantage that she paid for goods in foreign exchange which the Latins could use where they willed, and her naval, army and aviation missions were popular in several countries. Such was the situation when Hull and his associates appealed at Lima for loyalty to democratic ideals.

The Declaration of Lima advanced slightly beyond the Buenos Aires agreement but did not bind the powers to collective security for democracy in the American hemisphere. Brazil and Peru prevented use of the term "democracy." The Argentine prevented a denunciation of totalitarianism. The economic, political and moral declarations obtained by Hull included no sanctions. While they expressed disapproval of racial and religious persecution and approval of the principle of reciprocal trade agreements on a most-favored-nation basis, they laid down no concrete program for ending the persecution or establishing the reciprocity. While they reaffirmed loyalty to republicanism and a common concern over new dangers, they agreed to nothing to prevent adoption of Fascism by any country converted to it. The Declaration pledged the powers to consult together with a view to solidarity of action in event of threat to their peace, security or territorial integrity, but the consultation was to be at the request of the threatened nation. Hull had obtained somewhat less than his hopes, but there was gratification in February of 1939 when the finance ministers of the Argentine, Brazil, Paraguay and Uruguay announced a far-reaching program for lowering trade barriers among themselves. In September following, after Germany invaded Poland, the twenty-one Americas unanimously agreed to the Panama Pact. It set aside the offshore waters, from Canada's southern border to Cape Horn and extending seawards 250 to 1,250 miles at various points, as a "safety belt" closed to warring powers. This was less likely to keep belligerents out than to cement hemispheric friendships, for Britain and Germany both were soon ignoring the belt.

Conflict Approaches

By the time of these modest steps toward collective security in the western hemisphere, it was evident that United States isolation was weakening. The majority had rejoiced when the Munich agreement prevented a war but disapproved of that pact because it acceded to German seizures. They thought better of Roosevelt for urging peace on all parties at that time instead of pledging his support of war measures, but they showed unmistakably that they no longer were neutral. Many already were boycotting German, Italian and Japanese goods and were coöperating in international refugee work and in lightening immigration restrictions, in order to afford refuge for Jews as well as some Catholics and Protestants persecuted by the Nazis.

The composite origin of the population and the loyalty of the vast majority to what they term "democracy" ensured abandonment of isolation. Every warring nation abroad had its little group of interventionists in the United States, where the maintenance of free institutions left them liberty to spread propaganda. Most aggressive on the totalitarian side were the German-American *Bund,* supporting the Hitler régime, and the Communist groups infiltrating part of WPA and the automobile, steel and some other unions of the CIO. Uneasiness at such influences inspired spy hunts by the Federal Bureau of Investigation and the Dies Committee and caused laws requiring aliens to register and barring them from the WPA.

Selfish profiteers and honest advocates of collective security also were breaking down isolationism. The former had an eye upon some 9 billions in foreign bank balances which had been attracted to these safer shores and which the foreigners might spend for American-made munitions. The latter joined president, cabinet and lesser officials in exposing the menace of totalitarianism. They welcomed two visits: in December 1938 one by Anthony Eden, a British leader conspicuous both for opposition to the Munich agreement and for insistence upon United States support of Britain and France; in June 1939 one by King George and Queen Elizabeth, the first British monarchs to visit the land of the Declaration of Independence. Congress revealed the turning tide during 1937-1938 by appropriating for unprecedented peacetime expansion of the army, navy and merchant marine. The President was acquiring a good margin of popular support for every possible aid to England and France "short of war."

The death-blow to isolation was dealt during 1939-1940 by a surprisingly swift extension of Hitler's power over Europe. In March 1939 he incorporated in his "Third Reich" the remainder of Czechoslovakia and the Polish port of Memel. In August he achieved an understanding with Russia and in October proceeded to conquer and divide Poland with her. Russia followed with a winter conquest of Finland and subjugation of the Baltic countries of Esthonia, Latvia and Lithuania. April of 1940 found Hitler subjugating Norway and Denmark, and in May the Netherlands, Luxembourg and Belgium fell.

Against these advances Great Britain and France had contrived no effective obstacles. Their declaration of war against Germany in September 1939, upon her onslaught against Poland, had been followed by a series of calamitous defeats due to German superiority in preparation, equipment and technique. The Nazis showed their ingenuity and timing skill in making what was called "Blitzkrieg," meaning lightning war. First, the area chosen for conquest was thoroughly surveyed by spies. Second, key points, such as railroad junctions, power stations and governmental centers, were suddenly overrun by parachute troops. Third, aerial bombs and mechanized land artillery rained destruction on the astounded and fleeing populace. Fourth, German soldiery moved in to mop up and take control. This was "total war," devastating an entire land and its people, not just forts and armies. During June of 1940 such technique placed a large section of northern and central France under Nazi control, and in July a terrific bombing of England and Scotland began which seemed likely soon to subdue Britain also.

By this time, however, the British Empire was getting under way with Canadian, Australian and South African aid in a huge, coöperative war effort which it was about to ask the government of the United States to underwrite. Clearly, Britain could not halt the Nazification of Europe without United States munitions and money. Britain counted first on moral indignation over the destruction of Europe's small nations to transform the isolationist majority into a minority. Moral indignation proving slow in its effects, she welcomed the rise of feelings of fear and hate, which moved more swiftly in the direction of "all-out aid to Britain" as the electorate came to sense the Axis threat to their democratic form of government, their possessions and their trade.

Aid to Britain became part of a gigantic defense drive which gathered momentum with no less than sixty-one pieces of defense legislation between June 7 1939 and October 17 1940 and which signified abandonment of isolation. The radio, newsreels and press were carrying into every nook and cranny of the nation stark descriptions of total war. So Congress passed the Neutrality Act of November 1939. Its two most significant provisions weakened neutrality; it abolished the arms embargo and gave president and Congress alike the right to announce a "state of war." It had also isolationist provisions. It placed all ocean trade with belligerents on a cash and carry basis, except in the case of non-munitions cargoes carried on neutral vessels to belligerent-owned areas far from the war zone. It kept the earlier prohibition against United States citizens traveling on belligerent ships or loaning funds to combatants, adding that neither they nor ships owned by them could enter danger zones. Again, the terms were declared inapplicable to wars between Latin American and European powers.

Further Congress authorized the President to call out the National Guard, provided for immediate conscription of all able-bodied men between the ages of twenty-one and thirty-five into military service for one year and out of total 1940 appropriations of 9 billions allotted 2.5 billions to defense. It lowered income tax exemptions from $1,000 to $800 for single persons and from $2,500 to $2,000 for married people.

The President anticipated the change in sentiment and utilized it to press his foreign program, with and without explicit constitutional authorization. At the end of August 1940 he announced that he was giving Britain fifty "over-age" destroyers in exchange for ninety-nine-year leases on sites for eight sea and air bases. These made an offshore defense line 4,500 miles long between Newfoundland and British Guiana, including also sites on Bermuda, the Bahamas, Jamaica, St. Lucia, Trinidad and Antigua. Britain in return promised not to surrender her fleet under any conditions. Also the President set up with Canada a Joint Defense Board.

Secretary Hull assured Latin America that the bases were for defense against Europe, not for aggression to the south, that all the Americas could use the new sites "on the fullest coöperative basis." This was designed to prevent the destroyer-bases deal from undermining hemispheric solidarity. In July the foreign ministers of twenty-one American republics had agreed to the Havana Convention, which provided machinery for collective administration of any European possessions in the western world threatened with transfer to another non-American power. The United States had no wish to see islands of the West Indies transferred to German control by the countries the Nazis had overrun.

The domestic defense problem had two main aspects, the military and the economic, the military being the more familiar. It was an extremely difficult task, on the other hand, to perfect defense of the nation's economic system, which was violently dislodged by Europe's total war. Nazi defeat of the Lowlands and France forced continental Europe under German economic domination. This change and Britain's blockade of her enemies abruptly destroyed, in mid-1940, the continental market for United States products. Trade with colonial North Africa and the East Indies also was dislocated.

Latin America became the active battleground for markets. After the blockade cut Germany off, she used Japan as her agent there, and the Nipponese used that position to develop their own influence and trade. Nor were Germans stranded in Latin America idle; they became agents of United States business concerns, using the funds therefrom to push totalitarian influence and to palm off United States-made goods as German in origin, in order to remain in the market. Britain also fought United States competitors; she obtained Europe's former markets in the Argentine and Uruguay, using the gains to expand United States munitions purchases. The Roosevelt administration tried to strengthen Latin ties by extending to twelve nations loans and credits designed to finance past and present purchases of United States materials, to aid internal development and to stabilize local currencies. It fought Japanese plans by abrogating the trade treaty with her.

These changes worked drastic effects upon western agriculture and industry. While Europeans starved on rations, American governments had to finance storage of excess foodstuffs; the quantity of United States agricultural exports shrank during the final months of 1940 to the lowest level since 1869. United States exports came to be limited almost entirely to war goods—airplanes, steel, iron, chemicals, etc.—and her European market came to belong almost wholly to Britain, whose power to finance purchases must surely and rapidly shrink. Could the nation be saved from the evils of an inflated munitions boom?

A Third Term to Defeat Dictators

Further attempts to solve world economic problems were postponed while the nation became engrossed in a domestic political question. The presidential contest of 1940 was notable as reflecting the instability which reigned in both domestic and foreign affairs. The Republicans, meeting at Philadelphia 24 June, adopted a platform which assured the farmers, laborers and unemployed that their recent legislative favors would not be taken away; but the corollaries to those favors—

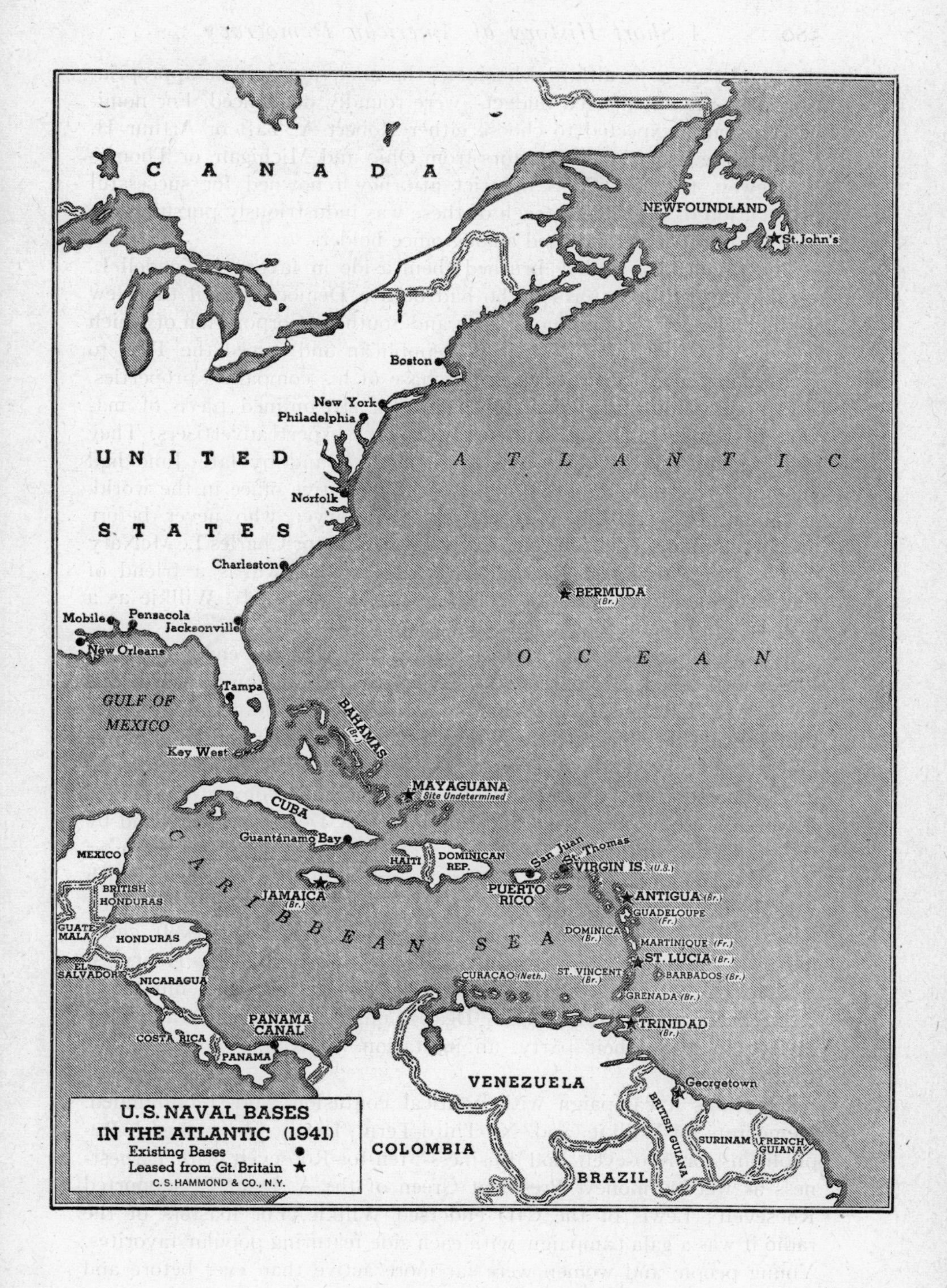

U. S. NAVAL BASES IN THE ATLANTIC (1941)

the regulation of wealth and business, the moderate defense appropriations and the unbalanced budget—were roundly denounced. For nominee the party expected to choose either Robert A. Taft or Arthur H. Vandenberg, isolationist senators from Ohio and Michigan, or Thomas E. Dewey, the New York district attorney renowned for successful prosecution of racketeers; each of these was industriously pursuing the prize in the manner accepted among office holders.

The Convention rudely brushed them aside in favor of Wendell L. Willkie, a utilities attorney who had been a Democrat until the New Deal challenged the Commonwealth and Southern Corporation of which he was president. He had turned Republican and forced the TVA to make unexpected concessions in purchase of his company's properties. The nomination-getting instrument was a streamlined piece of machinery run by political amateurs who were expert advertisers. They had begun charging their dynamo in March and by late June had enough power to nominate, for the highest elective office in the world, a comparatively little-known corporation lawyer who never before had been nominated or elected to any office. Senator Charles L. McNary of Oregon, a seasoned Republican wheelhorse known as a friend of the farmer and of TVA, was selected by the astute Mr. Willkie as a neat vice-presidential balance to his ticket.

The astounded Democrats speedily realized that the energetic Willkie, who proceeded to exceed Bryan's 1896 speech-making record, was out to win. The conservatives among them had been desperately hoping that Postmaster-General Farley or Vice-President Garner might prove able to deflect the third-term prospects of President Roosevelt, who had been endorsed by numerous primaries and state conventions. They, however, were mowed down by well-oiled New Deal machinery and by the well-founded fear of Willkie success. Convening in Chicago 15 July the Democrats named Roosevelt and adopted a platform which warmly defended the New Deal and reminded Republicans that they had obstructed welfare and defense appropriations. Roosevelt chose his own running mate, selecting Secretary of Agriculture Henry A. Wallace, son of Harding's secretary of agriculture and himself a Republican prior to the New Deal. Conservative Democrats were invited to leave their party, an invitation for which some had not waited.

Here was a campaign with political confusion worse confounded. Democrats-for-Willkie and No-Third-Term Democrats opposed Republicans-for-Roosevelt and Business-Men-for-Roosevelt with earnestness as well as money. President Green of the A. F. of L. supported Roosevelt; Lewis of the CIO endorsed Willkie. For masters of the radio it was a gala campaign, with each side featuring popular favorites. Young people and women were far more active than ever before and no expense was spared. The Hatch Act, with its expenditure limits of $3,000,000 for each national committee and $5,000 for individual gifts to that committee, was widely evaded by resourceful men and women who spread their gifts and loans among state committees for national purposes, raising total expenditure above $40,000,000.

Willkie made a whirlwind campaign which at first President Roosevelt ignored. While the Republican candidate promised to maintain the chief New Deal benefits to the farmer and to labor and to preserve social security, he would also restore much of the Old Deal. He exhorted the voters to a crusade to fight the "Battle of America." He would preserve the America of free enterprise against a government that cried scarcity, preached despair and throttled initiative by excessive regulation and taxation. The voters must not invite dictatorship by abandoning the "no-third-term" tradition.

His campaign and the results of straw-votes alarmed the Democrats. President Roosevelt, who had confined his campaigning chiefly to a few "defense inspection" tours, late in October took the stump in several eastern centers and at Cleveland. He dwelt on his achievements and the need of aid for Britain and accused the Republicans of obstructing defense. The Republican campaign he characterized as an alliance of the foes of the average man, and he called the voters to continue their march toward the vision of a new day. All this excitement, denunciation and outlay was followed November 7 by the peaceful casting of approximately 49 million votes: 27 million for the victor Roosevelt, and some 22 million for Willkie, besides a few small tallies for the minor parties which the main conflict had relegated to shadowy obscurity.

Careful analysis of the voting shows that had it not been for foreign diversions, the election would have fairly tested majority opinion on conservative and liberal principles, for the basic Republican appeal was to property, and the Democrats stood on the New Deal. Outside of the South (which Willkie made no attempt to electrify), the election revealed that Roosevelt's regrouping of voting classes had prevented restoration of old party lines. No longer was any state "safe," for they revealed similar politico-economic cross-sectioning, before which the stoutest state political machine well may quail. One-third of Roosevelt's former support in the upper-income and business groups left him. He retained the majority of labor and low-income votes, and he won the lion's share of unattached voters—those just of age and those formerly not in the habit of voting. He carried all but ten states.

Willkie's tally was significant for at least three reasons. He polled the largest popular vote ever given a defeated candidate; he obtained 45 per cent of the total, largely on an appeal to "restore freedom of enterprise"; and he did these things despite the fact that he also deserted his platform on diplomacy. His pledges of aid to Britain left isolationists little to choose between him and Roosevelt.

In the last analysis Hitler's Blitzkrieg decided the election of 1940; many an opponent of the New Deal supported the experienced political executive as preferable to the utilities attorney in dealing with international uncertainties. The people of the United States had conducted an orderly election under established rules of democracy. They had entrusted the victor in it with the task of defending democracy against totalitarianism.

CHAPTER L

PREPARATION

President Roosevelt's reëlection in 1940 had indeed assigned him the task of defending the Democracy against aggression; but defense involves preparation. The scope and type of his preparation were restricted as long as the majority believed neutrality need not necessarily be abandoned. Preparations would expand as the belief was relinquished. Post-election preparation for war had four main aspects: (1) economic warfare, carried on both in international trade and on the home front, (2) stepping up production, (3) preparation of armed forces and (4) diplomatic policy. In all four fields the defense legislation of 1939-1940 merged into belligerency in 1941.

Economic Warfare Before Pearl Harbor

The program of economic warfare, as applied in the field of international trade, had been designed originally as a substitute for military conflict. As difficulties developed, it was so extended into preparation for a "shooting" war that by late 1941 every foreign business transaction had been placed under some form of control "in the national interest." The program gave the nation an economic preparedness at least one year ahead of her preparedness in April of 1917. This advantage had been gained largely through two years of experiment with six weapons of economic warfare: (1) fund-freezing, (2) black-listing, (3) strategic purchasing, (4) export licensing, (5) lend-lease aid and (6) shipping control.

Fund-freezing had begun by executive order in April 1940 when Germany invaded Denmark and Norway. Funds pertaining to those areas and located in the United States were "frozen" to protect their owners from seizure of them by the invaders, and release of them required a license. Blocking of funds spread with the areas invaded, but assets of the invaders were by request of the State Department left unfrozen. This enabled Germany, Italy and Japan to finance propaganda and shipments, to move funds around and to purchase interests in United States firms abroad. Finally the barn door was locked after most of the horses were stolen; executive orders of June 1941 froze assets of all European states not frozen earlier. Following Japan's advance into Indo-China, her assets were also frozen; as Britain and the

Netherlands East Indies followed suit, Japan's export and import trade dried up. She felt severely the denial of access to aluminum, copper, lead, scrap iron and zinc. Blocking of Axis assets marked a shift from defensive to aggressive use of the fund-freezing weapon.

In fund-freezing, as in most other aspects of our economic warfare, the peculiar importance of Latin America in United States diplomacy quickly became evident. The freezing orders imposed heavy penalties for trading with nationals of any of the blocked states, wherever resident; and a large number of the Latin American leaders in banking, commerce and industry were nationals of the blocked nations or had Axis connections. United States exporters could scarcely determine which Latin American orders came from authentic natives and which from blocked sources. Trade and the "good neighbor" policy of the State Department were injured.

Black-listing, begun in July 1941, was the shield chosen to safeguard the fund-freezing weapon as applied to Latin America. The President began issuance of black-lists showing firms and persons believed to have German or Italian connections, and he forbade shipment of controlled exports to them. A gray-list was added to cover suspects pending investigation, while transactions with those not listed were permitted under an export license. Japanese firms were not black-listed until after Pearl Harbor. The lists put Inter-American trade on crutches, causing evasion, hardship and anger; but they helped to uncover the enemy. By midsummer of 1942 an Inter-American Committee was arranging uniform controls over Axis funds in this hemisphere.

Strategic purchasing was a weapon which was not well sharpened until Pearl Harbor brought painful awareness of a dearth of indispensable raw products. Fifteen months earlier Roosevelt had requested United States business men to end reëxport of strategic materials, but the speculators had not joined the regular traders in general obedience. The Army and Navy Munitions Board had long preached the necessity for stockpiles; and after their demands were reinforced by urgent OPM recommendations Congress finally made important purchasing possible. The act of 25 June 1940 authorized the RFC to form subsidiary corporations (which became the Metals Reserve Company, Rubber Reserves Company and Defense Supplies Corporation) for a program of acquisition of important stockpiles; price ceilings, however, robbed the act of much of its effectiveness. A broader act was passed the next year. Surplus buying began immediately in rubber, tin, tungsten, copper and platinum through contracts chiefly with the Far East, except for copper mainly from Latin America. The list lengthened. Unfortunately, bad management resulted in a stockpile fiasco. For strategic materials from distant ports that lay far beyond assured

United States control, a more aggressive policy was needed to assure adequate reserves. Too late the administration realized the colossal error.

Preclusive buying, aimed at forestalling Axis purchases, became an important branch of the strategic materials program beginning in May 1941. There began negotiation of overall agreements, principally with Latin American states. They forbade vendors to export except to the United States, to other American republics with satisfactory export control, or to Great Britain in some cases, our government agreeing to buy certain surpluses. The strategic purchasing program became world-wide, including nearly all the primary products in world trade. It ultimately led the United States into setting up with Britain a combined Raw Material Board for joint purchasing and caused heavy United States outlays in remote vendor areas for the improvement of production and transportation facilities.

Export licensing was a weapon used with more effectiveness than strategic purchasing. It began in earnest after the fall of France and the bombing of Britain early in 1940 aroused administration apprehensions. The Licensing Act of 2 July 1940 empowered the President to "prohibit or curtail" export of various materials useful in the manufacture of munitions, by means of granting or withholding export licenses; the system by December of 1941 embraced all but about 4 per cent of our exports. It was thoroughly integrated with our foreign policy. Exports to neutral areas like Spain and French North Africa were licensed in periods when the State Department hoped to turn foreign diplomatic policy.

Latin America again posed a difficult problem. She now had plenty of dollars with which to pay for imports because of our heavy purchases of her copper, wool and other products, and she resented her failure to get more liberal licensing. United States manufacturers, on the other hand, resented issuance of licenses for export of priority materials which they themselves were not allowed in plenty and which the foreign recipients could utilize without local priority restrictions. Our government thereupon promised equal treatment of domestic and Latin American users of priority materials. This placed civilian processors in both hemispheres where they received the remainders after the needs of the United States and of lend-lease had been met. As this sometimes meant no remainders Latin American buyers requested and obtained an "allocation" system, assuring them of fixed quotas of some commodities.

Economic warfare against the Axis reached a peak in the welding of the weapon of lend-lease by the act of 11 March 1941. It empowered the President to authorize any agency of the government to sell, transtransfer title, exchange, lease, lend or otherwise dispose of "any defense article for the government of any country whose defense the President deems vital to the defense of the United States." The term "defense article" was defined to include nearly anything; but procurement was limited to funds made available or contracts authorized by Congress, with procurement and payment the duty of the United States. On ultimate payment the law is a masterpiece of ambiguity, stating that "the terms under which any government receives aid shall be those satisfactory to the President" and the benefit to the United States may be payment or repayment "in kind or property, or any other direct or indirect benefit which the President deems satisfactory." Great Britain and thirty-two other countries were declared eligible for lend-lease aid. The more than 30 billion dollars of aid authorized by Congress up to June of 1942 went chiefly to the British Empire, with smaller amounts to Russia, China, Latin America and lesser powers.

Control of shipping developed when a shortage reached alarming proportions early in 1941. Legal ground for seizing foreign-owned ships lying idle in our harbors was afforded when Italian and German crews committed acts of sabotage on their vessels. Congress by law of 10 June 1941 empowered the President to use all idle foreign-owned ships for our merchant marine. This added comparatively little to the urgently needed tonnage; and the largest of the foreign ships, the French *Normandie,* was very badly damaged by fire through careless workmen converting her to our purposes. The far greater tonnage in United States-owned ships was commandeered through a Ship Warrants Act of 14 July; it required all vessels to have "priority" warrants from the Maritime Commission for the use of indispensable port facilities which automatically established federal control over their use. Most important was a vast ship-building program which after Pearl Harbor reached the proportions of 8 million deadweight tons of merchant ships for 1942 and 15 million for 1943. As will shortly be seen, steel shortages, naval building and submarine attacks complicated the transport problem.

Altogether, the restrictions upon trade, finance and communications set in motion before 7 December 1941 included some very formidable weapons. Thereafter Roosevelt, by invoking the 1917 Trading with the Enemy Act, was enabled to wield them more directly and forcefully.

Stepping Up Production

On the home front, meanwhile, domestic corollaries of economic warfare were put in operation. The accent was on defense. The Office of Production Management for Defense (OPM) was set up by Roosevelt 20 December 1940 with a four-man board. They were to administer actual production for war and defense, supervise equipment purchasing, decide what defense commodities should have priority in production, take over non-coöperating plants and allocate supplies as between the United States and Britain.

Strikes proved a very serious "bottleneck" in production, clogging the flow of ships, steel, ordnance, airplanes and other war material. Labor leaders were determined that the emergency should not weaken the prerogatives of their organizations, and management in some cases hoped to use the emergency to undermine the closed shop. The government with extreme difficulty sought the answer. The President tried various expedients. He appointed 19 March 1941 an eleven-person National Defense Mediation Board (NDMB) with three members representing the public, four labor and four management. They were to mediate defense industry strikes after the conciliation service of the Labor Department certified strikes to them.

Strikes continued, however. On 27 May the President declared an unlimited national emergency, supplementing a limited emergency proclaimed the previous September. This gave him technical control over labor and management and other elements in national life and expanded his authority to quell strikes and suppress subversive activities. He emphasized this move by making a declaration against defense strikes in a world broadcast before a distinguished audience. Thereupon the A. F. of L. executive council and some CIO leaders asked their memberships to defer defense strikes until conciliation was exhausted. Still striking persisted, with and without consent of union leaders. Sometimes CIO labor struck against the hiring of A. F. of L. labor; some strikebreakers struck against the re-hiring of strikers; some CIO groups pushed strikes outlawed by their own union heads. After the A. F. of L. was promised a monopoly of defense housing by Hillman, it struck against the use of prefabricated houses because the saving in time meant fewer employees.

Wages of labor rose, unemployment decreased and unionization advanced. Capital and workers suffered more than the labor organizations. The main loser seemed to be the worried public. The administration in a few cases used the army or navy department to take temporary control over idle plants; again, it refused to do this in some cases where labor desired it. The eight-hour day and some other peacetime restrictions on employment were suspended in the case of public defense works. Also, defense workers on strike were deprived of draft deferment.

One of the most important labor disputes came to a head in October. John L. Lewis, president of the United Mine Workers, ex-president of the CIO and a bitter opponent of Roosevelt since 1937, now defied him. He ordered a coal strike to make the "captive" coal mines, those operated by the steel companies for their own use, completely closed shop. He ignored two Roosevelt requests that he send the miners back and refused compliance with a third request. The NDMB rejected Lewis' proposition; and in chilly November the situation grew ugly. Roosevelt refused to order the closed shop and asked first that the issue be waived for the duration and second that management and labor promise to accept arbitration on it. They finally did so. An arbitral board consisting of Lewis, J. R. Steelman, head of the conciliator service of the Labor Department, and Benjamin Fairless, president of United States Steel, voted 2 to 1 for the closed shop; Lewis meanwhile promised there would be no more coal strikes before 1 April 1943.

Blame for the delay in fitting labor into the national defense picture was variously apportioned. Many citizens charged the strikes to racketeering and subversive activities, especially after lawsuits exposed outrageous political and financial practices by some union leaders. It was alleged that United States labor organizations now have an annual income of at least $500 million on which no taxes are paid or public accounting made. Various members of Congress introduced anti-strike bills which neither management, labor nor the administration wished to see enacted. Some senators and representatives made their support of Roosevelt's foreign policy contingent upon a firmer labor policy. The basic difficulty was threefold. There could be no united responsibility assumed by labor as long as two great rival groups existed, each free to fight each other, management and the government in its own way. Management leaders also failed to evolve a program with a chance of success. Furthermore, the administration delayed formulation of a consistent, understandable labor policy.

While the administration struggled with labor difficulties it worked also to secure control of strategic materials; priority and allocations powers were desired. First it had control over the order of filling army and navy contracts; then a Mandatory Priorities Act of 2 June 1941 gave it authority over the order of delivery of materials and machines under lend-lease. The OPM decreed priorities on such things as steel, iron, rubber, silk and automobiles; and Congress authorized the President to requisition defense materials. Among the new agencies were two others of great importance: an Office of Price Administration and Civilian Supply, headed by Leon Henderson, and an Office of the Coördinator of Commercial and Cultural Relations with Latin America, under a grandson of Senator Aldrich and of John D. Rockefeller, Nelson A. Rockefeller

As agencies multiplied and insisted upon diversion of materials to various priorities, chaotic conditions arose. To clarify matters Roosevelt set up 28 August 1941 the Supply Priorities and Allocations Board (SPAB) under Donald Nelson, executive vice-president of Sears Roebuck. This super-agency was to fix priorities and allocate supplies of all things essential to defense and civilian needs. There began a series of orders restricting and eventually ending various sorts of civilian manufacture and involving conversion of plants to war needs. Some concerns pooled their facilities on assurance from the Department of Justice and OPM that they should not be held liable under the anti-trust laws; but the existence of the statutes restricted contract makers. When Japan declared war, United States output in airplanes, tanks and ships had reached a point far higher than the strike headlines would have led one to expect.

Production of food, however, did not reach extraordinary proportions. There were still huge surpluses in storage accumulated under the AAA; and the realization that lend-lease and a shooting war might bring food shortages came very slowly. As late as May 1941 the farm lobby still considered the market too weak to ensure a fair income. Therefore the Crop Loan Act signed 26 May gave growers of wheat, corn, cotton, tobacco and rice the right to government loans up to 85 per cent of "parity"—parity being the purchasing power of non-farm commodities averaged for the period between August 1909 and July 1914. Farmers well remembered the bitter hardships of the last post-war slump; they would not again expand without legislation to safeguard their comparative status.

The large and rapid increase in industrial production for lend-lease and defense dislocated the price structure. Therefore control of prices to avoid inflation became another important job in the preparation for war. Limitations on instalment credit, on the price of raw sugar, on gasoline in the East and on anthracite coal were essayed by the President and the OPM but did not go very far. Bernard Baruch warned that experience in the First World War indicated a need for a price control law without exceptions, but Henderson urged partial control, with wages unaffected. Objections of labor and agriculture to a brake on rising wages and farm prices killed the chances for "overall" legislation. Prices rose rapidly. This worked particular hardship on the treasury. Congress by 26 December 1941 had appropriated more than 78 billions for preparedness, with the cost of particular items on it rising steeply. The sale of "defense" stamps and bonds, begun May 1941, was pushed as hard as consistent with non-compulsory buying; and after five months of debate, Congress in September passed the largest single revenue act to date. It added new excise and nuisance levies, an automobile "use tax" of $5 and higher corporation levies. Income tax exemptions were lowered and the rates raised; this increased the number of persons liable by about 5 million and more than doubled the levy on $10,000 incomes.

Military Preparations

In military preparations Pearl Harbor found the United States unready, although recent military advance had progressed considerable distance. The navy's status was:

	In Service	*Under Construction*
Battleships	17	15
Aircraft carriers	7	11
Cruisers	37	54
Destroyers	172	191
Submarines	113	73
Airplanes	5,000	15,000

Its personnel had been somewhat enlarged by a Knox order in July directing that naval reservists be retained for emergency purposes. A navy arrangement with the colleges enabled students who could meet the requirements for naval enlistment, to enlist, continue their college work and receive commissions later. This helped to meet the demand for officers, badly needed throughout the expanding military services.

The army did not enter the college field in like manner until 1942, although the R.O.T.C. originally established in 1918 began vigorous expansion in 1940. Congress in 1941 both strengthened and weakened the army program. The Selective Service Act of 1940 had stipulated that not more than 900,000 men, aged 21 to 36, should be under training simultaneously. Approximately 700,000 had been inducted by August; then Congress eliminated the 900,000 limitation and extended training from twelve months to a possible thirty, but provided for the deferment of men over 28. Some 200,000 draftees were selected for release during the second half of the year, on the grounds of dependents, hardship or for having fulfilled one year's training. In December the army numbered 1.6 million officers and men. In aviation the army had shown noteworthy foresight, for the air cargo service it established to help supply its depots was by 1940 carrying more than all commercial lines together; the navy did not create similar service until 1942.

In civilian aviation there were 100,000 active pilots, few compared with Germany and Japan, but an improvement over the 23,000 of early 1939 when Germany had 250,000 active plus 2.5 million in reserve. This rise was due largely to the zeal of Robert H. Hinckley, member of the Civilian Aeronautics Authority 1938-1940 and assistant secretary of commerce for air thereafter. Concluding that aviation had dictated the Munich Pact and was growing in stature every day, he led a crusade to teach American youth that they must live on a sphere without isolation, because aviation had destroyed the geographical distance on which isolationism was based. He pointed out that a whole generation of Germans had been pumped full of the doctrine of the German superman enslaving other peoples and had been taught from the sixth grade up that aviation was the means to enforce that doctrine. In 1934 when Henry Ford abandoned manufacture of tri-motor freight transports, the Germans were starting their production of them. Congress as late as 1937 refused to subsidize air freighters and public interest remained tepid. German glider clubs in those years were winning the battles in

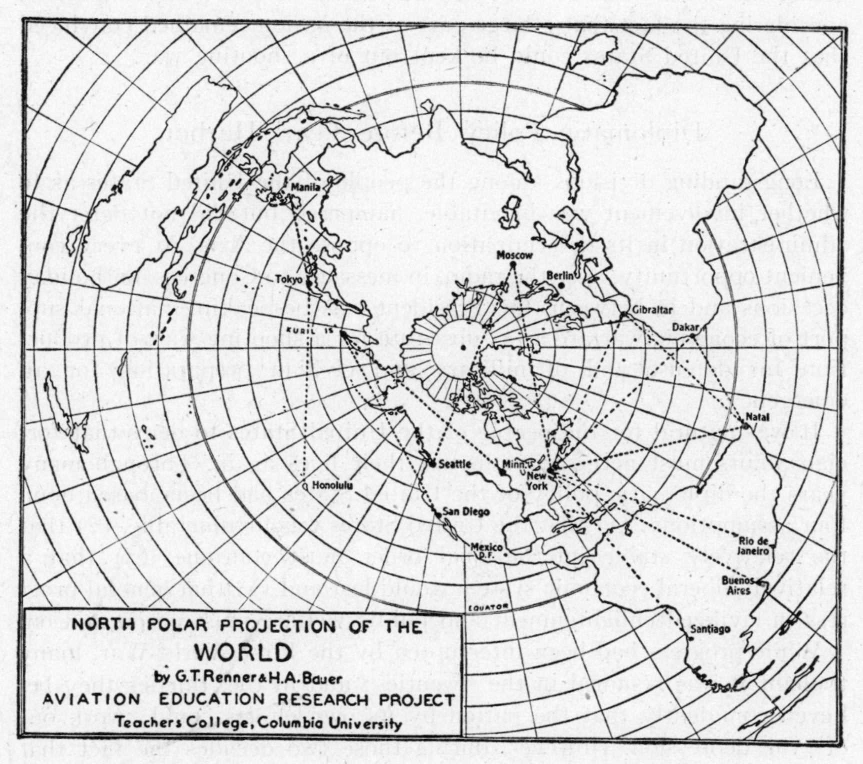

The dotted lines suggest some of the ways in which aviation can revolutionize world transit; for example, careful measurement shows that Tokyo is a little nearer to Minneapolis than to San Diego.

(Reprinted by permission.)

the war to come. By the time of Pearl Harbor the CAA had established aeronautics instruction at about 700 colleges.

Outside the army and navy an undetermined number of civilians, including approximately 215,000 air raid wardens, 5,500 volunteers for emergency food and housing and none knew how many auxiliary police and firemen, had been signed up by an Office of Civilian Defense (OCD), established at Washington in May 1941. OCD ultimately put most stress upon its protective services performed by six main groups. These are the firemen, policemen, air raid wardens (who had jurisdiction over emergency food and housing), public works units charged with repair, demolition and decontamination jobs and a utilities unit assigned to communications, light, power and water. The groundwork for part of OCD had been well laid by the Red Cross, which also included in its 1941 expansion a trained motor corps of women. Altogether the mlitary and civilian preparation for defense was remarkable, considering the fact that a large part of the nation remained convinced that the United States could be kept out of a shooting war.

Diplomatic Policy Before Pearl Harbor

Longstanding divisions among the people of the United States as to whether involvement was inevitable, hampered but did not deter the administration in its determination to oppose the Axis. At every convenient opportunity, over the radio, in messages to Congress, on holiday occasions and in between, the President was bespeaking national support of economic warfare as a substitute for a shooting war, of production for defense and of military and civilian preparation for an emergency.

It was natural for the people of the United States to deny that foreign affairs must necessarily disrupt their lives again. Through many years the diplomatic policy of the United States had been based upon four assumptions: (1) that the United States was invulnerable, (2) that the relatively stable international order must continue, (3) that a relatively liberal economic system would last and (4) that general progress in civilized enlightenment and public welfare must go on and on.

While progress had been interrupted by the First World War, many thought it was resumed in the 'twenties; and in the 'thirties they believed confidently that the nation by its own efforts could "work out of" the depression. However, during those two decades the fact that diplomatic policy clung to the old assumptions was making this power vulnerable and was proving a great advantage to aggressor powers. They were perfecting a military and naval technology upsetting the assumptions. As aviation developed, maintenance of the post-war European balance of power became important to American security; but only a small group at first realized it.

As the Second World War took its course the phenomenal success of the Axis increased the number of American interventionists. They advanced from the stage of emphasizing aid to Britain to that of ringing alarms for the safety of the United States—from "all aid short of war" to war. These "warmongers" as the isolationists described them, came to support the President's diplomatic policy, although many of them were Republicans. Organizing a Committee to Aid the Allies, a Bundles for Britain group and various others, they acquired wide propaganda influence. Refugees representing various fugitive governments applauded their efforts. The fact that they had close relations with British agents in the United States and were endorsed by some arms manufacturers made them doubly suspect to the isolationists. Opposing speakers on foreign policy went to violent extremes in mutual denunciation. As interventionists gained weight the isolationists charged unfair discrimination on the part of the press, the movies and the radio.

The isolationists also attracted adherents of divers political complexions. From the Democrats came Senators Walsh of Massachusetts, Wheeler of Montana and Clark of Missouri; from the conservative Republicans came Senator Taft of Ohio and Representative Fish of New York; from the independent Republicans came Senator Nye of North Dakota and ex-Governor Philip La Follette of Wisconsin. Support from some German-born Americans, some praise from Berlin, and ill-advised advocacy from the radio-priest, Father Charles E. Coughlin of the Church of the Little Flower, hampered the isolationists. Two sincere believers in isolationism, Charles A. Lindbergh and his wife, the former Anne Morrow, lost much of the popularity they had won for their aviation pioneering by warm espousal of isolation. After Hitler turned to attack Russia, 28 June 1941, many anti-Communists shrugged their shoulders and said, "Let them kill each other off; it'll be a good riddance."

Gradually Americans were questioning whether the old assumptions still protected them. Some of them were reading about an unfamiliar doctrine called "geopolitics," of late described in the magazines. Geopolitics appeared to be a diabolical plan for turning the New World, as well as the Old, upside down. It was presented as an involved body of theories, originating in divers countries through several centuries and given partial expression in Pan-Germanism before World War I. It added up to the doctrine that a nation's survival hangs upon its expansion into adequate life-giving space, "lebensraum," and that empires have always been the achievement of interior, continental peoples pushing out littoral, oceanic peoples. Interior nations can thrust out in all directions from their central resources because they possess "security in depth." They have resources so vast and so available as to assure self-sufficiency and easy aggrandizement. Each continent was bound to be ruled by the power holding the "heartland": a Pan-German, a Pan-Asiatic and a Pan-American superstate. In this scheme Great Britain, France, Spain, the Lowlands and of course all buffer states must fall victims to their undesirable location, especially in terms of modern warfare.

The leading apostle of geopolitics appeared presently to be Major General Karl Haushofer, who had taught military subjects to the Germans and Japanese and had communicated his philosophy to Hitler through Rudolph Hess. Chapter XXIV of *Mein Kampf,* embodying Hitler's version of lebensraum, was said to have been thus inspired. As editor of a monthly periodical, *Zeitschrift für Geopolitik,* and as head of the Geopolitical Institute at Munich, Haushofer was regularly supplying the Nazis with meticulous details on all countries, their strength, weakness and the right moment to overrun them. The mandate of geopolitics was that nothing could be allowed to obstruct the need of the superstate for space, neither religion, cultural aspirations, social institutions, historic traditions nor reverence for human life; and certainly the Nazis were showing no reverence.

This structure of political theory, erected upon a geographic base, posited the kind of world which the average American had no desire to see realized. Yet Hitler, and perhaps Japan, seemed on the way to realizing it. The spring of 1941 had brought more German successses. After an heroic effort to withstand Axis pressure, Jugoslavia was conquered in a twelve-day blitzkrieg, and Greece soon met a like fate; the vulnerability of these areas had long since been carefully explained by the staff of the Institute. Britain's spring offensive largely failed. Worse, her shipping losses reached a new high. German submarines and airplanes were scouring wider reaches of water and air. Britain under lend-lease now had ample resources available in the United States; but could she transport them safely overseas?

The government of the United States sought to protect shipping by various means. Besides operating the bases earlier secured from Britain, she took over the protection of Greenland by agreement 9 April with the minister of Denmark, who still remained in Washington. President Roosevelt removed the Red Sea from the status of a combat zone, as this was required under the neutrality law before American vessels could transport supplies around the Cape of Good Hope to Suez, and two weeks later the navy was ordered to extend its control across a "safety-zone" which included a large part of the Atlantic lanes used by the supply ships.

Intensification of the battle of the Atlantic meant increasing danger of a clash between German submarines and American shipping. June 9 brought word of the first sinking; the *Robin Moor,* an American freighter, had been sunk in the South Atlantic far outside any war zone. Early in July the President announced a wide extension of patrolling. The United States had garrisoned Iceland and it became apparent that the navy had relieved the British of patrol duty to within 700 miles of Scotland.

Meanwhile the tensity of the war situation had tightened tremendously. At 4 A.M. on 22 June Germany had suddenly begun an invasion 2,000 miles wide across the frontier of her erstwhile ally, Russia. With terrifying speed her blitzkrieg swept deep into Russia; Stalin turned to

Britain and the United States. Within a month he had from the one a declaration of military alliance and from the other a pledge of lend-lease aid. Japan was proceeding to complicate the situation. She had signed a Moscow Pact of April 1941 in which she and Russia pledged themselves to respect each other's territory and to maintain neutrality in any conflict as between either of them and third powers. This left Russia free from Japanese support of Germany and left Japan free from Russian interference with her Asiatic version of geopolitics. Japan's "new order" insisted upon her right to promote what she termed "the co-prosperity sphere of Greater East Asia." In mid-1941 she was widening her Chinese conquests and proceeding southwards into French Indo-China. She took control of its exports in June and obtained military sway in July. Roosevelt met Japan's advance with a fund-freezing decree and with an order absorbing the Philippine army into that of the United States.

Roosevelt and Churchill called for world support, issuing a 1941 appeal reminiscent of Wilson's "Fourteen Points." They met early in August in a "quiet bay" off the North American shore. Here they proclaimed the "Atlantic Charter," an eight-point program reiterating the ideals of democratic nationalism as a counter-foil to the Nazi superstate program. Their Charter declared that (1) the United Nations seek no aggrandizement, (2) boundaries should change only in response to the "freely expressed will of the peoples concerned," (3) self-government must be restored, (4) all must have access on equal terms to trade and raw materials, (5) economic collaboration must achieve improved labor standards and social security for all, (6) the peace must make all nations free from fear and want, (7) all must have freedom to traverse the seas, (8) force must be abandoned for a wider and permanent system of international security. Simultaneously, Roosevelt and Churchill pledged aid to Russia and gave notice to Japan that further aggression must cease.

Those were brave words in the Atlantic Charter, but they did not improve the safety of shipping. Early in September the United States destroyer *Greer,* carrying mail to Iceland, was attacked by a submarine (although without damage) on the American side of the Atlantic. Several days later the Navy Department released the news that the freighter *Sessa,* operated by the United States Maritime Commission under Panamanian registry, had been sunk with loss of life including one United States citizen. Thereupon the President announced that American warships had been ordered to "shoot at sight" if German attack seemed imminent. Secretary of the Navy Knox shortly revealed that United States vessels were convoying merchantmen. Consequences followed hard in October. The United States destroyer *Kearny* while off the coast of Iceland was hit and lost eleven of her crew; referring to this in his Navy Day speech of 27 October Roosevelt said: "The shooting has started." Three days later the destroyer *Reuben James,* on convoy duty, was sunk. The Atlantic progression from attacks to hits had culminated in a sinking. Defense work was speeded apace.

Meanwhile negotiations with Japan were approaching a Pacific crisis. She was still looking southward. The British and Dutch colonies in Malaya and the East Indies, indispensable sources of rubber, tin, valuable oils and other raw materials, were ill fixed to repel attack, and so were the Philippines. The President, however, had refused to abandon aid to China or otherwise tolerate Japan's version of the "new order." When Roosevelt and Churchill issued their warning of early August to Japan, they knew the vulnerability of the East Indies, but authorities differed as to whether Japan could afford to fight the United States or would prove a formidable foe. Negotiations seemed at an impasse. Yet Japan had a peace party which still was offering effective opposition to the rising militarist party there, and her premier, the liberal Prince Konoe, as late as 28 August caused a personal letter to be handed to Roosevelt opening the way for further negotiations; the President omitted explicit reference to Japan in his Labor Day speech condemning aggressors.

October and November brought a rise in war feeling in both countries. Prince Konoe resigned in October and was succeeded by a renowned militarist, General Tojo, who sent to the United States a special envoy known as "the trouble-shooter," identified with the peace group, Saburo Kurusu, to join their ambassador, Admiral Nomura, in the conduct of negotiations. On 10 November Britain pledged herself to stand by the United States in case of attack. Kurusu reached Washington the 15th. Two days later the United States was admitting the abandonment of what was left of neutrality. After a bitter debate between isolationists and interventionists of the two parties, a debate which conclusively showed that the nation was not united behind aid to Britain, Congress repealed sections 2, 3, and 6 of the Neutrality Act of 1939. Those sections had forbidden United States vessels to arm, to enter combat zones or to carry passengers or materials to belligerent states. The repeal was at once followed by openly doing the formerly forbidden acts. Also Roosevelt now sent troops to Dutch Guiana, a world-famous source of aluminum, to prevent Axis access to it.

Warlike acts increased, while neither side showed signs of retreat. United States proposals of 26 November insisted that Japan withdraw her troops from China and Indo-China, abandon aggression and adhere to a peaceful economic policy; these proposals were duly despatched to Tokyo. During the next two days the marines were embarked from Shanghai for the Philippines, and word was reaching Washington that Japan was sending heavy reinforcements into Indo-China. Concerning these the President on 2 December demanded an explanation from Japan. She replied that her troops were designed solely as a protection against the Chinese and on 5 December Tojo gave out assurances that negotiations would go on.

Quite unconvinced, the President next day sent a personal appeal to the Japanese Emperor to join him in maintaining the peace. The day following, 7 December, Nomura and Kurusu asked at one o'clock for an appointment to submit their government's reply to the proposals of 26 November. At 2:15 they handed Secretary Hull a document in effect refusing to make concessions and accusing the United States of plotting with Great Britain against Japan. Diplomacy at last had reached the breaking point. Isolation had been thoroughly undermined; only the explosion awaited.

THE SECOND WORLD WAR

1939-

CHAPTER LI

THE UNITED STATES ENTERS THE SECOND WORLD WAR

The explosion came. Almost at the instant that Nomura and Kurusu were handing Secretary Hull their government's rejection of American proposals, the President received unbelievable news from Hawaii which catapulted the United States into the war.

The Stimulus of Disaster

A carrier armada which must have been planned at least a week earlier had descended upon Pearl Harbor, Hawaii, where the United States had concentrated the might of her Pacific naval and air force. The enemy caught the base in all the somnolence of an early Sunday morning, excellent for golf. Although relations with Japan were known to be full of tension, the fact that negotiations were still in progress evidently had lulled the commanding officers into proceeding as if all were sweetness and light. None was alert. A non-commissioned officer who reported the sound of an air armada was reassured. Planes and warships were left quietly moored, neatly arrayed in rows shining and bright. The Japanese bombers, taking off from aircraft carriers and fueled with American gasoline, easily destroyed a great part of the Pearl Harbor armament and ended the lives of three thousand Americans. Almost simultaneously they were using land-based planes, which are more effective than carrier-based planes, to attack other strategic points in the Philippines, Malaya and Thailand, besides Hong Kong and the United States possessions of Guam and Wake Island, which were ultimately captured.

Congress assembled next day to hear President Roosevelt describe the "day of infamy" and speedily declared the existence of war forced upon the United States by Japan. Great Britain did likewise; and nine of the more northerly Latin American states followed suit, although Mexico delayed until 1 May. Various "governments in exile," the Free French, Netherlands and Greece, joined the United Nations later. On 11 December, Japan's allies, Germany and Italy, declared war on the United States, and signed a pledge with Japan not to make a separate peace with either the United States or Britain. The same day the United States declared war on Germany and Italy. Two days later the Axis satellites, Bulgaria, Hungary, and Rumania, declared war on the United States; but she did not reply in kind until the next June, when Russian lend-lease negotiations were pending.

The war effort was under severe handicaps. The main trouble was that the Axis powers were expertly prepared and acting on the offensive according to well-laid plans. Then there were so many fronts—all distant, in Europe, Africa, Australia, Asia, Alaska and innumerable remote islands. The advantages of Haushofer's ideal superstate—the comparatively short, interior lines reaching out from a convenient heartland—were possessed by the enemy, by Germany and Japan. The United States had instead a one-ocean navy scattered over seven seas with lines of communication as long as 8,000 miles; she stood committed to the most difficult task in the history of the world—to colossal effort to spread herself over the entire globe. Plans for the initial movement had been painstakingly made, at the ports, on the railroads and over sea and air channels; the result was that within the first three weeks of the war more than 600,000 American troops were despatched under naval escort, through submarine-infested waters, to battle stations scattered over six continents. This vanguard must be reinforced by others, continually maintained, equipped and directed.

American attention centered first on the Far East, where Japan was moving down the corridor between the Pacific Islands and China toward Australia and India, seizing control of mainland and islands on each side, en route. The Philippines, the Indies, Singapore and Burma around the bend of the continent were all part of Japan's carefully planned schemes. Conditions favored control by her of both sea and air in the corridor region. Her German ally had earlier disposed of two proud battleships, a battle cruiser and three huge carriers of the British navy, in European waters.[1] Using cheap bombers and submarines to supplement their battleships and carriers, the Axis had early perfected the technique of swiftly sinking costly enemy battleships. Now Japanese aircraft, within three days after Pearl Harbor, sent to the bottom of the South China Sea another giant British battleship and a cruiser, *H.M.S. Prince of Wales* and *H.M.S. Repulse.* As Japan's surprise air attacks upon Hawaii and the Philippines had sunk also the *U.S.S. Arizona* and *U.S.S. Oklahoma,* besides severely damaging other ships and destroying most of the army and navy air forces in the Hawaiian area, Japan's sea advance met no effective obstacles.

Likewise, on land, flooded rice fields and thick jungles, supposed by some British admirals and generals to be impenetrable, were quickly "infiltrated" by Nipponese warriors: thrusting through Thailand down to the tip of Malaya and pushing the British off the deep end, at the

[1] *H.M.S. Barham, Royal Oak, Hood, Courageous, Glorious* and *Ark Royal.*

CHURCHILL AND ROOSEVELT AT THE WHITE HOUSE

Conferring with United States, British and Filipino leaders

lost by reverses in Asia and in Africa. To help that same morale Roosevelt in April of 1942 had had Captain James Doolittle lead sixteen bombers from the carrier *Hornet* in a raid over military objectives at Tokyo, Yokohama, Kobe and Nagoya. It was wildly cheered—in America.

In Africa Germany's brilliant master of armored forces in desert warfare, Marshal Erwin Rommel, was trying to reach the Suez Canal from the west. Once beaten back to El Agheila, Libya, he regained the offensive, advancing 800 miles to within sixty-five miles of Alexandria, Egypt. Here, too, the supply question loomed. He had to get some of his supplies over 1,000 miles of desert from the Italian port of Tripoli and some by air across the Mediterranean. The British generals—since Axis submarines and planes took terrific toll in the Mediterranean—had to get most of theirs 14,000 miles by sea around Africa. Thus the United Nations during the black winter of 1941-1942 learned how the "interior lines," dear to Haushofer's philosophy, gave certain advantages to the Germans, the Japanese and, temporarily, to the Russians. They learned it the hard way, through setbacks and losses, through blood and tears.

Organizing for Victory

The teachings of Pearl Harbor, Bataan, the South China Sea, Russia and Africa were bitter lessons to learn. The greatest lesson taught by the Axis victories was coördination; in modern warfare unity of sea, land and air direction, and pooling of supplies are indispensable to success. Lack of coördination had been reported from Pearl Harbor, and charges of military ineffectiveness were rife in London and Washington. Over the ashes of repeated defeat rose the dreary wail, "Too little and too late."

Coördination was most difficult for the United Nations because vast distances stretch between them, and between their main theatres of war. Two weeks after Pearl Harbor, Prime Minister Churchill visited Washington—bringing leading members of the British army, navy and air forces—to lay plans. The visit was repeated six months later, and in January 1943 Roosevelt, Churchill and military advisors spent two weeks conferring in Casablanca, French Morocco. Key officials used airplanes to shuttle between Washington and London continually, Chungking and Moscow occasionally. The United States had the hardest problem of coördination, for Tojo was thousands of miles from Hitler.

To achieve unity the United States sponsored numerous boards, commissions and committees; their broad reach is revealed by the following list of the more important ones.

JOINT BOARDS, COMMISSIONS AND COMMITTEES BETWEEN THE UNITED STATES AND OTHER GOVERNMENTS

1. Seven with Great Britain, integrating policies concerning the Caribbean, chiefs of staff, food, Middle East, munitions, raw materials and shipping
2. Four with Canada, integrating plans for defense, economic arrangements, matériel and war production
3. One with Great Britain and Canada combining production and resources
4. Six with various groups of Pan American governments, for political and military defense, prevention of Axis sovereignty in the Americas, and for closer economic, juridical and maritime coöperation
5. One with Brazil for hemisphere defense
6. One with Mexico for common defense
7. Three with large groups of the United Nations for meeting post-war needs in food and raw materials, to cope with political refugees and to provide information
8. One with Australia coördinating plans and supplies
9. One with the United Nations of the Pacific area, as a Pacific War Council
10. Lend-lease working arrangements with Britain, China, Russia and lesser powers

The most important board is the "Combined Chiefs of Staff," sitting in Washington once weekly. It consists of the United States Joint Chiefs of Staff, of representatives of the British Chiefs of Staff and of a United States and a British secretariat, who together plan high strategy for Roosevelt-Churchill approval. Realizing that the old principle of "coöperation" among high commanders of equal rank in a theatre of war, was too divisive to defeat the Hitler-Tojo team, they substituted the principle of "single joint command." For example, they placed General MacArthur in supreme command of all United Nations land, air and sea forces in the Southwest Pacific.[1] Over the rest of that broad ocean they placed another American, Admiral Chester W. Nimitz. British officers were assigned in the Middle and Near East, India and the British Isles. An American, General Dwight D. Eisenhower, was made supreme commander in North Africa, between Dakar and Egypt, after British and United States units joined forces there in 1943 to oust Rommel.

Greater unity was achieved in military planning at Washington, also. Back in 1903 four members each of the army and navy high command had begun sitting as the "Joint Board," with Admiral Dewey as its leader. In 1942 emerged the smaller "Joint Chiefs of Staff," with two from the navy—the Chief of Staff to the Commander in Chief of the Army and Navy, Admiral William D. Leahy, and the Commander in Chief of the U. S. Fleet and Chief of Naval Operations, Admiral Ernest J. King—and with two from the army—the Chief of Staff of the

[1] Philippine-Australian area west of the 160th meridian up to the equator, thence west to the 130th meridian, north to the 20th latitude and westward to the Asiatic continent.

JOINT AND COMBINED CHIEFS OF STAFF

At the left of the table, United States officers, including General Marshall, Admiral Leahy and Admiral King (second fourth and fifth from front); on the right, British officers, among them Field Marshal Dill, Air Marshal Portal, General Brooke and Admiral Pound (third to sixth from front).

(Official U.S. Navy Photograph.)

U. S. Army, General George C. Marshall, and the Chief of the Army Air Forces, General Henry H. Arnold. They confer all day at least once weekly, select commanders for specific objectives and cut red tape short.

Administrative duties have been lessened for the Army Chief of Staff and the Chief of Naval Operations, freeing them for strategic direction of combat groups. These groups, profiting by war experience, have been developed into "task forces" which may combine infantry, sailors, airmen, amphibians, ski-troops, paratroops, motorized forces or whatever personnel or matériel may be needed to perform a particular task in winter or summer on land or sea. On all the far-flung battlefronts the army and navy endeavor to coöperate closely; for example, the army controls all the forces in the Panama Canal area, the navy those in the eastern Caribbean.

Within the United States Navy Department, which had to bear the first brunt of the global war, structure and tactics were modified. Responsibility was reallotted and concentrated; officers with aviation experience received assignments recognizing the fact that carrier groups and task forces now are the "shock troops" of the front line. This was a far cry from earlier days, when the late General "Billy" Mitchell was courtmartialed for demanding speedy establishment of aviation in the armed services. Airplane emphasis was shifted from flying boats to land-based bombers and reconnaissance planes operating together. Carriers became a vital part of the building program, which included additional battleships and tremendously increased submarine and anti-submarine construction. A carrier with compartments and a double or triple hull, with speed as high as thirty-four knots, with the largest and most diversified crew in the navy, with her top deck an airfield of half an acre and her next deck a hangar and repair shop resembling a gigantic armory, can catapault seventy-two planes into the air in eighteen minutes. Conversion of merchant and naval hulls into auxiliary carriers proceeds, with the United States carrier-building program the greatest in the world today. Henry J. Kaiser, by perfecting time-saving methods, became known as the wizard in mass production of shipping.

The army, meanwhile, achieved drastic reorganization, streamlining. The officers under the Secretary of War now are a Chief of Staff and Deputy Chief of Staff; under them are three commanding generals: of the Army Ground Forces, Air Forces and Service Forces. Special techniques are learned. Small, hard-hitting combat teams, some of them called "Rangers," train for guerrilla warfare, beach landing, river defending and anti-tank defense; they are taught to coöperate with other specialists in total war, such as the armored and air adjuncts. A new program of combat problems—closely simulating battle conditions likely to be encountered in the jungles, over the deserts, on mountains, on beaches, everywhere—toughened troops physically and mentally, to endure grueling warfare.

Noting that Germany and Britain had paid close attention to trans-ocean commercial air transport as a war aid, and confronted by a rapacious submarine wolf-pack, the United States went heavily into army air transport. Aviation became practically the sole link with China after Japan cut the Burma road artery of supply. Admiral Harry E. Yarnell, who had foreseen the Japanese attack and its methods as early as January 1939, warned that without air sustenance China could not continue offering opposition to Japan. General Claire L. Chennault was sent to China to head this work, while Japan scoured the China mainland for air bases to prevent American use of them. When the African campaign reached full swing early in 1943, the combined Atlantic and Pacific trans-ocean air transport averaged 500 flights weekly, or one take-off every twenty minutes, twenty-four hours a day, seven days a week. Some of the cargo was "V-mail," service letters reduced to microfilm form, whereby 1,000 letters weighing twenty-two pounds could travel as only four ounces.

Rapidly the army grew in size, by congressional law and by orders from the War Manpower Commission (WMC), established early in 1942. From about 1.5 million before Pearl Harbor, an enrollment of 10.8 million was projected for the end of 1943. The navy was to have about 2 million. Voluntary male enlistment in any of the branches was ended. All males 18-38 became subject to military drafting, with deferments limited to industrial, agricultural and hardship cases and the clergy. After a trial, drafting of 38-45 was ended, but all males 38-64 were registered. The powers of the War Manpower Commission became multiple, including besides Selective Service: the Employment Service, National Youth Administration, Roster of Scientific and Specialized Personnel, Apprenticeship Training, Training Within Industry and the War Training Programs of the Office of Education. Both the army and navy sent thousands of "selectees" to college for further training in science, mathematics, geography, English and history, the better to fit them for officers of war and of occupation.

Women, who had been employed to a limited extent for noncombatant duties by the navy and marine corps in the First World War, proved absolutely indispensable in the Second. The army, navy, air ferrying service, coast guard and marines one after another established, respectively, the WAACS, WAVES, WAFS, SPARS and Women Marines.[1] All but the WAACS began with pay equal to that of the

[1] Respectively the Women's Auxiliary Army Corps, Women Appointed for Voluntary Emergency Service, Women's Auxiliary Ferrying Squadron, *Semper Paratus* Always Ready Service, and the Women's Reserve of the Marine Corps, which last had been made a part of the navy before Pearl Harbor. Under the terms of a bill passed by Congress on 1 July 1943, the WAAC was reorganized into the WAC (Women's Army

men of equal rank; and as the base privates' pay was raised from $21 to $50, with very generous allowances for dependents, pay and allowances rose all along the line. Army and navy nurses became eligible for "relative rank" and pay, and women physicians and surgeons finally were admitted to the medical corps.

Furnishing the Supplies

While Americans of all ages were learning that aviation had shrunk the globe, they were learning also that the United States must expand production or lose the war. How supply the globe? How produce the goods and transport them over the seven seas? German submarines, cutting the "lifelines" to Britain, Russia and North Africa, seemed to win the "Battle of the Atlantic." Helped by spies and carelessness in the United States, they sank freighters far faster, during the first six months of 1942, than the United States could build them. Thereafter shore-line dim-outs and patrolling by planes, P-T boats and destroyers pushed the blockade further out; but it approached again the next spring in the form of gigantic submarines, possibly fueled from undersea "milk-cows." The trouble was dual: In France the RAF bombs could not penetrate the twelve-foot, concrete roofs of the Axis submarine bases; in America gasoline production, synthetic rubber and convoy ships all required oil or its derivatives, and the barrel was so low that the Petroleum Coördinator, Rubber Czar and Shipping Administrator all crowded round the spigot.

The overall problem of supply affected all sectors of the homefront: production, labor, agriculture, transportation, finance, politics and internal defense. It became a mad scramble for materials and manpower among the armed services, war plants, agriculture and essential civilian industry. Production could now proceed only under government fiat. A War Production Board (WPB) was set up in January 1942 with Donald Nelson of the SPAB installed as czar and supposedly given full authority in overall supervision of war production. A War Powers Bill of March set criminal penalties for violation of government priority orders and extended the President's property seizure powers. Accordingly the Alien Property Custodian was directed to seize all enemy patents, which were never to be returned; and the Department of Justice nullified patents agreements between United States and German firms which were fixing prices and restricting production of essential commodities.

To beat shortages it became essential to trace the flow of materials in terms of their final use; and the WPB in June substituted for gen-

Corps) in which women will have the same titles, pay, and privileges as their male counterparts in the army.

eral priorities a classified system of specific allocations of all strategic materials. Steel and rubber long had been doled out very carefully. Conversion to war manufactures and shortage of materials reached the point where very few companies survived, particularly in metal and mechanical fields, which did not have some part in the arms effort. Strong manufacturers of strategic materials like planes, tended to form pools. Conversion proved difficult for small concerns, although they received some government help in getting war orders. The "mortality" in businesses approached 100,000 annually, early in 1943.

The war reversed the labor problem of the depression, with war industries, government agencies and civilian concerns competing for workers. Pay and strike problems became more serious, as organized labor fought to preserve the 40-hour week principle, over-time pay and the right to strike and to shift jobs. The administration struggled with a very difficult situation. Roosevelt in February 1943 ordered the 48-hour week for war industries in certain regions but specified time-and-a-half for the extra eight hours, in effect a rise in earnings. To halt absenteeism, labor turnover, pirating and hoarding of labor, the WMC tried various expedients. It made the U.S. Employment Service the official agency for hiring skilled labor; it planned for "employment stabilization" by "freezing" labor in jobs and for shifting of labor to strategic centers. The WLB in July 1942 had adopted the "Little Steel" formula for increasing wages, setting a 15 per cent rise to fit estimated cost of living rises of January 1941-May 1942; but further increases were allowed to correct "inequalities." As production maladies remained serious, some people concluded that the crying need was for centralization of authority in a few people, with their functions better defined and with frequent conference among them to keep down disputes. Despite all these difficulties, national production [1] in 1942 exceeded that of 1941 by about 23.5 per cent, and exports exceeded by 50 per cent. The United States was showing the world the biggest war output in the history of mankind.

American agriculture, like labor, was thrown by the war into a state of confusion and fear and vowed to hold on to its depression winnings. As supplies available for civilians declined, the administration asked Congress for permission to sell some of its stock of wheat and corn for use as feed to meet wartime needs in dairy, meat and poultry products. The farm lobby resisted but the agricultural bloc split, allowing passage of a law permitting some sales. The government's loan, purchase and sale programs were adjusted to stimulate wanted products and Secretary Wickard called for substantial increases in output.

Inevitably the continuation of the war—with lend-lease, labor shortages, equipment priorities, the food needs of the armed services and the

[1] Estimated with August, 1939 as the base.

high earnings of labor—must make production lag far behind growing purchasing power. Many other supplies besides food must prove inadequate, and there was talk of a separate Office of Civilian Distribution. The work of the OPA grew very burdensome; it had attempted in May 1942 to "freeze" many prices at the highest level of the previous March; it thereafter tried to keep readjusting prices, to save sellers "squeezed" between frozen prices and the rising, uncontrolled prices of many products at their original source. The United States, like the other warring nations, had to adopt rationing; beginning in 1942 ration cards began to be issued for a succession of things, including gasoline, fuel oil, various foods and shoes. Families were urged to cultivate "victory gardens." The farmhand shortage was attacked by establishment of a "Land Army," by importation of Bermuda and Mexican labor and by special deferments of farm help from the draft. Food in 1943 became more of an international problem than munitions, for already there was talk of reconverting some plants to essential civilian goods. A United Nations conference was set for May at Hot Springs, Virginia, to meet the food emergency.

Farmers continued most concerned for their *relative* position in the national economy; as long as the administration allowed labor's earnings to rise, it should not restrict farm prices; allowance should be made for the cost of farm, as well as industrial, labor. In a price control law of 30 January 1942, projected to permit control of prices and rents, labor managed to remain unmentioned, and agriculture obtained provisions raising parity on some products to 110 per cent. An "anti-inflation" act of 2 October made special concessions to both labor and agriculture. However, when calculating parity, federal officials took into account federal payments to farmers, which kept the parity figure from rising so high. This practice the farm bloc undertook to forbid, in a Bankhead bill of March 1943. By this time foods, other farm products and raw materials were registering most of the gains in the wholesale price index; the farmers' net income of 1942 had exceeded 1941 by 55.5 per cent, and serious shortages had appeared in meat and potatoes with more general shortages a certain prospect.

The President tried to retard the upward spiral. He established an "Office of Economic Stabilization" in October 1942 and an Office of Food Distribution in the Agriculture Department in March following; in April he vetoed the Bankhead bill as inflationary. The agricultural interest proceeded to have the bill kept in committee as a sort of "club" over Roosevelt. He decided to confront labor and agriculture conjoined, especially as John L. Lewis and his United Mine Workers were demanding miners' wage increases beyond the "Little Steel" formula. On 8 April Roosevelt issued a "hold the line" order forbidding wage increases above the "Little Steel" formula, except where clearly necessary to correct substandards of living, and restricting prices to the maximum rise allowed by law. The WMC followed this up with regulations intended to "freeze" 27 million workers in war jobs. Farm and labor blocs were incensed. Organized labor talked of forgetting jurisdictional disputes in a united drive for retention of the right to increases arising out of "inequalities." The farm bloc considered attaching the Bankhead bill as a rider to some indispensable appropriation bill.

All products, whether agricultural or industrial, had to share the rails with the armed services and wartime workers of various sorts. An Office of Defense Transportation has been established to work for orderly transit and to try to prevent mounting charges.

Although inflation was, on the whole, proceeding less rapidly than in the First World War, the entire economy showed serious strain. In April of 1943 it became known that in the previous year the cost of living[1] had risen 7.6 per cent, while the national income rose 23.5 per cent. Stocks and bonds on the New York Stock Exchange boomed until the "hold the line" order. With more people earning more money than formerly, and with less goods for them to buy, prices were likely to rise. How high, depended on government controls and on taxation.

The war was now costing 7 billion monthly, making heavier taxes and bond sales imperative. The tax law of October 1942 had reduced exemptions and increased the individual normal and surtax rates as well as corporation rates; also it levied a 5 per cent "withholding" tax on wages earned in 1943, specifying 10 per cent withholdings in 1944, the amounts withheld to be credited against the income tax for the following year. Further increases were delayed by a bitter fight over an administration proposal to collect in 1943 both the taxes due on the previous year and these accruing from current income. The administration resisted a "Ruml" plan to "forgive" 1942 levies in order to reach a current basis without hardship.

Still lacking new levies in April 1943, the Treasury staged its Second War Loan drive, calling on the nation to subscribe for $13,475,000,000 in bonds. In the midst of this drive Congress renewed for two years the President's authority to maintain the 2 billion dollar stabilization fund but eliminated his right to revalue the dollar, asserting that possible devaluation clouded bond sales.[2] Somewhat earlier, lend-lease had been renewed with little difficulty, for people generally realized that it had become the essential agent among the United Nations for effective cooperation against the Axis. On the other hand, renewal of reciprocal trade agreements promised a fight.

[1] Estimated with August, 1939 as the base.

[2] Sales took an added spurt on the sudden revelation that some of the Tokyo bomber crew had been captured and executed by the Japanese, contrary to all rules of civilized warfare.

Thus stimulated by initial disaster the American people turned vigorously to operate the arsenal of democracy. They were arming to fight a global war, as President Roosevelt proclaimed, to maintain in the world the four freedoms: the freedom of speech and of religion, the freedom from want and fear.

CHAPTER LII

GLOBAL WARFARE

Because the nation was tackling with vigor the key jobs of (1) organizing the military services effectively and (2) furnishing the supplies abundantly, the global offensive needed for Axis defeat was beginning to materialize. The black months from Pearl Harbor to April 1942 were being followed by a year of brighter prospects. The United Nations were undertaking the offensive in four principal theatres: the Southwest Pacific, Eastern and Western Europe, and Northern Africa; elsewhere they simply tried to stand their ground.

Taking the Offensive

In the Pacific area Japan tried to sever the United Nations' lifeline; it ran from Hawaii through the fortified centers of the Samoan and Fiji islands, New Caledonia, and New Zealand to Australia. Japanese carriers sent into the Coral Sea east of Australia in May 1942 were routed by United States carriers, the first large-scale carrier engagement in history. Japan was stopped by the United States again in June, in a terrific air engagement near Midway Island. In the Aleutians Japan was not dislodged. These islands stretch out like a bowstring from Alaska to within 775 miles of Japan's Kurile Islands, along the route vital for air attack upon the United States. Japan in June bombed the strategic Dutch Harbor base and started air bases on the fog-bound, rocky islands of Kiska and Attu, in the "Rat" group, westernmost of the Aleutians. Thereupon the United States established planes on the Andreanofs, near the Rat group, the better to bomb Kiska with land-based planes. However, the Japs stuck tenaciously through a year of repeated attacks.

Japan, approaching Australia through the Solomon Islands, started a big airfield on Guadalcanal, an island ninety miles long and thirty wide. This region the United States chose for her first major offensive, taking the key airfield and smaller islands quickly. Unhappily, the jungle beyond the airfield took six months, from 7 August 1942 to 7 February 1943, of fighting by sea, land and air.

It is a story of the navy pounding Jap reënforcements approaching by sea: of army, navy and marine corps fliers bombing ships and strafing ground troops, of coast guardsmen plying in and out of danger-loaded zones delivering men and supplies. The Japs and the tropical climate kept the Americans under almost continual attack for five months, boiling out of the jungle, pouring out of the skies, shaking the ground with shell-quakes harder to endure than bombing, forcing the men into fox holes and slit trenches, making them sleep ready to fight, alongside their rifles. By qualitative superiority the outnumbering enemy were cut down—cut down because a man who won't surrender can't be taken prisoner.

Seven major sea battles punctuated the struggle; three night surface actions and four air-versus-surface actions. Most outstanding was the Battle of Guadalcanal, directed by Admiral William Halsey 13-15 November, in which the enemy lost no less than 2 battleships, 8 cruisers, 6 destroyers, 8 transports and 4 cargo ships sunk, besides 10 other vessels damaged. The total cost of the Solomon Islands offensive in United States ships was enormous: 2 carriers, 4 heavy cruisers, 3 light cruisers, 13 destroyers and 10 miscellaneous vessels sunk, besides 1 submarine lost and 5 other vessels damaged.

Nor was the end in sight. Lieutenant-General George C. Kenny's air forces annihilated a great Japanese transport group in March in the Bismarck Sea, with a loss of only four planes and nine men.[1] MacArthur's men with the Australians cleaned up part of New Guinea. But the Japs continued to operate from their magnificent naval base at Rabaul, New Britain, just 480 miles from Britain's Port Moresby on New Guinea and 700 from America's Guadalcanal. They were not waiting for the United States to receive the British aid which Churchill promised to deliver after Germany and Italy were defeated. Rather, they consolidated and strengthened their conquests. As MacArthur bluntly put it, deploring delay, "There is no such thing as 'holding' the Japanese. They require action." MacArthur and Halsey sent high officers to Washington to plead for more support. Major-General Doolittle, now an air commander in Africa, warned that Nippon could be defeated only by attacks on Japan proper.

In truth, the battle with Japan was a battle of supply routes—her short lines *versus* American long ones. Japan was determined that American lines should not be shortened by use of Chinese airfields; she made further advances in China. The United Nations did not succeed in reopening the Burma road, and China's plight became so desperate that the American-educated wife of her Generalissimo, Madame Chiang Kai-shek, toured the United States in the spring of 1943 with a plea for supplies and more supplies. Little but air-borne matériel could surmount the wall of inaccessibility with which Japan had surrounded China.

[1] Japan lost 3 light cruisers, 7 destroyers, 12 merchantmen and 15,000 men; she had expected cloudy weather to substitute for an air umbrella over the convoy. The weather cleared and American planes swooped down for the kill.

The few supplies reaching China had to enter by air from the eastern edge of seething India. There was Britain's serious political problem in the persons of Mahatma Gandhi and the "All India Congress." They, with native competitors of British business houses in India, refused to be content with less than immediate independence, which Churchill refused. The independence party, only one of several in India, won numerous American sympathizers on this very complicated issue. They cited the "four freedoms"—freedom from want and fear, freedom of speech and religion—which the President was wont to stress as the United Nations' ideal. It was anybody's guess as to what might happen to the British and American forces stationed at strategic centers in India if Indians helped Japan get a foothold there. Thus politics put a question mark on some battle fronts, and news of the one affected the other.

The fate of the United States, Britain and China was being determined in no small part by the course of events on the eastern edge of Europe. While the United Nations were inaugurating 1942 offensives in the Solomons, Germany was retaking a part of what she had lost in Russia the previous winter. In five months of favoring weather she seized about 150,000 square miles, chiefly along the southern half of the 1,500-mile front from Leningrad to Sevastopol. This time Hitler's forces penetrated the Caucasus, taking Maikop in the oil fields. They continued to hold Kharkov and Kursk and regained Rostov. They lengthened to 515 days the epic siege of Leningrad. Worse, they besieged Stalingrad, on the Volga and near the great bend in the Don. Their occupation of the Donetz basin (a tributary of the Don) and of the Rostov region inflicted severe losses on the coal and metal industries of the USSR. Also important railway and machine shops were added to the sugar, meat and grain assets earlier won by Germany.

Hard-pressed Stalin begged for an Anglo-American second front in Europe. A British trial raid on the channel coast at Dieppe proved disastrous. However the United States, despite considerable dislike for past Soviet policy on religion, private property, Finland and Poland, extended a helping hand in the form of lend-lease. The shipments had to run the German submarine gauntlet north to Murmansk or clear around to Iran or across the Pacific; they took precious time.

The Bolsheviks, however, had created a party government which by now had remained in power longer than any other major party in the world; it had built Russia into one of the great industrial powers and had knit her masses in a great loyalty. So Stalingrad in September almost fell, but not quite; "cold-mouthed" Fedor von Bock, the German general, did not gain the Volga's east bank. His whole army was captured or destroyed; Germany declared three days of official mourning for this disaster. Leningrad held. With winter weather the Russians retook 50,000 square miles, including Maikop, Rostov, Kharkov, Kursk and Rzhev—an amazing recovery. That winter about 29 per cent of the United States lend-lease was allotted Russia. The engagements of American-equipped Russians with Hitler's planes, tanks and infantry moderated the United Nations' situation in the Mediterranean and on the African and Atlantic coasts. Stalin had ruined Hitler's plan to become master of Europe by 1942.

Yet was the issue far from resolved. Come spring, the Germans in a fortnight pushed the Russians back 80 miles along a 200-mile front, retaking Kharkov. Russia had yet to regain the vital Orel-Sevastopol railroad line, which afforded the enemy mobility along the main front. The question remained: would the United States and Britain be able to establish a second front in time to keep Russia an effective opponent of Hitler?

Air warfare was stepped up. Hitler's channel fortifications could not intercept bombers; his home front was accessible via the stratosphere. So, by the end of May 1942 the United Nations had inaugurated mass air raids to wreak havoc on industrial targets of the European Axis. Germany, Italy and occupied France learned what it meant to have 1,000 planes come over at once to drop "block-busters" on their factories, railroads, harbors, submarine bases and munitions centers. "Round the clock" bombing was perfected by the next March, when destruction descended on the Axis every day of the month but three and sometimes through both night and day. The British preferred the night shift, aiming by the light of incendiary bombs. The United States crews preferred the day shift, doing high-level, precision bombing.

By this time the American masters of supply were outdoing themselves, for continual raiding requires superior skill in coördination. They were allotting about one-third of United States-made bombers, tanks and fighting planes to other nations; and American troops were receiving "reciprocal lend-lease," in the form of food and small ship-craft, at stations in Britain, New Zealand and Australia. Germany perfected her anti-aircraft defenses and for her warmaking drafted man, woman and child-power, rolling stock, heavy industry, *all* resources of her subject and "allied" peoples. Yet Hitler could not retaliate on Britain in equal measure, because his *Luftwaffe* was heavily engaged in Africa, as well as Russia.

In Africa, meanwhile, was being staged an offensive which reads like a romantic novel; it held surprise, intrigue, secret entry by submarine, men of mystery, assassination and a successful coup d'état by heroes. Roosevelt, Churchill and the Combined Chiefs of Staff had decided, during Churchill's visit to Washington in June of 1942, that the second front should begin with an offensive thrust into Italy, the "soft belly" of the Axis. In London during July United States and British generals and admirals planned the main points of supply and procedure. In August a date was selected and Churchill flew to Moscow to inform Stalin. Stalin aided the scheme by continuing his loud protests at delay in the second front, the protests which Willkie heatedly endorsed.

STALIN AND WILLKIE IN MOSCOW
(Press Association, Inc.)

The approach to Italy lay through North Africa, where were the Vichy provinces of Morocco, Algeria and Tunisia. Opposition from this quarter was forestalled by a series of clever and dangerous moves. In August the United States resumed lend-lease aid to French North Africa, which could be done because relations with the Laval government had not been severed upon Leahy's recall to Washington. In Algiers the United States Minister was Robert Murphy, personally chosen by the President for delicate diplomacy; Algiers was a hotbed of intrigue between Vichites and Free French followers of General de Gaulle. Shortly, the Vichy faction there had a secret visitor, brought by submarine in the night; he was Lieutenant General Mark W. Clark, of the staff of General Dwight Eisenhower, who was resident in London as commander of American forces in the European theatre.

In France Admiral Jean François Darlan, associate of Pétain and Laval in German appeasement, was growing uneasy. He flew from the French naval base of Toulon to Africa, to "inspect" French forces there. The popular French hero General Henri Honoré Giraud was also busy;

he had escaped to Vichy from a German prison camp and he had declined a British overture, but he met a United Nations submarine which took him to Gibraltar, where he conferred quite agreably with General Eisenhower. Back in Washington, Roosevelt was drafting appropriate reassuring letters to be sent Pétain, Generalissimo Franco of Spain and others when the time came, and was recording a speech in French for ultimate broadcast over the radio as reassurance of the French people.

The day of 7 November came. It brought American and British forces to African points near Casablanca, Oran and Algiers; the guns of the United States Navy neatly covered all landings on the Atlantic Coast, the British those on the Mediterranean shores of Morocco and Algeria. On the 9th Vichy broke off relations with the United States. Next day, German troops moved in to occupy the Vichy area, while Darlan, strangely enough, appeared "in the hands of" the United Nations. He became "protector" of North Africa, with Giraud as commander in chief, and at the end of two weeks announced that the military and naval forces of French North Africa adhered to the United Nations. So turned the rest of France's African empire also, including French West Africa which had been pro-Vichy, French Somaliland and French Equatorial Africa which had been Free French. Their peoples, starved and stripped by the Germans, received from the United States, food, arms and clothing.

This was not all. Britain occupied the great French island of Madagascar, east of Africa, and the United States secured from Admiral Robert, Vichy High Commissioner for Martinique and the other French possessions in the Caribbean area, a compact that they and their military and naval strength should be immobilized. Admiral Darlan directed his former sailors to scuttle what they could of the immobile Toulon fleet and flee to African ports with what would move.[1] Thus it happened that New York City and Philadelphia later saw strange sights; the proud battleship *Richelieu*, the heavy cruiser *Montcalm* and several French destroyers came into those ports for repairs to fit them for fighting the Axis.

The fly in the African ointment was that Darlan's German appeasement record made him anathema to the British-supported Free French, led from London by General Charles De Gaulle. After Darlan had brought over the French African possessions to the United Nations with practically no cost to them, he paid for his daring with his life. The assassin's bullet, Christmas eve of 1942, placed the far more popular General Giraud in the succession. He was endorsed by General Eisenhower and sought to concentrate on defeating the Axis. The De

[1] Secretary of the Navy Knox reported that 15 warships and 5 tankers were left afloat at Toulon.

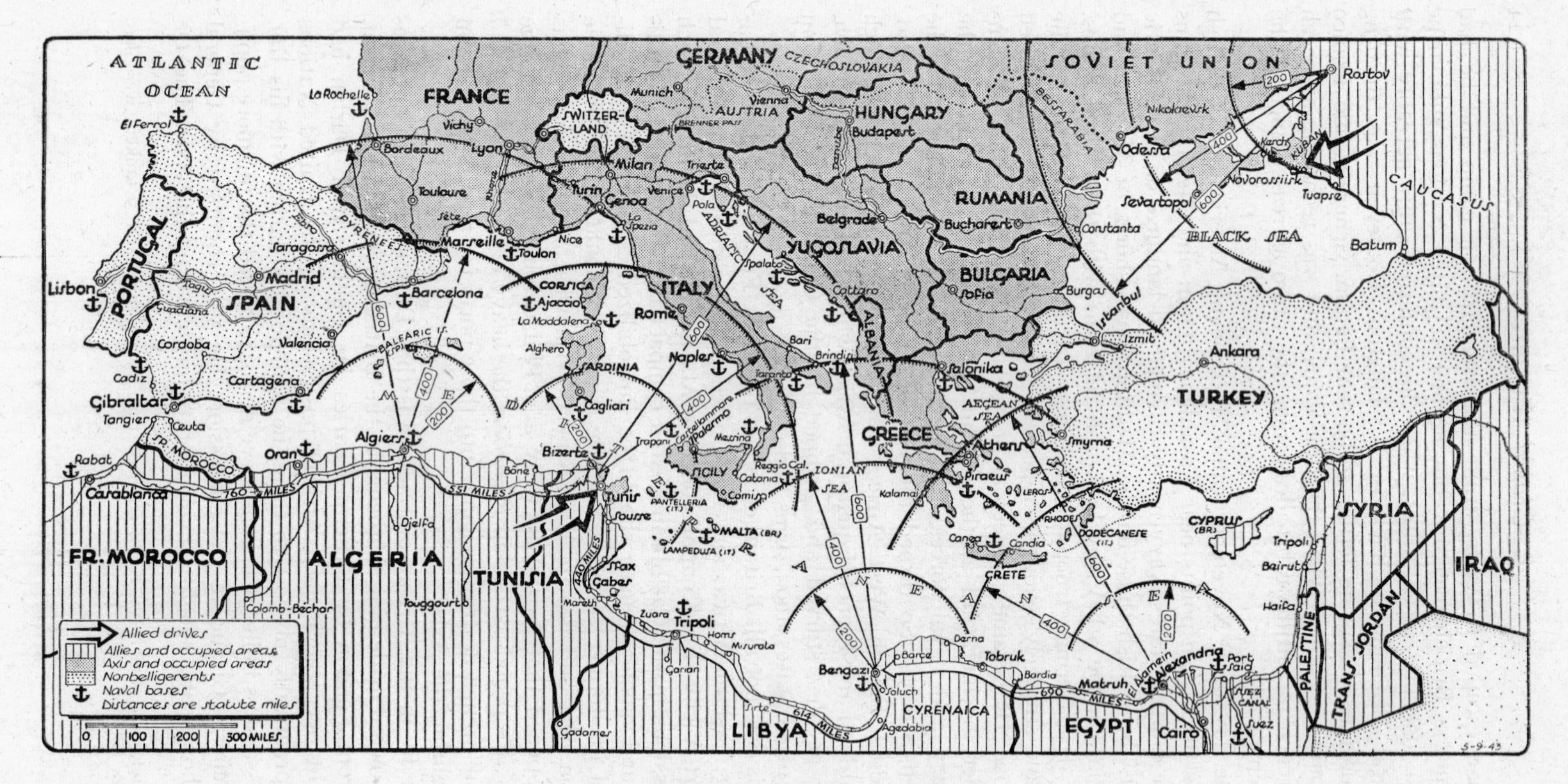

THE AFRICAN APPROACH TO EUROPE

(Courtesy of the New York *Times.*)

Gaullists feared they would lose the leadership, and to an appeasement group at that.

So delicate a political situation might dynamite military prospects. So Roosevelt, Churchill and their advisers conferred at Casablanca, under an umbrella of fighter planes, for a fortnight in January 1943.[1] They emerged with the declaration, reassuring to those fearing appeasement, that the United Nations would not stop short of "unconditional surrender" of the Axis. Pictures were taken of Giraud and De Gaulle shaking hands; but De Gaulle was hustled back to London to avoid political strife.

While obstacles thus confronted the political front, the military front was the first consideration. Two German generals, Von Arnim in northern Tunisia and Rommel in Egypt, had held the wide area between them. Von Arnim and Rommel would have to be cleaned out before the United Nations could cross the Mediterranean. The British general, Sir Bernard Montgomery, broke through Rommel's lines in Egypt, 26 October 1942, and during the next thirteen weeks chased him, his Afrika Korps and his Panzer divisions westward along the coast line 1,300 miles. Each attempt of Montgomery to outflank and surround Rommel was defeated, for the "desert fox" succeeded in withdrawing westward until finally he reached the fortified Mareth Line within Tunisia facing Libya. Here again Rommel evaded an enveloping manoeuver brilliantly conceived and executed by Montgomery. The American Second Corps and French troops had entered Tunisia, but Rommel held them in the mountain passes on his right flank while he retired to a junction with Von Arnim. The United Nations seized air control, sinking Germain reinforcements and hoping for an Axis Dunkerque. Hitler, however, strove to remove his best troops by air and to stand them behind newly built fortifications on the northern shore of the Mediterranean.

This effort at delaying action was futile. The Americans, the French and the British First and Eighth Armies closed in, fought through the mountainous defenses of Bizerte and Tunis and descended to the plains. A terrific and incessant air attack by American craft, bombardment by the Allied navies and direct assault by the armies won a great triumph. The first week in May 1943 saw the fall of these two cities and within a week a hundred thousand German and Italian troops had surrendered. North Africa was cleared of the Axis and the invasion of the continent of Europe was imminent.

[1] Roosevelt was the first president since Lincoln to visit a battle theatre, was the first to leave the United States in wartime, to visit Africa and to travel in an airplane.

Planning for Peace

From the beginning of the war, a desire for an intelligently planned peace was apparent. The utter lack of a terminal date did not deter peace-planners. Conferences large and small, committees and commissions sprouted over the land. The older generation had been keenly disappointed when Wilson's "war to end war" had bred another; they vowed to plan better than Versailles. The younger generation, most aviation-minded, sensed that aviation had become both servant and master in world affairs; as it made all nations vulnerable, they must plan to control it. Young and old had become more world-conscious; their kinsfolk were gone so far afield that a victory or defeat, as far east as Africa or as far west as Guadalcanal, could bring personal joy or grief into a kitchen in Kansas. Their hearts took their minds on a circle of the globe. They knew, too, that the products of their own hands in fields and factories were moving globe-wise, carried by the machinery of lend-lease and other wartime international arrangements. They knew much less about the "army of occupation in the United States," that is, the resident refugees engrossed in schemes for restitution; but these also added to the ferment. Altogether, by 1943 many persons of many minds were planning for peace in a fashion foreshadowing confusion when the guns were silenced.

Germany and Japan sent out their own peace feelers occasionally. For example, Germany in 1940 had offered a peace based on recognition of her "new order" in Europe; Britain had been too sure of United States aid to be compelled to accept it. Japan in 1943 was rumored to be willing to end war if the United States accepted her "new order" in Asia; the United States was too sure of her own strength to accept any such thing.

All Americans agreed with Roosevelt that it must be a peace based upon the "unconditional surrender" of the enemy; but there unanimity ended. Ex-President Hoover and Prime Minister Churchill warned that experience taught the need for regional groups of nations, within any world federation, to care for local differences; but some educators and clergymen feared that regional groups would divide and destroy a global union. Sir William Beveridge of England and the National Resources Planning Board of the Roosevelt administration argued that social security in each country was indispensable for world peace; but the American plan accepted much more world responsibility than the British.

Lord J. M. Keynes of the Bank of England and Mr. H. D. White of the United States treasury produced monetary plans for post-war use. Both utilized features of the tripartite agreement of 1936 and attempted to link world trade with the gold supply; the United States has the most gold and Britain's South Africa is the principal producer of it. But the British wished to apportion monetary influence according to pre-war trade importance, in which they had led. The United States would apportion it in reference to capital, in which they were foremost. An international conference on monetary issues was projected.

Senators spawned numerous plans, and a bipartisan group of four,[1] significantly an inland group, sought Roosevelt's approval for a detailed plan. They hoped to put the Senate on record as favoring a United Nations organization for five purposes: to finish the war, to establish temporary governments in Axis-controlled countries, to administer post-war rehabilitation, to set up machinery to settle future disputes and to provide for a United Nations world police. Such particularity guaranteed acrimonious debate; the President avoided it by expressing approval only "in theory" and by deprecating hasty action. A simpler proposition, that the Senate pledge support for the principle of collective security, had its opponents also. The House of Representatives for its part was sure that its judgment could not be ignored in peace-planning. Roosevelt well remembered how Wilson's ideals had failed of fulfilment for lack of coöperation from the Senate and from foreign powers; he wanted to know much more on both sectors before committing himself to any plan.

The Axis exploited any differences of opinion among its enemies. It tried to cut United Nations aid to Russia by proclaiming Germany as the world's defense against Communism and by encouraging Christian and Jewish resentment of Soviet policy on the church and in Poland and Finland. It advertised trade differences between the United States and Britain. This was indeed a sore subject. Britishers feared United States supremacy in air transport, and American exporters resented administration agreements to displace United States goods with British products in some areas. These and other frictions delighted the Axis.

The great, unifying idea, to the American mind, was that of the superiority of the democratic way of life. Idealists dreamed of implementing the Atlantic Charter and the Four Freedoms speedily, throughout the world. However, the *Basic Field Manual* issued by the War Department to United States commanders in all areas emphasized that no one formula would fit all countries; all officers in occupied zones must remember that military government "must suit the people, the country, the time and the tactical and strategic situation." Civil Officer staffs were being trained for armies of occupation. By the time that victory was won, the régimes set up under American control would

[1] Joseph H. Ball of Minnesota and Harold Burton of Ohio, Republicans; Lester Hill of Alabama and Carl Hatch of New Mexico, Democrats.

differ widely. Accomplished facts more imperious than theories would confront the planners.

Peace prospects and United Nations unity were somewhat strengthened by pledges extracted during dire emergencies. For example, the United States required recipients of lend-lease aid to pledge themselves to the multilateral, "most-favored-nation" principle, in contradistinction to Hitler's bilateral, barter principle. This looked to a united, post-war economic front, on the democratic rather than the geopolitical basis. Likewise, when Russia in her retreating June of 1942 had sought from Britain and the United States agreements upon a "second front" in Europe and lend-lease, the United States caused them to join in denials of territorial ambitions and of aggressive intentions. China, whose continued resistance to Japan was very important to the United Nations, extracted from the United States and Britain the abandonment of the principle of "extra-territoriality" under which foreign powers formerly had maintained their own jurisdiction in certain areas of China's domain.

Most peace-planners realized that there were serious obstacles to peace in the German and Japanese faith in the superman and divine-origin doctrines, which had been ingrained in their youth for generations; planners differed as to whether the enemy could be effectively "reëducated" for democracy and permanent peace.

SUGGESTIONS FOR FURTHER READING

American history may be considered in its relationship to history in general in Barnes, H. E., *History of Historical Writing*, 1937. The writing of American history itself has had an interesting history detailed in Kraus, M., *History of American History*, 1937, and Bassett, J. S., *Middle Group of American Historians*, 1917, which show how the ideas of the meaning of national growth have changed. Further insight into the development of American history is gained by reading the biographies of the historians which may be found conveniently in Hutchinson, W. T., ed., *Marcus W. Jornegan Essays in American Historiography*, 1937. An effective introduction to the problems of history and their study is Nevins, A., *Gateway to History*, 1938.

The standard general histories of the United States by individuals are Channing, E., *History of the United States* (6 vols. extending to 1865), 1905-1925, and McMaster, J. B., *History of the People of the United States* (9 vols. covering 1783-1865), 1883-1927. Coöperative series by various scholars are Hart, A. B., ed., *The American Nation: A History* (28 vols. extending to 1917), 1904-1928, and Johnson, A., ed., *Chronicles of America* (50 vols.), 1919-1921. The changing interpretation of American history, illustrating the turn from political to social and economic, is shown in the coöperative work edited by Schlesinger, A. M., and Fox, D. R., *History of American Life* (projected in 12 vols.), 1927- , in Beard, Charles A., and Mary R., *Rise of American Civilization* (4 vols.), 1927-1942 and Carman, H. J., *Social and Economic History of the United States* (projected in 3 vols.), 1930- . American history has been effectively illustrated in Gabriel, Ralph H., ed., *Pageant of America*, 1929. The key to American biography is found in Johnson, A. and Malone, D., ed., *Dictionary of American Biography*, 1928-1936.

Convenient works of reference are Adams, J. T., *Dictionary of American History* (6 vols.), 1940; Jameson, J. F., *Dictionary of United States History* (rev. ed.), 1931; Seligman, E. R. A., and Johnson, A., *Encyclopedia of Social Sciences* (15 vols.), 1934.

The most important periodicals are *American Historical Review*, 1895- ; *Mississippi Valley Historical Review*, 1915- ; *Hispanic American Historical Review*, 1918- ; *New England Quarterly*, 1928- ; *Journal of Southern History*, 1935- ; *Agricultural History*, 1927- ; *Annals of American Academy of Political and Social Sciences*, 1890- ; *Political Science Quarterly*, 1886- ; *Quarterly Journal of Economics*, 1886- ; *American Economic Review*, 1911- ; *American Journal of Sociology*, 1895- ; *Social Forces*, 1922- .

The richest mine of information on the development of the United States is in the official publications of federal and state governments. They reveal the remarkable expansion in socially useful functions required of government agencies. The various units publish, in addition to annual reports, a huge number of bulletins, often including excellent statistical graphs, maps and illustrations, and readily obtainable. Federal publications are described in Schmeckebier, L. F., *Government Publications and their Use*, 1936. State publications are ascertainable through the Library of Congress *Monthly Check List* and *Annual Index*. A convenient compilation is Richardson, J. D., comp., *A Compilation of the Messages and Papers of the Presidents,* 1896 (since enlarged).

The following suggestions for further reading have been divided into two groups. The first includes specialized works which are not confined to any particular period in American history or which cover several. The second group is arranged to correspond with the chronological divisions of the text and contains titles which pertain entirely to the particular period or which are most important for the epoch in question. This method of organization has been adopted to save a frequent repetition of titles.

Specialized Works

The history of the sections is described in Turner, F. J., *Frontier in American History,* 1921; and *Significance of Sections in American History,* 1932; Paxson, F. L., *History of the American Frontier,* 1924; Clark, D. E., *West in American History,* 1937; Brown, W. G., *Lower South in American History,* 1902; Hawk, E. Q., *Economic History of the South,* 1934; Hesseltine, W. B., *A History of the South,* 1936. The environment and people of the United States and their relationship may be studied in Bowman, I., *Forest Physiography,* 1911; Brigham, A. P., *Geographic Influences in American History,* 1903; Calhoun, A. W., *Social History of the American Family* (3 vols.), 1917-1919; Hulbert, A. B., *Soil,* 1930; Huntington, E., *Civilization and Climate,* 1915; Semple, E. C., *American History and its Geographic Conditions,* 1933; Stephenson, G. M., *History of American Immigration,* 1926; Wissler, C., *American Indian,* 1922. Much interesting comment upon American society has been made by foreign observers. Illustrations of such comment can be found in Mesick, J. L., *English Traveller in America, 1785-1835,* 1922; Monaghan, Frank, *French Travellers in the U. S., 1765-1932,* 1933; Nevins, A., *American Social Life as Seen by British Travellers,* 1923.

Thought and expression are described in Blair, Walter, *Native American Humor, 1800-1900,* 1937; Blankenship, R., *American Literature as an Expression of the American Mind,* 1931; Bleyer, W. G., *Main Currents in the History of American Journalism,* 1927; Cargill, O., ed., *American Literature: A Period Anthology* (5 vols.), 1933; Gabriel, R. H., *Course of American Democratic Thought,* 1939; Hall, T. C., *Religious Brackground of American Culture,* 1930; Lee, A. M., *Daily Newspaper in America,* 1937; Lee, J. M., *History of American Journalism,* 1923; Mencken, H. L., *American Language,* 1936; Mott, F. L., *A History of American Magazines* (3 vols.), 1930-1938; O'Neill, E. H., *A History of American Biography,* 1935; Parrington, V. L., *Main Currents in American Thought* (3 vols.), 1927-1930; Pattee, F. L., *First Century of American Literature,* 1935; and *History of American Literature Since 1870,* 1915; Quinn, A. H., *A History of the American Drama* (2 vols.), 1923-1927; and *American Fiction,* 1936; Riley, Woobridge, *American Thought,* 1923; Rowe, H. K., *History of Religion in the United States,* 1924; Sweet, W. W., *Story of Religions in America,* 1930; Taylor, W. F., *History of American Letters,* 1936; Townsend, H. G., *Philosophical Ideas in the United States,* 1934; Trent, W. P., et al., *Cambridge History of American Literature* (4 vols.), 1917-1921; Warfel, H. R., Gabriel, R. H., and Williams, S. T., *The American Mind,* 1937. Histories of individual newspapers are listed under the respective periods in which they were published.

American interest in and contribution to the arts are described in Caffin, C. H., *Story of American Painting,* 1907; Elson, L. C., *History of American Music,* 1904; Howard, J. T., *Our American Music,* 1931; Isham, S., *History of American*

Painting, 1903; Kimball, F., *Domestic Architecture of the American Colonies and of the Early Republic,* 1922; La Follette, S., *Art in America,* 1929; Mumford, L., *Sticks and Stones: A Study of American Architecture and Civilization,* 1924; Sonneck, O. G., *Early Opera in America,* 1915; Taft, L., *History of American Sculpture,* 1924; Tallmadge, T. E., *Story of Architecture in America,* 1927.

American interest in science and education are discussed in Cubberly, E. P., *Public Education in the United States,* 1934; Curti, M. E., *Social Ideas of American Educators,* 1935; Dana, E. S., et al., *A Century of Science in America,* 1918; Dexter, E. G., *A History of Education in the United States,* 1904; Packard, F., *History of Medicine in the United States* (2 vols.), 1931; Shryock, R. H., *Development of Modern Medicine,* 1936; Thwing, C. F., *A History of Higher Education in America,* 1906; Woody, T., *A History of Women's Education in the United States* (2 vols.), 1929.

Convenient general histories of American economic enterprise are: Cochran, T., and Miller, W., *Age of Enterprise,* 1942; Faulkner, H. U., *American Economic History* (4th ed.), 1938; Kirkland, E. C., *History of American Economic Life,* 1932; Shannon, F. A., *Economic History of the People of the United States,* 1934. Various phases of economic activity are described in Beard, Mary R., *Short History of the American Labor Movement,* 1920; Bidwell, P. W., et al., *History of Agriculture in the Northern United States, 1620-1860,* 1925; Clark, V. S., *History of Manufactures* (3 vols.), 1916-1928; Commons, J. R., et al., *History of Labor in the United States* (4 vols.), 1918-1935; Dewey, D. R., *Financial History of the United States,* 1922; Gray, L. C., *History of Agriculture in the Southern States to 1860* (2 vols.), 1933; Gras, N. S. B., *History of Agriculture in Europe and America,* 1925; Johnson, E. R., et al., *History of Domestic and Foreign Commerce of the United States* (2 vols.), 1915; Meyer, B. H., MacGill, C. E., et al., *History of Transportation in the United States before 1860,* 1917; Perlman, S., *History of Trade Unionism in the United States,* 1923; Shultz, W. J., and Caine, M. R., *Financial Development of the United States,* 1937; Taussig, F. W., *Tariff History of the United States* (8th ed.), 1931.

American political and diplomatic history are described in: Bailey, T. A., *Diplomatic History of American People,* 1940; Bemis, S. F., *Diplomatic History of the United States,* 1936, *American Secretaries of State* (10 vols.), 1927-1929, and *Latin-American Policy of the United States,* 1943; Bryce, James, *American Commonwealth,* 1886; Channing, E., *History of the United States* (6 vols.), 1905-1925; Ewing, Cortez A. M., *Judges of the Supreme Court,* 1938; McLaughlin, A. C., *Constitutional History of the United States,* 1935, Schouler, J., *History of the United States 1783-1877* (7 vols.), 1880-1889; Stanwood, E., *History of the Presidency, 1788-1916* (2 vols.), 1924; Swisher, C. B., *American Constitutional Development,* 1943; Warren, C., *Supreme Court in United States History,* 1928.

Convenient documentary source collections are: Callendar, G. S., *Selections from the Economic History of the United States,* 1900; Commager, H. S., *Documents of American History,* 1943; Commons, J. R., et al., *Documentary History of American Industrial Society* (10 vols.), 1910-1911; Flügel, F., and Faulkner, H. U., *Readings in the Social and Economic History of the United States,* 1929; Hart, A. B., ed., *American History told by Contemporaries* (5 vols.), 1899-1923; MacDonald, Wm., *Documentary Source Book of American History,* 1916.

Maps are found in: Adams, J. T., *Atlas of American History,* 1943; Fox, D. R., ed., *Harper's Atlas of American History,* 1920; Paullin, C. O., and Wright, J. K., *Atlas of Historical Geography of the United States,* 1932.

Guides to further search are Channing, Hart and Turner, *Guide to the Study and Reading of American History,* 1912, to be superseded by *Harvard Guide to American History* (to be published); Griffin, G. G., *Writings on American History,* 1906- ; Edwards, E. E., *Bibliography of the History of Agriculture in the United States,* 1930; Bemis, S. F., and Griffin, G. G., *Guide to the Diplomatic History of the United States,* 1935; Allison, W. H., et al., *Guide to Historical Literature,* 1931.

Colonies

1492-1763

The colonial period has been analyzed by three historians in extensive works: Andrews, C. M., *Colonial Period of American History* (4 vols. to date), 1934- ; Gipson, L. H., *British Empire before the American Revolution* (5 vols.), 1942; Osgood, H. L., *American Colonies in the Seventeenth Century* (3 vols.), 1904-1907; *American Colonies in the Eighteenth Century,* 1924. One-volume surveys are: Becker, C., *Beginnings of the American People,* 1915; Chitwood, P., *History of Colonial America,* 1931; Greene, E. B., *Foundations of American Nationality,* 1922; Jernegan, M. W., *American Colonies,* 1929; Nettels, C. P., *Roots of American Civilization,* 1938.

The period has been covered by volumes in the three series. In the *American Nation Series* are Cheyney, E. P., *European Background of American History;* Tyler, L. G., *English in America;* Andrews, C. M., *Colonial Self-Government;* Greene, E. B., *Provincial America.* In the *Chronicles of America* are Wood, W., *Elizabethan Sea-Dogs;* Johnson, M., *Pioneers of the Old South;* Andrews, C. M., *Fathers of New England;* Goodwin, M. W., *Dutch and English on the Hudson;* Fisher, S. G., *The Quaker Colonies;* Andrews, C. M., *Colonial Folkways.* In the *History of American Life* are Wertenbaker, T. J., *First Americans;* Adams, J. T., *Provincial Society.*

The English background is described in: Cheyney, E. P., *A History of England from the Defeat of the Armada to the Death of Elizabeth,* 1914-1926; Read, Conyers, *Tudors,* 1936; Scott, W. R., *Constitution and Finance of English, Scottish and Irish Joint Stock Companies to 1720,* 1912.

The planting and organizing of the colonies are detailed in: Adams, J. T., *Founding of New England,* 1921; and *Revolutionary New England, 1691-1776,* 1923; Beer, G. L., *Origins of the British Colonial System, 1578-1660,* 1922; and *Old Colonial System,* 1912; and *British Colonial Policy, 1754-1765,* 1907; Brown, A., *The Genesis of the United States* (2 vols.), 1891; Crane, V. W., *The Southern Frontier,* 1929; Dodd, W. E., *The Old South: Struggles for Democracy,* 1937; Johnson, A., *Swedish Settlements on the Delaware, 1638-1664,* 1911; Mereness, N. D., *Maryland as a Proprietary Province,* 1901; Morison, S. E., *Builders of the Bay Colony,* 1930; Wertenbaker, T. J., *Patrician and Plebeian in Virginia,* 1910; and *Virginia under the Stuarts, 1607-1688,* 1914; Wrong, G. M., *Rise and Fall of New France* (2 vols.), 1928; Wuorinen, J. H., *The Finns on the Delaware,* 1938.

Economic conditions are analyzed in: Abernethy, T. P., *Western Lands and the American Revolution,* 1937; Bining, A. C., *Pennsylvania Iron Manufacture in the 18th Century,* 1938; Bruce, P. A., *Economic History of Virginia in the Seventeenth Century,* 1896; Harrington, V. D., *The New York Merchant on the Eve of the Revolution,* 1935; Jernegan, M. W., *Laboring and Dependent Classes in Colonial America,* 1931; McFarland, R., *History of the New England Fisheries,*

1911; Stevens, W. E., *The Northwest Fur Trade,* 1928; Weeden, W. B., *Economic and Social History of New England,* 1890.

Some phases of social development are considered in: Bridenbaugh, C., *Cities in the Wilderness,* 1938; Morison, S. E., *The Puritan Pronaos,* 1936; and *Founding of Harvard College,* 1935; Schneider, H. W., *The Puritan Mind,* 1930; Spruill, J. C., *Women's Life and Work in the Southern Colonies,* 1938; Wertenbaker, T. J., *Founding of American Civilization: the Middle Colonies,* 1938.

Convenient biographies are: Chidsey, D. B., *Sir Humphrey Gilbert,* 1932; Fox, D. R., *Caleb Heathcote,* 1926; Ettinger, A. A., *James Edward Oglethorpe, Imperial Idealist,* 1936; Dobrée, B., *William Penn,* 1932, Waldman, M., *Sir Walter Raleigh,* 1928; Ernst, J. E., *Roger Williams,* 1932.

Independence
1763-1823

Two extensive works cover part of this period: McMaster, J. B., *History of the People of the United States, 1783-1865* (9 vols.), 1883-1927; Adams, H., *History of the United States during the Administrations of Jefferson and Madison* (9 vols.), 1890-1891. The volumes in the *American Nation Series* are Howard, G. E., *Preliminaries of the Revolution;* Van Tyne, C. H., *American Revolution;* McLaughlin, A. C., *Confederation and the Constitution;* Bassett, J. S., *Federalist System;* Channing, E., *Jeffersonian System;* Babcock, K. C., *Rise of American Nationality;* in the *Chronicles of America* are Becker, C., *Eve of the Revolution;* Wrong, G. M., *Washington and his Comrades in Arms;* Farrand, M., *Fathers of the Constitution;* Ford, H. J., *Washington and his Colleagues;* Johnson, A., *Jefferson and his Colleagues;* Corwin, E. S., *John Marshall and the Constitution;* Paine, R. D., *Fight for a Free Sea;* Skinner, C. L., *Pioneers of the Old Southwest;* Ogg, F. L., *Old Northwest.*

Accounts of the various phases of the Revolution are contained in: Alvord, C. W., *Mississippi Valley in British Politics,* 1916; Becker, C. L., *Declaration of Independence,* 1922; East, R. A., *Business Enterprise in the American Revolutionary Era,* 1938; Faÿ, B., *Revolutionary Spirit in France in America,* 1927; Jameson, J. F., *American Revolution Considered as a Social Movement,* 1920; McIlwain, C. H., *American Revolution,* 1923; Nevins, A., *American States During and After the Revolution,* 1924; Paullin, C. O., *Navy in the American Revolution,* 1906; Schlesinger, A. M., *Colonial Merchants and the American Revolution,* 1918; Trevelyan, Sir G. O., *American Revolution,* 1899-1907; Van Tyne, C. H., *Causes of the War of Independence,* 1922; *War of Independence,* 1929; and *Loyalists in the American Revolution,* 1902.

The formation of the Constitution is described in: Beard, C. A., *An Economic Interpretation of the Constitution of the United States,* 1913; Farrand, M., *Framing of the Constitution of the United States,* 1913; Jensen, M., *Articles of Confederation,* 1941; Schuyler, R. L., *Constitution of the United States,* 1923; Warren, C., *Making of the Constitution,* 1928.

Details of the political and diplomatic problems of the new nation are found in: Beard, C. A., *Economic Origins of the Jeffersonian Democracy,* 1915; Bemis, S. F., *Jay's Treaty,* 1923, and *Pinckney's Treaty,* 1926; Bowers, C. G., *Jefferson and Hamilton,* 1925; and *Jefferson in Power,* 1936; Cox, I. J., *West Florida Controversy,* 1918; Fox, D. R., *Decline of Aristocracy in the Politics of New York,* 1918; Lyon, E. W., *Louisiana in French Diplomacy,* 1934; Mahan, A. T., *Sea*

Power in its Relation to the War of 1812, 1905; McCaleb, W. F., *Aaron Burr Conspiracy,* 1903; Perkins, D., *Monroe Doctrine, 1823-1826,* 1927; Pratt, J. W., *Expansionists of 1812,* 1925; Sears, L. M., *Jefferson and the Embargo,* 1927; Updike, F. A., *Diplomacy of the War of 1812,* 1915; Whitaker, A. P., *Mississippi Question, 1795-1803,* 1934, and *Spanish-American Frontier, 1783-1795,* 1927.

Social and economic conditions are analyzed in: Bond, B. W., *Civilization of the Old Northwest,* 1934; Curti, M. E., *Social Ideas of American Educators,* 1935; Hinsdale, B. A., *Old Northwest,* 1899; Jones, H. M., *America and French Culture, 1750-1848,* 1927; Mathews, L. K., *Expansion of New England,* 1909; Miller, J. M., *Genesis of Western Culture,* 1938; Morison, S. E., *Maritime History of Massachusetts,* 1922; Roosevelt, T., *Winning of the West* (4 vols.), 1894-1896; Treat, P. J., *National Land System, 1785-1820,* 1910.

Some biographies of importance are: Adams, J. T., *Adams Family,* 1930; Miller, J. C., *Sam Adams,* 1936; Harlow, R. V., *Samuel Adams,* 1923; James, J. A., *Life of George Rogers Clark,* 1928; Van Doren, C., *Benjamin Franklin,* 1938; Fay, B., *Franklin, the Apostle of Modern Times,* 1929; Adams, H., *Life of Albert Gallatin,* 1879; Oliver, F. S., *Alexander Hamilton,* 1906; Monaghan, F., *John Jay,* 1935; Chinard, G., *Thomas Jefferson,* 1929; Hirst, F. W., *Life and Letters of Thomas Jefferson,* 1926; Muzzey, D. S., *Jefferson,* 1918; Beveridge, A. J., *Life of John Marshall* (4 vols.), 1916-1919; Morison, S. E., *Life and Letters of H. G. Otis,* 1913; Fitzpatrick, J. C., *George Washington Himself,* 1933; Hughes, R., *George Washington* (3 vols.), 1926-1930; Little, S., *George Washington,* 1929; Sears, L. M., *George Washington,* 1932.

Growth and Sectional Conflict

1823-1865

Part of this period is covered in the extensive work of J. F. Rhodes, *History of the United States from the Compromise of 1850* (9 vols.), 1893-1922. Volume surveys are: Adams, J. T., *America's Tragedy,* 1934; Randall, J. G., *Civil War and Reconstruction,* 1937; Turner, F. J., *United States, 1830-1850,* 1935. The *American Nation Series* contains Turner, F. J., *Rise of the New West;* Hart, A. B., *Slavery and Abolition;* MacDonald, W., *Jacksonian Democracy;* Garrison, G. P., *Westward Extension;* Smith, T. C., *Parties and Slavery;* Chadwick, F. E., *Causes of the Civil War;* Hosmer, J. K., *Appeal to Arms,* and *Outcome of the Civil War.* The appropriate volumes in the *Chronicles of America* are Ogg, F. A., *Reign of Andrew Jackson;* Hulbert, A. B., *Paths of Inland Commerce;* Skinner, C. L., *Adventurers of Oregon;* White, S. E., *Forty-Niners;* Hough, E., *Passing of the Frontier;* Dodd, W. E., *Cotton Kingdom;* Macy, J., *Anti-Slavery Crusade;* Stephenson, N. W., *Texas and the Mexican War,* and *Abraham Lincoln and the Union,* and *Day of the Confederacy;* Wood, W., *Captains of the Civil War.* In the *History of American Life Series* are Fish, C. R., *Rise of the Common Man;* Cole, A. C., *Irrepressible Conflict.*

Sectionalism and politics are discussed in: Adams, J. T., *New England in the Republic, 1776-1850,* 1926; Barker, E. C., *Mexico and Texas, 1821-1835,* 1928; Barnes, G. H., *Anti-Slavery Impulse,* 1933; Billington, R. A., *Protestant Crusade, 1800-1860,* 1938; Boucher, C. S., *Nullification Controversy in South Carolina,* 1916; Bowers, C. G., *Party Battles of the Jackson Period,* 1922; Carpenter, J. T., *South as a Conscious Minority,* 1930; Cole, A. C., *Whig Party in the South,* 1913; Craven, A., *Coming of Civil War,* 1942; Dumond, D. L., *Secession Movement,*

1860-1861, 1931; Goodwin, C., *Trans-Mississippi West,* 1922; Nichols, R. F., *Democratic Machine, 1850-1854,* 1923; Perkins, D., *Monroe Doctrine, 1826-1867,* 1933; Ray, P. O., *Repeal of the Missouri Compromise,* 1909; Russel, R. R., *Economic Aspects of Southern Sectionalism, 1840-1861,* 1924; Schaper, W. A., *Sectionalism and Representation in South Carolina,* 1901; Shryock, R. H., *Georgia and the Union in 1850,* 1926; Smith, J. H., *War with Mexico* (2 vols.), 1919; Van Deusen, J. G., *Economic Bases of Disunion in South Carolina,* 1928.

The economic background of the struggle is described in: Benns, F. L., *American Struggle for the West India Carrying Trade 1815-1830,* 1923; Buck, N. S., *The Development of the Organization of Anglo-American Trade, 1800-1850,* 1925; Carter, C. E., *When Railroads were New,* 1909; Catterall, R. C. H., *Second Bank of the United States,* 1903; Chittenden, H. M., *American Fur Trade in the Far West* (3 vols.), 1902; Clark, A. H., *Clipper Ship Era, 1843-1869,* 1910; Cole, A. H., *American Wool Manufacture* (2 vols.), 1926; Coman, K., *Economic Beginnings of the Far West* (2 vols.), 1912; Craven, A. O., *Soil Exhaustion as a Factor in the Agricultural History of Virginia and Maryland, 1660-1860,* 1925; Cutler, C. C., *Greyhounds of the Sea: The Story of the American Clipper Ship,* 1930; Flanders, R. B., *Plantation Slavery in Georgia,* 1932; Harlow, A. F., *Old Towpaths,* 1926; and *Old Waybills,* 1934; Hungerford, E., *Story of the Baltimore and Ohio Railroad, 1827-1927* (2 vols.), 1928; Kaempffert, W., *History of American Inventions* (2 vols.), 1924; McGrane, R. C., *Foreign Bondholders and American State Debts,* 1935; and *Panic of 1837,* 1924; Paine, R. D., *The Old Merchant Marine,* 1919; Phillips, U. B., *Life and Labor in the Old South,* 1929, and *American Negro Slavery,* 1918; Quick, H., *Mississippi Steamboatin',* 1926; Robert, J. C., *Tobacco Kingdom, 1800-1860,* 1938; Shotter, H. W., *Growth and Development of the Pennsylvania Railroad,* 1927; Stephenson, G. M., *Political History of the Public Lands from 1840 to 1862,* 1917; Sydnor, C. S., *Slavery in Mississippi,* 1933; Ware, C. F., *Early New England Cotton Manufacture,* 1931; Ware, N. J., *Industrial Worker, 1840-1860,* 1924; Wellington, R. G., *Political and Sectional Influence of the Public Lands, 1828-1842,* 1914.

Social and cultural phases of the period are analyzed in: Adams, W. F., *Ireland and Irish Immigration to the New World from 1815 to the Famine,* 1932; Blegen, T. C., *Norwegian Migration to America,* 1931; Branch, E. D., *Sentimental Years,* 1934; Brooks, V., *Flowering of New England,* 1936; Faust, A. B., *German Element in the United States* (2 vols.), 1909; Ford, H. J., *Scotch-Irish in America,* 1915; Janson, F. E., *Background of Swedish Immigration, 1840-1930,* 1931; Krout, J. A., *Origins of Prohibition,* 1925; Minnigerode, M., *Fabulous Forties,* 1924; Mumford, L., *Golden Day,* 1926; Pierce, B. L., *A History of Chicago,* 1937; Tewksbury, D. G., *Founding of American Colleges and Universities before the Civil War,* 1932.

The Civil War is treated in: Adams, E. D., *Great Britain and the American Civil War* (2 vols.), 1925; Baxter, J. P., 3rd, *Introduction of the Ironclad Warship,* 1933; Fite, E. D., *Social and Industrial Conditions in the North during the Civil War,* 1910; Lonn, E., *Desertion during the Civil War,* 1928; Owsley, F. L., *King Cotton Diplomacy,* 1931; Randall, J. G., *Constitutional Problems under Lincoln,* 1926; Schwab, J. C., *Confederate States of America: A Financial and Industrial History,* 1901; Simkims, F. B., and Patton, J. W., *Women of the Confederacy,* 1936; Wesley, C. H., *Collapse of the Confederacy,* 1937; Wiley, B. I., *Southern Negroes, 1861-1865,* 1938.

Biographies of the period are: Clark, B. C., *John Quincy Adams,* 1932; Porter, K. W., *John Jacob Astor, Business Man* (2 vols.), 1931; Smith, W. E., *Francis Preston Blair Family in Politics,* 1933; Meigs, W. M., *John C. Calhoun* (2 vols.),

1917; Mayo, B., *Henry Clay,* 1937; Van Deusen, G. G., *Henry Clay,* 1937; Cutting, E., *Jefferson Davis,* 1930; McElroy, R., *Jefferson Davis,* 1937; Milton, G. F., *Eve of Conflict: Life of Stephen A. Douglas,* 1934; James, M., *Andrew Jackson* (2 vols.), 1933-1937; Bassett, J. S., *Andrew Jackson* (2 vols.), 1911; Freeman, D. S., *R. E. Lee: a Biography* (4 vols.), 1934-1935; Beveridge, A. J., *Abraham Lincoln* (2 vols.), 1928; Stephenson, N. W., *Lincoln,* 1922; Hutchinson, W. T., *Cyrus Hall McCormick* (2 vols.), 1930-1935; Commager, H. S., *Theodore Parker,* 1936; Nichols, R. F., *Franklin Pierce,* 1931; McCormac, E. I., *James K. Polk,* 1922; Bancroft, F., *William H. Seward* (2 vols.), 1900; Pendleton, L., *Alexander H. Stephens,* 1908; Swisher, C. B., *Roger B. Taney,* 1936; Phillips, U. B., *Robert Toombs,* 1913; Fuess, C. M., *Daniel Webster* (2 vols.), 1930; Waterman, W. R., *Frances Wright,* 1924.

Reconstruction and Large-Scale Organization 1865-1900

The most extensive treatment of the period from 1865 to the present is Oberholtzer, E. P., *History of the United States since the Civil War, 1865-1901* (5 vols.), 1917-1936. Convenient one volume presentations are: Beard, C. A., *Contemporary American History,* 1914; Hacker, L. M., and Kendrick, B. B., *United States since 1865* (3rd edition), 1939; Lingley, C. R., and Foley, A. R., *Since the Civil War* (3rd edition), 1935; Mead, N. P., *Development of the United States since 1865,* 1930; Paxson, F. L., *Recent History of the United States* (Revised and enlarged edition), 1938; Stephenson, G. M., *American History since 1865,* 1938.

Surveys of the period 1865-1879 are found in the *American Nation Series,* the *Chronicles of America* and the *History of American Life,* respectively: Dunning, W. A., *Reconstruction, Political and Economic;* Fleming, W. L., *Sequel to Appomattox;* Nevins, A., *Emergence of Modern America.* Reference should also be made to Bowers, C. G., *Tragic Era,* 1929; Fleming, W. L., *Documentary History of Reconstruction* (2 vols.), 1906-1907; Henry, R. S., *Story of Reconstruction,* 1938.

For conditions in the South, special studies are: Caskey, W. M., *Secession and Restoration of Louisiana,* 1938; Coulter, E. M., *Civil War and Readjustment in Kentucky,* 1926; Davis, W. W., *Civil War and Reconstruction in Florida,* 1913; Eckenrode, H. J., *Political History of Virginia during Reconstruction,* 1904; Fleming, W. L., *Reconstruction in Alabama,* 1905; Garner, J. W., *Reconstruction in Mississippi,* 1901; Hamilton, J. G. de R., *Reconstruction in North Carolina,* 1914; Lonn, E., *Reconstruction in Louisiana after 1868,* 1918; Patton, J. W., *Unionism and Reconstruction in Tennessee,* 1934; Ramsdell, C. W., *Reconstruction in Texas,* 1910; Simkins, F. B., and Woody, R. H., *South Carolina during Reconstruction,* 1931; Staples, T. S., *Reconstruction in Arkansas,* 1923; Thompson, C. M., *Reconstruction in Georgia,* 1915; Dunning, W. A., *Essays in Civil War and Reconstruction,* 1910; Beale, H. K., *Critical Year: A Study of Andrew Johnson and Reconstruction,* 1930; Buck, P. H., *Road to Reunion,* 1937; Lewinson, P., *Race, Class and Party,* 1932; Lester, J. C., and Wilson, D. L., *Ku Klux Klan,* 1905. Significant biographies include Milton, G. F., *Age of Hate* (Andrew Johnson), 1930; Stryker, L. P., *Andrew Johnson, A Study in Courage,* 1929; Winston, R. W., *Andrew Johnson: Plebeian and Patriot,* 1929; Haynes, G. H., *Charles Sumner,* 1909; Woodley, T. F., *Great Leveler: The Life of Thaddeus Stevens,*

1937; Mitchell, S., *Horatio Seymour,* 1938; Coulter, E. M., *William G. Brownlow,* 1937; Pearce, H. J., *Benjamin H. Hill,* 1928; Cate, W. A., *L.Q.C. Lamar,* 1935.

For Eastern dominance, reference should be made to: Seitz, D. C., *Dreadful Decade, 1869-1879,* 1926; Ross, E. D., *Liberal Republican Movement,* 1919; Barclay, T. S., *Liberal Republican Movement in Missouri,* 1926; Barrett, D. C., *Greenbacks and Resumption of Specie Payments, 1862-1879,* 1931; Haworth, P. L., *Hayes-Tilden Disputed Presidential Election of 1876,* 1906; Adams, C. F., Jr., *Chapters of Erie,* 1886; Hungerford, E., *Men and Iron: The History of the New York Central,* 1938; Giddens, P. H., *Birth of the Oil Industry,* 1938; Hesseltine, W. B., *U. S. Grant, Politician,* 1935; Woodward, W. E., *Meet General Grant,* 1928; Nevins, A., *Hamilton Fish and the Grant Administration,* 1936; Eckenrode, H. J., *Rutherford B. Hayes,* 1930; Larson, H., *Jay Cooke,* 1936; Nevins, A., *Abram S. Hewitt: With some Account of Peter Cooper,* 1935; Seitz, D. C., *Horace Greeley: Founder of the New York Tribune,* 1926; Stone, C., *Dana and the Sun,* 1938; Fuller, R. H., *Jubilee Jim: The Life of Colonel James Fisk, Jr.,* 1928; Smith, A. D., *Commodore Vanderbilt,* 1927; White, B., *The Book of Daniel Drew,* 1910; Josephson, M., *Robber Barons,* 1934.

The advance of the West is particularly studied in: Branch, E. D., *Westward, the Romance of the American Frontier,* 1930; Caughey, J. W., *History of the Pacific Coast,* 1933; Foreman, G., *Advancing the Frontier,* 1933; Fuller, G. W., *Inland Empire* (3 vols.), 1928; Richardson, R. N., and Rister, C. C., *Greater Southwest,* 1934; Riegel, R. E., *America Moves West,* 1930, and *Story of the Western Railroads,* 1926; Hedges, J. B., *Henry Villard and the Railways of the Northwest,* 1930; Lewis, O., *Big Four,* 1938; Trottman, N., *History of the Union Pacific,* 1923; Debo, A., *Rise and Fall of the Choctaw Republic,* 1934; Foreman, G., *Five Civilized Tribes,* 1934; Vestal, S., *Sitting Bull,* 1932; Dale, E. E., *Range Cattle Industry,* 1930; Dick, E., *Sod House Frontier,* 1937; Garland, H., *Son of the Middle Border,* 1917; Gates, P. W., *Illinois Central Railroad and Its Colonization Work,* 1934; Henry, S., *Conquering Our Great American Plains,* 1930; Lyman, G. D., *Saga of the Comstock Lode,* 1934; Osgood, E. S., *Day of the Cattleman,* 1929; Pelzer, L., *Cattlemen's Frontier, 1850-1890,* 1936; Rister, C. C., *Southwestern Frontier, 1865-1881,* 1928, and *Southern Plainsmen,* 1938; Webb, W. P., *Great Plains,* 1931, and *Texas Rangers,* 1935; Buck, S. J., *Granger Movement,* 1913; and *Agrarian Crusade,* 1921; Hubbart, H. C., *Older Middle West,* 1936.

For general surveys of the years 1878-1900 see the appropriate volumes in the three series. In the *American Nation Series* are Sparks, E. E., *National Development;* Dewey, D. R., *National Problems;* Latané, J. H., *America as a World Power.* In the *Chronicles of America* are Thompson, H., *Age of Invention;* Moody, J., *Railroad Builders;* Hendrick, B. J., *Age of Big Business;* Orth, S. P., *Armies of Labor,* and *Boss and the Machine;* Moody, J., *Masters of Capital;* Thompson, H., *New South;* Ford, H. J., *Cleveland Era.* In the *History of American Life* are Schlesinger, A. M., *Rise of the City,* Tarbell, I. M., *Nationalizing of Industry.* Also see Peck, H. T., *Twenty Years of the Republic,* 1905; and Beer, T., *Mauve Decade,* 1926.

For industrial development see: Casson, H., *Romance of Steel,* 1907; and *History of the Telephone,* 1910; Collins, J. H., *Story of Canned Foods,* 1924; Glasscock, C. B., *War of the Copper Kings,* 1935; James, F. C., *Growth of Chicago Banks,* 1938; Jerome, H., *Mechanization in Industry,* 1934; Martin, T. C., and Coles, S. L., *Story of Electricity,* 1919; Moody, J., *Truth About Trusts,* 1904; Rickard, T. A., *History of American Mining,* 1932; Ripley, W. Z., *Railway Prob-*

lems, 1913, and *Railroads; Rates and Regulation,* 1913; Shinn, C. H., *Story of the Mine,* 1896; Tarbell, I. M., *History of the Standard Oil* (2 vols.), 1904; Leech, H., and Carroll, J., *Armour and His Times,* 1938; Hendrick, B. J., *Andrew Carnegie* (2 vols.), 1932; Carnegie, A., *Triumphant Democracy,* 1886; Dyer, F. L., and Martin, T. C., *Edison, His Life and Inventions,* 1929; Harvey, G., *Henry Clay Frick: The Man,* 1928; Tarbell, I. M., *Life of Elbert H. Gary,* 1928; O'Connor, H., *Guggenheims,* 1938; Kennan, G., *E. H. Harriman,* 1922; Pyle, J. G., *Life of James J. Hill,* 1917; Corey, L., *House of Morgan,* 1930; Flynn, J. T., *God's Gold: Life of John D. Rockefeller,* 1931; Nevins, A., *John D. Rockefeller,* 1940.

For labor, see: Adamic, L., *Dynamite: The Story of Class Violence in America,* 1931; Childs, H. L., *Labor and Capital,* 1930; David, H., *History of the Haymarket Affair,* 1936; Gompers, S., *Seventy Years of Life and Labor* (2 vols.), 1925; Harris, H., *American Labor,* 1938; Lorwin, L. L., *American Federation of Labor,* 1933; McMurray, D. L., *Coxey's Army,* 1929; Powderly, T. V., *Thirty Years of Labor,* 1889; Ware, N. J., *Labor Movement in the United States, 1860-1895,* 1929; Wolman, L., *Growth of American Trade Unions, 1880-1923,* 1924.

For agrarian conditions, see: Arnett, A. M., *Populist Movement in Georgia,* 1922; Brooks, R. P., *Agrarian Revolution in Georgia, 1865-1912,* 1914; Clark, J. B., *Populism in Alabama,* 1927; Haynes, F. E., *Third Party Movements since the Civil War,* 1916; Hicks, J. D., *Populist Revolt: A History of the Farmers' Alliance and the People's Party,* 1931; Kendrick, B. B., and Arnett, A. M., *The South Looks at Its Past,* 1935; Mitchell, B., *Industrial Revolution in the South,* 1930, and *Rise of the Cotton Mills in the South,* 1921; Odum, H.. *Southern Pioneers,* 1925; Sheldon, W. D., *Populism in the Old Dominion,* 1935; Simkins, F. B., *Tillman Movement in South Carolina,* 1926; Thompson, H., *From the Cottonfield to the Cotton Mill,* 1906; Woodward, C. V., *Tom Watson, Agrarian Rebel,* 1938.

For social and cultural progress, see: Mumford, L., *Brown Decades, A Study of the Arts in America, 1865-1895,* 1931; Wecter, D., *Saga of American Society,* 1937; Dondore, D. A., *Prairie and the Making of Middle America,* 1926; Hazard, L., *Frontier in American Literature,* 1927; Seldes, G. V., *Stammering Century,* 1928; Cushing, H., *Life of Sir William Osler* (2 vols.), 1925; James, H., *Charles W. Eliot, President of Harvard University, 1869-1909,* 1930; Winkler, W. R., *Hearst, An American Phenomenon,* 1928; Seitz, D. C., *Joseph Pulitzer, His Life and Letters,* 1924; Josephson, M., *Portrait of the Artist as American,* 1930; Cargill, O., *Intellectual America,* 1941.

For politics, see: Bryan, W. J., *First Battle,* 1896; Fish, C. R., *Civil Service and the Patronage,* 1904; Josephson, M., *Politicos, 1865-1896,* 1938; Laughlin, J. L., *History of Bimetallism in the United States,* 1897; Merriam, C. E., *American Party System,* 1923; and *American Political Ideas, 1867-1917,* 1920; Overacker, L., *Money in Elections,* 1932; Stanwood, E., *American Tariff Controversies in the 19th Century,* 1903; Tarbell, I. M., *Tariff in Our Times,* 1911; Walker, A. H., *History of the Sherman Law,* 1910. Influential figures include Barnard, H., *Eagle Forgotten, The Life of John Peter Altgeld,* 1938; Howe, G. F., *Chester A. Arthur,* 1934; Muzzey, D. S., *James G. Blaine,* 1934; Hibben, P., *Peerless Leader: William Jennings Bryan,* 1929; Barnes, J. A., *John G. Carlisle,* 1931; Nevins, A., *Grover Cleveland,* 1932; Chidsey, D. B., *Gentleman from New York: the Life of Roscoe Conkling,* 1935; Smith, T. C., *Life and Letters of James A. Garfield,* 1925; Caldwell, R. G., *James A. Garfield,* 1931; Croly, H., *Marcus Alonzo Hanna,* 1912; Beer, T., *Hanna,* 1929; Dennett, T., *John Hay,* 1933; Olcott, C. S., *William McKinley* (2 vols.), 1916; Gosnell, H. F., *Boss Platt and the New York Machine,*

1924; Trimble, B. R., *Chief Justice Waite,* 1938; Haynes, F. E., *James Baird Weaver,* 1919.

For foreign relations, see: Dennett, T., *Americans in Eastern Asia,* 1922; Millis, W., *Martial Spirit: A Study of our War with Spain,* 1931; Perkins, D., *Monroe Doctrine, 1867-1907,* 1937; Pratt, J. W., *Expansionists of 1898,* 1936; Ryden, G. F., *Foreign Policy of the United States in Relation to Samoa,* 1933; Tansill, C. C., *United States and Santo Domingo, 1798-1873,* 1938; Russell, H. B., *International Monetary Conferences,* 1898.

Perfection of Democracy

1900-1919

General treatments of this period are found in Sullivan, Mark, *Our Times* (5 vols.), 1926-1935; Dumond, D. L., *Roosevelt to Roosevelt,* 1937; Nichols, J. P., *Twentieth Century United States,* 1943; and Paxson, F. L., *American Democracy and the World War* (2 vols.), 1939. The appropriate volumes in the three series are: in the *American Nation Series,* Latané, J. H., *America as a World Power;* Ogg, F. A., *National Progress, 1907-1917;* in the *Chronicles of America,* Fish, C. R., *Path of Empire;* Howland, H., *Theodore Roosevelt and His Times;* Seymour, C., *Woodrow Wilson and the World War;* in the *History of American Life,* Faulkner, H. U., *Quest for Social Justice.*

For the spirit of reform, see: Addams, J., *Forty Years at Hull House,* 1930; Barton, A. O., *La Follette's Winning of Wisconsin, 1894-1904,* 1922; Bok, E. W., *Americanization of Edward Bok,* 1920; Brooks, V., *America's Coming of Age,* 1915; Chamberlain, J., *Farewell to Reform,* 1933; Croly, Herbert, *Promise of American Life,* 1909; DeWitt, B. P., *Progressive Movement,* 1915; Harriman, Mrs. J. B., *From Pinafores to Politics,* 1923; Haynes, F. E., *Social Politics in the United States,* 1924; Hillquit, M., *History of Socialism in the United States,* 1903; Howe, F. C., *Wisconsin, An Experiment in Democracy,* 1912; Regier, C. C., *Era of the Muckrakers,* 1932; Seager, H. R., and Gulick, C. A., Jr., *Trust and Corporation Problems,* 1929; Steffens, L., *Shame of the Cities,* 1904; Stahl, R. M., *Ballinger-Pinchot Controversy,* 1926; Warburg, P. M., *Federal Reserve System* (2 vols.), 1930; Weyl, W. E., *New Democracy,* 1912; Willis, H. P., *Federal Reserve System,* 1923. Significant biographies are Stephenson, N. W., *Nelson W. Aldrich: A Leader in American Politics,* 1930; Bowers, C. G., *Beveridge and the Progressive Era,* 1932; Howe, F. C., *Confessions of a Reformer,* 1925; Dennett, T., *John Hay,* 1933; Johnson, T., *My Story,* 1911; La Follette, R. M., *La Follette's Autobiography,* 1913; McClure, S. S., *My Autobiography,* 1914; Coolidge, L. A., *An Old-Fashioned Senator, Orville H. Platt of Connecticut,* 1910; *Selections from the Correspondence of Theodore Roosevelt and Henry Cabot Lodge* (2 vols.), 1925; Pringle, H. F., *Theodore Roosevelt,* 1931; Jessup, P. C., *Elihu Root,* 1938; Steffens, L., *Autobiography of Lincoln Steffens* (2 vols.), 1931; Pringle, H. F., *William Howard Taft,* 1939, and *Taft and Roosevelt: The Intimate Letters of Archie Butt* (2 vols.), 1930; Dorfman, J., *Thorstein Veblen and His America,* 1934; Veblen, T., *Theory of the Leisure Class,* 1899; Nevins, A., *Henry White: Thirty Years of American Diplomacy,* 1930; Whitlock, B., *Forty Years of It,* 1913.

For the responsibilities of world power, see: Chapman, C. C., *History of the Cuban Republic,* 1927; Curti, M., *Peace or War: the American Struggle,* 1936; Dennis, A. L. P., *Adventures in American Diplomacy, 1896-1906.* 1928; Dennett,

T., *Theodore Roosevelt and the Russo-Japanese War,* 1925; Diffie, B. W., and J. W., *Porto Rico: A Broken Pledge,* 1931; Forbes, W. C., *Philippine Islands* (2 vols.), 1928; Knight, M. M., *The Americans in Santo Domingo,* 1928; Hill, H. C., *Roosevelt and the Caribbean,* 1927; Jenks, L. H., *Our Cuban Colony: A Study in Sugar,* 1928; Lockmiller, D. A., *Magoon in Cuba,* 1938; Nearing, S., and Freeman, J., *Dollar Diplomacy,* 1925; Nichols, J. P., *Alaska,* 1924; Rippy, F. J., *Capitalists and Colombia,* 1931, and *United States and Mexico* (revised ed.), 1931; Hayden, J. R., *The Philippines: A Study in National Development,* 1942; Williams, M. W., *Anglo-American Isthmian Diplomacy, 1815-1915,* 1916.

Barnes, H. E., *Genesis of the World War,* 1929; and *World Politics and Modern Civilization,* 1930; Bassett, J. S., *Our War with Germany,* 1919; Borchard, E., and Lage, W., *Neutrality for the United States,* 1937; Clarkson, G. B., *Industrial America in the World War,* 1923; Creel, G., *How We Advertised America,* 1920; Crowell, B., and Wilson, R. F., *How America Went to War* (6 vols.), 1921; Dixon, F. H., *Railroads and Government, Their Relations in the United States,* 1922; Fay, S. B., *Origins of the World War* (2 vols.), 1928; Grattan, C. H., *Why We Fought,* 1929; Harbord, J. G., *American Army in France,* 1936; Hendrick, B. J., and Sims, W. S., *Victory at Sea,* 1920; Keynes, J. M., *Economic Consequences of the Peace,* 1919; Lippmann, W., *Liberty and the News,* 1920; McMaster, J. B., *United States in the World War* (2 vols.), 1918-1920; Millis, W., *Road to War,* 1935; Schmitt, B. E., *Coming of the War* (2 vols.), 1930; Seymour, C., *American Diplomacy during the World War,* 1934, and *American Neu*trality, 1935; Slosson, P. W., *Great Crusade—and After,* 1930; Tansill, C. C., *America Goes to War,* 1938; Willoughby, W. F., *Government Organization in War Time and After,* 1919.

Important leaders include Palmer, F., *Newton D. Baker: America at War* (2 vols.), 1931; Bernstorff, J. H., *My Three Years in America,* 1920; Bryan, W. J., *Memoirs,* 1925; Arnett, A. M., *Claude Kitchin and the Wilson War Policies,* 1937; Seymour, C., ed., *Intimate Papers of Colonel House* (4 vols.), 1926-1928; Houston, D. F., *Eight Years with Wilson's Cabinet,* 1926; McAdoo, W. G., *Crowded Years,* 1931; Hendrik, B. J., *Life and Letters of W. H. Page* (3 vols.), 1922-1925; Pershing, Gen. J. J., *My Experiences in the World War* (2 vols.), 1931; Baker, R. S., *Life and Letters of Woodrow Wilson* (8 vols.), 1927-1939; Seymour, C., *Woodrow Wilson and the World War,* 1921; Tumulty, J. P., *Woodrow Wilson As I Knew Him,* 1925; Wilson, E. B., *My Memoir,* 1939.

Between World Wars

1919-1939

General accounts are: Allen, F. L., *Only Yesterday,* 1931; Hacker, L. M., *American Problems of Today,* 1938; Malin, J. C., *United States after the World War,* 1930.

For politics, see: Anonymous, *Washington Merry-Go-Round,* 1931; Anonymous, *Mirrors of 1932,* 1933; Feldman, H., *Prohibition, Its Economic and Industrial Aspects,* 1927; Merz, C., *Dry Decade,* 1931; Myers, W. S., and Newton, W. H., *Hoover Administration,* 1936; O'Connor, H., *Mellon's Millions,* 1933; Odegard, P., *Pressure Politics: The Story of the Anti-Saloon League,* 1928; Pringle, H. F., *Alfred E. Smith: A Critical Study,* 1927; White, W. A., *Masks in a Pageant,* 1928, and *A Puritan in Babylon* (*Calvin Coolidge*), 1938.

For foreign relations, see: Bassett, J. S., *League of Nations,* 1928; Buell, R. L.,

Washington Conference, 1922; Clark, J. R. (prepared by U. S. State Dept.), *Memorandum on the Monroe Doctrine,* 1930; Hudson, M. O., *Permanent Court of International Justice and the Question of American Participation,* 1925; Miller, D. H., *Peace Pact of Paris,* 1928.

For the general mad whirl, see: Adams, J. T., *Our Business Civilization,* 1929; Berle, A. A., Jr., and Means, G. C., *Modern Corporation and Private Property,* 1932; Bonbright, J. C., and Means, G. C., *Holding Company,* 1932; Carver, T. N., *Present Economic Revolution in the United States,* 1925; Chase, S., *Men and Machines, The Tragedy of Waste,* 1929; Donald, W. J. A., *Trade Associations,* 1933; Dunn, R. W., *American Foreign Investments,* 1926; Epstein, R. C., *Automobile Industry,* 1928; Gellerman, W., *American Legion as Educator,* 1938; Hamilton, J. G. de R., *Henry Ford,* 1927; Lynd, R. S., and H. M., *Middletown,* 1929; Mumford, L., *Technics and Civilization,* 1934; Ripley W. Z., *Main Street and Wall Street,* 1927; President's Conference on Unemployment, *Recent Economic Changes* (2 vols.), 1929; President's Research Committee on Social Trends, *Recent Social Trends in the United States* (2 vols.), 1933; Rugg, H., *Culture and Education in America,* 1931; Seldes, G. V., *Years of the Locust: America, 1929-1932,* 1933; Tugwell, R. G., *Industry's Coming of Age,* 1927; Turlington, E., *Mexico and Her Foreign Creditors,* 1930; Warner, A. G., et al., *American Charities and Social Work,* 1930; Winkler, M., *Foreign Bonds, An Autopsy,* 1933, and *Investments of United States Capital in Latin America,* 1929.

For the plight of the farmer and the laborer, see: Black, J. D., *Agricultural Reform in the United States,* 1930; Brissenden, P. F., *History of the I.W.W.,* 1920; Fossum, P. R., *Agricultural Movement in North Dakota,* 1925; Gaston, H. E., *Non-Partisan League,* 1920; Frankfurter, F., and Green, N., *Labor Injunction,* 1930; Gambs, J. S., *Decline of the I.W.W.,* 1932; Nourse, E. G., *American Agriculture and the European Market,* 1924; Ostrolenk, B., *Surplus Farmer,* 1932; Russell, C. E., *Story of the Non-Partisan League,* 1920; True, A. C., *History of Agricultural Extension Work in the United States,* 1928.

The political phases of the New Deal are described in: Alsop, J., and Catledge, T., *168 Days,* 1937; Anonymous, *New Dealers,* 1934; Backman, J., *Government Price Fixing,* 1938; Berle, A. A., Jr., and others, *America's Recovery Program,* 1934; Buck, A. E., *Reorganization of State Governments in the United States,* 1938; Chase, S., *Rich Land, Poor Land,* 1936; Christensen, A. M., "Agricultural Pressure and Governmental Response," *Agricultural History,* 11:33-42 (Jan. 1937); Clark, J. P., *Rise of a New Federalism,* 1938; Corwin, E. S., *Twilight of the Supreme Court,* 1934; Douglas, P. H., *Social Security in the United States,* 1936; Epstein, A., *Insecurity: A Challenge to America,* 1933; Farley, J. A., *Behind the Ballots,* 1938; Hansen, A. H., *Full Recovery or Stagnation,* 1938; Holcombe, A. N., *New Party Politics,* 1934; Hoover, H., *Challenge to Liberty,* 1934; Lindley, B., and E. K., *A New Deal for Youth,* 1938; Lindley, E. K., *Roosevelt Revolution, First Phase,* 1933, and *Half Way with Roosevelt,* 1936; Nourse, E. G., and others, *Three Years of the Agricultural Adjustment Administration,* 1937; Nourse, E. G., *Marketing Agreements under the AAA,* 1935; Ogburn, W. F., ed., *Social Change and the New Deal,* 1934; Pearson, D., and Allen, R. S., *Nine Old Men,* 1936; Raushenbush, H. S., *Power Fight,* 1932; Raushenbush, H. S., and Laidler, H. W., *Power Control,* 1928; Rogers, L., "Reorganization: Post-Mortem Notes," *Pol. Sci. Quarterly,* 53:161-172 (June, 1938); Social Security Board, *Social Security in America,* 1937; Straus, M. W., and Wegg, T., *Housing Comes of Age,* 1938; Tugwell, R. G., *Battle for Democracy,* 1935; Wallace, H. A., *America Must Choose,* 1934.

Economic conditions during the New Deal may be found described in: Beard,

C. A., *The Future Comes,* 1933, *Idea of National Interest,* 1934, and *Open Door at Home,* 1934; Buell, R. L., "Death by Tariff," *Fortune,* Aug., 1938; Burns, A. R., *Decline of Competition,* 1936; Corey, L., *Decline of American Capitalism,* 1934, and *Crisis of the Middle Class,* 1935; Daniels, J., *A Southerner Discovers the South,* 1938; Goodrich, C., et al., *Migration and Economic Opportunity,* 1936; Leven, M., and others, *America's Capacity to Consume,* 1934; Lundberg, F., *America's Sixty Families,* 1937; Melder, F. E., "Economic War Among Our States," *Events,* Aug., 1938; Mills, F. C., *Economic Tendencies in the United States,* 1933; Moulton, H. G., *Financial Organization of Society* (rev. ed.), 1938; Nathan, R. R., *Income in the United States, 1929-1937,* 1938; National Resources Committee, *Consumer Income in the United States,* 1938; Nixon, H. C., *Forty Acres and Steel Mules,* 1938; Nourse, E. G., and associates, *America's Capacity to Produce,* 1934; Odum, H. O., *Southern Regions of the United States,* 1936; Rogers, J. H., *Capitalism in Crisis,* 1938; Rose, M. A., "States Get Together," *Current History,* May, 1938; Thomas, D. S., *Migration Differentials,* 1938; Twentieth Century Fund, *Big Business: Its Growth and Place,* 1937, and *How Profitable Is Big Business?,* 1937; Vance, R. B., *Population Redistribution within the United States,* 1938.

For labor conditions, see: Brooks, R. R. R., *When Labor Organizes,* 1937; and *Unions of Their Own Choosing,* 1939; U. S. Dept. of Labor, *Characteristics of Company Unions,* 1935; Levinson, E., *Labor on the March,* 1938; Stolberg, B., *Story of the C.I.O.,* 1938; Vorse, M. H., *Labor's New Millions,* 1938; Walsh, J. R., *C.I.O.: Industrial Unionism in Action,* 1937.

Foreign relations are treated in: Beals, C., *Coming Struggle for Latin America,* 1938; Bisson, T. A., *Japan in China,* 1938; Bruntz, G. G., *Allied Propaganda and the Collapse of the German Empire in 1938,* 1938; Dulles, A. W., and Armstrong, H. F., *Can We Be Neutral?,* 1936; Eliot, M., *Ramparts We Watch,* 1938; Fleming, D. F., *United States and World Organization,* 1938; *The German Reich and Americans of German Origin,* 1939; Griswold, A. W., *The Far Eastern Policy of the United States,* 1938; Gunther, J., *Inside Europe* (rev. ed.), 1938; Lewis, C., *America's Stake in International Investments,* 1938; Quigley, H. S., and Blakeslee, G., *The Far East,* 1938; Savage, C., *Policy of the United States Toward Maritime Commerce in War,* 1936; Thirteen Correspondents of the *N. Y. Times, We Saw It Happen,* 1938; Young, E. J., *Looking Behind the Censors,* 1938.

Some significant phases of the contemporary scene are described in: Anderson, J., *American Theatre,* 1938; Atkeson, M. M., *The Woman on the Farm,* 1924; Bardèche, M., and Brasillach, R., *History of Motion Pictures,* 1938; Burlingame, R., *March of the Iron Men,* 1938; Flexner, E., *American Playwrights, 1918-1938,* 1938; Grooch, W. S., *Winged Highway,* 1938; Hampton, B. B., *A History of the Movies,* 1931; Harlow, A. F., *Old Wires and New Waves,* 1936; Hicks, G., *The Great Tradition,* 1933; Lynd, H. M., *Middletown in Transition,* 1937; Mumford, L., *Culture of Cities,* 1938; National Resources Committee, *Our Cities: Their Role in the National Economy,* 1937; Pidgeon, M. E., *Women in the Economy of the United States,* 1937.

The era of isolation is described in Borchard, E., and Lage, W. P., *Neutrality for the United States,* 1937; Buell, R. L., *Isolated America,* 1924; Engelbrecht, H. C., and Hanighen, F. C., *Merchants of Death,* 1937; Jessup, P. C., *Elihu Root,* 1938; Lippmann, W., and others, *United States in World Affairs,* 1931, 1932, 1933; Wheeler-Bennett, J. W., *The Pipe Dream of Peace: The Story of the Collapse of Disarmament,* 1935. Japan's position is treated in Bisson, T. A., *American Policy in the Far East, 1931-1940,* 1940; Dulles, F. R., *Forty Years of American-Japanese Relations,* 1937; and Kirk, G. L., *Philippine Independence,* 1936.

Relations with Latin America receive particular attention in: Williams, M. W., *People and Politics of Latin America,* 1940; James, P. E., *Latin America,* 1942; Munro, D. G., *Latin American Republics,* 1942; Wilgus, A. C., *Development of Latin America,* 1941; Brown, F. J., and others, *Contemporary World Politics,* 1940; and Spykman, N J., *America's Strategy in World Politics,* 1942.

The undermining of isolation is discussed in: Alsop, J., and Kintner, R., *American White Paper,* 1940; Beard, C. A., *A Foreign Policy for America,* 1940; Davis, G. T., *A Navy Second to None,* 1940; Fields, H., *The Refugee Problem in the United States,* 1938; Lavine, H., and Wechsler, J., *War Propaganda and the U. S.,* 1940.

Economic warfare before Pearl Harbor is set forth by: Bidwell, P. W., in *Self Containment and Hemisphere Defense,* 1941; Holmes, H. N., *Strategic Materials and National Strength,* 1942; Spiegel, H. W., *Economics of Total War,* 1942; and Lary, H. B., "War Influences Dominate Foreign Trade" and "International Trade and Finance in 1941," published in *Survey of Current Business,* Oct., 1941, and Feb., 1932.

Preparations on the civilian and military fronts caused violent controversy over the direction of events, as indicated in: Agar, H., *A Time for Greatness,* 1942; Burnham, J., *The Managerial Revolution,* 1941; Kernan, W. F., *Defense Will Not Win the War,* 1942; Miller, D., *You Can't Do Business with Hitler,* 1941; Baldwin, H. W., *Strategy for Victory,* 1942; and McFarlane, C. T., *War with the Axis,* 1942.

The course of diplomatic policy before Pearl Harbor is revealed in: U. S. Dept. of State, *Peace and War,* 1942; and Roosevelt, F. D., *Roosevelt's Foreign Policy,* 1942. The American way of looking at things is developed in Beard, C. A., and Beard, M. R., *The American Spirit,* 1942; and Mead, M., *And Keep Your Powder Dry,* 1942. Geopolitical doctrines concern Dorpalen, A., *The World of General Haushofer,* 1942; Mackinder, H. J., *Democratic Ideals and Reality,* 1942; Weigert, H. W., *Generals and Geographers,* 1942; Hitler, A., *Mein Kampf,* 1940, and *My New Order,* 1941; and Ziemer, G., *Education for Death,* 1941.

The events culminating in Pearl Harbor have been described from various vantage points. The Washington view is found in: Bemis, S. F., *Diplomatic History,* 1942; and in Davis, F., and Lindley, E. R., *How War Came,* 1942. The Japanese view is in Matsuo, K., *How Japan Plans to Win,* 1942; Taylor, G. E., *America in the New Pacific,* 1942; Grew, J. C., *Report from Tokyo,* 1942; Newman, J., *Goodbye Japan,* 1942; and Tolischus, O., *Tokyo Record,* 1943. The German view is in Dodd, W. E., *Ambassador Dodd's Diary,* 1942; Shirer, W. L., *Berlin Diary,* 1941; and Smith, H. K., *Last Train from Berlin,* 1942. The Italian, Spanish and Russian precursors to American participation are discussed in Borghese, G. A., *Goliath,* 1937; Hamilton, J. J., *Appeasement's Child,* 1943; and Davies, J. E., *Mission to Moscow,* 1941. On Latin America see Quintanilla, L., *A Latin American Speaks,* 1943.

The Second World War

1939-

The severe losses involved in learning the hard way are described with reference to the Philippines in: Porter, C., *Crisis in the Philippines,* 1942; Quigley,

H. S., *Far Eastern War,* 1942; Belden, J., *Retreat with Stilwell,* 1943; Redmond, J., *I Served on Bataan,* 1943; White, W. L., *They Were Expendable,* 1942; and Abend, H., *Ramparts of the Pacific,* 1942. Understanding of the general course of the conflict is aided by Horrabin, J. F., *Atlas History,* 1940-1942; American Library Association, *Public Documents of World War II;* and Javsicas, G., *Shortage of Victory,* 1943. On Russia see Werth, A., *Moscow War Diary,* 1942.

The work of organizing for victory is described in Roosevelt and others, *America Organizes to Win the War,* 1942; Brown, F. J., *Organizing for Total War,* 1942; Van Valkenberg, S., *America at War,* 1942; Bargeron, C., *Confusion on the Potomac,* 1941; Kiplinger, F., *Washington is Like That,* 1942; Schubert, P., *Sea Power in Conflict,* 1942; Potter, J. C., *Alaska Under Arms,* 1942; and University of Pennsylvania, *Education in a Nation at War,* 1942. Coöperation with Britain is emphasized in Angell, N., *Let the People Know,* 1943; and Brogan, D. W., *The English People,* 1943. The part played by aviation is stressed in Levine, I. D., *Mitchell,* 1943; Huie, W. B., *Fight for Air Power,* 1942; Lissitzyn, O. J., *International Air Transport,* 1942; Steinbeck, J., *Bombs Away,* 1942; and Seversky, A. P., *Victory Through Air Power,* 1942.

The problem of furnishing supplies is elaborated in: Low, A. M., *Submarine at War;* Krout, J. A., *Transportation in Wartime,* 1943; Lorwin, L. L., *International Economic Developments,* 1943; Steiner, G. A., *Economic Problems of War,* 1942; Childs, M. W., *This is Your War,* 1942; Ware, C. F., *The Consumer Goes to War,* 1942; and Cherne, L. M., *Your Business Goes to War,* 1942. The fight against inflation stands forth in Kemmerer, E. W., *A B C of Inflation,* 1942; and Crum, W. L., *Fiscal Planning for Total War,* 1942. Political diversions and radio propaganda concern Young, R. A., *This is Congress,* 1943; and Rolo, C. J., *Radio Goes to War,* 1942.

The global offensive in general concerns Patterson, E. M., *Winning Both the War and the Peace,* 1942; Michie, A., *The Air Offensive,* 1943; and Morton, H. V., *Atlantic Meeting,* 1943. Russia's offensive is summarized in Dean, V. M., *Russia at War,* 1942. Experiences in the Pacific offensive are described in Johnston, S., *Queen of the Flat-tops,* 1942; Tregaskis, R., *Guadalcanal Diary,* 1943; Rickenbacker, E., *Seven Came Through,* 1943; Trumbull, R., *The Raft,* 1942; Bayler, L. J., *Last Man Off Wake Island,* 1943; Driscoll, J., *War Discovers Alaska,* 1943; Morrill, J., and Martin, P., *South from Corregidor,* 1943; Wolfert, Ira, *Battle for the Solomons,* 1943; Zanuck, D. F., *Tunis Expedition,* 1943.

Planning for peace is encouraging prolific authorship. The broader aspects of the problem are discussed in: Hoover, H., and Gibson, H., *Problems of a Lasting Peace,* 1942; and Willkie, W., *One World,* 1943. Far Eastern aspects concern Buck, P. S., *American Unity and Asia,* 1942; Abend, H., *Pacific Charter,* 1943; and Peffer, N., *Bases for Peace,* 1942. A radical view is Browder, E. R., *Victory and After,* 1942. British proposals are set forth in Carr, E. H., *Conditions of Peace,* 1942. The United Nations concern Straight, M. W., *Make This the Last War,* 1943. Economic aspects of post-war planning concern Corey, L., *The Unfinished Task,* 1942; Galloway, G. B., *Post-War Planning,* 1942; Harris, S., *Post-War Economic Developments,* 1943; and Jordan, H. D., *Problems of Post-War Reconstruction,* 1942. The various outstanding plans are conveniently summarized in Millspaugh, A. C., *Peace Plans and American Choices,* 1943.

APPENDIX

DECLARATION OF INDEPENDENCE

When, in the Course of human events, it becomes necessary for one people to dissolve the political bands which have connected them with another, and to assume among the powers of the earth, the separate and equal station to which the Laws of Nature and of Nature's God entitle them, a decent respect to the opinions of mankind requires that they should declare the causes which impel them to the separation.

We hold these truths to be self-evident, that all men are created equal, that they are endowed by their Creator with certain unalienable Rights, that among these are Life, Liberty and the pursuit of Happiness. That to secure these rights, governments are instituted among Men, deriving their just powers from the consent of the governed. That whenever any Form of Government becomes destructive of these ends, it is the Right of the People to alter or to abolish it, and to institute new Government, laying its foundation on such principles and organizing its powers in such form, as to them shall seem most likely to effect their Safety and Happiness. Prudence, indeed, will dictate that Governments long established should not be changed for light and transient causes; and accordingly all experience hath shewn, that mankind are more disposed to suffer, while evils are sufferable, than to right themselves by abolishing the forms to which they are accustomed. But when a long train of abuses and usurpations, pursuing invariably the same object, evidence a design to reduce them under absolute Despotism, it is their right, it is their duty, to throw off such Government, and to provide new Guards for their future security. Such has been the patient sufferance of these Colonies; and such is now the necessity which constrains them to alter their former Systems of Government. The history of the present King of Great Britain is a history of repeated injuries and usurpations, all having in direct object the establishment of an absolute Tyranny over these States. To prove this, let Facts be submitted to a candid world.

He has refused his Assent to Laws, the most wholesome and necessary for the public good.

He has forbidden his Governors to pass Laws of immediate and pressing importance, unless suspended in their operation till his Assent should be obtained, and when so suspended, he has utterly neglected to attend to them.

He has refused to pass other Laws for the accommodation of large districts of people, unless those people would relinquish the right of Representation in the Legislature, a right inestimable to them and formidable to tyrants only.

He has called together legislative bodies at places, unusual, uncomfortable, and distant from the depository of their public Records, for the sole purpose of fatiguing them into compliance with his measures.

He has dissolved Representative Houses repeatedly, for opposing with manly firmness his invasions on the rights of the people.

He has refused for a long time, after such dissolutions, to cause others to be elected; whereby the Legislative powers, incapable of Annihilation, have returned to the People at large for their exercise; the State remaining in the meantime exposed to all the dangers of invasion from without, and convulsions within.

He has endeavored to prevent the population of these States; for that purpose obstructing the Laws for Naturalization of Foreigners; refusing to pass others to encourage their migrations hither, and raising the conditions of new Appropriations of Lands.

He has obstructed the Administration of Justice, by refusing his Assent to Laws for establishing Judiciary powers.

He has made Judges dependent on his Will alone, for the tenure of their offices, and the amount and payment of their salaries.

He has erected a multitude of New Offices, and sent hither swarms of Officers to harass our people, and eat out their substance.

He has kept among us, in times of peace, Standing Armies, without the Consent of our legislatures.

He has affected to render the Military independent of and superior to the Civil power.

He has combined with others to subject us to a jurisdiction foreign to our constitution and unacknowledged by our laws; giving his Assent to their Acts of pretended Legislation: For quartering large bodies of armed troops among us: For protecting them by a mock Trial from punishment for any Murders which they should commit on the Inhabitants of these States: For cutting off our Trade with all parts of the world: For imposing Taxes on us without our Consent: For depriving us in many cases of the benefits of Trial by Jury: For transporting us beyond Seas to be tried for pretended offenses: For abolishing the free System of English Laws in a neighbouring Province, establishing there an Arbitrary government, and enlarging its Boundaries so as to render it at once an example and fit instrument for introducing the same absolute rule into these Colonies: For taking away our Charters, abolishing our most valuable Laws and altering fundamentally the Forms of our Governments: For suspending our own Legislatures and declaring themselves invested with power to legislate for us in all cases whatsoever.

He has abdicated Government here by declaring us out of his Protection and waging War against us.

He has plundered our seas, ravished our Coasts, burnt our towns, and destroyed the lives of our people.

He is at this time transporting large Armies of foreign Mercenaries to complete the works of death, desolation and tyranny, already begun with circumstances of cruelty and perfidy scarcely paralleled in the most barbarous ages, and totally unworthy the Head of a civilized nation.

He has constrained our fellow Citizens taken Captive on the high Seas to bear Arms against their Country, to become the executioners of their friends and Brethren, or to fall themselves by their Hands.

He has excited domestic insurrections amongst us, and has endeavoured to bring on the inhabitants of our frontiers, the merciless Indian Savages, whose known rule of warfare is an undistinguished destruction of all ages, sexes and conditions. In every stage of these Oppressions We have Petitioned for Redress in the most humble terms. Our repeated Petitions have been answered only by repeated injury. A Prince, whose character is thus marked by every act which may define a Tyrant, is unfit to be the ruler of a free people. Nor have We been wanting in attention to our British brethren. We have warned them from time to time of attempts by their legislature to extend an unwarrantable jurisdiction over us. We have reminded them of the circumstances of our emigration and settlement here. We have appealed to their native justice and magnanimity, and we have conjured them by the ties of our common kindred to disavow these usurpations, which would inevitably interrupt our connections and correspondence. They too have been deaf to the voice of justice and of consanguinity. We must, therefore, acquiesce in the necessity, which denounces our Separation, and holds them, as we hold the rest of mankind, Enemies in War, in Peace Friends.

WE, THEREFORE, the Representatives of the United States of America, in General Congress, Assembled, appealing to the Supreme Judge of the world for the rectitude of our intentions do, in the Name, and by authority of the good People of these Colonies, solemnly publish and declare, That these United Colonies are, and of Right ought to be, Free and Independent States: that they are Absolved from all Allegiance to the British Crown, and that all political connection between them and the State of Great Britain is and ought to be totally dissolved: and that as Free and Independent States, they have full Power to levy War, conclude Peace, contract Alliances, establish Commerce, and to do all other Acts and Things which Independent States may of right do. And for the support of this Declaration, with a firm reliance on the protection of Divine Providence, we mutually pledge to each other our Lives, our Fortunes, and our sacred Honor.

THE CONSTITUTION *

PREAMBLE

We, the people of the United States, in order to form a more perfect Union, establish justice, insure domestic tranquillity, provide for the common defence, promote the general welfare, and secure the blessings of liberty to ourselves and our posterity, do ordain and establish this Constitution for the United States of America.

ARTICLE I.

Section 1—(Legislative powers; in whom vested:)

All legislative powers herein granted shall be vested in a Congress of the United States, which shall consist of a Senate and House of Representatives.

Section 2—(House of Representatives, how and by whom chosen. Qualifications of a Representative. Representatives and direct taxes, how apportioned. Enumeration. Vacancies to be filled. Power of choosing officers, and of impeachment.)

1. The House of Representatives shall be composed of members chosen every second year by the people of the several States, and the electors in each State shall have the qualifications requisite for electors of the most numerous branch of the State Legislature.

2. No person shall be a Representative who shall not have attained to the age of twenty-five years and been seven years a citizen of the United States, and who shall not, when elected, be an inhabitant of that State in which he shall be chosen.

3. Representatives and direct taxes shall be apportioned among the several States which may be included within this Union according to their respective numbers, which shall be determined by adding to the whole number of free persons, including those bound to service for a term of years, and excluding Indians not taxed, three-fifths of all other persons. The actual enumeration shall be made within three years after the first meeting of the Congress of the United States, and within every subsequent term of ten years, in such manner as they shall by law direct. The number of Representatives shall not exceed one for every thirty thousand, but each State shall have at least one Representative; and until such enumeration shall be made, the State of New Hampshire shall be entitled to choose 3; Massachusetts, 8; Rhode Island and Providence Plantations, 1; Connecticut, 5; New York, 6; New Jersey, 4; Pennsylvania, 8; Delaware, 1; Maryland, 6; Virginia, 10; North Carolina, 5; South Carolina, 5, and Georgia, 3.

4. When vacancies happen in the representation from any State, the Executive Authority thereof shall issue writs of election to fill such vacancies.

5. The House of Representatives shall choose their Speaker and other officers, and shall have the sole power of impeachment.

Section 3—(Senators, how and by whom chosen. How classified. State Executive, when to make temporary appointments, in case, etc.

* The explanation and the information as to ratification are taken from the *World Almanac.*

Qualifications of a Senator. President of the Senate, his right to vote. President pro tem., and other officers of the Senate, how chosen. Power to try impeachments. When President is tried, Chief Justice to preside. Sentence.)

1. The Senate of the United States shall be composed of two Senators from each State, chosen by the Legislature thereof, for six years; and each Senator shall have one vote.

2. Immediately after they shall be assembled in consequence of the first election, they shall be divided as equally as may be into three classes. The seats of the Senators of the first class shall be vacated at the expiration of the second year, of the second class at the expiration of the fourth year, and of the third class at the expiration of the sixth year, so that one-third may be chosen every second year; and if vacancies happen by resignation or otherwise, during the recess of the Legislature of any State, the Executive thereof may make temporary appointment until the next meeting of the Legislature, which shall then fill such vacancies.

3. No person shall be a Senator who shall not have attained to the age of thirty years, and been nine years a citizen of the United States, and who shall not, when elected, be an inhabitant of that State for which he shall be chosen.

4. The Vice President of the United States shall be President of the Senate, but shall have no vote unless they be equally divided.

5. The Senate shall choose their other officers, and also a President pro-tempore, in the absence of the Vice President, or when he shall exercise the office of the President of the United States.

6. The Senate shall have the sole power to try all impeachments. When sitting for that purpose, they shall be on oath or affirmation. When the President of the United States is tried, the Chief Justice shall preside; and no person shall be convicted without the concurrence of two-thirds of the members present.

7. Judgment in cases of impeachment shall not extend further than to removal from office, and disqualification to hold and enjoy any office of honor, trust, or profit under the United States; but the party convicted shall nevertheless be liable and subject to indictment, trial, judgment, and punishment, according to law.

Section 4—(Times, etc., of holding elections, how prescribed. One session in each year.)

1. The times, places and manner of holding elections for Senators and Representatives shall be prescribed in each State by the Legislature thereof; but the Congress may at any time make or alter such regulations, except as to places of choosing Senators.

2. The Congress shall assemble at least once in every year, and such meeting shall be on the first Monday in December, unless they shall by law appoint a different day.

Section 5—(Membership, Quorum, Adjournments, Rules. Power to punish or expel. Journal. Times of adjournments, how limited, etc.)

1. Each House shall be the judge of the elections, returns, and qualifications of its own members, and a majority of each shall constitute a quorum to do business; but a smaller number may adjourn from day to day, and may be authorized to compel the attendance of absent members in such manner and under such penalties as each House may provide.

2. Each House may determine the rules of its proceedings, punish its members for disorderly behavior, and with the concurrence of two-thirds expel a member.

3. Each House shall keep a journal of its proceedings, and from time to time may publish the same, excepting such parts as may in their judgment require secrecy; and the yeas and nays of the members of either House on any question shall, at the desire of one-fifth of those present, be entered on the journal.

4. Neither House, during the session of Congress shall, without the consent of the other, adjourn for more than three days, nor to any other place than that in which the two Houses shall be sitting.

Section 6—(Compensation. Privileges. Disqualifications in certain cases.)

1. The Senators and Representatives shall receive a compensation for their services to be ascertained by law, and paid out of the Treasury of the United States. They shall in all cases, except treason, felony, and breach of the peace, be privileged from arrest during their attendance at the session of their respective Houses, and in going to and returning from the same; and for any speech or debate in either House they shall not be questioned in any other place.

2. No Senator or Representative shall, during the time for which he was elected, be appointed to any civil office under the authority of the United States which shall have been created, or the emoluments whereof shall have been increased during such time; and no person holding any office under the United States shall be a member of either House during his continuance in office.

Section 7—(House to originate all revenue bills. Veto. Bill may be passed by two-thirds of each House, notwithstanding, etc. Bill not returned in ten days, to become a law. Provisions as to orders, concurrent resolutions, etc.)

1. All bills for raising revenue shall originate in the House of Representatives, but the Senate may propose or concur with amendments, as on other bills.

2. Every bill which shall have passed the House of Representatives and the Senate shall, before it becomes a law, be presented to the President of the United States; if he approve, he shall sign it, but if not, he shall return it, with his objections, to that House in which it shall have originated, who shall proceed to reconsider it. If after such reconsideration two-thirds of that House shall agree to pass the bill it shall be sent, together with the objections, to the other House, by which it shall likewise be reconsidered; and if approved by two-thirds of that House it shall become a law. But in all such cases the votes of both Houses shall be determined by yeas and nays, and the names of the persons voting for and against the bill shall be entered on the journal of each House respectively. If any bill shall not be returned by the President within ten days (Sundays excepted) after it shall have been presented to him, the same shall be a law in like manner as if he had signed it, unless the Congress by their adjournment prevent its return; in which case it shall not be a law.

3. Every order, resolution, or vote to which the concurrence of the Senate and House of Representatives may be necessary (except on a question of adjournment) shall be presented to the President of the United States, and before the same shall take effect shall be approved by him, or being disapproved by him, shall be repassed by two-thirds of the Senate and the House of Representatives, according to the rules and limitations prescribed in the case of a bill.

Section 8—(Powers of Congress.)

1. The Congress shall have power:

To lay and collect taxes, duties, imposts, and excises to pay the debts and provide for the common defense and general welfare of the United States; but all duties, imposts, and excises shall be uniform throughout the United States.

2. To borrow money on the credit of the United States.

3. To regulate commerce with foreign nations, and among the several States and with the Indian tribes.

4. To establish a uniform rule of naturalization and uniform laws on the subject of bankruptcies throughout the United States.

5. To coin money, regulate the value thereof, and of foreign coin, and fix the standard of weights and measures.

6. To provide for the punishment of counterfeiting the securities and current coin of the United States.

7. To establish post-offices and post-roads.

8. To promote the progress of science and useful arts by securing for limited times to authors and inventors the exclusive rights to their respective writings and discoveries.

9. To constitute tribunals inferior to the Supreme Court.

10. To define and punish piracies and felonies committed on the high seas, and offenses against the law of nations.

11. To declare war, grant letters of marque and reprisal, and make rules concerning captures on land and water.

12. To raise and support armies, but no appropriation of money to that use shall be for a longer term than two years.

13. To provide and maintain a navy.

14. To make rules for the government and regulation of the land and naval forces.

15. To provide for calling forth the militia to execute the laws of the Union, suppress insurrections, and repel invasions.

16. To provide for organizing, arming, and disciplining the militia, and for governing such part of them as may be employed in the service of the United States, reserving to the States respectively the appointment of the officers, and the authority of training the militia according to the discipline prescribed by Congress.

17. To exercise exclusive legislation in all cases whatsoever over such district (not exceeding ten miles square) as may, by cession of particular States and the acceptance of Congress, become the seat of Government of the United States, and to exercise like authority over all places purchased by the consent of the Legislature of the State in which the same shall be, for the erection of forts, magazines, arsenals, drydocks, and other needful buildings.

18. To make all laws which shall be necessary and proper for carrying into execution the foregoing powers and all other powers vested by this Constitution in the Government of the United States, or in any department or officer thereof.

Section 9—(Provision as to migration or importation of certain persons. Habeas Corpus. Bills of attainder, etc. Taxes, how apportioned. No export duty. No commercial preference. Money, how drawn from Treasury, etc. No titular nobility. Officers not to receive presents, etc.)

1. The migration or importation of such persons as any of the States now existing shall think proper to admit shall not be prohibited by the Congress

prior to the year one thousand eight hundred and eight, but a tax or duty may be imposed on such importation, not exceeding ten dollars for each person.

2. The privilege of the writ of habeas corpus shall not be suspended, unless when in cases of rebellion or invasion the public safety may require it.

3. No bill of attainder or ex post facto law shall be passed.

4. No capitation or other direct tax shall be laid, unless in proportion to the census or enumeration hereinbefore directed to be taken.

5. No tax or duty shall be laid on articles exported from any State.

6. No preference shall be given by any regulation of commerce or revenue to the ports of one State over those of another, nor shall vessels bound to or from one State be obliged to enter, clear, or pay duties to another.

7. No money shall be drawn from the Treasury but in consequence of appropriations made by law; and a regular statement and account of the receipts and expenditures of all public money shall be published from time to time.

8. No title of nobility shall be granted by the United States. And no person holding any office of profit or trust under them shall, without the consent of the Congress, accept of any present, emolument, office, or title of any kind whatever from any king, prince, or foreign state.

Section 10—(States prohibited from the exercise of certain powers.)

1. No State shall enter into any treaty, alliance, or confederation, grant letters of marque and reprisal, coin money, emit bills of credit, make anything but gold and silver coin a tender in payment of debts, pass any bill of attainder, ex post facto law, or law impairing the obligation of contracts, or grant any title of nobility.

2. No State shall, without the consent of the Congress, lay any impost or duties on imports or exports, except what may be absolutely necessary for executing its inspection laws, and the net produce of all duties and imposts, laid by any State on imports or exports, shall be for the use of the Treasury of the United States; and all such laws shall be subject to the revision and control of the Congress.

3. No State shall, without the consent of Congress, lay any duty of tonnage, keep troops or ships of war in time of peace, enter into agreement or compact with another State, or with a foreign power, or engage in war unless actually invaded, or in such imminent danger as will not admit of delay.

ARTICLE II.

Section 1—(President: his term of office. Electors of President; number and how appointed. Electors to vote on same day. Qualification of President. On whom his duties devolve in case of his removal, death, etc. President's compensation. His oath of office.)

1. The Executive power shall be vested in a President of the United States of America. He shall hold his office during the term of four years, and together with the Vice-President, chosen for the same term, be elected as follows:

2. Each State shall appoint, in such manner as the Legislature thereof may direct, a number of electors equal to the whole number of Senators and Representatives to which the State may be entitled in the Congress; but no Senator or Representative or person holding an office of trust or profit under the United States shall be appointed an elector.

3. The electors shall meet in their respective States and vote by ballot for two persons, of whom one at least shall not be an inhabitant of the same State

with themselves. And they shall make a list of all the persons voted for, and of the number of votes for each, which list they shall sign and certify and transmit, sealed, to the seat of the Government of the United States, directed to the President of the Senate. The President of the Senate shall, in the presence of the Senate and House of Representatives, open all the certificates, and the votes shall then be counted. The person having the greatest number of votes shall be the President, if such number be a majority of the whole number of electors appointed, and if there be more than one who have such a majority, and have an equal number of votes, then the House of Representatives shall immediately choose by ballot one of them for President; and if no person have a majority, then from the five highest on the list the said House shall in like manner choose the President. But in choosing the President, the vote shall be taken by States, the representation from each State having one vote. A quorum, for this purpose, shall consist of a member or members from two-thirds of the States, and a majority of all the States shall be necessary to a choice. In every case, after the choice of the President, the person having the greatest number of votes of the electors shall be the Vice-President. But if there should remain two or more who have equal votes, the Senate shall choose from them by ballot the Vice-President.

4. The Congress may determine the time of choosing the electors and the day on which they shall give their votes, which day shall be the same throughout the United States.

5. No person except a natural born citizen, or a citizen of the United States at the time of the adoption of the Constitution, shall be eligible to the office of President; neither shall any person be eligible to that office who shall not have attained to the age of thirty-five years and been fourteen years a resident within the United States.

6. In case of the removal of the President from office, or of his death, resignation, or inability to discharge the powers and duties of the said office, the same shall devolve on the Vice-President, and the Congress may by law provide for the case of removal, death, resignation, or inability, both of the President and Vice-President, declaring what officer shall then act as President, and such officer shall act accordingly until the disability be removed or a President shall be elected.

7. The President shall, at stated times, receive for his services a compensation which shall neither be increased nor diminished during the period for which he shall have been elected, and he shall not receive within that period any other emolument from the United States or any of them.

8. Before he enter on the execution of his office he shall take the following oath or affirmation:

"I do solemnly swear (or affirm) that I will faithfully execute the office of President of the United States, and will, to the best of my ability, preserve, protect, and defend the Constitution of the United States."

Section 2—(President to be Commander-in-Chief. He may require opinions of Cabinet Officers, etc., may pardon. Treaty-making power. Nomination of certain officers. When President may fill vacancies.)

1. The President shall be Commander-in-Chief of the Army and Navy of the United States, and of the militia of the several States when called into the actual service of the United States; he may require the opinion, in writing, of the principal officer in each of the executive departments upon any subject relating to the duties of their respective offices, and he shall have power to grant

reprieves and pardons for offenses against the United States except in cases of impeachment.

2. He shall have power by and with the advice and consent of the Senate to make treaties, provided two-thirds of the Senators present occur: and he shall nominate and by and with the advice and consent of the Senate shall appoint ambassadors, other public ministers and consuls, judges of the Supreme Court, and all other officers of the United States whose appointments are not herein otherwise provided for, and which shall be established by law; but the Congress may by law vest the appointment of such inferior officers as they think proper in the President alone, in the courts of law, or in the heads of departments.

3. The President shall have power to fill up all vacancies that may happen during the recess of the Senate by granting commissions, which shall expire at the end of their next session.

Section 3—(President shall communicate to Congress. He may convene and adjourn Congress, in case of disagreement, etc. Shall receive Ambassadors, execute laws, and commission officers.)

He shall from time to time give to the Congress information of the state of the Union, and recommend to their consideration such measures as he shall judge necessary and expedient; he may, on extraordinary occasions, convene both Houses, or either of them, and in case of disagreement between them with respect to the time of adjournment, he may adjourn them to such time as he shall think proper; he shall receive ambassadors and other public ministers; he shall take care that the laws be faithfully executed, and shall commission all the officers of the United States.

Section 4—(All civil offices forfeited for certain crimes.)

The President, Vice-President, and all civil officers of the United States shall be removed from office on impeachment for and conviction of treason, bribery or other high crimes and misdemeanors.

ARTICLE III.

Section 1—(Judicial powers. Tenure. Compensation.)

The judicial power of the United States shall be vested in one Supreme Court, and in such inferior courts as the Congress may from time to time ordain and establish. The judges, both of the Supreme and inferior courts, shall hold their offices during good behavior, and shall at stated times receive for their services a compensation which shall not be diminished during their continuance in office.

Section 2—Judicial power; to what cases it extends. Original jurisdiction of Supreme Court Appellate. Trial by jury, etc. Trial, where.)

1. The judicial power shall extend to all cases in law and equity arising under this Constitution, the laws of the United States, and treaties made, or which shall be made, under their authority; to all cases affecting ambassadors, other public ministers and consuls; to all cases of admiralty and maritime jurisdiction; to controversies to which the United States shall be a party; to controversies between two or more States, between a State and citizens of another State, between citizens of different States, between citizens of the same State claiming

lands under grants of different States, and between a State, or the citizens thereof, and foreign states, citizens, or subjects.

2. In all cases affecting ambassadors, other public ministers, and consuls, and those in which a State shall be a party, the Supreme Court shall have original jurisdiction. In all the other cases before mentioned the Supreme Court shall have appellate jurisdiction both as to law and fact, with such exceptions and under such regulations as the Congress shall make.

3. The trial of all crimes, except in cases of impeachment, shall be by jury, and such trial shall be held in the State where the said crimes shall have been committed; but when not committed within any State the trial shall be at such place or places as the Congress may by law have directed.

Section 3—(Treason defined. Proof of. Punishment of.)

1. Treason against the United States shall consist only in levying war against them, or in adhering to their enemies, giving them aid and comfort. No person shall be convicted of treason unless on the testimony of two witnesses to the same overt act, or on confession in open court.

2. The Congress shall have power to declare the punishment of treason, but no attainder of treason shall work corruption of blood or forfeiture except during the life of the person attainted.

ARTICLE IV.

Section 1—(Each State to give credit to the public acts, etc., of every other State.)

Full faith and credit shall be given in each State to the public acts, records, and judicial proceedings of every other State. And the Congress may by general laws prescribe the manner in which such acts, records, and proceedings shall be proved, and the effect thereof.

Section 2—(Privileges of citizens of each State. Fugitives from justice to be delivered up. Persons held to service having escaped, to be delivered up.)

1. The citizens of each State shall be entitled to all privileges and immunities of citizens in the several States.

2. A person charged in any State with treason, felony, or other crime, who shall flee from justice, and be found in another State, shall, on demand of the Executive authority of the State from which he fled, be delivered up, to be removed to the State having jurisdiction of the crime.

3. No person held to service or labor in one State, under the laws thereof, escaping into another shall in consequence of any law or regulation therein, be discharged from such service or labor, but shall be delivered up on claim of the party to whom such service or labor may be due.

Section 3—(Admission of new States. Power of Congress over territory and other property.)

1. New States may be admitted by the Congress into this Union; but no new State shall be formed or erected within the jurisdiction of any other State, nor any State be formed by the junction of two or more States, or parts of States, without the consent of the Legislatures of the States concerned, as well as of the Congress.

2. The Congress shall have power to dispose of and make all needful rules and regulations respecting the territory or other property belonging to the United States; and nothing in this Constitution shall be so construed as to prejudice any claims of the United States, or of any particular State.

Section 4—(Republican form of government guaranteed. Each State to be protected.)

The United States shall guarantee to every State in this Union a Republican form of government, and shall protect each of them against invasion, and, on application of the Legislature, or of the Executive (when the Legislature cannot be convened) against domestic violence.

ARTICLE V.

(Constitution: how amended. Proviso.)

The Congress, whenever two-thirds of both Houses shall deem it necessary, shall propose amendments to this Constitution, or, on the application of the Legislatures of two-thirds of the several States, shall call a convention for proposing amendments, which in either case, shall be valid to all intents and purposes, as part of this Constitution, when ratified by the Legislatures of three-fourths of the several States, or by conventions in three-fourths thereof, as the one or the other mode of ratification may be proposed by the Congress, provided that no amendment which may be made prior to the year one thousand eight hundred and eight shall in any manner affect the first and fourth clauses in the Ninth Section of the First Article; and that no State, without its consent, shall be deprived of its equal suffrage in the Senate.

ARTICLE VI.

(Certain debts, etc., declared valid. Supremacy of Constitution, treaties, and laws of the United States. Oath to support Constitution, by whom taken. No religious test.)

1. All debts contracted and engagements entered into before the adoption of this Constitution shall be as valid against the United States under this Constitution as under the Confederation.

2. This Constitution and the laws of the United States which shall be made in pursuance thereof and all treaties made, or which shall be made, under the authority of the United States, shall be the supreme law of the land, and the judges in every State shall be bound thereby, anything in the Constitution or laws of any State to the contrary notwithstanding.

3. The Senators and Representatives before mentioned, and the members of the several State Legislatures, and all executives and judicial officers, both of the United States and of the several States, shall be bound by oath or affirmation to support this Constitution; but no religious test shall ever be required as a qualification to any office or public trust under the United States.

ARTICLE VII.

(What ratification shall establish Constitution.)

The ratification of the Conventions of nine States shall be sufficient for the establishment of this Constitution between the States so ratifying the same.

THE AMENDMENTS

The Bill of Rights was ratified by the States as follows—New Jersey, (Nov. 20, 1789); Maryland, (Dec. 19, 1789); North Carolina, (Dec. 22, 1789); South Carolina, (Jan. 19, 1790); New Hampshire, (Jan. 25, 1790); Delaware, (Jan. 28, 1790); Pennsylvania, (March 10, 1790); New York, (March 27, 1790); Rhode Island, (June 15, 1790); Vermont, (Nov. 3, 1791); Virginia, (Dec. 15, 1791); Massachusetts, (March 2, 1939); Georgia, (March 18, 1939); Connecticut (April 19, 1939).

ARTICLE I.

(Religious Establishment Prohibited. Freedom of Speech, of the Press, and Right to Petition.)

Congress shall make no law respecting an establishment of religion, or prohibiting the free exercise thereof; or abridging the freedom of speech or of the press; or the right of the people peaceably to assemble and to petition the Government for a redress of grievances.

ARTICLE II.

(Right to Keep and Bear Arms.)

A well-regulated militia being necessary to the security of a free State, the right of the people to keep and bear arms shall not be infringed.

ARTICLE III.

(No Soldier to be Quartered in Any House, Unless, etc.)

No soldier shall, in time of peace, be quartered in any house without the consent of the owner, nor in time of war but in a manner to be prescribed by law.

ARTICLE IV.

(Right of Search and Seizure Regulated.)

The right of the people to be secure in their persons, houses, papers, and effects, against unreasonable searches and seizures, shall not be violated, and no warrants shall issue but upon probable cause, supported by oath or affirmation, and particularly describing the place to be searched, and the persons or things to be seized.

ARTICLE V.

(Provisions Concerning Prosecution, Trial and Punishment—Private Property Not to Be Taken for Public Use Without Compensation.)

No person shall be held to answer for a capital or other infamous crime unless on a presentment or indictment of a Grand Jury, except in cases arising in the land or naval forces, or in the militia, when in actual service, in time of war or public danger; nor shall any person be subject for the same offense to be twice put in jeopardy of life or limb; nor shall be compelled in any criminal case to be a witness against himself, nor be deprived of life, liberty, or property, without due process of law; nor shall private property be taken for public use without just compensation.

ARTICLE VI.

(Right to Speedy Trial, Witnesses, etc.)

In all criminal prosecutions, the accused shall enjoy the right to a speedy and public trial, by an impartial jury of the State and district wherein the crime shall have been committed, which districts shall have been previously ascertained by law, and to be informed of the nature and cause of the accusation; to be confronted with the witnesses against him; to have compulsory process for obtaining witnesses in his favor, and to have the assistance of counsel for his defense.

ARTICLE VII.

(Right of Trial by Jury.)

In suits at common law, where the value in controversy shall exceed twenty dollars, the right of trial by jury shall be preserved, and no fact tried by a jury shall be otherwise re-examined in any court of the United States than according to the rules of the common law.

ARTICLE VIII.

(Excessive Bail or Fines and Cruel Punishment Prohibited.)

Excessive bail shall not be required, nor excessive fines imposed, nor cruel and unusual punishments inflicted.

ARTICLE IX.

(Rule of Construction of Constitution.)

The enumeration in the Constitution of certain rights shall not be construed to deny or disparage others retained by the people.

ARTICLE X.

(Rights of States Under Constitution.)

The powers not delegated to the United States by the Constitution, nor prohibited by it to the States, are reserved to the States respectively, or to the people.

ARTICLE XI.

(Judicial Powers Construed.)

The following amendment was proposed to the Legislatures of the several States by the Third Congress on the 4th of March, 1794, and was declared to have been ratified in a message from the President to Congress, dated Jan. 8, 1798.

It was on Jan. 5, 1798, that Secretary of State Pickering received from 12 of the States authenticated ratifications, and informed President John Adams of that fact.

As a result of recent research in the Department of State, it is now established that the Eleventh Amendment became part of the Constitution on Feb. 7, 1795, for on that date it had been ratified by twelve States as follows:

(1) New York, (March 27, 1794); (2) Rhode Island, (March 31, 1794); (3) Connecticut, (May 8, 1794); (4) New Hampshire, (June 16, 1794); (5)

Massachusetts, (June 25, 1794); (6) Vermont, (between Oct. 9, 1794, and Nov. 9, 1794); (7) Virginia, (Nov. 18, 1794); (8) Georgia, (Nov. 29, 1794); (9) Kentucky, (Dec. 7, 1794); (10) Maryland, (Dec. 26, 1794; (11) Delaware, (Jan. 23, 1795); (12) North Carolina, (Feb. 7, 1795).

On June 1, 1796, more than a year after the Eleventh Amendment had become part of the Constitution (but before anyone was officially aware of this), Tennessee had been admitted as a State; but not until Oct. 16, 1797, was a certified copy of the resolution of Congress proposing the amendment sent to the Governor of Tennessee (John Sevier) by Secretary of State Pickering, whose office was then at Trenton, New Jersey, because of the epidemic of yellow fever at Philadelphia; it seems, however, that the Legislature of Tennessee took no action on the Eleventh Amendment, owing doubtless to the fact that public announcement of its adoption was made soon thereafter.

Besides the necessary twelve States, one other, South Carolina, ratified the Eleventh Amendment, but this action was not taken until Dec. 4, 1797; the two remaining states, New Jersey and Pennsylvania, failed to ratify.

The Eleventh Amendment is as follows:

The judicial power of the United States shall not be construed to extend to any suit in law or equity, commenced or prosecuted against one of the United States, by citizens of another State, or by citizens or subjects of any foreign state.

ARTICLE XII.

(Manner of Choosing President and Vice-President.)

The following amendment was proposed to the Legislatures of the several States by the Eighth Congress (Dec. 12, 1803), and was declared to have been ratified in a proclamation by the Secretary of State (September 25, 1804). It was ratified by 12 of the 17 States, and was rejected by Connecticut.

The Electors shall meet in their respective States and vote by ballot for President and Vice-President, one of whom at least shall not be an inhabitant of the same State with themselves; they shall name in their ballots the person voted for as President, and in distinct ballots the person voted for as Vice-President; and they shall make distinct list of all persons voted for as President, and of all persons voted for as Vice-President, and of the number of votes for each, which list they shall sign and certify, and transmit, sealed, to the seat of the Government of the United States, directed to the President of the Senate; the President of the Senate shall, in the presence of the Senate and House of Representatives, open all the certificates and the votes shall then be counted; the person having the greatest number of votes for President shall be the President, if such number be a majority of the whole number of Electors appointed; and if no person have such majority, then from the persons having the highest number, not exceeding three, on the list of those voted for as President, the House of Representatives shall choose immediately, by ballot the President. But in choosing the President, the votes shall be taken by States, the representation from each State having one vote; a quorum for this purpose shall consist of a member or members from two-thirds of the States, and a majority of all the States shall be necessary to a choice. And if the House of Representatives shall not choose a President, whenever the right of choice shall devolve upon them, before the fourth day of March next following, then the Vice-President shall act as President, as in the case of the death or other constitutional disability of the President. The person having the greatest number of votes as Vice-President shall be the Vice-President if such number be a majority of the whole number of Electors appointed, and if no person have a majority, then, from the two highest numbers on the list the Senate shall choose the Vice-President; a quorum for the purpose shall consist of two-thirds of the whole number of Senators, and a majority of the whole number shall be necessary to a choice. But no person constitutionally ineligible to the office of President shall be eligible to that of Vice-President of the United States.

ARTICLE XIII

(Slavery Abolished.)

The following amendment was proposed to the Legislatures of the several States by the Thirty-eighth Congress (Feb. 1, 1865), and was declared to have been ratified in a proclamation by the Secertary of State (Dec. 18, 1865). It finally was ratified by 33 of the 36 States, and was rejected by Delaware (Feb. 8, 1865), ratified (Feb., 1901) and Mississippi.

President Lincoln signed the joint resolution of Congress proposing the 13th amendment, although such resolutions (proposing amendments) are not submitted to the President. The U. S. Supreme Court decided, in 1798, that the President has nothing to do with the proposing of amendments to the Constitution, or their adoption.

1. Neither slavery nor involuntary servitude, except as a punishment for crime whereof the party shall have been duly convicted, shall exist within the United States, or any place subject to their jurisdiction.

2. Congress shall have power to enforce this article by appropriate legislation.

ARTICLE XIV

(Citizenship Rights Not to Be Abridged.)

The following amendment was proposed to the Legislatures of the several States by the Thirty-ninth Congress (June 13, 1866), and was declared to have been ratified in a proclamation by the Secretary of State (July 28, 1868). The amendment got the support of 23 Northern States: it was rejected by Delaware (Feb. 7, 1867), ratified (Feb., 1901), Kentucky, Maryland, and 10 Southern States. California took no action. Subsequently it was ratified by the 10 Southern States.

The 14th amendment was adopted only by virtue of ratification subsequent to earlier rejections. Newly constituted legislatures in both North Carolina and South Carolina, respectively (July 4 and 9, 1868), ratified the proposed amendment, although earlier legislatures had rejected the proposal. The Secretary of State issued a proclamation which, though doubtful as to the effect of attempted withdrawals by New York and New Jersey, entertained no doubt as to the validity of the ratification by North and South Carolina. The following day (July 21, 1868), Congress passed a resolution which declared the 14th amendment to be a part of the Constitution and directed the Secretary of State so to promulgate it. The Secretary waited, however, until the newly constituted legislature of Georgia had ratified the amendment, subsequent to an earlier rejection, before the promulgation of the ratification of the new amendment.

1. All persons born or naturalized in the United States, and subject to the jurisdiction thereof, are citizens of the United States and of the State wherein they reside. No State shall make or enforce any law which shall abridge the privileges or immunities of citizens of the United States, nor shall any State

deprive any person of life, liberty, or property without due process of law, nor deny to any person within its jurisdiction the equal protection of the laws.

Apportionment of Representatives in Congress

2. Representatives shall be apportioned among the several States according to their respective numbers, counting the whole number of persons in each State excluding Indians not taxed. But when the right to vote at any election for the choice of Electors for President and Vice-President of the United States, Representatives in Congress, the executive and judicial officers of a State, or the members of the Legislature thereof, is denied to any of the male inhabitants of such State, being twenty-one years of age, and citizens of the United States, or in any way abridged, except for participation in rebellion, or other crime, the basis of representation therein shall be reduced in the proportion which the number of such male citizens shall bear to the whole number of male citizens twenty-one years of age in such State.

Power of Congress to Remove Disabilities of United States Officials for Rebellion

3. No person shall be a Senator or Representative in Congress, or Elector of President and Vice-President or hold any office, civil or military, under the United States, or under any State, who, having previously taken an oath, as a member of Congress, or as an officer of the United States, or as a member of any State Legislature or as an executive or judicial officer of any State, to support the Constitution of the United States, shall have engaged in insurrection or rebellion against the same, or given aid and comfort to the enemies thereof. But Congress may, by a vote of two-thirds of each House, remove such disability.

What Public Debts Are Valid

4. The validity of the public debt of the United States, authorized by law, including debts incurred for payment of pensions and bounties for services in suppressing insurrection and rebellion, shall not be questioned. But neither the United States nor any State shall assume or pay any debt or obligation incurred in aid of insurrection or rebellion against the United States, or any claim for the loss or emancipation of any slave; but all such debts, obligations, and claims shall be held illegal and void.

5. The Congress shall have power to enforce by appropriate legislation the provisions of this article.

ARTICLE XV

(Equal Rights for White and Colored Citizens.)

The following amendment was proposed to the Legislatures of the several States by the Fortieth Congress (Feb. 26, 1869), and was declared to have been ratified in a proclamation by the Secretary of State (March 30, 1870). It was ratified by 31 of the 37 States, and was rejected by California, Delaware (March 18, 1869) ratified (Feb., 1901) and Kentucky. New York rescinded its ratification (Jan. 5, 1870). New Jersey rejected it in 1870, but ratified it in 1871.

1. The right of the citizens of the United States to vote shall not be denied or abridged by the United States or by any State on account of race, color, or previous condition of servitude.

2. The Congress shall have power to enforce the provisions of this article by appropriate legislation.

ARTICLE XVI

(Income Taxes Authorized.)

The following amendment was proposed to the Legislatures of the several States by the Sixty-first Congress (July 12, 1909) and was declared to have been ratified in a proclamation by the Secretary of State (Feb. 25, 1913). The amendment was ratified by 42 of the 48 States, and was rejected by Connecticut, Rhode Island, and Utah.

The Congress shall have power to lay and collect taxes on incomes, from whatever sources derived, without apportionment among the several States, and without regard to any census or enumeration.

ARTICLE XVII

(United States Senators to Be Elected by Direct Popular Vote.)

The following amendment was proposed to the Legislatures of the several States by the Sixty-second Congress (May 16, 1912) and was declared to have been ratified in a proclamation by the Secretary of State (May 31, 1913). The amendment was adopted by 37 of the 48 states, but was rejected by Utah.

1. The Senate of the United States shall be composed of two Senators from each State, elected by the people thereof, for six years and each Senator shall have one vote. The electors in each State shall have the qualifications requisite for electors of the most numerous branch of the State Legislatures.

2. When vacancies happen in the representation of any State in the Senate, the executive authority of such State shall issue writs of election to fill such vacancies: Provided, That the Legislature of any State may empower the Executive thereof to make temporary appointment until the people fill the vacancies by election as the Legislature may direct.

3. This amendment shall not be so construed as to affect the election or term of any Senator chosen before it becomes valid as part of the Constitution.

ARTICLE XVIII

(Liquor Prohibition Amendment.)

The following amendment was proposed to the Legislatures of the several States by the Sixty-fifth Congress (Dec. 18, 1917), and (Jan. 29, 1919) the United States Secretary of State proclaimed its adoption by 36 States, and declared it in effect (Jan. 16, 1920).

The total vote in the Senates of the various States was, 1,310 for, 237 against —84.6% dry. In the lower houses of the States the vote was, 3,782 for, 1,035 against—78.5% dry.

The amendment ultimately was adopted by all the States except Connecticut and Rhode Island.

1. After one year from the ratification of this article the manufacture, sale, or transportation of intoxicating liquors within, the importation thereof into, or the exportation thereof from the United States and all territory subject to the jurisdiction thereof for beverage purposes is hereby prohibited.

2. The Congress and the several States shall have concurrent power to enforce this article by appropriate legislation.

3. This article shall be inoperative unless it shall have been ratified as an amendment to the Constitution by the Legislatures of the several States, as pro-

vided in the Constitution, within seven years from the date of the submission hereof to the States by the Congress.

ARTICLE XIX

(Giving Nation-Wide Suffrage to Women.)

The following amendment was presented to the Legislatures of the several States by the Sixty-fifth Congress having been adopted by the House of Representatives (May 21, 1919) and by the Senate (June 4, 1919). The Secretary of State (Aug. 26, 1920) proclaimed it in effect, having been adopted (June 10, 1919-August 18, 1920) by three-quarters of the States. In West Virginia, despite Senate rules of procedure which forbade reconsideration of a measure during the sessions in which it was defeated, the Senate ratified the proposed 19th amendment, subsequent to a rejection in the same session. The amendment was rejected by Alabama, Maryland, and Virginia.

1. The right of citizens of the United States to vote shall not be denied or abridged by the United States or by any State on account of sex.

2. Congress shall have power, by appropriate legislation, to enforce the provisions of this article.

ARTICLE XX

(Terms of President and Vice-President to Begin on Jan. 20; Those of Senators and Representatives, on Jan. 3.)

The following amendment was proposed to the Legislatures of the several States by the Seventy-second Congress (March, 1932), a joint resolution to that effect having been adopted, first by the House, and then (March 2) by the Senate. The Secretary of State (Feb. 6, 1933) proclaimed it in effect, 39 of the 48 States having ratified. By Oct. 15, 1933, it had been ratified by all of the 48 States.

Section 1.—The terms of the President and Vice-President shall end at noon on the 20th day of January, and the terms of Senators and Representatives at noon on the 3rd day of January, of the years in which such terms would have ended if this article had not been ratified; and the terms of their successors shall then begin.

Section 2.—The Congress shall assemble at least once in every year, and such meeting shall begin at noon on the 3rd day of January, unless they shall by law appoint a different day.

Section 3.—If, at the time fixed for the beginning of the term of the President, the President elect shall have died, the Vice-President elect shall become President. If a President shall not have been chosen before the time fixed for the beginning of his term, or if the President elect shall have failed to qualify, then the Vice-President elect shall act as President until a President shall have qualified; and the Congress may by law provide for the case wherein neither a President elect nor a Vice-President elect shall have qualified, declaring who shall then act as President or the manner in which one who is to act shall be selected, and such person shall act accordingly until a President or Vice-President shall have qualified.

Section 4.—The Congress may by law provide for the case of the death of any of the persons from whom the House of Representatives may choose a President whenever the right of choice shall have devolved upon them, and for the case of the death of any of the persons from whom the Senate may choose a Vice-President whenever the right of choice shall have devolved upon them.

Section 5.—Sections 1 and 2 shall take effect on the 15th day of October following the ratification of this article (Oct., 1933).

Section 6.—This article shall be inoperative unless it shall have been ratified as an amendment to the Constitution by the legislatures of three-fourths of the several States within seven years from the date of its submission.

ARTICLE XXI

(Repeal of the Eighteenth (Prohibition) Amendment by Conventions in the States.)

The following proposed amendment in the Constitution, embodied in a joint resolution of the 72nd Congress (Senate, Feb. 16, 1933, by 63 to 23; House, Feb. 20, 1933, by 289 to 121), was transmitted to the Secretary of State on Feb. 21 and he at once sent to the governors of the States copies of the resolution. The amendment went into effect on Dec. 5, 1933, having been adopted by 36 of the 48 States—three-quarters of the entire number. The amendment is:

Section 1.—The eighteenth article of amendment to the Constitution of the United States is hereby repealed.

Section 2.—The transportation or importation into any State, Territory, or Possession of the United States for delivery or use therein of intoxicating liquors, in violation of the laws thereof, is hereby prohibited.

Section 3.—This article shall be inoperative unless it shall have been ratified as an amendment to the Constitution by convention in the several States, as provided in the Constitution, within seven years from the date of the submission hereof to the States by the Congress.

PROPOSED CHILD LABOR AMENDMENT

The following amendment was proposed to the Legislatures of the several States by the Sixty-eighth Congress, having been adopted as a joint resolution by the House of Representatives (297 to 69) on April 26, 1924, and by the Senate (61 to 23) on June 2, 1924.

It was ratified by Arizona (1925); Arkansas (1924); California (1925); Colorado (1931); Idaho (1935); Illinois (1933); Indiana (1935); Iowa (1933); Kansas (1937); Kentucky (1937); Maine (1933); Michigan (1933); Minnesota (1933); Montana (1927); Nevada (1937); New Hampshire (1933); New Jersey (1933); New Mexico (1937); North Dakota (1933); Ohio (1933); Oklahoma (1933); Oregon (1933); Pennsylvania (1933); Utah (1935); Washington (1933); West Virginia (1933); Wisconsin (1925); Wyoming (1935); total, 28. —Ratifications by 36 States is necessary.

The U. S. Supreme Court, in 1921 (Dillon vs. Glass, 256 U. S. 368) ruled that proposed amendments of 1789, 1810, and 1861 were no longer pending. "We conclude," said the Court, "... that the ratification must be within some reasonable time after the proposal."

Section 1.—The Congress shall have power to limit, regulate, and prohibit the labor of persons under eighteen years of age.

Section 2.—The power of the several States is unimpaired by this article except that the operation of State laws shall be suspended to the extent necessary to give effect to legislation enacted by the Congress.

THE PRESIDENTIAL

President and Vice-President	*Secretary of State*	*Secretary of Treasury*	*Secretary of War*
George Washington-John Adams. 1789 Fed.	T. Jefferson......1789 E. Randolph......1794 T. Pickering......1795	Alex. Hamilton. 1789 Oliver Wolcott. 1795	Henry Knox......1789 T. Pickering......1795 Jas. McHenry..1796
John Adams-Thomas Jefferson....1797 Fed.	T. Pickering......1797 John Marshall...1800	Oliver Wolcott. 1797 Samuel Dexter. 1801	Jas. McHenry..1797 John Marshall..1800 Sam'l Dexter...1800 R. Griswold....1801
Thomas Jefferson-Aaron Burr....1801 Dem. Rep. George Clinton 1805	James Madison...1801	Samuel Dexter. 1801 Albert Gallatin. 1801	H. Dearborn...1801
James Madison-George Clinton...1809 Dem. Rep. Elbridge Gerry 1813	Robert Smith ....1809 James Monroe....1811	Albert Gallatin. 1809 G. W. Campbell 1814 A. J. Dallas....1814 W. H. Crawford 1816	Wm. Eustis...1809 J. Armstrong...1813 James Monroe..1814 W. H. Crawford 1815
James Monroe-D. D. Tompkins..1817 Dem. Rep.	J. Q. Adams......1817	W. H. Crawford 1817	Isaac Shelby ...1817 Geo. Graham ..1817 J. C. Calhoun..1817
John Q. Adams-John C. Calhoun. 1825 Nat'l Rep.	Henry Clay.......1825	Richard Rush ..1825	Jas. Barbour...1825 Peter B. Porter. 1828
Andrew Jackson-John C. Calhoun. 1829 Dem. Martin Van Buren 1833	M. Van Buren...1829 E. Livingston....1831 Louis McLane....1833 John Forsyth.....1834	S. D. Ingham..1829 Louis McLane..1831 W. J. Duane...1833 Roger B. Taney 1833 Levi Woodbury 1834	John H. Eaton. 1829 Lewis Cass ....1831 B. F. Butler....1837
Martin Van Buren-R.M. Johnson. 1837 Dem.	John Forsyth......1837	Levi Woodbury. 1837	J. R. Poinsett..1837
Wm. H. Harrison-John Tyler....1841 Whig	Daniel Webster ..1841	Thos. Ewing ...1841	John Bell 1841
John Tyler ....1841 Whig	Daniel Webster ..1841 Hugh S. Legaré...1843 Abel P. Upshur...1843 John C. Calhoun. 1844	Thos. Ewing ...1841 Walter Forward 1841 J. C. Spencer..1843 Geo. M. Bibb..1844	John Bell ......1841 John McLean...1841 J. C. Spencer..1841 Jas. M. Porter..1843 Wm. Wilkins...1844
James K. Polk-George M. Dallas. 1845 Dem.	James Buchanan. 1845	R. J. Walker...1845	Wm. L. Marcy. 1845
Zachary Taylor-Millard Fillmore. 1849 Whig	John M. Clayton. 1849	W.M. Meredith 1849	G. W. Crawford 1849
Millard Fillmore ....1850 Whig	Daniel Webster...1850 Edward Everett ..1852	Thomas Corwin. 1850	C. M. Conrad..1850
Franklin Pierce-William R. King. 1853 Dem.	W. L. Marcy......1853	James Guthrie .1853	Jefferson Davis. 1853
James Buchanan-J. C. Breckinridge Dem. 1857	Lewis Cass.......1857 J. S. Black.......1860	Howell Cobb...1857 P. F. Thomas..1860 John A. Dix....1861	John B. Floyd..1857 Joseph Holt....1861
Abraham Lincoln-Han. Hamlin..1861 Rep. Andrew Johnson 1865 Union	W. H. Seward....1861	S. P. Chase....1861 W.P. Fessenden 1864 H. McCulloch..1865	S. Cameron ....1861 E. M. Stanton..1862

ADMINISTRATIONS

Secretary of Navy	*Secretary of Interior*	*Postmaster-General*	*Attorney-General*
	Established March 3, 1849.	Samuel Osgood .1789 Tim. Pickering.1791 Jos. Habersham.1795	E. Randolph...1789 W. Bradford...1794 Charles Lee...1795
Benj. Stoddert..1798		Jos. Habersham.1797	Charles Lee....1797 Th. Parsons....1801
Benj. Stoddert..1801 Robert Smith..1801		Jos. Habersham.1801 Gideon Granger.1801	Levi Lincoln...1801 J. Breckinridge.1805 C. A. Rodney..1807
Paul Hamilton.1809 William Jones..1813 B. W. Crowninshield 1814		Gideon Granger.1809 R. J. Meigs,Jr..1814	C. A. Rodney..1809 W. Pinkney....1811 Richard Rush..1814
B. W. Crowninshield 1817 S. Thompson...1818 S. L. Southard..1823		R. J. Meigs, Jr..1817 John McLean..1823	Richard Rush..1817 William Wirt...1817
S. L. Southard..1825		John McLean..1825	William Wirt...1825
John Branch...1829 Levi Woodbury.1831 M. Dickerson..1834		Wm. T. Barry.1829 Amos Kendall..1835	J. M. Berrien..1829 R. B. Taney...1831 B. F. Butler...1833
M. Dickerson..1837 J. K. Paulding.1838		Amos Kendall..1837 John M. Niles..1840	B. F. Butler...1837 Felix Grundy..1838 H. D. Gilpin..1840
Geo. E. Badger.1841		Francis Granger 1841	J. J. Crittenden '41
Geo. E. Badger.1841 Abel P. Upshur.1841 David Henshaw 1843 T. W. Gilmer..1844 John Y. Mason.1844		Francis Granger 1841 C. A. Wickliffe.1841	J. J. Crittenden '41 Hugh S. Legaré.'41 John Nelson...1843
Geo. Bancroft..1845 John Y. Mason.1846		Cave Johnson..1845	J. Y. Mason...1845 Nathan Clifford..'46 Isaac Toucey..1848
W. B. Preston..1849	Thomas Ewing.1849	Jacob Collamer.1849	R. Johnson....1849
W. A. Graham.1850 J. P. Kennedy.1852	A. H. H. Stuart.1850	Nathan K. Hall 1850 S. D. Hubbard.1852	J. J. Crittenden '50
Jas. C. Dobbin.1853	R. McClelland.1853	James Campbell 1853	Caleb Cushing.1853
Isaac Toucey...1857	J. Thompson...1857	A. V. Brown...1857 Joseph Holt...1859 Horatio King...1861	J. S. Black....1857 E. M. Stanton..1860
Gideon Welles..1861	Caleb B. Smith.1861 John P. Usher..1863	M'gomery Blair 1861 Wm. Dennison.1864	Edward Bates..1861 James Speed...1864

THE PRESIDENTIAL

President and Vice President	*Secretary of State*	*Secretary of Treasury*	*Secretary of War*
Andrew Johnson (R) 1865	W. H. Seward 1865	Hugh McCulloch 1865	E. M. Stanton 1865 U. S. Grant 1867 L. Thomas 1868 J. M. Schofield 1868
Ulysses S. Grant (R) 1869 Schuyler Colfax 1869 Henry Wilson 1873	E. B. Washburne 1869 Hamilton Fish 1869	G. S. Boutwell 1869 W. A. Richardson 1873 B. H. Bristow 1874 L. M. Morrill 1876	J. A. Rawlins 1869 W. T. Sherman 1869 W. W. Belknap 1869 Alph. Taft 1876 J. D. Cameron 1876
Ruth. B. Hayes (R) 1877 W. A. Wheeler 1877	W. M. Evarts 1877	John Sherman 1877	G. W. McCrary 1877 Alex. Ramsey 1879
James Garfield (R) 1881 Chester A. Arthur 1881	J. G. Blaine 1881	William Windom 1881	R. T. Lincoln 1881
Chester A. Arthur 1881	F. Frelinghuysen 1881	C. J. Folger 1881 W. Q. Gresham 1884 Hugh McCulloch 1884	R. T. Lincoln 1881
Grover Cleveland (D) 1885 T. A. Hendricks 1885	T. F. Bayard 1885	Daniel Manning 1885 C. S. Fairchild 1887	W. C. Endicott 1885
Benjamin Harrison (R) 1889 L. P. Morton 1889	J. G. Blaine 1889 J. W. Foster 1892	William Windom 1889 Charles Foster 1891	R. Proctor 1889 S. B. Elkins 1891
Grover Cleveland (D) 1893 A. E. Stevenson 1893	W. Q. Gresham 1893 Richard Olney 1895	J. G. Carlisle 1893	D. S. Lamont 1893
William McKinley (R) 1897 G. A. Hobart 1897 Theodore Roosevelt 1901	John Sherman 1897 W. R. Day 1897	L. J. Gage 1897	R. A. Alger 1897 Elihu Root 1899
Theodore Roosevelt (R) 1901 C. W. Fairbanks 1905	John Hay 1901 Elihu Root 1905 Robert Bacon 1909	L. J. Gage 1901 L. M. Shaw 1902 G. Cortelyou 1907	Elihu Root 1901 W. H. Taft 1904 L. E. Wright 1908
William H. Taft (R) 1909 J. S. Sherman 1909	P. C. Knox 1909	F. MacVeagh 1909	J. M. Dickinson 1909 H. L. Stimson 1911
Woodrow Wilson (D) 1913 T. R. Marshall 1913	W. J. Bryan 1913 Robert Lansing 1915 Bainbridge Colby 1920	W. G. McAdoo 1913 Carter Glass 1918 D. F. Houston 1920	L. M. Garrison 1913 N. D. Baker 1916
Warren G. Harding (R) 1921 Calvin Coolidge 1921	C. E. Hughes 1921	A. W. Mellon 1921	J. W. Weeks 1921
Calvin Coolidge (R) 1923 C. G. Dawes 1925	C. E. Hughes 1923 G. B. Kellogg 1925	A. W. Mellon 1923	J. W. Weeks 1923 D. F. Davis 1925
Herbert Hoover (R) 1929 Charles Curtis 1929	H. L. Stimson 1929	A. W. Mellon 1929 O. L. Mills 1932	J. W. Good 1929 P. J. Hurley 1929
F. D. Roosevelt (D) 1933 J. N. Garner 1933 H. A. Wallace 1941	Cordell Hull 1933	W. H. Woodin 1933 H. Morgenthau 1934	G. H. Dern 1933 H. A. Woodring 1936 H. L. Stimson 1940

ADMINISTRATIONS

Secretary of Navy	*Secretary of Interior*	*Postmaster General*	*Attorney General*	*Recent Departments*
Gideon Welles 1865	J. P. Usher 1865 James Harlan 1865 O. H. Browning 1866	Wm. Dennison 1865 A. W. Randall 1866	James Speed 1865 H. Stanbery 1866 W. M. Evarts 1868	*Sec. of Agr.* est. 11 Feb., 1889 N. J. Colman 1889 J. M. Rusk 1889 J. S. Morton 1893 James Wilson 1897 James Wilson 1901 James Wilson 1909 D. F. Houston 1913 E. T. Meredith 1920 H. C. Wallace 1921 H. M. Gore 1924 W. M. Jardine 1925 A. M. Hyde 1929 H. A. Wallace 1933 C. R. Wickard 1940 *Sec. of Com. & Lab.* est. 14 Feb., 1903 G. Cortelyou 1903 V. H. Metcalf 1904 O. S. Straus 1907 Charles Nagel 1909 Dept. divided 1913 *Sec. of Com.* est. 4 Mar., 1913 W. C. Redfield 1913 J. W. Alexander 1919 H. C. Hoover 1921 H. C. Hoover 1925 W. F. Whiting 1928 R. P. Lamont 1929 R. D. Chapin 1932 D. C. Roper 1933 H. L. Hopkins 1939 J. H. Jones 1940 *Sec. of Lab.* est. 4 Mar., 1913 W. B. Wilson 1913 J. J. Davis 1921 W. N. Doak 1930 F. Perkins 1933
A. E. Borie 1869 G. M. Robeson 1869	J. D. Cox 1869 C. Delano 1870 Zach. Chandler 1875	J. A. J. Creswell 1869 J. W. Marshall 1874 M. Jewell 1874 J. N. Tyner 1876	E. R. Hoar 1869 A. T. Ackerman 1870 G. H. Williams 1871 E. Pierrepont 1875 Alph. Taft 1876	
R. W. Thompson 1877 Nathan Goff 1881	Carl Schurz 1877	D. M. Key 1877 Hor. Maynard 1880	Charles Devens 1877	
W. H. Hunt 1881	S. J. Kirkwood 1881	T. L. James 1881	W. MacVeagh 1881	
W. H. Hunt 1881 W. E. Chandler 1882	S. J. Kirkwood 1881 H. M. Teller 1882	T. O. Howe 1881 W. Q. Gresham 1883 Frank Hatton 1884	B. H. Brewster 1881	
W. C. Whitney 1885	L. Q. C. Lamar 1885 W. F. Vilas 1888	W. F. Vilas 1885 D. M. Dickinson 1888	A. H. Garland 1885	
B. F. Tracy 1889	J. W. Noble 1889	J. Wanamaker 1889	W. H. Miller 1889	
H. A. Herbert 1893	Hoke Smith 1893 D. R. Francis 1896	W. S. Bissell 1893 W. L. Wilson 1895	R. Olney 1893 J. Harmon 1895	
J. D. Long 1897	C. N. Bliss 1897 E. A. Hitchcock 1899	J. A. Gary 1897 C. E. Smith 1898	J. McKenna 1897 J. W. Griggs 1897 P. C. Knox 1901	
J. D. Long 1901 W. H. Moody 1902 Paul Morton 1904 C. J. Bonaparte 1905 V. H. Metcalf 1907 T. H. Newberry 1908	E. A. Hitchcock 1901 J. R. Garfield 1907	C. E. Smith 1901 H. C. Payne 1902 R. J. Wynne 1904 G. Cortelyou 1905 G. von L. Meyer 1907	P. C. Knox 1901 W. H. Moody 1904 C. J. Bonaparte 1907	
G. von L. Meyer 1909	R. A. Ballinger 1909 W. L. Fisher 1911	F. H. Hitchcock 1909	G. W. Wickersham 1909	
Jos. Daniels 1913	F. K. Lane 1913 J. B. Payne 1920	A. S. Burleson 1913	J. McReynolds 1913 T. W. Gregory 1914 A. M. Palmer 1919	
Edwin Denby 1921	A. B. Fall 1921 Hubert Work 1923	W. H. Hays 1921 Hubert Work 1922 H. S. New 1923	H. M. Daugherty 1921	
Edwin Denby 1923 C. D. Wilbur 1924	Hubert Work 1923 R. O. West 1928	H. S. New 1923	H. M. Daugherty 1923 H. F. Stone 1924 J. G. Sargent 1925	
C. F. Adams 1929	R. L. Wilbur 1929	W. F. Brown 1929	W. D. Mitchell 1929	
C. A. Swanson 1933 Charles Edison 1940 Frank Knox 1940	H. L. Ickes 1933	J. A. Farley 1933 F. C. Walker 1940	H. S. Cummings 1933 Frank Murphy 1939 Robert Jackson 1940 F. Biddle 1941	

INDEX